BTEC National
Sport

BTEC National
Sport

Development, Coaching and Fitness

Jennifer Stafford-Brown
Simon Rea

HODDER
EDUCATION
PART OF HACHETTE LIVRE UK

endorsed by
edexcel

This high quality material is endorsed by Edexcel and has been through a rigorous quality assurance programme to ensure that it is a suitable companion to the specification for both learners and teachers. This does not mean that its contents will be used verbatim when setting examinations nor is it to be read as being the official specification – a copy of which is available at www.edexcel.org.uk

Orders: please contact Bookpoint Ltd, 130 Milton Park, Abingdon, Oxon OX14 4SB. Telephone: (44) 01235 827720. Fax: (44) 01235 400454. Lines are open from 9.00 to 5.00, Monday to Saturday, with a 24 hour message answering service. You can also order through our website www.hoddereducation.co.uk

If you have any comments to make about this, or any of our other titles, please send them to educationenquiries@hodder.co.uk

British Library Cataloguing in Publication Data
A catalogue record for this title is available from the British Library

ISBN: 978 0 340 94082 2

First Edition published 2007
Impression number   10 9 8 7 6 5 4 3
Year   2011 2010 2009 2008

Copyright © Jennifer Stafford-Brown, Simon Rea

Cover photo by Digital Vision/Getty Images

Typeset in 11/13 Minion by Fakenham Photosetting Limited, Fakenham, Norfolk

Printed in Italy for Hodder Education, a part of Hachette Livre UK, 338 Euston Road, London NW1 3BH.

Contents

Acknowledgements

Jennifer Stafford-Brown

I would like to thank my friend and co-author Simon Rea for all of his hard work and enthusiasm and for agreeing to spend another summer in front of the computer writing! I would also like to thank Tamsin and Bianca from Hodder Arnold for their input, my colleagues from Edexcel and, of course, the contributing authors for their hard work and advice. As always, particular thanks go to my husband Matt, our children Ellie and Alex and my parents Ann and Brian Stafford for their continued support, encouragement, patience and understanding. I would also like to thank my friends for their help and support and especially Grace Whitehead and Avril Young for their encouragement, help and child care and never-ending supply of coffee!

Simon Rea

I would like to give special thanks to Gavin Hughes, Sue Pinson and Rebecca Woodard for their invaluable help during the writing period. Thanks also go to my fellow author, Jenny Stafford-Brown, for her patience and never-ending support, as well as to the staff and students at Oxford and Cherwell Valley College and Uxbridge College and to all my personal training clients for the inspiration and fun they have brought over the year, Thank you to my parents, Tony and Pam for their love, support and sustenance during this adventure! In loving memory of Daryl Hughes, a true sportsman and a family man, who took sport and life to their very limit.

Contributing authors

Chris Manley has ten years' teaching experience in FE colleges. He has been a National League Basketball Coach and Referee and is currently Divisional Leader at North West Kent College. Chris wrote the chapters 'Principles of sports coaching', 'Practical individual sports and practical team sports', 'Sports leadership', and 'Rules, regulations and officiating in sport'.

Vicki McQuaid has taught sport in schools and FE colleges for 11 years. She has also worked for local authorities in various sport and physical activity roles. She is currently the Business Development and Special Projects Manager for the Hertfordshire Sports Partnership. Vicki wrote the 'Sports development' chapter.

Michael Robinson has a degree in Physiotherapy and has since focused on musculoskeletal therapy. He clinically specialises in shoulder and spinal conditions and recently attained an MSc in Practice Development. He currently manages the orthopaedic service for Bolton PCT. Michael wrote the 'Sport and exercise massage' chapter.

Julie Hancock is a Lead Verifier and trainer for a major examination board. She has been teaching for 18 years in schools, further education and, presently, in higher education at Huddersfield University as a Senior Lecturer and Course Leader within the Division of Sports & Health Studies. She is also a HSE Approved First Aid trainer. Julie wrote the 'Sports injuries' chapter.

Richard Horner has spent many years teaching in FE colleges. He is now a Conditioning Coach at Chelsea FC working within their Academy, as well as the Course Tutor for the ever-increasing football excellence at West Herts College. Richard wrote the 'Talent identification and development in sport' chapter in conjunction with David Pears.

David Pears has a BSc (Hons) with QTS in Physical Education and an MSc in Coaching Science. He works as a coaching science lecturer at the University of Bedfordshire and as a football coach. David co-wrote the 'Talent identification and development in sport' chapter with Richard Horner.

Every effort has been made to trace and acknowledge ownership of copyright. The publishers will be glad to make suitable arrangements with any copyright holders whom it has not been possible to contact.

The authors and publishers would like to thank the following for the permission to use the following photographs in this book:

p37 Getty Images/Hamish Blair, **p39** © imagebroker/Alamy, **p40** SPL/Steve Allen, **p44** Mark Baker/AP Photo/Empics, **p45** (left) Adrian Dennis/AFP/Getty Images, **p45** (right) Nigel French/Empics, **p62** Clive Brunskill/Getty Images, **p67** © iStockphoto.com/Ana Abejon, **p73** Michelangelo Gratton/Digital Vision/Getty Images, **p77** © Adrian Muttitt/Alamy, **p79** © ImageState/Alamy, **p80** Steve Bardens/Action Plus, **p81** © Real World People/Alamy, **p85** © View Pictures Ltd/Alamy, **p110** Glyn Kirk/Action Plus, **p116** Shelly Gazin/The Image Works/TopFoto, **p121** © iStockPhoto.com/Ben Blankenburg, **p124** Neil Tingle/Actionplus, **p137** Action Plus/Steve Bardens, **p138** Rex Features/Peter Burian, **p145** SPL/Steve Allen, **p148** © Ashley Cooper/Corbis, **p150** © iStockPhoto.com/Lisa Thornberg, **p151** © iStockPhoto.com/Galina Barskaya, **p155** (top) © Comstock Select/Corbis, (bottom) © Philip Wilkins/Antony Blake Picture Library, **p159** (top) Photolibrary.com, (bottom) © Maximilian Stock Ltd/Anthony Blake Photo Library, **p209** © John Norris/Corbis, **p210** © Andersen Ross/Blend Images/Corbis, **p211** Empics/Gabriel Piko, **p212** Darren Walsh/Empics/Chelsea FC, **p213** © John Elk III/Alamy, **p216** Glyn Kirk/Actionplus, **p219** Sparky/The Image Bank/Getty Images, **p220** © iStockPhoto.com/Simon Podgorsek, **p221** ©www.purestockX.com, **p227** Jed Leicester/Empics Sports Photo Agency, **p234** Dr P. Marazzi/Science Photo Library, **p235** Arthur Glauberman/Science Photo Library, **p237** (top) Martin M. Rotker/Science Photo Library, (bottom) CNRI/Science Photo Library, **p244** © iStockPhoto.com/Oleg Kozlov, **p266** Glyn Kirk/Actionplus, **p275** © www.purestockX.com, **p276** © Ace Stock Limited/Alamy, **p280** Donna Day/Workbook Stock/Jupiter Images, **p281** © www.purestockX.com, **p286** © Nucleus Medical Art, Inc./Alamy, **p323** (left) Action Images/Nick Potts, (right) © Pete Leonard/zefa/Corbis, **p327** (left) Alex Bartel/Science Photo Library, (right) Dr M.A. Ansary/Science Photo Library, **p348** Neil Tingle/Actionplus, **p374** Action Images/Andrew Couldridge, **p375** Neil Tingle/Actionplus, **p377** Steve Bardens/Actionplus, **p378** Mel Evans/AP/Empics, **p384** (left) © Marc Serota/Reuters/Corbis, (right) © Joe Fox/Alamy, **p412** © Rick Becker-Leckrone/Corbis, **p425** © Richard Sheppard/Alamy

Artwork by Cactus Design and Illustration Ltd from McGuinness, H. (2006) *Anatomy and Physiology*, 3rd edn, Hodder Arnold: **p10, p11**

Artwork by Kate Nardoni, Cactus Design and Illustration Ltd: **p3, p4, p6, p13, p33, p34, p51, p55, p56** Fig 3.14a, **p57, p99, p100, p101, p102, p103, p108** Fig 6.09, **p167, p186, p237, p251, p252, p257, p258, p262, p264, p280, p282, p283, p284, p285, p300** Fig 15.04, **p349, p400**

Artwork by David Graham from Wesson, K. *et al.* (2005) *Sport & PE*, 3rd edn, Hodder Arnold : **p8, p9** Fig 1.11, **p14, p15, p16, p17, p18, p49, p50, p56** Fig 3.13, **p114**

Artwork by Tony Jones, Art Construction from Stafford-Brown, J. *et al.* (2005) *BTEC First Sport*, Hodder Arnold: **p9** Fig 1.12, **p21** Figs 1.44, 1.45, **p24, p107, p108** Fig 6.08, **p110, p112, p141, p147**

Artwork from Stafford-Brown, J. *et al.*, (2003) *BTEC National in Sport and Exercise Science*, Hodder Arnold: **p5, p20, p23, p234, p320, p324, p325, p331, p332, p370, p371**

Study skills

The course you are studying has no externally set exams. Instead, you will be assessed in a variety of ways including practical work, presentations, case studies and other written formats.

This chapter is designed to help you with your assessments. By the end of this chapter you should:

- understand the grading criteria
- know how to use a range of research sources
- understand how to take notes
- know how to use, quote and reference your work
- know how to avoid plagiarism
- know what to do if you are absent.

Understanding the grading criteria

You will be studying a number of units and in order to pass this course you have to show that you have understood each part of each unit. The units are broken down into separate learning outcomes, each of which has different grading criteria allocated to it. The grading criteria start at pass (P), merit (M) and then distinction (D). Distinction is the highest grade you can attain. Each P, M and D criterion is split into smaller, numbered parts – P1, P2, P3, M1, M2, M3, D1, D2, etc. The number in each P, M and D varies depending on the unit. The grade that you are awarded for your work is based upon the work you present in your assessments.

An example of part of a grading grid is shown in the box below.

Once you have completed all the assessments for one unit you will be awarded a final grade for that particular unit. This grade is determined by all the grades you achieve for that unit's work. In order to pass the unit, you must meet every one of the P grading criteria. In order to attain an M you must meet every one of the P grading criteria and also all the M grading criteria. In order to attain a D you

Grading criteria

To achieve a pass grade the evidence must show that the learner is able to:	To achieve a merit grade the evidence must show that, in addition to the pass criteria, the learner is able to:	To achieve a distinction grade the evidence must show that, in addition to the pass and merit criteria, the learner is able to:
P1 describe skills, techniques and tactics required in two different team sports	**M1** explain skills, techniques and tactics required in two different team sports	**D1** analyse identified strengths and areas for improvement, and justify suggestions made in relation to personal development
P2 demonstrate appropriate skills, techniques and tactics in two different team sports	**M2** explain the application of the rules and regulations of two different team sports, in three different situations for each sport	
P3 describe the rules and regulations of two different team sports, and apply them to three different situations for each sport	**M3** explain identified strengths and areas for improvement, and make suggestions relating to personal development	

must meet all the P grading criteria, all the M grading criteria and all the D grading criteria.

You may be given a number of small assessments that cover all the unit grading criteria (usually between two and four) or you may be given one large assessment that covers all the unit grading criteria. Your assessment should include details of the grading criteria it is addressing. These may be placed in the task, on a separate grading grid or on the front sheet. If you are unsure where to find them, ask your tutor.

The grading criteria contain verbs to explain what you need to do. If you know what each of these verbs means exactly, you then know what you need to do to gain the grading criteria you are aiming for.

Pass verbs

The following verbs are found in the pass grading criteria.

Describe	Give a detailed account of something; think of it as painting a picture with words
Define	To give a brief meaning of something
Outline	A brief description of something that concentrates on the main topic or item
Illustrate	Give examples or diagrams to help show what you mean
Identify	Point out (choose the right one) or give a list of the main features or prove something as being certain
Interpret	Give the meaning of something
Plan	Write a plan of how you intend to carry out the activity
State	Give a full account
Summarise	Give the main points or essential features of an idea or a discussion; do not include unnecessary details that could confuse the main topic of concern
List	A record that includes an item-by-item record of relevant information

Merit verbs

The following verbs are often found in the merit grading criteria.

Explain	Give a detailed account to give the meaning of something with reasons; include the 'how' and 'why' of the topic of interest
Compare/ contrast	Show the similarities between the two areas of interest and also the differences between the two, or the advantages and disadvantages
Discuss	Examine the advantages and disadvantages of the subject of interest and then try to complete the discussion with a conclusion
Account for	Explain the process or give a reason to explain the reason for something being the way it is
Demonstrate	Give a number of related examples or details from a variety of sources to support the argument you are making; in a practical situation, this means that you must practically carry out the activity or skill while being observed
Distinguish	Explain the differences
Examine	Inspect something closely
Interpret	Explain the meaning of something by giving examples, diagrams and/or opinions

Distinction verbs

In order to achieve a distinction, you will usually need to carry out research so that you have examined a minimum of at least two sources of information. So will need to obtain other people's views and see where they agree and disagree.

Analyse	Explore the main ideas of the subject, stating how they are related, why they are important and how each one contributes to the main area of interest
Critically analyse	Give your opinion of the subject of interest, both the advantages and disadvantages, after having considered all the evidence
Conclude	After having given evidence to support your opinion or argument give a reasoned judgement
Assess	Give your judgement on the importance of something
Criticise	Analyse a topic or issue objectively – give both the advantages and disadvantages and then make a decision based upon the evidence you present
Evaluate	Give evidence to support the good and bad points of the topic and then give your opinion based upon the evidence
Justify	Give supported reasons for your view to explain how you have arrived at these conclusions

Research sources

You will be given a great deal of information in your lectures and lessons and that, together with this textbook will give you all the information you need to pass this course. However, if you wish to attain a higher grade than a pass you will need to carry out more research to develop your understanding of the subject area.

There is a large range of resources available to you. This section will help guide you towards the appropriate resources and explain how to use them effectively.

Textbooks

Textbooks are a reliable source of information, which means that you can be certain that the information they contain is accurate. They have usually been written by subject specialists and are then reviewed by experts to ensure the work is accurate. If the textbook is endorsed by an examining board it means that its content is in line with the specifications of the course.

There is a range of textbooks available for this specific course and they may be in your library for you to look through. There are also more 'specific' textbooks available that concentrate purely on a particular topic. For example, if you are studying the anatomy unit, you may wish to refer to textbooks that are written purely about anatomy.

Internet

There is a huge array of internet sites out there, but not all are credible sources. Anybody is able to set up a website and write about whatever they want to, so you cannot be certain that the information they have written is accurate. However, sites set up by governing bodies and government information sites (e.g. British Food Foundation) are reliable and the information given should be accurate.

Journals

Journals are written by subject specialists, reviewed by subject experts and come out at regular intervals throughout the year. As they are published so frequently, the information they contain is up to date and will contain current facts and trends. Most libraries stock a range of relevant journals and you can also access some journals via the internet (some charge a subscription cost – check to see if your centre has a subscription). If you are hoping to achieve distinction grades, journals are a very good source of information to help you attain this level of understanding.

Taking notes

In order to remember all the information you are hearing or researching, it is a good idea to take notes. For some people the very act of writing something down will help them to remember that information. Note taking also means that you do not have to reread a whole chapter or section of a journal if you have forgotten it. All you will need to do is read your notes.

Taking notes in lectures and lessons

Do not attempt to write everything down that your tutor or teacher says – listen to the parts that you feel are most relevant and jot them down on paper.

You will always find it easier to take notes if you have some knowledge about the subject area. If your tutor gives you reading prior to a lecture it is a very good idea to carry out this work as you will find the lecture much more useful and learn more from it. Here is some guidance:

- you should always place the title and date at the top of your page and number each page so that your notes will make sense when you come to read them later
- make sure you can read your own writing
- read through your notes at the end of the lecture to check that you understand them.

There is a range of methods of taking notes that you can try in order to determine which one is best for you:

- shorthand – use your own shorthand, such as E = energy, F = football, MS = motor skill, and so on; the more you use this shorthand the more effective it becomes
- structured lists – these have a main heading with relevant information below; for example:

Health and Safety at Work Act 1974
Occupational factors
Environmental factors
Human factors
RIDDOR 1995

- diagrams – spider diagrams (like that in the diagram, top right), pattern notes, mind maps; with these you write the main topic in the middle of the page and then information is linked to this by lines. Underline any information that you think is very important.

Taking notes from research materials

Remember to keep to the topic in question. You can best do this by keeping the task or question close by so that you can keep checking that you are sticking to the task at hand and not researching work that is irrelevant. For example, if the task asks you to explore the aerobic energy system, research only this topic. You will not get extra marks for writing about the anaerobic energy system because the question did not ask for that. Here is some guidance:

- skim through the information to check that it is suitable for your work

An example of a spider diagram

- make a note of the details of the book or article that you are using
- actively read the work – have a pen in your hand and start to make notes
- write down any relevant quotes that you think you may use in your work
- summarise information in your own words.

Using quotes

Once you have read through a range of resources you should try to put this information into your own words. To help justify what you say, it is a good idea to include quotes in your work. A quote is a sentence or two taken from one of your research sources, which is written word for word. To show that you are quoting the material, you must place the quote in speech marks and then state the name of the authors of the source in brackets after the quote. For example:

> **Journals are written by subject specialists, reviewed by subject experts and come out at regular intervals throughout the year.**
>
> *Stafford-Brown and Rea (2007)*

This is good practice and should be encouraged. Quotes are used to help to substantiate what you have written. For example:

People are taking much less exercise these days, more people drive to work or school and spend more time pursuing sedentary leisure activities.

> **The average adult watches over 26 hours of television each week.**
>
> *Stafford-Brown and Rea (2007)*

If you have written a summary of information that has come from more than one textbook, then you can write the summary **in your own words** with no speech marks and then quote the authors at the end of the paragraph. For example:

Aerobic fitness training has been shown to have many cardiovascular benefits. Resting heart rate decreases, stroke volume increases, hypertrophy of the left ventricle occurs, new capillaries form (capillarisation) and there is an increase in haemoglobin content of the blood due to an increase in the number of red blood cells (Stafford-Brown *et al.* (2007), Wesson *et al.* (2006)).

You will notice that when there is more than one author, it is possible to write the name of the lead author (the first one printed on the book) and then write '*et al.*', which literally means 'and the rest'. However, when you come to write your bibliography or reference page, you must list the names of every author involved in writing the book you have used.

Your quote should not really be any longer than around two sentences. It is not good practice to quote large chunks of text. That shows that you are able to copy work but does not demonstrate your understanding of that work!

Referencing your work

Any sources that you have used quotes from or have used to help you to research your assessment activity should be included in a reference section or bibliography located at the back of your work.

The types of source you have used will determine the way in which the source is referenced, below are the most conventional formats.

Book

Author. Year *Book Title (in italics)*. Edition (if not the 1st), Publisher: Publisher location, Pages used.

e.g. Stafford-Brown, J. and Rea, S. (2007) *BTEC National in Sport,* 2nd edn., Hodder Arnold: London, pp116–20.

Journal

Author. Year Article title. *Journal (in italics)*, Volume, Issue no., Pages used.

e.g. Swaine, I. (1997) Cardiopulmonary response to exercise in swimmer using a swim bench and a leg-kicking ergometer. *International Journal of Sports Medicine*, 18, pp359–62.

Website

Author. Year – look for the © at the bottom of the page *Web page title (in italics)*, Full web page address, Date you accessed the page.

McKenzie, B. (2002) *Cardiovascular tests*, www.brianmac.demon.co.uk/cvtesting.htm, accessed 22 February 2006.

Newspaper

Author. Year Article title, *Newspaper (in italics)*, Pages used.

Layer, G. (2004) Wide of mark on participation, *Times Higher Education Supplement*, p76.

How to avoid plagiarism

Plagiarism is a term given to a situation where a person has copied work from another person or another source and passed it off as their own. This is a form of cheating and any person found to have plagiarised work in their assignments will not pass that assignment and will usually face further questioning from their tutor or quality manager.

Examples of plagiarism include copying:

- work from another student
- work from a textbook
- text from the internet
- diagrams from the internet.

Any information you would like to use should be put into **your own words** or presented as a quote. If you would like to copy diagrams from the internet, again you must acknowledge that the work is not your own and give details of the website next to the diagram you have used.

> **LEARNER ACTIVITY**
> - Make a list of all your weekly commitments.
> - Make a list of all the leisure activities you like to do.
> - Place all this information on a weekly planner and then highlight times that you could put aside for course work.

Organising yourself

The very nature of your course means that you will be faced with a lot of coursework to complete. For each unit you study you will have between two and four assessments. As a result, you will probably find that there are times when you have a number of assessments set at a similar time. You must learn to organise yourself and plan your time effectively so that you are able to complete the assessment(s) to the best of your ability and still meet the deadline set for handing in the work.

Design a weekly plan that includes all of your commitments, similar to the one shown at the bottom of the page.

You are then able to see which days and times you can dedicate to coursework.

For each assessment, spend some time making a list of tasks that you will need to complete in order for you to finish the work. Here is an example:

- Go to library to find suitable books and journals.
- Draw and illustrate a diagram of the heart.
- Research the structure and function of blood vessels.
- Type up information on the structure and function of blood vessels.
- Find out how the cardiovascular system responds to exercise.
- Type up work on how the cardiovascular system responds to exercise.

Date Week beginning 20 Sept	Mon	Tue	Wed	Thur	Fri	Sat	Sun
Day	College 9.00–15.30	Part-time shop work 10.00–17.00	College 9.00–12.00 Football game – away 12.00–17.00	College 10.00–15.00	College 10.00–15.00	Football practice 10.00–12.00	Football game – home 12.00–16.00
Evening	Football practice 18.30–20.00			Circuit training 20.00–21.00	Cinema 19.00–23.00		

An example of a weekly plan

The list of tasks is complete once you have included everything you need to do in order to finish the assessment.

Try to estimate how long you think each task will take and then allocate a time period on your weekly day planner for each of these tasks. Days on which you have very few commitments should be your main coursework days where you aim to complete a number of tasks. Always ensure that you plan to complete the assessment with some time to spare – you may find that some tasks take longer than expected.

Speak to your tutor if you are unsure about any aspect of the task or would benefit from having certain aspects of the task explained to you again. You will find that most tutors will be happy to spend time with you in lectures or even outside of directed study times (as long as you have made an appointment and the meeting takes place in good time prior to the actual hand-in deadline) so that you are able to understand the subject and achieve a good grade.

Absence from college or school

In most centres if you are absent from lectures you are expected to catch up with the work in your own time. You should always speak to your tutor as soon as you return to your centre so that she/he can give you any handouts and/or directed reading to help you to catch up.

You may find that a 'buddy system' works well for you too, in addition to tutor support. At the start of the course, find a person that you get on with and exchange contact details such as mobile phone numbers, email, etc. If you are absent from college, your buddy will know to collect any handouts or coursework for you, give you copies of their notes, pass on details of directed reading, give you homework and also let you know if an assessment has been handed out. If you meet up with your buddy as soon as possible after the lecture you have missed, you will have more time to catch up with the work you have missed and get back on track.

You are usually expected to contact the centre to let them know that you are not able to attend and give them an idea of when you think you will be able to return. If you need to be absent for any length of time and your absence has been approved, your tutor may be able to make arrangements so that you are able to keep up to date with work while away from the centre.

Core Units

Goals

By the end of this chapter you should understand:

- the structure and function of the skeletal system and how it responds to exercise
- the structure and function of the muscular system and how it responds to exercise
- the structure and function of the cardiovascular system and how it responds to exercise
- the structure and function of the respiratory system and how it responds to exercise
- the different energy systems and their use in sport and exercise.

This chapter explores the foundations of anatomy and physiology. Human movement is produced by the integration of the different systems of the body working together, allowing us to take part in a wide range of activities, including sport and exercise. In particular, movement involves the integration of the skeletal, muscular, cardiovascular, respiratory and energy systems, which are the subjects this chapter will examine.

The skeleton

The skeleton is the central structure of the body and provides the framework for all the soft tissue to attach to, to giving the body its defined shape. The skeleton is made up of bones, joints and cartilage and enables us to perform simple and complex movements such as walking and running.

Axial and appendicular skeleton

The axial skeleton (Fig 1.01) is the central core of the body or its axis. It consists of the skull, the vertebrae, the sternum and the ribs. It provides the core which the limbs hang from.

The appendicular skeleton (Fig 1.02) is the parts hanging off the axial skeleton. It consists of the shoulder girdle (scapula and clavicle), the pelvic girdle, upper and lower limbs.

Functions of the skeleton

The skeleton performs the following functions.

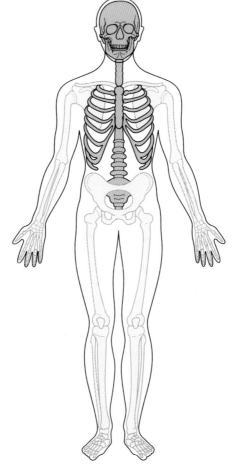

Fig 1.01 Axial skeleton

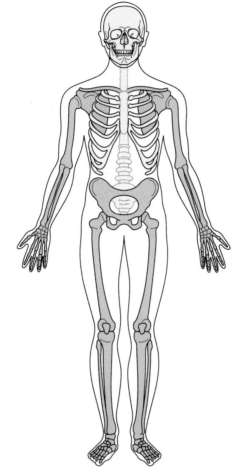

Fig 1.02 Appendicular skeleton

- **Provides a bony framework for the body** – the bones give the body a distinctive shape and a framework to which to attach muscles and other soft tissue to. Without bones we would just be a big sac of fluids.
- **Allows movement of the body as a whole and its individual parts** – the bones will act as levers and by forming joints they will allow muscles to pull on them and produce joint movements. This will enable us to move in all directions and perform the functions we need on a daily basis.
- **Offers protection to the organs found within the skeleton** – the bones will support and protect the vital organs they contain. For example, the skull will protect the brain, the ribs offer protection to the heart and lungs, the vertebrae protect the spinal cord and the pelvis offers protection to the sensitive reproductive organs.
- **Production of blood cells** – certain bones will contain red bone marrow and the bone marrow will produce red blood cells, white blood cells and

platelets. The bones that contain marrow are the pelvis, sternum, vertebrae, costals, cranial bones and clavicle.
- **Storage of minerals and fats** – the bones themselves are made of minerals stored within cartilage; therefore, they act as a mineral store for calcium, magnesium and phosphorous, which can be given up if the body requires the minerals for other functions. The bones will also store dietary fats (triglycerides) within the yellow bone marrow.
- **Attachment of soft tissue** – bones provide surfaces for the attachment of soft tissue such as muscles, tendons and ligaments. This is why they are often irregular shapes and have bony points and grooves to provide attachment points.

Major bones of the body

The skeleton consists of 206 bones, over half of which are in the upper and lower limbs. Babies are born with around 300 bones and over time these fuse together to reduce the number.

Cranium

The cranium consists of eight bones fused together which act to protect your brain. There are 14 other facial bones which form the face and jaw.

Sternum

This is the flat bone in the middle of the chest which is shaped like a dagger. It protects the heart and gives an attachment point for the ribs and the clavicles.

Ribs or costals

Adults have 12 pairs of ribs, which run between the sternum and the thoracic vertebrae. The ribs are flat bones that form a protective cage around the heart and lungs. An individual will have seven pairs of ribs that attach to both the sternum and vertebrae (true ribs), three that attach from the vertebrae to a cartilage attachment on the sternum and two that attach on the vertebrae but are free as they have no second attachment (floating ribs).

Clavicle

This bone connects the upper arm to the trunk of the body. One end is connected to the sternum and the other is connected to the scapula. The role of the clavicle is to keep the scapula at the correct distance from the sternum.

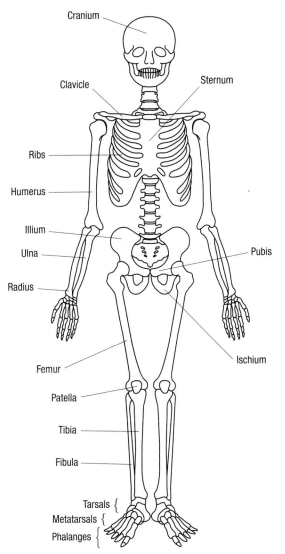

Fig 1.03 Anterior view of a skeleton

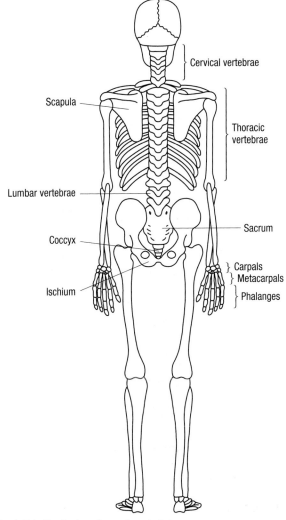

Fig 1.04 Posterior view of a skeleton

Scapula

This bone is situated on the back of the body. The scapula provides points of attachment for many muscles of the upper back and arms.

Arm

This consists of three bones: the humerus (upper arm), the radius and the ulna (lower arm). The ulna forms the elbow joint with the humerus and runs to the little finger. The radius is positioned beside the ulna and runs to the thumb side. When the hand moves, the radius moves across the ulna.

Hand

The hand has three areas made up of different types of bones. First, the wrist is made up of eight carpals, which are small bones arranged in two rows of four; the five long bones between the wrist and fingers are the metacarpals and the bones of the fingers are called phalanges. There are 14 phalanges altogether with three in each finger and two in the thumb. There are a total of 30 bones in the upper limb.

Pelvis

The pelvis protects and supports the lower internal organs, including the bladder, the reproductive organs and also, in pregnant women, the developing foetus. The pelvis consists of three bones, the ilium, pubis and ischium, which have become fused together to form one area.

The leg

The leg consists of four bones: the femur is the longest bone in the body and forms the knee joint with the tibia, which is the weight-bearing bone of the lower leg; the fibula is the non-weight bearing bone of the lower leg and helps form the ankle; the patella is the bone which floats over the knee, it lies within the patella tendon and smoothes the movement of the tendons over the knee joint.

Foot

Like the hand, the foot has three areas: the seven tarsals which form the ankle, the five metatarsals which travel from the ankle to the toes and the 14 phalanges which make up the toes. There are three phalanges in each toe with only two in the big toe. Again the lower limb has 30 bones; it has one less tarsal but makes up for it with the patella.

Vertebrae

The spine is made up of five areas:

- cervical – 7
- thoracic – 12
- lumbar – 5
- sacrum – 5
- coccyx – 4.

The seven cervical vertebrae make up the neck and run to the shoulders. The twelve thoracic vertebrae make up the chest area, and the five lumbar vertebrae make up the lower back. The sacrum consists of five vertebrae which are fixed together and form joints with the pelvis, and the coccyx is four bones joined together, which are the remnants of when we had a tail.

Structure of a long bone

- **Epiphysis** – this is the ends of the bone.
- **Diaphysis** – this is the long shaft of the bone.
- **Hyaline cartilage** – this is the thin layer of bluish cartilage covering each end of the bone.
- **Periosteum** – this is the thin outer layer of the bone. It contains nerves and blood vessels that feed the bone.
- **Compact bone** – this is hard and resistant to bending.

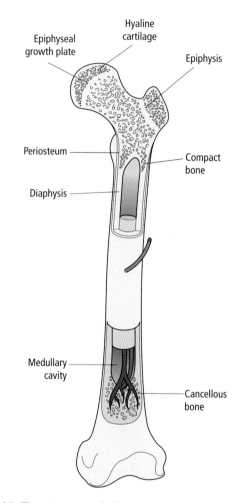

Fig 1.05 The structure of a long bone

- **Cancellous bone** – this lies in layers within the compact bone. It has a honeycomb appearance and gives the bones their elastic strength.
- **Medullary cavity** – this is the hollow space down the middle of the compact bone and contains bone marrow. There are two types of bone marrow: red marrow, which produces blood cells, and yellow marrow, which stores fat.

Bone growth

In a fetus, most of the skeleton consists of cartilage, which is a tough flexible tissue; as the foetus develops minerals are laid down in the cartilage and the bones become harder and less flexible. This process is called ossification and it continues until we are adults. Bones keep growing until between the ages of 18–30, depending upon the bone and the body part. When a bone grows it occurs at the epiphyseal plate, which is an area just behind the head of the bone at each epiphysis; as a bone grows, its two ends are slowly pushed away from each other.

Bones are very much alive and full of activity. We know bones are living material because they can repair if they are damaged, grow when we are young and they produce blood cells. Bones contain blood vessels and nerves.

Bone is continually being broken down and replaced; this process is done by different cells, osteoblasts and osteoclasts:

- **osteoblasts** are cells that will build bone
- **osteoclasts** are cells that destroy or clean away old bone.

Osteoclasts and osteoblasts will replace around 10 per cent of bone every year; this means that no matter how old we are our skeleton is no older than ten years of age!

> **definition**
>
> Ossification: the process of cartilage turning into bone.

Connective tissue

There are connective tissues in the body to connect tissue and stabilise joints. There are three types of connective tissue:

- cartilage
- ligament
- tendon.

Cartilage is a dense and tough tissue which cushions joints. It comes in three types:

- hyaline (found at the ends of bones)
- fibro (thick chunks found in the knee and between vertebrae)
- elastic (gives shape to structures such as the ear and the nose).

Ligaments:

- attach bone to bone
- act to give stability to joints
- are tough, white and inelastic.

Tendons:

- attach muscle to bone
- carry the force from muscle contraction to the bone
- are tough, greyish and inelastic.

All these types of connective tissue have a very poor blood supply, hence their whitish colour, and will take a long time to repair if they become damaged.

Key learning points

- The functions of the skeleton are shape, movement, protection, blood production and mineral storage.
- A bone is made up of a periosteum, compact bone, cancellous bone and bone marrow.
- Bones grow at their growth plates.

Joints

> **definition**
>
> Joint: a place where two bones meet.

The place where two or more bones meet is called a joint or an articulation. A joint is held together by ligaments, which give the joints their stability.

Joints are put into one of three categories depending upon the amount of movement available.

1 **Fixed joints/fibrous** – these joints allow no movement. These types of joints can be found between the plates in the skull.
2 **Slightly moveable/cartilaginous** – these allow a small amount of movement and are held in place by ligaments and cushioned by cartilage. These types of joints can be found between the vertebrae in the spine.
3 **Moveable/synovial** – there are six types of these joints and all allow varying degrees of movement. The six types of synovial joint are: hinge, ball and socket, pivot, condyloid, sliding, and saddle.

Hinge joint

These can be found in the elbow (ulna and humerus) and knee (femur and tibia). They allow flexion and extension of a joint. Hinge joints are like the hinges on a door, and allow you to move the elbow and knee in only one direction.

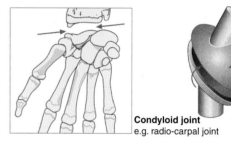

Fig 1.06 Hinge joint

Ball and socket joint

These types of joint can be found at the shoulder (scapula and humerus) and hip (pelvis and femur) and allow movement in almost every direction. A ball and socket joint is made up of a round end of one bone that fits into a small cup-like area of another bone.

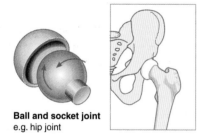

Fig 1.07 Ball and socket joint

Pivot joint

This joint can be found in the neck between the top two vertebrae (atlas and axis). It allows only rotational movement – for example, it allows you to move your head from side to side as if you were saying 'no'.

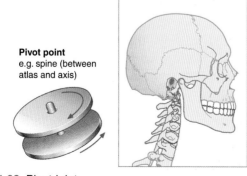

Fig 1.08 Pivot joint

Condyloid joint

This type of joint is found at the wrist. It allows movement in two planes; this is called biaxial. It allows you to bend and straighten the joint, and move it from side to side. The joints between the metacarpals and phalanges are also condyloid.

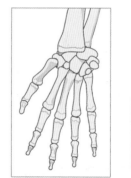

Fig 1.09 Condyloid joint

Saddle joint

This type of joint is found only in the thumbs. It allows the joint to move in three planes, backwards and forwards, and from side to side and across. This is a joint specific to humans and gives us 'manual dexterity', enabling us to hold a cup and write, among other skills.

Fig 1.10 Saddle joint

Gliding joint

This type of joint can be found in the carpal bones of the hand. These types of joint occur between the surfaces of two flat bones. They allow very limited movement in a range of directions.

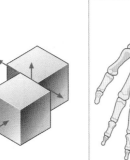

Gliding joint
e.g. carpals

Fig 1.11 Gliding joint

Structure of a synovial joint

Figure 1.12 shows the structure of a synovial joint, which is made up of the following components.

- **Synovial capsule** – keeps the contents of the synovial joint in place.
- **Synovial membrane** – releases synovial fluid onto the joint.
- **Synovial fluid** – a thick 'oil like' solution which lubricates the joint and allows free movement.
- **Articular cartilage** – a bluish-white covering of cartilage which prevents wear and tear on the bones.

Key learning point

- There are three types of joint: fixed, slightly moveable and moveable/synovial.

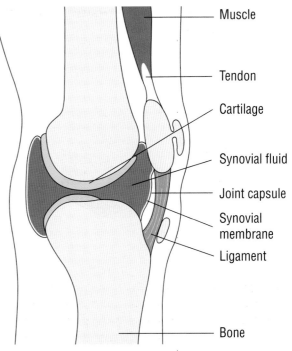

Fig 1.12 Structure of a synovial joint

Types of joint movement

To enable us to understand sporting movements we need to be able to describe or label joint movements. Joint movements are given specific terms (see Table 1.01 and below).

General movements

General movements apply to more than one joint.

Table 1.01 Different types of joint

Type of joint	Type of movement	Examples in the body
Hinge	Flexion and extension	Elbow, knee
Ball and socket	Flexion and extension Abduction and adduction Circumduction and rotation	Hips and shoulders
Pivot	Rotation	Neck
Condyloid	Flexion and extension Abduction and adduction	Wrist
Saddle	Flexion and extension Abduction and adduction	Thumb
Gliding	Limited movement in all directions	Carpals

- **Flexion** – this occurs when the angle of a joint decreases. For example, when you bend the elbow it decreases from 180 degrees to around 30 degrees.

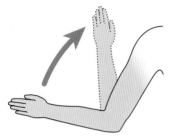

Fig 1.13 Flexion

- **Extension** – this occurs when the angle of a joint increases. For example, when you straighten the elbow it increases from 30 degrees to 180 degrees.

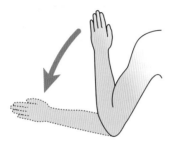

Fig 1.14 Extension

- **Adduction** – this means movement towards the midline of the body.

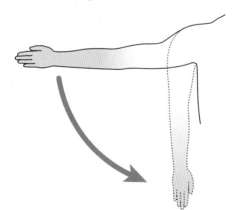

Fig 1.15 Adduction

- **Abduction** – this means movement away from the midline of the body. This occurs at the hip during a star jump.

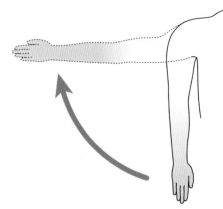

Fig 1.16 Abduction

- **Circumduction** – this means that the limb moves in a circle. This occurs at the shoulder joint during an overarm bowl in cricket.

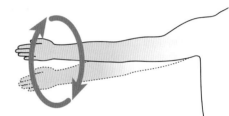

Fig 1.17 Circumduction

- **Rotation** – this means that the limb moves in a circular movement towards the middle of the body. This occurs in the hip in golf while performing a drive shot.

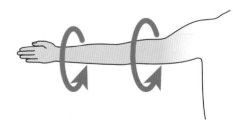

Fig 1.18 Rotation

Specific movements

Specific movements apply to a specific joint.

- **Pronation** – this means when the hand is facing down while the elbow is flexed. Pronation occurs as the hand moves from facing up to facing down and is the result of the movement of the pivot joint between the ulna and radius. This would happen when a spin bowler delivers the ball in cricket.

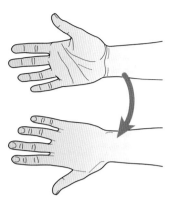

Fig 1.19 Pronation

- **Supination** – this means when the palm of the hand is facing up. Supination occurs as the hand moves from facing down to facing up and is the result of the movement of the pivot joint between the ulna and radius. You can remember this by thinking that you carry a bowl of soup in a supinated position. Throwing a dart involves supination of the forearm.

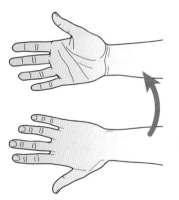

Fig 1.20 Supination

- **Plantarflexion** – this means that the foot moves away from the shin bone and you will be pointing your toes or raising onto your tiptoes. It is specific to your ankle joint and occurs when you walk.

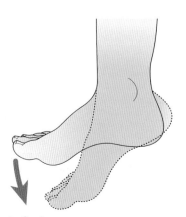

Fig 1.21 Plantarflexion

- **Dorsiflexion** – this means that the foot moves towards the shin as if you are pulling your toes up. It is specific to the ankle joint and occurs when you walk.

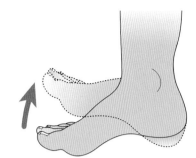

Fig 1.22 Dorsiflexion

- **Inversion** – this means that the soles of the feet are facing each other. It occurs at the gliding joints between the tarsals rather than at the ankle joint.

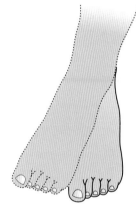

Fig 1.23 Inversion

- **Eversion** – this means that the soles of the feet are facing away from each other. It occurs at the gliding joints between the tarsals rather than at the ankle joint.

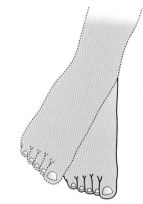

Fig 1.24 Eversion

- **Hyperextension** – this is the term given to an extreme or abnormal range of motion found within a joint – for example, at the knee or elbow.

> ## LEARNER ACTIVITY
>
> Give examples of other sporting movements in which you would see the sportsperson perform each of the above types of movement.

Effects of exercise on the skeletal system

If we train for a period of around three months we will start to experience adaptations to the skeletal system:

- increase in bone density
- stronger ligaments
- thickening of the hyaline cartilage at the ends of bones.

The bones become denser if we perform weight-bearing exercise, which is where we put a force through a bone. For example, walking and running put forces through the tibia, fibula and femur, and the body will respond by laying down more cartilage and calcium in the bones to strengthen them. Weight-bearing exercise will actually increase osteoblast activity, which means more bone is built or laid down. As the ligaments become stronger due to more collagen being laid down they also increase the stability of the joints and make them less prone to injury.

The muscular system

The muscular system will work in conjunction with the skeleton to produce movement of the limbs and body. The muscular system always has to work with the nervous system because it will produce a nervous impulse to initiate movement. There are three types of muscle tissue: smooth, cardiac and skeletal.

1 **Smooth muscles** – smooth muscles are also called involuntary muscles because they are out of our conscious control. They can be found in the digestive system (large and small intestine), the circulatory system (artery and vein walls) and the urinary system. Smooth muscles contract with a peristaltic action in that the muscle fibres contract consecutively rather than at the same time and this produces a wavelike effect. For example, when food is passed through the digestive system it is slowly squeezed through the intestines.

2 **Cardiac muscle** – the heart has its own specialist muscle tissue which is cardiac muscle; it makes up the heart muscle or myocardium and is also an

> ## LEARNER ACTIVITY
>
> | Ossification | Calcium | Flexion | The leg | Bone marrow |
> |---|---|---|---|---|
> | Ribs | Abduction | Bone marrow | Immovable | Pivot |
>
> Choose a word from the boxes above to answer each of the following questions.
>
> 1 What is the main mineral stored in bones?
> 2 Where are blood cells produced?
> 3 Which bones protect the heart and lungs?
> 4 Which limb consists of four bones?
> 5 What is the name given to the process of cartilage turning into bone?
> 6 Which joint allows only this type of movement and no other?
> 7 Which term describes movement away from the body?
> 8 This type of joint can be found in the neck.
> 9 This type of joint can be found in the skull.
> 10 This part of the bone produces new blood cells.

involuntary muscle. The heart has its own nerve supply via the sino-atrial node and it works by sending the nervous impulse through consecutive cells. The heart will always contract fully – that is, all the fibres contract – and contracts around 60–80 times a minute. The function of the myocardium is to pump blood around the body.

3 **Skeletal muscle** – skeletal muscle is the muscle that is attached to the skeleton across joints. It is under voluntary control as we decide when to contract muscles and produce movement. Skeletal muscle is arranged in rows of fibres and is also called striated, or striped, due to its appearance. The coordinated contractions of skeletal muscle allow us to move smoothly and produce sports skills. There are over 700 skeletal muscles in the human body and they make up around 40 per cent of our body weight (slightly less for a female).

Skeletal muscle is responsible for the following functions:

- producing movement
- maintaining body posture
- generating heat to keep us warm
- storage of glycogen for energy.

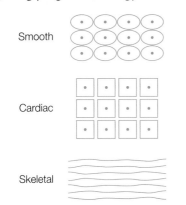

Fig 1.25 Types of muscle fibre under the microscope

Types of skeletal muscle

Within our muscle we actually have two types of muscle fibre which are called fast twitch and slow twitch fibres due to the speed at which they contract (see Table 1.02 overleaf). If we look at the evolution of humans we were originally hunters and gatherers; this meant that we had to walk long distances to find animals to eat and then, when we saw one, we would have to chase after it as fast as we could. Therefore, we adapted slow twitch muscle fibres to walk long distances and fast twitch muscle fibres to run quickly after our prey.

Slow twitch fibres (type 1)

Slow twitch fibres will be red in colour as they have a good blood supply. They have a dense network of blood vessels, making them suited to endurance work and they are slow to fatigue. They also contain many mitochondria to make them more efficient at producing energy using oxygen.

Mitochondria: the energy-producing organelles within cells.

Fast twitch fibres (type 2)

Fast twitch fibres will contract twice as quickly as slow twitch fibres and are thicker in size. They have a poor blood supply, are whiter in appearance and, due to the lack of oxygen, they will fatigue fairly quickly. Their faster, harder contractions make them suitable for producing fast, powerful actions such as sprinting and lifting heavy weights.

Within the group of fast twitch fibres there are two types: 2A and 2B. The type which is used depends upon the intensity of the chosen activity. Type 2B fibres work when a person is working very close to their maximum intensity, while type 2A work at slightly lower intensities but at higher intensities than slow twitch fibres are capable of. For example, a 100 m runner would be using type 2B fibres while a 400 m runner would be using type 2A fibres.

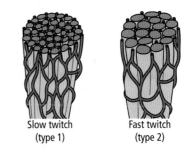

Fig 1.26 Slow and fast twitch fibres

Training effect on muscle fibres

The type 1 and type 2B fibres will always retain their distinctive features. However, type 2A fibres can take on characteristics of the type 1 or type 2B fibres, depending upon the training that is done. If you were to do endurance training, the type 2A fibres would develop more endurance, or if you were to do speed training they would develop more speed. They do not change their fibre type but they do take on different characteristics.

Every muscle in the body will contain a mixture of fast and slow twitch fibres depending upon its role in the body. Postural muscles, which keep us standing upright, such as the muscles in the legs, back and abdominal areas, will be predominantly slow twitch. For example, 90 per cent of the muscles in the back are slow twitch. Postural muscles need to produce low forces over a long period of time. The arms tend to be more fast twitch as they will need to move quickly but over much shorter periods of time. The types of muscle found in the legs will determine whether we are more suited to sprinting or endurance running; you will know which you have most of based on your own athletic performances. According to Bursztyn (1997), well-trained middle-distance runners will have around 80 per cent slow twitch fibres while well-trained sprinters may have up to 75 per cent fast twitch.

Key learning points

Involuntary muscle	Smooth muscle and cardiac muscle
Voluntary muscle	Skeletal muscle

Table 1.02 Summary of muscle fibre types

Slow twitch (type 1)	Feature	Fast twitch (type 2)
Red	Colour	White
Slow	Contraction speed	Fast
High	Endurance	Low
Low	Intensity used	High
Many	Blood vessels	Few
Smaller	Size	Larger
Many	Mitochondria	Few

Major muscles of the body

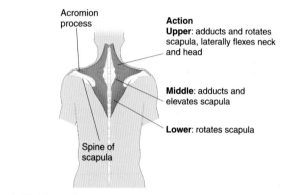

Fig 1.27 Trapezius
Position: upper back **Origin:** base of skull, cervical and thoracic vertebrae **Insertion:** clavicle and scapula **Action:** elevation, retraction and depression of shoulder girdle **Exercise:** bent-over rows

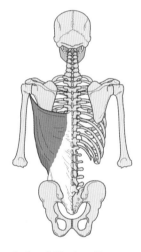

Action Adduction of humerus

Fig 1.28 Latissimus dorsi
Position: lower back **Origin:** lower six thoracic and all lumbar vertebrae, ilium **Insertion:** humerus **Action:** adduction and extension of shoulder **Exercise:** lateral pulldown

Anterior view

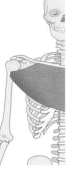

Action
Medial rotation of the humerus. Flexes the shoulder and horizontally adducts humerus

Fig 1.29 Pectoralis major
Position: chest **Origin:** clavicle and sternum **Insertion:** humerus **Action:** horizontal flexion and adduction of shoulder **Exercise:** bench press

Posterior deltoid
Anterior deltoid

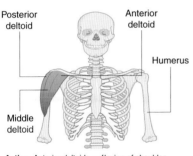

Humerus

Middle deltoid

Action Anterior deltoids – flexion of shoulder
Middle deltoid – abduction of shoulder
Posterior deltoid – extension of shoulder

Fig 1.30 Deltoid
Position: shoulder **Origin:** clavicle and scapula **Insertion:** humerus **Action:** abduction, flexion and extension of shoulder **Exercise:** lateral raises

Anterior view

Long head
Short head

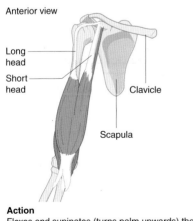

Clavicle

Scapula

Action
Flexes and supinates (turns palm upwards) the forearm

Fig 1.31 Biceps brachii
Position: front of upper arm **Origin:** scapula **Insertion:** radius **Action:** flexion of elbow and shoulder, supination of forearm **Exercise:** bicep curls

Posterior view
Clavicle

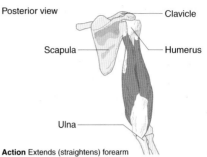

Scapula
Humerus

Ulna

Action Extends (straightens) forearm

Fig 1.32 Triceps brachii
Position: back of upper arm **Origin:** humerus and scapula **Insertion:** ulna **Action:** extension of elbow and shoulder **Exercise:** triceps extension

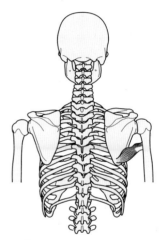

Fig 1.33 Teres major
Position: shoulder **Origin:** scapula **Insertion:** humerus **Action:** medial rotation of shoulder **Exercise:** cable shoulder rotation

Action
Transverse: constricts abdominal contents, assists in forcing air out of lungs
Rectus: gives anterior support to lumbar spine, holds ribcage and pubis together
Internal/external obliques: flex, rotate and side-bend trunk

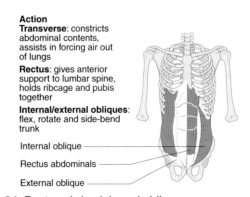

Internal oblique
Rectus abdominals
External oblique

Fig 1.34 Rectus abdominis and obliques
Position: front of abdomen and sides of the abdomen **Origin:** pubis and ribs, ilium **Insertion:** sternum and ilium, pubis, ribs **Action:** flexion of vertebrae and rotation of vertebrae **Exercise:** swiss ball sit-ups and side bends

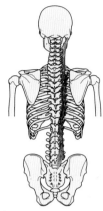

Fig 1.35 Erector spinae
Position: up and down the spine **Origin:** sacrum, ilium and vertebrae **Insertion:** ribs, vertebrae, base of skull **Action:** extension of vertebrae **Exercise:** dorsal raises

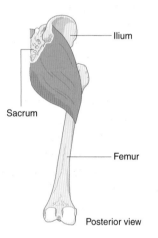

Action Extends hip, laterally rotates femur

Fig 1.36 Gluteus maximus
Position: bottom **Origin:** ilium **Insertion:** femur **Action:** extension of hip **Exercise:** squats

*The quadriceps are made up of four muscles. The rectus femoris acts on **both** the hip and knee joint. The vasti muscles (medialis, intermedialis and lateralis) act on the knee joint only.*

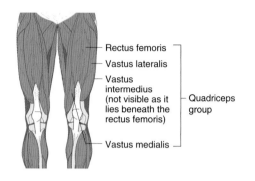

Action
Extends lower leg at the knee, flexes femur at the hip

Fig 1.37 Quadriceps group
Rectus femoris **Position:** front of upper leg **Origin:** ilium, femur **Insertion:** tibia **Action:** extension of knee **Exercise:** leg extension
Vastus lateralis **Position:** front of upper leg **Origin:** femur **Insertion:** tibia **Action:** extension of knee **Exercise:** leg extension
Vastus medialis **Position:** front of upper leg **Origin:** femur **Insertion:** tibia **Action:** extension of knee **Exercise:** leg extension
Vastus intermedius **Position:** front of upper leg **Origin:** femur **Insertion:** tibia **Action:** extension of knee **Exercise:** leg extension

Posterior view

Semitendinosus
Semimembranosus
Biceps femoris

The hamstrings consist of three muscles

Action
Flexes the knee, extends the femur of the hip

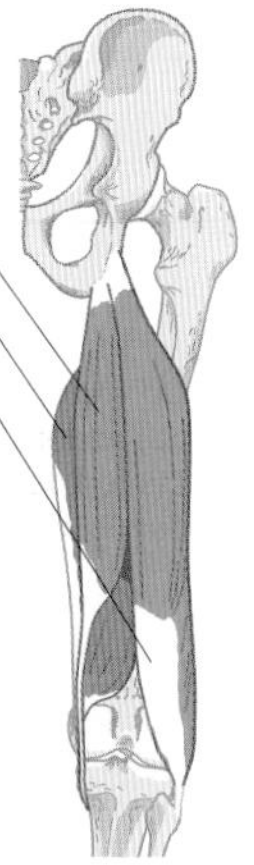

Fig 1.38 Hamstring group
Semimembranosus **Position:** back of upper leg **Origin:** ischium **Insertion:** tibia, fibula **Action:** flexion of knee **Exercise:** leg flexion
Semitendinosus **Position:** back of upper leg **Origin:** ischium **Insertion:** tibia, fibula **Action:** flexion of knee **Exercise:** leg flexion
Biceps femoris **Position:** back of upper leg **Origin:** ischium, femur **Insertion:** tibia, fibula **Action:** flexion of knee **Exercise:** leg flexion

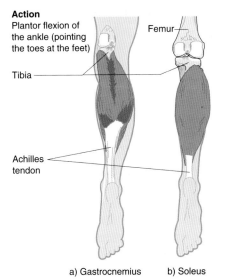

Action
Plantor flexion of the ankle (pointing the toes at the feet)

Femur

Tibia

Achilles tendon

a) Gastrocnemius   b) Soleus

Fig 1.39 Gastrocnemius and soleus
Position: back of lower leg **Origin:** femur and tibia **Insertion:** calcaneus **Action:** plantarflexion of ankle, knee flexion and plantarflexion of ankle **Exercise:** calf raises

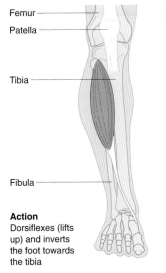

Femur
Patella

Tibia

Fibula

Action
Dorsiflexes (lifts up) and inverts the foot towards the tibia

Fig 1.40 Tibialis anterior
Position: front of lower leg **Origin:** tibia **Insertion:** tarsals and metatarsals **Action:** dorsiflexion of ankle **Exercise:** walking

Muscle movement

Tendons are responsible for joining skeletal muscles to your skeleton. Skeletal muscles are held to the bones with the help of tendons.

Tendons are cords made of tough tissue; they work to connect muscle to bones. When the muscle contracts, it pulls on the tendon, which in turn pulls on the bone and makes the bone move.

definition

Tendons: **these join muscles to the skeleton.**

Group action of muscles

When muscles contract they work as a group in that the muscle contracting is dependent on other muscles to enable it to do its job. A muscle can play one of four roles, as outlined below.

- **Agonist (or prime mover)** – this muscle contracts to produce the desired movement.
- **Antagonist** – this muscle relaxes to allow the agonist to contract.
- **Synergist** – this muscle assists the agonist in producing the desired movement.
- **Fixator** – these muscles will fix joints and the body in position to enable the desired movement to occur.

An antagonistic muscle pair is the muscle which contracts to produce the movement and the muscle which relaxes to produce the movement. For example, when you perform a bicep curl the biceps brachii will be the agonist as it contracts to produce the movement, while the triceps brachii will be the antagonist as it relaxes to allow the movement to occur.

definition

Antagonistic muscle pairs: **as one muscle contracts the other relaxes.**

Types of muscle movement

Muscles can contract or develop tension in three different ways.

1 **Concentric contraction** – a concentric contraction involves the muscle shortening and developing tension. The origin and insertion of the muscle move closer together and the muscle becomes fatter. To produce a concentric contraction a movement must occur against gravity.

2 **Eccentric contraction** – an eccentric contraction involves the muscle lengthening to develop tension. The origin and the insertion move further away from each other. An eccentric contraction provides

the control of a movement on the downward phase and it works to resist the force of gravity.

If a person is performing a bench press (as in Fig 1.41) they will produce a concentric contraction to push the weight away from their body. However, on the downward phase they will produce an eccentric contraction to control the weight on the way down. If they did not, gravity would return the weight to the ground and hurt them in the process. The agonist muscle will produce concentric and eccentric contractions, while the antagonist muscle will always stay relaxed to allow the movement to occur.

3   **Isometric contraction** – if a muscle produces tension but stays the same length then it will be an isometric contraction. This occurs when the body is being fixed in one position, e.g. a gymnast on the rings in the crucifix position. Also when we are standing up our postural muscles will produce isometric contractions.

Concentric contraction

Eccentric contraction

Fig 1.41 Bench press

LEARNER ACTIVITY
Think of three other sporting examples for each type of muscle contraction.

Effects of exercise on the muscular system

When we work the muscles with resistance or aerobic training we will start to overload them. When a muscle is overloaded it can experience low-scale damage in that some of the muscle fibres become damaged. We know this occurs because we experience muscle soreness the day after. The body adapts by laying down more protein in the muscle fibre because it thinks it is weak and needs strengthening. If we keep producing this response we will see that the muscle becomes firmer and may become larger. A body builder will aim to keep damaging the muscle so more muscle is laid down and produces the effect called hypertrophy where the muscle becomes larger.

Exercise will have other effects on the muscular system:

- increase in strength of muscle contraction
- increase in power produced (strength at speed)
- increase in muscular endurance
- increase in muscle mass
- increased range of motion
- improved coordination of muscles and nervous system
- increased metabolic rate
- increased strength of ligaments and tendons.

definition

Hypertrophy: increase in size of skeletal muscle.

The respiratory system

The respiratory system is responsible for transporting the oxygen from the air we breathe into our body. Our body then uses this oxygen in combination with the food we have eaten to produce energy. This energy is then used to keep us alive by supplying our heart with energy to keep beating and pumping blood around the body, which in turn allows us to move and take part in sports and many more different types of activities. Each person has two lungs running the length of the ribcage; the right lung is slightly larger than the left lung. The left lung has to make space for the heart in an area called the cardiac notch.

Structure of the respiratory system

The aim of the respiratory system is to provide contact between the outside and internal environments so that oxygen can be absorbed by the blood and carbon dioxide can be given up. It is made up of a system of tubes and muscles delivering the air into two lungs. The average person takes around 26,000 breaths a day to deliver the required amount of oxygen to the cells of the body.

Composition of air

The air that is inspired is made up of a mixture of gasses; the air exhaled is different in its composition of gases (see Table 1.03).

Oxygen is extracted from the air and replaced by carbon dioxide. However, most of the oxygen stays in the air and this is why mouth-to-mouth resuscitation works, because there is still 17 per cent available to the casualty.

Functions of the respiratory system

The aim of breathing is to get oxygen into the bloodstream where it can be delivered to the cells of the body. At the cells it enters the mitochondria where it combines with fats and carbohydrates to produce energy with carbon dioxide and water produced as waste products. This energy is used to produce muscular contractions, among other things.

Fats/carbohydrates + oxygen → energy + carbon dioxide and water

It is important to say that when the body produces more energy the amount of carbon dioxide increases in the body and it becomes dissolved in water to produce a weak acid. The body does not like the acidity of the blood to increase so the respiratory centre in the brain speeds up the rate of breathing to get rid of the excess carbon dioxide. Therefore, the breathing rate increases because carbon dioxide levels rise, rather than as a result of the cells demanding more oxygen.

Diffusion of gases

Gases will move around through a process of diffusion. Diffusion is how gases move in the open air. For example, if a person is wearing perfume it will diffuse around a room so that everyone can smell it. This is because the person is in an area of high concentration and the gas moves to areas of low concentration.

definition

> Diffusion: the movement of a gas from an area of high concentration to an area of low concentration.

In the respiratory system diffusion takes place in the lungs and the muscles.

- **Diffusion in the lungs** – in the lungs we have a high concentration of oxygen and in the muscles we have a high concentration of carbon dioxide, and they will diffuse across the semipermeable membrane. Oxygen is attracted into the blood by the haemoglobin, which is a protein in the red blood cells, and it attaches to this haemoglobin.
- **Diffusion in the muscles** – in the muscles we have a high concentration of carbon dioxide and a low concentration of oxygen due to the process of energy production. As a result the oxygen diffuses into the muscles and is attracted by the myoglobin in the muscles and the carbon dioxide diffuses into the bloodstream. It is then taken to the lungs to be breathed out.

Anatomy of the respiratory system

Figure 1.42 shows the respiratory system in which the following processes occur.

1 Air enters the body through the **mouth and nose**.

Table 1.03 Composition of inhaled and exhaled air

Inhaled air	Gas	Exhaled air
79.04%	Nitrogen	79%
20.93%	Oxygen	17%
0.03%	Carbon dioxide	4%

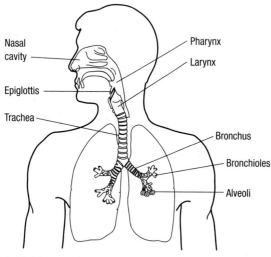

Nasal cavity

Pharynx

Larynx

Epiglottis

Trachea

Bronchus

Bronchioles

Alveoli

Fig 1.42 The respiratory system

2 It passes through the **pharynx**, which is the back of the throat area.

3 It then passes through the **larynx**, which is responsible for voice production.

4 Air passes over the **epiglottis**. The epiglottis closes over the trachea when we swallow food to stop the food going down 'the wrong way' into our trachea and down into our lungs.

5 The air enters the **trachea**, which is a membranous tube that delivers air to the lungs.

6 The trachea will divide into two **bronchi**, one into each lung.

7 The two main bronchi will divide into **bronchioles** which will further subdivide 23 times and result in 8 million terminal bronchioles in each lung.

8 Around the bronchioles you will find the groups of air sacs called **alveoli**. There are around 600 million alveoli in each lung and it is here that the exchange of gases (oxygen and carbon dioxide) occurs. Each alveolus is in contact with a capillary where the blood is present.

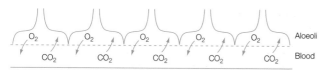

O_2 O_2 O_2 O_2 O_2 Aloeoli

CO_2 CO_2 CO_2 CO_2 CO_2 Blood

Fig 1.43 Exchange of gases in the alveoli and blood

Respiratory muscles

The respiratory system also includes two types of muscles which work to move air into and out of the lungs.

- The **diaphragm** is a large dome-shaped muscle which covers the bottom of the ribcage. At rest it is dome shaped but when contracted it flattens and pushes the two sides of the ribcage away from each other.
- The **intercostal** muscles attach between the ribs; when they contract they push the ribs up and out and increase the size of the chest cavity, drawing air in. If you put your hands on your ribs and breathe in you will feel your ribs push up and out; this is the action of the intercostal muscles.

LEARNER ACTIVITY

In groups of three work as follows.

- Person one explains the composition of air and why we need to breathe.
- Person two explains the seven structures that air passes through to reach the blood in the capillaries.
- Person three explains the process of diffusion.

Mechanisms of breathing

Breathing is the term given to inhaling air into the lungs and then exhaling air out. The process basically works on the principle of making the **thoracic cavity** (chest) larger, which decreases the pressure of air within the lungs. The surrounding air is then at a higher pressure, which means that air is forced into the lungs. Then the thoracic cavity is returned to its original size, which forces air out of the lungs.

Breathing in (inhalation)

At rest
The diaphragm contracts and moves downwards; this results in an increase in the size of the thoracic cavity and air is forced into the lungs.

Exercise
During exercise, the diaphragm and intercostal muscles contract, which makes the ribs move upwards and outwards, and results in more air being taken into the lungs.

Breathing out (exhalation)

At rest
The diaphragm relaxes and returns upwards to a domed position. The thoracic cavity gets smaller,

which results in an increase in air pressure within the lungs so air is breathed out of the lungs.

Exercise
During exercise, the intercostal muscles contract to help decrease the size of the thoracic cavity, which results in a more forcible breath out.

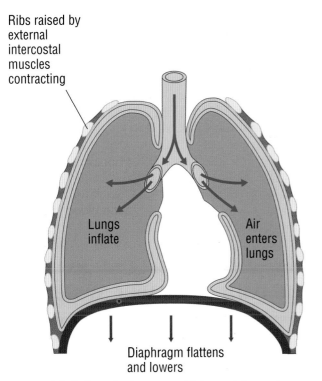

Ribs raised by external intercostal muscles contracting

Lungs inflate

Air enters lungs

Diaphragm flattens and lowers

Fig 1.44 Inhalation, diaphragm and intercostal muscles

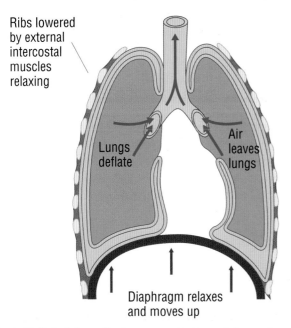

Ribs lowered by external intercostal muscles relaxing

Lungs deflate

Air leaves lungs

Diaphragm relaxes and moves up

Fig 1.45 Exhalation, diaphragm and intercostal muscles

Respiratory volumes

In order to assess an individual's lung function we use a spirometer. An example of the readings given by a spirometer is shown in Fig 1.46.

An individual will have a lung capacity of around 5 litres, which is about the amount of air in a basketball. It will be slightly lower for a female and slightly higher for a male, due to the differing sizes of the male and female ribcages.

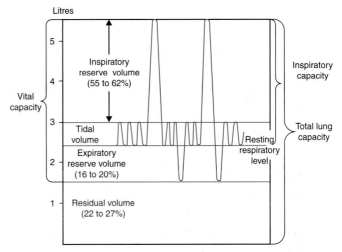

Fig 1.46 Lung volumes as shown on a spirometer trace

Tidal volume
This is the amount of air breathed in with each breath.

Inspiratory reserve volume
This is the amount of space that is available for air to be inhaled. If you breathe in and stop and then try to breathe in more this extra air inhaled is the inspiratory volume.

Expiratory reserve volume
This is the amount of air that could be exhaled after you have breathed out. If you exhale and then stop and try to exhale more the air that comes out is the expiratory reserve volume.

Vital capacity
This is the maximum amount of air that can be breathed in and out during one breath. It is the tidal volume plus the inspiratory reserve volume plus the expiratory reserve volume.

Residual volume

This is the amount of air left in the lungs after a full exhalation. Around 1 litre will always remain or else the lungs would deflate and breathing would stop.

Total lung volume

This is the vital capacity plus the residual volume, and measures the maximum amount of air that can be present in the lungs at any moment.

Breathing rate

This is the number of breaths taken per minute.

Respiratory volume

This is the amount of air that is moving through the lungs every minute:

Respiratory volume = breathing rate × tidal volume

For example, at rest a person may have a tidal volume of 0.5 litres per minute and a breathing rate of 12 breaths per minute. But during exercise both of these will rise and at high intensities tidal volume may rise to 3 litres per minute and breathing rate to 35 breaths per minute.

At rest respiratory volume:

> 0.5 litres × 12 = 6 litres/minute

During exercise respiratory volume:

> 3 litres × 35 = 105 litres/minute

Effects of exercise on the respiratory system

In the short term, exercise will have the following effects on the respiratory system:

- increase in breathing rate
- increase in tidal volume
- increase in respiratory volume.

In the long term, exercise will have the following effects on the respiratory system:

- increased strength of the respiratory muscles
- decrease in breathing rate
- increase in tidal volume
- increase in vital capacity
- decrease in residual volume.

The lungs do not actually get larger; however, as the respiratory muscles become stronger and more effective they will increase the efficiency of the respiratory system.

LEARNER ACTIVITY

1 Count your breathing rate at rest for one minute.
2 Take part in one minute of aerobic exercise and count your breathing rate again.
3 Explain why there is a difference between the two breathing rates.

Key learning points

- Air travels into the body through the mouth and nose, down the trachea and into the bronchus. It then passes into the bronchioles and down into the alveoli. In the alveoli gaseous exchange takes place, which takes oxygen into the body and passes carbon dioxide out of the body.
- The diaphragm and intercostal muscles contract to allow you to breathe in and out.

The cardiovascular system

The cardiovascular system is made up of three parts:

- heart
- blood vessels
- blood.

The heart is a muscular pump that pumps the liquid, which is blood, through the pipes, which are the blood vessels.

The cardiovascular system is responsible for the following actions:

- delivering oxygen and nutrients to every part of the body
- carrying hormones to different parts of the body
- removing the waste products of energy production such as carbon dioxide and lactic acid
- maintaining body temperature by re-directing blood to the surface of the skin to dissipate heat.

Structure of the heart

The heart is a large muscular pump which is made up of thick walls. The heart muscle is called the myocardium and is divided into two halves which are separated by the septum. The right-hand side of the heart is responsible for pumping deoxygenated blood to the lungs and the left-hand side pumps oxygenated blood around the body. Each side of the heart consists of two connected chambers. Each side will have an atrium and a ventricle. The top chambers – the atria (plural of atrium) – are where the blood collects when it enters the heart. (Atrium is Latin for 'hall' and is where visitors used to wait before being accepted into a villa.) The lower chambers are called the ventricles and are the large pumps which send the blood up to the lungs or around the body. Once the blood has entered the heart from the veins it will be sucked into the ventricles as they relax and there follows powerful contraction of the ventricles. The left ventricle is the largest and most muscular because it has to send the blood to the furthest destinations and thus has to produce the most pressure.

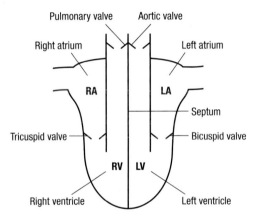

Fig 1.47 The heart

Blood flow through the heart

Blood flows through the heart and around the body in one direction. This one-way 'street' is maintained due to special valves placed within the heart and within the blood vessels leading from the heart.

The heart is sometimes called a 'double pump' because the right-hand side of the heart pumps blood to the lungs and the left-hand side of the heart pumps blood to the body.

Right-hand side

1 When the heart is relaxed, deoxygenated blood from the body enters the heart via the **vena cavae**.
2 Blood enters the right atrium.
3 The right atrium contracts and pushes blood down through the **tricuspid** valve and into the right ventricle.
4 The right ventricle contracts, the tricuspid valve closes, and blood is pushed up and out of the heart

through the **semilunar** valve and into the **pulmonary artery** which takes the blood to the lungs.
5 The heart relaxes and the semilunar valves close to prevent blood flowing back into the heart.
6 The blood flows to the lungs where it becomes oxygenated and ready to be returned to the heart for distribution around the body.

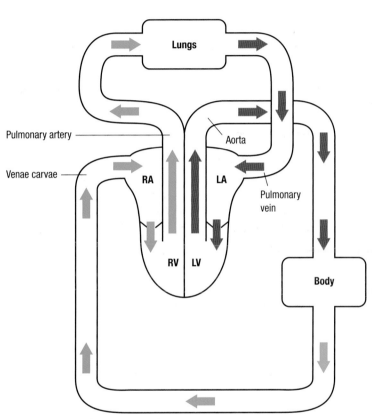

Fig 1.48 Blood flow through heart

Left-hand side

1 When the heart is relaxed, oxygenated blood from the lungs enters via the **pulmonary vein**.
2 Blood enters the **left atria**.
3 The left atria contracts and pushes blood down through the **bicuspid** valve and into the left ventricle.
4 The left ventricle contracts; the bicuspid valve closes to prevent blood flowing back into the heart. Blood is then pushed up and out of the heart through the **semilunar** valve and into the **aorta**, which is the large artery leaving the heart, taking blood to the rest of the body.
5 The heart relaxes and the semilunar valves close to prevent blood flowing back into the heart.

Terminology

Resting heart rate

The resting heart rate (RHR) is the number of beats the heart will take at rest. It is measured in beats per minute (bpm).

Stroke volume

Stroke volume is the amount of blood leaving the heart with each beat. It is measured in millilitres.

Cardiac output

Cardiac output is the amount of blood leaving the heart each minute and is measured in litres/minute. It depends upon heart rate and stroke volume:

Cardiac output = stroke volume × heart rate

LEARNER ACTIVITY

Working in groups of three each student explains to the others one of the following:

- the functions of the cardiovascular system
- the flow of blood through the right side of the heart
- the flow of blood through the left side of the heart.

Function of the heart

The cells of the body need a steady and constant supply of oxygen. Blood is responsible for carrying and delivering oxygen to all the body's cells, and this blood is pumped around the body and to the lungs by the heart. The left-hand side of your heart pumps the oxygenated blood to the cells of the muscles, brain, kidneys, liver and all the other organs. The cells then take the oxygen out of the blood and use it to produce energy. This is called metabolism and it produces waste products, such as carbon dioxide. The deoxygenated blood then continues its journey back to the heart, enters the right-hand side and is pumped out of the right ventricle to the lungs. At the lungs, the blood becomes oxygenated and the waste product carbon dioxide is 'unloaded' and breathed out.

Blood vessels

In order to make its journey around the body, blood is carried through five different types of blood vessels:

- arteries
- arterioles
- capillaries
- venules
- veins.

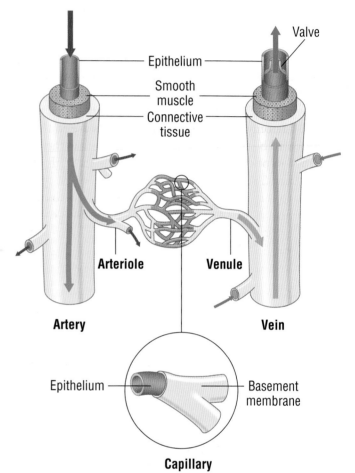

Fig 1.49 The five linked blood vessels

Arteries and arterioles

Arteries are the large blood vessels which leave the heart. They have thick, muscular walls which contract and relax to send blood to all parts of the body. The main artery leaving the heart is the aorta and it quickly splits up into smaller vessels which are called the arterioles. Arterioles mean 'little arteries'. Artery walls contain elastic cartilage and smooth muscle. This flexible wall allows the vessels to expand and contract, which helps to push the blood along the length of the arteries. This action is called peristalsis and is how smooth muscle contracts.

Arteries do not contain any valves as they are not required and they predominantly carry oxygenated blood. The exception to this is the pulmonary artery which carries deoxygenated blood away from the heart.

- Arteries carry blood away from the heart.
- Arteries have thick, muscular walls.
- Arteries carry predominantly oxygenated blood.
- Arterioles are the small branches of arteries.

Capillaries

Once the arteries and arterioles have divided, they will eventually feed blood into the smallest blood vessels, called capillaries. These are found in all parts of the body, especially the muscles, and are so tiny that their walls are only one cell thick. As the walls are so thin there will be tiny spaces in them which allow the diffusion of oxygen and other nutrients through the cell walls. The blood flows very slowly through the capillaries to allow for this process. In the capillaries the blood will also pick up the waste products of metabolism: carbon dioxide and lactic acid. There are more capillaries than any other type of blood vessel in the body.

- Capillaries are tiny blood vessels one cell thick.
- Small spaces in the thin walls of capillaries allow for diffusion.
- Oxygen and nutrients will diffuse into the cells.
- Carbon dioxide and lactic acid will flow from the cells into the capillaries.

Veins and venules

The capillaries will eventually feed back into larger blood vessels called venules, which are the smallest veins, and they eventually become veins. These veins are thinner and less muscular than arteries and they carry blood back to the heart. They also contain smooth muscle and contract to send the blood back to the heart. The veins are generally acting against gravity so they contain non-return valves to prevent the blood flowing back once the smooth muscle has relaxed. These valves prevent the pooling of blood in the lower limbs. Veins will predominantly carry deoxygenated blood, with the exception of the pulmonary vein, which carries oxygenated blood to the heart from the lungs.

- Veins always take blood towards the heart.
- Veins have thin, muscular walls.
- Veins have non-return valves to prevent backflow.
- Veins predominantly carry deoxygenated blood.
- Venules are the smaller branches which feed into veins.

Blood

Blood is the medium in which all the cells are carried to transport nutrients and oxygen to the cells of the body. Among other things, blood will transport the following: oxygen, glucose, proteins, fats, vitamins, hormones, enzymes, platelets, carbon dioxide and electrolytes.

Blood is made up of four components:

- red blood cells
- white blood cells
- platelets
- plasma.

Blood can be described as a thick, gloopy substance due to the high concentration of solids it carries. Blood is made up of 55 per cent plasma and 45 per cent solids, which is a very high concentration.

Red blood cells

Of the blood cells in the body around 99 per cent of them are red blood cells or erythrocytes. They are red in colour due to the presence of a red-coloured protein called haemoglobin. Haemoglobin has a massive attraction for oxygen and thus the main role of the red blood cells is to take on and transport oxygen to the cells. There are many millions of red blood cells in the body; for example, there are 5 million red blood cells for 1 mm^3 volume of blood.

White blood cells

White blood cells are colourless or transparent and are far fewer in number (1:700 ratio of white to red blood cells). The role of white blood cells, or leucocytes, is to fight infection; they are part of the body's immune system. They destroy bacteria and other dangerous organisms and thus remove disease from the body.

Platelets

Platelets are not full cells but rather parts of cells; they act by stopping blood loss through clotting. They become sticky when in contact with the air to form the initial stage of repair to damaged tissue. Platelets also need a substance called factor 8 to enable them to clot. A haemophiliac is a person whose blood does not clot; this is not because they are short of platelets but rather factor 8, which enables the platelets to become active.

Plasma

Plasma is the liquid part of the blood, which is straw-coloured in appearance. It is the solution in which all the solids are carried.

Effects of exercise on the cardiovascular system

In the short term when you start to train, your cardiovascular system will start to respond immediately and after about ten minutes you will notice the following have happened:

- increased heart rate
- increased stroke volume
- increased cardiac output
- redistribution of blood to the working muscles and away from other organs
- blood vessels in the skin start to dilate
- increased blood pressure.

If we take part in regular aerobic endurance exercise (which means the exercise session should last for at least 20 minutes and we should take part in it three to five times a week), after about two to three months you will notice the following changes:

- decreased heart rate at rest
- increased stroke volume
- heart muscle becomes larger (cardiac hypertrophy)
- fall in blood pressure
- increased red blood cell count
- increased size of blood vessels
- increased blood volume.

LEARNER ACTIVITY

List five sports performers who you think would have low resting heart rates; explain your answer.

Key learning points

- The heart has four chambers, two atria and two ventricles.
- The ventricles pump blood to the body and lungs.
- Valves in the heart make sure blood flows in one direction.
- Blood travels through five different types of blood vessels, arteries, arterioles, capillaries, venules and veins.
- The heart adapts to aerobic training by becoming bigger and stronger.

Energy systems

The body needs a steady supply of energy to enable it to perform the functions it needs to stay alive:

- muscular contractions and movement
- circulation
- transmission of nerve impulses
- digestion of foods
- repairing and replacing tissue.

ATP

The only form of energy that the body can use is called ATP, or adenosine triphosphate. In the muscles ATP will provide the energy to enable the muscle fibres to shorten and develop tension. As long as there is a supply of ATP then the muscles will be able to contract. To supply this energy the body has three different energy systems:

- creatine phosphate system
- lactic acid system
- aerobic system.

ATP is produced by breaking down the foods that we eat in our diet. The food types which contain energy in the form of kilocalories (kcals) are:

- carbohydrate   1 g gives 4 kcals
- fat   1 g gives 9 kcals
- protein   1 g gives 4 kcals

ATP is a high-energy compound made up of one adenosine molecule attached to three phosphate molecules. These molecules are bound together by high-energy bonds.

The adenosine and phosphate molecules do not contain any energy; the energy is stored in the high-energy bonds and therefore to liberate energy we need

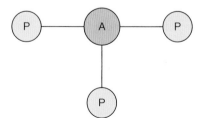

Fig 1.50 ATP

to break down the bonds attaching the molecules. To break one of the bonds we need an enzyme called ATPase. When ATP has been broken down we are left with a second compound called adenosine di phosphate (ADP). A loose phosphate will also be created by the reaction.

Unfortunately, we have very limited stores of ATP in the muscles and ADP cannot be broken down any further. To allow further production of energy we need to remake or resynthesise ATP. We have the ingredients in ADP and the spare phosphate, and what is needed is energy to reattach the phosphate to the ADP. It is the three-energy system which provides the energy for this reaction to happen.

Creatine phosphate system

If energy is needed for an activity of high intensity and low duration, such as 100 m sprinting or jumping in basketball, it will be needed very rapidly to produce a muscular contraction. The cells contain a small amount of ATP (about 3 seconds' worth) and a small amount of a second high-energy compound called creatine phosphate (CP). There is enough CP to provide a further 5 to 7 seconds' worth of energy. The CP will be broken down to provide the energy to resynthesise the ATP.

This system will last until the stored CP has run out. Along with breaking down the stores of ATP in the muscles this system will last for around 8 to 10 seconds and is used for high-intensity activities.

Lactic acid system

When stores of ATP and PC have run out, the body has a second way of providing energy quickly. This is used when activity is intense and lasts around 1 to 3 minutes. This system relies upon the breakdown of glucose which has been stored in the muscles (this is called glycogen). Energy for muscular contraction is still needed rapidly and the body does not have time to deliver oxygen to the working muscles; therefore, the glucose has to be broken down without oxygen. This is called anaerobic (absence of oxygen) and is referred to as anaerobic glycolysis.

As glucose is broken down in the muscles to provide the energy to resynthesise ATP, a by-product, lactic acid, is produced. This lactic acid can produce a burning, uncomfortable feeling in the muscles and limit performance. In reality the glucose is first broken down into pyruvic acid and then into lactic acid. This process will produce 3 ATP per glucose molecule.

Glucose → Pyruvic acid   no oxygen → Energy + Lactic acid

Aerobic system

This system differs from the other two because it requires oxygen to break down glucose or fat and produce energy for the resynthesis of ATP. It will be used when the intensity of an activity is lower and the duration longer. It tends to be used during rhythmical, repetitive activities such as long-distance running, cycling and swimming.

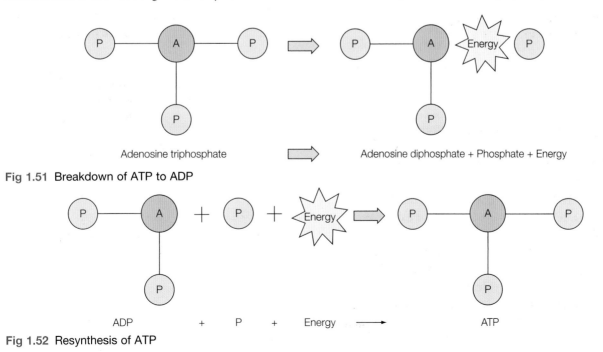

Adenosine triphosphate ⟹ Adenosine diphosphate + Phosphate + Energy

Fig 1.51 Breakdown of ATP to ADP

ADP + P + Energy ⟶ ATP

Fig 1.52 Resynthesis of ATP

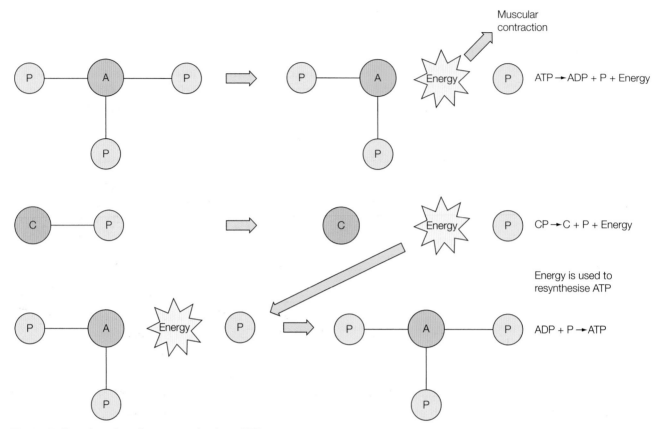

Fig 1.53 Creatine phosphate resynthesises ATP

The aerobic system will produce carbon dioxide, water and heat as waste products of the aerobic breakdown of glucose and fats. Carbon dioxide is breathed out with some of the water which can also be lost as sweat when the heat is dissipated from the body.

The aerobic system can produce energy by breaking down glucose (from carbohydrates) or fat. Fat is a much richer store of energy for ATP resynthesis but can be used only in low-intensity exercise because it is a lengthy process. At the higher intensities fuel is needed more quickly and glucose will be used to provide this energy.

The fuel used also depends upon the fitness of the individual because fitter people become more effective at burning fats. The result of this is that their glycogen stores will go further and last longer. For example, Paula Radcliffe can run a marathon without any discernible loss of performance towards the end of the race.

The aerobic system provides the most plentiful supply of oxygen in that if 1 molecule of glycogen is broken down aerobically it will provide 38 ATP; while 1 molecule of fat will provide 128 ATP.

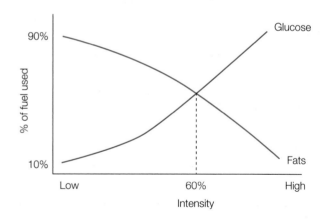

Fig 1.54 Fuel used for the aerobic system depends upon the intensity of the activity

Application to sport

Different sports will utilise different energy systems depending upon the demands of the sport and the speed at which energy is required (see Table 1.04 and the continuum opposite).

The sports of football and tennis may appear to use the aerobic system because they last for a long time; however, they predominantly use the anaerobic system due to the fact that they involve bursts of energy followed by periods of recovery, rather than consistent movement.

Anaerobic   **Aerobic**

Creatine phosphate   Lactic acid   Oxygen

Weight lifting	Tennis	800 m run	1500 m run	Marathon
100 m run	Football	200 m swim	400 m swim	Skating 10 k
Shot-put	Rugby	Boxing		50 k walk
Golf swing	400 m run			50 k cycle

Fig 1.55 Energy continuum

Table 1.04 Summary of energy systems

Criteria	Creatine phosphate	Lactic acid	Aerobic
Speed of energy production	Very fast	Fast	Slow
Energy source	Creatine phosphate	Glycogen	Glycogen and fat
Amount of ATP produced	Very limited	Limited	Unlimited
Production of waste products	None	Lactic acid is produced as a by-product	Carbon dioxide and water which are eliminated
Duration of energy production	8–10 seconds	1–3 minutes	Up to 2 hours
Intensity used as % of maximum intensity	High intensity (95–100%)	Moderate to high intensity (60–95%)	Low intensity (<60%)
Length of time to recover	30 seconds to 4 minutes	20 minutes to 2 hours	Time to rest and replace glycogen stores

Review questions

1. What is the purpose of the skeleton?
2. Why do we have joints?
3. Examine the skeletal and muscular systems and then describe how our body is able to move.
4. Explain how our heart and lungs work together to supply our muscles with oxygen.
5. Draw a diagram to show how blood travels around the body and to the lungs. Include the blood vessels and a labelled heart.
6. Explain why taking part in exercise is good for your skeleton, your muscular system, your respiratory system and your circulatory system.
7. Think of your favourite sport, then describe how your skeletal system, muscular system, cardiovascular system, respiratory system and energy systems work together to allow you to take part in this activity.

References

Beashel, P. and Taylor, J. (1996) *Advanced Studies in Physical Education and Sport,* Nelson.

Bursztyn, P. G. (1997) *Physiology for Sportspeople: A Serious User's Guide to the Body,* Manchester University Press.

Kapit, W. and Elson, L. (2001) *The Anatomy Coloring Book,* Benjamin Cummings.

Stafford-Brown, J., Rea, S. and Chance, J. (2003) *BTEC National in Sport and Exercise Science,* Hodder Arnold.

Stafford-Brown, J., Rea, S., Janaway, L. and Manley, C. (2006) *BTEC First Sport,* Hodder Arnold.

Wesson, K. Wiggins-James, N., Thompson, G. and Hartigan, S. (2005) *Sport and PE: A Complete Guide to Advanced Level Study,* Hodder Arnold.

Goals

By the end of this chapter you should:

- know the key factors that influence health and safety in sport
- be able to carry out risk assessments
- know how to maintain the safety of participants and colleagues in a sports environment
- be able to plan a safe sporting activity.

Safety is a very important factor to consider when taking part in sports or leading sporting events. If sports leaders fail to ensure that health and safety guidelines are adhered to this could result in a charge of 'negligence' being brought against them through the civil courts. It is therefore important that learners understand the legislative factors, regulations and legal responsibilities involved while working in sporting situations.

This chapter will cover ways in which a sports leader can plan and carry out a sporting activity safely under the overall supervision of a more experienced person. It includes how to carry out risk assessments, preparation of the site and participants for the activity, and maintaining the safety of participants while taking part in the activity. The chapter closes with ideas on how to plan a safe sporting activity.

Key factors that influence health and safety in sport

Legislative factors

> **Legislation:** a generic term for laws, which includes acts, regulations, orders and directives.
> **Directive:** legislative acts passed by the European Union that its member states must adhere to.

A number of laws and acts have been devised in order to try to ensure all safety precautions are taken into account while at work and during sports participation. Any person who works should be aware of these acts and be sure they do everything possible to adhere to the legislation.

The Health and Safety at Work Act 1974

The Health and Safety at Work Act became law in 1974 in response to thousands of accidents and near misses in the workplace. Its purpose is to ensure that employers take reasonable steps to ensure the health, safety and welfare of their employees while they are at work. These steps include:

- making sure the working environment and equipment are up to the necessary standard
- ensuring regular and appropriate safety checks are carried out
- ensuring safe use, handling and storage of equipment and substances
- providing information, training and supervision to ensure employees can do their job safely
- regular monitoring of the working environment to ensure it is hygienic and that no toxic contaminants are present.

The Health and Safety at Work Act also requires the employee to take reasonable steps to ensure their own safety. They are expected to cooperate with the employer to meet legal obligations and use the equipment provided appropriately.

Both the employer and employee benefit from this act because:

- fewer accidents equals better health for the employees
- fewer accidents equals more regular earning for the employee
- less sickness equals money saved by the employer and the NHS.

The majority of accidents caused in the workplace are due to the following actions and circumstances:

- lifting and carrying
- slips, trips and falls
- being hit by moving objects or vehicles
- moving machinery
- harmful substances.

Some illness and diseases can be work-related, for example occupational deafness, back pain and stress.

The following three factors can affect health and safety in the work place.

1 **Occupational factors** – people may be at risk from injuries or illnesses because of the work they do.
2 **Environmental factors** – the conditions in which people work may cause problems.
3 **Human factors** – poor attitudes and behaviour can contribute to accidents.

It is the responsibility of both the employer and employees to ensure that health and safety is maintained.

After the Health and Safety at Work Act was passed in 1974, 'RIDDOR' was added in 1995. RIDDOR stands for the Reporting of Injuries, Diseases and Dangerous Occurrences Regulations, which came into force on 1 April 1996. It means that all work-related accidents, diseases and dangerous occurrences should be reported to the Incident Contact Centre (ICC). These include:

- deaths
- major injuries
- over-three-day injuries
- injuries to members of the public where they are taken to hospital
- work-related diseases
- dangerous occurrences – where something happens that does not result in a reportable injury but which could have done.

Personal Protective Equipment Regulations 2002

Personal protective equipment should be used when a hazard cannot be sufficiently controlled by other health and safety measures.

definition

Personal protective equipment (PPE): clothes and other items worn to protect the wearer against hazards.

A range of PPE exists to protect various parts of the body, for example goggles for the eyes, a helmet for the head, ear plugs for the ears, etc.

LEARNER ACTIVITY

1 Think of PPE for the following body parts that you have used or may use for a range of sporting activities:

- head
- eyes
- lower leg
- feet
- hands.

2 Name the piece of PPE, the sport and how a person might be harmed if they did not wear this piece of equipment.

Control of Substances Hazardous to Health Regulations (COSHH) 2002

Hazardous substances can cause a wide range of health problems, e.g. dermatitis and asthma; they may also cause other problems, e.g. explosions or fires.

definition

Hazardous substance: any material or substance with the potential to cause illness or injury to the people who come into contact with it.

In the sports industry you may be exposed to a range of hazardous substances, such as cleaning fluids or chlorine which is used in swimming pools. All hazardous substances should have labels that detail the nature of the hazardous substance, e.g. corrosive, irritant, poison.

You must ensure that you have been trained in how to use the equipment properly and that you wear the appropriate PPE when dealing with these substances. All hazardous substances should be kept in a locked cabinet.

Manual Handling Operations Regulations 1992

definition

Manual handling: using the body to lift, carry, push or pull a load.

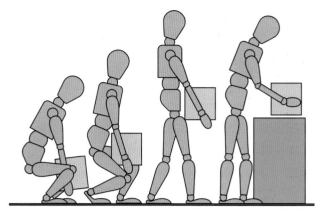

Fig 2.01 Manual handling guide

In the sports industry you will probably find yourself having to lift, move and set up sporting equipment. Therefore it is important that you learn safe lifting techniques and how to lift each item safely. Maintaining a straight back at all times is the proper way to lift items, as shown in Figure 2.01. Typical injuries from incorrect manual handling are back sprains and strains, cuts, bruises, crushing, fractures, hernias and trapped nerves.

Health and Safety (First Aid) Regulations 1981

These regulations require companies and organisations to have sufficient first-aid facilities and equipment in case of illness or injury to employees. The number of qualified first aiders will be related to the number of employees working in the organisation.

The Fire Safety and Safety of Places of Sport Act 1987

This act was drawn up after the Bradford City football ground fire tragedy in 1985. It requires that all sports arenas and stadiums have sufficient means of escape in the event of a fire. Venues must also provide adequate equipment for fighting fire.

The Adventure Activities Licensing Authority (AALA)

The Adventure Activities Licensing Authority was founded in 1996 and is an independent, government-funded organisation that is responsible for inspecting activity centres and other outdoor and adventurous activity providers on behalf of the Department for Education and Skills (DfES).

If the Adventure Activities Licensing Authority is satisfied that the provider meets nationally accepted standards of good practice, then it will issue a licence. This helps provide the public with assurances that the activities are not exposing the participants to unnecessary danger or risks of injury.

Fig 2.02 Health and Safety legislation

Despite all of this legislation, there are still fatalities in the workplace: in 2005–6, 220 workers were killed and 361 members of the public fatally injured. This should remind you to remain vigilant in maintaining your own and your co-workers' health and safety while at work.

LEARNER ACTIVITY

Select a health and safety act of your choice. Design a piece of promotional material that could be used in a place of work to remind employees to be vigilant about your chosen piece of health and safely legislation.

Safety signs

There are four types of safety sign (see Fig 2.03). Each type has a certain shape, colour and meaning.

LEARNER ACTIVITY

Walk around your place of learning and your sports facility. Try to find at least two of each of the types of signs shown in Fig 2.03.

● Draw each.
● Explain what they mean.
● State the location of each sign.

Legal factors

The court system within Britain has a structure that all legal cases have to pass through. There are a range of courts that deal with different types of charges.

● **Magistrates Court** – this is the lowest court in England and deals mainly with minor criminal matters.
● **Crown Court** – this deals with serious criminal charges, such as murders, with a judge and jury.
● **House of Lords** – this is the highest court in England and deals with appeals on important issues from the Court of Appeal.
● **European Court of Justice** – this is the supreme law court in Europe. The decisions of this court have to be enforced by all member states.

Prohibition
These signs tell you what you are not allowed to do, e.g. No smoking
Shape: Circular
Colour: White with red border and red crossbar running from top left to bottom right

Warning
These signs warn you of a danger
Shape: Triangular
Colour: Yellow with black border and letters

Mandatory
These signs tell you what you *must* do, e.g. wear ear protectors
Shape: Circular
Colour: Blue background with white symbol and letters

Warning
These signs tell you about safe areas or equipment, e.g. fire exit
Shape: Square or oblong
Colour: Green background with white symbol and letters

Fig 2.03 Safety signs

Statutory law

This is a written law set down by a governing authority. Any person breaking these laws is liable to be arrested by the police and prosecuted accordingly.

Civil law

Civil law deals with the rights of private citizens and does not involve the police. An example of civil law would be when a person is suing a company or an individual for some form of negligence. Another example of civil law is when a partner in a marriage wishes to divorce the other person.

If a company does not abide by the Health and Safety at Work Act and a person is injured as a result of this negligence, the company can be prosecuted because it has broken a statutory law. Also, the employee who is injured can take out a civil case and sue the company for compensation.

Case law

Case law is when a similar case has previously occurred which then results in the guilty party being prosecuted and/or sued in a similar manner to the previous case.

In loco parentis

In loco parentis basically means 'in place of the parent'. This means that a person or organisation has to take on the functions and responsibilities of a parent. An example of this would be a teacher supervising a student on a school trip. The teacher has overall responsibility for the child's health and safety. A person taking on a role in loco parentis is expected to apply the same standard of care as would a 'reasonable parent' acting within a range of reasonable responses.

Negligence

Negligence is the name given to a situation in which a person in a supervisory role basically fails to meet a 'standard' of care. The supervisor may be careless in their actions or lack of actions, such as not carrying out a full risk assessment which then resulted in a person taking part in the activity suffering from an injury or even death.

If a person is deemed to be negligent they may be held liable for any injuries or damages to the people involved.

Regulatory bodies

A number of regulatory bodies have been set up to help 'police' employers and facilities so that they adhere to appropriate legislation. The Health and Safety Commission is in charge of health and safety regulation in the UK. The Health and Safety Executive and local authorities are responsible for enforcing these regulations. Staff from these organisations will inspect facilities and speak to staff to ensure the facility is being run appropriately. If the facility is not being run in accordance with

legislation, it will be given actions to address within a set time period, or the facility may even be closed down until it is able to show that it meets health and safety guidelines.

Key learning points

- A range of laws is in place in order to protect the employee and employer in the workplace; these include: Health and Safety at Work Act, Personal Protective Equipment Regulations, Control of Substances Hazardous to Health Regulations, Health and Safety (First Aid) Regulations, Manual Handling Operations Regulations, Fire Safety and Safety of Places of Sport Act, Adventure Activities Licensing Authority.
- Statutory law is where a person is prosecuted, and involves the police.
- Civil law does not involve the police.
- Case law is where a case in the past is referred to.
- The Health and Safety Executive enforces regulations in the workplace.

Risk assessment

Risk assessment is a technique for preventing accidents and ill health by helping people to think about what could go wrong and ways to prevent problems. Risk assessment is good practice and it is also a legal requirement. It often enables organisations to reduce the costs associated with accidents and ill health, and to decide their priorities, highlight training needs and assist with quality assurance programmes. A risk assessment is usually performed by the manager or instructors working in the sports centre. It allows people to take time to consider what could go wrong while taking part in their activity. The risk assessment examines the possible hazards that may occur, the risks involved, the likelihood of them happening and how the hazards could be prevented.

Risk assessments should be logged, kept and reviewed regularly to see if they are up to date and to ensure that any of the details have not changed.

Hazard

> Hazard: a potential source of danger.

A hazard is anything with the potential to cause harm. A range of hazards can be found in any workplace. Examples include:

- fire
- electricity
- harmful substances
- damaged/wet flooring
- unfastened shoelaces
- jewellery worn during sports participation
- water in a swimming pool.

Risk

> Risk: this is the possibility of something bad happening.

A risk is linked to the chance of somebody being harmed by the potential hazard. Risks are often categorised into how likely they are to happen. Something that is a low risk means that the likelihood of it happening is low, whereas something that is high risk means that it is likely to happen. Examples of risks include:

- slipping on a wet floor and twisting your ankle
- drowning in a swimming pool
- tripping over your shoelaces and cutting your knee
- your earring catching on clothing or an opponent's hand and ripping your ear.

LEARNER ACTIVITY

Make a list of three sporting activities. Try to determine at least five hazards and five risks you may encounter while taking part in each.

Undertaking a risk assessment

Once you have highlighted the hazard, the easiest way to assess the potential problems that may arise is to use the following formula:

Likelihood $\times$ Severity
Likelihood – is it likely to happen:

1 unlikely
2 quite likely
3 very likely.

Severity – how badly someone could be injured:

1 no injury/minor incident
2 injury requiring medical assistance
3 major injury or fatality.

For example, Table 2.01 attempts to assess the risk of capsizing in a kayak.

By multiplying the likelihood against the severity you will be able to draw up a chart that looks at the potential problems and make a decision on whether you want to take the risk or not (see Table 2.02).

In the example in Table 2.01, the likelihood times the severity is $2 \times 1 = 2$.

Control measures

Hazards in the workplace should be removed whenever possible. Sometimes, however, there is no alternative but to keep a hazard. In such cases, it is important to reduce the risk – the likelihood of an accident – by introducing appropriate control measures. If some flooring is wet or damaged, for

Table 2.01 Capsizing in a kayak

Likelihood of happening	Severity
2 Quite likely	1 No injury

Table 2.02 Is the risk worth taking?

Likelihood × Severity	Is the risk worth taking?
1	Yes, with caution
2	Yes, possibly with caution
3	Yes, possibly with extreme caution
4	Possibly, but with extreme caution
5 or above	No

example, this could include placing a barrier around the damage or putting up warning signs.

Other control measures could include participants wearing/using specialist protective clothing and/or equipment to help minimise the risk of injury.

Fig 2.04 Protective clothing worn for playing cricket

LEARNER ACTIVITY

Choose three of your favourite sporting activities. Make a list of all the safety equipment you need in order to reduce the risk of injury.

The risk assessment process

1 Identify area to be assessed, e.g. resistance equipment in the gym.
2 List the hazards that you can identify, e.g. free weights incorrectly stored, wet floor.
3 Identify the risks and the people who are at risk from the hazards listed, e.g. first-time users, inexperienced users.
4 Assess the likelihood of an accident happening. For example, if a person comes to the gym for the first time to use free weights, what is the likelihood that they may suffer from a lower back injury through an incorrect lifting technique? Give the likelihood of this risk happening of between 1 and 3.
5 How severe will the outcome of the accident be, 1–3?
6 Work out the level of risk.
7 Is the risk worth taking? Look at what control measures can be put in place to reduce the risk of injury, e.g. ensure all gym users are given an induction prior to using the equipment.

LEARNER ACTIVITY

Copy and complete the risk assessment form on page 8 for a sports activity of your choice.

Example of a risk assessment form

Location of risk assessment:
Risk assessor's name:
Date:

Hazard	People at risk	Likelihood	Severity	Level of risk	Control measures

Key learning points

- A hazard is something that has the potential to cause injury or compromise safety.
- A risk is the likelihood of something unpleasant happening.
- A risk assessment is a list of possible hazards that states the likelihood of them happening, and ways of controlling them.
- Level of risk is worked out by multiplying likelihood of risk by severity. A risk level of five or more means that either more safety precautions should be introduced or the activity should not take place.

Maintaining the safety of participants and colleagues in a sports environment

The general manager and his team of managers of a sport or leisure facility are responsible for running a safe and secure environment. They will ensure every member of staff receives training on how the facility operates, and two manuals that provide information on how every part of the facility should operate under normal conditions and also what to do in an emergency situation – usually referred to as 'Normal Operating Procedures' (NOP) and 'Emergency Operating Procedures' (EOP).

The NOP give instructions on how to deal with everyday situations, whereas the EOP give instructions on how to deal with minor and major emergency situations such as disorderly behaviour from customers or dealing with a drowning incident.

Normal Operating Procedures (NOP)

This document contains details of all the services the leisure facility provides, e.g. swimming pool dimensions, squash courts and their dimensions, and is specific to that individual facility.

The manual will indicate any potential risk factors and hazards that staff should be aware of, some of which may include:

- **known hazards** – e.g. unruly behaviour by the customer, customers with prior health problems, misuse of equipment
- **pool hazards** – e.g. slippery pool side, diving in shallow water, blind spots in the pool
- **customers at risk** – e.g. weak swimmers, elderly customers, customers under the influence of alcohol or drugs.

There follow instructions on how to carry out risk assessments so that these hazards and risks can be minimised.

Methods of dealing with the public will be included in the manual, which incorporates forms of communication and rules and regulations the customers must adhere to; an example of this is the pool-side rules – no running on the pool side, no pushing, no ducking, etc.

Staff duties and responsibilities are also covered. The manual will contain details of what is expected from them, e.g. they should wear the uniform provided, lifeguards must always carry a whistle, they must never leave a pool area unattended. There are usually details of staff training requirements too, e.g. a lifeguard will usually be required to attend training sessions at least once a month so that their skills are up to date and have been practised recently.

Details of staffing requirements for a range of situations are usually included within this document, examples of these include the number of lifeguards required on pool side in relation to the number of swimmers (the more swimmers there are, the more lifeguards there need to be on duty), supervision of diving, etc.

Pool, sports hall and changing room hygiene is also an area that should be covered in this document, which gives instructions on how to carry out everyday cleaning duties. Details of first-aid supplies and how to locate a first aider will also be in this document.

All leisure facilities will have some form of alarm system to summon help or warn people of a fire; the NOP will contain details of where these alarms are located and how to use them.

Emergency Operating Procedures (EOP)

This manual details how staff should respond to a range of emergency situations. It will give details on how staff should respond if they were to encounter any of the situations listed below:

- fire
- customer suffering from a minor injury (e.g. grazed knee)
- customer suffering from a major injury (e.g. knocked unconscious with a head injury)
- how to deal with a drowning incident
- bomb threat
- emission of a toxic gas
- structural failure
- spinal injury
- how to deal with blood, vomit and faeces.

Staff training

Most centres will ensure their staff are up to date with their role requirements and their qualifications are up to date by either running in-house training events or

paying for their staff to attend relevant training events. Pool lifeguards will often be expected to attend weekly training events to ensure they are able to carry out all the different rescue techniques. In most centres all staff will be expected to have a basic first-aid award, and again be expected to attend regular training events to ensure their first-aid skills are up to date. Staff meetings are often held on a weekly basis to update staff on any centre changes or staffing changes, etc.

Checking facilities

There should be regular inspections to ensure the facility is functioning as it should be; these checks may be required on a regular basis throughout the day, or some may need to be performed at the start and end of the day. For example, examining the changing facilities to ensure they are clean and tidy and testing the swimming pool water to assess the chlorine levels should be carried out once every few hours; however, checking all the lights are working inside and outside the building only really needs to be carried out once or twice a day.

All sports and leisure facilities have regular inspections from various authorities to ensure that the organisation is maintaining a high level of health

Fig 2.05 A person from the fire department checking equipment

and safety. For example, the fire department will check such things as the number and functioning of fire extinguishers and that the fire exits are easily accessible.

Equipment should be checked regularly; although there is not a legal requirement to inspect the equipment, a centre could be prosecuted if there was an accident due to faulty equipment. A typical pro forma for checking equipment should have the following headings:

- name of equipment
- when checked
- name of person checking equipment
- any action taken
- signature of the inspector
- results of check.

Key learning points

- All staff have a job specification to work to, and must follow normal procedures and emergency procedures as documented in their work handbook.
- People working in a leisure or sport facility must maintain a secure and safe environment for their customers and staff.

Planning a safe sporting activity

When planning a sporting activity you will need to determine the roles and responsibilities of each member of the group.

Roles and responsibilities

The leader of the activity is responsible for the planning and preparation, and the smooth running of the event.

Prior to the activity, the leader should:

- determine who will be taking part in the activity
- undertake a risk assessment of the proposed activity
- determine the staffing requirements of the activity; this should include an appropriate number of qualified first aiders
- ensure that you or your centre has adequate insurance to run the activity
- plan transport arrangements if required

- visit the site or facility where you plan to hold the activity
- plan contingency and emergency arrangements
- if the activity is for children then you or your centre must inform parents and obtain parental and medical consent.

The site, equipment and first-aid provision

The site chosen must be suitable for the activity. If it is an indoor event then you must ensure that the facility is an appropriate size, has suitable lighting, suitable changing facilities, first-aid provision, all the equipment you require, etc. Basically it has to suit the needs of the chosen activity and the needs of the participants and still adhere to health and safety guidelines. If the activity is to be held outside, then you should always take into account environmental factors that may adversely affect your activity. For example, a lot of rain could waterlog a sports field, which could then become dangerous to play on. Always have a contingency plan that allows you to still run an activity but does not put the participants' health at risk. For example, a football game that was due to be played outside could be changed to a five-a-side match inside.

It is important that all equipment is checked prior to being used to ensure that it is complete, in working order and not faulty or damaged.

Adequate arrangements must be made for first aid, including responsible people, equipment and facilities.

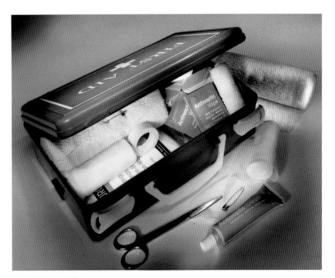

Fig 2.06 A first-aid kit

You should always carry a basic first-aid kit with you or ensure you have access to one when you are running a sports activity.

A basic first-aid kit should contain:

- ten plasters in various sizes
- two large sterile dressings for management of severe bleeding
- one medium sterile dressing for care of larger wounds
- four triangular bandages to support suspected broken bones, dislocations or sprains
- one eye pad in case of a cut to the eye
- four safety pins to secure dressings
- disposable gloves.

Suitability of participants to the activity

One of the main factors to help determine the suitability of a participant is to consider their age. If the participants are people of a different age from yourself then you should always speak to a person who has experience of dealing with this age group. You can then discuss your idea for your activity and determine whether it is suitable. From this you will be able to gauge what sort of equipment you should use, any adaptions required to make the activity more suitable and the staffing ratio required.

For example, if you wanted to run a cricket activity with (a) primary-school-aged children or (b) a group of 18 year olds, you would have very different plans.

For the primary-school-aged children you would use soft balls because hard balls would be more likely to cause injuries as the children are less experienced in throwing and catching compared with most adults. You would probably adapt the game so that more people are active more of the time; for example, you may have four teams of eight children playing quick cricket. You would need more staff to supervise the children to ensure their health and safety.

For a group of 18 year olds you would use the usual cricket equipment, the game would be played to the usual cricket rules, and the only staffing required would be to umpire the event and to ensure there is appropriate first-aid provision.

Health and safety review

After an event has taken place, you should always review your health and safety planning and procedures to see whether they were effective or if they could be improved. Examine if there were any injuries or near misses, how they occurred and if you could have done anything to reduce the likelihood of that incident happening. Determine if the participants were a suitable group for the activity, were they the right age, of the right ability, etc. Did the staff receive a suitable briefing so that they were able to carry out their roles and responsibilities effectively? Was the equipment suitable, could you have used anything else to improve the health and safety of the participants during the activity?

This information will help you to improve your awareness of health and safety, and to ensure that you are doing everything possible to reduce risks and maintain the health and safety of yourself and others.

LEARNER ACTIVITY

1 In groups of two or more make plans for a sporting activity. Your plan could actually take place, or you could use it as a 'trial run' to prepare you for when you do wish to plan an actual sporting activity.
2 Determine the roles of each member of the team and then make plans to help ensure your activity can be carried out safely. Things that you should consider include:

- the types of activity
- equipment
- site
- participants
- first-aid provision
- risk assessment.

Key learning points

- In order to pay full attention to health and safety, a sporting activity should be planned effectively with attention given to risk assessments, equipment, the site, the participants, first-aid provision, contingency plans, and the roles and responsibilities of each team member.

Review questions

1 Why and when was the Health and Safety at Work Act developed?
2 How does the employer and the employee benefit from the Health and Safety at Work Act?
3 What is the Adventurous Activities Licensing Authority (AALA)?
4 What does 'loco parentis' mean?
5 Describe what a risk is.
6 What is a risk assessment and why are they performed?
7 List the factors that should be taken into consideration when performing a risk assessment.
8 Describe a Normal Operating Procedures document and give examples of what it contains.
9 Write out a list of roles and responsibilities that leaders should take into account when planning an event.
10 What should a basic first-aid kit contain?

References

Stafford-Brown, J., Rea, S., Janaway, L. and Manley, C. (2006) *BTEC First Sport*, Hodder Arnold.

Websites

www.hse.gov.uk – Health and Safety Executive
www.rospa.com – Royal Society for the Prevention of Accidents

Goals

By the end of this chapter you should:

- understand the fitness requirements of different sporting activities
- understand different methods of physical fitness testing
- be able to plan a fitness training programme
- be able to monitor and evaluate a fitness training programme.

Developing the correct training programme is vital to the success of the individual athlete and the team. Top-class athletes build their life around the requirements of their fitness training and have a dedicated coach for this purpose. Fitness will be important to any individual who is involved in physical activity to give them the best chances to succeed.

Components of fitness

Fitness can mean different things to different people and has been defined in different ways. When we examine fitness we need to ask 'What does this person have to be fit for?' or 'What functions does this person have to perform?' From this starting point we can build up a picture of their fitness requirements and then look at what can be done to develop their fitness.

Fitness is defined by the American College of Sports Medicine (ACSM) (1990) as:

> a set of attributes that people have or achieve that relate to their ability to perform physical activity.

Fitness is clearly related to performance and developing the attributes to achieve this performance.

Physical fitness

Physical fitness can be seen to be made up of the following factors.

Aerobic endurance is also called cardiovascular fitness or stamina. It is the individual's ability to take on, transport and utilise oxygen. It is a measure of how well the lungs can take in oxygen, how well the heart and blood can transport oxygen and then how well the muscles can use oxygen. When working aerobically we tend to perform repetitive activities using large muscle groups in a rhythmical manner for long periods of time.

Muscular endurance is how well the muscles can produce repeated contractions at less than maximal (submaximal) intensities. When training for muscular endurance we usually do sets of 15 to 20 repetitions. Most movements we produce in sport and everyday activities will be at submaximal intensities and all people will benefit from muscular endurance training.

Flexibility is the range of motion that a joint or group of joints can move through. Flexibility is often not given the amount of attention it should have in a training programme because people do not always see its importance. However, improving flexibility can improve performance because a greater range of motion will result in greater power development and

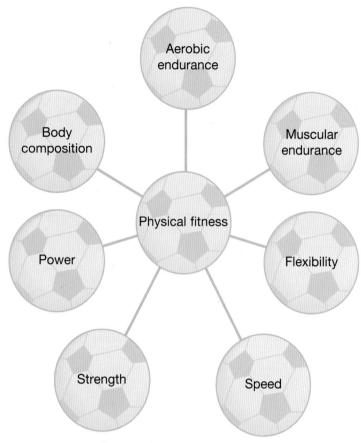

Fig 3.01 Physical fitness

will help to prevent injury and pain caused through restrictions in movement.

Speed is the rate at which the body or individual limbs can move.

Strength is the maximum force a muscle or group of muscles can produce in a single contraction. Heavy weight lifting or moving a heavy object will require strength. For example, if you have to push-start a car the success or failure of this effort will be an expression of your muscular strength. To train for strength we usually do sets of 1 to 5 repetitions.

Power is the production of strength at speed and can be seen when we throw an object or perform a sprint start. To move a heavy load quickly we need to use our power. Activities such as jumping to head a ball or a long jump will require us to express our power.

Body composition

Although not strictly a component of fitness, body composition has a direct impact on sports

performance and the ability to perform certain activities.

The shape of the body is defined by three factors:

- the skeleton
- the amount of fat
- the amount of muscle.

Somatotyping is a method for describing an individual's body type or shape. 'Somatotype' describes which of these three factors are most dominant in the individual.

- **Ectomorphs** are mainly thin with low body fat and less muscle mass. They tend to have long levers and are suited to aerobic events such as long-distance running and cycling.
- **Endomorphs** are predominantly fat and may be apple or pear shaped. Some endomorphs will have a fair amount of muscle and may be found in sports such as shot-put and sumo wrestling.
- **Mesomorphs** will be predominantly muscular with low levels of body fat. They tend to have broad shoulders and narrow hips. Mesomorphs will be found in team sports such as football and rugby.

Fig 3.02 Ectomorph

Fig 3.04 Mesomorph

Fig 3.03 Endomorph

Skill-related fitness

This aspect of fitness relates to the production of skilled movement. This is the coordination between the brain, nervous system and muscles. All movement starts in the brain as it produces a nervous impulse which is transferred to the muscles through the nerves. The nervous impulse travels down the spinal cord and out through the nerves that shoot off the spinal cord. These nerves bring the nervous impulse to the muscles which then contract to produce movement.

When we learn a skill the brain sends the message to the muscles, but at the start it may not be the right message and may not produce a skilled performance. However, as we learn the skill we learn to send the right message and we develop a 'pathway' between the brain, nerves and muscles. All these skills need to have a strong pathway between the brain, nerves and muscular system.

Agility is a measure of how well you can control your body while moving through space. It is particularly important when you have to quickly change direction, such as a goalkeeper saving a deflected shot.

Balance is how well you can keep your body weight over a central base of support. It is important for us to stay on our feet during quick changes of direction.

Coordination is how well we can produce the skilled movement that is required of us.

Reaction time is how quickly you can pick up information, make a decision and then produce a reaction to it.

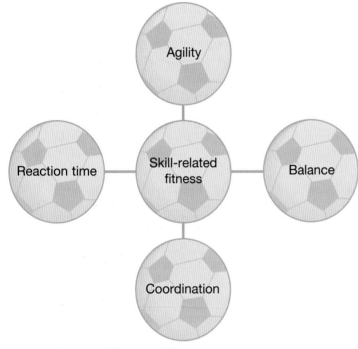

Fig 3.05 Skill-related fitness

Fitness requirements of a range of sports

In order to safely and effectively take part in sports it is necessary to have all the basic components of health-related fitness. Depending on the sport, some components need to be trained more than others. Different sports also have different skill-related component requirements, which also need to be trained for a player to excel in their sport.

Key learning points

- Aerobic endurance is a measure of how well the lungs can take in oxygen, how well the heart and blood can transport oxygen and then how well the muscles can use oxygen.
- Muscular endurance is how well the muscles can produce repeated contractions at low intensities.
- Flexibility is the range of motion that a joint or group of joints can move through.
- Speed is the how quickly the body or individual limbs can move.
- Strength is the maximum force a muscle or group of muscles can produce once.
- Power is the production of strength at speed.
- Body composition is the ratio of fat to lean body weight a person possesses.
- Agility is a measure of how well you can control your body while moving through the air.
- Balance is how well you can keep your body weight over a central base of support.
- Coordination is how well you can produce the skilled movement that is required of you.
- Reaction time is how quickly you can pick up information, make a decision and then produce a reaction to it.

There are a number of key aspects that need to be considered when planning a training programme for a sportsperson:

- the length of the activity
- the strength required
- the flexibility required
- the skills required.

If the activity lasts for a period of less than 30 minutes, aerobic fitness and muscular endurance tend not to be major components that need to be trained. Weight lifting involves short bursts of intense activity for which the sportsperson does not need high levels of aerobic fitness or muscular endurance. However, a marathon runner needs to be able to run for continuous periods of two hours and over, so aerobic fitness and muscular endurance are key areas that need to be trained.

Some sports require the athlete to have high levels of strength, speed and power so that they are able to exert high levels of force against a resistance, as in the throwing events such as the shot-put and javelin. Strength training is also necessary to build muscle mass in order to increase a person's sprinting speed.

Some flexibility is required by all sportspeople in order to avoid injury. However, some sports demand that the athlete has particularly high levels of flexibility in order to carry out the movements involved. Examples of these sports are gymnastics, martial arts and diving.

A number of sports involve a variety of the skill-related components of fitness. In order for athletes to improve in their sports they must take part in specific training practices to refine these skills. For example, a rugby player needs good hand/ball and foot/ball co-ordination, so they must take part in drills to practise these skills. Sprinters need good reaction times in order to get off to a good start in a race.

Football

Footballers need to train in a variety of the health-related and skill-related components of fitness. A player's position also influences their training programme – a goalkeeper needs quite a different training programme to that of a striker. The main components of fitness footballers need to train are as follows.

- **Anaerobic fitness**: football involves short bursts of speed and then periods of rest or walking. It is not really an aerobic activity because movement occurs at different speeds and is not steady-state or repetitive. Football and other team sports predominantly use the anaerobic system.
- **Strength, speed and power**: their training should include some resistance work in order to allow them to jump high, kick the ball hard and sprint, to reach the ball quickly, dodge and mark opponents.
- **Skill-related components**: with the agility to beat players and run after the ball as well as foot to ball coordination.

Swimming

Swimming uses all the major muscle groups of both the upper and the lower body. In this respect it is also known as a whole-body exercise. The type of fitness a swimmer needs depends on which stroke and at what distance they compete. Both sprint and distance swimmers need the following.

- **Muscular endurance**: to ensure that their muscles are able to continue to function and propel the body through the water for periods of time.
- **Flexibility**: to allow them to complete the stroke effectively. The butterfly stroke especially requires the swimmer to have a good range of movement in the shoulder joint in order to perform the stroke efficiently and effectively.

LEARNER ACTIVITY Different sports and their fitness requirements

Investigate the following sports by considering the amount of each component of fitness that is required to perform at the highest level for each one. Give each component a score of between 1 and 10 where 1 is the lowest and 10 is the highest.

	Aerobic endurance	Muscular endurance	Flexibility	Speed	Strength	Power	Agility	Balance	Coordination	Reaction time
Gymnastics										
Rowing										
Boxing										
Salsa dancing										
Archery										
Squash										
Rock climbing										

- **Aerobic endurance**: for the distance swimmer to complete long-distance swims.
- **Muscular strength**: for the sprint swimmer to increase their speed through the water.

Cycling

For long-distance cycling, such as the Tour de France, an athlete needs extremely high levels of aerobic fitness and muscular endurance. For hill work and sprint finishes they also need to train for muscular strength.

Racket sports

Tennis, squash and badminton involve bursts of intense activity for short periods. However, because these games usually last longer than 20 minutes, a player also needs to have high levels of aerobic fitness and muscular endurance. Some strength training should be carried out to hit the ball/shuttlecock with force. In tennis, some players may concentrate on improving their strength specifically to improve their serve. If the ball is hit with more strength it will travel faster, making it less likely to be reached by the opponent. There is quite a lot of skill required for these sports as the players need to have good racket/ball or racket/shuttlecock coordination. They also need to have high levels of agility in order to get to the ball/shuttlecock.

Rugby

Rugby players need a range of health-related and skill-related components of fitness, but their specific training programme will vary in accordance with their playing position. All rugby players need to train the following components of fitness.

- **Aerobic fitness and muscular endurance**: because a game of rugby lasts at least 80 minutes.
- **Strength and power**: to be able to tackle opponents, sprint and dodge opponents.
- **Good hand/ball and foot/ball coordination and high levels of agility to get to the ball**.

Methods of physical fitness training

Flexibility

Flexibility is the 'range of motion available at a joint' and is needed in sports to:

- enable the athlete to have the range of motion to perform the movements needed
- prevent the athlete from becoming injured
- maintain and improve posture
- develop maximum strength and power.

What happens to muscles when we stretch?

The stretching of muscles is under the control of the sensory nerves. There are two types of sensory nerves which are involved in allowing muscles to stretch and relax. They are muscle spindles and Golgi tendon organs (GTOs). The sensory nerves work to protect the body from becoming injured and will contract if they think a muscle is at risk of becoming damaged. This is one of our basic survival instincts because when we were hunter-gatherers injury would render us incapable of finding food and our families would starve.

The muscle spindles are sensory receptors which become activated as the muscle lengthens (due to its potential danger). When the muscle has reached a certain length they tell the nervous system to contract the muscle and prevent it being stretched any further. This protects the muscle against damage. If you perform the patella knee tap test this activates the muscle spindles. When this test is conducted, the knee extends due to the contraction of the quadriceps muscle activated by the muscle spindle. This is also called 'the myotatic stretch reflex'.

When we stretch a muscle we try to avoid this by stretching in a slow and controlled manner. The muscle spindles contract the muscle, which makes it feel uncomfortable or slightly painful. This is called the 'point of bind' where the muscle has contracted to avoid any damage.

When the point of bind is reached the stretch should be held for around ten seconds. This is because after ten seconds the muscle will relax and the pain will disappear. This relaxation is brought on by the action of the GTOs. GTOs are found in tendons and they sense how much tension there is in the muscle. Once the GTOs sense that the muscle is not in danger of damage they will override the muscle spindles and cause the muscle to relax. This is the effect that you want a stretch to have; it is called 'the inverse stretch reflex'. Once the muscle has relaxed you can either stop the stretch there or stretch the muscle a bit more until the point of bind is reached again and the process starts again.

There are various methods of stretching muscles.

Static stretching

This is when a muscle is stretched in a steady, controlled manner and then held in a static or still position. It is taken to the point where the muscle contracts and a slight pain is felt. This is called 'the point of bind'. At this point the stretch is held until the muscle relaxes and the discomfort disappears.

A static stretch can be a maintenance stretch or a developmental stretch. A maintenance stretch is held until the discomfort disappears and then the stretch is stopped. A developmental stretch is different because when the muscle relaxes and the discomfort disappears the stretch is applied further to a second point. It is taken to a point when the discomfort is felt again, it is held until the muscle relaxes and then applied again. It lasts for around 30 seconds while a maintenance stretch will last for around 10 seconds.

Proprioceptive neuromuscular facilitation

This type of stretching, known as PNF, is an advanced type of stretching in order to develop the length of the muscle. It needs two people to be involved: one person to do the stretching and one to be stretched.

It is carried out in the following way.

- The muscle is stretched to the point of bind by the trainer.
- At this point the trainer asks the athlete to contract the muscle and push against them at about 40 to 50 per cent effort.
- This contraction is held for 10 seconds.
- When the muscle is relaxed the trainer stretches the muscle further.
- Again a contraction is applied and then the muscle is re-stretched.
- This is done three times.

This is a more effective way of developing the length of the muscle as the contraction will actually cause the muscle to relax more quickly and more deeply.

Ballistic stretching

This means a 'bouncing' stretch as the muscle is forced beyond its point of stretch by a bouncing movement. Ballistic stretches are performed in a rapid, repetitive bouncing movement. It is a high-risk method of stretching due to the risk of muscular damage but it may be used in specific sports such as gymnastics. It must never be used on people training for health and fitness reasons rather than sports.

Resistance training

Resistance training means using any form of resistance to place an increased load on a muscle or muscle group. Resistance training can be used to develop muscular endurance, strength and hypertrophy (muscle bulk). Resistance can be applied through any of the following:

- free weights
- resistance machines
- cable machines
- gravity
- medicine balls
- air
- water
- resistance bands
- manually.

The following are popular methods of resistance training:

- resistance machines
- free weights
- cables
- plyometrics
- circuit training.

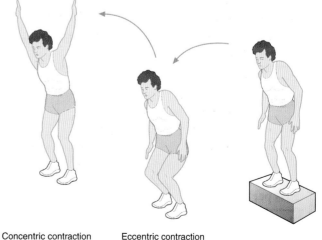

Concentric contraction taking place in the quadriceps muscle group

Eccentric contraction taking place in the quadriceps muscle group

Fig 3.06 A plyometric exercise

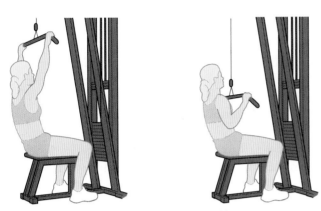

Fig 3.07 Resistance training with a machine

A range of **resistance machines** have been developed to train muscle groups in isolation. They were originally developed for body builders but their ease of use and safety factors make them a feature of every gym in the country. These machines target individual muscles and replicate the joint actions these muscles produce.

Free weights involve barbells and dumbbells and are seen to have advantages over resistance machines. Mainly, they allow a person to work in their own range of movement rather than the way a machine wants them to work. Also, when a person does free weights they have to use many more muscles to stabilise the body before the force is applied. This is particularly so if the person performs the exercise standing up. They also have more 'functional crossover' in that they can replicate movements that will be used in sports and daily life. This is seen as a huge advantage.

Cable machines are becoming increasingly popular because again they involve the use of many more muscles than resistance machines, and therefore burn up more calories. Once again, they can produce movements that are not possible on machines. For example, a golfer will need to perform rotation-type movements and can do these on cable machines.

The box at the bottom of the page shows the repetition ranges for targeting components of fitness.

Plyometrics

Plyometric training develops power, which is producing strength at speed. It usually involves moving your body weight very quickly through jumping or bounding. Any sport that involves jumping in the air or moving the body forwards at pace will need power training. Examples of plyometric training include:

- jumping on to boxes and over hurdles
- depth jumping
- vertical jumps and standing long jump
- medicine ball throws
- hopping
- bounding
- squat and jump
- press-up and clap.

It is a very strenuous type of training and an athlete must have well-developed strength before performing plyometrics. Before you take a plyometric session you must make sure the athlete is well warmed up and that you have checked the equipment and the surfaces

Objective	Muscular strength	Muscle hypertrophy	Muscular endurance	Power
Repetitions or duration	1–5	6–12	12–20	1–2 for single-effort events 3–5 for multiple-effort events
Recovery period	3–5 mins	1–2 mins	30–60 secs	2–5 mins
Sets per exercise	2–6	3–6	2–3	3–5
Frequency per week	1–2 on each muscle group	1–2 on each muscle group	2–3 on each muscle group	1–2 sessions a week

(Adapted from Baechle and Earle, 2000)

thoroughly. Ideally, you should use a sprung floor or a soft surface.

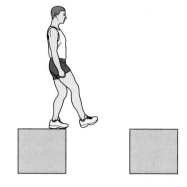

Start

Descent

Push off

Fig 3.08 Squat jump

Fig 3.10 Depth jump

Fig 3.09 Chest pass

Aerobic fitness or pulse raisers	Shuttle runs Skipping Box step-ups Box jumps Jumping jacks Star jumps Spotty dogs Grapevines
Upper body	Press-ups Bench press with dumbbells Cable seated rows Bent-over row Shoulder press Bicep curls Tricep dips Lateral raises Dumbbell pullovers Medicine ball chest passes Medicine ball chest pass and press-up Medicine ball overhead throws
Lower body	Squats Lunges Split squats Side lunges Squat thrusts Hurdle jumps Ladder work Step-ups with dumbbells
Core exercises	Swiss ball curls Swiss ball back extension Plank Bridge Superman Rotations with medicine ball Medicine ball rotate and throw

Circuit training

Circuits have been popular in this country since the 1950s, particularly in the army! A circuit is a series of exercises arranged in a specific order and performed one after the other. There are normally eight to twelve stations set out and organised so that each muscle group is worked in rotation. Each exercise is performed for a certain number of repetitions or a set time period. Circuits can be performed for a range of fitness gains but are usually done to develop aerobic fitness or a general fitness base. They can be made specific to various sports by including exercises for the muscles used in that sport and some of the skills specific to that sport.

When planning a circuit you need to ask several questions:

- What is the objective of the session?
- How many participants will I have?
- What is their level of fitness?
- How much space have I got?
- What equipment is available?

A basic circuit session should contain exercise to improve aerobic fitness or raise the pulse rate, exercises to work the upper body, lower body and the core. When designing the circuit layout be careful not to place all the exercises for the same muscle group beside each other as this will cause undue fatigue. The circuit should follow the normal structure of a routine:

- warm-up
- main session
- cool-down
- flexibility.

The warm-up will include a pulse raiser, mobility and dynamic stretches. For example:

- walk
- walk with bicep curls and shoulder presses
- slow jog with shoulder circles
- jog
- dynamic stretches such as squat and press, step back and chest stretch
- jog with knee raises and heel flicks
- run
- jumps and hops
- sprint.

The main session should include eight to twelve exercises from the box on page 180.

The cool-down should progressively lower the pulse, but it can be combined with some stretching as well. It could follow this example:

- run (1 minute)
- jog (1 minute)
- brisk walk and stretch trapezius, pectoralis major, latissimus dorsi, triceps, deltoids
- standing stretches of adductors, calves and quads
- kneeling stretches of hip flexors and lower back
- lying stretches of hamstrings and gluteus medius and minimus.

LEARNER ACTIVITY Circuit training session

Design a circuit session of eight stations for 16 people who will work in pairs. Choose a target audience and consider the amount of space and equipment you have available. Also design a warm-up and cool-down specific to the session.

Aerobic training

Continuous training is also called 'steady-state' training and involves an individual maintaining a steady pace for a long period of time. To be effective it needs to be done for a period of over 20 minutes. It is useful for developing a strong base of aerobic fitness, but it will not develop speed or strength.

While continuous training has a role to play it can be limited in its benefits, particularly if the athlete does the same session each time they train. While initially it will have given them fitness gains there will be limited benefits after about four weeks once the body has adapted to the work. It may also produce boredom and a loss of motivation to train.

Interval training is described as having the following features: 'a structured period of work followed by a structured period of rest'. In other words, an athlete runs quickly for a period of time and then rests at a much lower intensity before speeding up again. This type of training has the benefit of improving speed as well as aerobic fitness. Interval training also allows the athlete to train at higher intensities than they are used to, and thus steadily increase their fitness level and the intensity they can work at. The theory is that you will be able to run faster in competition only if you train faster – and interval training allows this to occur. Intervals can be used to improve performance for athletes and fitness levels for people involved in exercise.

Interval training can be stressful to the systems of the body and it is important to ensure that an individual has a good aerobic base before raising the intensity of the training.

Once an athlete has reached the limit of their aerobic system they will start to gain extra energy from their anaerobic system (lactic acid system); this is demonstrated by an increased accumulation of lactic acid in the blood. The point where blood lactic acid levels start to rise is called the lactate threshold. Interval training can be designed to push an athlete beyond their lactate threshold and then reduce the exercise intensity below the lactate threshold. This has the effect of enabling the athlete to become better at tolerating the effects of lactic acid and also increasing the intensity they work at before lactic acid is produced. Well-designed interval training sessions can produce this desirable effect.

The intensity of interval training is higher than continuous work and thus there will be more energy production to sustain this high-intensity work. More energy production equals more calories burnt during training, which could lead to a faster loss of body fat (if the nutritional strategy is appropriate). As the intensity is higher more waste products are built up, resulting in a greater oxygen debt and a longer period of recovery. This longer period of recovery results in more oxygen being used post-exercise and more energy used to recover. Therefore, more energy is used during exercise and also after exercise, multiplying the potential effects of fat loss.

The main benefits of interval training are:

- improved speed
- improved strength
- improved aerobic endurance
- improved ability to tolerate the effects of lactic acid
- increased fat burning potential
- increased calorie output
- improved performance.

Interval training can be used to develop aerobic fitness as well as anaerobic fitness. When designing interval training sessions you need to consider how long the periods of work are in relation to the periods of rest. The following are recommended guidelines for training with each of the three energy systems.

- **Aerobic interval**: 1 or half a unit of rest for every unit of work.
- **Lactic acid intervals**: 2 to 3 units of rest for 1 unit of work.
- **ATP/CP intervals**: 6 units of rest for 1 unit of work.

As the intensity increases, more rest is required to guarantee the quality of each interval. If you were training for aerobic fitness you may do four minutes' work then have two minutes' rest (1:1/2). If you were training for lactic acid intervals you would have one minute's work and two or three minutes' rest.

Sample aerobic interval session

First estimate the maximum heart rate as 220 minus age and then you can work out the percentage of maximum heart rate.

For a 20 year old:

Maximum heart rate = 220 − 20 = 200 bpm
70% of max HR = 200 × 0.7 = 140 bpm
80% of max HR = 200 × 0.8 = 160 bpm
90% of max HR = 200 × 0.9 = 180 bpm

You will need to find out what workload (speed) produces each heart rate when you are running.

Basic interval

Work = 4 minutes   Rest = 2 minutes

4 sets of 4 minutes at 70% effort with 2 minutes' rest in between

Pyramid interval

Work = 3 minutes   Rest = 1.5 minutes

Warm-up

3 mins @ 80% of max HR
Rest
3 mins @ 85% of max HR
Rest
3 mins @ 90% of max HR
Rest
3 mins @ 85% of max HR
Rest
3 mins @ 80% of max HR
Cool-down

Treadmill hills pyramid

Find the speed that produces 70% of max HR and stay at this speed throughout the interval programme; then vary the gradient on the treadmill.

Work = 2 mins   Rest = 1 min

Warm-up
2 mins @ 2% gradient
Rest
2 mins @ 4% gradient
Rest
2 mins @ 6% gradient
Rest
2 mins @ 4% gradient
Rest
2 mins @ 2% gradient
Cool-down

Alternately the gradients could be set at 3%, 6%, 9%, 6% and 3%.

Sample anaerobic session
Lactic acid system

6 sets of 45 seconds (or 300 m) at 90–95% effort with 90 seconds' rest

4 sets of 75 seconds (or 500 m) at 80–85% effort with 150 seconds' rest

ATP/PC system

10 sets of 50 metres at 100% effort with 1 minute rest

Fartlek is a Swedish term; it literally means 'speed play' and it involves an athlete going out and running at a range of different speeds for a period of 20 to 30 minutes. This type of training is excellent for replicating the demands of a sport such as football, rugby or hockey where different types of running are required at different times. It can be used to develop aerobic or anaerobic fitness depending on the intensity of the running. It can also be used in cycling or rowing training. Fartlek running involves finding a base speed at around 60 to 70 per cent of maximum intensity and then fast bursts of work at 75, 80, 85 and 90 per cent mixed up into longer or shorter time periods. It can be used to challenge the different energy systems and demands of sports as well as reducing the boredom of training for long periods of time.

Core stability

If we were to take our arms and legs off our body we would be left with the body's core, which can be said to be the working foundation of the body and is responsible for providing the base to develop power. If we have a strong core we will be able to generate more force and power through the arms and legs; this is important when we kick a football or hit a tennis ball.

> definition
>
> Core stability: 'the ability of your trunk to support the effort and forces from your arms and legs, so that muscles and joints can perform in their strongest and most effective positions.'
>
> (Elphinston and Pook, 1999)

The body is made up of layers of muscles and the abdominal area is no different as it has deep, middle and outer layers which work together to provide stability.

The outer layer of muscles are the best known abdominal muscles with the rectus abdominis at the front, the erector spinae at the back and the internal and external obliques at the sides.

The middle layer is deeper muscle, which forms a cylinder or unit around the vertebrae. At the top we

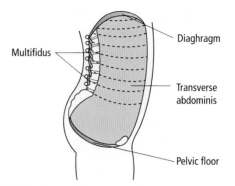

Fig 3.11 Outer layer of core muscles

have the diaphragm and at the bottom the pelvic floor muscles, while across the back we have the multifidus, and around the front and sides we have the transverse abdominis (TVA). The TVA is the key muscle here and is described as being 'the natural weight belt' because a weight belt replicates its shape and function.

The role of the inner muscles is to stabilise the vertebrae, ribs and pelvis to provide the stable working base or foundation. These muscles contract a fraction of a second before the arms or legs are moved when the body is functioning correctly. If this does not happen the chances of damaging the spine are increased.

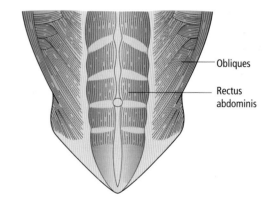

Fig 3.12 Inner layer of core muscles

The deep layer is tiny muscles which sense the position of the vertebrae and control their movement to keep them in the strongest position and prevent injury.

Activating the core muscles can be done in two ways. First, by hollowing or pulling in the abdominals or by bracing, which means contracting the muscles without them moving out or in. Different trainers will recommend different techniques depending upon their own experiences and training.

Abdominal training

The concepts of abdominal training are changing rapidly. The traditional method has been to do hundreds of sit-ups in pursuit of a perfect six-pack and then, in the late 1990s, abdominal cradles were introduced into gyms to aid people further. The 2000s have seen the introduction of Swiss balls and functional abdominal exercises into training programmes. There is still some confusion over what is the best way to train the abdominals. We need to look at a couple of misconceptions first before looking at what is the best way to train.

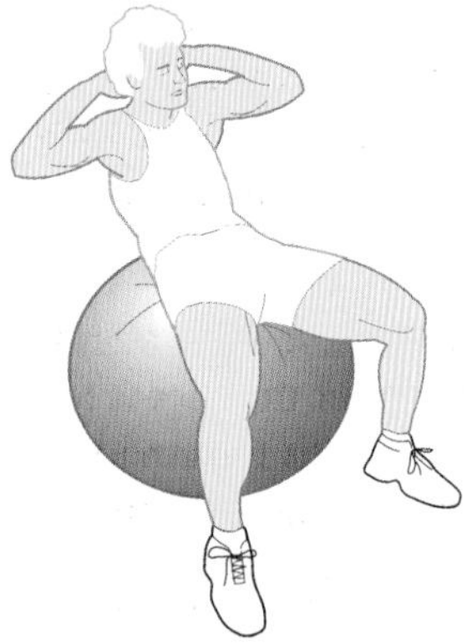

Fig 3.13 Swiss ball abdominal crunches

> **Sit-ups will help me lose fat in the abdominal area**

No, you cannot spot-reduce fat because the muscle below the abdominal fat is separate from the fat itself and you can never be sure from where the losses in fat due to exercise will come. The way to lose abdominal fat is to increase activity level and have a correct nutritional strategy.

> **Sit-ups will give me the six-pack I want**

Not necessarily, because overdoing abdominal work can cause a shortening of the abdominal muscles and pull your posture forwards, making the abdominal area shorter, squeezing the fat together and making you look fatter. In fact, if you perform back extensions it will make your posture more upright and help to keep the abdominals contracted and make them look more toned.

> **Sit-ups are the best abdominal exercise**

This is debatable because sit-ups produce concentric and eccentric muscular contractions. The abdominals will contract isometrically when we train and move around in daily life. Therefore, surely we should replicate this isometric contraction when we train as it will have the best 'functional crossover' to daily life.

LEARNER ACTIVITY
Abdominal exercises

Work in pairs for this exercise.

Stand up and let your abdominals relax. Your shoulders may fall forward slightly and you may slump. Then get your partner to push you back gently from the shoulders and observe the effect this has.

Then either suck your belly button towards your vertebrae slightly or contract your abdominals and repeat the gentle push. What do you observe happens to your upper body in each case and how does the contraction of the abdominals change the way you hold yourself (your posture)?

When we train the core muscles we need to target the deeper muscles; this is done by producing isometric or static contractions.

Any exercise where you are standing up or supporting your body weight will be a core exercise. For example, a press-up is an excellent core exercise because the core muscles work to keep the back straight and the back will start to sag when these muscles become fatigued. All standing free weight and cable exercises require the core to stabilise the vertebrae while they are being performed. However, there are some specific core exercises which can be performed (see Fig 3.14).

The use of a Swiss ball to perform exercises requires an extra load on the core muscles and works them harder, as will using cables to exercise.

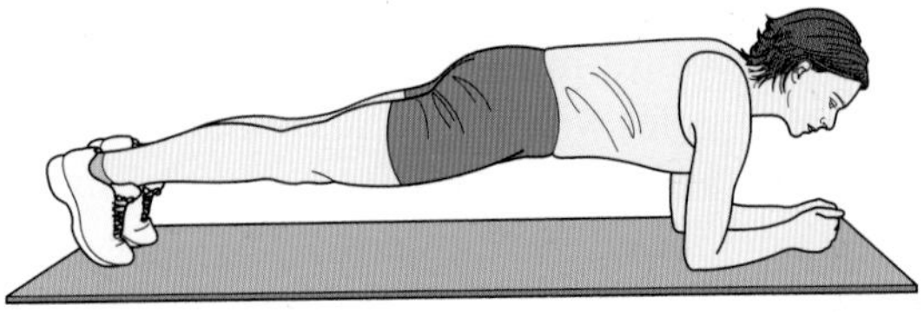

Fig 3.14a Plank

Fig 3.14b Side plank

Fig 3.14c Bridge

Planning physical fitness training programmes
Principles of training

To develop a safe and effective training programme you will need to consider the principles of training. These principles are a set of guidelines to help you understand the requirements of programme design. The principles of training are:

- **F**requency
- **I**ntensity
- **T**ime
- **T**ype
- **O**verload
- **R**eversibility
- **S**pecificity.

Frequency means how often the athlete will train per week, month or year. It is recommended that a beginner trains three times a week while a competitive athlete may train ten or twelve times a week.

Intensity is how hard the athlete works for each repetition. It is usually expressed as a percentage of maximum intensity. Intensity can be increased by adding more weight to be lifted, or increasing speed or gradient on the treadmill.

Time indicates how long they train for in each session. The recommended length of a training session is around 45 minutes before fatiguing waste products build up and affect training technique.

Type shows the type of training they will perform and needs to be individual to each person. A training effect can be achieved by varying the exercises an individual does – moving them from a treadmill to a rower, or a seated chest press to a free weight bench press.

Key learning points

Flexibility training is to develop the 'range of motion available at a joint'. There are various methods of stretching muscles: static stretching; ballistic stretching and PNF stretching.

Resistance training means using any form of resistance to place an increased load on a muscle or muscle group. Resistance can be applied through any of the following:

- free weights
- resistance machines
- cable machines
- gravity
- medicine balls
- air
- water
- resistance bands
- manually.

Plyometric training develops power by overcoming a resistance at speed. It can include jumping, throwing, hopping and bounding.

Circuit training is performing a series of exercises in sequence to achieve muscular and aerobic endurance, strength or speed.

Aerobic training aims to develop the efficiency of the heart, lungs and working muscles. It can be of three types: continuous training, interval training and Fartlek training.

Core stability is the strength of the muscles in the abdominal region, which act as the power base of the body. The most important muscle is the transverse abdominis.

Overload shows that to make an improvement a muscle or system must work slightly harder than it is used to. The weight that produces overload depends upon what the individual is currently used to at that moment. This may be as simple as getting a sedentary person walking for ten minutes or getting an athlete to squat more weight than they have previously. Overload can be achieved by changing the intensity, duration, time or type of an exercise.

Reversibility says that if a fitness gain is not used regularly the body will reverse it and go back to its previous fitness level. Any adaptation which occurs is not permanent. The rule is commonly known as 'use it or lose it'.

Specificity states that any fitness gain will be specific to the muscles or system to which the overload is applied. Put simply, this says that different types of training will produce different results. To make a programme specific you need to look at the needs of the athletes in that sport and then train them accordingly. For example, a footballer would need to run at different speeds and have lots of changes of direction. A golfer would need to do rotational work but sprinting speed would not be so important. A runner would need to do running predominantly, and they may get some aerobic gain from swimming or cycling but it would not achieve the best result.

There are other principles too.

Progressive overload

To ensure an athlete continues to gain fitness they need to keep overloading their muscles and systems. This continued increase in intensity (how hard they work) is called progressive overload. If you keep training at the same intensity and duration the body will reach a plateau where no further fitness gains are made. Therefore, it is important to keep manipulating all the training variables to keep gaining adaptations.

Periodisation

Periodisation means a progressive change in the type of training that is being performed to gain maximum fitness benefits. It needs to be carefully planned and would show progression from one type of training to another. For example, a sprinter will focus on developing their strength base and muscular endurance in the autumn before working on improving power and speed as they get closer to the competitive season. All training for sports performance needs to be periodised.

Macrocycle, mesocycle and microcycle are terminology specific to periodisation. The macrocycle is the largest unit of the training cycle and would cover the overall objective of the training. It will last for the length of a season or a training year. It is broken down into smaller units or mesocycles. A mesocycle is an individual phase of training and would cover a period of around a month depending upon the objective of the phase of training. A microcycle would represent each individual training session and its content. The plan would be periodised by looking at the big picture, or the macrocycle, then broken down into mesocycles, each contributing to the big picture and then the small detail of each session would be to consider how to achieve the aim of each mesocycle.

Collecting information

As an effective fitness coach it is important to be able to write an appropriate fitness training programme. There is a process that you need to go through to write an effective training session for a client.

Stage 1 – Gathering information: the first step is to gain relevant information about the person so that you can plan a personal training programme. The key is to build up a picture of the individual and what their life is like. Then you can look at what exercises you will plan for them. This is done through a questionnaire which the client will fill out on your first meeting. (See Chapter 6: Fitness testing for sports performance, for a sample questionnaire.)

What a person does or does not do in their life will have an effect on their health and fitness levels as well as their chances of being able to keep the training programme going. The following factors need to be taken into consideration.

- Occupation – hours worked and whether work is manual or office-based.
- Activity levels – amount of movement they do on a daily basis.
- Leisure time activities – whether these are active or inactive.
- Diet – what, how much and when they eat.
- Stress levels – either through work or their home life and how they deal with it.
- Alcohol intake – how much they consume and how often.

- Smoking – whether they are a smoker or ex-smoker and the amount they smoke.
- Time available – the client needs to fit the training into their schedule and the fitness trainer needs to be realistic when planning the programme.
- Current and previous training history – this will give an idea of the current fitness level of the client and also their skill level.

> ## LEARNER ACTIVITY
> ### Fitness questionnaire
> Prepare a questionnaire of ten questions to enable you to gather the relevant information you need to design a training programme.

Stage 2 – Establishing objectives: to ensure the success of the fitness programme it needs to be specific to the outcome a person wants. Once we have found this out we can establish goals. Their objective could be any of the following:

- cardiovascular fitness
- flexibility
- muscular strength
- muscular size
- muscle tone
- power.

Once the objectives have been established it is time to set goals to achieve these objectives.

Stage 3 – Goal setting: when setting goals it is important to ensure they follow the SMART principle – that they are specific, measurable, achievable, realistic and time-constrained. These goals should be set for the year or season, then for three months, one month and down to one week or one day.

This goal-setting information should be kept in the training diary along with records of each training session.

Monitoring and evaluating a fitness training programme

The programme is planned out in detail and implemented with great energy and enthusiasm; likewise it must be evaluated in an organised manner. The athlete must keep a training diary for every session, whether it covered physical training, technical development or mental skills. Only then can it be accurately and systematically evaluated.

A training diary

A training diary should include the following details:

- date of each session
- detail of what was done in each session
- a record of the performances in training
- notes on how the athlete felt
- reasons as to why the athlete felt that way
- competition results
- fitness testing results
- performance reviews with their coach.

This can then be used to demonstrate progress, keep the athlete motivated and then to understand any improvements which have been made (or not).

The athlete can evaluate the success and effectiveness of their training in three ways:

- repeating their fitness tests
- evaluating performances
- reviewing their training diary.

Based on all this information the next stage of the training programme can be developed.

The diary can also be used to evaluate the reasons why the athlete did or did not achieve their goals, and any modifications or interventions can then be planned.

Key learning points

- Before designing a training programme you need to draw up a comprehensive questionnaire. It must cover the following: medical history, activity history, goals and outcomes required, lifestyle factors, nutritional status and other factors that will affect fitness.
- Frequency means how often the athlete will train per week.
- Intensity is how hard the athlete will work.
- Time is how long they will train for in each session.

- Type is the type of training they will perform; this needs to be individual to each person.
- Overload is working a muscle or system slightly harder than it is used to.
- Reversibility says that if a fitness gain is not used regularly the body will reverse it and go back to its previous fitness level.
- Specificity states that any fitness gain will be specific to the muscles or system to which the overload is applied.

Review questions

1 Define fitness and explain what it means for you in your sport.
2 Explain what is meant by aerobic endurance, muscular endurance and muscular strength.
3 Give four components of skill-related fitness.
4 Explain why you have to stretch in a slow, controlled manner.
5 Give five ways in which resistance can be applied in training.
6 What are the repetition ranges and rest periods for muscular strength, muscular endurance and muscle hypertrophy?
7 Explain the benefits that interval training has over continuous training.
8 Why may performing sit-ups not be the best method of abdominal training?
9 What is meant by the terms overload, reversibility and specificity?
10 When planning a training programme give five factors you need to consider to do with an individual's lifestyle and briefly explain why they are important.

References

Baechle, T. and Earle, R. (2000) *Essentials of Strength Training and Conditioning*, Human Kinetics.

Dalgleish, J. and Dollery, S. (2001) *The Health and Fitness Handbook*, Longman.

Elphinston, J. and Pook, P. (1999) *The Core Workout: a Definitive Guide to Swiss Ball Training for Athletes, Coaches and Fitness Professionals*, Core Workout.

Stafford-Brown, J., Rea, S., Janaway, L. and Manley, C. (2006) *BTEC First Sport*, Hodder Arnold.

Wesson K., Wiggins-James, N., Thompson, G. and Hartigan, S. (2005) *Sport and PE: A Complete Guide to Advanced Level Study*, Hodder Arnold.

Goals

By the end of this chapter you should:

- understand the role, responsibilities and skills of a coach
- understand the techniques used by coaches to improve the performance of athletes
- be able to plan a coaching session
- be able to deliver a coaching session.

Sports coaches are vital to the success of a number of programmes across a range of sports. They are at the heart of participation and performer development. Whether the coach of an after-school club or a top international coach with support staff, coaches are at the very centre of the development of sport.

This chapter will assist those starting on the coaching ladder to learn the rules and responsibilities, the qualities and characteristics of sports coaches. It will provide an understanding of the role of the coach in promoting a positive coaching experience.

The role of the coach

Effective coaches tend to find new ways of improving existing practices or theories. Some adapt the way in which they practise, others deal with how to play specific strategies in differing situations. Other coaches integrate new developments or technologies to improve performance. Consider the trampoline coach who adapts a harness that supports a performer for use while learning somersaults, allowing them the freedom to twist at the same time and add to the range of skill and techniques achievable. Performers who work with innovative coaches speak about how they are never bored and always trying something new.

Trainer, educator and instructor

The difference between a teacher, educator and instructor is hard to discern. Teaching implies a transfer of learning through demonstration, modelling or instruction. Coaches can also teach emotional and social skills. Young performers in particular can be encouraged to increase their social awareness, learn to cope with losing and winning, and develop self-confidence. Good coaches will be aware that people learn in different ways. They then adapt and use a range of techniques to ensure that learning takes place.

In some cultures trainers and coaches are taken to mean the same thing. Since all sport requires some kind of physical exertion, it is important that these physical demands are recognised and that allowance for these demands is incorporated into coaching programmes.

A sound knowledge of anatomy, physiology and fitness theory is essential for coaches. In the role of trainer, you might expect to design and implement training programmes for your performers.

LEARNER ACTIVITY
Training programme

You are assisting an experienced coach in your sport. The coach asks you to put together a typical six-week pre-season training programme for your athletes specific to your sport. Using a recognised training plan format, plan a typical pre-season session plan for a sport of your choice.

Motivator

Motivation can come merely by providing a stable environment in which to learn, in a positive and safe atmosphere. Performers who constantly find negativity are certain at some point to become despondent and suffer a reduction in self-confidence and improvement.

Evidence suggests that performers who receive praise and positive feedback are likely to get more from their performances. When providing feedback to performers you would employ the following technique: KISS, KICK, KISS.

This technique would be applied in providing feedback such as in skill learning. When communicating with performers, the emphasis with this technique would be to start your feedback with a positive comment. There is nearly always something that is positive in any performance. Second, a corrective comment can be presented in as positive a manner as possible. Finally, leave the interaction with a positive comment and possibly an action plan. Consider a tennis player struggling to make a particular shot:

KISS – 'Good positioning prior to the shot and you watched the ball well.'
KICK – 'You should consider how you back lift the racket, you could prepare your grip earlier.'
KISS – 'If you practise these changes you will almost certainly improve.'

Role model

In almost every coaching situation players will look mostly, if not entirely, to the coach as their source of inspiration and knowledge, never more so than when working with children. Children often imitate the behaviour and manner of their coach. For this reason it is vital that coaching is safe and responsible, and that behaviour is considered good practice.

The coach can influence player development in a number of ways.

- Social – sport offers a code of acceptable social behaviour, teamwork, citizenship, cooperation and fair play.
- Personal – players can be encouraged to learn life skills, promote their own self-esteem, manage personal matters like careers or socialising, and develop a value system including good manners, politeness and self-discipline.
- Psychological – coaches can create environments that help performers control emotions and develop their own identities. Confidence, mental toughness, visualisation and a positive outlook on life can be developed or improved.

- Health – in taking care to design coaching or training sessions to include sufficient physical exercise, good health and healthy habits can be established and maintained.

Fig 4.01 A tennis coach and player

The responsibilities of a coach

Many expectations are put upon a coach. Some of these responsibilities are clear-cut, others less so. Coaching and playing sport should always be enjoyable, and to that end coaches should not be overburdened by expectation. Common sense and a good knowledge of safety and ethics will provide the basis of a responsible coach.

As coaching is now considered a profession, so coaches will increasingly be measured and assessed, whether paid or voluntary, and increasingly expected to work to a code of practice.

A coaching code of practice

So that performers achieve their potential, coaches should:

- remain within the bounds of adopted codes of practice
- maintain safe and secure coaching environments
- make best use of all facilities and resources
- establish good working relationships with all involved
- control the behaviour of participants where possible.

Many sports governing bodies and sports coach UK have established a code of conduct for sports coaches, which includes the following sections.

- Rights – coaches must respect and champion the right of every individual to participate in sport. Coaches should ensure that everyone has the opportunity to participate regardless of age, gender, race, ability, faith or sexual orientation.

For example, you would organise sessions in a place that has childcare arrangements, and you would be sensitive to religious festivals of all denominations and make allowances for the absences of performers on notable religious dates.

Coaches also have a responsibility to ensure that no discriminating behaviour occurs during their working sessions. Every member of the coaching group should have the right to feel part of the group, free from prejudice.

- Relationships – coaches need to establish relationships with performers that are based on openness, trust and mutual respect. This is not just about effective communication. Good coaches understand how their performers think and what is best for them. Performers will also learn better in an atmosphere of trust and respect for their coach. Involving performers in the decision-making process is an excellent way of establishing an effective relationship with a performer. When deciding what is best for a performer or group of performers, an example could be a situation where the coach presents the performers with information about their performance, such as a particular phase of play in a tennis competition.

Having supplied that information and perhaps offering their opinion, the coach could present the performer with a range of options that relate to the best course of action – how to improve on the last period of play. The performer who has an input into the decision in this process will come to appreciate the knowledge and analytical skills of the coach and over time their relationship will develop based on trust and respect.

Coaches should also anticipate and deal with potential relationship problems such as:

- dealing with parents
- dropping players from squads
- assuming control as a carer.

Personal standards

Coaches should demonstrate model behaviour at all times. Their influence should always be positive and would usually mean working to a code.

> ## LEARNER ACTIVITY
> ## Club policy or code
>
> Write a policy or code for coaches at your sports club regarding the following issues:
>
> - abusive language
> - equal interest in participants
> - professionalism
> - respect for officials and opponents
> - accepting defeat.
>
> Your club wants you to make the points clear for all of the club's new and existing coaches.

Professional standards

It is not enough to achieve a coaching qualification. Coaches should have a commitment to continual and ongoing learning or professional development. This could include:

- attaining higher-grade qualifications
- attending workshops and seminars
- being aware of changes to their sport.

LEARNER ACTIVITY Decision-making

Imagine yourself as a coach in the following examples and suggest how you could best present the options to a performer and include them in the decision-making process. You can choose from the strategies below or devise one of your own:

- a trampolinist who is struggling to learn a particular skill
- a basketball player who asks you how to improve an aspect of tactical awareness
- a fencer who refuses to believe that they are making critical technical mistakes, when it is obvious that they are.

Strategies
- Demonstrate your technical understanding in the form of a series of choices to achieve the desired outcome.
- Show them a video tape, followed by some suggestions to choose from.
- Ask the performer to reflect on how the skill 'felt', what their opinion of their execution is and how they might improve.

Skills of sports coaches

The essential skills required of a sports coach are illustrated in Fig 16.01.

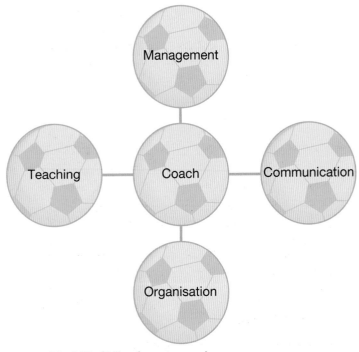

Fig 4.02 Skills of sports coaches

Management

The key ways to demonstrate good leadership in coaching are:

- checking that participants are well prepared and organised

- checking that participants and appropriate others are well deployed
- safe management and coordination of equipment and facilities
- safe and well-delivered sessions
- maintaining support and guidance to participants
- establishing and maintaining effective communication with appropriate others within the coaching environment.

It is important that coaches motivate participants by ensuring that they remain interested and challenged. Coaches will get the best from their sport if they are self-motivated and working in an atmosphere that allows them to:

- enjoy their coaching sessions
- share their experiences with others and socialise with peers and friends
- compete in a safe and non-threatening environment
- achieve negotiated goals
- remain fit and healthy
- achieve success or reward
- please others and receive praise
- create a positive self-image.

Organisation

Planning and organisation are critical to the success of coaching. When planning a session there is much to consider, but the main points are to:

- have identified a set of goals for the session
- have an awareness of the resources available
- have enough information about the participants
- have developed a plan that allows participants to achieve.

During a session coaches need to be constantly making judgements about the following.

- Is the practice working?
- What could be adapted and how?
- Are the facilities being used to full advantage?

Many coaches now keep records, usually in the form of logbooks. Many coaching qualifications require candidates to complete logbooks as part of the formal assessment process. Few coaches have the privilege of just turning up, coaching and going home. Often coaches are also involved in booking facilities, arranging equipment or contacting participants, which involves a great deal of organisation. Some coaches delegate these responsibilities as in the example for a senior women's volleyball team shown at the top of the opposite page.

In some clubs such as this, some or all of these responsibilities and others are undertaken by appropriate others, usually with the coach in control of exactly who is capable and most responsible for the task.

Communication

Perhaps the single most valuable skill is the ability to convey your thoughts and ideas in such a way as to be easily understood. It is not enough to just present your opinions: you must be able to send effective messages – these are mostly non-verbal signals. Consider the body language of a coach in a variety of scenarios. The main feedback a performer receives in almost every sport is non-verbal body language from their coaches.

Talking too much can lead to confusion. The pace, tone and volume of the spoken word will all have a marked effect on participants. The coach who spends most of their time shouting abuse will quickly lose the respect of their participants and will be less likely to be successful.

You must also be able to receive incoming messages. This particular skill is concerned with understanding and interpreting the signs and signals of others, player, officials, etc. You must also listen to opinions from players regarding tactical decisions, drills in practice or perhaps even concerning opponents.

You must also be able to check message reception. Good coaches will question their players and check their understanding. If an instruction is not understood, this is either the fault of the performer lacking concentration or the coach in the quality of the message. One way of ensuring understanding is to ask players to explain a concept in their own words.

Role/responsibilities

Coach: team selection

Assistant coach: warm-up, cool-down and general preparation

Player 1: telephone players to arrange meeting place for away fixtures

Player 2: washing and looking after kit

Player 3: contacting officials prior to games

Player 4: maintaining website and making travel arrangements

Player 5: all communication with league

Player 6: introducing new players and schools liaison

Player 7: seeking sponsorship

LEARNER ACTIVITY
Non-verbal communication

Read the following scenarios.

- An angry basketball coach infuriated because players have failed to understand their instruction.
- The badminton coach who appears confused at the tactic that one of their players has employed.
- The trampoline coach who is pleased with the performer's execution of a difficult routine.

In each case describe gestures, facial expressions and body language that would be typical. Then suggest what effect this would have on the participants in each case.

Devise a list of gestures, facial expressions and body language that you would employ as a coach and, where possible, state in what situations you would use them in your own sport.

Teaching

One of the key processes of teaching is an understanding of how people learn. Drills and practices need to be designed in a way that allows participants to progress at an appropriate pace. As a rule of good practice, the following model is useful when teaching skills:

- introduce and explain the technique
- demonstrate the technique
- practise (allow performers to experience the technique)
- observe and analyse the participants
- identify and correct errors.

It is vital that learning is achieved in simple, short and logical steps. The most valuable knowledge that a coach can gain is through learned experience, judging for themselves and from their performers what is effective and what is not.

Coaching is a continuous process which lends itself to self-reflection and evaluation. Since the knowledge and skills required to be a successful coach are constantly changing and developing with the sport, it is unlikely that coaches will ever reach the point where they will know all that there is to know!

Techniques to improve performance

Coaches in all sports have a number of techniques at their disposal that they can use to improve the performance of their athletes.

Coaching diaries/logbooks

Diaries come in different sizes, paper or electronic. They can be used to record personal thoughts, make appointments or log training sessions. Diaries can be useful in aiding self-reflection, planning and evaluation of coaching sessions.

Guidelines for getting the most from your diary are as follows.

- Complete the diary soon after the coaching session.
- Write down what happened in order.
- Focus on what went well first.
- Describe what needs improvement.
- Action plan to develop what needs to be improved.

The benefits of diaries are that they can show progress over a period of time and are usually honest and describe how you felt about a situation at that time.

Performance profiles

If a trampolinist is not performing a somersault correctly or is not coping with the physical demands of the sport, the coach or trainer can design a suitable exercise or coaching programme. But, what if the trampolinist has trouble with their nerves before the start of the competition or they have some kind of mental block that stops them from executing a skill?

Although not always obvious, the following psychological factors can affect sporting performance.

- Confidence: belief in yourself and your abilities.
- Concentration: the ability to attend to relevant cues, not being distracted.
- Control: the extent to which you feel able to influence events.
- Commitment: the level to which you apply yourself.

Key learning points

The roles of a sports coach are many and varied, and include teacher, trainer, motivator and instructor.

Coaches can have a direct influence on the lives of their performers in terms of their social, psychological, personal and health development.

Most coaches in the UK work to a code of conduct or practice that is established to set the parameters of acceptable behaviour and effective coaching.

The essential skills toolkit of a successful sports coach includes:

- management
- communication
- teaching
- organisation.

- Re-focusing after errors: the ability to adjust to negative outcomes in a positive way.
- Enjoyment: the amount of fun that you can have.

To use a performance profile you would talk with the performer and ask them to tell you how they feel about their sport. Do they ever feel anxious, and if so when? Do they understand the terms above and, if so, how do they rate them?

In the box below a performer has been asked to rate out of ten the importance of each of the factors and then rate their own proficiency in that factor.

Performance factors	Importance to performer	Self-assessment
Confidence	9	9
Commitment	10	10
Concentration	9	6
Control	9	8
Re-focusing after error	10	6
Enjoyment	7	9

Fig 4.03 Coaching the team

It seems that the performer's main emphasis for any intervention should be focused on the areas that they identify as a weakness, in this case re-focusing after errors and concentration.

In the same way, coaches can adapt this approach and apply it to their own coaching (as in the example overleaf).

Intervention: an interruption that brings about change (in sporting performance).

Observation and analysis

It is possible to be observed and analysed by your team or club mates, your coach and by yourself, particularly if you have access to a video of your performance.

Interviews

It is possible to get a great deal of information from an interview. You could ask a performer about what they consider to be their strengths and weaknesses, or you could ask them about what tactics they might use against a particular opponents.

SWOT analysis

This is a subjective analysis of a performance or a performer's ability. Table 4.01 overleaf shows an example of a SWOT analysis carried out on a golfer.

Simulation or conditioned practice

This is about artificially creating a competition-like situation in a practice session, or a particular condition that may be likely to happen in a competitive situation. A basketball coach might consider the merits of initially removing defenders, or outnumbering them in a practice situation that is aimed at improving a particular attacking focus. Defenders can be added when the techniques are well practised. Or, conversely, extra defenders could be added so that the attacking technique could be practised under greater pressure. Similarly, defenders in these practices could be asked to take one of three roles according to the conditions required by the coach:

- passive, offering little resistance other than presence
- active, playing under normal conditions, tempo, intensity
- pressure, playing with extra intensity.

Conditioned games are used when a coach wants to create a situation that is likely to happen in a game, such as practising defending free kicks in football. Or simply adding a condition that emphasises a teaching point, such as choosing a target area on a tennis court with a chalk circle or hoop where the player is expected to return the balls in a practice drill.

Coaching factors	Importance to coach	Self-assessment
Planning and preparation	9	9
Needs of participants considered	10	10
Technical progression and sequencing	9	6
Health and safety observed	9	8
Goals defined at start of session	10	6
Technically accurate instructions/ demonstrations	7	9
Appropriate content and structure		
Variety of drills		
Monitored progress		
Skills related to game situation		
Errors identified and corrected		
Control and behaviour of group		
Time management		
Debrief and feedback to participants		
Checked player understanding		
Stopped and brought group	together	
	Evaluated against objectives set	
	Made provisions for future planning	

Table 4.01 SWOT analysis of a golfer

Strengths	Weaknesses
A good relaxed swing	Not accurate with driving clubs
Excellent body positioning in relation to the ball	Putting is inconsistent
A low-risk safety-first approach	Poor technique in short iron game (head up too early)

Opportunities	Threats
Opponent has no knowledge of the course	Environment – windy day
Short game practice has been improved in recent weeks	Opponent is a better player
Has learnt how to mentally rehearse	Can be prone to getting annoyed easily and letting it spoil their game

LEARNER ACTIVITY SWOT analysis

Interview a performer using the SWOT analysis form below and progressing through the following steps.

- Ask your performer what they consider to be their own personal strengths and weaknesses.
- Watch them in competitive situations and see if you can add to their strengths and weaknesses. It would help to research what the perfect model for their position/sport is, or simply imagine who you would consider to be the best in the world in their position.
- Identify any potential opportunities that they may have in their performance, such as extra training time or access to a scouting report on their opponent.
- Identify any threats to their performance, such as a stronger opponent, difficulty concentrating, a slippery surface or poor equipment.
- Draw up a brief action plan that shows what they might practise or change before their next performance.

Strengths	Weaknesses
Opportunities	Threats

Video analysis

Video gives the person who watches it an objective record of a performance. The greatest benefit of video is the playback feature, including slow motion, which can be used to demonstrate skill execution, tactical efficiency or a more general generic performance evaluation.

Here are some guidelines on the use of video analysis in sport.

- Do not try to film your performers and coach them at the same time. Ask someone reliable to do the filming and brief them on what you want – follow the player or the ball, try and capture tactics or specific techniques, etc.
- Try to pick up all of the sound as it can provide useful feedback.
- Start the recording before the action and end it well after, judging players' body language before and after performance.
- Label and date the film immediately, to keep a record.

Notation

Notation is a way of collecting data and can be done by hand or with a computer. Hand notation is a system of recording detailed analysis of a sport and literally noting the data on a sheet of paper using a pre-defined set of symbols. Systems like this exist for many sports, such as tennis, archery and football.

The advantage of these systems is that they are inexpensive and, if completed by a skilful recorder, will produce quick information in real time, so that the coach or performer can have instant access to detailed information. The main disadvantages of this system are that it is open to human error, can be difficult to interpret and can be difficult in certain conditions such as bad weather.

On the next page there is an example of a match analysis sheet for a team sport. This could be filled in by the performer, a peer or a neutral observer, scoring 1 to 10 for both achieved and target scores.

Team sport match analysis

Date:	Opponent:		Result:	
Analysis area			**Mark**	**Target**
Positional play				
Tactical awareness/decision-making				
Fitness levels				
Skills/techniques				
Cooperation/teamwork				
Concentration/psychological factors				
Diet/nutrition				

LEARNER ACTIVITY Conditioned practice

For each scenario below suggest a condition that a coach might use in a practice session. Note how they might organise the practice, and what the condition/s would be.

- You are a tennis coach and the junior players that you coach are playing in their first tournament at the weekend. Most of them are very nervous, to the extent that you think their performance may suffer. There will be spectators, including their parents.
- You are a rugby coach responsible for a team that is not very good at tackling or covering break-away plays. In your next fixture you play a team that handles the ball well, switches the ball well in either direction and is particularly strong at exploiting gaps in defensive lines. Think of practices that encourage communication and decision-making.
- You are a kayak instructor responsible for a group who are reasonably experienced paddlers. They are about to embark on their first overnight expedition, much of which requires them to be in remote areas with no means of external contact. You need to satisfy yourself that all the participants are aware of their role in a variety of emergency situations.

Key learning points

- Coaches can make good use of reflective diaries in order to improve their coaching performance.
- Performance profiles can be used for performers and coaches alike.
- Coaches are expected to make interventions to improve performance having identified areas for development.
- Coaches can condition games to facilitate the teaching of a specific skill or tactic.

Plan a coaching session

Planning can be separated into the following stages:

- collecting and reviewing relevant information
- identifying participant needs
- goal setting
- identifying appropriate resources
- identifying appropriate activities to enable goals to be achieved
- planning coaching sessions and/or programmes.

Before you coach any session you need to answer the following questions.

- What is the starting point, what are their skill levels, who are they?
- Where do they want to be and what do they want from you?
- How will you achieve this?
- What will you need to do this – facilities, equipment, etc.?
- How will you/they know if they have improved?

To plan an effective coaching session or programme of sessions, the coach needs to establish:

- the number of participants, as this will affect the kinds of practices that the coach can employ
- the age of participants, as this will affect the kinds of practices that the coach can use, and even how they might approach coaching that group
- the level of experience and ability of the participants

- whether the participants have any special requirements relating to diet, health, culture or language.

An example of a session planner is reproduced in the box below.

Setting SMART goals

It is a good idea to use the SMART principle when planning your sessions or season.

Specific: this means that the session meets what you want it to meet, and is specific to the sport. For example, you could focus a cricket batting session on dealing with short-pitched, fast deliveries, thus being explicit and specific.

Measurable: this is the way in which you measure your results. If you have identified that you want to improve a basketball player's jump shooting, then you might measure this by counting how many shots are successful in a training or game situation and then measure again after the training programme.

Session Planner	
Date:	Venue:
Time:	Duration:
Group:	No. of participants:
Equipment required:	Aims of session:
Safety checks required:	
TIME	CONTENT
	Warm-up:
	Fitness work:
	Main technical skills work:
	Game play/tactical work:
	Cool-down:
Injuries/issues arising:	
Evaluation of session:	

Achievable: what you set out to improve must be possible. It would not be fair to ask a beginner in trampolining to complete a complicated routine with multiple somersaults.

Realistic: it must be possible and realistic to achieve what you intend to achieve.

Time-constrained: there should be a reasonable amount of time to achieve the learning goal. Some goals will be short term in nature and established to be achieved in the next session, others more long term and established for the entire season.

Health and safety

The health and safety of all involved in sport should be the most important of considerations of the coach. In most cases it is necessary to ensure that facilities and equipment are safe and well maintained, and that performers are adequately aware of key health and safety issues, particularly relating to their own safety and the safety of others.

Coaches should consider the following as a checklist, though it is by no means exhaustive.

- The context in which the sport will take place – the facilities and equipment. Does the provider have a normal operating procedure and emergency action plan? This should cover number of players allowed, coach:learner ratio, conduct and supervision, hazardous behaviours, fire and evacuation procedures.
- The nature of the sport, for playing and training:
  - what to do when rules are not observed
  - what to do with injured players
  - not teaching activities beyond the capabilities of the performers
  - in competitive situations matching performers where appropriate by size, maturity or age.
- The players:
  - Are you aware of any special individual medical needs, and the types of injuries common to the sport?
  - Safety education – informing players of inherent risks and establishing a code of behaviour.
  - Team-mates and opponents to be aware of their responsibilities to each other.
  - Players should be discouraged from participating with an existing injury.
- The coach:

- safe practices
- safe numbers for the area
- arranging appropriate insurance
- dealing with and reporting accidents
- being aware of emergency actions.

Risk assessments

Risk assessments are not just forms to fill out. A risk assessment is a skill that helps prevent accidents or serious events. You need to consider what could go wrong and how likely it is.

Risk assessments should be kept and logged, and stored in a safe place. Examples of risk assessments for sporting activities are wide ranging and will depend upon who they are prepared for, the nature of the sport and the competence of the person making the assessment.

LEARNER ACTIVITY
Session plan
As part of your job, you have been asked to coach some sessions in your own sport with a group of beginner adults at the local leisure centre. Design a sample session plan and complete six session plans indicating:

- participant details
- your objectives for all six sessions
- a risk assessment for your activity.

Contingency planning

Nothing ever goes completely to plan and for that reason it is good practice to plan for the unexpected so that everyone remains safe and continues to learn. Consider the following as examples of what can happen and what you could plan for.

- Weather threatens your outside session.
- You fall ill and are no longer able to continue as coach.
- There are not enough participants for the session.
- The facility is double-booked when you arrive for the session.
- The group are not responding to your style of coaching or the practices that you have chosen.

The components of a session

While the demands of the structure of sessions for different sports are quite different, the general rules for the layout of sessions are common to all sports.

Warm-up: to physically and mentally prepare and focus the performers.

Skill learning phase: the objectives of the session are established and employed through a series of drills or practices, perhaps with a competition, followed by an evaluation.

Cool-down: the final and often ignored phase that is concerned with restoring normality to body functions and that has a role to play in injury prevention and emotional control.

Fig 4.04 A coach working with skiers

Key learning points

- Planning is the first stage of coaching and requires the gathering of information relating to performers, facilities and resources.
- Effective coaches use session planners to show what they have planned for a session and to maintain a record.
- Health and safety is the most important consideration in the planning and delivery of coaching sessions.
- Contingency plans are back-up plans that can be used in the event of an unforeseen circumstance that threatens the safety or quality of the coaching session.

Deliver a coaching session

This is concerned with the actual 'doing' part of coaching, and will help with the principles of coaching sessions.

Like the planning of a session, delivering a session follows a logical path.

- Ensure the session plan fits all.
- Identify any risks to the delivery of the session.
- Introduce and start planned activities.
- Manage the behaviour of all involved.
- Monitor and adapt the session as it progresses.
- Summarise and conclude the coaching session.

Once the session is under way, the coach should work to maintain what is going well, and the role of the coach changes to become more of a manager/supervisor.

Skills should be introduced, followed by an explanation which could help performers understand their relevance and when they could be used in a competitive situation.

A competent demonstration should follow, which could be from the coach or with the aid of a video model. This must be a technically correct example and should be thorough, without too much explanation. There should be a balance between verbal instruction and visual demonstration. There will also need to be a balance between activity, instruction and discussion depending on the age, experience and maturity of performers. It is essential for the coach to note the differing rates of learning of individuals.

Performers will then need time to practise the skill or technique. Coaches can use questions to check understanding. The role of the coach changes again to become one of observer/analyst, and it is here that the coach will be looking to assist learners and correct any faults.

To improve performance the coach must have highly developed awareness relating to how to identify errors, compare to a perfect model example and, most importantly, knowledge of how to bridge the gap using feedback, observation and application of a range of suitable techniques.

There is no substitute for practice at this stage. A session that is continually interrupted by a coach for whatever reason is less likely to be successful. It is also important that a coach does not attempt too much in one session.

Most coaches enjoy this part of the coaching process the most, but it is too easy to forget what the aims of the session are and how to keep track of achievement.

> ## LEARNER ACTIVITY
> ## Skill introduction
>
> Using the following as a process, describe how you would choose to introduce a skill or technique from a sport of your choice:
>
> - explain
> - demonstrate
> - practise
> - observe
> - analyse.
>
> Explain your reasoning where appropriate.

Reviewing a session

It is important to consider that coaching does not end at the end of a session when everyone has cooled down or even gone home. Coaching is a continuous process, and the best coaches reflect on what happened and, more importantly, how to improve. A well-considered evaluation should aid the improvement of subsequent sessions.

The process is as follows.

- Collect, analyse and review – information about the session from feedback, self-reflection and from others.
- Session effectiveness – identify the effectiveness of the session in achieving objectives.
- Review key aspects – drills or practices.
- Identify development needs and take steps to action them.

When evaluating a session a coach should consider the following.

- **Performance against pre-set goals**: effective coaches will be familiar with the goals for the season, both long and short term. There should be an opportunity to decide to what extent, if at all, the session objectives were met and to what extent this matched the other goals.
- **Participants' progress**: the review will enable coaches to monitor the performer's progress over a period of time, and help plan for future sessions. Typical review questions could be:

  - How well did the performers learn the skills or techniques introduced to them?
  - What performance developments were evident for each participant?
  - Are the performers ready to progress to the next session?
- **Coaching ability:** this is the part where the coach can review their own performance:
  - What went well?
  - What went less well?
  - How did the performers respond?
  - Were the performers bored or restless?
  - Did the coach behave acceptably?
- **Future targets:** this is all about planning for future goals and objectives based on achievements and progress made by participants.

Tools for the review process

There are a number of tools that coaches can use.

- Videos – an excellent way of improving your coaching effectiveness. Videos can be used to judge coaching actions, interaction with your performers, facial expressions and gestures, as well as what you say.
- Critical analysis and self-reflection – self-reflection allows you to explore your perceptions, decisions and subsequent actions to work out ways in which performers can improve technical, tactical or physical ability.
- A mentor – a mentor coach can help provide you with a role-model figure who can offer you practical solutions, work as a sounding board and generally provide you with a range of support.
- Coaching diaries – these can act as a permanent source of information to record your own thoughts and feelings, and serve as a true account of what happened and when. Diaries or logs can certainly help with self-reflection and form the basis of action plans for improvement.

Formative and summative reviews

A formative review occurs during the process of coaching and changes can be made immediately. A summative review is done at the end of the coaching session as you reflect on the process overall.

Key learning points

- Delivery of a coaching session starts with an effective warm-up related to that activity or sport, and finishes with a cool-down and evaluation.

- Coaches could structure the skill-learning phase to include an introduction, explanation, demonstration, practice and review.

- At the end of a session the coach should take time to reflect on the quality of the session and plan for future improvements.

Review questions

1 Describe the role of motivator for a coach.
2 In what ways can a coach influence the development of individuals?
3 Provide examples of what a code of practice for coaches should include.
4 What are the advantages of a coaching diary or log?
5 What is a coaching intervention and describe one?
6 What is a conditioned game?
7 What kind of information would be essential to a coach prior to starting a first session with a group of beginners?
8 Describe the process of teaching a particular skill from any sport, e.g. basketball lay-up shot, assuming that you do not need to consider warm-up and cool-down.
9 When evaluating a coaching session, what do you need to focus on?
10 Describe the role of a mentor in the coaching process.

References

Crisfield, P. (2001) *Analysing your Coaching*, Coachwise.

Miles, A. (2004) *Coaching Practice*, Coachwise.

Stafford-Brown, J., Rea, S., Janaway, L. and Manley, C. (2006) *BTEC First Sport*, Hodder Arnold.

Goals

By the end of this chapter you should:

- understand the key concepts in sports development
- know about the key providers of sports development
- understand how quality is measured in sports development
- know about sports development in practice.

Sports development, as we understand the term today, has been evolving over the last 25 years. It now has a wider national importance, which is demonstrated in its positive links with other important national issues such as health, crime reduction, lifelong learning and economic regeneration.

The chapter starts by looking briefly at the background to the evolvement of sports development. Models of sports development and their uses will be considered, as will the use of target groups within sports development work. An understanding of the barriers that there are to sports participation will be provided and the difference between provision and enablement in sports development will be discussed.

The key providers of sports development are then explored, and the structures and functions they use to deliver their work are discussed. The many different roles that exist for sports development workers will also be examined.

Methods often used to measure quality in sports development are discussed, together with the purpose of these quality measures along with their relative advantages and disadvantages.

Finally, the chapter will look at sports development in practice. The importance of working in partnership will be demonstrated, as will some examples of current initiatives. The overall effectiveness of sports development will be discussed.

Understand the key concepts in sports development

Sports development is defined as:

> Ultimately about provision of more and better quality opportunities for people, irrespective of age, gender or level of ability/disability, to access sport

(Eady, 1993)

Sports development is a broad term that has itself developed over time. It is used to describe the work undertaken by a range of organisations that try to ensure a positive change in sporting behaviour or physical activity throughout the community.

Fig 5.01 Enjoying sport

Sports development was first accepted as a term in the Wolfenden Report of 1960. The recommendations of the Wolfenden Report led to more sports facilities being developed in the UK and to financial support being given to governing bodies for sport. It also led to government funds being used for sporting initiatives and for national councils for sport. In essence the outcomes of the report provided the principal framework for sports development until 1998. The scope of sports development was then widened by 'New Labour'. This will be considered in more detail later.

LEARNER ACTIVITY

There have been a number of national sports development campaigns. An understanding of them is key to your understanding of sports development.

Research and make brief notes in your own words on the following:

- 1970s Sport for All? campaign
- 1980s Action Sport
- 2005 Everyday Sport campaign.

Sports development continuum

The sports development continuum is used widely by many sporting organisations in the UK to help inform strategies and policies on sports development. It locates the development of sport on a hierarchical basis from foundation, participation and performance to excellence (see Fig 5.02).

- **Foundation** – encouraging young people into the exercise habit and developing basic movement and sports skills (for example, throwing, catching and hand–eye coordination) to provide a foundation for personal development and future participation in the sport of their choice.
- **Participation** – opportunities for all members of the community to take part in a sport, whether for reasons of enjoyment, fitness, social contact or simply to get involved in the sport for its own sake.
- **Performance** – opportunities for those already participating to improve their performance from whatever base they start, where the desire to improve is the key factor for involvement.
- **Excellence** – opportunities for those with the interest and ability to achieve publicly measured levels of excellence.

The model implies that individuals move upwards through the continuum until they find their preferred level or the limit to their ability. It is a simple but useful model as it demonstrates the integration of different forms of involvement in sport.

This traditional model has been refined over time to take into account the rather more complex methods via which an individual may move along the continuum (see Fig 5.03).

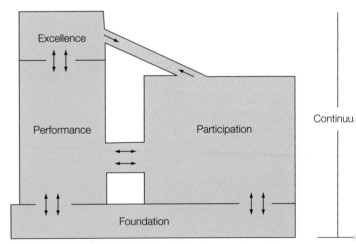

Fig 5.03 Model 2 of the sports development continuum (Source: Sport England)

The final model (see Fig 5.04) is flexible enough to allow an individual to remain at a particular level of performance for the time being if they choose, or to allow the individual to leave and re-enter the sport (and the level at which they participate) over time.

In addition to these models of the sports development continuum, other stages have sometimes been added. For example, a stage has often been added after 'participation' to show that many

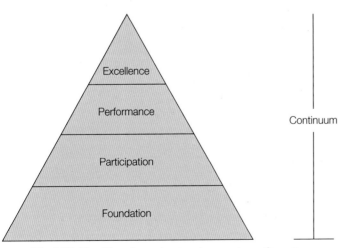

Fig 5.02 Traditional sports development continuum

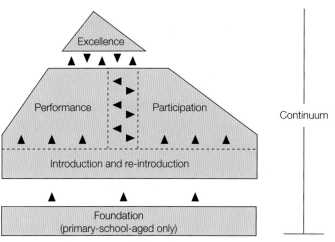

Fig 5.04 Revised model 2 of the sports development continuum

participants become 'committed participants' before they move on to become performers:

Foundation → participation → committed participation → performance → excellence

Target goups

Fig 5.05 Older people participating in sport

Inequalities have traditionally existed within sport, particularly in relation to gender, race and disability.

Sport England identified 'target groups' in sport in the 1980s. These were groups of people who were under-represented in terms of participation in sport. These target groups included:

- women
- people aged 50+
- people with a disability
- young people
- black and minority ethnic groups.

definition

Sport England (the brand name of the English Sports Council): established by Royal Charter in 1972, Sport England is responsible for promoting and investing in sport thereby helping the government meet its sporting objectives. At present it is the principal deliverer of government and Lottery funding to sport.

Sport can and does play a big role in promoting the inclusion of all groups in society. Therefore, many different campaigns and activities have been organised across the UK in order to try to increase the number of people from these target groups participating in sport and physical activity. The two case studies on the next page demonstrate initiatives aimed at target groups.

In sport these target groups are not the only population groups that are under-represented. As in society in general, many population groups may feel discriminated against. Today the main organisations involved in sports development have moved away from using the term 'target groups' and instead use the term 'sports equity'.

> Sports equity is about fairness in sport, equality of access, recognising inequalities and taking steps to address them. It is about changing the culture of sport to ensure that it becomes equally accessible to everyone in society, whatever their ethnic origin, age, gender, impairment, social and economic status or level of ability

(Sport England Equity Statement)

All organisations involved in sports development are now encouraged to ensure equal opportunities are at the heart of all their policies. This is demonstrated in Sport England's publication *The Framework for Sport in England*, published in 2004, which sets out the strategic direction and policy priorities for sport in England. Within the framework, sports equity and variations in access are given a high priority. Visit www.sportengland.org to find out more.

LEARNER ACTIVITY

Carry out research to find out where the nearest 'inclusive' gym is in relation to where you live.

Case study

Football Unites Racism Divides

In Sheffield, Football Unites Racism Divides (FURD), in partnership with Millennium Volunteers, runs a football academy for four hours on a Sunday with Sheffield United Football Club. This academy, which has been running since 1995, has increased the number of people from black and minority ethnic groups who are involved in organised football at a grassroots level. It has been very successful, attracting well over 100 youngsters aged from six upwards each week. It has also attracted a number of volunteers, from very diverse backgrounds, who help to deliver the football programme each week.

Fig 5.06 Football unites, racism divides

Case study

Inclusive Fitness Initiative

The English Federation of Disability Sports piloted the Inclusive Fitness Initiative in 1998. The aim of the initiative was to include equipment in gyms that could be used by people with a disability. The pilot was successful so Sport England awarded the initiative £5m of Lottery funds to extend it further. There are now 150 'inclusive' gyms all across England.

Barriers to participation

Even though there has been a huge growth in the number of sports facilities open for public use since the 1970s, there has not been the same increase in participation. A number of barriers have been identified that can affect an individual's ability to participate in sport. These include the following.

- **Cultural barriers** – the beliefs and knowledge of individuals and communities about sport and physical activity may prevent them participating in some or all sports. For example, women's rates of participation in sport are consistently lower than those experienced by men in England. Different cultures also put different values on sport. In some countries, such as the USA, sport has a high profile, whereas in others it is not valued.
- **Social barriers** – the social class of a person can have a major bearing on their sports participation. People in the 'professional' social class are three times more likely to participate in sport than those in the 'unskilled manual' group.

- **Economic barriers** – sports participation for many people is out of reach because they simply cannot afford the membership fees, equipment or clothing required. They may also not be able to get to the sporting facility of their choice because they do not own a car or cannot afford public transport.
- **Historical barriers** – many sports have been around for a long time and have often been played by predominantly one type of population group. It is, therefore, often hard to change these sports.
- **Fitness/health barriers** – some people who do not participate in sport do have genuine health reasons why they should not. Health professionals try to encourage most people to participate in sport for the many associated physical and mental health benefits. However, many people do not take part in sport because they think they will not be any good at it, or because they are simply too embarrassed.

LEARNER ACTIVITY

Choose a sport you are currently participating in. Answer the following questions.

- Are there any barriers that affect your participation in this sport at the moment?
- What barriers do you think may affect your participation in this sport in the future, i.e. in 10 or 20 years' time?
- Compare your answers to those of a partner and highlight any similarities or differences.

Cross-cutting agendas

The focus of sports development was widened in the late 1990s when Labour was elected to government. In particular, it wanted to use the wider benefits of sports participation to tackle 'social exclusion'.

> There are so many reasons to invest in sport. It helps our children become fit and healthy. It diverts many young people from crime and disorder. They do better at school.
>
> *(Tessa Jowell MP, Secretary of State for Culture, Media and Sport, 2004)*

definition

Social exclusion: social exclusion is a term used to describe what can happen when people or areas suffer from a combination of linked problems such as unemployment, poor skills, low incomes, poor housing, high crime, bad health and family breakdown.

The wider benefits of sporting participation include the following.

- Improving the health of the nation. By participating in sport and physical activity certain mental and physical health problems can be reduced. For example, 30 minutes of moderate activity five times a week can reduce the risk of cardiovascular diseases, some cancers, strokes and obesity.

Fig 5.07 Regular gym use increases fitness

- Reduction of crime and drug use. There has been some evidence that sports participation has a positive effect on crime reduction and drug use.
- Raising educational standards.
- More cohesive, sustainable communities.

Provision and enabling

There are many different ways of providing sports development activities.

- Many organisations directly provide courses on specific sports. For example, swimming lessons are run by many different organisations including schools, local authority sports centres and private/commercial providers. These organisations may run 'taster sessions' to encourage participants to try out a sport before they commit to paying for more sessions.
- Some organisations in sports development, such as sports coach UK, do not directly provide sports

Case study

⚽ Positive Futures programme

This programme is aimed at 10–16 year olds at risk. Its aim is to reduce youth offending and drug use, and increase regular participation in sport and physical activity.

The programme has operated in 24 locations, one of which is on the Gascoigne estate in Barking. In Barking this programme has worked in partnership with Leyton Orient Football Club's community sports programme to set up a football scheme on the estate that has mushroomed into a community sports club for teenagers. Police statistics show that the number of offences in this ward had decreased by 77 per cent in June to August 2001 compared with the same quarter in 2000 immediately prior to the start of this programme.

development activities. They instead enable and facilitate the activities being run by other organisations by providing, for example, coach education courses. Many sports development organisations may also give grants or help with the provision of sports equipment or facilities to enable sports development activities to take place.

- Partnership working (two or more organisations working together) in sports development is very common. This may include, for example, a local authority sports development department joining forces with a Primary Care Trust to deliver initiatives such as a GP referral scheme.

Key learning points

- Sports development is a broad term used to describe the work undertaken by a range of organisations that try to ensure a positive change in sporting behaviour or physical activity throughout the community.
- There are four main stages in the sports development continuum: foundation, participation, performance and excellence.
- The key target groups that have been highlighted as being under-represented in terms of participation in sport are:
  - women
  - people aged 50+
  - people with a disability
  - young people
  - black and minority ethnic groups.
- Sports equity is the 'in vogue' term used today to describe how all sports should be accessible to everyone.
- There are a number of barriers to people participating in sport. These include social, economic, cultural, historical and health barriers.
- There are different ways of providing sports development activities, including directly providing an activity, enabling another organisation to provide an activity or working in a partnership.

The key providers of sports development

There are many different organisations involved in the provision of sports development today. These include national organisations such as UK Sport, and voluntary organisations such as sports coach UK. Most local authorities have a sports development unit or department. There are also a number of professional and private-sector sports development providers. We will now look at some of these in more detail.

National organisations

> **definition**
>
> Department of Culture, Media and Sport (DCMS): the DCMS is the government department responsible for policy direction in sport (as well as tourism and creative industries). It aims to improve the quality of life for its people through cultural and sporting activities and through the strengthening of the sport, tourism and creative industries. Visit www.culture.gov.uk for more details of its work.

UK Sport

UK Sport was established by Royal Charter in 1996. It has a strategic role in sports development. It focuses on high-performance sport in the UK, with the aim of achieving sporting excellence on the world stage. It works in partnership with the sports councils (i.e. Sport England, Sport Wales and Sport Scotland) and other agencies. It is responsible for managing and distributing public funds (approximately £29 million annually) and is a distributor of funds raised by the National Lottery.

UK Sport is responsible to the Department for Culture, Media and Sport (DCMS). Its work is directed by a board, to which the DCMS appoints members. This board meets every two months. It also has various committees that report to the board on different matters.

For more details on its work visit www.uksport.gov.uk.

Sport England

County Sports Partnership (CSP): there are 49 CSPs across England, whose core funding comes from Sport England. A County Sports Partnership is a partnership of agencies that seek to make the connections between national planning and local delivery. They aim to provide 'one voice for sport' in each county. Their main goals are to:

- put together pathways for young people to move on in sport
- help club development in their area
- develop the workforce involved in sport.

Sport England also has a strategic role in sports development. It is responsible for promoting and investing in sport and helping the government meet its sporting objectives in England.

Sport England's vision is to make England an active and successful sporting nation. It aims to achieve this by getting people to:

- **start in sport** – to improve the health of the nation, particularly for disadvantaged groups
- **stay in sport** – through a thriving network of clubs, coaches and volunteers, and a commitment to equity
- **succeed in sport** – via an infrastructure capable of developing world-class performers.

Since 1994 it has invested £2bn in sport in England. This money comes from the Lottery and from government funds.

The main board of Sport England has overall responsibility for its performance. It deals with strategy, finance, major projects and performance management. Its board members are appointed by the DCMS. Its chief executive is responsible to the main board for the day-to-day running of Sport England. It also has a number of committees that focus on specific tasks, strategies or policies. They report back to the main board.

Sport England works through nine regional offices, along with their regional sports boards. It also funds County Sports Partnerships throughout England.

Visit www.sportengland.org for more details on its work.

Voluntary organisations

There are a number of voluntary, independent agencies that are outside the influence of the government organisations mentioned above. They also have a great influence on policies and strategies for sport, though. These include:

- the Central Council for Physical Recreation (CCPR)
- the Youth Sport Trust (YST)
- sports coach UK (SCUK).

The Central Council for Physical Recreation

The Central Council for Physical Recreation (CCPR) has existed since 1944. It is the 'umbrella organisation' for the national governing and representative bodies of sport and recreation in the UK. It works on behalf of:

- 270 national governing and representative bodies of sport and recreation
- 150,000 voluntary sports clubs
- millions of individuals who participate in sport and recreation.

The CCPR:

- speaks and acts to **promote, protect and develop** the interests of sport and physical recreation at all levels

- is at the **forefront** of sports politics, providing support and services to those who participate in and administer sport and recreation

- is **completely independent** of any form of Government control

- has **no responsibility** for allocating funds

- is strictly **non-party** and will support or oppose proposed measures only on the basis of their perceived value to sport and recreation

(Source: www.ccpr.org.uk)

Sports National Governing Bodies

All major sports in Britain have a National Governing Body (NGB); for example, the Football Association is the governing body for football, the All England Netball Association is the governing body for netball and the Lawn Tennis Association is the governing body for tennis. There are over 265 governing bodies in the UK.

LTA
TENNIS NATION

Teams and clubs normally pay a subscription to their sport's governing body, which administers the sport nationally and organises competitions and the national team.

Most sports governing bodies receive funding and resources from Sport England. To receive this funding each NGB has to produce a whole sport plan (see definition below).

The NGB for each sport may also receive funding and resources for its elite athletes from UK Sport.

definition

Whole sport plan: these are plans for the whole of a sport from grassroots to performance (at a county level). They will identify the help and resources they need to deliver their plans; for example, partners such as county sports partnerships, and programmes such as PE, School Sport and Club Links (PESSCL).

The Youth Sport Trust

The Youth Sport Trust was established in 1994 as a registered charity and supports the education and development of all young people through physical education (PE) and sport. It believes that all young people have the right to:

YOUTH SPORT TRUST

- experience and enjoy PE and sport
- a quality introduction to PE and sport suited to their own level of development
- the best teaching, the best coaching and the best resources
- experience and benefit from positive competition
- develop a healthy lifestyle
- progress along a structured pathway of sporting opportunities
- fulfil their sporting potential.

LEARNER ACTIVITY

Visit the Youth Sport Trust's website (www.youthsporttrust.org) and find out more about some of the initiatives it is involved in, such as:

- TOP programme
- PE, School Sport and Club Links (PESSCL)
- Specialist Sport Colleges and School Sport Partnerships.

sports coach UK

sports coach UK was established in 1983 (it was originally named the National Coaching Foundation) as a sub-committee of the Sports Council but became a separate charitable organisation in 1989. It works at a strategic level, its main aim being to guide the development and implementation of a coaching

Great Coaches...Great Sport

system for all coaches at every level in the UK. Its main activities include:

- providing coaching resources
- running coaching courses
- administering coaching qualifications
- working with governing bodies to raise the quality of coaching schemes.

A board of directors who are responsible for policy direction runs sports coach UK. The management team implements these policies on a day-to-day basis. The organisation also has a network of Coach Development Officers (one per county) who work on these activities at a local level.

Local authorities

Local authorities are extremely important to the sports development industry. They spend approximately £1bn per year on sport and leisure – more than 50 per cent of the total resources available to sport. They follow the national lead in developing sport.

> There is a need for all local authorities to 'take the lead' individually or in partnership with neighbouring authorities for overseeing the strategic planning for structured sport, physical education and lifelong learning through sport ...
>
> *(Sport England, 2004)*

Local authorities recognise the benefits of developing sport for their population. Most local authorities employ at least one Sports Development Officer, while many will have a whole team. They will tend to focus on sports participation trends within their area and will then target their resources at any apparent inequalities that exist.

Local authorities in the UK directly provide many public leisure facilities, including sports halls, swimming pools, golf courses and football pitches. They, therefore, provide most of the facilities used to facilitate sports development activities. Many operate concessionary schemes or special initiatives within these facilities in order to encourage as many of their population to use their facilities as possible. They also have important links to schools in terms of sporting facilities and policies on sport.

Fig 5.08 Local authority-owned swimming pool

Many local authorities also support local organisations in their development of sports facilities, sometimes with financial help, but mainly with advice on strategy and building regulations.

Private and professional organisations

There are many private organisations involved in directly providing sports development activities. For example, many private leisure or health clubs run activities for their paying members, such as swimming, golf or tennis lessons.

There are also many small businesses within the sports development industry that run sports coaching sessions for a fee. They may provide, for example, football coaching sessions for children.

Sport development roles

Sports development is one of the fastest-growing areas of the sports industry and just as there are many different organisations involved in sports development, there are also many different roles. The decision to award the 2012 Olympics to London means that there is likely to be an increase in opportunities for Sports Development Officers (SDOs) over the coming years.

SDOs aim to improve access to sport and physical activity for people of all ages and ability. They may promote sport in general, working for a County Sports Partnership or local authority, or may be Sports Specific Development Officers (SSDOs), concentrating on a specific sport and working for an NGB.

Generally an SDO's work can include anything from organising events for communities, devising and implementing sports programmes, ensuring people can get access to activities, linking into local and regional sports initiatives, as well as speaking to schools, clubs, governing bodies and individuals. They may work with the local community, liaising with clubs and schools, as well as agencies such as the police and sports' National Governing Bodies.

They may also work closely with specific groups, including those who may not have had access to sporting opportunities before, such as the socially excluded, young people, disabled people, or people from disadvantaged backgrounds.

Much of their work involves formulating and implementing strategies aimed at increasing participation and improving standards.

There are currently approximately 100,000 paid SDOs working in the UK. There are, however, many more people working in sports development who are volunteers i.e. in a non-paid capacity. A recent study by Sport England (Sport Volunteering in England, 2002) estimated that there are 5.8 million volunteers in sport. Their roles range from coaching and officiating in local clubs to sitting on regional sports boards.

Case study

London Borough of Enfield: free swims for 0–18 year olds

As part of its target to increase the number of attendances at leisure centres by young people (aged 0–18), the London Borough of Enfield, in partnership with Enfield Leisure Centres Ltd (ELCL), the operator of the Council's leisure facilities, agreed a free swims programme during public swimming sessions for several weeks during school holidays in 2006. The cost to the Council was £18,000.

The free swims were located in Council-owned facilities in the eastern corridor of the borough, which is one of the more deprived areas in Enfield and where many young people are not currently taking part in sporting activities. The scheme was extremely successful, with approximately 20,000 extra swims by young people taking place during this period in comparison with similar periods in 2005.

The aim is that the free swims initiative will encourage the young people who have taken part to continue to take part regularly in swimming or other physical activity in the future and to make physical activity a habit in their lives.

> ... 47% of young people's volunteering takes place in sport. The sport sector accounts for 26% of all volunteers and volunteers are vital to the success of our national sporting life – the London Marathon relies on 6000 volunteers. The Manchester Commonwealth Games involved 10,000 volunteers and the role of volunteers will be integral to the 2012 Olympics ... [and Paralympic Games]

(Russell Commission, 2005)

Many sports clubs are run entirely by volunteers. Volunteers are now recognised by the main organisations involved in sports development as making an extremely important contribution. As a result, a number of initiatives have been set up to try to encourage more people to volunteer in sport, e.g. Sport England's 'Step into Sport' initiative.

LEARNER ACTIVITY

Answer the following questions on the 'Step into Sport' initiative by visiting www.sportengland.org.uk.

- What is the initiative about?
- Who is it for?
- How does it work?

Key learning points

- There are a number of key providers in sports development including:
  - national organisations such as UK Sport and Sport England
  - voluntary organisations such as sports coach UK and National Governing Bodies of sports
  - local authorities
  - private and professional organisations.
- There are currently approximately 100,000 people in paid employment in the sports development industry. They are employed in a variety of roles but are collectively known as sports development officers.
- There are a vast number of volunteers (i.e. non-paid) working in the sports development industry. They have a variety of roles, ranging from coaching at a local club to sitting on a regional sports board.

Quality measurement in sports development

definition

Quality: displaying excellence in an organisation.

Methods of quality measurement in sports development

Traditionally many different methods have been used to try to measure quality in sports development, such as attendances at sporting activities or local participation levels. These methods have not provided consistency across the sports development industry because not all organisations have measured the same outputs or used the same methods to do so. As a result of this, and to gain the benefits listed below, a number of schemes have been developed to measure quality in sports development. The main idea behind these schemes is that by putting together a clear set of quality standards that are appropriate to the industry sector, performance in the sector can be measured more realistically. The main quality measures that have been developed, and are appropriate to sports development, include those described below.

Towards an Excellent Service (TAES)

This quality scheme was originally developed by Sport England for local authority sport and recreation services. An additional modified version was created to be used by County Sports Partnerships (CSPs) within the sports development industry. This scheme is based on good practice taken from other quality schemes used across the sports industry. TAES aims to provide a clear measurement of the present and future health of 'how' a CSP is functioning through an assessment that defines its strengths and areas for improvement.

In practice, each CSP has to complete a self-assessment on different areas of its work and grade itself as either poor, fair, good or excellent. External assessors then carry out their own assessment of the CSP. The results of these two assessments are combined to create an improvement plan where the CSP identifies its improvement priorities. It will then measure its progress towards these priorities over a specified time period.

Quest

This quality management system is aimed at sports development units in local authorities, governing bodies and voluntary organisations. The Quest quality management system defines what the industry standards in sports development are and what good practice is. It encourages organisations to apply and develop these standards in all areas of their work: management, operations, customer relations and staffing, etc.

To achieve Quest accreditation organisations must have both a self-assessment improvement programme and the opportunity for an independent external assessment. Here is an example.

1   To complete a self-assessment improvement programme an organisation must look at all the work it currently does and assess how well it thinks it is doing. It then has to put together an action plan of how and when it is going to improve on certain areas. This action plan has to be monitored and evaluated regularly so that the organisation is constantly striving for improvement. This promotes continuous improvement within its work.
2   External assessment/audits are completed by an industry professional who carries out an independent audit of the organisation's work.

There are a number of other quality awards that are used within the sports development industry, such as:

- ISO 9001:2000
- Investors In People
- Charter Mark
- Green Flag (for grass pitches).

LEARNER ACTIVITY

In pairs, each select two of the quality awards listed below:

- ISO 9001:2000
- Investors In People
- Charter Mark
- Green Flag (for grass pitches).

Using a variety of sources, find out more about them, write a brief summary of each and then share your findings with your partner.

National Governing Body schemes

Many sports' National Governing Bodies have themselves developed their own quality schemes or quality marks that are open for their members to achieve. One good example is the Amateur Swimming Association's (ASA) Swim 21 Accreditation scheme, which is its own 'quality mark' scheme. It recognises nationally and regionally the swimming clubs that are committed to providing safe, effective and high-quality services for the benefit of their members.

To gain this quality mark, swimming clubs must work towards attaining a series of outcomes. These are seen as essential if the right level of support is to be provided at each stage of a swimmer's development.

The Swim 21 scheme is really a planning tool, based on the principles of Long Term Athlete Development (see below), enabling swimming clubs to help athletes, teachers, coaches and administrators to achieve their full potential. It focuses mainly on the needs of swimmers – looking to provide them with the best possible support and environment.

> **definition**
>
> Long Term Athlete Development (LTAD): **the principle used to achieve optimal training, competition and recovery throughout an athlete's career.**

Other examples of quality marks or schemes used by sports' governing bodies include the Football Association's Charter Standard and the Amateur Athletic Association of England Clubmark award.

An added benefit of gaining a quality mark or award is that many are recognised by Sport England as a Clubmark accredited scheme. Swim 21 is one such award and therefore all clubs gaining Swim 21 accreditation will automatically receive Clubmark status. Clubmark is a Sport England quality accreditation scheme, which will eventually be accessible to all sports. It seeks to ensure that young people are participating within a safe and friendly environment.

Why measure quality in sports development?

There are a number of important reasons why quality should be measured in sports development. These include the following.

1 All organisations should be constantly striving to improve their service – this is known as 'continuous improvement'. For example, by being involved in Quest or TAES, organisations are having to continually evaluate how they are performing and put in place systems to measure their performance. This can bring many benefits to organisations, such as:
- increasing their customer focus
- improving their consultation with users
- improving their staff morale
- developing better internal systems of work and procedures
- developing more effective service delivery
- an improvement in complaints handling
- delivering more cost-effective services.

2 Recognition: by achieving a quality mark sports development organisations can use this to promote the service they provide.

3 When sports development organisations apply for additional funding, external agencies will be able to tell by the quality marks the organisation holds that it provides a successful service. This is looked upon favourably by most funding bodies.

4 Standardisation: it is easier to measure the performance of one sports development organisation against another when they achieve a quality accreditation.

There are some disadvantages in measuring quality in any sports development organisation. Applying for and then going through the process of achieving quality accreditation can be both costly and time consuming. This is mainly because most organisations will need to pay for some expert help in order to achieve the quality accreditation. They will also have to spend a great deal of time collecting evidence themselves from within their organisation.

LEARNER ACTIVITY

Choose a sport you are currently participating in and find out if it has its own quality mark or scheme. Explain what the clubs within your chosen sport have to do to qualify for their governing body's quality mark or scheme. Share your findings with your group.

Key learning points

- Quality is about displaying excellence in an organisation.
- Traditional methods of measuring quality in sports development have been inconsistent and difficult to compare from one organisation to another.
- Quality awards such as TAES and Quest are used by many sports development organisations.
- There are a number of benefits to a sports development organisation of gaining a quality award, such as continuous improvement in its service.
- The process of gaining a quality award can be both time consuming and costly to sports development organisations.

Sports development in practice

We have already looked at some of the key providers in sports development. They range from national organisations at one end of the spectrum to local sports clubs at the other. The way that they operate in practice and their effectiveness will now be considered.

Sports development organisations working in partnership

The interaction of sports development organisations has been the subject of a number of recent Sport England documents. In the past, many sports development organisations have worked in isolation and as a result there has been a lot of duplication of effort. This duplication has wasted valuable resources.

As a result of this, all the main organisations involved in the delivery of sport are now committed to supporting the new Delivery System for Sport (see Fig 5.09).

The Delivery System for Sport has two aims: to increase the number of people taking part in sport and recreation, especially amongst the hard-to-reach; and to build clear pathways for people with sporting talent to achieve their full potential. Figure 5.09 shows the relationship between the key components of the system and how the national and regional partners connect to the sub-regional and local components of the system. The two key elements of the Delivery

System at the local levels are the County Sport Partnerships (CSPs) and the Community Sport Networks (CSNs).

> The ambition of Sport England is to lead and support the development of a holistic, coherent and quality-assured delivery system that ensures everybody, no matter where they live or their personal circumstances, is able to access high quality sporting opportunities that truly meet their personal needs.
>
> *(Sport England, 2006)*

definition

Community Sports Network (CSN): these are locally coordinated networks of organisations with an interest in sport. They identify local sporting needs and develop a shared vision for sport and physical activity in their area. A CSN's geographical boundaries are often the same as those of a local authority.

Partnerships in practice

As mentioned before, sports development organisations often work together in partnerships with other sports development organisations or with other types of organisation. For example, in the case study on page 80, 'Football Unites Racism Divides', the Millennium Volunteers organisation worked with Sheffield United Football Club and the Football Unites Racism Divides organisation, to offer football to girls and boys from black and minority ethnic groups.

Working in partnerships can have a number of benefits to all those involved, including the pooling of resources so that more can be achieved than if the organisations were working alone. Inevitably, there are often a number of barriers that have to be overcome in partnership working. For example, differing opinions or ideas as to how a project should be set up or delivered.

However, joint strategies can be devised so that the partners adopt a coordinated approach. This often informs others about the targets of the partnership and how they expect to achieve these targets. This then enables the partnership to measure its level of success.

LEARNING ACTIVITY

Find out more about your county's County Sports Partnership and answer these questions:

● What are its main aims?
● How many staff does it employ and what are their roles?

Local authority sports development in practice

Each local authority provides sports development work in different ways. For example, many local authorities will have a small section within a Leisure Department devoted to sports development. This may consist of only one Sports Development Officer or many Sports Development Officers. Some local authorities have 'contracted out' their sports development work along with the management of their sport and leisure facilities.

The effectiveness of sports development organisations in practice

There are a number of criteria that organisations involved in sports development use to help them measure their effectiveness.

● **Quality measures** (as detailed above) – can be used to measure the effectiveness of organisations.

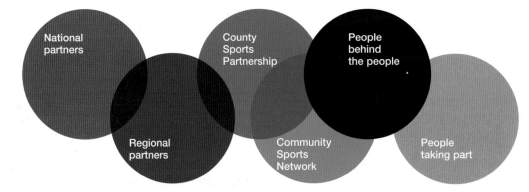

Fig 5.09 The Delivery System for Sport (Sport England, 2006)

Case study

 Herts Sports Partnership

The Herts Sports Partnership (HSP) was established in 2004 as one of 49 County Sport Partnerships in England, as part of the Sport England delivery system. The HSP is led by a voluntary representative executive board and has a core team of full- and part-time paid sports development officers.

The core team works alongside partners bringing together knowledge, ideas and expertise from the sports world in Hertfordshire; providing a central and coordinated 'sports authority' for the county.

Its key purposes for Hertfordshire are:

- to increase the number of people taking part in sport and physical activity
- to develop the sports infrastructure
- to increase the quality of provision.

The HSP offers services and support at all levels to those who:

- take part in sport or physical activity
- deliver sport or physical activity
- are involved with the strategic development of sports and physical activity.

Examples of the services and support offered include: planning schemes to increase participation, such as school–club link programmes and 'Get Active' campaigns; workshops for clubs, coaches, officials, administrators and volunteers; providing advice and guidance on writing funding applications, and coordinating countywide projects.

Sport can also contribute to the improvement of a number of community priorities such as healthier communities, safe, strong and sustainable communities, economic vitality and workforce development, and meeting the needs of children and young people. The HSP forges partnerships across a range of industries and organisations to create sport schemes designed, for example, to tackle anti-social behaviour and the fear of crime.

More information about this partnership can be found by visiting www.sportinherts.org.uk.

Case study

Manchester City Council

Established in 1992, Manchester Leisure is the department within Manchester City Council responsible for sports development and parks. The Sports Development Team employs over 60 people. This includes:

- Sports Development Managers such as a Strategic Sports Development Manager and administrative staff
- Sports Specific Development Officers who represent 13 sports including badminton, cricket and swimming
- Community Sports Development Officers who work within specific communities citywide
- Sports Officers with a remit to work with targeted sectors of the community such as refugees, disabled people and people aged over 50.

Manchester Leisure's team of Sports Development Officers has two main objectives. These are:

- to maximise participation in sport by all sectors of the community within Manchester
- to provide pathways to excellence that enable every person to fulfil their real sporting potential.

The sports development team has put together a number of strategies and action plans to guide its work. It also provides advice and guidance on funding issues, hosts both national and local events and runs a coach education scheme in the City of Manchester. It works in partnership with many other organisations, such as NGBs.

- **Achievement of stated aims and objectives** – most organisations involved in sports development produce a business or development plan. This should clearly set out the aims and objectives that the organisation wants to achieve. It will then state how these aims and objectives are going to be achieved, i.e. what resources are going to be needed and how long it will take to achieve them.
- **Customer feedback** – this may take many forms, i.e. customer complaints cards, questionnaires, interviews or mystery visit results. The results will give a good indication of whether the customer is satisfied with an organisation.
- **Value for money** – this can be hard to quantify because not all benefits of sports participation can be reliably measured. However, generally a cost/benefit analysis based on human and financial resources can be carried out.
- **Consultation** – valuable feedback can be gained from those involved in delivering sports development, i.e. SDOs and other organisations and partners.

Good-quality monitoring and evaluation is necessary so that delivery organisations, partners and funders know whether sport and physical activity projects have been efficiently run and effective in achieving their aims.

Key learning points

- Most sports development organisations, in practice, work in partnership with other organisations.
- In practice, Sport England along with other key sports development organisations, is committed to providing a single delivery system for sport.
- Each local authority, in practice, will provide its sports development work in a different way.
- In practice, there are a number of ways a sports development organisation can measure its effectiveness, e.g. by achieving its stated aims and objectives.

Review questions

1 Explain in your own words what the term 'sports development' means.
2 Describe the four main stages of the sports development continuum.
3 What does the term 'sports equity' mean?
4 How does participating in sport lead to wider benefits? Use examples in your answer.
5 Explain the different ways there are of providing sports development activities.
6 Describe who the key providers are in sports development.
7 Describe one type of quality scheme/mark used by a National Governing Body of sport.
8 List the advantages and disadvantages of a sports development organisation gaining a quality accreditation.
9 Describe what a County Sports Partnership is and what its main areas of work are.
10 How can sports development organisations measure how effective they are?

References

Eady, J. (1993) *Practical Sports Development*, Pitman.

Houlihan, B. and White, A. (2002) *The Politics of Sports Development*, Routledge.

Hylton, K., Bramham, P., Jackson, D. and Nesti, M. (2001) *Sports Development: Policy, Process and Practice*, Routledge.

Joint DCMS/Strategy Unit Report (2002) 'Game Plan: a strategy for delivering Government's sport and physical activity objectives'.

Russell Commission (2005) 'A National Framework for Youth Action and Engagement'.

Sport England (1996) 'The value of sport to Local Authorities'.

Sport England (2004) 'The Framework for Sport in England'.

Websites

www.ccpr.org.uk – The Central Council for Physical Recreation

www.connexions-direct.com – Connexions Direct

www.culture.gov.uk – The Department for Culture, Media and Sport

www.furd.org – Football Unites, Racism Divides

www.ilam.co.uk – now www.ispal.org.uk, Institute for Sport, Parks and Leisure

www.isrm.co.uk – Institute for Sport and Recreation Management

www.nasd.uk.com – now www.ispal.org.uk, Institute for Sport, Parks and Leisure

www.skillsactive.com – Skills Active

www.sportengland.org – Sport England

www.youthsporttrust.org.uk – Youth Sports Trust

Goals

By the end of this chapter you should:

- understand a range of laboratory- and field-based fitness tests
- understand the practice of health screening
- be able to prepare for, and conduct, appropriate fitness tests
- be able to analyse the results of fitness tests.

The ability to conduct fitness testing is a vital skill for the sport scientist to possess. All athletes and people starting exercise need to know where they are at any point in time so they can work out how close they are to where they want to be. The aims of fitness testing are to:

- ensure that the person is safe to exercise
- find out their current position in terms of fitness
- identify their strengths and weaknesses
- gain information to inform the process of writing a training programme
- be able to monitor any changes in fitness
- show a professional and caring approach.

Understanding the practice of health screening

Before you start to conduct fitness tests with an athlete or a person who wants to start exercise you will need to conduct a detailed fitness consultation. This will consist of the following:

- health screening questionnaire
- informed consent form
- identification of coronary heart disease risk factors
- identification of any causes for medical referral.

Health screening questionnaire

You will need to have prepared a detailed questionnaire to cover areas such as medical conditions, illnesses and injuries, as well as past history of exercise and lifestyle factors. A sample questionnaire is shown below.

Informed consent

An informed consent form lets a client know what to expect during the exercise test, and the associated risks involved in exercise or training. It also stresses that any participation in the tests is voluntary and you have the choice to stop at any point.

An example of an informed consent form is given in Table 6.01 on page 99.

Section 1: Personal details

Name

Address

Home telephone _____ Mobile telephone

Email

Occupation

Date of birth

Section 2: Sporting goals

1 What are your long-term sporting goals over the next year or season?

2 What are your medium-term goals over the next three months?

3 What are your short-term goals over the next four weeks?

Section 3: Current training status

1 What are your main training requirements?

✓ Muscular strength
✓ Muscular endurance
✓ Speed
✓ Flexibility
✓ Aerobic fitness
✓ Power
✓ Weight loss or gain
✓ Skill-related fitness
✓ Other (please state) _____

2 How would you describe your current fitness status?

3 How many times a week will you train?

4 How long have you got for each training session?

Section 4: Your nutritional status

1 On a scale of 1 to 10 (1 being very low quality and 10 being very high quality) how would you rate the quality of your diet?_____

2 Do you follow any particular diet?

✓ Vegetarian
✓ Vegan
✓ Vegetarian and fish
✓ Gluten-free
✓ Dairy-free

3 How often do you eat? Note down a typical day's intake.

4 Do you take any supplements? If so, which ones?

Section 4: Your lifestyle

1 How many units of alcohol do you drink in a typical week? _____
2 Do you smoke? _____ If yes, how many a day? _____
3 Do you experience stress on a daily basis? _____
4 If yes, what causes you stress (if you know)?

5 What techniques do you use to deal with your stress?

Section 5: Your physical health

1 Do you experience any of the following?

✓ Back pain or injury
✓ Knee pain or injury
✓ Ankle pain or injury

✓ Swollen joints
✓ Shoulder pain or injury
✓ Hip or pelvic pain or injury
✓ Nerve damage
✓ Head injuries

2 If yes, please give details

3 Are any of these injuries made worse by exercise? _____
4 If yes, what movements in particular cause pain?

5 Are you currently receiving any treatment for any injuries? If so, what?

Section 6: Medical history

1 Do you or have you had any of the following medical conditions?

✓ Asthma
✓ Bronchitis
✓ Heart problems
✓ Chest pains
✓ Diabetes
✓ High blood pressure
✓ Epilepsy
✓ Other _____

2 Are you taking any medication (If yes, state what, how much and why)

Name: Signature:
Trainer's name: Trainer's signature:
Date:

Risk of coronary heart disease

Coronary heart disease (CHD) is a leading cause of death in all industrialised countries. It is caused by a narrowing of the coronary arteries, which limits the amount of blood flowing through the artery.

definition

Coronary arteries: blood vessels that brings oxygenated blood to nourish the muscle cells of the heart muscle.

Table 6.01 Example of an informed consent form

1 Explanation of the tests

You will perform a series of tests which will vary in its demands on your body. Your progress will be observed during the tests and stopped if you show signs of undue fatigue. You may stop the test at any time if you feel unduly uncomfortable.

2 Risks of exercise testing

During exercise certain changes can occur, such as raised blood pressure, fainting, raised heart rate, and in a very small number of cases heart attacks or even death. Every effort is made through screening to minimise the risk of these occurring during testing. Emergency equipment and relevantly trained personnel are available to deal with any extreme situation which occurs.

3 Responsibility of the participant

You must disclose all information in your possession regarding the state of your health or previous experiences of exercise as this will affect the safety of the tests. If you experience any discomfort or unusual sensations it is your responsibility to inform your trainer.

4 Benefits to expect

The results gained during testing will be used to identify any illnesses and the types of activities that are relevant for you.

5 Freedom of consent

Your participation in these tests is voluntary and you are free to deny consent or stop a test at any point.

I have read this form and understand what is expected of me and the tests I will perform. I give my consent to participate.

Client's signature_____

Print name_____

Date _____

Trainer's signature_____

Print name_____

Date _____

Arteries losing their elasticity is part of the ageing process. However, there are many lifestyle factors that cause damage or narrowing of the arteries. Obstructions are created as cholesterol and fatty plaques are laid down in the artery causing a narrowing of the artery space.

The coronary arteries are found only in the heart and they supply the heart with oxygen to enable it to pump. When these arteries narrow or become blocked the blood supply to the heart is reduced. As a result, carbon dioxide builds up in the heart muscle and this causes pain, which is called angina. Angina feels like a crushing pain on the chest. If this pain becomes a shooting pain into the left arm and the neck the person is having a heart attack.

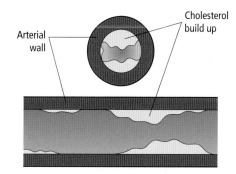

Fig 6.01 Build-up of cholesterol in an artery

The following lifestyle factors will increase an individual's chance of having CHD:

- diet high in fat (particularly deep fat fried foods)
- diet high in table salt (sodium chloride)
- obesity (particularly abdominal fat)
- smoking
- excess alcohol consumption
- older age
- male gender
- high blood pressure
- type 2 diabetes.

Fig 6.02 Smoking will increase an individual's chance of having CHD

If you consider that a person has a high risk of CHD it is best to refer them for GP clearance before you start to train them.

Medical referral

To ensure that you offer a proper 'duty of care' to your client you will need to refer them to a GP if you have any doubt regarding their safety to exercise. If your client has any of the following they must be referred to their GP:

- high blood pressure (over 160/100)
- poor lung function
- excess body fat (40%+ for a female, 30%+ for a male)
- high resting heart rate (100+ bpm)
- medication for a heart condition (e.g. beta blockers).

Or if they experience any of the following:

- muscle injuries
- chest pain or tightness
- light-headedness or dizziness
- irregular or rapid pulse

- joint pain
- headaches
- shortness of breath.

Health monitoring tests

Tests can split into two clear categories: those that measure health and those that measure fitness. Health tests are done to see if the individual is healthy enough to do the fitness tests or whether they need to receive GP clearance. Health tests will be static in nature while fitness tests will be dynamic and involve bodily movement and exertion.

Key learning points

- Before a fitness test is conducted a health screening form and informed consent form must be completed.
- A client must be screened for risk of CHD; risk factors include poor diet, obesity, smoking, excess alcohol intake, male gender and type 2 diabetes.

The health tests conducted are:

- heart rate
- blood pressure
- lung function
- waist to hip ratio
- body mass index (BMI).

When testing people it is important that the tests are safe for the client; also that the conditions the tests are performed in are consistent and stable.

The following should be taken into consideration in relation to the client.

- They should have medical clearance for any health conditions.
- They should be free of injuries.
- They should be wearing appropriate clothing.
- They should not have had a heavy meal within three hours of the test.
- They should have had a good night's sleep.
- They should not have trained on the day and should be fully recovered from previous training.
- They should have avoided stimulants such as tea, coffee or nicotine for two hours before the test.

The following should be taken into consideration regarding the environment.

- Heating in the area should be at room temperature (around 18°).
- The room should be well ventilated.
- The room should be clean and dust-free.

Validity and reliability

These two terms must be considered before a test is conducted. The two questions you must ask yourself are:

- Does this test actually test what I say it tests?
- If this test were to be repeated would I get the same results?

The first question tests its validity. For example, a speed test using a shuttle run may actually test a person's ability to turn, which is more about agility than speed.

The second question tests its reliability. The conditions of the test must always be identical so that it is most likely that the same results will be produced. However, there are many factors that may change, such as the temperature of the environment, the physical state of the athlete and the technique of the tester. All these may alter the results produced.

Test sequence

The order in which tests are conducted must be considered because it may change the accuracy of the results you produce. You may even have to do different tests on different days to produce the best results.

Our knowledge of sport science can help to decide which tests should be done first and for how long the athlete will have to rest between tests. For example, a test which requires effort over a long period of time or works to failure will require one to two hours of recovery. Also a test requiring a high level of skill or coordination needs to be done first because skill level goes down when a person is tired. The correct order to follow would be:

- sedentary tests – height, weight, body composition, flexibility
- agility tests
- maximum power and strength tests
- sprint tests
- muscular endurance test
- aerobic endurance tests.

Resting heart rate

To measure the resting heart rate you can use a heart rate monitor or do it manually. The best time to take resting heart rate is before the person gets out of bed and experiences the stresses of the day. To perform it manually complete the following steps.

1 Let your client sit down and rest for about five minutes.
2 Find their radial pulse (wrist) or brachial pulse (front of elbow).
3 Using the middle and index fingers place them over the pulse. The thumb has a pulse of its own and will produce an inaccurate reading.
4 Count the pulse for 60 seconds and record the result before repeating for another 60 seconds.
5 If there is a large variation in readings then take a third reading.

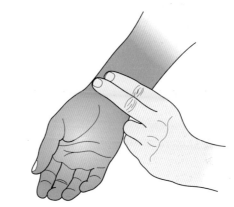

Fig 6.03 Taking a pulse rate

Here is a reference for resting heart rates for men and women:

Category	Males (bpm)	Females (bpm)
Normal	60–80	60–80
Average	70	76
Proceed with caution	90–99	90–99
GP referral	100+	100+

(Adapted from Franklin, 2000)

Blood pressure

Blood pressure is the pressure blood exerts on the artery walls and is a clear indication of general health. It is vitally important to measure blood pressure before a client exercises because it will tell you whether they are at risk of having a heart attack.

We need to split this up into the short term and long term. Short term means the blood pressure rises for a period and then falls again, while long term means that the blood pressure remains high all the time.

Factors that raise blood pressure in the short term:

● stress, anxiety and arousal
● exercise
● heavy weight training
● isometric exercises
● eating (process of digestion)
● smoking
● caffeine
● stimulant drugs.

Factors that raise blood pressure in the long term:

● inactivity
● obesity
● high-fat diet
● high salt (sodium) intake
● excessive alcohol
● smoking
● stress and anxiety
● stimulant drugs.

Blood pressure is taken by a blood pressure meter and stethoscope, or it can be done using an electronic blood pressure meter.

1 Allow the client to be relaxed for about five minutes.
2 Sit the client down with their left arm resting on a chair arm; their elbow should be at 45 degrees with the palm of the hand facing up.
3 Find the brachial pulse – it should be on the inner side of the arm just under the biceps muscle.
4 Place the cuff just clear of the elbow (about 2–3 cm above the elbow). The bladder of the cuff (the part which inflates) should be directly over the pulse.
5 Place the earpieces of the stethoscope in your ears and place the microphone over the brachial pulse.
6 Inflate the cuff up to 200 mmHg.
7 Slowly open the valve by turning it anti-clockwise and release the pressure.

8 Listen out for the first time you hear the thud of the heart beat and make a mental note of it. This is the systolic blood pressure reading.
9 Keep deflating the cuff and when the heart beat becomes muffled or disappears this is your diastolic reading.
10 Keep deflating the cuff and, if necessary, repeat after around 30 seconds.

This is a classification of blood pressure readings:

Classification	Systolic blood pressure (mmHg)	Diastolic blood pressure (mmHg)
Low	90	60
Normal	120	80
Proceed with caution	140–159	90–99
High	160+	100+

(Adapted from Franklin, 2000)

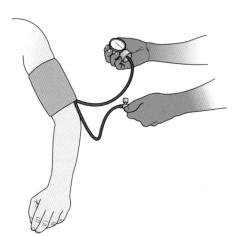

Fig 6.04 Taking a blood pressure reading

Lung function

We need to assess lung function to see whether the airways between the mouth and the alveoli are clear and conducive to good air flow. Poor lung function will limit the amount of oxygen which can be delivered to the bloodstream and the tissues.

Lung function can be measured using a microspirometer or a hand-held peak flow meter.

To use a peak flow meter proceed through the following steps.

1 Ask the client to hold the peak flow meter directly in front of their mouth.
2 Ask them to turn their head to the side and take three deep breaths.
3 On the third breath ask them to put their mouth around the end of the tube and, ensuring a good lip seal, blow as hard as they can into the tube.
4 Say that it should be a short, sharp blow as if they were using a pea shooter.
5 Repeat twice more and take the highest reading. This is called their peak expiratory flow rate (PEFR).

Fig 6.05 Peak flow meter

Factors affecting lung function:

- asthma
- bronchitis
- smoking
- environmental pollution
- gender
- age
- height
- size of ribcage.

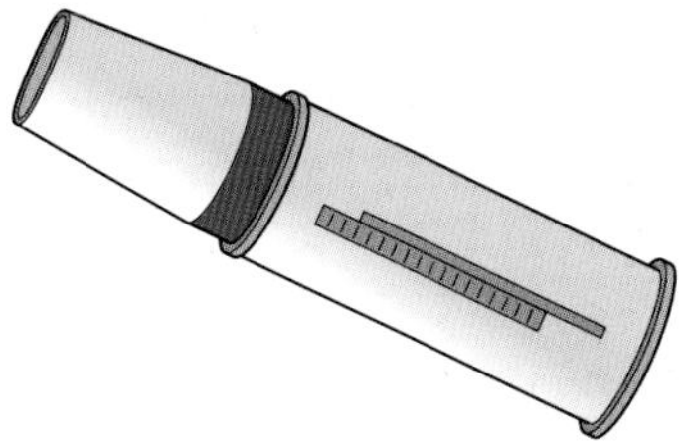

The PEFR is a measurement of the power of the lungs. It is a hypothetical figure which tells us how much air would pass through our lungs if we breathed in and out at our maximum power for a minute. It is hypothetical because it cannot really be measured as we would faint after about 15 seconds of breathing at maximum power.

You will need to know the gender, age and height of the client to work out their acceptable score.

The PEFR for males is shown below.

The PEFR for females is shown overleaf.

If your client's score is 100 below the acceptable figure this classifies as poor lung function and they should be referred to their GP before they exercise.

PEFR for males:

Age	1.55 m	1.60 m	1.65 m	1.70 m	1.75 m	1.80 m	1.85 m	1.90m
25	515	534	552	570	589	607	625	644
30	502	520	539	557	576	594	612	632
35	489	508	526	544	563	582	600	619
40	476	495	513	531	550	568	586	606
45	463	482	501	519	537	556	574	593
50	450	469	487	505	524	543	561	580
55	438	456	475	493	511	530	548	567
60	424	443	462	480	498	517	535	545
65	412	430	449	460	486	504	522	541
70	399	417	436	454	472	491	509	528

(Adapted from Franklin, 2000)

PEFR for females:

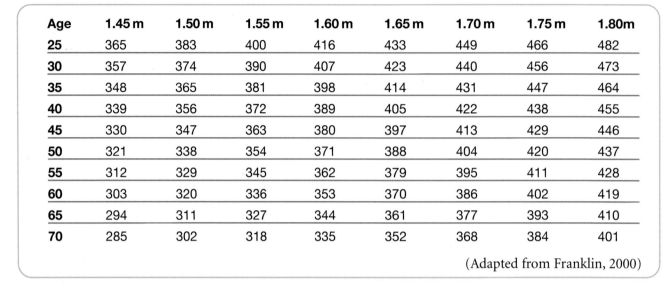

Age	1.45 m	1.50 m	1.55 m	1.60 m	1.65 m	1.70 m	1.75 m	1.80m
25	365	383	400	416	433	449	466	482
30	357	374	390	407	423	440	456	473
35	348	365	381	398	414	431	447	464
40	339	356	372	389	405	422	438	455
45	330	347	363	380	397	413	429	446
50	321	338	354	371	388	404	420	437
55	312	329	345	362	379	395	411	428
60	303	320	336	353	370	386	402	419
65	294	311	327	344	361	377	393	410
70	285	302	318	335	352	368	384	401

(Adapted from Franklin, 2000)

Body mass index

Body mass index (BMI) is used to give us an idea of whether a client is obese. It then gives the extent of their obesity.

This is worked out by using the following formula:

$$\text{Body mass index (BMI)} = \frac{\text{Weight (in kg)}}{\text{Height in m} \times \text{height in m}}$$

For male who is 75 kg and 1.80 m tall:

$$\frac{75}{1.80 \times 1.80} = 23.1$$

Thus his body mass index will be 23.1 kg/m^2.

What does this mean? The chart below shows the classification of overweight and obesity:

	Obesity class	BMI (kg/m2)
Underweight		< 18.5
Normal		18.5–24.9
Overweight		25–29.9
Obesity	I	30–34.9
Obesity	II	35–39.9
Extreme obesity	III	> 40

> **LEARNER ACTIVITY Your own BMI**
> Using the formula on the left, work out your body mass index.

The body mass index has serious limitations because it does not actually measure body composition. It can be used as a quick measure to see if a person is over-fat, but it is inaccurate because it does not make a distinction between muscle and fat. Thus, someone with a lot of muscle may come out as fat!

Hip to waist ratio

Hip to waist ratio is taken as an indicator of the health risks associated with obesity and in particular the risk of coronary heart disease (CHD). Fat stored in the abdominal area is a greater risk factor for CHD because it is closer to the heart and can more easily be mobilised and taken to the heart.

Hip to waist ratio is calculated in the following way using a tape measure.

- Waist measurement is taken at the level of the navel with the stomach muscles relaxed and after a normal expiration. The tape measure is put around the waist and a horizontal reading is taken.
- Hip measurement is taken with the client standing up and is the widest measurement around the hips. It is usually taken at the level of the greater trochanter, which is at the top of the femur.

Key learning points

- Tests can be split up into two types: those which test health and are static in nature and those which test fitness and are dynamic in nature.
- Before conducting a test you must consider that both the client and the environment are in an appropriate state for the test to take place.
- A valid test is one that tests what it says it will test.
- A reliable test is one that would yield the same results if it were to be repeated.

The ratio is worked out by dividing the waist measurement by the hip measurement.

$$\frac{\text{Waist measurement}}{\text{Hip measurement}}$$

A male with a 26" waist and 30" hips would be:

$$\frac{26}{30} = 0.66$$

What do these scores mean? The chart below shows the classification for hip to waist ratio:

Classification	Males	Females
High risk	> 1.0	> 0.85
Moderate risk	0.90–0.99	0.80–0.85
Low risk	< 0.90	< 0.8

(Adapted from Franklin, 2000)

A male with a score above 0.90 and a female with a score above 0.80 will have an increased risk of developing CHD.

LEARNER ACTIVITY Hip to waist ratio

Working with a partner calculate each other's hip to waist ratio. Work out where you fall on the above table.

Preparing, conducting and analysing fitness tests

Tests are conducted to assess each different component of fitness. It is important to choose the components of fitness relative to the person you are working with. This will depend upon their own goals and the activities they are involved in, be it sport or exercise.

Performance-related fitness

Performance in sport and exercise is dependent upon a range of components of fitness. These are shown in Fig 6.06.

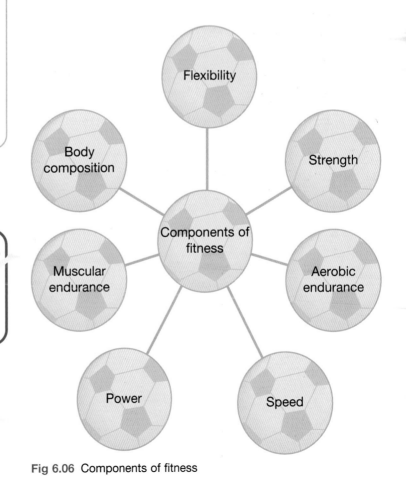

Fig 6.06 Components of fitness

LEARNER ACTIVITY Components of fitness

The following table shows a list of sports and the various components of fitness. Take each component of fitness and give it a score between 1 and 10 depending on how important it is for successful participation in that sport: 1 is not at all important and 10 and is vitally important.

Activity	Flexibility	Strength	Aerobic endurance	Speed	Power	Muscular endurance	Body composition
Rugby Union							
Basketball							
Netball							
Cricket							
100 m sprinting							
400 m sprinting							
Marathon running							
Long-distance cycling							
Tennis							
Football							
Squash							

Test protocols

The following is a list of test protocols:

- sit and reach
- 1 repetition maximum
- grip strength dynamometer
- multi-stage fitness test
- step test
- 40-yard sprint
- vertical jump
- wingate test
- one-minute press-up test
- one-minute sit-up test
- skinfold assessment
- bioelectrical impedance
- hydro densitometry.

We will now look at each of these in turn.

Flexibility

The **sit and reach test** measures the flexibility of the muscles in the lower back and hamstrings. This test is safe to perform unless the athlete has a lower back injury, particularly a slipped disc. The test is performed in the following way.

1 Warm the athlete up with five minutes' jogging or cycling.
2 Ask the athlete to take off their shoes and any clothing which will limit movement.
3 The athlete sits with their legs straight and their feet against the board. Their legs and back should be straight.
4 The client reaches as far forward as they possibly can and pushes the marker forward.
5 Record the furthest point the marker reaches.

What do these results mean? These are the categories for males and females:

Category	Males (cm)	Females (cm)
Elite	> 27	> 30
Excellent	17 to 27	21 to 30
Good	6 to 16	11 to 20
Average	0 to 5	1 to 10
Fair	−8 to −1	−7 to 0
Poor	−9 to −19	−8 to −14
Very poor	< −20	< −15

(Adapted from Franklin, 2000)

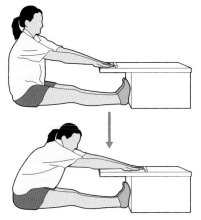

Fig 6.07 Sit and reach test

Strength

The **1 repetition maximum** (1 RM) is a measure of absolute strength and is the maximum weight that can be moved once with perfect technique.

This is clearly a dangerous test to perform unless the client is of an advanced skill level and is very well conditioned. The test will also require a thorough warm-up prior to its performance.

The test is performed in the following way.

1 Choose an exercise requiring the use of large muscle groups – e.g. a bench press or a leg press.
2 Warm up with a light weight for ten repetitions.
3 Give one minute rest.
4 Estimate a resistance that can be used for three to five repetitions.
5 Give two minutes' rest.
6 Estimate a load that can be used for two to three repetitions.
7 Give two to three minutes' rest.
8 Decide upon a load that can be used for one repetition.
9 If successful then give two to four minutes' rest.
10 Add a little more weight and complete one repetition.
11 Weight is gradually added until the client fails.
12 1 RM is the last weight that can be completed successfully.

There are no normative tables for 1 RM tests as they are used to monitor progress and strength gains. They can also be used to decide upon training loads for the individual.

The **grip strength dynamometer** is a static test to assess muscular strength in the arm muscles. Unfortunately, it will give no indication as to the strength of other muscle groups. The test involves squeezing a hand grip dynamometer as hard as possible. The test is conducted in the following way.

1 Adjust the handle to fit the size of your hand.
2 Hold the dynamometer in your strongest hand and keep the arm hanging by your side with the dynamometer by your thigh.
3 Squeeze the dynamometer as hard as you can for around five seconds.
4 Record the results and repeat after about a minute.
5 Take your best recording.

What do the results mean?

Rating	Males (kg)	Females (kg)
Excellent	> 64	> 38
Very good	56–64	34–38
Above average	52–56	30–34
Average	48–52	26–30
Below average	44–48	22–26
Poor	40–44	20–22
Very poor	<40	<20

(Adapted from Franklin, 2000)

Fig 6.08 Hand grip dynamometer

Aerobic endurance

The **multi-stage fitness test** was developed at the University of Loughborough and is known as the 'bleep' test because athletes have to run between timed bleeps. The test will give you an estimation of your VO_2max which is the measure of your aerobic fitness level. You will need the pre-recorded CD or tape and a flat area of 20 metres with a cone at either end. This test can be used with large groups as all the athletes will run together. The procedure is as follows:

1 Mark out a length of 20 metres with cones.
2 Start the tape and the athletes run when the first bleep sounds. They will run the 20 metres before the second bleep sounds.
3 When this bleep sounds they turn around and run back.
4 They continue to do this and the time between the bleeps gets shorter and shorter so they have to run faster and faster.
5 If an athlete fails to get to the other end before the bleep on three consecutive occasions then they are out.
6 Record at what point the athlete dropped out.
7 Using the tables provided you find out your predicted VO_2max.

How did you score?

Category	Males (mm/O$_2$/kg/min-1)	Females (mm/O$_2$/kg/min-1)
Extremely high	70+	60+
Very high	63–69	54–59
High	57–62	49–53
Above average	52–56	44–48
Average	44–51	35–43

(Adapted from Baechle and Earle, 2000)

The **Canadian step test** is a simple and straightforward test to perform and measures how heart rate increases with steady-state exercise.

You need a 30 cm high step, a heart rate monitor and a stopwatch. This test is carried out in the following way.

Fig 6.09 Canadian step test

1 The client steps up and down for three minutes while you monitor their heart rate.
2 You keep the client at a steady state by saying 'up, up, down, down' at a normal speech rate. The client should complete 24 steps per minute.
3 At the end of the third minute record their heart rate.
4 Compare the result to the normative data for males and females.

What does this mean?

This is the classification for males measured in bpm:

Age	18–25	26–35	36–45	46–55	56–65	65+
Excellent	< 79	< 81	< 83	< 87	< 86	< 88
Good	79–89	81–89	83–96	87–97	86–97	88–96
Above average	90–99	90–99	97–103	97–105	98–103	97–103
Average	100–105	100–107	104–112	106–116	104–112	104–113
Below average	106–116	108–117	113–119	117–122	113–120	114–120
Poor	117–128	118–128	120–130	123–132	121–129	121–130
Very poor	> 128	> 128	> 130	> 132	> 129	> 130

This is the classification for females measured in bpm:

Age	18–25	26–35	36–45	46–55	56–65	65+
Excellent	< 85	< 88	< 90	< 94	< 95	< 90
Good	85–98	88–99	90–102	94–104	95–104	90–102
Above average	99–108	100–111	103–110	105–115	105–112	103–115
Average	109–117	112–119	111–118	116–120	113–118	116–122
Below average	118–126	120–126	119–128	121–129	119–128	123–128
Poor	127–140	127–138	129–140	130–135	129–139	129–134
Very poor	> 140	> 138	> 140	> 135	> 139	> 134

(both charts adapted from Franklin, 2000)

This is a safe test to use with clients and gives us a useful means to monitor progress. It will not provide any information regarding their maximal aerobic capacity.

Speed

The **40-yard sprint** is a test for pure speed. You will need a flat running surface and a tape measure to ensure the distance is correct. You also require a stopwatch and a person who can time the run. The test is conducted in the following way.

1 The athlete warms up for several minutes.
2 They will then do the 40-yard run at a speed less than their maximum.
3 The athlete starts the test behind the line with one or two hands on the ground.
4 The starter will shout 'go' and the athlete sprints the 40 yards as quickly as possible.
5 This run should be repeated after two or three minutes and the average of the two runs taken.

What do these scores mean? Here are the categories for males and females:

Category	Males (seconds)	Females (seconds)
Elite	< 4.6	< 5.5
Excellent	4.6–4.7	5.5–5.7
Good	4.8–5.0	5.8–6.3
Average	5.1–5.5	6.4–6.7
Below average	5.6+	6.7+

(Adapted from Franklin, 2000)

Fig 6.10 Vertical jump test

Power

The **vertical jump** is a test of power with the aim being to see how high the athlete can jump. It is important that you find a smooth wall with a ceiling higher than the athlete can jump. A sports hall or squash court is ideal. The test is conducted in the following way.

1 The athlete rubs chalk on their fingers.
2 They stand about 15 cm away from the wall.
3 With their feet flat on the floor they reach as high as they can and make a mark on the wall.
4 The athlete then rubs more chalk on their fingers.
5 They then bend their knees to 90 degrees and jump as high as they can up into the air.
6 At the top of their jump they make a second chalk mark with their fingertips.
7 The trainer measures the difference between their two marks; this is their standing jump score.
8 This test is best done three times so the athlete can take the best of their three jumps.

What do the results mean? Here are the ratings for males and females:

Rating	Males (cm)	Females (cm)
Excellent	> 70	> 60
Very good	61–70	51–60
Above average	51–60	41–50
Average	41–50	31–40
Below average	31–40	21–30
Poor	21–30	11–20
Very poor	< 21	< 10

(Adapted from Franklin, 2000)

Fig 6.11 Wingate test

Anaerobic capacity

The **Wingate test** is a maximal test of anaerobic capacity and is thus suitable only for highly conditioned clients. It is used to measure peak anaerobic power and anaerobic capacity.

It is carried out in the following way.

1 The client warms up for around two to three minutes at increasing intensities until their heart rate is 180 bpm.
2 Once they are ready the client cycles as fast as they can for 30 seconds at a calculated load.

The load is calculated for use on the Monark cycle ergometer. For a person aged under 15 the load is their body weight in kg × 0.35 g. For an adult it is their body weight in kg × 0.75 g.

A 70 kg adult's workload would be worked out in the following way:

70 × 0.75 = 52.5 kg

3 The client is instructed to start and then given two seconds to achieve their maximum speed at which point the workload is added.
4 The client pedals for 30 seconds as fast as they can and the tester needs to count the number of revolutions of the flywheel every five seconds.
5 There needs to be a second tester who records the scores as they are called out for each five seconds.
6 At the end of the 30 seconds the client cools down at a light workload.

To work out the power for each five-second interval you need to use the following equation:

Power = load (kg) × revolutions of flywheel in five seconds × radius of flywheel × 12.33

This score is then divided by their body weight in kg to calculate the power per kg of body mass.

To analyse the results you need to do the following.

- Plot a graph with power in watts (y-axis) against time in seconds (x-axis).
- The peak anaerobic power is the highest power score in a five-second period.
- The minimum anaerobic power is the lowest score in a five-second period.

- The power decline can be calculated in the following way:

$$\text{power decline} = \frac{\text{peak power} - \text{minimum power}}{\text{peak power} \times 100}$$

You will need to use the table shown at the bottom of this page to record the results and then to work out the power achieved.

Muscular endurance

The **one-minute press-up test** is a test of muscular endurance in the chest and arms. You will need a mat and a stopwatch.

It is carried out in the following way.

1 This test involves the male starting in the press-up position with their hands facing forwards and below the shoulders, back straight and pivoting on their toes. Females will perform the test from their knees with their knees, hips and shoulders all in line and their lower legs resting on the ground.
2 The subject will go down until their chest is 2 cm off the floor and push up to a straight elbow. They must maintain a straight back.
3 The number of press-ups performed in one minute without rest is recorded.
4 If a client is unable to maintain good technique or shows undue fatigue the test must be stopped.

Time	Number of revolutions of fly wheel	Power (watts)	Power per kg of body mass
0–2s			
2–7s			
7–12s			
12–17s			
17–22s			
22–27s			
27–32s			

What do these scores mean? These are the categories for males measured in the number of completed press-ups:

Age	20–29	30–39	40–49	50–59	60–69
Excellent	36	30	25	21	18
Very good	29–35	22–29	17–24	13–20	11–17
Good	22–28	17–21	13–16	10–12	8–10
Fair	17–21	15–20	8–12	7–9	5–7
Needs improvement	< 17	< 15	< 8	< 7	< 5

(Adapted from Franklin, 2000)

These are the categories for females measured in the number of completed press-ups:

Age	20–29	30–39	40–49	50–59	60–69
Excellent	30	27	24	21	17
Very good	21–29	20–26	15–23	11–20	12–16
Good	15–20	13–19	11–14	7–10	5–11
Fair	10–14	8–12	5–10	2–6	2–4
Needs improvement	< 10	< 8	< 4	1	1

(Adapted from Franklin, 2000)

The **one-minute sit-up test** is a test of muscular endurance in the abdominals. You will need a mat and a stopwatch.

The test procedure is as follows.

1 The athlete lies on the floor with their fingers on their temples and their knees bent.
2 On the command of 'go' the athlete sits up until their elbows touch their knees.
3 They will return to the start position with the back of their head touching the floor. That will be one repetition.
4 The athlete does as many as they can in one minute.

Fig 6.12 One-minute sit-up test

What do these results mean? Here are the classifications for males and females measured in the number of completed sit-ups:

Males				Females		
Age	**17–19**	**20–29**	**30–39**	**17–19**	**20–29**	**30–39**
High	49 +	44 +	39 +	42 +	36 +	30 +
Above average	44–48	39–43	34–38	32–41	27–35	22–29
Average	37–43	32–38	27–33	25–31	21–26	17–21
Below average	24–36	20–31	16–26	19–24	15–20	11–16
Low	< 24	< 20	< 16	< 19	< 15	< 11

(Adapted from Franklin, 2000)

Body composition

In very simple terms a person's body weight or mass can be split into two categories: fat mass and lean body weight (all that is not fat).

Fat mass	Lean body weight
Fat (adipose tissue)	Muscle Water Bone Organs Connective tissue

This table shows that you can lose weight by reducing any of the components of the body. However, lean body weight could be seen as healthy weight as it contributes to the performance of the body. Fat weight in excess would be unhealthy weight as it would cause a loss in performance as it requires oxygen without giving anything back to the body.

It is necessary to take a body fat measurement to show that the weight loss is fat and not muscle.

It is impossible to turn muscle into fat or fat into muscle. This is because they are completely different types of tissue in the body. A good training programme will produce a loss of fat or excess fat and a gain in muscle tissue. So while it may look like one is turning into the other this is not the case. This particularly happens when an athlete does weight training.

The **skinfold assessment** test is done using skinfold calipers. It is done using the Durnin and Wormsley sites which are as follows:

Area	Description of site
Triceps	This is taken halfway between the shoulder and elbow on the back of the arm. It is a vertical pinch.
Biceps	This is taken 1 cm above the site for the triceps on the front of the arm. It is a vertical pinch.
Subscapular	This is taken 2 cm below the lowest point of the shoulder blade. It is taken at a 45-degree angle.
Suprailiac	This is taken just above the iliac crest (hip bone), directly below the front of the shoulder.

It is carried out as follows.

1. **Triceps brachii**
   With the client's arm hanging loosely, a vertical fold is raised at the back of the arm, midway along a line connecting the acromion (shoulder) and olecranon (elbow) processes.

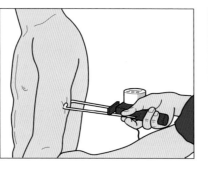

2. **Biceps brachii**
   A vertical fold is raised at the front of the arm, opposite to the triceps site. This should be directly above the centre of the cubital fossa (fold of the elbow).

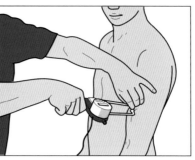

3. **Subscapular**
   A fold is raised just beneath the inferior angle of the scapula (bottom of the shoulder-blade). This fold should be at an angle of 45 degrees downwards and outwards.

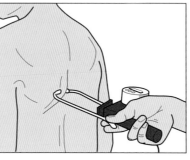

4. **Anterior suprailiac**
   A fold is raised 5–7 cm above the spinale (pelvis), at a point in line with the anterior axillary border (armpit). The fold should be in line with the natural folds downward and inwards at up to 45 degrees.

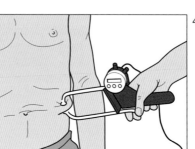

Fig 6.13 Body fat measurement

1 Take the measurements on the left-hand side of the body.
2 Mark the client up accurately.
3 Pinch the skin 1 cm above the marked site.
4 Pull the fat away from the muscle.
5 Place the calipers halfway between the top and bottom of the skinfold.
6 Allow the calipers to settle for one or two seconds.
7 Take the reading and wait 15 seconds before repeating for accuracy.
8 Add up the total of the four measurements.
9 Calculate body fat percentage using the table on the opposite page.

The **bioelectrical impedance** technique involves placing electrodes on one hand and one foot and then passing a very small electrical current through the body. The theory is that muscle will conduct the electricity while fat will resist the path of the electricity. Therefore, the more electricity that comes out of the body the more muscle a person has, and the less electricity that comes out the more fat a person has.

This technique has benefits over skinfold measurement because it is easier to do and does not mean that the client has to remove or adjust any clothing. However, it has been shown to be not such an accurate measure of body fat percentage.

Hydro densitometry or underwater weighing is a technique which is based on the Archimedes principle. It involves a person being weighed on land and then when fully submerged in water. Muscle and bone are denser than water while fat is less dense. A person with more bone and muscle will weigh more in water, have a higher body density and therefore less fat. Once the weight on land and weight in water are taken, a formula is used to work out percentage body fat.

This technique involves the use of a large pool of water and significant amounts of equipment. It is impractical for use outside a sport science laboratory.

Reasons to terminate a fitness test

There will be occasions where it becomes unsafe to continue with a test due to physiological changes within the client. The following is a list of specific situations when a test should be stopped:

- chest pains or angina-like symptoms
- excessive increase in blood pressure (250/115)
- shortness of breath and wheezing
- leg cramps or pain
- light-headedness, nausea, or pale, clammy skin
- heart rate does not rise with exercise intensity
- irregular heart beat
- client requests to stop
- signs and symptoms of severe exhaustion
- equipment fails.

Males		Females	
Sum of skinfolds	Body fat %	Sum of skinfolds	Body fat %
		14	9.4
		16	11.2
		18	12.7
20	8.1	20	14.1
22	9.2	22	15.4
24	10.2	24	16.5
26	11.2	26	17.6
28	12.1	28	18.6
30	12.9	30	19.5
35	14.7	35	21.6
40	16.3	40	23.4
45	17.7	45	25.0
50	19.0	50	26.5
55	20.2	55	27.8
60	21.2	60	29.1
65	22.2	65	30.2
70	23.2	70	31.2
75	24.0	75	32.2
80	24.8	80	33.1
85	25.6	85	34.0
90	26.3	90	34.8
95	27.0	95	35.6
100	27.6	100	36.3
110	28.8	110	37.7
120	29.9	120	39.0
130	31.0	130	40.2
140	31.9	140	41.3
150	32.8	150	42.3
160	33.6	160	43.2
170	34.4	170	44.6
180	35.2	180	45.0

(Adapted from Franklin, 2000)

Then using the following table you can categorise your body fat percentage:

Classification	Males (% body fat)	Females (% body fat)
Under-fat	< 6%	< 14%
Athletes	6–13%	14–20%
Fitness	14–17%	21–24%
Acceptable	18–25%	25–30%
Overweight	26–30%	31–40%
Obese	> 30%	> 40%

(Adapted from Franklin, 2000)

Fig 6.14 Underwater weighing

LEARNER ACTIVITY Fitness profile

Choose a sport which you are involved in and develop a fitness profile of an athlete in that sport. You will need to look at which components of fitness are important for that sport. For example, a sprinter will need to do well in the 40-yard run and vertical jump test but the multi-stage fitness test may be irrelevant.

Using a checklist, compare your own test results to the profile that would be needed for success. Analyse the results and draw up a list of your strengths and weaknesses.

Feedback on fitness testing

Once you have completed a fitness test it is important to give detailed feedback to the individual. Before you conduct a test you need to say what you are testing and explain how the test will be conducted. Feedback is given once you have conducted the test, written down the result and then worked out how the result compares to the normative tables.

Feedback should be given in the following format:

- repeat the component of fitness that has been tested
- tell them what the result of the test was
- explain what you have tested and what the score represents
- tell them how they fit in within the population norms

- tell the what the implications of the result are in terms of their health and fitness
- discuss what recommendations you would make for the future.

If you have done a blood pressure test you would give feedback in this specific way:

- 'I have just taken your blood pressure.'
- 'Your blood pressure was 120/80 mmHg.'
- 'Blood pressure is the pressure of blood in the arterial system; 120 mmHg is the pressure during the contraction phase of the heart beat and 80 mmHg is the pressure during the relaxation phase of the heart beat.'
- 'This score is within the normal healthy range.'
- 'It means you are healthy enough to take part in sport and exercise.'

The scores of all fitness tests must be recorded in writing to ensure you have the information available in the future when you come to retest.

Recommendations

Once you have completed all the tests you may write an action plan or a report on the individual; this would cover the following information:

- current situation, highlighting strengths and weaknesses
- the client's aims and objectives
- changes to be made, with options
- actions – a step-by-step guide to achieving aims
- timescale for review.

Key learning points

- Blood pressure, resting heart rate, lung function, body mass index and hip to waist ratio are all static tests which are performed to see if the client is healthy enough to perform the dynamic fitness tests.
- Performance-related fitness is made up of the following components: flexibility, strength, aerobic endurance, speed, power, muscular endurance and body composition.
- Flexibility is measured by a sit and reach test.
- Strength is measured by 1 repetition maximum and grip strength dynamometer.
- Aerobic endurance is measured by the multi-stage fitness test and the step test.
- Anaerobic capacity is measured by the Wingate test.
- Speed is measured by the 40-yard sprint test.
- Power is measured by the vertical jump test.
- Muscular endurance is measured by the one-minute press-up test and the one-minute sit-up test.
- Body composition is measured by skinfold assessment, and bioelectrical impedance and hydro densitometry tests.

Revision questions

1 Give four reasons why we might conduct fitness tests.
2 What five areas should be covered in a health screening questionnaire?
3 What is the aim of an informed consent form?
4 Briefly explain what is meant by coronary heart disease (CHD) and what factors may cause it.
5 Give five situations where you would refer a client to their GP for clearance before training.
6 The client should be in a certain state to make sure we get accurate results. What four pieces of advice would you give a client before they come for a fitness test?
7 What is meant by validity and reliability?
8 Why is the order in which you perform the tests important?
9 Why is it important to take a person's blood pressure prior to exercise?
10 What five factors will affect an individual's lung function?
11 What does hip to waist ratio give us an indication of?
12 What do the following tests measure?
- Wingate test
- Skinfold assessment
- Multi-stage fitness test
- 1 repetition max
- Sit and reach
- One-minute press-up test
13 Which test for body composition would you choose for your clients and why?
14 Give five situations where you would terminate a test.

References

Baechle, T. and Earle, R. (2000) *Essentials of Strength Training and Conditioning*, Human Kinetics.

Davis, R., Bull, C., Roscoe, J. and Roscoe, D. (2005) *Physical Education and the Study of Sport*, Elsevier Mosby.

Franklin, B. (2000) *American College of Sports Medicine's (ACSM) Guidelines for Exercise Testing and Prescription*, 6th edn, Lippincott, Williams and Wilkins.

Stafford-Brown, J., Rea, S., Janaway, L. and Manley, C. (2006) *BTEC First Sport*, Hodder Arnold.

Wesson K., Wiggins-James, N., Thompson, G. and Hartigan, S. (2005) *Sport and PE: A Complete Guide to Advanced Level Study*, Hodder Arnold.

Practical individual sports and practical team sports

Goals

By the end of this chapter you should:

- be able to use a range of skills, techniques and tactics in selected team and/or individual sports
- understand the rules and regulations of selected team and/or individual sports
- be able to assess your own performance in selected team and/or individual sports
- be able to assess the performance of a team in two selected team sports or other individuals in selected individual sports
- be able to use a range of skills, techniques and tactics in selected team and individual sports.

Sport and sports participation are on the increase in the UK. Sport has many purposes: to improve health, for enjoyment and the natural human urge to compete among others. There are many different types of sports, and this chapter includes details of how to improve your performance in sport and your knowledge of the rules and regulations, as well as the ways in which you can measure and assess performance.

Team and individual sports

Team sports are those in which two or more players compete together with a single aim. They include sports such as football, rugby, netball and lacrosse.

Individual sports are those in which the competitor usually competes on their own and is solely responsible for their own actions. It includes sports such as gymnastics, judo, trampolining and golf.

Sports can be further classified as follows.

- **Invasion sports**: these are games such as football, netball, basketball and rugby where the object of the sport is to invade the opponent's territory.

- **Court sports**: these are non-contact sports because opponents are normally on opposite sides of a net, such as badminton, volleyball and tennis.
- **Target sports**: these involve the use of marksmanship and include golf and archery.
- **Striking/fielding**: these games have a batting and a fielding team, and include cricket, baseball and rounders.
- **Martial arts**: these come from different ancient fighting methods, many of which originated in the Far East, such as judo, tae kwon do and karate.
- **Water sports**: these are activities undertaken on or in water, including swimming, sailing and water polo.
- **Field sports**: hunting sports associated with the outdoors, such as shooting and fishing.

Skills and techniques in team and individual sports

Technique is a way of undertaking a particular skill. If a basketball player is able to perform a jump shot well, it is said that they have a good technique in playing the shot.

There are many shared skills in different team sports, and having the awareness and ability to undertake them will be an advantage to your team. These include:

- passing – moving the ball around your team-mates
- receiving – being able to receive a pass from a team-mate
- shooting – aiming at a specific target such as a goal or a basket
- dribbling – moving around with the ball
- throwing – there are many ways of throwing an object, normally specific to the sport being played
- intercepting – this is where a player stops the ball from reaching its intended place; this could be through a block or a tackle
- creating space – this means moving away from opponents so that you are in a position in which you can receive a pass or create a shooting opportunity.

In addition to the skills and techniques required of a sport, players may also be judged on other criteria such as their performance over the duration of a game. Below are two case studies: one for a team sport and the other for an individual sport.

All sports are made up of a range of specific skills. In tennis there are a number of different shots that you can play at different times during a game. Playing these effectively will allow you to win points. These include:

- forehand drive with spin variation
- forehand volley
- the service
- the lob
- the smash
- return of service.

Case study

Skills and techniques in football	
Outfield	**Goalkeeper**
Ball control with both feet	Dealing with crosses
Running with the ball	Shot stopping
Passing	Narrowing angles
Heading in attack and defence	One on one
Turning with the ball	Organising a defence
Shooting with preferred foot	Defending free kicks
Crossing from wide positions	Distribution – throwing
Tackling	Distribution – kicking
Jockeying	Dealing with back passes

All these skills can be compared with technical models and can be assessed with regard to:

- preparation – body position/alertness
- execution – technique/timing
- result – consistency/recovery.

Case study

Skills and techniques in snow boarding:

- front side sliding
- back side sliding
- toe carving
- heel carving
- swing to the hill from steep traverse
- carved turns
- controlled descent of a slalom course.

Fig 7.01 Snowboarding

Tactics

definition Tactics: these are plans and actions to achieve a goal.

Tactics in sport are usually focused directly or indirectly on winning. Tactics can depend upon the opposition, players of the other team or opponents, the importance of the competition and maybe the weather. Tactics can be:

- pre-event tactics – a particular plan before the event
- in-event tactics – a plan implemented during the game such as switching from man-to-man to zone defence in basketball.

Tactics can fail if the opposition work them out too easily, if the tactic is employed too late or if the player or players are simply not able to understand or execute the necessary tactic(s).

Consider the range of options that a tennis player has at their disposal. First, where should they stand while waiting for their opponent's return? If the ball is likely to come over the net in the middle and low, then the player might consider standing close to the net to make a volley. In this way the player has selected a tactical position and shot selection. The same player might also consider serving the ball to the forehand or backhand of their opponent, some with spin, some without and some faster than others. This is known as variation.

If the conditions of the match are that the player is losing, that player might start to play defensive shots in an attempt to prevent them from falling further behind.

Tactics can include playing precise formations against specific opponents. Football teams may play more defensively away from home and opt to play with more defending players rather than strikers. In certain sports opposing players may be marked to stop them having a positive effect for their team.

Other tactics may include working on specific set plays such as line-outs in rugby, and corners and free kicks in football.

In order to improve your performance, it is a good idea to actually watch yourself perform the skill. Have a friend or a coach video you while you perform a set skill. You can then analyse your performance and see what you are doing. You may be surprised and realise your body is not doing what you thought it was doing! You will then need to amend the skill, practise it and video yourself again to check that you are now performing the skill properly.

Rules and regulations

The rules and regulations of any sport are normally set and amended by its national governing body (NGBs) and international sports federations (ISFs). These are set to ensure that the sport is played fairly and that the opponents are aware of how to win.

LEARNER ACTIVITY Tactics

- For the following tactics give a description and when they might be applied. An example would be full-court pressure defence in basketball – defenders of a team pressurise their opponents across the whole of the court. It could be applied to force the opposition to make mistakes and to score points quickly from steals.

Team sports	Individual sports
Man marking in football	Slowing down between points in tennis
Setting an attacking field in cricket	Three shots to the green on a par 5 hole
Kicking for touch in rugby	Repeated drop shots in badminton

- For one of the tactics above, or another from a sport of your choice, explain the tactical significance of these strategies, detailing in what conditions they may be employed.
- Describe two other tactics from the same sport, again detailing the conditions in which they can be applied.

Key learning points

- Sports can be divided into invasion, court, target, striking and fielding, martial arts, water and field sports.
- Tactics are plans and actions to achieve a goal. Tactics in sport are usually focused directly or indirectly on winning.
- Team and individual sports are different not just in terms of numbers, but also in terms of the skills and techniques to be developed and assessed.

International sports federations and national governing bodies may change the rules and regulations periodically as they look to improve the sport. For example, FIBA, the international governing body for basketball meets every four years at a world congress with a view to changing or clarifying rules to the benefit of the sport.

Time

Many team sports have time constraints and are split into periods of play.

- Ice hockey has three periods of 20 minutes.
- Basketball has four periods of 10 minutes.
- Rugby union has two halves of 40 minutes.

Usually the team with the most points or goals is declared the winner, and if the scores are tied the game is normally declared a draw. For sports like rugby and football the timing is described as real time since the start and finish times are exact (except for added time), whereas basketball and ice hockey are played in artificial time because the game clock is stopped on a regular basis for a variety of reasons, meaning that the whole of the running game time is spent on the court/field of play.

In some sports a winner can be declared before the allocated time has elapsed. Often in test match cricket, a team will have bowled out a team twice and scored the required number of runs before the five days are completed.

Few individual sports are constrained by time, the outcome of the event usually being determined by the success of the competition, and usually by accruing points to a critical point.

Scoring

Each sport has a different scoring system, with the team or individual with the most points usually being declared the winner. An exception to this is golf where the player who has taken the fewest strokes is the winner. Scoring may include putting the ball into a goal in football and handball.

LEARNER ACTIVITY National governing bodies

Name as many of the governing bodies for sport as you can in the table below, both national and international. Two examples are given.

Team sports

Sport	NGB	ISF
Cricket	England and Wales Cricket Board (ECB)	International Cricket Council (ICC)
Rugby union		
Hockey		
Netball		
Rugby league		
Volleyball		
Ice hockey		

Individual sports

Sport	NGB	ISF
Tennis	Lawn Tennis Association (LTA)	International Tennis Federation (ITF)
Trampolining		
Badminton		
Table tennis		
Swimming		
Squash		
Fencing		

Facilities and equipment

Specific sports require certain facilities to enable play to take place. Different surfaces can be used for different sports, and often sports are played on a range of surfaces. Tennis is a good example as it can be played on grass, clay and hard surfaces, and can be played inside or outdoors. Occasionally rules may be adapted for sports played on different surfaces.

Many sports require the participants to wear or use specialist equipment. In football the laws of the game insist that all players must wear shin guards to protect their lower legs. In sports such as hockey, rugby and cricket, players may wear specific equipment to reduce the risk of injury. This could include arm guards, helmets and padding.

You can find the rules and regulations of each sport via its national governing body. The NGB looks after many aspects of a sport, including organising major competitions, running coaching schemes and dealing with the development of the sport at all levels.

Fig 7.02 A cricket umpire indicating a leg bye

Unwritten rules and etiquette

Unwritten rules cover those situations in sports where the normal rules of the sport are unclear or require the discretion or cooperation of the competitors. Examples include the following.

- **Football:** when a player appears to be injured the opposition often put the ball out of play, and in an act of fair play the other team returns the ball to its generous opponents.
- **Fencing:** points in fencing are scored when an opponent strikes another. In a fast-moving sport the electronic scoring apparatus can misinterpret an inaccurate contact, such as the blade contacting the floor. Sporting opponents often either concede the point or suggest that the contact was not eligible for scoring.
- **Cricket:** a batsman can choose to 'walk' on appeal. In other words, if a fielder appeals for a dismissal decision, the batsman can choose to walk from the

field of play, effectively admitting that they were out.

- **Golf:** players can 'give' competitors shots, usually when their opponent's ball is very close to the hole. In doing so, they allow them to score that shot without actually playing it.

Officials

Officials in sport have wide-ranging roles and duties, from football fourth officials, trampoline judges, athletics markers, cycle marshals and netball umpires to cricket third umpires. The role of these officials varies in terms of their physical nature, their proximity to the event and the support that they receive from their co-officials.

Playing surfaces

The amount and type of surface played on in sports is many and varied. While some surfaces can be used for

> **LEARNER ACTIVITY** Surfaces
>
> Complete the grid below, suggesting the kinds of surfaces that each sport is usually competed on.
>
> | | |
> |---|---|
> | Basketball | |
> | Hockey | |
> | Ice hockey | |
> | Rugby union | |
> | Cricket | |
> | Golf | |
> | Badminton | |
> | Tennis | |
> | Squash | |
> | Gymnastics (floor routine) | |

a variety of sports, others are more specialised. The level of competition can also have a bearing. Artificial surfaces also come in many varieties – with rubber crumbs or sand drainage.

Situations

Rules and regulations are often used to describe what should be done in certain situations, such as what to do if a player handles the ball in football, or when a ball is out of bounds in golf. Where rules are broken, officials have a predetermined course of action and a penalty may follow.

LEARNER ACTIVITY Situations

State what action the appropriate official should take in the following situations. You may need to speak with an expert from that sport or look on the governing body website for that sport.

Sport	Situation	Outcome/action
Football	Player tackles another from behind and makes no contact with the ball	
Basketball	With the ball at their disposal from out of bounds at the halfway line, the player passes the ball to a team-mate in their back court	
Baseball	Pitcher hits the batter with a stray pitch	
Rugby union	Ball is accidentally fumbled forwards while being passed between team-mates	
Cricket	Batter hits ball, which then hits a fielder's helmet left behind the stumps in the correct place	
Golf	Player swings a club while attempting to play the ball; no contact is made with the ball, and the player records their card counting only the shots where the ball was hit	
Badminton	Player stretches to reach a shot, cannot reach, so throws their racket to the shuttlecock, which causes the shuttle to cross the net successfully	
Tennis	Player running wide of the court plays a shot that does not go over the net but lands on the opponent's side	
Squash	Player accidentally gets in the way of another, causing him to lose the point	
Swimming	Relay team having completed their four legs celebrate by jumping into the pool before the last team completes	

Football rules

Football rules are known as the 'laws of the game'. There are 17 laws, which have changed marginally over the years. The international sports federation, FIFA, adapts them as it considers necessary. Recent examples of this include changing the offside law to encourage more attacking football.

The following is a summary of the 17 laws.

- **The field of play:** this law looks at the surface, dimensions, layout and markings of the football pitch.
- **The ball:** the shape and dimensions of the football are covered, as well as replacing the ball should it burst during a match.
- **The number of players:** there should be 11 players at the start of a match, including a designated goalkeeper; the use of substitutions is also looked at.
- **The players' equipment:** the health and safety considerations of what players wear is mentioned. No jewellery should be worn and all players must wear shin guards. The goalkeeper must also wear a top that distinguishes him from the other players.
- **The referee:** this law looks at the responsibilities of the referee, which include enforcing the laws, taking responsibility for the safety of the players, acting as a timekeeper, punishing serious offences and providing a match report to the relevant authority.
- **The assistant referees:** assistant referees assist the referee to control the game, signalling when the ball goes out of play and any offences that the referee may miss.
- **Duration of the match:** a football match is played over two equal periods of 45 minutes. This time may be reduced for youth football. Time can be added for substitutions, injuries and time wasting, at the referee's discretion.
- **The start and restart of play:** the team that wins the toss of a coin can choose which goal they want to attack; the game starts with a kick-off, where all players must be in their own half of the pitch; this method is also used after a goal has been scored.
- **The ball in and out of play:** the ball is out of play when the whole ball crosses one of the perimeter lines or when the referee blows his whistle to stop play.
- **The method of scoring:** the rule states that a goal is scored when the ball crosses the line between the posts and under the crossbar. The team with the most goals wins.
- **Offside:** a player is offside if 'he is nearer to his opponent's goal line than both the ball and the second last opponent' and receives a pass from one of his team-mates. The player also needs to be in his opponent's half and interfering with the game. However, you cannot be offside if you receive the pass from a goal kick or throw-in.
- **Fouls and misconduct:** fouls and misconduct are penalised by either a direct or indirect free kick. There are ten offences that result in a direct free kick, including kicking, tripping or pushing an opponent. Indirect free kicks are given for infringements such as a goalkeeper picking up a back pass or throw-in, or for impeding an opponent. Direct free kicks are given for offences that are committed by a player in their own penalty box and are awarded as a penalty kick.
- **Free kicks:** following a foul, a free kick is awarded, which will be either direct or indirect. Opponents must be a minimum of ten yards away from the ball. A direct free kick shot directly into the opponent's goal will be awarded a goal, while a goal can be scored from an indirect free kick only if it has touched another player before going into the goal. A referee will signal an indirect free kick by raising one arm into the air above their head.
- **The penalty kick:** awarded when an offence is committed by a player in their own penalty area. The goalkeeper must remain on their line until the ball has been kicked. A penalty taker cannot touch the ball until it has touched another player if they miss.
- **The throw-in:** the ball is thrown back on to the pitch when the ball goes out of play on either side of the pitch. A throw-in is taken with two hands on the ball and the ball must be released from behind the player's head.
- **The goal kick:** the ball is kicked back into play from within the goal area when the ball crosses the goal line and was last touched by an attacking player. The ball must leave the penalty area before it can be played again.
- **The corner kick:** a corner is awarded when the ball crosses the goal line and was last touched by a defending player. The kick is taken from within the corner arc. A goal can be scored direct from a corner kick.

The FA has set a number of regulations to help the running of football in England. Regulations are rules controlled by the organising bodies.

Key learning points

- Rules are established and controlled by national governing bodies (NGBs), such as the Rugby Football Union (RFU).
- Sports can be played in real time, like one-day cricket, or in artificial time, like basketball.
- Unwritten rules are situations that can occur when players and officials can choose to demonstrate fair play.

- Governing bodies are responsible for any necessary changes to rules or changes to interpretations of rules.

The FA has included regulations on:

- the control of youth football
- the doping control programme
- disciplinary procedures.

Assessing the performance of a team or individual

Performance assessment

Performances can all be assessed. Assessment should always be done with a mind to improve future performances.

Some assessors try to correct errors in performance by simply shouting instructions like 'You are not trying hard enough' or 'Get more aim on your shot' in basketball. These instructions give the sportsperson an idea of what they should be doing but not how to achieve this. To analyse techniques from a coach's viewpoint it is important to:

- sort the effective technique from the less effective
- break down complete movements into simple parts
- concentrate on the techniques that need the most improvement, in the right order.

There are many different factors to consider when evaluating a team's or individual's performance.

- How well do they perform specific skills?
- Are they using the correct techniques?
- Are they using appropriate tactics?
- Are they successful at employing these tactics?

There are several ways in which to assess performance.

- Assessment can be completed by the individual, known as self-assessment.

- Peer assessment is the assessment of an individual or a group of individuals on performance.
- Other observers could be teachers, coaches or judges.

Here are some key terms in assessing performance.

- **Observation** – involves watching sporting performances.
- **Analysis** – deciding what has happened.
- **Evaluation** – the end-product of observation and analysis. It is the final process where decisions are made and feedback is given to the performer.
- **Qualitative analysis** – largely subjective, meaning that it is open to personal interpretation and is therefore subject to bias or error. The more knowledge the observer has the more valid the observations.
- **Quantitative analysis** – more involved and scientific, and involves the direct measurement of a performance or technique. Match statistics recorded while the game is in progress are called 'real-time', while match statistics recorded after the events are called 'lapsed-time' analysis.

There are a number of methods of assessment that can be used to assess performance.

Video analysis

Video gives the person who watches it an objective record of a performance. The greatest benefit of video is the playback feature, including slow motion, which can be used to demonstrate skill execution, tactical efficiency or a more general generic performance evaluation.

Here are some guidelines on the use of video analysis.

- Do not try to film your performers and coach them at the same time. Ask someone reliable to do the filming, and brief them on what you want – follow the player or the ball, try to capture tactics or specific techniques, etc.

- Try to pick up all the sound, as it can provide useful feedback.
- Start the recording before the action and end it well after, judging players' body language before and after performance.

- Label and date the film immediately to keep a record.

Here is an example of a match analysis sheet for a team sport. This could be filled in by the performer, a peer or a neutral observer, scoring 1 to 10 for both achieved and target scores.

Date	Opponent	Result	
		Mark	Target
Analysis area			
Positional play			
Tactical awareness/decision-making			
Fitness levels			
Skills/techniques			
Cooperation/teamwork			
Concentration/psychological factors			
Diet/nutrition			

Here is an example of a match analysis sheet for an individual sport. Again, this could be filled in by the performer, a peer or a neutral observer, scoring 1 to 10 for both achieved and target scores.

Date	Opponent	Result	
		Mark	Target
Analysis area			
Positional play			
Tactical awareness/decision-making			
Fitness levels			
Skills/techniques			
Self-discipline			
Concentration/psychological factors			
Diet/nutrition			

Notation

Notation is a way of collecting data and can be done by hand or with a computer.

Hand notation is a system of recording detailed analysis of a sport and literally noting the data on a sheet of paper using a pre-defined set of symbols. Systems like this exist for many sports, such as tennis, archery and football.

The advantage of these systems is that they are inexpensive and, if completed by a skilful recorder, produce quick information in real-time, so that the coach or performer can have instant access to detailed information. The main disadvantages of this system are that it is open to human error, can be difficult to interpret and can be difficult in certain conditions, such as bad weather.

Here is an example of a profile of a hockey player's skills and techniques. The darker column is the assessment of the level of performance by the performer and the lighter column is the assessment of the level of performance as identified by the coach.

If you look at the results, it is clear that there are differences in opinion as to level of performance. It is important that, if there are differences, the coach and performer discuss the issues and decide on what needs development in practice and game situations and how that can be achieved.

LEARNER ACTIVITY
Peer assessment

Arrange a session in a team or individual sport of your choice. Ask a fellow competitor or team-mate to complete an evaluation of your performance using an analysis sheet.

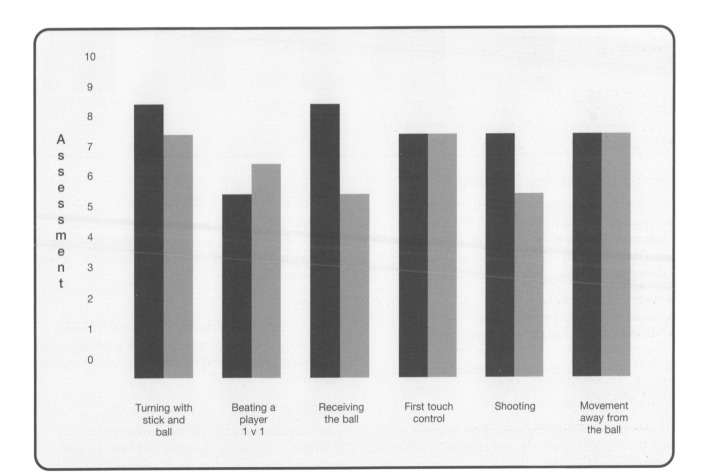

Here is an example of a profile of a basketball player's tactical awareness. The darker column is the assessment of the level of tactical awareness identified by the performer and the lighter column is the assessment by the coach.

Looking at the profile produced, it would seem that there is a difference in how the coach perceives the player is able to recognise the opponent's tactics. A discussion could follow where the coach and performer discuss their differences of opinion openly, providing examples that will help improve the understanding between coach and performer.

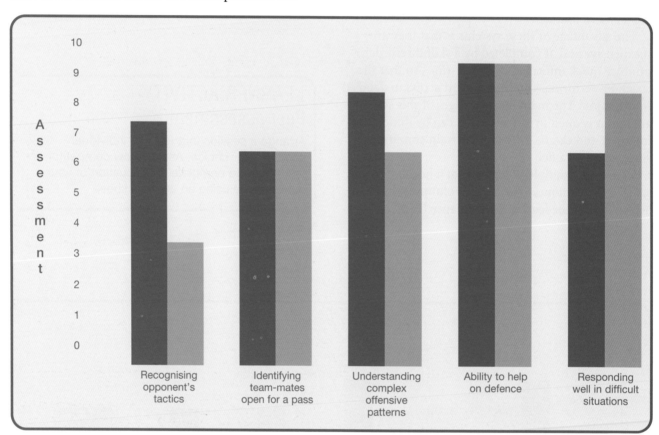

Technology in performance analysis

As video and sound technology improve, new software packages have been developed that can analyse all physical activities. Packages such as Kandle and Dartfish are capable of producing a range of exciting analysis tools including:

- video delay systems
- distance and angle measurement
- overlays and comparators that compare other performances
- multi-frame sequencing that breaks down complex skills
- drawing and annotation tools.

Thanks to ever decreasing costs these packages have become available in schools and colleges as well as at professional sports clubs.

Critical analysis and self-reflection

Self-reflection allows a performer to explore their perceptions, decisions and subsequent actions to work out ways in which they can improve technical, tactical or physical ability.

A mentor

A mentor should be someone who is a role-model figure, who can help provide practical solutions, work as a sounding board and generally provide a range of support.

Coaching diaries

Coaching diaries can act as a permanent source of information to record thoughts and feelings, and serve as a true account of what happened and when.

LEARNER ACTIVITY SWOT analysis

Interview a performer using the SWOT analysis form below and progressing through the following steps.

- Ask your performer what they consider to be their own personal strengths and weaknesses.
- Watch them in competitive situations and see if you can add to their strengths and weaknesses. It would help to research what the perfect model for their position/sport is, or simply imagine who you would consider to be the best in the world in their position.
- Identify any potential opportunities that they may have in their performance, such as extra training time or access to a scouting report on their opponent.
- Identify any threats to their performance, such as a stronger opponent, difficulty concentrating, a slippery surface or poor equipment.
- Draw up a brief action plan that shows what they might practise or change before their next performance.

Strengths	Weaknesses
Opportunities	**Threats**

Table 7.01 SWOT analysis of a golfer

Strengths	Weaknesses
A good relaxed swing	Not accurate with driving clubs
Excellent body positioning in relation to the ball	Putting is inconsistent
A low-risk safety-first approach	Poor technique in short iron game (head up too early)

Opportunities	Threats
Opponent has no knowledge of the course	Environment – windy day
Short game practice has been improved in recent weeks	Opponent is a better player
Has learnt how to mentally rehearse	Can be prone to getting annoyed easily and letting it spoil their game

Diaries or logs can certainly help with self-reflection and form the basis of action plans for improvement.

SWOT analysis

An example of a SWOT analysis carried out on a golfer is shown in Table 7.01.

Performance profiling

Performance profiling is a method that can be used by a performer or, more typically, applied by a coach or observer. Put simply, it is an inventory of attributes, skills and techniques that form the basis of an assessment grading model.

Performance profiling can be used to analyse and record technical or tactical factors as well as psychological attributes.

Scouting

This is a process where an expert observer can identify either a talented individual or produce a report about an opponent. In the first case it could result in bringing a new player to a team to strengthen the existing squad. The second aspect, gaining knowledge of how your opponent performs, is an underused approach in this country. A simple observation and a few notes can be very useful in deciding how to prepare for the next match. If a tennis player knows that their opponent has a fast, hard service but is poor on their backhand, then their preparation should have a greater emphasis on service returns under pressure and returning the ball to their opponent's weaker side.

Development

The last stage is what to do once performance has been assessed. In other words, what to do about what you have discovered, be they strengths or points for improvement.

Aims and objectives

Following analysis it is important to collate the information relating to the performance improvement. Having done this, there needs to be an established set of priorities that will form the basis of the plan of action. These aims or objectives need to be the foundation of the targets to be set.

It is a good idea to use the SMART principle in designing an action plan. SMART stands for:

- Specific
- Measurable
- Achievable
- Realistic
- Time-constrained.

Specific: this means that the action plan meets what you want it to meet. For example, instead of saying that attacking play is a technical weakness in football, you could say that running off the ball, pass completion and beating a defender are weaknesses.

Measurable: this is the way in which you measure your results. If you have identified that you want to improve a basketball player's jump shooting, then you might measure this by counting how many shots are successful in a training or game situation, and then measure again after additional training sessions.

Achievable: what you set out to improve must be possible. It would not be fair to ask a beginner in trampolining to complete a complicated routine with multiple somersaults.

Realistic: it must be possible and realistic to achieve what we intend to achieve.

Time-constrained: there should be a reasonable amount of time to complete an action plan or achieve a goal.

Key learning points

- Performances can be analysed by the performer themselves, their peers, and observers such as coaches.
- Video capture and analysis is a very effective performance assessment tool, especially features like slow motion, freeze frame and video playback.
- SMART goals should be used to establish action for the improvement of performance.

Review questions

1 What is an invasion sport? Give three examples.
2 In team sports creating space is essential. Explain with the aid of three examples how this is achieved in these sports.
3 Describe a range of skills that could be assessed in an individual sport of your choice.
4 Identify how you could go about becoming an official in your sport. Find out how much the course costs, how long it takes and how you are assessed.
5 What is the difference between qualitative and quantitative analysis?
6 Describe four capabilities of advanced technological packages such as Kandle or Dartfish.
7 What is a mentor?
8 What is a performance profile and how does it work in performance analysis?

References

Crisfield, P. (2001) *Analysing your Coaching*, Coachwise.

Galligan, F., Crawford, D. and Maskery, C. (2002) *Advanced PE for Edexcel, Teacher's Resource File*, Heinemann.

Miles, A. (2004) *Coaching Practice*, Coachwise.

Stafford-Brown, J., Rea, S., Janaway, L. and Manley, C. (2006) *BTEC First Sport*, Hodder Arnold.

Specialist Units

Goals

By the end of this chapter you should:

- know about the organisation and provision of outdoor and adventurous activities
- understand the safety and environmental considerations associated with outdoor and adventurous activities
- be able to participate in outdoor and adventurous activities
- be able to review your own performance in outdoor and adventurous activities.

Outdoor and adventurous activities are very popular these days. Many of these activities require people to work as a team, which helps them to learn social skills and leadership skills.

The aim of this chapter is to introduce outdoor and adventurous activities and to help give tips in developing skills and techniques in these activities. The chapter explores the organisations and range of provision for outdoor activities including governing bodies and the places in which these sports can take place. As most outdoor and adventurous activities do involve an element of risk, safety considerations are also covered. The effect of these activities on the environment is also explored so that outdoor pursuits participants can be made aware of how to protect the environment and still enjoy their activities.

Provision of outdoor and adventurous activities

Outdoor and adventurous activities normally take place in an outdoor rural environment and often contain an element of danger or risk. These activities can be placed into two main categories: land based and water based.

Land-based activities

As the name suggests, these types of outdoor and adventurous activities take place on land. Examples include the following.

- **Rock climbing:** this involves using a range of methods to climb vertical rock faces. Climbers use harnesses, ropes and safety equipment to help them climb.
- **Mountain walking:** this is basically the practice of hiking and navigating mountains. In Britain the classification of a mountain is that it has to be 2000 ft above sea level.
- **Caving:** caving involves exploring caves. It may involve some potholing whereby the person has to manoeuvre their body through small passage ways.
- **Orienteering:** this sport uses a map and compass to determine the correct travel route. It is often performed competitively whereby people have to navigate across challenging terrain from point to point aiming to arrive at the finish first.
- **Mountain biking:** this is basically off-road cycling which uses specially designed mountain bikes. It can be performed recreationally or competitively.

Fig 8.01 Mountain biking

Water-based activities

These sports are carried out in or on water. Types of water include the sea, rivers, canals, lakes, etc. Activities include the following.

- **Canoeing:** people often mistake kayaking for canoeing. A canoe is an open-top boat and is usually paddled by kneeling up and using a single paddle.
- **Kayaking:** a kayak is similar to a canoe, except the paddler is fully enclosed, and uses a double-bladed paddle from a sitting position.
- **Wind surfing:** this is more correctly known as sail boarding. Windsurfing uses a small board and is powered by wind acting on a single sail, which is connected to the board via a flexible joint.
- **Sailing:** this is done in a wind-propelled boat. A rudder helps to steer the boat and a sail is used to harness the wind and propel the boat across the water.

Fig 8.02 Kayaking

LEARNER ACTIVITY Outdoor activities of interest

Make a list of all the outdoor activities you would like to try and explain what it is about them that interests you.

National governing bodies

definition

National governing body: the people or committee who make up a team for the purpose of administering and running the operations of their chosen sporting activity.

There are many providers of outdoor and adventurous activities in the UK. Most activities have their own governing bodies that are responsible for the activity in Great Britain.

The governing bodies promote their activity, liaise with other agencies to try to improve the access and availability of their activity and also offer personal development and coaching qualifications. Many governing bodies provide job opportunities either through coaching and educating or in administration.

The British Orienteering Federation

The British Orienteering Federation (BOF) is the official governing body for orienteering in the UK. Its responsibilities include overseeing development and coordinating a range of orienteering events.

The BOF has a national badge scheme, which awards badges on the basis of performance over a series of events. It also runs five coaching awards, which specialise in teaching orienteering in a range of different environments, and caters for beginners through to experts.

The British Canoe Union

Canoeing is the most popular watersport in the UK. The British Canoe Union (BCU) is the governing body for canoeing and kayaking in the UK, with a membership of 60,000. Its prime aim is to encourage and provide opportunities for people to be able to participate in canoeing. The BCU is currently working on improving access to more rivers in England and Wales.

The BCU operates a widespread range of coaching and education courses. These courses are designed to ensure that coaches and participants are sufficiently prepared to take part in the sport and that the coaches have the relevant qualifications to instruct participants in all aspects of technique, skills and safety.

The Royal Yachting Association

The Royal Yachting Association (RYA) is Britain's national association for all forms of recreational and competitive boating. This includes sailing, motor cruising, sports boats, sail boarding, inland boating, powerboat racing and personal watercraft.

It helps to organise competitions and offers a range of training schemes. Around 185,000 people per year complete RYA training courses in 20 different countries. Other aims of the RYA include:

- to increase boating participation
- to promote safety while afloat
- to protect boaters' rights to enjoy their activity in a responsible way
- to achieve international competitive success.

Mountain Leader Training UK (MLTUK)

Mountain Leader Training UK (MLTUK) is the coordinating body responsible for improving the nation's education and training in the skills required for leadership and instruction for safe rural walking, hill and mountain walking, rock and ice climbing, and other associated activities that take place in cliff and mountainous environments.

Where appropriate, MLTUK works in conjunction with other bodies to help their cause. MLTUK is the coordinating body for all mountain training schemes in Great Britain. It oversees the training and assessment of approximately 6000 leaders, instructors and guides, and is the awarding body of the Mountaineering Instructor Award (summer), Mountaineering Instructor Certificate and European Mountain Leader Awards. MLTUK also has direct links with the mountaineering councils (the British Mountaineering Council, Mountaineering Council of Ireland and Mountaineering Council of Scotland), enabling the training schemes to support the needs of the sport as a whole.

The British Caving Association

The British Caving Association (BCA) is the governing body for underground exploration in the UK. It represents people with either a sporting interest or a scientific interest in caves. Some of its aims are to:

- maintain and seek to improve access to caves and sites of special interest
- seek to achieve a better public understanding of all matters to do with caves and caving
- promote and advise on training, equipment, science and safety
- promote and administer caver training
- provide necessary services and information on behalf of cavers in general
- organise and/or support meeting and events, including training, conservation, science and education.

Statutory bodies

There are many organisations that have an effect on the running of outdoor and adventurous activities. Examples of these include the Countryside Agency, which is responsible for looking after the British countryside and running England's national parks.

National parks

There are currently 12 national parks in England and Wales:

- the New Forest
- the Norfolk Broads
- Snowdonia
- the Pembrokeshire Coast
- the Brecon Beacons
- Dartmoor
- Exmoor
- Northumberland
- the Peak District
- the Lake District
- the North York Moors
- the Yorkshire Dales.

They all provide excellent opportunities to participate in a range of outdoor and adventurous activities.

National sports centres, managed by Sport England, also exist to provide top-level participants with the opportunity to train and prepare for competition. Holme Pierrepont in Nottingham is the National Water Sports Centre, and has a regatta lake and slalom course amongst its facilities. Plas y Brenin is the National Mountain Centre and is located near Snowdonia in North Wales. Its location means that it can it offer some of the best places to participate in mountaineering, climbing and canoeing. It also has a climbing practice wall, ski slope and indoor canoe pool.

Voluntary bodies

The Ramblers' Association is Britain's biggest charity working to promote walking and improve conditions for all walkers. It has 143,000 members in the UK and has been in place for 70 years. Its aims are to:

- safeguard Britain's network of public paths
- provide information to help plan walks and enjoy them in safety and comfort
- increase access for walkers – its work helps to establish statutory rights of access to the outdoors

- protect the countryside and green spaces from unsightly and polluting developments
- educate the public about their rights and responsibilities, and the health and environmental benefits of walking.

Urban outdoor pursuit centres

Due to the increase in the number of people living in more urban areas (built-up towns and cities) there has been an increase in the number of facilities offering alternative opportunities to participate. Somebody who participates in rock climbing and lives in London will find it difficult to get to natural rocks regularly to practise.

As technology has advanced, there have been many manmade facilities created that replicate natural resources. Indoor climbing walls and manmade lakes have meant that more people gain the opportunity to participate in a wider range of activities. An example of modern technology is seeing artificial ski slopes being replaced by real snow indoor skiing facilities. Xscape, in Milton Keynes and Castleford, near Leeds, is a company that has built indoor skiing arenas, with slopes containing real snow.

Therefore the construction of manmade facilities has increased participation in many activities, which otherwise would not be easily accessible to some people.

LEARNER ACTIVITY Provision for outdoor activities

Select four outdoor activities of your choice.

Research places where you may participate in these activities that are:

- close to you
- some distance away from you
- based in an urban environment.

Safety considerations

The Adventure Activities Licensing Authority is a non-departmental public body (NDPB) currently sponsored by the Department for Education and Skills (although, in 2007, this is due to be transferred to the Department for Work and Pensions).

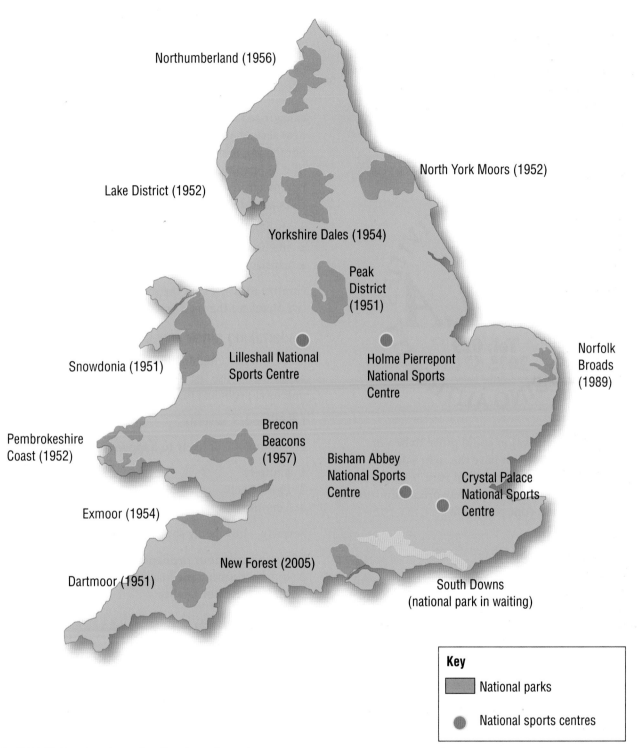

Northumberland (1956)

North York Moors (1952)

Lake District (1952)

Yorkshire Dales (1954)

Peak District (1951)

Norfolk Broads (1989)

Snowdonia (1951)

Lilleshall National Sports Centre

Holme Pierrepont National Sports Centre

Pembrokeshire Coast (1952)

Brecon Beacons (1957)

Bisham Abbey National Sports Centre

Crystal Palace National Sports Centre

Exmoor (1954)

Dartmoor (1951)

New Forest (2005)

South Downs (national park in waiting)

Key

National parks

National sports centres

Fig 8.03 National parks and national sports centres

If it is satisfied that the provider meets nationally accepted standards of good practice, it will issue a licence. This helps provide the public with assurances that the activities are not exposing the participants to unnecessary danger or risks of injury. (Details of when, what and how can be found on its website, at www.aala.org.uk.)

Taking part in outdoor activities can be immensely beneficial, as well as great fun. You can often find yourself miles away from the roads, shops and other

Key learning points

- Each outdoor activity has a governing body which administers and runs the operations of its chosen sporting activity.
- National parks and national sports centres provide opportunities for outdoor activity participation.
- Urban outdoor pursuit centres allow outdoor activities to take place in urban environments.

people. But this isolation could prove to be very dangerous if you do not have the right safety awareness if you or a member of your team get into difficulty. You should follow safety precautions to help keep yourself and your party safe.

Risk assessments

A risk assessment is a procedure used to help prevent any potential accidents and injuries. This process is usually performed by the manager or instructors working in the outdoor pursuit centre. The assessment allows people to take time to consider what could go wrong when taking part in their activity. The risk assessment examines the possible hazards that may occur, the risks involved, the likelihood of them happening and how the hazards are being prevented. Risk assessments should be logged, kept and reviewed regularly to see if they are up to date and none of the details has changed.

An example of a hazards would be:

- a strong current in the sea, used for windsurfing
- ice on a footpath.

A risk is linked to the chance of somebody being harmed by the potential hazard. Risks are often

definition

Hazard: a potential source of danger which has the potential to affect someone's safety or cause an injury.
Risk: the possibility of something bad happening.

categorised into how likely they are to happen, and how serious they are likely to be if they do happen. Something that is a low risk means that the likelihood of it happening is low, whereas something that is high risk means that it is likely to happen. Examples of risks include:

- slipping on ice and twisting your ankle
- the boom hitting your head while sailing
- capsizing while kayaking.

Control measures are the measures taken to control (i.e. manage) the risks (see below).

Undertaking a risk assessment

Once you have highlighted a hazard the easiest way to assess it is to use the following formula to assess any potential problems that may arise:

Likelihood $\times$ severity

Likelihood – is it likely to happen?

1 Unlikely
2 Quite likely
3 Very likely

Severity – how badly someone could be injured.

1 No injury/minor incident
2 Injury requiring medical assistance
3 Major injury or fatality

Here is an example: Capsizing in a kayak

Likelihood of happening	Severity
2. Quite likely	1. No injury

By multiplying the likelihood against the severity you will be able to draw up a chart that looks at the potential problems and make a decision on whether you want to take the risk or whether it is too much of a hazard. The example above would be $2 \times 1 = 2$

Likelihood × severity	Is the risk worth taking?
1	Yes with caution
2	Yes possibly with caution
3	Yes possibly with extreme caution
4	Yes possibly with extreme caution
6	No
9	No

Control measures

Control measures reduce the likelihood of an accident happening. This could include specialist protective equipment to help minimise the risk of injury.

- Mountain bikers wear helmets in case they fall off their bike.
- Safety ropes are used in climbing to minimise the risk of falling.
- Hiking boots are worn when mountain walking to minimise the risk of slipping and twisting an ankle.
- Life jackets or buoyancy aids are worn for most water sports to minimise the risk of drowning.

LEARNER ACTIVITY Hazards and risks

Make a list of three outdoor activities. determine at least five hazards and five risks you may encounter while taking part in each of these activities, and five corresponding control measures.

LEARNER ACTIVITY Safety equipment

Choose three of your favourite outdoor activities. Make a list of all the safety equipment you need in order to reduce the risk of injury.

An example of a risk assessment form is given on the next page.

LEARNER ACTIVITY Risk assessment

Copy and complete the risk assessment form on page 144 for an outdoor activity of your choice.

Contingency plans

A contingency plan is about expecting the unexpected. It is planning for any event that might happen. In this way it is possible to imagine and then calculate what you would do in any given situation. You or your instructor should have devised a contingency plan for every activity so that they know what to do should such a situation arise.

When planning an activity you could ask yourself a series of 'What would I do if ...' questions:

- What would I do if someone become seriously injured?
- What would I do if the minibus breaks down?
- What would I do if the weather becomes really bad?
- What would I do if a participant gets lost?
- What would I do if we run out of food and drink?
- What would I do if the leader is unable to continue?

Emergency procedures

When an emergency occurs it is important that you remain calm. If there are casualties it is important to

Key learning points

- A hazard is something that has the potential to cause injury or compromise safety.
- A risk is the likelihood of something happening.
- A risk assessment is a list of possible hazards that states the likelihood of them happening, and ways of controlling them.
- The level of risk is worked out by multiplying likelihood or risk by severity. A risk level of 6 or more means that either more safety precautions should be introduced or the activity should not take place.

Risk assessment

Location of risk assessment: _____

Risk assessor's name:_____

Date: _____

Hazard _____

People at risk _____

Likelihood _____

Severity _____

Level of risk _____

Control measures_____

definition

Casualty: a person injured or killed as a result of an incident.
Emergency: a serious incident that happens suddenly or unexpectedly and is likely to require different forms of assistance.

summon assistance as soon as possible. Use either a mobile or public phone to dial 999 and ask for an ambulance (and possibly the mountain rescue team, depending on where you are located). You will need to give them the following details:

- the name and age of the casualty, and a description of their injuries
- the exact location of the injured person – grid references and the map sheet number
- the time and nature of the accident
- the weather conditions.

You should then stay on the phone until you are met by the emergency services.

If the injury is life-threatening a rescue helicopter may have to be brought in. If this is the case, there are a few precautions that you will need to follow before and during its arrival.

- Secure all loose equipment; this can be done with stones or rucksacks.
- Raise your arms in a V shape as the helicopter approaches; this will signal to the helicopter that you are the casualty group. Do not wave to the helicopter as this is the signal for everything is OK.
- Shelter the injured person from the rotor downdraught.
- Do not approach the helicopter unless directed.

If you do not have a mobile phone or there is no signal, you would have to send a distress signal. If you have a whistle with you, give a series of six loud blasts followed by one minute's silence. Continue this process until you receive a response. If you are in an area where it may be difficult for other people to hear this sound, you should use a visual signal. Smoke from a fire gives a good visual signal. If you hear or see an aircraft, you should try to attract its attention with a mirror, glass or any other shiny object. You should also try to spread out any bright clothing you have on the floor which will help draw attention to yourselves.

At night you should use a torch to signal the code SOS. This is done by giving three short flashes, three long flashes followed by another three short flashes.

LEARNER ACTIVITY
Emergency procedures role play

In groups of four imagine one of you has injured themselves on a mountain. Two people carry out a role play to determine how they will get help. The fourth person should observe and give feedback to the group on what they thought they did well and how they could improve.

Safety equipment

You should always carry a basic first aid kit with you on any outdoor activities. If you are taking part in water-based activities, make sure the following pieces of safety equipment are kept in a sealed watertight container:

- ten plasters in various sizes
- two large sterile dressings for management of severe bleeding
- a medium sterile dressing for care of larger wounds
- four triangular bandages to support suspected broken bones, dislocations or sprains
- an eye pad in case of a cut to the eye
- four safety pins to secure dressings
- disposable gloves.

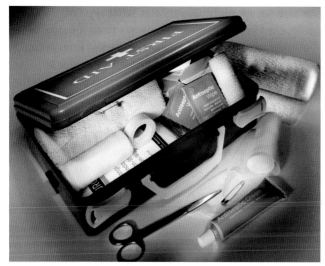

Fig 8.04 A first-aid kit

You should also carry the following:

- a survival bag – a large heavy-duty bag that you can climb into to keep you insulated against the cold
- a torch and spare batteries in your rucksack so that you can see where you are going and give distress signals if required
- a whistle in your pocket or on a string around your neck so that you can give distress signals
- enough food for your journey as well as emergency rations (energy-dense foods such as Kendal mint cake or a Mars bar) just in case you find yourself trapped or having to spend longer out on the activity than you intended.

Environmental considerations

When enjoying walking in the outdoors it is essential that you respect the environment to preserve its beauty. Some of the areas you choose to explore may be subject to special protection, such as Areas of Outstanding Natural Beauty (AONBs). An area of natural beauty is an area with a greatly valued landscape that should be preserved. There are 41 in England and Wales, and they include coastlines, meadows and moors.

There are also National Nature Reserves (NNRs), which are places designated to putting wildlife first. They help to protect, preserve and study wildlife and their habitat. Nearly every rural county has an NNR. The majority of NNRs have access for visitors.

The Countryside Rights of Way Act 2000 (known as CRoW) was put in place in order to increase the public's ability to enjoy the countryside. It allows the public access to open country and registered common land whereas before some people were restricting access. It aims to modernise the rights of way system, provide better management for AONBs and strengthen wildlife enforcement legislation. Wherever you walk in the countryside you should always adhere to the Countryside Code:

- Always close and secure gates after yourself.
- Leave property as you find it.
- Protect plants and animals – do not damage or move plants, trees or rocks from their natural habitat.
- Do not leave litter of any type, take it home with you and dispose of it properly.
- Keep dogs under close control.
- Consider other people – do not make too much noise and do not block entrances and driveways with your vehicle.

Key learning points

- Distress signals: six loud blasts on the whistle followed by one minute of silence, to be repeated until help arrives.
- Torchlight flashes: three short flashes, three long flashes, three short flashes, break and repeat.
- Enjoy, but always respect, the environment in which you participate in your outdoor activity. Always follow the Countryside Code.

Participate in outdoor and adventurous activities

There is a host of skills and techniques required for each outdoor activity you choose to take part in. As there is not enough room in this book to detail every skill and technique required for each activity we will explore only map reading, navigation and route planning, as these skills are required for a number of outdoor and adventurous activities.

Maps

Maps give an accurate representation of the ground as seen from above. They are then scaled down to different sizes. Most maps you will use are Ordnance Survey (OS) maps, with a scale of 1:25,000. This means one unit of length represents 25,000 units on the ground. So, if one unit was 1 cm, 1 cm would cover 250 m on the ground. Maps contain different symbols to show different landmarks on the ground. They also contain the following useful information:

- map title – the area of ground that the map covers
- key to the symbols
- the year the map was made
- the sheet number – the whole of the UK is covered by 203 sheets
- adjoining sheet numbers
- grid numbers
- a scale line to measure distances.

Measuring distance

There are a two main methods you can use to measure the distance of your route. The cheapest method uses only a piece of string. Take a piece of string and place it along the exact route on the map. Place the string on the scale line and count the distance it covers. This should give you an idea of the route you are planning. You could also use a commercially made map measurer which you run along your route and it will tell you the distance covered.

Navigation

Navigation: the process of plotting and following a route from one place to another.

There are a number of different methods you can use to navigate your journey. The best one to use will be determined by the lay of the land, the weather and the time of day or night. No matter what type of navigation you use, you will always need a map.

Across an OS map you will see a series of lines going up and across the map, dividing it into 1 km block squares. These lines are blue; the ones that run across the map are known as Eastings and those that run up and down the map are Northings. The lines are numbered and allow you to pinpoint your exact location on a map. When giving a grid reference you should always give the Eastings first. A good way to remember this is to think 'Go along the corridor and then up the stairs.'

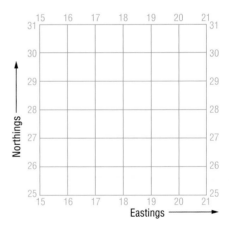

Fig 8.05 A grid showing Eastings and Northings

LEARNER ACTIVITY
Route planning

- Look at an OS map and plan a route from an area that contains water or forest to another area that contains a building of some sort. Work out the distance using a piece of string and the scale line on your map.
- If you have one available, carry out the same exercise using a map measurer.
- Compare the distances you get and try to explain why there may be any differences.

LEARNER ACTIVITY
Grid references

Look at a map and choose three features. Give the grid references of these three different features.

Contour: lines on a map that show you the height of the land.

Most areas that you plan to walk through will not be totally flat. Therefore, contour lines are drawn on to maps to show the height of the land above sea level. The height between contour lines on OS maps is 10 m. The height is written into some of these lines. The numbers are written with the top of the number facing uphill.

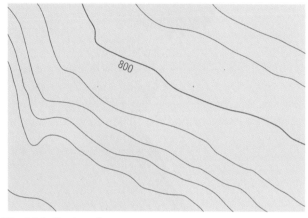

Fig 8.06 Contour lines

Contour lines also give you a good impression of the shape of the land. Areas of the map that contain lots of closely packed contour lines show that the land has a steep slope. Valleys and ridges can also be shown by these lines.

Fig 8.07 Contour lines showing valleys and ridges

LEARNER ACTIVITY Contours
Look at a map and choose an area with contours. Now try to draw the formation of the land in relation to the contours.

Setting the map
Setting the map is a method of placing the map in a position so that all the features are lined up and your location is at the central point. So, if you were to look to your left, you would see the same features on the ground as you would on the map, and the same would be true for looking ahead or to your right. You may find the writing on the map is upside down when you have set it.

This process can be carried out without any problems if there is good visibility. Look for a prominent feature on the map such as a church, a hill or a village then turn the map so that the features on the ground are in line with you at the central point. If visibility is poor – fog or night-time – you will have to use your compass to set the map. The compass will show you where magnetic north is. Then you will need to line up north on the map with north on the compass. While you are walking, ensure that you keep the map set (i.e. change its position) as you change direction so, if you turn right, turn the map in the same direction so that it remains set.

Using a compass
You need to carry your compass in such a way that it is accessible at all times and you are able to move it in any direction. You must also be able to let it go without losing it. The best method of carrying a compass is to attach a long cord to it and carry it over one shoulder.

Fig 8.08 A compass

definition

Bearing: a direction of travel, between 0 and 360 degrees from north in a clockwise direction.

Taking a bearing

When you are walking in poor visibility you will need to take bearings from your map and walk on a bearing. Place the compass on the map so that the arrow is pointing in the direction you wish to travel. Then line up the baseplate with where you want to travel to. Then turn the compass housing so that the north arrow is pointing to the north on the map. Ensure the lines within the compass housing are running parallel to the grid lines running northwards.

Now you need to convert the bearing to a magnetic bearing by adding magnetic variation, which is 5 degrees. Hold the compass horizontally in front of you. Change your direction until the red end of the compass needle is over the orienteering arrow and parallel to the lines in the bottom of the housing. Look in the direction of the travel arrow to see if you can see a feature on the landscape that it lines up with. You can then walk towards this feature. When you have reached the feature, stop and repeat the process until you have reached your desired location. If you do not see a feature to walk towards, hold the compass in front of you and keep walking in the direction of the travel arrow.

Measuring distance travelled

There are two methods of estimating the distance you have covered: timing and pacing.

Timing

This process works on the principal of estimating your walking speed and knowing how long you have been walking for. The speed that you walk at will vary depending on whether you are walking uphill or on flat terrain. Most fit people walk at a speed of about 5 km per hour on flat ground. You then need to add ten minutes for every 100 m of height gained or one minute for every 10 m gained (Naismith's rule). Walking down steep hills will take longer than walking on the flat, so you should add 1 minute for every 30 m descent.

Pacing

This process uses the principle of counting the number of steps you have taken and estimating the distance covered from these steps. It takes an average-sized male about 60 double steps to cover 100 m. From this you can then work out how far you have

travelled. You need to be aware that the size of your pace will vary depending on whether you are travelling uphill or downhill.

Fig 8.09 Taking a bearing

> ## LEARNER ACTIVITY Pacing your distance
> Work out your own paces by counting how many double steps you take when walking along a 100 m athletics track.

Planning your route

This process should be thought through carefully and planned properly. If you do not give it full attention you may find yourself walking up some very steep mountains or having to walk through boggy ground when you really just wanted to have a fairly easy walk. Think about what you want to accomplish on your expedition and the features you would like to see, such as lakes or forests. Think about how far you would like to walk and the time it will take you, or if you are in a group, how long it would take your slowest walker.

You will also need to factor in meal breaks. You may wish to aim to eat lunch at a certain place by a river or in a cafe. If you are planning an overnight expedition, make sure you have given yourself enough time to reach your campsite or have chosen an appropriate place to pitch your tent for the night. You should then prepare a route card and make sure you leave a copy of it with someone, preferably a police officer at the nearest police station to your route or a person at the nearest mountain centre. This is very important as it will not only aid your navigation, but if you get into difficulty, this route card can be used to locate and rescue you.

An example of a route card is shown below.

Use of equipment

The equipment used for taking part in outdoor activities is often very specialised and specific to the activity. There are, however, some generic items that are worn for both water-based and land-based activities.

Water-based activities

For most water-based activities you will usually need to wear either a wetsuit or a drysuit and a buoyancy aid.

Wetsuits are used to try to protect your body from the cold water and are used during the warmer seasons – late spring, summer and early autumn. They use your own body heat to keep you warm by trapping air, and then the neoprene of the wetsuit helps to keep you warm by acting as an insulator for your body heat. When you fall in the water or capsize, you will feel cold for a short while as your body heat warms up the layer of water trapped in the wetsuit. For a wetsuit to work effectively, it is essential that it fits the wearer snugly.

An alternative to wetsuits are drysuits. These are worn during the colder seasons such as late autumn, winter and early spring. They are designed to keep the wearer dry, even when the person is totally submerged in water. Underneath the drysuit, a person usually wears thermal clothing to keep them warm. A drysuit does not need to fit as snugly as a wetsuit because it is airtight so it sucks the suit closer to your body.

A buoyancy aid is different from a life jacket. A buoyancy aid will help to keep you afloat if you fall into the water, whereas a life jacket will not only help to keep you afloat, but is designed to help keep your head up and out of the water should you fall unconscious during your time submerged. Buoyancy aids are usually worn for windsurfing, kayaking and small dinghy sailing because they allow greater mobility than life jackets. Life jackets are usually worn on larger sailing boats as these tend to be used for sailing further out into the water and further away from help and rescue.

Team leader: R. Ambler Starting point: GR 328800 ETD: 0800
Date: 26.10.06 Finishing point: GR 337621 ETA: 1800

Leg	From	From	To	To	Bearing	Bearing	Distance	Remarks, hazards, etc.
	Location	GR	Location	GR	Grid	Mag		
1	River	327645	Stile	337644	342	347	500m	Cairns
2	Stile	337644	Xroads	341044	54	59	1700m	Steep slope

Fig 8.10 A life jacket

Land-based activities

For most land-based activities, one of the most important pieces of equipment you will buy is your footwear. If you choose the wrong type or if they do not fit you properly it could mean your activity has to be ended prematurely due to blisters or injury. Both hiking boots and shoes are available. Boots give ankle support which helps prevent twisting ankles on uneven ground. The top of the boot or shoe should be waterproof or water repellent. The soles should be able to give good grip on all walking surfaces you may face. The soles should also provide some cushioning from the impact of walking.

LEARNER ACTIVITY Footwear

Look through outdoor pursuits catalogues or on internet sites. Read through the information on the footwear they have to offer.

Decide which footwear you would buy for:

● a hike on a summer day on low land in Britain
● a hike in winter in the Lake District
● orienteering
● rock climbing.

Explain why you have chosen each particular pair.

Key learning points

Ensure you can demonstrate an understanding of the following:

● know how to read and set a map
● ensure you are able to read and give grid references
● know how to use a compass
● know how to take and follow bearings
● know how to write a route card.

The equipment you use for your outdoor activity is necessary to ensure your safety and enjoyment. Always find out exactly what you need to wear and take with you. Research the different types of equipment available and then determine what is best for you, based on the time of year and the location of your activity.

Review performance in outdoor and adventurous activities

Having completed an activity, it is important to gain some feedback on how to improve performance. Feedback can come from a number of sources.

All of the above can be improved. You should develop your own self-assessment techniques, paying particular attention to what needs to be improved and in what order.

Target setting

Once a decision has been made about your areas of development, it is an appropriate time to think about setting targets. Remember that you may not be able to achieve your desired skill levels immediately and while these remain your long-term goal it is important to set realistic short-term targets to lay the pathway to achieving your skills. When you have identified areas for development, it is good practice to apply the SMART principle. This stands for the following:

- **Specific**
- **Measurable**
- **Achievable**
- **Realistic**
- **Time-constrained**.

Specific: the target must be specific to what you want to achieve. For example, you may need to improve your paddle position in order to complete an Eskimo roll.

Measurable: targets must be stated in a way that is measurable, so they need to include figures. For example, I want to be able to hike 15 km in eight hours.

Achievable: it must be possible to actually achieve the target.

Realistic: we need to be realistic in our setting and look at what factors may stop us achieving the target.

Time-constrained: there must be a timescale or deadline on the target. This means you can review your success. It is best to state a date by which you wish to achieve the goal.

From this information you can then determine your aims and objectives. Do you want to be able to complete certain awards for your chosen outdoor activity? If this is the case, you will have to investigate whether there are any clubs in your area that run the activity or perhaps you could go on a residential course at an outdoor pursuits centre. From this information you will be able to continue developing your skills and techniques in your chosen outdoor activities and possibly eventually take on instructing qualifications and pursue a career in these sports.

Fig 8.11 A buoyancy aid

- From yourself: a log book, how the activity felt, did you complete the skill effectively, etc.
- From your peers: verbal feedback, comparison of ability, how well you work as a team, etc.
- An assessor: did you achieve the set target?
- An instructor: verbal feedback, video footage.

Strengths and areas for development

Information about strengths and weaknesses provides us with a template for improvement. You should be able to learn something new about your abilities after every activity session. Examples of development feedback could be:

- poor or ineffective stroke (canoeing or kayaking)
- ineffective/unsafe knots used (climbing)
- ineffective communication with the group
- inaccurate pacing technique (hiking).

LEARNER ACTIVITY Finding out about clubs

Select two outdoor activities that you have taken part in. Find out:

- the nearest clubs that cater for these activities
- the award scheme for each activity
- what you need to be able to do to achieve your first or next qualification in this activity.

Review questions

1. Select four outdoor activities of your choice; for each, name the governing body and the main objectives of that body.
2. Explain the purpose of a risk assessment.
3. Explain how you would get help should an emergency situation arise while taking part in an outdoor activity.
4. What does SMART mean in relation to setting targets?
5. What is the purpose of planning an escape route?
6. Explain the purpose of the Countryside Code and give examples of what it includes.
7. Describe how you would set a map.

References

Cox, D. (2002) *The Sailing Handbook*, New Holland Publishers.

Hanson, J. and Hanson, R. (1997) *Ragged Mountain Press Guide to Outdoor Sports*, McGraw-Hill.

Lockren, I. (1998) *Outdoor Pursuits*, Nelson Thornes.

Long, S. (2003, revised 2004) *Hill Walking*. Mountain Leader Training UK.

Rowe, R. (1989) *Canoeing Handbook, Official Handbook of the British Canoe Union*, Chameleon Press.

Websites

www.bcu.org.uk – British Canoe Union

www.thebmc.co.uk – British Mountaineering Council

www.ramblers.org.uk – Ramblers Association

www.rya.org – Royal Yachting Association

Nutrition for sport 09

Goals

By the end of this chapter you should:

- understand the concepts of nutrition and digestion
- understand energy intake and expenditure in sports performance
- understand the relationship between hydration and sports performance
- be able to plan an appropriate diet for a selected sports activity.

As we seek to gain an extra edge in our sporting performances and to maximise the effects of our training, so the spotlight has fallen on areas other than training. Nutrition has been shown to be an area of increasing interest. We know that training brings benefits and we know that eating properly brings benefits. So if we combine the correct training with the correct nutritional strategy the gains are multiplied. Nutrition is as important for people who are seeking to improve their performance as it is for those seeking fitness gains or weight-management objectives.

Nutrients

> **definition**
>
> Nutrients: chemical substances obtained from food and used in the body to provide energy, as well as structural materials and regulating agents to support growth, maintenance and repair of the body's tissues.

Nutrients can be divided into two main groups: macronutrients and micronutrients. The three macronutrients are:

- carbohydrate
- protein
- fat.

Macronutrients are needed in large amounts in the diet and all provide energy for the body. They are also used to build the structures of the body and produce functions needed to sustain life.

The two micronutrients are:

- vitamins
- minerals.

They are needed in smaller amounts in the diet and contain no energy themselves. They work in conjunction with the macronutrients to produce life-sustaining functions and are needed to unlock the energy present in the macronutrients.

There are other food groups such as water and fibre. Water is not usually regarded as a nutrient because it has no nutrient value despite being highly important in sustaining life. Fibre is a type of carbohydrate so it would be part of that food group.

Carbohydrate

Almost every culture relies on carbohydrate as the major source of nutrients and calories – rice in Asia, wheat in Europe, the Middle East and North Africa, corn and potato in the Americas.

Carbohydrate should provide between 50 and 60 per cent of calorie intake and its main role is to supply energy to allow the body to function. The energy content of carbohydrate is 1 g provides 4 kcals.

There are many sources of carbohydrate, such as bread, rice, pasta, potatoes, fruit, vegetables, sweets and biscuits. They all differ in form slightly but are all broken down into glucose because that is the only way the body can use carbohydrate.

The functions of carbohydrate are to provide energy for:

- the brain to function
- the liver to perform its functions
- muscular contractions at moderate to high intensities.

When carbohydrate foods are digested they are all broken down into glucose which is then absorbed in the small intestine and enters the bloodstream. From the bloodstream it can either be used immediately as energy or stored in the liver and muscles. Glucose is stored in the form of glycogen which is bound to water (1 g of glucose needs 2.7 g of water) for storage. However, the glycogen molecule is bulky and difficult to store in large amounts. The body can store around 1600 kcals of glycogen, which would enable us to run for around two hours.

definition

Glucose: the smallest unit of a carbohydrate. Glycogen: stored glucose in the muscles and liver attached to water molecules.

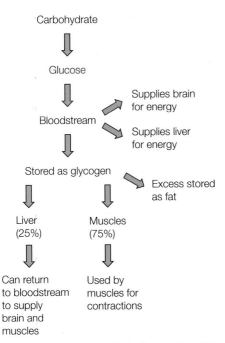

Fig 9.01 What happens to carbohydrate when it is digested

Forms of carbohydrate

Carbohydrates come in a variety of forms, but they are all made up of molecules of sugar. These molecules of sugar are called saccharides; they come in different forms depending upon the foods in which they are found. Eventually through the process of digestion they all become glucose. These saccharides are found as one of the following:

- monosaccharides
- disaccharides
- polysaccharides.

Monosaccharides are one saccharide molecule on its own. There are three types of monosaccharide:

- glucose – occurs naturally in most carbohydrate foods
- fructose – occurs in fruit and honey
- galactose – does not occur freely but is a component of the sugars found in milk products.

Disaccharides are two saccharide molecules joined together by a bond:

- sucrose = glucose + fructose – most commonly found as table sugar
- lactose = glucose + galactose – found in milk and milk products
- maltose = glucose + glucose – found in malt products, beers and cereals.

Mono- and disaccharides are commonly known as simple carbohydrates because they are in short simple chains – existing as individual molecules.

LEARNER ACTIVITY
Simple carbohydrates

The following are sources of simple carbohydrates. Put them in order of how healthy a choice you think each one would be.

biscuits	jelly babies
tinned fruit	Jaffa cakes
dried fruit	fruit smoothies
cakes	fruit juice
sweets	sports energy drinks
fresh fruit	

Give three reasons why you have ranked the foods in this order.

Polysaccharides are long, complex chains of glucose molecules containing ten or more molecules. Due to their complicated structures they are called 'complex carbohydrates'.

To digest polysaccharides, the bonds need to be broken down through the process of digestion so that they can become individual glucose molecules and be absorbed into the bloodstream. If a complex carbohydrate is processed or cooked in any way these

Monosaccharides

Disaccharides

Polysaccharides

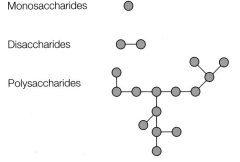

Fig 9.02 Structure of saccharides

Fig 9.03 Unrefined brown foods

bonds will start to be broken down before they enter the digestive system.

Polysaccharides or complex carbohydrates can come in either their natural or refined forms. Wheat and rice are naturally brown in colour due to their high levels of fibre, vitamins and minerals. Therefore, the brown varieties of bread, rice and pasta are of greater nutrient value than their white, refined varieties.

Good sources of polysaccharides:

- wholemeal, wholegrain or granary breads
- wholemeal pasta
- wholegrain rice
- potatoes
- sweet potatoes
- vegetables
- pulses.

Poorer choices of polysaccharides:

- white bread
- white pasta
- white rice
- rice cakes.

Glycaemic index

The rate at which carbohydrate foods are broken down and how quickly they raise blood glucose levels is measured via the glycaemic index. It is a ranking system which shows how quickly the carbohydrate is broken down and enters the blood as glucose in comparison to the speed glucose would enter the blood if consumed. Foods with a high glycaemic index break down quickly and rapidly increase blood glucose levels. Table sugar is a good example. Pasta would have a lower glycaemic index, breaking down into glucose more slowly. It would also have less of an immediate effect on blood glucose levels, causing a slower increase over a longer period.

Fig 9.04 Refined white foods

The glycaemic index is one of the most important principles in nutrition currently. We deal best with foods of a low glycaemic index which release their energy slowly and over time. Foods of a high glycaemic index cause a rapid release of glucose into the bloodstream, followed by a rapid drop in blood glucose causing hunger and fatigue. The person who eats high glycaemic index foods will experience fluctuating blood glucose levels and be tempted to overeat the wrong type of food. High glycaemic index foods, such as sweets, cakes, biscuits, fizzy drinks, white breads and sugary cereals, are linked to obesity and the development of type 2 diabetes. If a person eats low glycaemic index foods they will find that their stable blood glucose levels give them energy and enable them to concentrate throughout the day.

In the glycaemic index foods are either high, moderate or low.

High	Moderate	Low
Above 85	60–84	Below 60

The speed at which a food is broken down and enters the bloodstream is dependent on a range of factors. The following will lower the speed glucose enters the bloodstream:

- the presence of fibre in the food
- the presence of fat in the food
- the presence of protein in the food
- the type of saccharides present in the food*
- the amount of carbohydrate eaten.

* Fructose and galactose have to be converted into glucose before they can be used as energy. This process happens in the liver and takes a long time, so they enter the blood as glucose more slowly.

LEARNER ACTIVITY Glycaemic index (part 1)

Conduct an internet search using the key words 'glycaemic index' and print off a table showing the glycaemic index of a range of food types.

The following will increase the speed glucose enters the bloodstream:

- the length of the cooking process
- the amount the food has been refined or processed
- the riper the fruit has become.

LEARNER ACTIVITY Glycaemic index (part 2)

Using the table you found for part 1 look up the glycaemic index of the following foods:

- oranges
- French baguette
- baked potatoes
- muesli
- ice cream
- baked beans
- wholemeal bread
- bananas
- French fries
- wholemeal spaghetti

Using the factors which affect glycaemic index, explain why each food has the glycaemic index it does.

Fibre

Dietary fibre is the part of a plant that is resistant to the body's digestive enzymes. It is defined as 'indigestible plant material', and although it is a carbohydrate and contains calories the digestive system cannot unlock them from the plant. As a result, fibre moves through the gastrointestinal tract and ends up in the stool. The main benefit in eating fibre is that it retains water, resulting in softer and bulkier stools that prevent constipation and haemorrhoids. Research suggests that a high-fibre diet also reduces the risk of colon cancer. All fruits, vegetables and grains provide some fibre.

There are two types of fibre – soluble and insoluble – that perform slightly different functions.

Soluble fibre dissolves into a gel in water and is found in the fleshy part of fruit and vegetables, oats, barley and rice. For example, when you make porridge the oats partly dissolve into a sticky gel and this is the soluble fibre. Soluble fibre has two main roles to play:

- it slows down how quickly the stomach empties and how quickly glucose enters the bloodstream
- it binds to fat and blood cholesterol, thus decreasing the risk of heart disease.

Insoluble fibre will not dissolve in water and is found in the skin of fruit and vegetables, wheat, rye, seeds and pips of fruit. Insoluble fibre passes through the digestive system without being altered in any way. Its main roles are as follows.

- It adds bulk to faeces and speeds its passage through the large intestine.
- It helps to keep the large intestine clean and prevent bowel disease.
- It stretches the stomach and makes you feel full for longer.
- It slows down the release of glucose into the bloodstream.

It is recommended that we eat around 18 g of fibre a day. This can be done by eating foods in their natural form rather than in their processed or refined states.

Recommended daily intake of carbohydrate

A minimum recommended daily intake of at least 50 per cent of total kilocalories consumed should come from complex carbohydrate sources. The British Nutrition Foundation found that in Britain the average intake of carbohydrate is 272 g for men and 193 g for women, providing just over 43 per cent of the energy in the diet.

As with most nutrients, eating excess amounts can lead to problems. Excessive consumption of sugar (e.g. sucrose) can lead to tooth decay and is linked to a number of major diseases, such as diabetes, obesity and coronary heart disease. Excess carbohydrate in the diet will be converted to and stored as fat. Thus it is possible to gain body fat even on a low-fat diet.

Key learning points

Carbohydrate provides energy for:

- brain function
- liver function and digestion
- muscular contractions.

Carbohydrates are made up of saccharides of which there are three types:

- monosaccharides – single units of saccharides known as 'simple sugars'
- disaccharides – two units of saccharides joined by a bond called 'simple sugars'
- polysaccharides – long chains of saccharides called 'complex carbohydrates'.

Glycaemic index (GI) is the rate at which a carbohydrate food enters the bloodstream as glucose:

- high GI = above 85
- moderate GI = 60–85
- low GI = less than 60.

Fibre is 'indigestible plant material' which cannot be digested. It protects against heart disease and diseases of the colon by keeping the colon clean and the waste moving through quickly.

Protein

The word 'protein' is derived from Greek and means 'prime importance'. Proteins are of prime importance because they are the building blocks which make up the structures of the body. Muscle, skin, bones, internal organs, cartilage and ligament all have a

LEARNER ACTIVITY Carbohydrate category

Copy out the table below and place the foods listed into their correct carbohydrate category.

table sugar   sweetcorn   baked potato   strawberry jam
cola   orange   pasta   honey
apple   milkshake   bread   All-bran

Monosaccharide	Disaccharide	Polysaccharide	Fibre

protein component. We gain our protein by eating protein-rich foods such as red meat, fish, chicken, eggs and dairy products.

The diet should consist of between 10 and 20 per cent protein depending upon the specific needs of the individual. Protein also provides a source of energy: 1 g of protein provides 4 kcals.

Amino acids

The smallest unit of a protein is an amino acid. Proteins are made up of long chains of amino acids which are formed into structures. Amino acids are the smallest unit of a protein and there are 20 amino acids in total. Amino acids can be seen to be like the alphabet. In the English language we have 26 letters from which we can make up millions of words. The protein alphabet has 20 amino acids from which can be produced approximately 50,000 different proteins present in the body. Just as different words are made up of different orders of letters so different structures are made up of different orders of amino acids.

They can be split into essential and non-essential amino acids. An essential amino acid is one which must be gained through eating it in the diet, while a non-essential amino acid can be made in the liver if all essential amino acids are present. This means to produce all the structures of the body we must gain all the essential amino acids on a daily basis.

There are eight **essential amino acids** to be gained from the diet:

- isoleucine
- leucine
- lysine
- methionine
- phenylalanine
- threonine
- tryptophan
- valine.

There are 12 **non-essential amino acids** which are synthesised in the liver if all eight essential amino acids are gained from the diet:

- cystein
- tyrosine
- histidine
- glutamine
- glutamic acid
- glycine

- alanine
- serine
- proline
- aspartic acid
- asparagine
- arginine.

Foods which contain all eight essential amino acids are described as being complete, while a food which is missing one or more essential amino acid is described as being incomplete.

The following are sources of complete and incomplete proteins:

Complete protein	Incomplete protein
Chicken	Wheat
Eggs	Oats
Fish	Rice
Red meat	Pulses
Dairy products	Nuts
Soya bean	Vegetables

With the exception of the soya bean, the sources of complete protein are from animals, while incomplete proteins come from plant sources. To gain all eight essential amino acids from incomplete protein sources you need to eat a range of sources or combine protein sources. This is called 'complementary protein' and examples are:

- wheat and pulses (beans on toast)
- nuts and vegetables (nut roast)
- rice and lentils (vegetarian chilli).

All protein sources contain different amounts of amino acids. The greater the quantity of the essential amino acids in the food the higher the biological value. Eggs have the highest quality or biological value of all foods and are given a protein rating of 100. All other proteins are compared to eggs in terms of their quality and quantity of amino acids. This is shown in the box on the opposite page.

Functions of protein

When we eat protein it is digested in the digestive system and then delivered to the liver as individual

Fig 9.05 Complete protein

Fig 9.06 Incomplete protein

Food	Protein rating
Eggs	100
Fish	70
Beef	69
Cow's milk	60
Brown rice	57
White rice	56
Soya beans	47
Wheat	44
Peanuts	43
Beans	34

(Adapted from McArdle, Katch and Katch, 1999)

amino acids. The liver then rebuilds the amino acids into long chains to make up proteins. The proteins that the liver produces depend upon the needs of the body at that time. If we need to replace muscle the liver will produce the relevant proteins to replace muscle tissue.

Proteins have three specific roles in the body:

- to build structures (structural)
- to perform functions (functional)
- to provide fuel.

Protein forms a part of the following structures:

- muscle (skeletal, smooth and cardiac)
- bone
- internal organs (heart, kidneys, liver)
- connective tissue (tendons and ligaments)
- hair
- nails.

Protein forms part of the following structures which perform specific functions in the body:

- hormones (which send messages to cells – insulin and adrenaline)
- enzymes (biological catalysts which speed up reactions in cells)
- part of the immune system (white blood cells are made partly of protein)
- formation of lipoproteins (these help to transport fats around the body).

Protein is not the body's first choice of fuel but it can be used as energy. It is heavily used during endurance training and events, or at times of starvation.

Recommended intakes of protein

The average daily intake of protein in the UK is 85 g for men and 62 g for women. The recommended daily amount of protein for healthy adults is 0.8 g per kilogram of body weight, or about 15 per cent of total kilocalories. Protein needs are higher for children, infants and many athletes.

Key learning points

Proteins are long chains of amino acids. There are 20 amino acids in total: eight are essential amino acids which need to be eaten in the diet, and 12 are non-essential amino acids which can be synthesised by the liver if all eight essential amino acids are present.

Foods containing all eight essential amino acids are described as being complete protein. Foods missing one or more essential amino acid are described as being incomplete.

Protein has the following main functions:

- to build structures of the body
- to perform specific functions
- to provide fuel.

Macronutrient	Kcals per gram
Carbohydrate	4
Protein	4
Fat	9

Fats

Fats are often perceived as being bad or a part of the diet to be avoided. In fact, fats are vital to health and perform many important functions in the body. The intake of certain fats does need to be minimised and excess consumption of fats will lead to health problems.

The functions of fat are as follows:

- formation of the cell membrane
- formation of the myelin sheath which coats the nerves
- a component of the brain and nervous system
- protection of internal organs (brain, kidneys, liver)
- production of hormones (oestrogen and testosterone)
- transportation and storage of vitamins A, D, E and K
- constant source of energy
- store of energy
- heat production.

Fats and oils belong to a family called 'lipids' and they perform a variety of important roles in the body. Predominantly fats supply energy for everyday activities and movement. They are described as being 'energy-dense' because they contain a lot of energy per gram: 1 g of fat provides 9 kcals.

If we compare this figure to the 4 kcals which carbohydrates and protein provide (see box, top right) then we can see that it is significantly higher.

The difference between a fat and an oil is that a fat is solid at room temperature while an oil is liquid at room temperature.

The smallest unit of a fat is called a 'fatty acid'. There are different types of fatty acid present in the foods we ingest. In particular, a fatty acid can be saturated or unsaturated; this is important because they will be shaped differently. In chemistry shape matters because it influences the function performed. Therefore, different fatty acids perform different functions in the body.

Triglycerides

Triglycerides are dietary fats in that they are how the fats we ingest are packaged. A triglyceride is defined as 'three fatty acids attached to a glycerol backbone'. Glycerol is actually a carbohydrate which the fatty acids attach to. During digestion the fatty acids are broken off from the glycerol backbone to be used by the body as required. The glycerol is used as all carbohydrates are used, to produce energy.

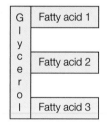

Fig 9.07 Structure of a triglyceride

Types of fatty acid

Fatty acids can be divided into:

- saturated fatty acids
- monounsaturated fatty acids
- polyunsaturated fatty acids.

A fatty acid consists of long chains of carbon atoms with an acid group (COOH) at one end and a methyl group (CH_3) at the other. The structure of the chains of fatty acids attached to the glycerol molecule determines whether the fat is classed as saturated, monounsaturated or polyunsaturated. If you think of different types of fats, such as butter, lard, sunflower oil and olive oil, you will notice that they differ in terms of their colour, texture and taste. This is because of the different types of fatty acids attached to the glycerol backbone.

A **saturated fat** is one where all the carbon atoms are attached to hydrogen molecules. The chain is said to be saturated with hydrogen.

$$CH_3 - \overset{\displaystyle H}{\underset{\displaystyle H}{C}} - \overset{\displaystyle H}{\underset{\displaystyle H}{C}} - \overset{\displaystyle H}{\underset{\displaystyle H}{C}} - \overset{\displaystyle H}{\underset{\displaystyle H}{C}} - \overset{\displaystyle H}{\underset{\displaystyle H}{C}} - \overset{\displaystyle OH}{C} = O$$

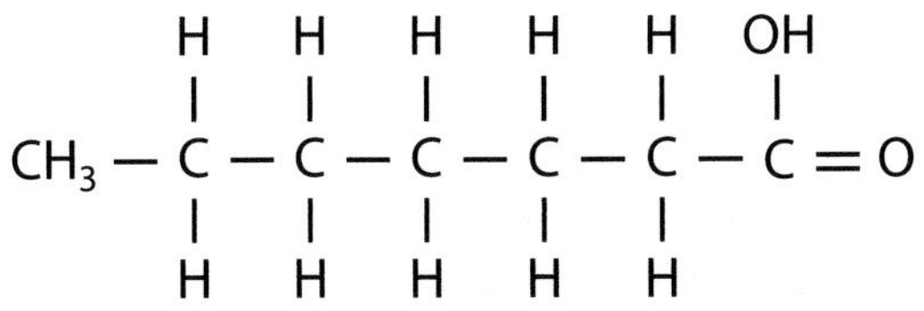

Fig 9.08 Saturated fatty acid

We can see that the carbon atoms each have single bonds between them and each carbon atom has four bonds. The hydrogen atoms possess a very slight charge and gently push away from each other. This has the effect of making the chain straight in shape. In chemistry shape matters as it affects function and it also makes the saturated fat solid at room temperature. This is because the fatty acids can pack tightly together with little space between each one. Saturated fats are also described as being stable or inert. This means that their structure will not change when they are heated. They will melt but the structure of the fatty acid chain stays the same.

The majority of saturated fats come from animal sources.

Animal sources:	Plant sources:
● red meat	● coconut oil
● poultry	● palm oil.
● eggs	
● dairy products.	

The Department of Health recommends a person should have a maximum of 10 per cent of daily kilocalories from saturated fat.

An **unsaturated fat** is one where there are hydrogen atoms missing from the carbon chain, causing the carbon atoms to attach to each other with double bonds. This is because carbon has to have four bonds and if there is no hydrogen present they will bond to each other. In this case the carbon chain is not saturated with hydrogen atoms and is therefore 'unsaturated'.

A monounsaturated fat is one where there is just one double bond in the carbon chain (see Fig 9.09).

Due to the slight charge the hydrogen atoms contain they push each other away. Now that there are hydrogen atoms missing it causes the chain to bend and become curved. The curved fatty acids cannot

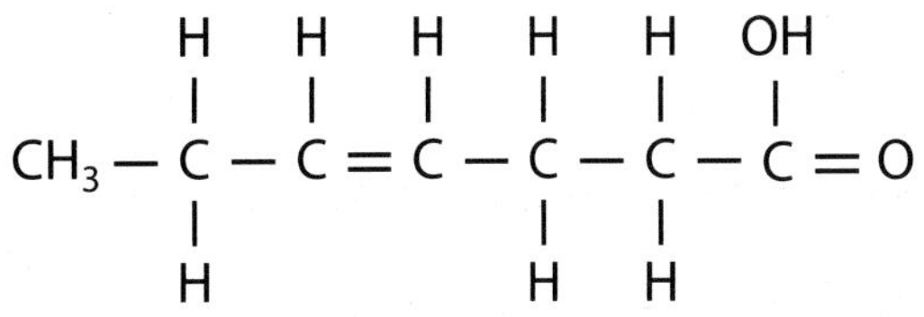

$$CH_3 - \overset{\displaystyle H}{\underset{\displaystyle H}{C}} - \overset{\displaystyle H}{C} = \overset{\displaystyle H}{C} - \overset{\displaystyle H}{\underset{\displaystyle H}{C}} - \overset{\displaystyle H}{\underset{\displaystyle H}{C}} - \overset{\displaystyle OH}{C} = O$$

Fig 9.09 Monounsaturated fatty acid

pack so tightly together so their appearance changes and they will be in liquid or oil form. They will also be less stable or more reactive. This is because of the double bonds between the carbon atoms. Carbon attaches to itself only if there is nothing else to be attached to and it will take the opportunity to break off and attach to something else if it can. If monounsaturated fats are heated they change their structure.

Examples of monounsaturated fats are:

● olive oil
● peanut oil
● avocados
● rapeseed oil (canola oil)
● almond oil.

The Department of Health recommends a person should have a maximum of 12 per cent of daily kilocalories from monounsaturated fat.

A **polyunsaturated fat** is one where there are many double bonds in the carbon chain due to a shortage of hydrogen ions in the chain.

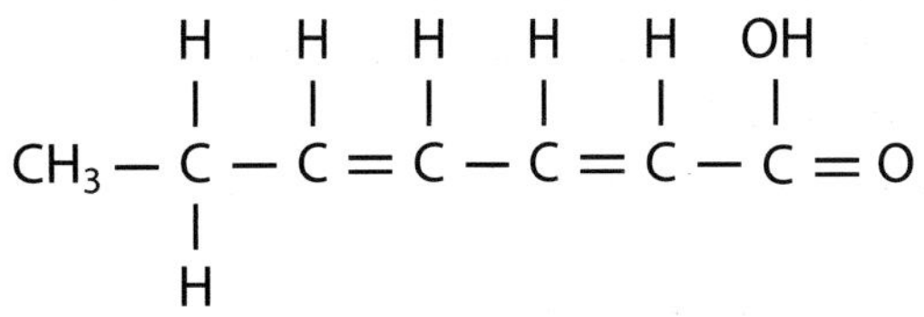

$$CH_3 - \overset{\displaystyle H}{\underset{\displaystyle H}{C}} - \overset{\displaystyle H}{C} = \overset{\displaystyle H}{C} - \overset{\displaystyle H}{C} = \overset{\displaystyle H}{C} - \overset{\displaystyle OH}{C} = O$$

Fig 9.10 Polyunsaturated fatty acid

This has the effect of making the fatty acid even more curved and highly reactive in nature. They are also in oil or liquid form. Polyunsaturated fats are highly unstable when heated to high temperatures and will change their structure.

Examples of polyunsaturated fats are:

● sunflower oil
● safflower oil
● corn oil
● fish oils
● nuts
● seeds.

The Department of Health recommends a person should have a maximum of 10 per cent of daily kilocalories from these polyunsaturated fats.

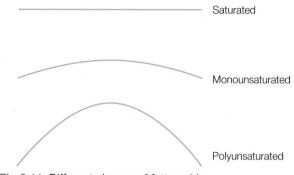

Fig 9.11 Different shapes of fatty acids

Saturated versus unsaturated fats

Saturated fats have always received bad press until recently when people realised that they have an important role in the diet. Due to their stable nature they always retain their structure. This is important because when they enter the fat cells the cells will recognise them and know what to do with them. Saturated fats are always stored as fat in the fat cells.

Naturally occurring unsaturated fats, such as olive oil, have very beneficial effects when they are stored in fat cells – they improve circulation, lower cholesterol levels and improve the health of hair, skin and nails. The problem comes when unsaturated fats are heated or processed in any way because they then change their structure and start to look like saturated fats. They become 'hydrogenated' or altered structurally and when they enter the body they are accepted into the fat cells because they look like saturated fats. Once inside the fat cells they start to cause damage to the cell and stop positive reactions occurring. The two most dangerous types of fats are:

- hydrogenated vegetable oil
- trans fats.

These have been linked to heart disease and cancer and are present in processed foods and deep-fat-fried foods.

Butter versus margarine?

In terms of fat content these two products are pretty similar. However, due to the margarine being an unsaturated fat (sunflower oil), it would appear to be beneficial to health. Sunflower oil is naturally a liquid and margarine is a solid product, which means it has

been processed in some way and thus changed structurally.

The butter will not be changed structurally because it is predominantly saturated fat. For these reasons the butter is a better health choice because it is a more naturally occurring product. In particular, it is the cheap margarines which need to be avoided. If choosing a margarine check the contents for hydrogenated vegetable oil and trans fats.

LEARNER ACTIVITY Fatty acid

Look in your cupboards at home and find the fats and oils that you use to cook with. Choose three sources and look at the fatty acid content of each. Make a note of the breakdown of saturated, monounsaturated and polyunsaturated fatty acids in each source. What have you found?

Essential fatty acids

The body can make all the fatty acids it needs except for two, the essential fatty acids (EFAs), which must be supplied in the diet. These fatty acids are omega 3 and omega 6.

Sources of omega 3 and 6 are as follows.

Omega 3 fatty acids:

- oily fish (salmon, mackerel, herring)
- flax oil
- walnuts
- soya beans.

Omega 6 fatty acids:

- sunflower oil
- pumpkin seeds
- sesame seeds
- safflower oil.

Research into omega 3, and in particular fish oils, has shown that eating oily fish protects against heart disease. This is because the omega 3s may prevent the formation of blood clots on the artery walls and lower the levels of triglycerides circulating in the bloodstream.

The essential fatty acids are also thought to improve the function of the brain and promote learning as well as being beneficial for arthritics because they reduce swelling in the joints.

Cholesterol

Cholesterol can either be ingested or made in the body. It is found only in animal products and never in plants. It has some useful functions including building cell membranes and helping the function of various hormones.

There are two types of cholesterol: low-density lipoproteins (LDLs) and high-density lipoproteins (HDLs). LDLs are responsible for the deposits lining the walls of arteries and lead to an increased risk of coronary heart disease. HDLs actually reduce this risk by transporting cholesterol away to the liver and so are beneficial to health.

Recommended daily intake of fat

Fat intake should make up no more than 30 per cent of total kilocalories. Only 10 per cent of kilocalories should come from saturated fat. Dietary cholesterol should be limited to 300 mg or less per day.

There are many health problems related to eating an excess of fat, especially saturated fats. These include obesity, high blood pressure and coronary heart disease, although it is important to distinguish between the different types of fat eaten in a person's diet. Consumption of certain fatty acids (omega 3 fish oils found in tuna) is linked to a decreased risk of coronary heart disease.

As fat provides just over twice as much energy per gram as carbohydrate, a diet high in fat can make over-consumption more likely. It is thought that excess dietary fat may be more easily converted to body fat than excess carbohydrate or protein. Research suggests that more people are obese today than ever before. Obese people are more likely to suffer from a range of illnesses including coronary heart disease, adult-onset diabetes, gallstones, arthritis, high blood pressure and some types of cancer. However, most of the health problems associated with obesity are removed once the extra weight is lost.

LEARNER ACTIVITY Your own daily intake (part 1)

Using the food groups discussed, work out how many servings of each you ate yesterday.

Determine areas in you diet that you could make improvements to, suggesting alternative foods that you could eat.

Vitamins

Vitamins are organic substances that the body requires in small amounts. The body is incapable of making vitamins for its overall needs, so they must be supplied regularly by the diet.

Vitamins are not related chemically and differ in their physiological actions. As vitamins were discovered, each was identified by a letter. Many of the vitamins consist of several closely related compounds of similar physiological properties.

Vitamins may be subdivided into:

- water soluble – C and B (complex)
- fat soluble – A, D, E and K.

The water-soluble vitamins cannot be stored in the body so they must be consumed on a regular basis. If excess quantities of these vitamins are consumed, the body will excrete them in the urine. Fat-soluble vitamins are stored in the body's fat so it is not necessary to consume these on such a regular basis. It is also possible to overdose on fat-soluble vitamins, which can be detrimental to health.

LEARNER ACTIVITY Your own daily intake (part 2)

Draw a table like the one shown below on a separate piece of paper. Write down the last ten foods you ate. Now place these foods into their correct category in the table.

Simple sugars	Complex carbohydrate	Saturated fat	Unsaturated fat (mono or poly)	Protein

Key learning points

Fat performs some vital functions in the body:

- formation of the cell membrane
- formation of the myelin sheath which coats the nerves
- a component of the brain and nervous system
- protection of internal organs (brain, kidneys, liver)
- production of hormones (oestrogen and testosterone)
- transportation and storage of vitamins A, D, E and K
- constant source of energy
- store of energy
- heat production.

Saturated fats occur when all the carbon atoms are saturated with hydrogen. They are solid at room temperature, stable and unreactive. Examples of saturated fats include:

- animal fats
- fat of red meat and poultry
- dairy products
- eggs
- coconut oil
- palm oil.

Unsaturated fats occur when there is a double bond in the carbon chain due to a shortage of hydrogen. They are liquid at room temperature, unstable and reactive. There are two types of unsaturated fats:

- monounsaturated fats, which have one double bond in the chain and include olive oil and peanut oil
- polyunsaturated fats, which have more than one double bond and include sunflower oil and fish oils.

Varying amounts of each vitamin are required. The amount needed is referred to as the recommended daily allowance (RDA).

Fat-soluble vitamins

Vitamin A

- Function – to help maintain good vision, healthy skin, hair and mucous membranes, and to serve as an antioxidant; also needed for proper bone and tooth development
- Source – liver, mackerel and milk products
- RDA – 1.5 mg

Vitamin D (calciferol)

- Function – essential for calcium and phosphorus utilisation; promotes strong bones and teeth
- Source – sunlight, egg yolk, fish, fish oils and fortified cereals
- RDA – 0.01 mg

Vitamin E

- Function – antioxidant, helps prevent damage to cell membranes
- Source – wheat germ, nuts, whole grains and dark green leaf vegetables
- RDA – 15 mg

Vitamin K

- Function – used in the formation of blood clots
- Source – leafy green vegetables
- RDA – 70 mg

Water-soluble vitamins

B vitamins are not chemically related, but often occur in the same foodstuff. Their main function is to aid in metabolism of food.

Vitamin B1 (thiamine)

- Function – helps convert food to energy and aids the nervous and cardiovascular systems
- Source – rice bran, pork, beef, peas, beans, wheat germ, oatmeal and soya beans
- RDA – 1.5 mg

Vitamin B2 (riboflavin)

- Function – aids growth and reproduction, and helps to metabolise fats, carbohydrates and proteins; promotes healthy skin and nails
- Source – milk, liver, kidneys, yeast, cheese, leafy green vegetables, fish and eggs
- RDA – 1.7 mg

Vitamin B3 (niacin)

- Function – helps to keep the nervous system balanced and is also important for the synthesis of sex hormones, thyroxine, cortisone and insulin
- Source – poultry, fish, peanuts, yeast extract (e.g. Marmite), rice bran and wheat germ
- RDA – 20 mg

Vitamin B5 (pantothenic acid)

- Function – helps in cell building and maintaining normal growth and development of the central nervous system; helps form hormones and antibodies; also necessary for the conversion of fat and sugar to energy
- Source – wheat germ, green vegetables, whole grains, mushrooms, fish, peanuts and yeast extract (e.g. Marmite)
- RDA – 10 mg

Vitamin B6 (pyridoxine)

- Function – helps in the utilisation of proteins and the metabolism of fats; also needed for production of red blood cells and antibodies
- Source – chicken, beef, bananas, yeast extract (e.g. Marmite), eggs, brown rice, soya beans, oats, whole wheat, peanuts and walnuts
- RDA – 2 mg

Vitamin C (ascorbic acid)

- Function – essential for the formation of collagen; helps to strengthen tissues, acts as an antioxidant, helps in healing, production of red blood cells, fighting bacterial infections and regulating cholesterol; also helps the body to absorb iron
- Source – most fresh fruits and vegetables
- RDA – 60 mg

Folic acid (folacin)

- Function – helps the body form genetic material and red blood cells, and aids in protein metabolism; also acts as an antioxidant; research has shown that if folic acid is taken on a daily basis 30 days before conception, the fetus is less likely to suffer from birth defects such as spina bifida
- Source – green vegetables, kidney beans and orange juice
- RDA – 400 mg

Minerals

There are several minerals required to maintain a healthy body. Some are needed in moderate amounts others only in very small amounts; the latter are referred to as trace minerals.

Calcium

- Function – needed to build strong bones and teeth, helps to calm nerves and plays a role in muscle contraction, blood clotting and cell membrane upkeep; correct quantities of calcium consumption have been shown to significantly lower the risk of osteoporosis
- Source – milk and milk products, whole grains and unrefined cereals, green vegetables and fish bones
- RDA – adults 1200 mg
- Deficiency – fragile bones, osteoporosis, rickets, tooth decay, irregular heartbeat and slowed nerve impulse response; vitamin D is essential for proper calcium absorption and utilisation

Magnesium

- Function – aids the production of proteins and helps regulate body temperature; helps lower blood pressure and assists with the proper functioning of nerves and muscles
- Source – whole grain foods, wheat bran, dark green leafy vegetables, soya beans, fish, oysters, shrimp, almonds and peanuts
- RDA – 350 mg
- Deficiency – decreased blood pressure and body temperature, nervousness, interference with the transmission of nerve and muscle impulses

Phosphorus

- Function – essential for metabolism of carbohydrates, fats and proteins; aids growth and cell repair, and is necessary for proper skeletal growth, tooth development, proper kidney function and the nervous system
- Source – meat, fish, poultry, milk, yoghurt, eggs, seeds, broccoli and nuts
- RDA – 800 mg
- Deficiency – bone pain, fatigue, irregular breathing and nervous disorders

Potassium

- Function – in conjunction with sodium helps to maintain fluid and electrolyte balance within cells;

important for normal nerve and muscle function and aids proper maintenance of the blood's mineral balance; also helps to lower blood pressure
- Source – bananas, dried apricots, yoghurt, whole grains, sunflower seeds, potatoes, sweet potatoes and kidney beans
- RDA – 2500 mg
- Deficiency – decreased blood pressure, dry skin, salt retention and irregular heartbeat

Sodium

- Function – works in conjunction with potassium to maintain fluid and electrolyte balance within cells
- Source – virtually all foods contain sodium, e.g. celery, cheese, eggs, meat, milk and milk products, processed foods, salt and seafood
- RDA – 2500 mg
- Deficiency – confusion, low blood sugar, dehydration, lethargy, heart palpitations and heart attack

Trace minerals

Copper

- Function – assists in the formation of haemoglobin and helps to maintain healthy bones, blood vessels and nerves
- Source – barley, potatoes, whole grains, mushrooms, cocoa, beans, almonds and most seafoods
- RDA – 2 mg
- Deficiency – fractures and bone deformities, anaemia, general weakness, impaired respiration and skin sores

Iron

- Function – required for the production of haemoglobin
- Source – liver, lean meats, eggs, baked potatoes, soyabeans, kidney beans, whole grains and cereals, and dried fruits
- RDA – males 10 mg, females 18 mg
- Deficiency – dizziness, iron deficiency anaemia, constipation, sore or inflamed tongue

Selenium

- Function – a powerful antioxidant, aids normal body growth and fertility
- Source – seafood, offal, bran and wheat germ, broccoli, celery, cucumbers and mushrooms

- RDA – 1 mg
- Deficiency – heart disease, muscular pain and weakness

Zinc

- Function – necessary for healing and development of new cells; an antioxidant, plays an important part in helping to build a strong immune system
- Source – beef, lamb, seafood, eggs, yoghurt, yeast extract (e.g. Marmite), beans, nuts and seeds
- RDA – 15 mg
- Deficiency – decreased learning ability, delayed sexual maturity, eczema, fatigue, prolonged wound healing, retarded growth and white spots on nails

Key learning points

- Vitamins and minerals play key roles in sustaining life and the health of the body.
- Vitamins B and C are water soluble.
- Vitamins A, D, E and K are fat soluble.

Water

One of the major chemicals essential to life is water although it has no nutritional value in terms of energy. Water is used by the body to transport other chemicals. It also plays a major role in maintaining the body at a constant temperature. About 2.5 litres a day are needed to maintain normal functions in adults. This amount depends heavily on environmental conditions and on the amount of energy expenditure. In the heat a greater amount of water is needed, and exercise requires an increased intake of water due to the loss of fluid via sweating.

Only half of the body's water requirement comes in the form of liquid. The other half is supplied from food (especially fruit and vegetables) and metabolic reactions (the breakdown of food results in the formation of carbon dioxide and water).

Digestion

The digestive system is where foods are broken down into their individual nutrients, absorbed into the bloodstream and the waste excreted. It works through processes of mechanical and chemical digestion.

Mechanical digestion starts before the food enters the mouth as we cook the food and then cut it up or mash it to make it more palatable. In the mouth we chew the food to tear it apart further, then digestive juices continue this process. The chemical digestion of foods occurs through the presence of digestive enzymes which are present in the mouth and the other organs the food passes through. Enzymes are defined as biological catalysts which break down the large molecules of the nutrients into smaller molecules which can be absorbed.

The aim of the digestive system is to break the nutrients down into their smallest units:

Nutrient	Smallest unit
Carbohydrate	Glucose
Protein	Amino acid
Fats	Fatty acid

The digestion, absorption and elimination of nutrients take place in the gastrointestinal tract, which is a long tube running from the mouth to the anus. It includes the mouth, oesophagus, stomach, small intestine and large intestine.

Mouth

The technical term for the mouth is the buccal cavity and this is where the journey of the food begins. The teeth and jaw produce mechanical digestion through a process of grinding and mashing up the food. The jaw can produce forces of up to 90 kg on the food. Saliva acts to soften and moisten the food, making it easier to swallow and more like the internal environment. Saliva contains the digestive enzyme amylase, which starts the breakdown of carbohydrates. The tongue is also involved in helping to mix the food and then produce the swallowing action.

Oesophagus

When the food has been swallowed it enters the oesophagus, which delivers the food to the stomach through a process of gravity and peristalsis. Amylase continues to break down the carbohydrates.

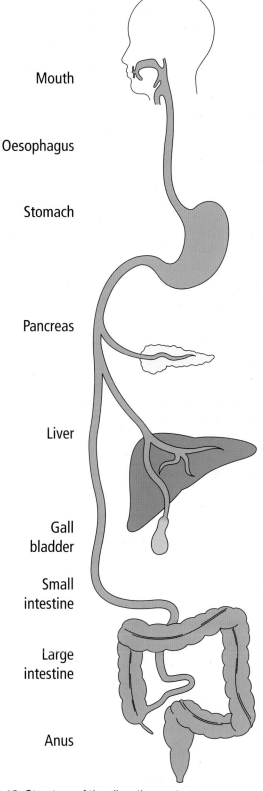

Fig 9.12 Structure of the digestive system

Mouth

Oesophagus

Stomach

Pancreas

Liver

Gall bladder

Small intestine

Large intestine

Anus

Stomach

The stomach is situated in the upper left of the abdominal cavity and is behind the lower ribs. The stomach continues the process of chemical digestion, but no absorption of nutrients occurs in the stomach because the pieces are still too large. The only substance absorbed in the stomach is alcohol, which can enter the bloodstream here. The stomach is made up of three layers of smooth muscle which help to mix up the food. The parietal cells that line the inside of the stomach release hydrochloric acid which helps to dissolve the food and kill off the bacteria present. These cells also release another digestive enzyme, pepsinogen, which produces protein breakdown. The stomach takes around one to four hours to empty completely, depending upon the size of the meal. Carbohydrates leave the stomach most quickly, followed by proteins and then fats.

Small intestine

Around 90 per cent of digestion occurs in the upper two-thirds of the small intestine with help from the pancreas, liver and gall bladder. The small intestine is between five and six metres long and consists of three areas:

- the duodenum, the first 25 cm
- the jejunum, the next 2 m
- the ileum, around 3 to 4 m long.

The partly digested foods (called chime) move through the small intestine partly by gravity and mainly through the peristaltic action of the smooth muscle present in the intestine walls. The peristaltic action is also aided by the action of the villi and microvilli, which push the food along. These structures line the walls of the intestine and absorption of nutrients occurs between the villi. Any waste is passed into the large intestine.

Pancreas

The pancreas is an important organ in digestion because it secretes around 1.5 litres of a juice which contains three digestive enzymes. These are amylase to digest carbohydrates, lipase to digest fats and trypsin to digest protein.

Liver

The liver is bypassed by the food but it does secrete bile, which helps to emulsify and digest fats. Bile is synthesised in the liver and is stored in the gall bladder, which sits just below the liver.

Large intestine

The large intestine, or colon, performs the following functions:

- storage of waste before elimination
- absorption of any remaining water
- production of vitamins B and K
- breakdown of any toxins that might damage the colon.

The colon contains many millions of bacteria which work to keep the colon healthy through detoxifying the waste and producing vitamins. They are intestinal micro-flora and there are as many of these present in the colon as there are cells in the body. These can be supplemented by yoghurt drinks that promote and increase the number of friendly bacteria.

Anus

The anus is the end of the gastrointestinal tract and is the opening to allow the elimination of waste products of digestion.

Energy intake and expenditure

Energy intake and expenditure can be measured in either calories or joules. One calorie is defined as the amount of energy, or heat, needed to raise the temperature of one litre of water by 1°C. A calorie should be referred to as a kilocalorie (kcal). While in Britain we use calories, the international unit for energy is a joule or, more specifically, a kilojoule. To convert a kcalorie into a kjoule you need to use the following calculation: 1 kcal = 4.2 kjoules.

Key learning points

The aim of the digestive system is to produce the mechanical and chemical breakdown of the nutrients into their smallest units.

- Carbohydrates are broken down into glucose.
- Proteins are broken down into amino acids.
- Fats are broken down into fatty acids.

The main structures of the digestive tract are:

- mouth
- oesophagus
- stomach
- small intestine (duodenum, jejunum, ileum)
- large intestine
- anus.

Other organs are vital in releasing digestive juices to aid in the chemical breakdown of foods.

- The pancreas releases amalyase to digest carbohydrates, lipase to digest fats and trypsin to digest proteins.
- The liver produces bile to digest fats.

Energy value of foods

To discover how much energy foods contain a scientist in a laboratory would use a bomb calorimeter which is used to burn foods completely and see how much energy is liberated. We know that different nutrients provide different amounts of energy:

1 g of carbohydrate = 4 kcals
1 g of protein = 4 kcals
1 g of fat = 9 kcals

Measurement of the energy produced by the body

The amount of energy produced by the body can be measured through direct and indirect calorimetry. Direct calorimetry involves having an athlete working in an airtight chamber or human calorimeter. There are coils in the ceiling which contain water circulating at a specific temperature. The athlete has a mouthpiece leading outside the chamber to enable them to breathe. As they work the circulating water heats up, dependent on the amount of heat and energy the athlete gives off during their activity.

Indirect calorimetry is done by working out how much oxygen an athlete consumes. This works because all reactions in the body which produce energy need oxygen to be present.

Basal metabolic rate

Basal metabolic rate (BMR) is the minimal caloric requirement needed to sustain life in a resting individual. This is the amount of energy your body would burn if you slept all day or rested in bed for 24 hours. A variety of factors affect your basal metabolic rate. Some speed it up so you burn more kilocalories per day just to stay alive, whereas other factors slow your metabolic rate down so that you need to eat fewer kilocalories just to stay alive.

- Age: as you get older you start to lose more muscle tissue and replace it with fat tissue. The more muscle tissue a person has, the greater their BMR, and vice versa. Hence, as you get older this increased fat mass will have the effect of slowing down your BMR.
- Body size: taller, heavier people have higher BMRs. There is more of them so they require more energy.
- Growth: children and pregnant women have higher BMRs. In both cases the body is growing and needs more energy.
- Body composition: the more muscle tissue, the higher the BMR, and the more fat tissue, the lower the BMR.
- Fever: fevers can raise the BMR. This is because when a person has a fever, their body temperature is increased, which speeds up the rate of metabolic reactions (to help fight off an infection) and results in an increased BMR.
- Stress: stress hormones can raise the BMR.
- Environmental temperature: both heat and cold raise the BMR. When a person is too hot, their body tries to cool down, which requires energy. When a person is too cold they shiver, which again is a process that requires energy.
- Fasting: when a person is fasting, as in dieting, hormones are released which act to lower the BMR.
- Thyroxin: the thyroid hormone thyroxin is a key BMR regulator – the more thyroxin produced, the higher the BMR.

Hydration and sports performance

It is possible to survive for six or seven weeks without food because the body stores energy in the form of fat, protein and a small amount of carbohydrate. However, you could survive for only two or three days without drinking water. Every day we lose roughly two litres of water through breathing, sweating and urine production. This is increased if we train or compete as water is sweated out to control the heat produced as a waste product of energy production. Therefore, we need to drink at least two litres of water a day – and more if we train or drink caffeinated or alcoholic drinks. The advice is that we should continually sip water throughout the day or take two or three mouthfuls of water every 15 minutes.

Dehydration

Dehydration is a condition which occurs when fluid loss exceeds fluid intake. The signs and symptoms of dehydration are:

- thirst
- dizziness
- headaches
- dry mouth
- poor concentration
- sticky oral mucus
- flushed red skin
- rapid heart rate.

Dehydration causes a significant loss of performance. This is because dehydration, also called hypo hydration, causes a loss of blood plasma affecting blood flow and the ability to sweat. Thus temperature starts to increase steadily. When we sweat it is predominantly blood plasma that is lost and thus cardiac output (the amount of the blood leaving the heart per minute) is reduced. Therefore, dehydration affects the circulation of the blood and the body's ability to control temperature.

Hyper hydration

Hyper hydration is when an athlete drinks extra water before exercising. This is done when they are exercising in a hot environment to prevent the negative effects of dehydration and to minimise the rise in body temperature. The advice is to increase fluid intake over the preceding 24 hours and then drink around 500 ml of water 20 minutes before the event starts. This does not replace the need to continually top up water levels during the competition.

Fluid intake

It is advised that an athlete continually take on enough fluid to cover the 'cost' of their training or competition. This may involve them consuming around 2.5 to 3 litres of water a day. It should be taken on continually and then some extra taken on 20 minutes before the event. During the event they should top up their water levels when they have a chance. Finally, they should drink water steadily for around one to two hours after their performance depending upon the demands of the event.

Choices of fluid intake

Water is a good choice, particularly bottled water served at room temperature. Chilled drinks, although refreshing, need to be warmed up in the stomach before they can leave the stomach to be absorbed in the small intestine. This slows down the speed of their absorption.

Sports drinks have a benefit over water in that they provide energy as well as fluid replacement. They are now a common sight at all sports grounds and there are three types of sport drink.

- **Isotonic:** these drinks have a similar concentration of dissolved solids as blood and as a result are absorbed very quickly. They contain 6 mg of carbohydrate per 100 ml of water and thus provide a good source of fuel as well as being good for hydration. These drinks are useful before, during and after performance, and are the most commonly used.
- **Hypotonic:** these drinks have a lower concentration of dissolved solids than blood and are absorbed even more quickly than isotonic drinks. With only 2 g of carbohydrate per 100 ml of water they are a relatively poor source of energy. They are used to hydrate after performance.
- **Hypertonic:** these drinks have a higher concentration of dissolved solids than blood and are absorbed relatively slowly. They contain 10 g of carbohydrate per 100 ml of water and are a very good source of energy but relatively poor for

hydration. They are mostly used in endurance events of over an hour and a half.

These drinks also contain the correct amounts of the electrolytes, which ensure optimum speed of absorption. On the negative side they often contain additives such as sweeteners and colourings which have a negative effect on health. They are also relatively expensive when compared with water.

An easy and cheaper alternative is to make your own sports drinks by taking 500 ml of unsweetened fruit juice, 500 ml of water and a pinch of salt to aid absorption. You will have made yourself an isotonic sports drink which is cheaper and without the additives.

LEARNER ACTIVITY
Sports drinks

Name as many different sports drinks as you can. Look through magazines, on the internet or in sports shops to help you. Note down the prices of these drinks and any claimed benefits of consuming them.

Key learning points

We need to drink at least 2 litres of water a day to keep hydrated and 2.5 to 3 litres if we are active. It is best to regularly sip water, taking two or three mouthfuls every 15 minutes.

There is a range of sports drinks available to provide fuel and rehydration.

- Isotonic drinks are of the same concentration as blood and provide good fuel and good hydration.

- Hypotonic drinks are less concentrated than blood and provide good hydration but will be a poor source of fuel.

- Hypertonic drinks are more concentrated than blood and provide a good source of fuel but will be poor for hydration.

Planning a diet for a selected sports activity

A balanced diet consists of the following quantities:

- 50–60 per cent of kcals from carbohydrates
- 10–20 per cent of kcals from proteins
- 30 per cent of kcals from fats
- a plentiful supply of vitamins and minerals from fruit and vegetables
- 2 litres of water.

When choosing foods there are some guidelines that will help you make a good choice:

- eat foods which are naturally occurring rather than processed
- eat foods that look as they occur in nature
- limit processed or take-away foods
- the best foods will not have a label containing ingredients
- avoid additives or E numbers
- eat organic foods where possible as they will contain more vitamins and minerals.

Basically what you eat will become a part of your body or affect the way your body functions so be very particular about what you choose to eat.

When deciding upon a nutritional strategy for any person you need to look at the physiological demands placed upon them and the effect these have on their body structures and fuel consumption. You may also have to make a decision about whether to use food alone or to combine food with supplements, protein shakes or multi-vitamins.

Aerobic athletes

The physiological demands on the aerobic athlete are considerable and you will have to consider the following:

- replacing the energy lost during training
- maintaining high energy levels
- repairing any damage done to the body's structures during training
- the need for vitamins and minerals to ensure correct functioning of all the body's systems
- replacement and maintenance of fluid levels.

LEARNER ACTIVITY Designing a sports drink

The aim of this practical is to make a sports drink. You need to decide which athletes you are making the drink for and when it should be consumed (i.e. if you want to make an isotonic, hypertonic or hypotonic drink).

For this experiment, if you are using equipment taken from the science lab, it must have been thoroughly sterilised. You will need:

- measuring cylinders
- beakers
- weighing scales
- glucose
- sweeteners
- flavourings – your choice
- colourings – your choice
- tasting cups
- drinking water
- salt

Method
Isotonic drink

- If you are designing an isotonic drink, you need to ensure that the carbohydrate content of your drink is between 6 and 8 per cent. To do this, for every 100 ml of water, you need to add between 6 to 8 g of glucose.
- You can then add other flavourings to your drink to make it taste better. These flavourings should not contain any carbohydrates, so use things that contain sweeteners, such as reduced-sugar squash.

Hypertonic drink

- If you are designing a hypertonic drink, it should contain at least 9 per cent carbohydrates. This means for every 100 ml of water, you need to add at least 9 g of glucose.
- You can then add other flavourings which can contain carbohydrates.

Hypotonic drink

- If you are designing a hypotonic drink, it should contain 5 per cent or less carbohydrates. To do this, to every 100 ml of water add 5 g of glucose or less.
- You can then add other flavourings, but these should not contain any carbohydrates, so you could use things that contain sweeteners.

Experiment with different flavours and quantities of flavour. Ensure that, each time, you write out exactly how much of each ingredient you use. When you have made a drink that you think tastes acceptable place it in a beaker.

Results
Go around the class and sample other people's sports drinks. Do this by pouring their drink from the beaker into your own tasting cup. Ensure that you rinse out your cup after each tasting. Draw up a table for your findings.

Conclusion
In your conclusion answer the following questions.

1 Who was your drink designed for?
2 Did your drink taste acceptable?
3 Would people buy your drink?
4 What could you have done to improve the taste of your drink?
5 Out of the class tasting session, which drinks tasted the best and why?

Anaerobic or power athletes

The physiological demands on the anaerobic athlete differ from the aerobic athlete and they will be:

- repairing the considerable damage occurring to the muscles and other structures of the body during training
- replacing the energy lost during training
- the need for vitamins and minerals to ensure correct functioning of all the body's systems
- replacement and maintenance of fluid levels.

Catabolism and anabolism

Catabolism refers to the breaking down of the structures of the body. Training, especially weight training, is catabolic in nature because it causes damage to the muscles being trained. We know this has occurred because we tend to feel sore and stiff the next day until the body has repaired itself. The process of catabolism releases energy.

Anabolism refers to the building up of the structures of the body. When the body is resting and recovering it will be in an anabolic state. Eating also promotes anabolism. While training is the stimulus to improving our fitness and strength of the body's structures it is actually when we rest that the body builds up and becomes stronger. The process of anabolism requires energy.

When looking at different athletes' diets we need to give advice on two of the nutrients specifically. They are carbohydrate to replace the energy used and protein to repair the damage which has occurred to the structures. Each performer will still require around 30 per cent of kcals to come from fats with 10 per cent from saturated fats, 10 per cent from monounsaturated and 10 per cent from polyunsaturated. They will each require at least five to nine portions of fruit and vegetables a day and enough water to replace their fluid loss.

Recommended protein intake

The amount of protein recommended is dependent upon the activity in which the individual is involved. The box top right gives estimated recommended amounts.

Therefore, if you have a sedentary person of 70 kg you would work out their requirements in the following way:

70 × 0.8 = 56 g of protein

Activity	Grams of protein per kg of body weight
Sedentary adult	0.8 g
Recreational exerciser	0.8–1.5 g
Endurance athlete	1.2–1.6 g
Speed/power athlete	1.7–1.8 g
Adult building muscle (hypertrophy)	2 g

(Adapted from Franklin, 2000)

Or a body builder at 90 kg:

90 × 2.0 = 180 g of protein

Protein is best utilised if it is taken on in amounts of 30 to 35 g at a time. If any more is taken on it is either excreted in the urine or stored as body fat. A chicken breast, tin of tuna or a small steak gives 30 g of protein. The best advice for the body builder would be to consume six portions of 30 g of protein rather than three large protein meals.

Recommended carbohydrate intake

The amount of carbohydrate recommended is based on the activity level of the individual in terms of its length and intensity.

Activity level	Recommended amount of carbohydrate in grams per kilogram of body weight
Light (less than 1 hour a day)	4–5 g
Light to moderate (1 hour a day)	5–6 g
Moderate (1–2 hours a day)	6–7 g
Moderate to heavy (2–4 hours a day)	7–8 g
Heavy (4 hours a day)	8–10 g

An endurance athlete would need 10 g a day, mainly from complex carbohydrate sources.

The continuum in Fig 9.13 shows an estimated calorie intake and clearly depends upon the size and weight of the individual.

Daily intake of carbohydrate, protein and fat

The box on the opposite page shows a summary of the studies done into male and female athletes.

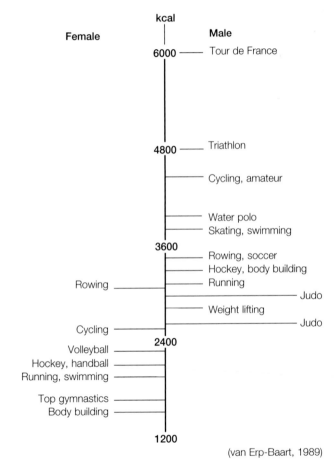

Fig 9.13 Daily energy expenditure

Protein shakes

Recently there has been a boom in the use of protein shakes as a supplement to training. They are employed by athletes who want to lay down more muscle and need to gain more protein on a daily basis. Protein shakes are usually high in whey protein because it contains high levels of three essential amino acids: leucine, isoleucine and valine. These are important because they are the amino acids which are broken down most during training.

Protein shakes contain plentiful supplies of amino acids and are quick and convenient to use. However, there are several issues to consider.

- The human body has evolved to gain its protein from natural rather than processed sources (meats rather than powders).
- They often contain additives such as sweeteners, sugars and colourings.
- The process of drying the proteins into powder form damages the structure of the amino acids, making them unusable by the body.
- They are often very expensive.

Diet plans

If the amount of energy taken in (via food) equals the amount expended (physical activity and BMR) then a person will remain at the same weight. To lose weight, energy intake must be less than energy expenditure and to gain weight energy intake must exceed expenditure. Therefore, in order to lose weight a person needs to reduce intake (eat less) and increase expenditure (do more physical activity).

Athlete group	Carbohydrate %	Protein %	Fat %	Kcals per kg of body weight
Triathlete				
M	66.2	11.6	21.2	62.0
F	59.2	11.8	29	57.4
Cyclists				
M	54.3	13.5	31.7	46.2
F	56.5	14.0	29.5	59.1
Swimmers				
M	50.3	15.0	34.7	45.3
F	49.3	14.2	36.5	55.6
Runners				
M	48.0	14.0	38.0	42.2
F	49.0	14.0	36.0	42.9
Basketball				
M	49.0	15.0	36.0	32.0
F	45.3	16.0	34.7	45.6
Gymnasts				
M	49.8	15.3	34.9	37.8
F	44.0	15.0	39.0	53.3
Dancers				
M	50.2	15.4	34.4	34.0
F	38.4	16.5	45.1	51.7
Rowers				
M	54.2	13.4	23.7	
F	55.8	15.3	30.3	
Soccer				
M	47	14	39	
Weight lifters				
M	40.3	20.0	39.7	46.5
Marathon runners				
M	52	15	32	51

To lose one pound in body weight (approximately 0.45 kg) the energy deficit needs to be around 3500 kcals per week. If you expended 250 kcals per day and consumed 250 kcals less you would have a daily deficit of 500 kcal. In seven days you would have a deficit of 3500 kcals (500 × 7) and hence you would have lost eleven pounds in body weight.

Weight loss

We have established that in order to lose weight it is necessary to consume fewer calories than your body needs. Athletes may not be overweight, but may need to lose excess weight to compete in a lower weight category. Excess weight in the form of fat usually acts to hinder a person's performance because a heavier body requires more energy for transport. Therefore, athletes may diet to get rid of any unessential fat. The best type of diet to help the person lose weight but still have enough energy to train seems to be a low-fat diet.

Low-fat diets

A low-fat diet recommends low-fat options whenever possible, plus regular consumption of complex carbohydrates like potatoes and brown bread. Low-fat diets are usually quite filling because they involve eating large amounts of complex carbohydrates, which include fibre. Weight loss is steady at about 1.5 to 2 pounds per week. Most experts agree that faster weight loss is not sustainable as the weight lost is from the glycogen stores and not from the fat stores of the body.

Here is an example of what you might eat on a low-fat diet.

A typical breakfast:

- glass of freshly squeezed orange
- large bowl of cereal with fat-free milk
- toast with no margarine, and yeast extract (e.g. Marmite) or jam
- tea/coffee.

A typical lunch:

- large brown bread sandwich with lean meat, and large salad with low-fat dressing
- low-fat yoghurt.

A typical dinner:

- 4 oz lean chicken with potatoes (no butter) and two helpings of vegetables
- chopped fruit topped with low-fat ice cream or low-fat fromage frais.

Typical snacks:

- fruit
- low-fat yoghurts
- whole-wheat sandwiches
- cereal.

Review questions

1 Name the three macronutrients and the two micronutrients.
2 Give the energy content that can be derived from 1 g of each of the nutrients.
3 What is the smallest unit of each of the macronutrients?
4 Explain what happens to carbohydrate foods when they are digested.
5 Name the three monosaccharides and the three disaccharides.
6 Explain the difference between refined and unrefined polysaccharides in terms of their nutrient content.
7 What is the glycaemic index and why is it important in nutrition?
8 What factors will affect the glycaemic index of a food?
9 What is fibre and why is it important to have fibre in the diet?
10 What functions does protein perform in the body?
11 What is an essential amino acid?
12 Define a complete protein and an incomplete protein and give four sources of each.
13 Give five functions of fats.
14 What are the three types of fatty acids and how are they different?
15 What is a triglyceride?
16 Give three sources of saturated, monounsaturated and polyunsaturated fatty acids.
17 Name the water-soluble and fat-soluble vitamins.
18 What is the aim of the digestive system?
19 Name the main structures of the digestive tract and briefly explain what happens in each.
20 Name and summarise five factors which will affect BMR.
21 Give five symptoms of dehydration.
22 List three ways to keep well hydrated.
23 What advice would you give an aerobic and an anaerobic athlete about their diet?
24 How much protein and carbohydrate would you recommend an individual consume on a daily basis?
25 If an athlete wanted to take a protein shake what advice would you give them?

References

Burke, L. and Deakin, V. (1994) *Clinical Sports Nutrition*, McGraw-Hill.

Clark, N. (2003) *Sports Nutrition Guidebook*, Human Kinetics.

Eisenman, P., Johnson, S. and Benson, J. (1990) *Coaches' Guide to Nutrition and Weight Control*, Leisure Press.

Franklin, B. (2000) *American College of Sport Medicine's (ACSM) Guidelines for Exercise Testing and Prescription*, 6th edn, Lippincott, Williams and Wilkins.

McArdle, W. D., Katch, F. I. and Katch, V. L. (1999) *Sports and Exercise Nutrition*, Williams & Wilkins.

McArdle, W. D., Katch, F. I. and Katch, V. L. (2001) *Exercise Physiology: Energy, Nutrition and Human Performance*, Williams & Wilkins.

van Erp-Baart, A., Saris, W., Binkhorst, R., Vos, J. and Elvers, J. (1989) Nationwide survey on nutritional habits in elite athletes. *International Journal of Sports Medicine*, 10, 53.

Goals

By the end of this chapter you should:
- understand how the development of sport has influenced how it is organised
- know about the sports industry in the UK today
- understand how contemporary issues affect sport
- understand cultural influences and barriers that affect participation in sports activities.

The state of current sport and the issues prevalent in sport today can be understood and interpreted only if we examine the society they are played in and how sports have developed. Sport in some way affects the lives of most people in our society whether it is through playing or watching sport, getting caught up in the excitement of a tournament or supporting the activities of others. Sport in Britain has developed as a result of the development of our society, and the values and features prevalent in sport are also reflected in the values and features of our society. Sport has also been used to address some of the problems in society and improve the quality of the society in which we live.

The development of modern sports

Pre-industrial sports

There are two distinct periods in Britain: sport before the Industrial Revolution and sport after it. The Industrial Revolution covers a specific period of time from 1780 to 1850. In 1800 only one in five people lived in towns, but by 1851 for the first time over 50 per cent of the population lived in urban environments. By the 1880s this had risen to 75 per cent of the population.

This was a period of major development in society because the ways people lived and worked were changing. Rather than being a country where people lived predominantly in the countryside and farmed areas of land, Britain became a society of city dwellers who worked for a wage in factories. This had a profound effect on leisure time and the form that sports took. It led to rapid changes in sports, with sports taking on the features we recognise in these activities today. Prior to the Industrial Revolution Britain was described as being an agricultural society where people lived in the countryside and farmed the land.

Mediaeval England (1066–1485)

The period from 1066 to 1485 is commonly known as the Middle Ages. At this time Britain's population mainly lived in rural areas, although there were a growing number of townspeople who worked mainly as lawyers, doctors and merchants. Society was split into three specific social groups: the nobility, the bourgeoisie (business people who were gaining wealth) and peasants. It was a period of growing prosperity because trade between merchants was booming due to the lack of conflict between lords and landowners.

Sports were played for two reasons. First, for functional reasons – to prepare men to defend their country. Archery and hunting were a way for the nobility to practise their skills. Second, as Christianity became more widespread and religious customs replaced pagan festivals as 'holy days' or holidays, more time was put aside for recreational activities. Holidays included Easter, Shrove Tuesday and Ash Wednesday, and would involve sports such as folk football, wrestling, skittles and bowls. Other entertainment was provided by musicians, dancers and acrobats.

Tudor and Stuart periods (1485–1714)

Henry Tudor's victory at the Battle of Bosworth Field is the event that signalled the end of the Middle Ages and started a period known as the Renaissance (1485–1640). Tudor rule ran from 1485 to 1617, when the Stuart's rule commenced. England during this period was still a rural, agricultural society with London as the only recognised city, with a population of 300,000. Around 10 per cent of people lived in the towns and the main source of income was farming. Society was becoming more commercial as the feudal lords who had become landlords started to see their estates as sources of income. Henry VIII (1509–47) was the best known king of this period. He reigned during a period of greater prosperity and he was able to develop cultural and sporting interests. He enjoyed literature and the theatre. He would participate in all-day hunts and had a 'real tennis' court built at Hampton Court where it can still be seen.

Sport was still used to maintain distance between social groups. The upper class had hunting on their private land, predominantly of red deer, boar and hares. Other popular sports activities were hawking and jousting. All these activities were used to prepare for war and sharpen the men's combat skills.

The peasants were involved in sport in the role of servicing the sports of the upper classes. They also had their own activities, such as mob football and baiting animals. These sports were characterised by high levels of violence which allowed the peasants an avenue to channel their energies.

When James I came to the throne in 1603 the reign of the Stuarts began and it was built on religious grounds. In 1617 he issued the 'Book of Sports', which stated that sport should be encouraged as long as it did not affect attendance at church. This era saw the development of Puritanism with influential leaders such as Oliver Cromwell, who had been made Protector of Britain. The Puritans were opposed to playing sports on a Sunday, cruelty inflicted to animals in the name of sport, and heavy drinking and its associated idleness, foul language and blasphemy.

They believed that the focus of people's lives should be on praying for the salvation of their souls and working hard rather than participating in activities that had pagan roots and diverted attention away from more worthy pursuits. However, the Puritans were only partially successful and under the rule of Charles II and the Restoration period sports started to flourish again but without ever regaining their previous popularity. Charles II enjoyed a leisurely lifestyle in which he and his courtiers were actively involved in sports and other leisurely activities.

Hanoverian period (1714–90)

This phase from 1714 to 1790 saw a change in how people earned their living. The movement from the spacious environment of the countryside to the cramped conditions of urban living was brought on by a decline in farming and a growth in the production of consumer goods. Factories were offering better wages and promising a better standard of living.

The Industrial Revolution (1780–1850)

From around the mid-eighteenth century the English economy underwent a vast transformation. It had been based on agriculture, with particularly busy periods of work for planting and harvesting. Working hours varied and there were long periods of free time available for workers to enjoy leisure activities.

The Industrial Revolution saw the development of factories producing a wide range of consumer goods. Factory owners required their workers to accept longer hours and less free time. Typically, a worker would have a six-day week, working from 7 in the morning to 7 at night. There may also have been a night shift; this was to maximise the output of factories and reduce their unit costs. Overhead costs were high and could be reduced only if machinery was being worked for as many hours as possible. The second issue was that there was a shortage of people living in the towns and cities where these factories were based, so they had to attract workers from their countryside homes. This was done by offering better wages and the lure of consumer goods to raise standards of living.

The reality was a little different from the promise because these workers traded increased wages for longer working hours and less leisure time. Also, the standards of housing were much worse than in the countryside where they enjoyed plenty of space. The perceived rise in spending and standard of living never occurred because it was more expensive to live in cities. In the cities families and workers were herded into 'slum' accommodation with little space.

Leisure activities became a problem because the violent sports could result in serious injuries, the excessive drinking led to hangovers and absenteeism, and gambling undermined the work ethic. Leisure cost the factory owners money and affected output. Factory owners supported the middle-class efforts to clean up society and impose a new form of morality. Campaigns were mounted against excessive drinking, idleness, sexual promiscuity, gambling, violent sports and the excessive holidays. The aim of the middle classes was to impose a work ethic on the population and make behaviour more polite and respectable.

The agricultural industry also underwent a parallel revolution with the scope and quantity of production increasing. This meant that the population of England became better fed, healthier and had more energy for work.

The economic forces contributed to changes in traditional sports because the employees had to bow to their employers' demands and, moreover, they had little time or energy to play aggressive contact sports. These demands were supplemented by the efforts of religious reformers, who believed violent sports led to moral corruption, and sport on the Sabbath was eventually banned. The Royal Society for the Protection of Animals (RSPCA) put pressure on the authorities to ban sports involving cruelty to animals. The Industrial Revolution led to a growth in the size of towns and cities and a reduction in the amount of space available for recreation. Folk football, which was played across vast swathes of countryside, was completely inappropriate for the urban setting. The result of all these changes was that sports slowly disappeared.

Key learning points

- The effects of the Industrial Revolution led to an increase in working hours and a decline in leisure time. Many activities were banned because they became costly in terms of working hours and productivity being lost.
- The workers had a low spending power in reality.
- The urban setting provided an inappropriate environment for playing sports.

Sports for the leisured upper classes and middle classes were still popular and carried on in pre-industrialised forms.

The 1830s and 1840s started to see an upturn in fortune for the workers, because the development of the railways led to an increased mobility. The sports of cricket and horse racing benefited from the easier access to the countryside, allowing the workers to go and watch meetings and matches. The 1840s saw a

genuine improvement in real wages (meaning an increased spending power), improving diets and standard of living. There was also money available to spend on entrance fees into sports events.

The 1860s saw the development of nationally agreed rules, known as the codification of sport, and a changing attitude of the middle-class factory owners to their employees' sports activities. Two groups promoted the benefits of sport. First, the industrialists, who saw sport as promoting values which would make their workers more productive, such as teamwork and loyalty. Second, the Muscular Christians took team sports to working-class communities to teach the Bible through sport and promote the value of a healthy mind in a healthy body.

Figures from the time suggest sport was still a minority activity, but spectating was growing, as was professionalism in the sports of football, cricket and horse racing. Social change included the urban population growing from 50.2 per cent in 1851 to 77 per cent in 1900. Working-class wages rose by 70 per cent and a half-day holiday was granted on Saturdays. This meant sport could be played and watched on Saturday afternoons and is the origin of the three o'clock kick-off in football matches.

Rationalisation and regulation

'Rational recreation' is the term given to the introduction of leisure activities which were seen as being productive and moral. Up until the 1860s and 1870s the workers had relied on their public houses for amusement and entertainment, which were often socially destructive. Rational recreations were brought in by various philanthropic groups, such as the Muscular Christians and other middle-class groups who introduced new alternatives. Thus, societies such as the Mechanics Society, the Boys Brigade and the Young Men's Christian Association developed, and facilities such as libraries, public baths and sports grounds offered more purposeful activities.

This is an example of using sport and leisure as a means of social control, whereby people are persuaded to take part in positive, socially acceptable activities to prevent them from participating in otherwise socially destructive activities such as drinking, gambling and fighting. The middle-class philanthropists wanted to provide better activities for the working class to improve their standard of living, but their ulterior motive was to make sure they were healthier, fitter and more productive workers.

Twentieth-century development

Globalisation of sport

The forms of sport that were established in England in the late nineteenth century quickly spread around the world, particularly through the influence of the British Empire. Officers and soldiers brought the new codified forms of sport to the countries in which they were stationed, and the sports in turn were adopted by the natives. By the end of the nineteenth century the Olympic movement, under the influence of the French, was finding its feet and starting to involve more and more nations.

The influence of sport by the end of the twentieth century can be seen by the fact that three of the four largest international organisations were sporting organisations:

- the IAAF (International Amateur Athletic Federation) with 184 member countries
- FIFA (Fédération Internationale de Football Association) with 178 members
- the IOC (International Olympic Committee) with 171 members.

The non-sporting organisation was the United Nations, with 180 member countries.

Professionalism

The increasing playing demands of the sports of rugby, football and cricket mean that players have had to devote increasing amounts of time and energy to their sports. By the end of the nineteenth century these three sports had all embraced professionalism. As the standards of the sports rose payments had to be made to players to compensate for the wages they would otherwise have earned. Professionalism was initially looked down upon because the upper classes thought that sport should be played purely for the enjoyment derived from the activity. A class distinction arose between the upper-class amateurs and the working-class professionals, which remained until the latter part of the twentieth century. By the end of the twentieth century, professionalism was an accepted part of all sports and necessary to uphold the high standards of play demanded by the sophisticated audiences.

The development of sport as a profitable industry

As sports have increasingly embraced professionalism, their expenditure has increased. As a result they have had to increase the amount of money coming into the sport to pay these expenses. Sports and their clubs have increasingly sought sponsorship as a source of income, along with trying to make the sport more attractive and increase the number of spectators coming to matches. As sports have become more popular and widely watched, they have increasingly drawn the attention of the media. This has opened up new sources of revenue to sports and has led to increased profits.

There is also an expanding industry in sport for non-competitive participants, and this has created a variety of opportunities for private companies to invest their money and make profits. It has also resulted in a growing industry with new, exciting employment opportunities.

The development of sport in education

The key element in the expansion of sport in the education system was the 1944 Education Act, which made it policy for local authorities to provide adequate facilities for the teaching of physical education. Sport and physical education became compulsory elements of children's education and are now key features in the National Curriculum. Added to that, there are now many more opportunities to study sport at GCSE, AS and A2 level, National Diploma and degree level.

Mid-twentieth-century developments

The two world wars had a major effect on the development of sport. During World War I, in which the Allies (Britain, France, Russia, Italy and the USA) defeated the central powers (Germany, Austria, Hungary and Turkey), all sports stopped at national and international level as young people were recruited for the war and many were then killed during the fighting. The Olympic Games scheduled for 1916 had to be cancelled.

Between the wars the upper classes returned to their leisure activities, playing tennis, golf and cricket, and also indulged in overseas holidays and nights of partying. The development of the railways allowed them to visit the seaside in the summer months. The working classes returned to watching football on Saturday afternoons and the first dog racing meeting was held in 1926 at Belle Vue in Manchester.

During the 1930s Great Britain experienced a series of financial and economic problems as a result of strikes and industrial unrest. Unemployment rose to three million and the development of Nazism and Fascism led the country to feel insecure, with a negative effect on national morale

World War II again saw the cessation of sporting activities as all energy went into the war effort and training the young troops for war. The training used by the troops started to appear in schools, forming an integral part of physical education lessons.

The organisation of sport in Britain

The government in Britain still plays a key role in influencing the direction sport takes and the opportunities for participation in sport. Rather than directly being involved in sport, the government has developed agencies to influence policy for sport and this is backed up by the provision of funding. In this way the government can keep sport 'at arm's length' but still maintain some control over it. The current government's major success has been to attract the Olympic Games to London in 2012.

Central government control of sport

Sport in central government is administered through the Department of Culture, Media and Sport (DCMS) under the control of a Secretary of State for Culture, Media and Sport and a Minister for Sport. The DCMS looks after the interests of world-class sportspeople and also ensures that everyone has an opportunity to take part in sport. The roles of the DCMS in relation to sport are to:

- widen access to sport for all citizens and offer Sport for All
- promote the achievement of excellence in national and international competition
- promote physical education and sport for young people and work with the Department for Education and Skills (DfES) to promote children's play through education

- attract major sporting events to Britain, such as the successful bid for the 2012 Olympic Games
- manage schemes to support the training of athletes, such as TASS (Talented Athletes Scholarship Scheme) which supports athletes in full-time education, and funding of athletes through Lottery money.

The DCMS is not the only department representing the interests of people playing sport in Britain. Sport in schools and developing the physical education syllabus is under the control of the DfES. Sports development departments are under the control of the local authorities within the Department for Communities and Local Government.

The CCPR – Central Council for Physical Recreation – represents the interests of national governing bodies (NGBs).

NGBs – national governing bodies – all sports clubs are members of the NGB, which runs the leagues, and provides officials and disciplinary measures. For example, the Football Association (FA) is football's NGB.

ISFs – International Sports Federations – in order to be involved in international competition the NGB needs to be affiliated to a relevant ISF.

The BOA – British Olympic Association – selects, funds and manages the team to represent Great Britain and Northern Ireland at the Olympic Games.

The IOC – International Olympic Committee – organises and manages each Olympiad.

Central Council for Physical Recreation

The Central Council for Physical Recreation (CCPR) (www.ccpr.org.uk) was set up against the bleak

---

LEARNER ACTIVITY
Government representatives

Find out the current Secretary of State for:

- the Department of Culture, Media and Sport
- the Department for Education and Skills
- the Department for Transport and the Regions
- the Home Office.

Find out the current Minister for Sport.

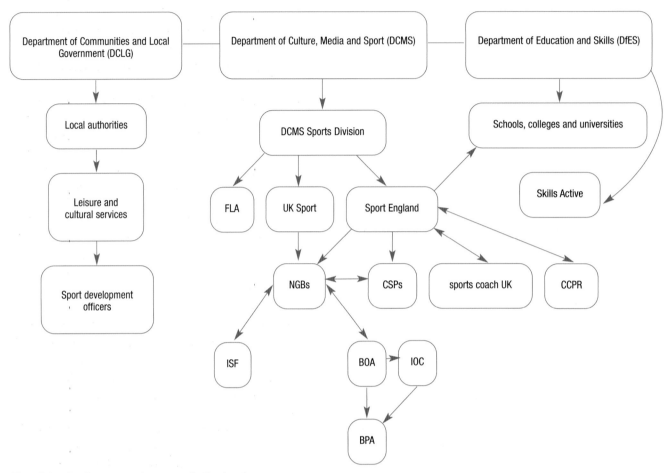

Fig 10.01 Bodies governing sport in England

backdrop of 1930s Britain, which was experiencing economic unrest and high levels of unemployment. The school leaving age was 14 and, with the exception of students in private education, this was when education stopped. There was little opportunity after school to play sport and even in state schools sport was limited.

The CCPR was the first attempt to provide government influence in sport and aimed to promote the benefits of sport. Initially the CCPR supported the work of the National Fitness Council to provide training for physical education teachers. In 1946 it was offered the use of Bisham Abbey at a low rent to be used as the national Physical Recreation Centre. Lilleshall was acquired in 1947, Plas y Brenin in 1955, and Crystal Palace was built in 1964 and Holme Pierrepoint in 1973. These national sports centres were the central facilities to provide high-quality, residential training facilities and venues for national and international competition.

The CCPR worked to gain the support of the national governing bodies and within six months of its inception 82 NGBs were signed-up members. The CCPR prepared an influential report into sport in Britain, called the Woolfenden Report, which was published in 1960. Among its main recommendations was the formation of a sports council to promote sport in Britain. The Sports Council was formed in 1965 in an advisory capacity and became an executive body in 1972 when it was decided that the CCPR should be taken over by the Sports Council and transfer all its staff and assets. This was not agreed and the CCPR still exists today representing the members of the NGBs.

UK Sport

UK Sport (www.uksport.gov.uk) was established in 1997 through a Royal Charter as the twin roles of the Sports Council were separated. The Sports Council had two remits: first, to promote excellence in sports

LEARNER ACTIVITY
Central Council for
Physical Recreation
Find out the following information on the CCPR.

- How is it funded?
- What services does it provide to its members?

achievements and, second, to promote participation in sport. These were seen as being radically different and it was decided to let the Sports Council (now Sport England) continue to promote participation in sport but to give the role of developing excellence to a new body with responsibility across the UK.

The role of UK Sport is to support athletes in becoming world-class performers. In 2003 it was granted around £25 million a year, mostly from Lottery funding, to spend on its aims, which are to:

- encourage, develop and support sporting excellence in UK athletes
- identify and implement policies with a UK-wide application
- in conjunction with NGBs and appropriate home country sports councils, to provide grants for athletes
- oversee the policy on the delivery of sport science, sports medicine, coaching and drug control over the UK
- coordinate the policy for attracting major sporting events to the UK
- represent the UK internationally and to increase the influence of the UK in sporting matters.

These roles are performed through four directorates.

- Performance development: provides advice to NGBs on planning applications, allocation of grants and funding, and advises on awards from the Lottery Sports Fund.
- UK Sports Institute: a central service based in London with a network of regional centres to cater for the needs of sportspeople from Olympic sports, including disabled athletes; the support services include sport science, sports medicine and lifestyle management services to create the correct environment for the development of excellence.
- International relations and major events: the UK needs to attract major sports events to gain the social, economic and cultural benefits of sport; the

2008 Olympics being held in Beijing is seen as the completion of China being accepted as a major force in world sport, while the 2012 Olympics in London is seen as being the return of the UK as an important force in world sport.

- Ethics and anti-doping: UK Sport manages and administers a wide-reaching programme of drug testing to ensure that the ethics of fair play and honesty are maintained in British sport; this work is done under the umbrella of the World Anti-Doping Authority, established in 2000 by the International Olympic Committee (IOC). In 2005/6 there were 55 positive drug tests in the UK with power lifting having the most at eight positive tests.

Sport England

Sport England (www.sportengland.org) was formed from the old Sports Council by Royal Charter in 1997 and is responsible to the Secretary of State for the Department of Culture, Media and Sport. Sport England also operates ten regional offices across England.

It has responsibility for promoting and investing in sport and helping the government to implement its sporting objectives through the distribution of Lottery funds. The vision of Sport England is 'to make England an active and successful sporting nation'. Sport England invested around £2 bn from 1994 to 2006 to achieve its objectives. The business objectives of Sport England are to allocate its resources to get people to:

- start – to participate in sport to improve the health of the nation, particularly within disadvantaged groups
- stay – keeping people active through a network of clubs, coaches and volunteers
- succeed in sport – achieving higher levels of performance through an infrastructure capable of developing world-class performances.

Regional offices

There are nine regional offices which administer the regional policies of Sport England and deliver local initiatives (see Fig 10.02):

- North East (A)
- North West (C)
- East Midlands (E)
- London (G)

- Yorkshire (B)
- West Midlands (D)
- East (F)
- South East (H)
- South West (I).

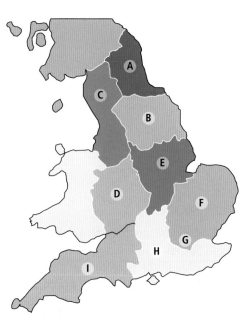

Fig 10.02 Sport England regions

There are also regional offices for the other three countries of the United Kingdom, as outlined below.

Sport Scotland

Sport Scotland (www.sportscotland.org.uk) is funded through and distributes Lottery funding to develop community links among schools and communities, and in particular to encourage participation in deprived areas and support the efforts of top athletes.

Sport Scotland runs three national sports centres:

- Inverclyde – a residential centre for training
- Cumbrae – a water sports centre
- Glenmore Lodge – an outdoor centre.

Sport Scotland developed a strategy called Sport 21 2003–2007 to shape Scotland's sporting future, with the aim of achieving:

- a country where sport is more widely available to all
- a country where sporting talent is recognised and nurtured
- a country achieving and sustaining world-class performances in sport.

The overall target is to get 60 per cent of adult Scots to participate in sport at least once a week.

The Sports Council for Wales

The Sports Council for Wales (www.sports-council-wales.co.uk) has been in action since 1972 and has its head office at the Welsh Institute of Sport in Cardiff. Its aim is to:

- provide opportunities for everyone to participate and enjoy the benefits of sport, whatever their background or ability
- develop those individuals with potential into competitors who generate national pride through Welsh sporting achievements
- gain international recognition for Wales as a nation with a sporting culture.

In 1999 it published its strategic plan: 'A Strategy for Welsh Sport – Young People First'. The aims of this strategy are:

- the creation of sporting opportunities for children, in schools and in the community
- recruitment and development of coaches, administrators and officials, raising standards of performance and achieving excellence
- the effective distribution of SPORTLOT funds for capital and revenue purposes, addressing issues of inclusion through sport
- increasing participation by women and girls.

Sports Council for Northern Ireland

The aims of the Sports Council for Northern Ireland (www.sportni.net) are to work with partners to:

- increase and sustain committed participation, especially among young people
- raise the standards of sporting excellence and promote the good reputation and efficient administration of sport
- develop the competencies of its staff, who are dedicated to optimising the use of its resources.

National governing bodies

To be recognised as a sport there must be a governing body to control the activities of the participants involved in that sport. Governing bodies are found at a local, national and international level.

If we look at football, for example, we find the following structure.

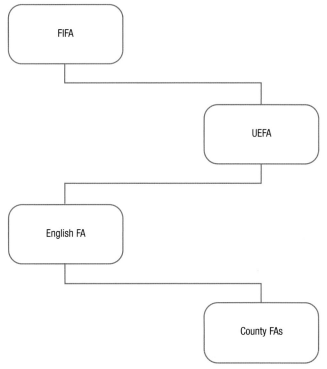

Fig 10.03 Football's governing bodies

Football has an international governing body (FIFA), a European governing body (UEFA), a national governing body (English FA) and county governing bodies (e.g. Herts FA), each of which has different responsibilities. You will find similar structures in all sports.

The roles of governing bodies are as follows:

● setting rules for the sport
● implementing the rules of the sport
● changing the rules of the sport
● finding ways of improving the sport through technology
● providing officials for matches
● organising competitions
● providing codes of conduct for players
● disciplining players who break the rules or codes of conduct
● fining or banning offending players
● providing a system of drug testing
● finding sponsorship for events and competitions
● selling the rights to show the sport on television
● raising money for the sport
● managing and developing the sport.

LEARNER ACTIVITY National governing bodies

In groups of two go to the library and find out three recent occasions when a national governing body has intervened in a sport in some way.

The Sports industry in the UK

The scale of the sports industry

In order to look at the economic importance of sport we need to examine the following factors:

● participation rates in sport
● consumer spending on sport
● employment in sport.

Participation in sport

Sport England has been looking at participation rates by area in a survey called 'The Active People Survey', published in December 2006. The results can be found on the Sport England website.

Research was done by Mori using a questionnaire. This revealed the percentage of adults participating in at least 30 minutes' moderate-intensity sport and recreation (including walking) on three or more days a week. A sample of the results is reproduced here as Table 10.01.

LEARNER ACTIVITY Active People Survey

● Go to the Sport England website and access the findings of the Active People research.
● Find out the number of people participating in sport in your region.
● Choose eight other areas from around the country and find out the participation rates in these areas.
● Compare them to the results for your area and write down three reasons why the results from your area are higher or lower than those from the other areas.

Table 10.01 Regional participation in sport

Area	% of adults participating in sport
Birmingham	20.1
Boston	11.2
City of London	19.5
Leeds	15.8
Liverpool	16
Manchester	22.2
Norwich	23.9
North Devon	21.5
Oxford	20.5
Sheffield	18.2
Southampton	18.2
Swindon	14.7
Watford	20.0

(Sports Council, 2006)

Consumer spending on sport

A key indicator of the value of an activity is its contribution to the economy. Table 10.02 shows the expenditure on sports participation and sports goods across three years.

These figures show the considerable worth of sport to the economy without looking at the value of sporting success. The figures show an increase in expenditure on sport of 31 per cent over a six-year period with a huge leap in the amount of money created by cable and satellite TV, plus the effect of the National Lottery on spending on football pools.

Employment in sport

In 2001 there were almost half a million people employed in the sports industry in Britain in the sectors listed in Tables 10.03, 10.04 and 10.05.

Table 10.02 Consumer expenditure on sport-related goods and services (£ million)

Category	1995	1998	2001
Participation sport (subs and fees)	2,060.29	2,541.93	3,663.39
Clothing sales	1,429.61	1,821.91	1,996.00
Footwear sales	898.00	1,049.00	1,059.00
Sports goods	707.45	852.95	1,287.16
TV, rental, cable and satellite subscriptions	692.37	1,212.13	1,656.21
Gambling (horse racing)	1,553.16	1,622.65	1,793.16
Gambling (pools)	469.30	166.70	74.80
Other consumer spending	2,470.32	3,150.66	3,447.26
Total	**10,278.50**	**12,417.93**	**14,979.98**

(Sports Council, 2004)

Table 10.03 Private-sector employment in sport

	Employment in '000s
Spectator clubs	41.94
Participation clubs	15.33
Retailers	80.84
Manufacturing	11.84
TV and radio	12.65
Subtotal	*162.59*
Voluntary sport	60.47
Commercial non-sport	157.92
Subtotal	*218.39*

(Sports Council, 2004)

Table 10.04 Public sector (central government)

	Employment in '000s
Transport	0.03
Administration	1.62
Subtotal	*1.65*

(Sports Council, 2004)

Table 10.05 Public sector (local government)

	Employment in '000s
Sports facilities	35.76
Education	25.16
Transport/police	6.13
Subtotal	*67.04*
Total for all sectors	***449.658***

(Sports Council, 2004)

Structure of the sports industry

When we look at provision for sport we look at three things:

- who provides the money to fund the sports
- why they provide this money
- what sports they provide for.

Sports provision is provided by three very different sectors (see Fig 10.04).
  What do these mean?

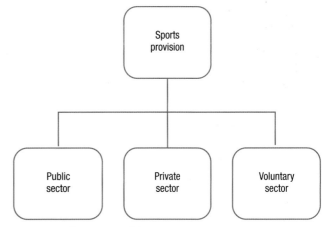

Fig 10.04 Sports provision

- Public sector: this is money spent by the government on sport. Public means the money is raised by charging the general public tax and then this money is invested in sport.
- Private sector: this means that money is invested by private individuals to provide sports facilities. These individuals invest their own money with the hope of making a profit for themselves.
- Voluntary sector: this means that sport is run and funded by volunteers to provide sporting opportunities for other people with the same interests. They do not want to make profit – they just want to play sport.

Public sector

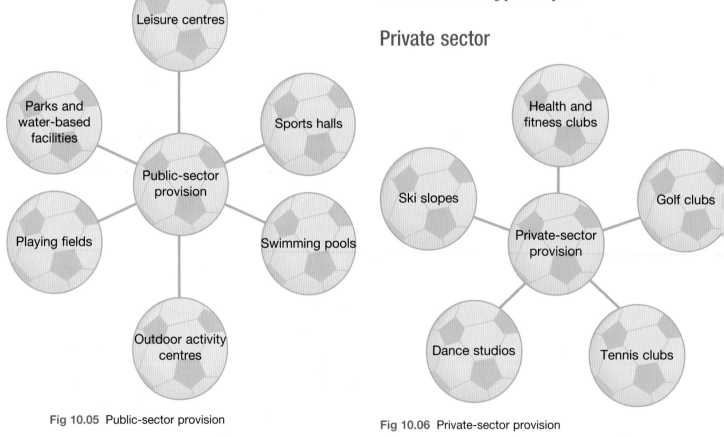

Fig 10.05 Public-sector provision

- They are usually named after the town, city or area.
- They are priced to be available to everyone rather than to exclude people.
- They offer facilities for team and individual sports.
- Their facilities offer sports opportunities rather than comfort or luxury.
- The people who work there are employed by the local authority.
- They often receive grants from Sport England or the national governing bodies of sport.

Public-sector facilities are provided by local authorities with the aim of offering people a positive activity to do in their leisure time. These facilities often lose money as they do not charge enough money for entrance or membership to make a profit. This is not important because their priority is to improve the quality of people's lives and offer them the benefits of taking part in sport.

Private sector

Fig 10.06 Private-sector provision

You can identify public-sector facilities by the following.

- They are funded by money from the local authority.
- They are large in size.

You can recognise private-sector facilities by the following.

- They are usually named after a person or given an attractive name.
- They mainly provide for individual sports.

- They offer exclusive memberships which are paid monthly or yearly.
- They are often expensive to join.
- They tend to be plush and luxurious.
- They are aimed at certain groups of people rather than the general public.

There are several large chains of health and fitness clubs in Britain which meet all these criteria. David Lloyd Leisure, Cannons, Next Generation, Esporta and Virgin Active clubs would all fit. These companies are interested in providing for sports and physical recreation with the aim of making money for the individuals or shareholders who have invested their money. As a result their membership fees are high to attract the more wealthy people. Their facilities are also more luxurious to attract these types of people and aim to keep them as members.

Voluntary sector

The voluntary sector includes sports clubs, which offer opportunities to play competitive sport.

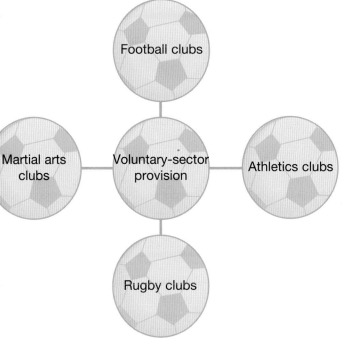

Fig 10.07 Voluntary-sector provision

You can identify voluntary-sector clubs by the following.

- They provide for competitive sports.
- They offer opportunities for only one sport.

- They are funded by members on a yearly membership basis and charge fees for individual matches as well.
- They rarely own their own facilities and hire facilities from the public sector.
- They may receive sponsorship from local businesses.
- They are managed by a committee voted for by the members.
- They are usually named after their town or city.
- They are not trying to make a profit.
- They have to be affiliated through the national governing body.

In summary, voluntary-sector clubs are funded and run by members for the benefit of all the members, with the aim of providing opportunities to be involved in sport on a competitive level. If you look at the sports you are involved in outside school or college it is very likely that it will be through the voluntary sector.

LEARNER ACTIVITY Local sports facilities

In groups of four or five complete a brainstorming session of all the sports facilities you have in your local area. Then, using the criteria set out above, divide them into public, private or voluntary sector.

Provision levels of sport

To have an organised and meaningful approach to sports provision we can see provision as addressing two areas:

- **sports development** – giving people the opportunity to learn the basics of sports and sports skills, and the opportunity to teach sports.
- **sports equity** – to examine the inequalities in sport and develop strategies to give people equal opportunity to participate in sport regardless of race, age, gender or ability.

Sport England has developed a sports development continuum, as follows.

- **Foundation**: learning and understanding basic movement skills and developing a positive attitude to physical activity.

- **Participation**: taking part in sport for a range of reasons – health, fitness and social.
- **Performance**: improving standards of performance through coaching, competition and training.
- **Excellence**: reaching national standards of performance.

How contemporary issues affect sport

The world of sport is an ever changing one. Every week there are new sets of results and every week it seems there are new issues that emerge. Take a look at the back (and front!) pages of any newspaper and you will find the latest scandal being dissected before an ever information-hungry public. When an athlete takes a banned substance or a football manager takes a bung, sport suffers and the authorities have to act if they want to maintain their credibility. To understand how contemporary issues affect sport we need to look at each one in turn and discuss the negative and positive aspects that arise.

Media

'The media' refers to the means of communication that reach large numbers of people. The happenings in sport are reported through a variety of media:

- newspapers
- television
- radio
- internet
- films
- books
- magazines
- teletext services.
- mobile phones.

Local and national press

Each area in the UK has its own local newspaper. The local newspaper has a small circulation compared with the national newspaper and its aim is to provide local information only. It will therefore print only local sports stories. It will give reports on the best local teams and will cover national news only if there is a local angle, such as 'Local girl wins national judo championships'. In the same way, national

newspapers report world events primarily if there is a UK angle, such as 'England win 2006 Women's World Team Squash Championship'.

It is the editors who make decisions about what news we receive. They decide which news is most important and which news is most relevant. An editor will always have one eye on whether people will be interested in a particular story and if they can relate to it.

Television

Television is the most important aspect of the media in sport. Since the first televised World Cup in football in 1970 to the Sky and Setanta deal with the Premiership to pay £1.7 billion for three years from 2007/8 it has often been about money. TV companies are prepared to pay high prices for the rights to show the best sporting events. The largest events are the FIFA World Cup, the Olympics and the Superbowl. Some 800 million people worldwide watch the Superbowl each year. And the Superbowl viewing figures occupy nine out of the ten most watched sporting events on television in the USA. Only the women's figure skating from the 1994 Winter Olympics can make it into the list, at number 10! With these types of viewing figures the TV networks are able to hike up their advertising rates and, at their peak in 2000, 30 seconds of airtime during the Superbowl could cost US$2.5 million!

In the UK, 20.4 million viewers tuned in to watch Italy win the 2006 World Cup final. During the match this figure dropped to as low as 13.6 million. But for the penalty shootout it rose back to the peak with 17 million watching BBC and 3.4 million watching ITV. In contrast, the Wimbledon men's tennis final which was shown earlier had an audience of 7.1 million on BBC watching Roger Federer take the title. The average Premiership football game shown on Sky TV in 2006 attracted audiences of 1.25 million. Pay-per-view games in 2006 attracted audiences of 215,000. The average crowd at a Premiership football match in 2006 was 34,000. In 2001 the Office for National Statistics reported that UK children aged between six and sixteen watch three hours of TV per day compared with two hours elsewhere in Europe.

Table 10.06 shows the viewing figures for one week in September 2006. It shows how terrestrial channels (BBC1 and 2, ITV, Channel 4 and five) still dominate overall viewing figures, but that channels like Sky Sports 1 have a relatively large share of viewers considering they show only sports programmes.

What is the effect of the media on sport? Table 10.07 lists some of the positive and negative effects.

Sport is presented on television in a 'mediated' form, meaning that television professionals have made decisions about how the sport is presented. It is usually done to make the sports event more attractive to the floating viewer. They know that the devoted sports fans will watch anyway, so they are seeking to attract the attention of viewers who are less committed to the sport, but may enjoy the sense of occasion. As a result, television changes sport to maximise its attractiveness and its number of viewers.

Table 10.06 Hours of viewing, share of audience and reach – multi-channel homes: including timeshift (week ending 24 September 2006)

Channel	Average daily reach		Weekly reach		Average weekly viewing	Share
	'000s	%	'000s	%	Hrs:mins per person	%
ALL/ANY TV	32,101	72.9	40,913	92.9	23:37	100.0
BBC1 (incl. Breakfast News)	20,232	46.0	35,294	80.2	4:33	19.2
BBC2	10,338	23.5	26,967	61.2	1:31	6.4
TOTAL BBC1/BBC2	22,567	51.3	36,815	83.6	6:04	25.7
ITV (incl. GMTV)	17,131	38.9	32,695	74.3	4:21	18.4
CHANNEL 4/S4C	11,037	25.1	28,137	63.9	1:39	7.0
five	7,502	17.0	22,632	51.4	1:05	4.6
TOTAL/ANY COMM. TERR. TV	22,534	51.2	37,056	84.2	7:05	30.0
Total terrestrial	27,764	63.1	39,195	89.0	13:09	55.7
Sky One	2,757	6.3	9,935	22.6	0:22	1.6
Sky Two	1,239	2.8	5,721	13.0	0:08	0.6
Sky Three	1,391	3.2	6,367	14.5	0:07	0.5
Sky News	1,367	3.1	4,591	10.4	0:07	0.5
Sky Sports 1	2,033	4.6	6,109	13.9	0:34	2.4
Sky Sports 2	1,752	4.0	5,795	13.2	0:18	1.3
Sky Sports 3	598	1.4	2,375	5.4	0:05	0.3
Sky Sports News	1,832	4.2	5,902	13.4	0:09	0.6
Sky Premiership Plus	82	0.2	523	1.2	0:01	0.1
Sky Sports Extra	264	0.6	1,329	3.0	0:02	0.1
All Sky Sports	4,284	9.7	10,625	24.1	1:08	4.0

(Broadcasters' Audience Research Board Ltd, 2006)

Table 10.07 Positive and negative effects of the media on sport

Positive	Negative
● More participation may result from the desire to emulate the superstars	● Less participation as people become couch potatoes, watching too much TV
● Increased amount of money in the sport which can go to help grassroots	● The majority of the money goes to players/clubs – very little goes to grassroots
● Allows the players to be full-time professionals and so raises standards	● Only certain sports get enough TV money to allow them to be professional
● Clubs can provide better facilities/ equipment/players	● The popular/successful clubs get richer and the poor clubs remain poor
● Positive role models can promote good behaviour	● Negative role models can promote poor behaviour
● Can bring different ethnic groups together – e.g. the multi-ethnic French World Cup squads in 1998 and 2006	● Increased media hype may lead to nationalism and 'anti' feelings towards others

The effects of increasing television coverage of sport are as follows.

● **Money**: increased sums of money come into the sport from television companies who pay for the rights to broadcast the sports. Also, sponsors become more willing to spend more money on sponsoring sport as they know it will receive national attention. Hence, sports' finances receive a boost on two fronts, and this enables them to spend more money on players, players' wages and stadiums. The development of football in the 1990s was based on increased income from television companies and firms offering sponsorship. This extra income enabled the owners of the clubs to spend money on players from overseas, who were superstars of the sport. In turn this makes the sport more attractive to the viewers, who are willing to pay more to watch sport on television and at the grounds. For world events the risks can be great as evidenced by some Olympics which did not turn a profit, but the earnings can also be huge. The 2006 World Cup made profits of £741 million, with the cost of staging the event outstripped by sales of tickets, merchandising, sponsorship and media rights.

● **Changes in the rules of the game**: in order to make sports more attractive, the rules can be amended to make the action faster or to penalise negative play. In Rugby Union the points for a try rose from four to five, bonus points are given to teams scoring four or more tries and losing by fewer than five points. One-day cricket has punished bowlers delivering no balls by offering batsmen a free hit on the next delivery from which they cannot be out. In hockey the offside rule was changed and in netball players no longer have to wait for the umpire's whistle to restart play.

● **Changes in the presentation of the sport**: as an example, cricket authorities addressed the problem of low attendances by introducing day–night cricket matches, which start at around 4.00 p.m. and run until around 10.30 p.m. This caters for people who are at work during the day, but are keen to watch a match in the evening. The matches themselves have been organised as part of family entertainment, where the players are introduced by music, and there is additional entertainment such as firework displays, bouncy castles and barbecues on offer. To make the game look more spectacular, the players wear coloured clothing and use a white ball with black stumps. More recently the introduction of 20/20 games has proved most popular, with cricket gaining some of its largest attendances for this fast-paced game, although its detractors argue that it bears no resemblance to the normal game of cricket and shouldn't be taken seriously.

● **Changes in starting times**: the start times of matches are regularly changed to suit the needs of the television audience. Football games may kick off any time between 11.00 a.m. and 10.00 p.m., depending on where the game is played and when the audience is available. This is great for the television viewers, but comes at a high cost to the spectators at the game, who become very inconvenienced. Televised games on a Sunday are shown at 4.00 p.m. and not 3.00 p.m. after an enforced change one week attracted a much larger audience. The Monday-night games are an attempt to generate the sort of audience loyalty seen in the USA where Monday-night football is watched religiously.

- **Sponsorship**: in the world of corporate sponsorship, how a brand performs off the pitch is just as important as how the players perform on the pitch. FIFA uses Sponsorship Intelligence, a company that researches the impact of events such as the 2006 World Cup. At this event it claims that Coca-Cola 'won the World Cup' in terms of successful promotion. Its research showed that out of the 15 World Cup sponsors the best remembered was Coca-Cola, something it says might be attributed to that company's support of the World Cup since Mexico 1970.

Other forms of media coverage

Radio is an increasingly popular medium and due to the wealth of radio stations on air, it is possible to devote stations entirely to sports coverage. BBC Radio Five Live is a current affairs and sports station that offers a viable alternative to television through its in-depth coverage.

Books are increasingly becoming an important source of media coverage, and they have the advantage of interpreting events we may not have fully understood at the time. Recently, Wayne Rooney signed a £5 million deal plus royalties to write five books over the next 12 years: a good example of how a player can make money off the field.

Visit any large newsagents and you will see the wide array of **sports magazines** available. The internet has also become a rich source of information for people following sports, and there is a vast number of websites dedicated to sport in general and to individual sports. The problem has been that much information has appeared in an unedited, unmediated format and often reflects the views of a minority.

Deviance

Deviance is a form of behaviour which is considered to violate society's norms and therefore to be unacceptable. In sport this manifests itself in a number of ways such as drugs, gamesmanship and violence. A sportsperson can exhibit positive and negative deviance.

Positive deviance equals over-commitment. For example, over-training or playing on through injury and pain and much of the 'no pain no gain' philosophy supports this behaviour. In many sports we applaud the images of athletes covered in blood but carrying on for their country.

Negative deviance equals either a desperate or calculated breaking of the rules or norms. This is the more recognisable side of deviance – e.g. using banned substances to win a race.

Drugs in sport

The most notorious drug cheat was probably Canadian sprinter Ben Johnson, who tested positive at the 1988 Seoul Olympics for an anabolic steroid called stanozolol. Johnson had been beaten by his nearest rival, Carl Lewis, about a month before in an emphatic manner. When the Olympic 100 m final came around, Johnson led from gun to finish and won easily in a new world record time of 9.79 seconds. Two days later he tested positive for drugs and was stripped of his medal and world record. It was common knowledge that Johnson had been using illicit drugs for years, but he maintains that the drug he was using was not stanozolol and that he had been set up.

But the problem hasn't gone away. Statistically speaking, Athens 2004 was twice as bad as the previous worst Olympic Games for doping offences. By the time the flame was extinguished in the Olympic Stadium, 24 doping violations had been uncovered. That is double the previous highest number of 12 at Los Angeles in 1984.

More recently we have seen sprinter Justin Gatlin, 100 m world record holder, testing positive for elevated levels of testosterone. And in the UK Dwain Chambers, the 25-year old European 100 m champion and record holder, was the first athlete in the world to be punished for taking tetrahydrogestrinone (THG), a previously undetectable steroid. Chambers' positive test caused his 4 × 100 m team to be stripped of their European gold in 2002 and silver in the World Championships in 2003. When he had served his ban and was reinstated in the 4 × 100 m team for the European Championships in 2006 and the team won gold again, Darren Campbell, who had lost both

LEARNER ACTIVITY Classification of drugs

To understand more about drugs, research the effects of drugs by completing the following table.

Name of drug	What they do	Sports associated	Side effects
Anabolic steroids			
Stimulants			
Narcotic analgesics			
Peptide hormones			
Blood doping			
Beta blockers			
Diuretics			

previous medals because of Dwain Chambers, refused to take part in the lap of honour. Under British Olympic Association rules Dwain Chambers can never compete at the Olympics for Team GB as it has imposed its own life ban for anyone who fails a drug test.

The World Anti-Doping Agency

The World Anti-Doping Agency (WADA) (www.wada-ama.org) has the following mission statement:

WADA is the international independent organization created in 1999 to promote, coordinate, and monitor the fight against doping in sport in all its forms. Composed and funded equally by the sports movement and governments of the world, WADA coordinated the development and implementation of the World Anti-Doping Code (Code), the document harmonizing anti-doping policies in all sports and all countries.

LEARNER ACTIVITY Drug use in sport

Think about the following statements and then decide whether you agree or disagree with each one.

	Agree	Disagree
1 Drug use in sport gives users an unfair advantage.	☐	☐
2 Sports are natural and drug use is unnatural.	☐	☐
3 Morally the issue of drug use in sport is clear-cut – the use of drugs is always wrong.	☐	☐
4 Sport is a healthy activity and should not be polluted by products that will potentially damage health.	☐	☐
5 There are no good reasons why athletes should use drugs.	☐	☐
6 Drugs are taken by choice and users should be severely punished.	☐	☐
7 If athletes relied more on the advice of doctors there would be less drug taking in sport.	☐	☐
8 Sporting bodies like the IOC, Sports Council and national governing bodies are doing everything they can to eliminate drug use in sport.	☐	☐

Gamesmanship

We often talk about sports performers playing fairly, but find it hard to define what playing fairly is. Is a player who appeals for every decision playing fairly or trying to influence the referee? Some definitions may help:

> **definition**
>
> Gamesmanship: **not playing within the unwritten rules of the game and destroying the ethics, spirit, goodwill, fairness, etc.**
> Letter of the game: **written rules of play.**
> Spirit of the game: **playing fairly and abiding by unwritten rules, and expressing the correct attitudes and ethics of the game.**
> Sportsmanship: **playing within both the written and unwritten rules.**

LEARNER ACTIVITY

Look at the examples below and think about how each behaviour fits into the definitions above:

- kicking the ball off the pitch when the opposition has an injury
- not 'walking' in cricket
- shaking hands with the opposition at the end of the game
- deliberately punching an opponent in a scrum
- pretending something has distracted you when your opponent is about to serve
- clapping someone who makes a century in cricket
- arguing with the referee after a decision has been made
- faking an injury to get another player booked
- taking a dive
- lending your opponents a practice ball to warm up with
- taking a banned substance.

As sport has become increasingly pressured with a 'win at all costs' approach taking over from the old ideals of athleticism (playing fairly as an amateur), so we have seen a rise in gamesmanship. Much sport is professional and the rewards for winning are great. There is pressure from fans, managers and, in world competitions, the nation, all desperate for a win. It is becoming less and less likely to find role models who will not compromise their ethical stance.

Sports initiatives

Sport has often been used as a power for good. It has been argued that sport is good for society and has a positive influence. For example, those who believe it is functional claim it can increase participation, reduce crime and anti-social behaviour, and improve the nation's health. The government certainly subscribes to this view. It spends millions each year to provide sport and leisure opportunities for all and is particularly interested in deprived areas or those with high incidences of crime. There are a number of anti-crime initiatives the government has introduced which use sport as a vehicle for providing an alternative to committing crime. Sport England (which receives money from government funds) has a representative within the Home Office who has been working closely with the Community Cohesion Unit to show how sport can unite communities, especially in deprived areas.

Social exclusion

To understand social exclusion it helps to look at occupations and income. Type of employment and income can be considered together as one is dependent on the other. This is addressed further in the next section.

Health

Sport England also believes it can make an important contribution to improving health and reducing the estimated £8.2 billion cost of inactivity to the NHS. The 'Everyday Sport' physical activity campaign encourages even the most inactive people to incorporate a little more activity into their daily lives, taking small steps that can make a big difference – from taking the stairs instead of the lift or getting off the bus a stop early, to joining a sports club. Other initiatives include 'Sporting Champions', a scheme that takes sports stars into schools and communities to inspire young people about sport.

Racism

If we look at Britain as a whole, we can see that some sports are more popular in some areas and less popular in others. One of the major factors influencing the sports we play is where we are brought up. For example, rugby league is more prevalent in the north of England and rugby union in the south of England and Wales. Scotland has its own sports, such as skiing, curling and its Highland Games, and Ireland has sports such as hurling and Gaelic football.

Britain has developed into a multi-racial society. Many members of the population are from African-Caribbean or various Asian and European backgrounds. Many were initially drawn to Britain by the need for jobs during the 1950s.

Some ethnic groups choose to retain separate cultural identities within British society, but black sportspeople participate successfully in most sports in Britain. However, racism does still occur in British sport, although it is not usually the overt racism that black footballers suffered in the 1980s and early 1990s.

definition

Race: the physical characteristics of a person.
Ethnicity: the cultural adherence of a person or group, characterised by their customs and habits (religious beliefs, diet, clothing, leisure activities and lifestyle).

Racism describes the oppression of a person or group by another person or group on the grounds of physical differences. Racism in British sport occurs in two ways, through racial stereotyping and stacking.

- **Stereotyping:** historically, racial discrimination has excluded black people from achieving in the workplace, so many black people entered sport as an arena where they could improve their life chances. Thus, many young black people spent more time improving their sporting ability at the cost of their academic abilities. This produced two stereotypes:
  - black people are naturally good at sport
  - black people are not intelligent.
- **Stacking:** black people tend to be guided into certain sports and certain positions within teams. They tend to predominate in sports such as track and field athletics, football, basketball and boxing. These sports tend to be inexpensive, requiring little specialist equipment, and can be practised relatively cheaply. Within these sports black people tend to dominate in certain positions or events, usually those requiring physical rather than intellectual or decision-making qualities, such as wingers in rugby rather than positions of centrality.

This stacking comes from a stereotype that black people have a natural, genetic ability to be quick and powerful, but lack high intellectual abilities. This stereotype has in the past been perpetuated by teachers and coaches of sports who, when choosing teams, place black people in a position or an event because they believe all black people are fast and powerful.

More recently black and Asian players have broken down these stereotypes. In football in the 1980s and 1990s the majority of black players were forwards. That stereotype no longer exists with players like Rio Ferdinand and Ashley Cole dominating in their defensive positions. However, an Asian football star is yet to emerge in the England football team.

LEARNER ACTIVITY Stacking and stereotyping

How does racism through stacking and stereotyping occur in the following sports in Britain?

cricket	athletics
tennis	swimming
golf	rugby

Racism has been tackled on the football terraces under the Football Offences Act 1991, which makes it illegal to take part in racist chanting. An arrest can be made only if there are one or more people chanting and if the chants are causing distress to the person they are aimed at.

The 'Kick it Out' campaign to combat racism in British football has been fairly successful and it is now less of an issue. However, there are constant allegations of racism against black players in British teams when they are involved in international competitions.

This is a very difficult area of sport to debate (see the 'Learner activity' on the opposite page). Many arguments can be made on each side. However, it is important to remember that social influences are as strong as other factors. Peer pressure, role models, historical success and society's norms all exert big pressures on young people looking for a sport and an identity. Concepts such as 'white flight' – the avoidance of seemingly black-dominated sports such as sprinting, may occur. In the same way financial implications may simply be at the root of it all. There is no one answer and looking for a simple 'yes' or 'no' is not the way to answer this question. You might like

LEARNER ACTIVITY Black athletes debate

Debate the following issue in a group: Are black athletes superior in sport?

Here are some points to help you discuss the question. Do some research and see if you can find some more.

For:

- the black population in Britain is approximately 5 per cent and yet 40 per cent of English Premiership players are black
- nearly every world record in athletics track events is held by an athlete of African origin, and in the Athens 2004 Olympics in the 100 m final there was not a single white competitor
- the vast majority of heavyweight boxing champions have been black.

Against:

- there is no scientific research that has been able to prove any genetic superiority
- many sprint events (such as swimming 50 m freestyle) are dominated by white athletes
- many sports, like tennis, are dominated by white players in the UK.

to look at the question in the activity again and think about how difficult it is to generalise about an entire population of people.

Sexism

Before starting a discussion of the relationship between sex and sports participation it is useful to examine the definitions of the terms we will use.

> **definition**
> Sex: the biological and therefore genetic differences between males and females.
> Gender: the learned social and cultural differences between males and females, in terms of their habits, personality and behaviour.

Here is a comparison of men's and women's sport (General Household Survey figures, 1996):

- 71 per cent of men participate in sport, compared with 57 per cent of women
- 42 per cent of men participate in outdoor sports, compared with 24 per cent of women
- twice as many men as women watch sport
- there are very few female professionals as compared with men
- the men's singles prize money at Wimbledon 2006 was £655,000 and the women's £625,000
- there are few women in administrative positions in sport; IOC members for GBR are HRH The Princess Royal, Craig Reedie, Matthew Pinsent and Phil Craven

- the history and growth of sport is documented mainly in terms of the development of male sport
- sport in the media is dominated by male sport.

> **definition**
> Sexism: sexism means different things to different people. The following definition gives us a framework to work within:
> 'Sexism is a practice based on the ideology that men are superior to women. The ideology is expressed through a system of prejudice and discrimination that seeks to control and dominate women. It is systematically embodied in the structures and organisations of that society.' (Hargreaves, 1994)

Here are some possible reasons why women's participation rates are lower than men's.

- Historically, women in partnerships with men have taken on domestic responsibilities and thus any sport is fitted in between responsibilities of childcare, cooking, working, cleaning, washing, and so on. Sport can be time-consuming and costly, especially if childcare is needed.
- Class inequalities accentuate gender inequalities. Middle-class women have much higher participation rates than working-class women, as they typically have more money and access to private transport. The fitness boom has mostly benefited middle-class women.
- The major biological difference between men and women is that women can bear children and this has psychological and social repercussions. Women

are allocated to reproductive, mothering and childcare roles, which limit the time and opportunity they have for sports activities. However, women are waiting longer now before having a family and this has improved their situation. Also, gender equality has meant that childcare and nurturing roles are more commonly shared between partners.

- Every society has a set of beliefs and values that dictate what is acceptable behaviour for women (and men) in all spheres of their lives, and sport is included in these values. Many people consider that some sporting activities can induce masculine traits in women, especially in competitive sports. Strong opinions are held as to what sports are acceptable or unacceptable for girls or women. Even strong peer pressure may prevent women from considering certain sports.

The conventional image of sport is based on chauvinistic values and male identity formation. Sport is the arena for the celebration of masculinity. To be successful at sport you need to show skill, power, muscularity, competitiveness, aggression, assertiveness and courage. To be successful at sport is to be successful as a man, and to be uninterested or not talented is to be less of a man.

However, more recently body image has changed to accept a fitter, stronger female. Successful sportswomen have broken the old stereotypes and fashion has changed to support the image of a toned body as opposed to a flabby unfit one. Of course, there is also the argument that successful female athletes are a threat to the male-dominated world of sport. The reticence of males towards female sport could be simply viewed as a threat to male hegemony.

What other reason could the British Board of Boxing Control (BBBC) have for not sanctioning women's professional boxing for so long? Its arguments at the time were based on possible breast cancer in female boxers and a weakened state during a woman's period – none of the potential brain damage arguments that all boxers face. It was not until 1998 when the Equal Opportunities Commission backed Jane Couch (world champion at the time) that the BBBC was forced to allow her to fight professionally. Then there was the landmark case of Theresa Bennett, an 11 year old who won her county court case to play alongside boys in her local football team, only to have the FA go against the wishes of her club and have the decision overturned at the Court of Appeal.

LEARNER ACTIVITY
Female participation

Discuss the following questions with a partner.

- Which sports are regarded as socially acceptable for females?
- Which sports are not so socially acceptable for women, and may conflict with the behaviour expected of them?

It could be argued that to be successful at sport a woman must show masculine traits that contrast with the so-called feminine traits of agility, balance, flexibility, coordination and gentleness. Successful sportswomen not only have to be exceptional athletes, they also have to retain their femininity.

Commercialisation of sport

Commercialisation refers to the practice of applying business principles to sport. The advantages and disadvantages of commercialisation are outlined in Table 10.08.

Advertising

This is the way a company makes itself known to the public. In sport this can be through using advertising boards around stadiums, placing an advert in the programme, TV commercials using sport stars, etc. Sponsorship, merchandising and endorsement all act as types of advertising.

Sponsorship

An agreement between a company and a team/governing body/stadium/competition. The company agrees to pay a certain amount to have its logo appear on kit or merchandising.

Merchandising

The sale of goods that are linked to the club, player or competition. Usually this is replica kits, flags, scarves, stickers, etc.

Table 10.08 The advantages and disadvantages of commercialisation

Advantages	Disadvantages
Sponsorship can help an event that would otherwise not happen without the money provided	The event becomes reliant on the sponsors and would not happen if they pulled out
Endorsements can help boost a performer's wages and sales of a product	The product may be unethical; the performer may not actually wish to use the product; the company may drop a performer who behaves badly or underperforms
Merchandising can help a club provide better facilities and buy better players	The fans could feel like they are being cheated, especially when shirts constantly change and prices are too high
Advertising can be a way for a performer to make extra income or back a worthy cause such as a charity	It can appear the performer has 'sold out', or may seem like they are not taking their sport seriously enough

Endorsement

When a player promotes the use of a product. Companies pay well for a sports star to say their product is worth buying.

> **LEARNER ACTIVITY**
> ## Commercialisation of sport
> List as many examples of commercialisation of sport as you can think of.

Commercialised sports do not work in all societies. They are predominantly found in developed societies where people have enough free time to be involved in watching sport, disposable income to spend on sport and means of private transport to travel to the venues.

Education and sport in schools

Sport in schools has often been controversial. When working-class schools first started in the 1870s children were drilled in military fashion so that they could be prepared for war. More recent controversy in the 1980s saw teacher strikes over pay lead to a withdrawal of teacher support for after-school sports fixtures when their pay demands were not met. When the National Curriculum started in the early 1990s the suggestion was that all school children should receive two hours of PE per week, but in reality many schools provided less. Alongside this in the 1990s was the scandal of many schools selling off their playing fields for redevelopment.

The government response in the mid-1990s was a report called 'Raising the Game', which promised funding and increased status for schools that could persuade their teachers to provide more after-school activities and raise money for new facilities. The result was Sportsmark status for many schools and new specialist sports colleges with PE teachers taking on new roles such as school sports coordinators. The future for schools PE in the UK will no doubt centre on the 2012 London Olympics. The first response to this has been the proposal for school 'Olympics' to be held across the country each year in the run-up to 2012.

Other issues centre on how we do things in the UK. For example, countries like Australia have talent identification programmes in schools, which test students and assess their suitability for different sports. In this way they have encouraged a number of school children to take up events they would previously not have thought of, such as rowing. In the UK we have been accused of having a laissez-faire approach to identifying talent. Although some might argue that this allows us to value all equally.

Child protection

Following a number of high-profile child abuse cases involving sports coaches, new legislation has been put in place. All people working with children must be police-checked for any convictions involving children, and child protection training is now mandatory on most coaching courses.

> ### LEARNER ACTIVITY
> ### Contemporary issues
>
> - Write a report that provides an in-depth understanding of the effects of four contemporary issues in sport.
> - Try to look at both sides of the argument for each issue.
> - Provide further examples to back up your arguments.
>
> Evaluation of contemporary issues
>
> - Extend your report by evaluating the importance of the arguments you have formulated in your report.
> - Make suggestions on the potential impact of each issue.
> - Draw conclusions on the outcomes of each issue, both actual and perceived.

Cultural influences and barriers that affect participation

While we can see that sport benefits people and fulfils needs in their lives it is important to point out that not all people have an equal access to sporting opportunities.

> ### LEARNER ACTIVITY Barriers to sport participation
>
> Ask yourself the following questions and then in groups discuss your answers and why that is the case.
>
> - Is sport played by men and women in the same numbers?
> - How many black British golfers do you see?
> - Why are there lots of Asian cricketers but very few Asian rugby players?
> - Why do British tennis players tend to be from wealthy families?

These may be issues you take for granted, but in reality these differences exist because of the way our society is organised and how it has developed. A range of factors affect participation in sport, including:

- gender
- ethnic origin
- age
- socio-economic classification.

Gender

Statistics prepared by Sport England clearly show that women have lower participation rates than men (see Table 10.09).

With the odd exception, we can clearly see that men are more active than women. The figures show that as a group 65 per cent of men and 53 per cent of women had participated in at least one sporting activity in the four weeks before the interview. The only discrepancies were in sports such as keep fit and yoga, which traditionally attract more females.

Ethnic origin

Recent statistics have shown a direct relationship between ethnic origin and participation in sport (see Table 10.10).

This and other research shows that:

- white ethnic groups have the highest participation rates
- people of Pakistani origin have the lowest participation rates
- women of Pakistani origin have particularly low rates of participation
- certain ethnic groups are well represented in some sports but very poorly represented in others.

Britain is now regarded as a multiracial society and we must work to meet the needs of all groups. Sports development officers are working hard to offer opportunities to people from all ethnic groups and meet their specific needs – e.g. offering women-only swimming sessions for Muslim women.

Age

Age and also an individual's stage in the life cycle are key factors in influencing the level of participation and also the choice of sports. Younger people tend to

Table 10.09 Percentage of men and women aged 16+ participating in sport in the four weeks before interview

Sport	Men	Women
Walking	34.6	33.7
Swimming	12.3	15.2
Keep fit/yoga	7.1	16.5
Weight training	8.6	3.5
Running	7.1	3.1
Golf	8.3	1.3
Soccer	9.8	0.5
Tennis	2.2	1.6
Badminton	2.2	1.5
Fishing	3.1	0.2

(Sport England, 2002)

choose more physical contact sports such as football and rugby, while older age groups will still be active but in more individual sports with less physical contact (see Table 10.11).

The relationship between participation and age is not always clear-cut, as swimming and keep fit have fairly stable levels of participation across the age groups. Fishing and golf increase slightly with age before falling off again, and soccer and running decline is related to age.

Socio-economic classification

Socio-economic classification is a system of classifying people based on their occupation and thus potential income (see Table 10.12).

Barriers to sports participation

The relationship between gender, ethnicity, age and socio-economic group and sports participation has

Table 10.10 Percentage of adults aged 16+ participating in the four weeks before interview, by ethnic origin

Ethnic group	Participation excluding walking	Participation including walking
White	44.1	59.4
Any minority ethnic group	34.6	45.5
Indian	30.4	46.3
Pakistani/Bangladeshi	21.7	25.9
Black (Caribbean, African, other)	33.2	43.7
Other (Chinese, none of the above)	45.1	56.5

(Sport England, 2002)

Table 10.11 Percentage of adults aged 16+ participating in the four weeks before interview, by age

Sport	16–19	20–24	25–29	30–44	45–59	60–69	70+
Walking	40.7	41.1	42.3	50.5	52.0	46.1	26.8
Swimming	46.2	46.3	47.6	48.2	33.3	19.8	8.1
Keep fit/yoga	29.8	33.2	33.3	27.9	19.8	10.7	6.2
Snooker	42.5	41.3	30.3	19.4	10.7	6.2	3.5
Weight training	18.6	19.8	20.4	12.3	5.6	1.4	0.5
Running	19.7	18.1	18.0	13.9	4.6	1.0	0.2
Golf	14.6	17.4	17.1	14.5	10.9	8.1	4.0
Soccer	33.5	26.1	20.2	10.9	2.1	0.3	0.1
Tennis	24.0	14.7	10.1	8.7	4.8	2.1	0.5
Fishing	8.1	5.2	5.2	6.1	6.3	4.9	1.6
At least one activity	90.1	88.3	88.3	85.1	77.2	64.4	39.4

(Sport England, 2002)

been clearly shown and these could be perceived as barriers to participation. All these under-represented groups have something in common: they all have special requirements. Sport is predominantly marketed at young, white males and this group is well represented in sport. So arrangements have to be made to ensure that sports activities are accessible to all.

There are other barriers which may have to be overcome:

- time
- resources
- fitness levels
- ability
- lifestyle
- medical conditions.

Time

Time is a major reason cited by people as a barrier. There are 24 hours in a day and we have to choose

Table 10.12 Participation in sport, by socio-economic classification

Sport	Large employers/ higher managerial	Higher professional	Lower managerial and professional	Intermediate	Small employers	Lower supervisory and technical	Semi-routine	Routine	Long-term unemployed
Walking	47.1	46.2	41.7	32.7	30.0	29.4	28.5	23.5	19.5
Swimming	24.0	19.9	17.7	13.7	11.9	11.2	8.8	7.8	7.4
Snooker	9.9	9.2	9.6	10.2	9.4	9.1	8.5	7.0	5.5
Keep fit/yoga	20.8	18.3	15.3	14.8	11.1	9.4	7.1	6.3	4.6
Weight training	11.4	8.5	7.3	6.9	5.1	4.0	4.0	2.5	2.0
Running	10.1	8.1	6.6	5.2	3.3	3.4	2.2	2.3	3.2
Golf	9.5	8.4	6.1	4.2	4.8	4.7	3.3	3.8	4.2
Soccer	6.1	5.4	5.5	4.2	4.9	3.6	1.8	1.7	0.0
Tennis	3.1	4.0	2.7	1.8	1.7	0.5	0.8	0.5	1.0
Fishing	1.1	1.1	1.2	1.5	2.5	2.3	1.6	1.5	0.8

(Sport England, 2002)

how to spend them. The management of time involves allocating time for work requirements, family responsibilities, activities for survival, such as eating and washing, sleep and time for relaxation. People need to find activities which fit in with their weekly schedule and put these times into their diary. They can then make arrangements for work and time to fit these activities in.

Resources

Resources include facilities, equipment and clothing. There is an uneven spread of facilities across the UK. Provision is dependent upon location (city or countryside), natural resources (such as water or mountains), the policy of the local authority on spending for sport and the demand from consumers. Equipment and clothing requirements can seriously deter people from sports – for example, the expense of going skiing or playing golf.

Fitness

It is perceived that people who play sport or take exercise are fit and will look down on those who are not. This perception puts people off because they see their current situation as being miles away from where most people are or want to be. It needs to be explained to these people that there are many activities which can be performed at their own pace and as they get fitter they can increase the intensity they work at. Walking would provide adequate exercise for an unfit person and they can then move on to brisk walking, jogging or even running in their own time.

Ability

Not having the required skills and ability is a concern for some people as they do not want to look foolish or show themselves up. It is important that relevant coaching is provided to enable people to acquire the skills needed and develop their ability. This is done through local sports development initiatives and government-sponsored schemes.

Lifestyle

Lifestyle issues, such as stress, smoking, alcohol and drug consumption, place barriers in front of people. All these activities will detract from attempts to do sport because smoking, alcohol and drug use all negatively affect health and make a person feel less likely to want to exercise. Stress and stressful situations mean a person is focusing on other issues and cannot contemplate playing a sport or taking exercise. These lifestyle issues need to be dealt with before a person can consider playing sport regularly and being successful.

Medical conditions

These are a serious consideration in a person playing sport, as if a person exercises inappropriately with a medical condition it can make the condition worse; in the case of heart disease it may lead to their death. Having said that, there is virtually no medical condition which does not benefit or improve through regular exercise. Before a person plays sport or exercises they will be screened by a qualified person and then appropriate interventions need to be put in place to ensure the person takes part in the activity safely.

Strategies and initiatives

Sport England and local authorities are well aware of the problems faced by people from different cultures and the barriers faced by the general population. Since its inception in 1972 the Sports Council (now Sport England) has run a series of campaigns which started with 'Sport for All' and included 'Ever thought of sport?' and '50+ and all to play for'. These campaigns were aimed at specific groups with low participation rates, such as women and older people.

Recent strategies have included:

- Game Plan
- Every Child Matters
- Sporting Equals
- TASS
- Plan for Sport 2001
- Active Sports
- Sportsmark.

Game Plan

Game Plan was published in December 2002 to present the government's vision for sport up to 2020 and the strategy to deliver this vision. It includes strategies for developing excellence in performance and promoting mass participation.

Every Child Matters

Every Child Matters is a national policy which is to be achieved through local initiatives. The aim is for school provision to improve the children's attainment and life chances involving the actions of pupils, parents, teachers and governors. Sport and leisure activities are a part of this scheme by using school facilities to deliver courses.

Sporting Equals

Sporting Equals is a strategy to promote racial equality in sport with the specific aims of developing a society where:

- people from minority ethnic groups can influence and participate equally in sport at all levels, as players, officials, coaches, administrators, volunteers and decision-makers, working with partners to develop awareness and understanding of racial equality issues that impact on sport
- governors and providers of sport recognise and value a fully integrated and inclusive society
- a sporting environment is established where cultural diversity is recognised and celebrated.

Talented Athlete Support Scheme

The Talented Athlete Support Scheme (TASS) aims to provide funds for talented athletes at schools, colleges and universities to gain access to support for the development of their excellence. Money is provided for equipment, travel costs and sport science support, such as nutritional advice, sport psychology and physiological testing, and medical support such as physiotherapy and sports massage.

Plan for Sport 2001

This document was published in 2001 under the title 'A sporting future for all' and was an action plan setting out the vision and how it will be delivered. The action plan covers initiatives to develop sport in

education and the community, and the modernisation of sporting organisations.

Active Sports

Active Sports is delivered on a local county basis and outlines the steps local authorities are taking to develop partnerships to deliver increased opportunities to participate in sport. For example, in Oxfordshire there is a network of partners working together to achieve the following aims:

- to increase participation in sport and active recreation
- to improve the levels of performance in sport
- to widen access to sport and active recreation
- to improve health and well-being.

Sportsmark

Sportsmark was introduced in 2004 as a partnership between the Departments for Education and Skills and for Culture, Media and Sport. It is an accreditation scheme for secondary schools to reward their commitment to developing out-of-hours sport provision as well as a well-designed PE curriculum. There are two levels of award: Sportsmark and Sportsmark Gold, at which a school can achieve a distinction award.

LEARNER ACTIVITY
National strategies
In groups of threes or fours research one of these initiatives further and present your findings to the rest of the group. Each group will have five minutes to present their topic.

Review questions

1 Why is it important to study sport in the context of the societies in which it is played?
2 When did sports start to appear in the forms we recognise today?
3 Why did sports have to change? Give three reasons.
4 Explain what happened to society during the Industrial Revolution.
5 What is meant by the term 'rational recreation'?
6 Discuss the four main themes in the development of sport in the twentieth century.
7 What is the government department responsible for sport?
8 What are the respective roles of Sport England and UK Sport?
9 How can we assess the economic importance of sport?
10 Explain the differing aims of the three sectors of provision for sport in Britain.
11 What is meant by the term 'media'?
12 How do the media affect sports events?
13 How is sport changed through its presentation on television?
14 Explain the positive and negative effects of the increasing amount of sport shown on television.
15 Name four types of drugs athletes may use and explain what effects each has.
16 What are the relationships between gender, ethnicity, age and socio-economic classification and sport?
17 Name three barriers to sports participation and explain why they are barriers.
18 What is TASS and how does it help athletes?
19 Explain the aim of the strategy 'Every Child Matters'.

References

Beashel, P. and Taylor, J. (1996) *Advanced Studies in Physical Education and Sport*, Nelson.

Beashel, P., Sibson, A. and Taylor, J. (2001) *The World of Sport Examined*, Nelson Thornes.

Cashmore, E. (2000) *Making Sense of Sport*, Routledge.

Clarke, J. and Critcher, C. (1985) *The Devil makes Work*, Macmillan.

Davis, R. J., Bull, C. R., Roscoe, J. V., Roscoe, D. A. (2000) *Physical Education and the Study of Sport*, Mosby.

Dunning, E. (1996) *Figurational Sociology and the Sociology of Sport*, University of Leicester, MSc in the Sociology of Sport, Module 5, Unit 8.

Dunning, E. (1996) *Notes on the Early Development of Soccer*, University of Leicester, CRSS.

Dunning, E. (1996) *The Civilizing Process*, University of Leicester, CRSS.

Dunning, E. and Sheard, K. (1979) *Barbarians, Gentlemen and Players*, Martin Robertson.

Haralambos, M. and Holborn, M. (1995) *Sociology: Themes and Perspectives*, Collins Educational.

Hargreaves, J. (1994) *Sporting Females – Critical Issues in the History of Women's Sport*, Routledge.

Haywood, L., Bramham, P., Capernhurst, J., Henry, I., Kew, F. and Spink, J. (1995) *Understanding Leisure*, Stanley Thornes.

Hodgson, D. (1996) *Anyone For Cocktails: Drugs, Sport and Morality*, University of Leicester, CRSS.

Polley, M. (1998) *Moving the Goalposts – A History of Sport and Society Since 1945*, Routledge.

Sport England (2001) *A Review of the Economic Importance of Sport.*

Stafford-Brown, J., Rea, S., Janaway, L. and Manley, C. (2006) *BTEC First Sport*, Hodder Arnold.

Torkildsen, G. (1999) *Leisure and Recreation Management*, E&FN Spon.

Vamplew, W. (1996) *Industrialisation and Popular Sport in the Nineteenth Century*, University of Leicester, CRSS.

Walvin, J. (1994) *The People's Game (the History of Football Revisited)*, Mainstream Publishing.

Wesson, K., Wiggins, N., Thompson, G. and Hartigan, S. (2005) *Sport and PE: A Complete Guide to Advanced Level Study*, Hodder Arnold.

Websites

www.ausport.gov.au – Australian Sports Commission

www.bbc.co.uk/sport – BBC Sport

www.ccpr.org.uk – Central Council of Physical Recreation

www.culture.gov.uk – Department for Culture, Media and Sport

www.olympics.org – Olympic Movement

www.oxonactivesports.co.uk – Oxfordshire Active Sports

www.skysports.com – Sky Sports

www.sportdevelopment.org.uk – Resources for Students

www.sportengland.org – Sport England

www.sportingequals.com – Sporting Equals

www.sports-drugs.com – Sports Drugs

www.tass.gov.uk – Talented Athlete Scholarship Scheme

Goals

By the end of this chapter you should:

- understand the qualities, characteristics and roles of effective sports leaders
- understand the importance of psychological factors in leading sports activities
- be able to plan sports activities
- be able to lead sports activities effectively.

Leadership has been defined as 'the behavioural process of influencing individuals and groups towards set goals'.

In sport and exercise, leadership has many dimensions, including decision-making processes, motivational techniques, giving feedback, establishing interpersonal relationships and directing a group or team effectively. A leader knows where the group is going (its goals and objectives), and provides the direction and resources to help it get there.

The qualities, characteristics and roles of effective sports leaders

Qualities of effective sports leaders
Knowledge of sports and rules/laws

A person leading a sports activity session will need to have a good knowledge of many areas. This process is not an instant one and requires a great deal of practice. First-hand experience and willingness to learn new things will give you a better understanding of delivering sports sessions. A sports leader will need to have a good understanding of the many health and safety factors associated with sports. This should include having a good understanding of emergency

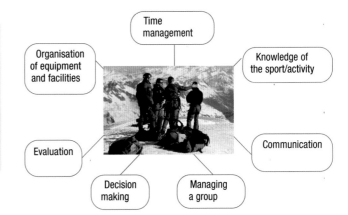

Fig 11.01 Qualities of effective sports leaders

procedures and awareness of the facilities being used, as well as having some basic first-aid knowledge.

Good fitness levels are linked with good sports performance. Therefore a sports leader will need to have a good understanding of the different components of fitness and how they can be improved.

A sports leader must also have an in-depth understanding of the sport itself. When delivering a session it is important to have an understanding of the rules, techniques and tactics required in the sport and how to deliver them. Most sports require the use of different equipment. A leader must first be able to use the equipment properly and safely themselves and be able to show others the correct way to use it.

It is also important to have some knowledge of the group of people you are working with. Knowing which people have specific circumstances such as illness, asthma or prior injuries is important in case of a potential incident. In sports matches it is useful to have some knowledge of your opponents so that you can expose their weaknesses.

Knowledge is gained through experience, but can be improved through undertaking a variety of external awards run by National Governing Bodies.

Communication

This is arguably the most important skill for any sports leader to have. The art of good communication is a difficult skill to learn. Communication is successfully sharing information with other people. There are many ways of communicating within a sporting environment, but for communication to be successful you must know that the message sent has been understood.

A sports leader can communicate to a group in many ways, these include:

- verbally
- non-verbally
- by listening
- by demonstrating
- by assisting.

1 **Verbal communication** – it is important to speak clearly to help the participants understand what it is you are telling them. Try to be concise and avoid any jargon that may confuse them. It is also important to be constructive and positive, as being negative or critical can upset the sports performers and affect motivation.

Fig 11.02 A sports leader

2 **Non-verbal communication** – sometimes it can be difficult to be heard in a sporting environment so we may need to use a range of non-verbal communication methods. These can include the use of body language, gestures, hand signals and facial expressions.
    Remember actions speak louder than words!
3 **Listening** – listening is a vital part of the communication process, however it is often

forgotten. A good sports leader will listen to their group, when appropriate.

4 **Demonstrations** – demonstrations are a method of communication that helps participants learn new skills. It is important when showing people demonstrations that they are kept simple and that they are done correctly, so that the participants do not pick up incorrect techniques.
5 **Assisting** – this is the part where the sports leader helps individuals who cannot perform a sports skill correctly. This method will include using a range of the previously mentioned techniques to help them understand what it is they should be doing.

LEARNER ACTIVITY

This is a role-play exercise that will test your listening skills. Each leader will leave the room, and on their return someone will give them a hurried and frantic message about an artificial emergency. Something like, 'Quick! Find a phone and get the police, a man fell off the pavement and hit his head, another man in a blue jumper grabbed his mobile phone and passed it on to his girlfriend who ran to a red car and drove off. I think he called her Sonia.'

Your tutor will give everyone the same message and ask each of you back in, one by one. For fun you could score points on who provides the best information in an imaginary call to the police. As an alternative the message could be passed on to the next person coming in, and you should note how the original message differs from the message that the last person gives to the police.

Managing a group

A sports leader may have to work with a large number of people in their group. There can often be conflict within a group of people, however a group leader must ensure that the group is able to work together. Effective management of the group will ensure that you get the best out of them.

Decision making

A sports leader will have to make many different types of decisions when working with sports performers. What to do, and why, will need to be considered when making decisions. Knowing how to make the right decision will come through relevant experiences.

LEARNER ACTIVITY

Communication is essential for an effective leader. Complete the following activity.

Memorise the phrase 'The field is fine; get a bat, a ball and a base.' You will be given a mood card, which will have one of the following moods on it:

- enthusiastic
- timid
- threatening
- assertive
- bored
- happy
- sad
- impatient
- with no speech.

Paying attention to where you stand and what you say, see if you can get the group to guess what mood you are giving that phrase in. Comment on the clarity of the instruction and any accompanying body language.

LEARNER ACTIVITY

What type of decisions will a sports leader have to make?

Evaluation

A good sports leader will take time to evaluate their own performance or that of their participants. Evaluating your own sessions will help you improve them in the future. Consider what worked well, what could be improved and how you can make your session more enjoyable in the future, what was the feedback from the participants, etc.

Organisation of sports equipment and facilities

It is important for sports leaders to be organised when arranging their sports sessions. They should consider what facilities are available when planning and organising a session. Once you know what facilities are available you can start to organise the sports equipment that you will need.

There are many equipment factors that a sports leader will need to consider before their session. These include what equipment is available and whether there is enough equipment for the group. It is important that any equipment that is to be used is in

Fig 11.03 A coach setting out equipment

a safe, working condition, and that it is returned in the same condition in which it was lent out.

Time management

Time management is an important skill to develop if you want to be successful. Sports leaders take on many responsibilities, so it is therefore important that they manage their time wisely. Time management is linked to having good organisational skills. It is also important that a sports leader can prioritise items when required.

A sports leader also needs many personal qualities in order to be successful. Such qualities include:

- a good personal appearance
- having ambition
- being positive
- showing empathy
- being motivated
- being confident
- having enthusiasm.

The personal appearance of a sports leader is very important. Sports leaders must remember that they are setting the standard. By dressing in the appropriate attire, you will gain the respect of the group, some of whom may see you as a role model. It is therefore very important to look smart. This can also make you feel more confident when delivering your session. What you wear can also differentiate you from the rest of the group so that you can easily be spotted.

Characteristics of effective sports leaders

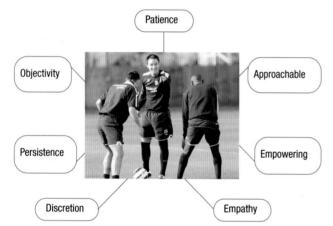

Fig 11.04 Characteristics of effective sports leadership

Patience

It is very important for leaders to be controlled and responsible in every situation, especially when their patience is tried. People can test the patience of leaders in a variety of ways:

- people who are particularly slow to learn
- people with annoying or anti-social habits
- people who disrupt the group.

Often leaders encounter problems that are beyond their control. It is essential that leaders develop a strategy for coping with such problems.

Approachable

It is very important that leaders are accessible to a range of different people; people who are in the group that is being led need to feel that they can approach the leader on a range of potential issues, such as:

- difficulty in learning a new technique
- a personal, health-related problem

- conflict between group members
- simply not understanding a task and requiring extra explanation.

Leaders should also consider how they appear to others, not just the group but others involved in the leadership process, such as parents, teachers, other instructors, and possibly authority figures such as governing bodies of sport or emergency services.

Empowering

Sports leaders must inspire and motivate their groups. In order to motivate others, leaders need to consider what methods they could use to inspire and encourage their participants, e.g. prizes, fun, targets or general praise.

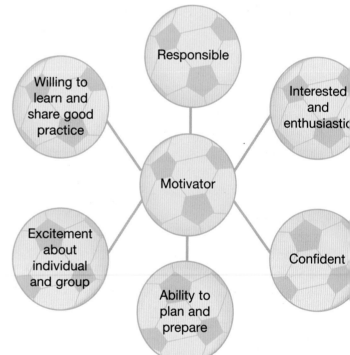

Fig 11.05 Characteristics of effective motivators

Empathy

Empathy is the ability to understand the needs of others. Most groups will have people of mixed ability. Some groups will have examples of different cultures, backgrounds and possibly health status.

Leaders must identify the needs of each member of the group and establish effective ways of ensuring that everybody gains from their activity experience.

Some organisations and good leaders gather information before activities in the form of questionnaires or perhaps even an interview.

Discretion

For the purpose of maintaining the rights of an individual it is absolutely necessary for leaders to develop policies and procedures that are completely confidential. It may be necessary for leaders to gather information about their group, such as personal details, names, addresses and health information.

Many organisations are required by law not to divulge personal information under the Data Protection Act, which makes the inappropriate use of personal information illegal, intended or otherwise.

Fig 11.06 Sea kayakers with a leader

Persistence

In many situations, it is necessary for a leader to be persistent. When participants or groups fail to meet objectives, leaders must re-evaluate the target or intended achievement. In many cases simply trying a different approach or a variety of approaches can be useful. Consider a group of kayakers who are tired and close to finishing their trip, but in order to do so, they must cross a stretch of water that is a busy shipping lane. While all members of the group are capable, some have become tired and are reluctant to cross the stretch of water. In this situation the leader must find a way of persuading these paddlers to complete what they are capable of, while ensuring that the safety of any member of the group is not compromised.

Objectivity

Being objective is simply about taking a range of factors into account. A leader may be presented with a great deal of information about a range of issues, such as:

- the capability of a group
- the weather or environment
- a conflict within the group.

It is very important that the leader carefully considers the facts and takes a 'bigger picture' view of all situations, particularly those concerning safety, when deciding on the most appropriate course of action.

The roles of effective sports leaders

Effective leaders tend to find new ways of improving existing practices or theories. Some adapt the way in which they practise, others develop specific strategies

for differing situations. Other leaders integrate new developments or technologies to improve performance.

Teacher/educator/instructor

The difference between these is hard to discern. Teaching implies a transfer of learning through demonstration, modelling or instruction. Leaders can also teach emotional and social skills. Young performers in particular can be encouraged to increase their social awareness, learn to cope with losing and winning, and develop self-confidence.

Good leaders will be aware that people learn in different ways, and will adapt and use a range of techniques to ensure that learning takes place.

Trainer

In some cultures trainers and leaders are taken to mean the same thing. Since all sport requires some kind of physical exertion, it is important that these physical demands are recognised and that allowance for these demands is incorporated into coaching programmes. A sound knowledge of anatomy, physiology and fitness theory is essential for coaches. In the role of trainer, you might expect to design and implement training programmes for your performers.

Motivator

Motivation can come merely by providing a stable environment in which to learn, creating a positive and safe atmosphere. Performers who constantly find negativity are certain at some point to become despondent and suffer a reduction in self-confidence and improvement.

LEARNER ACTIVITY

In a group of leaders divide yourself into four. A member of each of these groups should volunteer to be leader; each leader devises a short and fairly simple aerobics-style exercise routine or sporting activity, which contains between five and eight basic skills or moves. The whole routine should last no longer than three minutes. The rest of the group should not see the routine until the exercise begins.

Group A – The leader **describes** the whole routine to the rest of the group. The group cannot ask questions. The group then performs the routine. The leader may not interrupt the session while the group is performing. The leader may describe the routine again, before the group makes a second attempt.

Group B – The leader **draws** the whole routine for the rest of the group on a flip chart. No further explanation or demonstration is made. The group cannot ask questions. The group then performs the routine. The leader may not interrupt the session while the group is performing. The leader may amend diagrams or place them around the activity area, before the group makes a second attempt.

Group C – The leader **demonstrates** the whole routine to the rest of the group. The group cannot ask questions until the leader has finished the routine. The group then performs the routine. The leader may not interrupt the session while the group is performing. The leader may demonstrate the routine again, before the group makes a second attempt.

Group D – The leader **performs** the whole routine with the rest of the group. The group cannot ask questions. The group follows the leader, who may choose to perform the routine in stages before the group's second attempt.

A discussion should follow, centred on:

- how the groups performed
- which method, if any, was most effective
- asking each individual which would be the best method for them.

LEARNER ACTIVITY

Scenario

You are assisting an experienced coach in your sport. In order to get the best from you and knowing your sport science background, the coach asks you to put together a typical six-week pre-season training programme for your athletes that is specific to your sport.

Task

Using a recognised training plan format, plan a typical pre-season session plan for a sport of your choice.

Evidence suggests that performers who use praise and positive feedback are likely to get more from their performances.

When providing feedback to performers, for example in the case of skill learning, you could employ the following technique:

KISS

KICK

KISS

When communicating with performers, the emphasis with this technique is to start your feedback with a positive comment; there is nearly always something

that is positive in any performance. Second, a corrective comment can be presented in as positive a manner as possible. Finally, leave the interaction with a positive comment and possibly an action plan.

For example, consider a tennis player struggling to make a particular shot:

KISS – 'Good positioning prior to the shot and you watched the ball well.'

KICK – 'You should consider how you backlift the racket, you could prepare your grip earlier.'

KISS – 'If you practise these changes you will almost certainly improve.'

Role model

In almost every coaching situation, players will look mostly, if not entirely, to the leader as their source of inspiration and knowledge, never more so than when working with children. Children often imitate the behaviour and manner of their coach. For this reason, it is vital that leadership is safe and responsible and that behaviour is considered good practice.

The leader can influence player development in a number of ways.

1 **Social** – sport offers a code of acceptable social behaviour, teamwork, citizenship, cooperation and fair play.
2 **Personal** – players can be encouraged to learn life skills, promote their own self-esteem, manage personal matters like careers or socialising, and develop a value system that includes good manners, politeness and self-discipline.
3 **Psychological** – coaches can create environments that help performers control emotions and develop their own identities, confidence, mental toughness, visualisation and a positive outlook on life.
4 **Health** – in taking care to design coaching or training sessions to include sufficient physical exercise, good health and healthy habits can be established and maintained.

Leadership styles

Leaders will vary in the styles and methods that they use with their groups. This includes the way in which they deliver their outcomes and take responsibility for their groups.

The following leadership styles are commonly used in sports leadership.

- The **autocratic** style, which is sometimes known as the command style, is where the person leading the group makes all the decisions and imposes them on the group, who respond by doing what they are told. The leader concentrates more on the outcome, rather than the group. It is a method that is often used when dealing with large groups or in circumstances where there may be potential hazards.
- The **democratic** method is different to the autocratic style as the leader involves the group and asks for their opinions when making the decisions. This enables the group to take more responsibility for their actions. The leader, however, will have the final say.

- A **liberal** leader will look to use a combination of both autocratic and democratic methods.
- The **laissez-faire** method of leadership allows the group to make all the decisions required. This allows the group much freedom to do what they like. For this method to work, the group needs to be highly motivated as the leader does not provide any direction.

Key learning points

- Communication can be in the following forms:
  - verbal
  - non-verbal
  - listening
  - demonstrating
  - assisting.
- Leaders should have the following qualities:
  - a good personal appearance
  - having ambition
  - being positive
  - showing empathy
  - being motivated
  - being confident
  - having enthusiasm.
- There are several styles of leadership that can be employed in different situations and with different groups. The following leadership styles are commonly used in sports leadership:
  - the autocratic style
  - the democratic style
  - a liberal style
  - the laissez-faire style.

The importance of psychological factors in leading sports activities

Team dynamics

A group is two or more people interacting with one another so that each person influences and is influenced by the others. Groups have a collective identity and a sense of shared purpose involving mutual awareness and potential interaction with structured patterns of communication. For example:

- the crowd at a football match
- a soccer team
- parents watching their children swim.

Successful groups have a strong collective identity, members have an opportunity to socialise and share goals and ambitions, and also ownership of ideas. They also have members who are able to communicate effectively (on the same wavelength), have strong cohesion (see below), who value relationships within the group and have a successful leader who ensures that members' contributions to the group are valued.

Fig 11.07 The England Cricket Team in a huddle

Team cohesion

Players and coaches of teams often attribute team success or failure to how well the team works together as a cohesive unit.

Cohesion can be defined as the total field of forces that act on members to remain in a group. There are two major forces acting on members to remain in a group:

- the first class of forces, attractiveness of a group, refers to the individual's desire for interpersonal interactions with other group members and a desire to be involved in group activities
- the second class of forces, control, refers to the benefits that a member can derive by being associated with a group.

Several other definitions have since been proposed, all having the common idea that cohesion consists of two basic dimensions: task cohesion and social cohesion.

- **Task cohesion** reflects the degree to which members work together to achieve common goals.
- **Social cohesion** reflects the degree to which members in a team like each other and enjoy each other's company, and is often equated to interpersonal attraction. For example, in an exercise class a common goal would be to improve fitness, and it has been shown through research that such classes thrive and continue if the social cohesion of the group increases.

Carron (1982) redefined cohesion to include the task and social components, suggesting that cohesion is 'a dynamic process which is reflected in the tendency for a group to stick together and remain united in the pursuit of its goals and objectives'.

The following factors contribute to cohesiveness, which Carron describes as a dynamic rather than a static characteristic:

- environmental factors
- personal factors
- team factors
- leadership factors.

Improving team cohesion

One of the key roles of a leader is to keep teams together and to ensure that teams or groups work effectively together. Improving and maintaining cohesion is achieved in a variety of ways, some of which are illustrated in Table 11.01.

Group formation

A group of sports performers does not necessarily become a team. Realistically, teams evolve, usually through four stages (Tuckman, 1965).

1 **Forming** is a stage where the team members familiarise themselves with other members of the team. They try to determine if they belong in the group and, if so, in what role. Having found their place, the individual forms and tests interpersonal relationships with other members, including leaders. It is at this stage that a sense of team identity is important.

2 **Storming** is characterised by rebellion against the leader, resistance to control by the group and interpersonal conflict, which can even extend to fights as individual members vie for a spot on the team. Most of the in-fighting is, however, social and interpersonal in nature.

Table 11.01 The leader's role in group cohesion

Explaining individual roles in team success
Developing pride within any sub-units that might exist
Setting challenging team goals
Encouraging team identity
Avoiding the formation of social cliques
Avoiding excessive turnover of players
Conducting periodic team meetings to resolve conflicts
Knowing something personal about each member of the group
Staying in touch with the team's attitudes and feelings

3 **Norming** is the stage where hostility is replaced with solidarity and cooperation. The athletes work together for common goals. This is the stage where group cohesion occurs. This usually improves an individual's sense of satisfaction, and sets the foundations for future success. Team roles stabilise and respect develops for the unique role of team-mates. Instead of competing for status, members strive for economy of effort and task effectiveness.

4 **Performing** is the final stage where team members rally together to channel their energies towards team success. Structural issues and interpersonal relationships are stabilised. Roles are well defined and the players work for each other towards the primary goal – team success. The coach's job is to maintain this status by providing feedback about individuals' special contributions to the team performance, but omitting nobody.

Social loafing

Individual abilities do not make up a group or team performance, and there can be losses in group performance due to faulty processes. Ringelmann (1913) observed that groups of two, three and eight people pulling on a rope did not pull as much as their individual efforts suggested they should.

Later investigations concluded that the faulty processes involved are not due to a decrease in coordination, but rather a loss of motivation.

This **Ringelmann effect** has become known as '**social loafing**' – defined as the reduction of individual effort when working as part of a team or group.

Personality

Personality is how we present our self to the outside world. Each person is unique in this respect and while we compare ourselves to others we are not really like anyone else. However, although we are all different, we can still place people into certain categories which will give us an indication of how they may react in certain situations.

One method of categorising people is to decide if they are an introvert or extrovert. An introvert is a person who is shy, quiet and inward looking. They are not so good in social situations and like to spend time on their own. Many long-distance runners have been found to have such a personality and this makes sense as they spend a lot of time training on their own. An extrovert is someone who is outgoing, likes talking and mixing with people, and is good in social situations; they do not like to spend too much time on their own and are easily bored. People who take part in team sports are more likely to have an extrovert personality as such sports usually provide action and excitement.

Motivation

> **definition**
>
> Motivation: this is the stimulus for a sportsperson to continue training and competing in their chosen sport.

There are two main types of motivation: intrinsic and extrinsic.

Intrinsic motivation

Behaviour which is intrinsically motivated has the following features:

- behaviour is chosen for the pleasure of participating
- behaviour provides its own satisfaction
- there is no reward outside participating in the activity.

Extrinsic motivation

Behaviour which is extrinsically motivated has the following features:

- behaviour where the goal of participation is outside the activity
- behaviour in the activity is a means to an end rather than for the pleasure of being involved – this can be in the form of rewards such as a trophy, money or praise
- success is needed to ensure maximum results.

Stress, arousal and anxiety

Arousal and anxiety are terms related to stress. Arousal is seen as being a positive aspect of stress and shows how motivated we are by a situation. The more aroused we are, the more interested and excited we are by a situation. Anxiety can be seen as a negative aspect of stress, and it may accompany high levels of arousal. It is not pleasant to be anxious, and anxiety is characterised by feelings of nervousness and worry. Again, the stress and anxiety responses are unique to each individual. Arousal levels will have an influence on performance, in some cases as arousal levels increase, performance will also increase (drive theory) – this can be seen mainly in strength-related sports such as weight lifting. However, sports such as snooker or archery that require a lot of concentration and precision can be negatively affected by high levels of arousal.

The inverted U hypothesis suggests that arousal does improve performance, but only up to a point, and once arousal goes beyond this point performance starts to decline.

This theory's main point is that there is an optimum level of arousal before performance starts to diminish, and it is important for leaders to identify this at the right time.

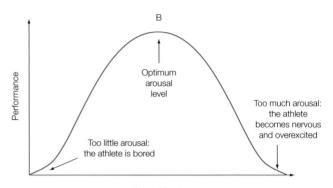

Fig 11.08 The inverted U theory of arousal

Key learning points

- A group is two or more people interacting with one another so that each person influences and is influenced by the others.
- Cohesion is 'a dynamic process which is reflected in the tendency for a group to stick together and remain united in the pursuit of its goals and objectives'.
- Social loafing is defined as the reduction of individual effort when working as part of a team or group.
- Motivation is the stimulus for a sportsperson to continue training and competing in their chosen sport.

Planning sports activities
Risk assessment

A risk assessment is a technique for preventing any potential accidents, injury or ill health by helping people to consider what could go wrong either in the workplace or on the sports field. A risk assessment looks at the possible hazards that may occur, the likelihood of them happening and how the hazards could be prevented.

In sporting activities and outdoor pursuits, risk assessments are important and need to be undertaken by a range of people: the manager of a sports centre, a basketball coach and a mountain walker would all need to ensure that they had undertaken a risk assessment prior to starting their activity.

Fig 11.09 A sports leader undertaking a risk assessment

everyday life. For example, a racing car driver, wishing to overtake, will make their decisions based on factors such as the speed at which they are travelling, the layout of the track and the weather conditions, so that they can overtake safely. By looking at these factors the driver is assessing the hazards, so as to minimise the risk of an accident.

After you have highlighted a potential hazard, the easiest way to assess any potential problems that may arise is to use the following formula:

Likelihood × severity.

Likelihood – is it likely to happen:

1 unlikely
2 quite likely
3 very likely.

Severity – how badly someone could be injured:

1 no injury/minor incident
2 injury requiring medical assistance
3 major injury or fatality.

For example, Table 11.02 attempts to assess the risk posed by broken glass on a park football pitch.

By multiplying the likelihood against the severity you will be able to draw up a chart that looks at the potential problems, and make a decision on whether you want to take the risk or not (see Table 11.03).

In the example in Table 11.02, the likelihood times the severity is $2 \times 2 = 4$.

Control measures

Control measures help reduce the likelihood of an accident happening. This could include having safety goggles for example, where a person is at risk of getting something in their eye. Having eyewash solution close by could also help somebody if they were to get something in their eyes. Cleaners often put up warning signs when they are mopping floors. This is a control measure to alert people that the floor may be wet, and helps reduce the risk of injury by bringing attention to the hazard. Control measures can also be known as precautions.

Risk assessments should be logged, kept and reviewed regularly to see if they are up to date, and to ensure that any of the details have not changed. Britain's Health and Safety Commission (HSC) and the Health and Safety Executive (HSE) are responsible for health and safety regulation in the workplaces of Britain. All major organisations in sport will have a health and safety policy.

Undertaking a risk assessment

We have established that a risk assessment is about identifying hazards and assessing the risks associated with them; however, how do we undertake a risk assessment? This is something we do informally in

Table 11.02 Broken glass on a park football pitch

Likelihood of happening	Severity
2 Quite likely	2 Injury requiring medical assistance

Table 11.03 Is the risk worth taking?

Likelihood × Severity	Is the risk worth taking?	What measures should be considered/taken prior to activity?
1	Yes, with caution	
2	Yes, possibly with caution	
3	Yes, possibly with extreme caution	
4	Possibly, with extreme caution	
5 or above	No	

Safety equipment

Specialist equipment is also sometimes used in sport to help minimise the risk of injury. This can include protective clothing, accessories and equipment.

Cyclists wear helmets in case they fall off, while a batsman would wear protective equipment such as a box and helmet to prevent injury from the ball. Safety ropes are often used in climbing and abseiling to minimise the risk of potential danger.

Fig 11.10 An amateur boxer wearing a head guard

LEARNER ACTIVITY

Choose three of your favourite sports or outdoor activities. Make a list of all the safety equipment you would need in order to reduce the risk of injury.

Reporting procedures

Health and safety is the responsibility of everyone. In the workplace everyone should be responsible, however in sports activities it is often the responsibility of the instructor, coach or leader. If an accident happens or there is a near miss, it needs to be reported and documented, so that it can be looked at, dealt with accordingly and hopefully stopped from happening again.

definition

Hazard: something that has the potential to cause injury or compromise safety.
Risk: the likelihood of something unpleasant happening.
Risk assessment: a list of possible hazards that states the likelihood of them happening, and ways of controlling them.

Reviewing a risk assessment

It is important that, once a risk assessment has been undertaken, it is reviewed and updated regularly. As equipment gets older it is more likely to go wrong and, therefore, become more hazardous. Undertaking an activity at a new venue or in a different environment also needs to be looked at, even if you are undertaking an activity you are familiar with.

LEARNER ACTIVITY

1 Create a blank risk assessment document.
2 Undertake a risk assessment in your sports hall or other area. Include:

● the hazards and risks
● what is the likely risk of injury and who is at risk
● does the hazard need to be controlled, if so how.

Activities

Leadership is more than simply being the person at the front of the room or area telling the others what to do. A variety of activities can be applied to each situation.

Warm-ups

Warm-ups are essential for all activities, and should be fun and relevant to the session and the participants. Here is an example of a warm-up useful with younger children:

Let's have an adventure
The leader sets a warm-up exercise to an exciting story. The participants follow the actions of the leader. For example the children go looking for pirate treasure. As the leader tells the story, the actions might include crawling along a tunnel, swimming across rivers, climbing up cliffs, jumping over volcanoes and running away from the pirate. The actions should become progressively more energetic and involve as many body parts as possible.

Small-sided games

The concept of small-sided games is that the game has more impact on individuals, it helps people learn and recognise rules and fair play, and it encourages the young to adapt their own games.

These games are typically versions of traditional sports such as basketball, netball or football. The games can be modified by restricting the playing area, changing the equipment (e.g. smaller balls in basketball), changing roles and positions (such as in the game of high five in netball) or adapting scoring to reward fair play.

Activities suitable for older people

In an increasingly ageing population there is a growing need for physical activities for older people. Older people still have a desire and a need to take part in physical activity. While some consideration should be made regarding physical capability the principles for leadership are the same as for any group.

Soft tennis
An adapted game of tennis, using plastic rackets, foam balls and a lower net. The game is usually played indoors using a badminton court.

To make the game easier you could serve nearer to the net, allow two bounces before returning the ball or even take the net away.

Fig 11.11 Older people exercising

Activities suitable for disabled people

Every effort should be made to include disabled people into mainstream sports, and to promote a general awareness and positive attitude towards disabled people in sport.

Table cricket
Table cricket is a game designed by the Youth Sport Trust for people with a range of disabilities. A large table, perhaps a table tennis table, is 'fenced' at the edges with the exception of one end where the batter attempts to score runs. Table cricket can be played with teams of mixed ability but is particularly suitable for young people with severe impairments.

Parachute games

Parachute games are ideal for a whole range of different groups, involving a wide variety of games and activities. These games expose people to many social skills such as cooperation, trust, problem solving and communication. Parachute games also help develop perceptual, physical and basic motor skills. Apart from all these benefits, they are also great fun!

Parachute games
Waves
This is the easiest game. All you have to do is hold the parachute at the sides and create a wave effect between each other.

Mushroom
Everyone kneels down and pulls the parachute tight. On a signal, everyone stands up, lifting the

parachute into the air high up over their heads. The parachute makes a large mushroom shape which can be allowed to settle again on the floor.

Jumbo mushroom
Just like the game above, but when the mushroom goes up everybody walks in a step or two, making the mushroom much bigger. If you keep walking towards the middle, the mushroom grows larger and larger and eventually everyone meets in the middle.

Parachute golf
Using a ball small enough to fit through the hole in the middle, everyone tries to make the ball go through the hole. This requires a great deal of teamwork and cooperation and is a lot harder than it sounds.

Parachute pass
All the players stand still and pass a bit of the parachute to their neighbour. The parachute is passed from hand to hand, but the players are not allowed to cross their arms. One hand must remain holding on at all times. The object is to try to pass faster than you receive.

Planning sports activities

Planning a session means that you will need to look at every detail of the activity and consider every possible eventuality. The time spent planning may be time consuming, however it will help ensure that you get the best out of your sessions.

Remember: Proper Planning Prevents Poor Performance!

There are many considerations to take into account when planning your activity session, however the first thing to consider should be what you want to get out of the activity session. It is important to set aims and objectives.

LEARNER ACTIVITY

What factors should be considered when planning a sports activity session?

There is an acronym for setting goals that is believed to motivate people in achieving their aims and objectives. These are known as SMARTER targets:

- **S**pecific – your aim must be specific
- **M**easurable – how can you measure it?
- **A**chievable – it must be possible to achieve the goal
- **R**ealistic – be realistic with your aims, are they achievable?
- **T**ime-constrained – set yourself a time period to do it
- **E**xciting – this will help motivate you to achieve your aims
- **R**ecorded – record your aims, this will help you stick to them.

This method should be used when setting potential aims and objectives for your session.

Following this you will need to consider the participants that the session is being planned for. How many participants will there be? Knowing the age and ability of the group is also important, as you can use this information in planning the types of activities that you wish to include. Leading an activity for a group of beginners is completely different to organising a session for more advanced performers. Also when planning your sports activity session, you might consider what the group has done prior to your session or what they have planned for the following sessions.

Another consideration you may have to take into account is if you have a mixed-sex group.

Lastly, it is important to know of any medical or special needs that any participants have, prior to running a session. A good way for a leader to know the medical backgrounds of their participants is to get them to complete a PAR-Q prior to taking part in exercise. A PAR-Q is a Physical Activity Readiness Questionnaire, which looks at an individual's medical history and highlights any major factors that could stop them from participating (see the example opposite).

Planning the resources

Planning and organising what equipment you will require for your activity should be done prior to the session. Time spent during the activity putting goals up or pumping up balls, and so on, eats into participants' time, therefore planning this in advance will help the session run more smoothly. You should also consider what facilities you will have to use for your session. These may well need to be booked in advance of the session

Physical Activity Readiness Questionnaire (PAR-Q)

1   Has a doctor ever said you have a heart condition and recommended only medically supervised physical activity?

2   Do you have chest pain brought on by physical activity?

3   Have you developed chest pain in the past month?

4   Do you tend to lose consciousness or fall over as a result of dizziness?

5   Do you have a bone or joint problem that could be aggravated by the proposed physical activity?

6   Has a doctor ever recommended medication for your blood pressure or a heart condition?

7   Are you aware through your own experience, or a doctor's advice, of any other physical reason against your exercising without medical supervision?

8   Have you had any operations?

9   Have you suffered any injuries?

10 Do you or have you suffered from back pain?

11 Are you pregnant?

12 Have you recently given birth?

If the person answered YES to one or more questions they should be instructed to talk with their doctor before beginning an exercise programme or taking part in fitness tests.

Here is a copy of a typical session planner:

Session planner

Date: Venue:

Time: Duration:

Group: No. of participants:

Equipment required: Aims of session:

Safety checks required:

TIME	CONTENT
	Warm-up:
	Fitness work:
	Main technical skills work:
	Game play/tactical work:
	Cool-down

Injuries/issues arising

Evaluation of session

and this is the responsibility of the activity leader. When planning your session you will need to ensure that you have enough material and activities to last the time allocated; it is a good idea to have a few more activities planned than you think you will need, then you will never run out of things to do during the session!

To sum up, the key points for planning an activity session are as follows.

- What space/facilities do you need?
- How many people are there participating in the session?
- How much equipment do you need?
- How long will the session last?

Many sports leaders will use a session planner to highlight the information above and the aims and content of the session.

Key learning points

- A risk assessment is a technique for preventing any potential accidents, injury or ill health by helping people to consider what could go wrong either in the workplace or on the sports field.
- Warm-ups are essential for all activities, and should be fun and relevant to the session and the participants.
- Proper Planning Prevents Poor Performance!
- A PAR-Q is a Physical Activity Readiness Questionnaire, which gives details of an individual's medical history and highlights any major factors that could stop them from participating.

Leading sports activities effectively

Leading a sports activity session

When delivering your session you will need to do many things to ensure that your participants understand what it is you are trying to cover.

First, you will need to explain and demonstrate the skills that you require them to undertake. Demonstrations should be kept simple and it is important that they are done correctly. This will help ensure that the group understand what it is that you are trying to teach them. Some participants will need additional support when teaching them new skills, so it is important that you move around your group and look at the different individuals' needs.

It is also important to look to progress the session. This will help motivate the participants and help prevent them from getting bored. Spending too much time on one activity can cause participants to switch off and start to do other things as they get bored. Progression also gives encouragement to performers as they can see their own achievement.

Sometimes you may need to adapt the session as things are not going to plan or changes may become necessary due to factors that are out of your control.

What components should go into your sports activity session?

The first thing to consider is what is the activity session that you wish to carry out?

Sessions could include:

- a fitness session such as a circuit
- a practical coaching session
- a sports event such as a competition or race
- a competitive match.

A typical sports coaching session will progress through the following stages.

1 **Warm-up** – this will typically involve pulse-raising activities, mobility and flexibility work, and some sports-specific skills that help prepare the performer for what they are about to do. It is important to consider what skill-related components of fitness will be used during the activity and how to integrate them into the warm-up. For example, volleyball players require both power and hand–eye coordination in their sport, so both should be included in their warm-up.

2 **Fitness work** – if time allows, participants should undertake some fitness and training methods that are relevant to their sport. Rugby players, for example, might incorporate aerobic conditioning and muscular endurance training into their sessions.

3 **Technical skills practice** – this is where you normally cover the main aims of your session. This will include your drill and routines that you have prepared. Remember to demonstrate the skills and give people the opportunity to practise them, while assisting those individuals who struggle.

4 **Tactical work** – once you have developed the skills, you should look at how and when you use them to gain an advantage over your opponents.

5 **Game play** – it is important to put the skills learnt into a game context.

6 **Cool-down** – this is used to help reduce the build-up of lactic acid and reduce the risk of DOMS (delayed onset of muscle soreness).

LEARNER ACTIVITY

Plan and lead a sports activity session for your class.

It is important that you record evidence of your sports activity session. You should use the feedback to help you evaluate the session. Evaluation is as important as the planning process, and it can help you with future sessions as you will know what has worked well, any problems that arose and what should be changed.

Reviewing a sports activity session

It is important to consider that leadership does not end at the end of a session when everyone has cooled down or even gone home. Leadership is a continuous process and the best leaders reflect on what happened and, more importantly, how to improve. A well-considered evaluation should aid the improvement of subsequent sessions.

LEARNER ACTIVITY

1 Design a feedback form that you could give to your fellow students to comment on how your sports activity session went.

2 Consider what were your strengths and weaknesses, and what actions you would need to undertake to improve your future sessions. You could give the sheet to your peers and teacher in order to get their feedback too. Videoing your session will also allow you to look back at how you performed and will mean that you will not have to rely on memory.

The process is something like this:

- **collect analyse and review** – information about the session from feedback and self-reflection, and from others
- **session effectiveness** – identify the effectiveness of the session in achieving objectives
- **review key aspects** – e.g. the drills or practices
- **identify development needs** – and take steps to action them.

When evaluating a session a leader should consider the following.

1 **Performance against pre-set goals** – effective leaders will be familiar with the goals for the session, both long and short term. There should be an opportunity to decide to what extent, if at all, the session objectives were met and to what extent this contributed to the achievement of all the goals.

2 **Participants' progress** – a review will enable leaders to monitor a performer's progress over a period of time and help plan for future sessions. Typical review questions could be:
   - How well did the performers learn the skills or techniques introduced to them?
   - What performance developments were evident for each participant?
   - Are the performers ready to progress to the next session?

3 **Leadership ability** – this is the part where the leader can review their own performance.
   - What went well?
   - What went less well?
   - How did the performers respond?
   - Were the performers bored or restless?
   - Did the leader behave acceptably?

4 **Future targets** – this is all about planning for future goals and objectives based on achievements and progress made by the participants.

Tools to help the review process

- **Videos** – an excellent way of improving your effectiveness. Videos can be used to judge leadership actions, interaction with your performers, facial expressions and gestures, as well as what you say.
- **Critical analysis and self-reflection** – self-reflection allows you to explore your perceptions, decisions and subsequent actions to work out ways in which performers can improve technical, tactical or physical ability.
- **A mentor** – a mentor leader can help provide you with a role model figure who can help you with practical solutions, work as a sounding board and generally provide you with a range of support.
- **Leadership diaries** – can act as a permanent source of information to record your own thoughts and feelings, and serve as a true account of what happened and when. Diaries or logs can certainly help with self-reflection and form the basis of action plans for improvement.

Using a diary or log

These can come in all shapes and sizes. Most people will have used a diary at some point and this will make them easy to use. Diaries can be useful tools in assisting self-reflection, planning and monitoring progress.

The major benefits of diaries are that they provide a written record over time of progress. It is also easy to record emotions, feelings, etc.

Tips for a good diary

- Write your diary soon after the event.
- Write in a form that suits you – notes, flow charts, etc.
- Write down what happened first, before attempting to analyse.
- Always focus on the positives first.
- Describe what was not so positive and how you might change it.
- Identify ways in which you could improve.
- Be patient with yourself.

Critical analysis and self-reflection

Everyone has experienced a certain amount of self-reflection. As a leader it is possible to think back over a competition, but in everyday life perhaps a driving test or an argument.

This can be a useful process if you review what happened and what you did and then suggest to yourself what you might have done better. This could lead you to determine what you might do in the future.

The process of reflection has several stages (as illustrated in Fig 11.12).

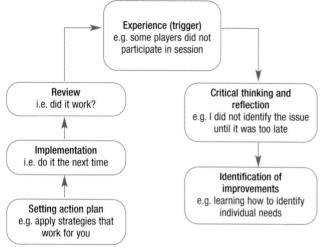

Fig 11.12 Example of the self-reflection process

Using video

Simply having your performance filmed will provide you with an objective record of what happened, with the advantage of being able to analyse in slow motion or real time. You will see yourself as you see others and there is no need to try and remember everything as in the case of a diary.

Videos can also be used to form a point of reference. Watching an elite official in action can be beneficial and help demonstrate the techniques required to improve.

Peer observation

Information from people in the same situation as you can be some of the most valuable information received. Often as a new leader it is easier for peers to relate to the kind of situations that you might be in, and offer you the benefit of their own experiences and ways in which they have dealt with challenging situations. It is very easy for an experienced leader to state the easiest way to deal with a difficult situation,

Fig 11.13 A leader surrounded by young rugby players

LEARNER ACTIVITY

Video a practical session with the camera focused on the leader/s and not the play. When you have completed filming, go to a quiet area and reflect on what went well and what may need development. You may need some help with this to start with, so don't be afraid to ask others to make comments on your performance.

You should be able to produce at least three action points for future developments.

Guidelines

- Make sure the person filming you is able to do so properly and understands what action they need to record.
- Picking up sound, particularly your voice, is an advantage.
- Camera positioning is crucial. It would be good to follow the leaders in the course of the activity, and try and pick up on body language, interaction with participants, etc.

but it should be borne in mind that what works for them is most likely based on the relationships that they have established through years of experience and that an appropriate course of action for you could be completely different from the one that they might take.

Qualifications

In improving as a leader it is necessary at some stage to become qualified. Qualifications such as the Duke of Edinburgh's Award Scheme and the Community and Higher Sports Leadership Awards are useful both in terms of your personal development and in introducing you to peers, who will want to update you with all the relevant issues and scenarios relating to leadership.

Message boards/chat rooms

One fairly recent development on the internet is the use of message boards or chat rooms as a means of communication between officials. It should be pointed out that while this medium may be very useful it is open to abuse and it is worth being cautious about all contact unless it is supported by a recognised governing body.

Development

Feedback

- **Formative** – this sort of feedback assists the leader in the improvement of their own performance, and provides corrective advice and guidance for improvement.
- **Summative** – this sort of feedback passes a judgement on performance and can be used as an assessment tool, such as in the assessment of a leaders' course or qualification, or in the formal assessment of leadership performance, measured against a specification authorised by the governing body, such as the British Sports Trust.

Having completed an activity it is important to gain some feedback on how to improve performance. Feedback can come from a number of sources:

- yourself
- your peers
- an assessor
- a supervisor
- an observer.

Whatever the nature and style of your leadership, and whatever the nature of your activity, no two leaders are identical. Information about strengths and weaknesses provides us with a template for improvement. A leader should learn something new from every session.

Examples of development feedback could be:

- poor or ineffective stroke demonstration
- unsafe activity
- ineffective/unsafe knots used (climbing)
- ineffective communication with the group
- lack of confidence and experience.

All the above can be improved. Leaders must review and develop their own self-assessment techniques, paying particular attention to what needs to be improved and in what order.

Target setting

When you have identified areas for development, it is good practice to apply the SMART principle:

- **S**pecific – e.g. test the effectiveness of your teaching, in this case to a group of beginners
- **M**easurable – e.g. test the effectiveness of your teaching; see if you can learn the skill well enough to produce an effective demonstration
- **A**chievable – i.e. know that you are capable of executing the skill well enough to demonstrate to a group of beginners
- **R**ealistic – is it possible?
- **T**ime-constrained – e.g. review the situation in one month.

Evaluating a session

Once a session is completed, it is important to review and record the practice, to improve the quality of your leadership and the quality of the experience for the learner.

LEARNER ACTIVITY

Organise and lead a simple sports activity, perhaps a football competition or a short walk. Having finished the activity complete an evaluation, as in the example below.

Leader activity evaluation
1 Aims and objectives – were they achieved?
2 Participants' performance – did it improve?
3 Were there any behaviour issues?
4 Health and safety issues – anything to report?
5 Organisation – were the skills taught and the techniques used appropriate?
6 What was my leadership like (communication, adaptations, style, etc.)?
7 Actions for the next session . . .

Key learning points

- A typical sports activity session will usually contain:
  - warm-up
  - fitness work
  - technical skills practice
  - tactical work
  - game play
  - cool-down.
- Sports sessions take many forms, e.g.:
  - a fitness session such as a circuit
  - a practical coaching session
  - a sports event such as a competition or race
  - a competitive match.
- Feedback may be: formative – assists the leader in the improvement of their own performance; or summative – passes a judgement on performance.
- Self-reflection allows you to explore your perceptions, decisions and subsequent actions to work out ways in which performers can improve technical, tactical or physical ability.

Review questions

1 Give a definition for sports leadership.
2 What qualities and characteristics does a sports leader require?
3 Describe three roles associated with being a sports leader.
4 Describe the different leadership styles that are commonly used.
5 What is team cohesion?
6 What are the four stages of group formation?
7 Why would you use SMARTER targets when setting aims and objectives for your sports activity?
8 What planning considerations should be made prior to running a sports activity session?
9 What are the stages of a typical sports activity session?
10 What are parachute games and who are they for?

References

Carron, A. V. (1982) Cohesiveness in sport group: interpretations and consideration. *Journal of Sport Psychology*, 4, 123–38.

Crisfield, P. (2001) *Analysing your coaching*, Coachwise.

Higher Sports Leader Award Resource Pack (2005) *Developing Leadership Through Community Sport*, British Sports Trust.

Miles, A. (2004) *Coaching Practice*, Coachwise.

Stafford-Brown, J., Rea, S., Janaway, L. and Manley, C. (2006) *BTEC First Sport*, Hodder Arnold.

Tuckman, B. W. (1965) Developmental sequence in small groups. *Psychological Bulletin*, 63, 384–99.

12

Exercise, health and lifestyle

Goals

By the end of this chapter you should:

- understand the importance of lifestyle factors in the maintenance of health and well-being
- be able to assess the lifestyle of a selected individual
- be able to provide advice on lifestyle improvement
- be able to plan a health-related physical activity programme for a selected individual.

A person's lifestyle can have a huge impact on their long-term health. Lifestyle plays a key role in the prevention of a large number of diseases including coronary heart disease, cancer and obesity. This chapter will give you the knowledge and skills to assess the lifestyle of an individual, provide advice on lifestyle improvement and plan a health-related physical activity programme.

Lifestyle factors

Physical activity

Physical activity: **the state of being active.**

Our lifestyle has become much more sedentary over the years. We now have methods of transport that require little physical exertion. Cars and buses have replaced walking and cycling. Recent studies have shown that 30 per cent of children go to school by car, and fewer than 50 per cent walk. This country has less time dedicated to PE lessons than any other country in the European Union. There are now relatively few

manual occupations, and the majority of people's careers are spent in an office-based environment. Everyday tasks such as laundry, cleaning and cooking require little effort as they are all aided by labour-saving devices. It is now even possible to go shopping by sitting in front of a computer and logging on to the internet. For entertainment, the average person spends less time participating in active leisure pursuits and prefers to sit in front of the TV. The average adult watches over 26 hours of television each week, which is a virtually totally sedentary activity.

Children also spend much less time pursing activity-based play and choose computer games, videos or the TV to occupy their free time. All these factors have led to many people taking part in very low levels of physical activity.

Physical activity can increase a person's basal metabolic rate by around 10 per cent. This elevated basal metabolic rate can last for up to 48 hours after the completion of the activity. By taking part in physical activity kilocalories will be expended. The number of kilocalories used depends on the type and intensity of the activity. The more muscles that are used in the activity and the harder you work, the more kilocalories will be used up to perform the activity. For example, swimming the front crawl uses both the arms and the legs and will therefore use more calories to perform than walking, which mainly uses the leg muscles.

The body weight of the person will also have an impact on the number of kilocalories burnt while taking part in a physical activity. The heavier the person, the more kilocalories are required to move the heavier weight. So a heavier person will burn more calories than a lighter person when performing the same activity at the same intensity.

National recommended guidelines

In order to gain the health benefits of physical activity adults should aim to participate in physical activity for 30 minutes at least five times a week. Our national recommended guidelines for children state that they should participate in moderate intensity exercise for 60 minutes per day, but the European Health Study 2006 found that they should be exercising for 90 minutes per day to gain the health benefits of physical activity.

Health benefits of physical activity

Taking part in regular exercise has consistently been shown to have many benefits to a person's physical and mental health. Many types of disease can be alleviated or prevented by taking part in regular exercise. Discussed below are the main types of ill-health that can be eased or prevented by taking part in regular exercise.

Coronary heart disease and physical activity

Coronary heart disease (CHD) is the leading cause of death in the western world. One-third of all deaths associated with CHD are due to not taking part in physical activity. Coronary heart disease is a narrowing of the coronary arteries, which are the blood vessels that pass over the surface of the heart and supply it with blood. CHD is usually a result of a build-up of fatty material and plaques within the coronary blood vessels. This is known as atherosclerosis.

definition

Atherosclerosis: build-up of fatty material in the coronary blood vessels, which makes their diameter smaller.

When a person with CHD takes part in a physically demanding task, the coronary arteries may not be able to supply the heart muscle with enough blood to keep up with the demand for oxygen. This will be felt as a pain in the chest (angina). If a coronary artery becomes completely blocked, the area of the heart muscle served by the artery will die, resulting in a heart attack.

Taking part in regular exercise appears to reduce the risk of heart disease directly and indirectly. Research has shown that exercise:

LEARNER ACTIVITY Activity diary

This activity is designed to determine how much time you spend each day taking part in physical activity and how much time is spent pursuing sedentary activities.

- Keep an activity diary for at least one full day.
- Copy and complete the table below.

Time of day	Activity	Time spent on activity

- In the middle column write an S next to the activity if it is sedentary or an A it if it requires physical activity.
- Total up the time spent on S activities and then total up the time spent on A activities.
- From your activity diary, do you think you are spending enough time pursing physically active tasks, or too long on sedentary tasks? Explain your answer.

- increases levels of HDL cholesterol
- decreases the amount of triglycerides in the bloodstream.

> **definition**
>
> HDL cholesterol: the 'good' cholesterol that acts to clean the artery walls, which in turn reduces atherosclerosis.

> **definition**
>
> Triglycerides: another type of fat; high levels in the bloodstream have been linked with increased risk of heart disease.

Hypertension and physical activity

> **definition**
>
> Hypertension: high blood pressure.

A person is deemed to have hypertension if their blood pressure consistently reads at 140/90 or higher. Hypertension is a very common complaint and around 15 to 25 per cent of adults in most western countries have high blood pressure. If a person with hypertension does not reduce their blood pressure they are more at risk of suffering from a stroke or a heart attack.

Diabetes and physical activity

Today more and more people are suffering from diabetes, a disease which places people at higher than average risk for heart disease. Diabetes is a disease in which the body does not produce or properly use insulin.

> **definition**
>
> Insulin: a hormone produced in the pancreas that controls the level of blood sugar.

The cause of diabetes is unknown, although genetics, obesity and a lack of exercise are thought to play a significant role.

There are two types of diabetes: one is insulin dependent (type 1) and the other is non-insulin dependent (type 2).

Type 1 diabetes means that the pancreas is no longer producing insulin, so it is necessary to inject insulin into the body every day to control blood sugar levels. It occurs most often in children and young adults. However, adults may become type 1 diabetic later on in life. Steve Redgrave, the British rower, became type 1 diabetic prior to taking part in the Sydney 2000 Olympics. Type 1 diabetes accounts for around 5 to 10 per cent of diabetes.

Type 2 diabetes means that a person's body is either unable to make enough insulin or it has become less sensitive to insulin. This results in elevated levels of glucose in the bloodstream. It is the most common form of the disease and accounts for 90 to 95 per cent of diabetes. Diet and exercise can often control type 2 diabetes, although insulin medication may also be necessary.

Today, type 2 diabetes is nearing epidemic proportions, due to an increase in obesity and a decrease in activity levels. It usually effects people later on in life, but because of inadequate activity and poor diet, children today are developing this disease.

There is good evidence to suggest that physical activity has a role in the prevention, and also in the treatment, of type 2 diabetes. Studies have shown that the risks of developing diabetes are lower in people who are physically active than in those who are sedentary. Exercise can also help to treat people with type 2 diabetes, as it improves a person's sensitivity to insulin.

People with uncontrolled diabetes should be referred to their doctor. They should not take part in strength training or high-impact exercises as they can strain weakened blood vessels in the eyes or injure blood vessels in the feet. People who are taking insulin should take special precautions before embarking on a workout programme because glucose levels vary dramatically during exercise. Type 1 diabetics may need to decrease insulin doses or take in more carbohydrates prior to exercise to help maintain blood glucose levels during the activity.

Obesity and physical activity

A person is classified as being obese if they are 20 per cent or more heavier than the correct weight for their height. The number of people who are obese is rising rapidly throughout the world, making obesity one of the fastest developing public health problems.

The World Health Organisation has described the problem as a 'worldwide epidemic' and has estimated

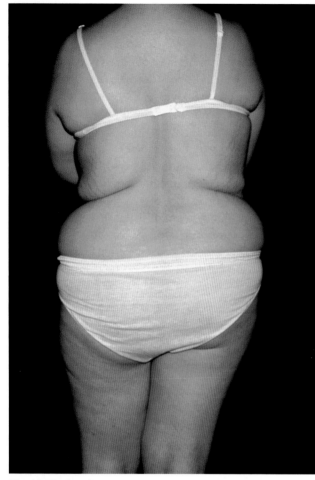

Fig 12.01 An obese person

that around 250 million people worldwide are obese, about 7 per cent of the adult population. Obesity takes years to develop and results from the amount of energy being consumed exceeding the amount of energy expended. This excess energy is then stored mainly as fat. Research to date suggests that in England over 50 per cent of the adult population are overweight and 17 per cent of men and 21 per cent of women are obese.

Obese people are at risk of developing a number of medical conditions which can cause poor health and premature death. These include:

- osteoarthritis
- rheumatoid arthritis
- some forms of cancer
- coronary heart disease (CHD)
- deep vein thrombosis (DVT)
- type 2 diabetes
- gall bladder disease
- gout

- hypertension
- stroke.

When a person takes part in exercise they burn up kilocalories, which results in the person being in a state of negative energy balance. This means that they will start to burn kilocalories from their fat stores and so lose weight.

The best forms of exercise to combat obesity are fat-burning exercises of low intensity and of long duration – walking is a very good type of exercise for obese individuals. This is because walking is a low-impact form of exercise and will therefore place less stress on the joints than a high-impact form of exercise. The person should aim to walk at a pace that increases their breathing rate and heart rate but still allows them to talk.

Arthritis and physical activity

Arthritis is a condition in which the synovial membrane of one or more joints has become inflamed. The two main forms of arthritis are:

- rheumatoid arthritis, a long-term inflammation of the synovial membrane lining the joints
- osteoarthritis, a condition in which the cartilage in the joints becomes diseased or damaged.

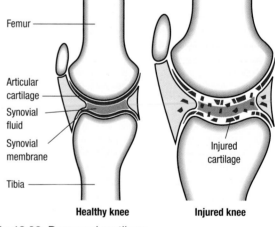

Fig 12.02 Damaged cartilage

Cartilage serves as a shock absorber, or cushion, between the bones and provides a smooth surface that allows the bones to move against each other with less friction. When this cartilage is damaged, the joint is inflamed as the cartilage becomes rougher and thinner, and the joint may swell up as there is increased production of synovial fluid. As the cartilage continues to wear away, growths of bone called bone spurs may form around the edges of the joint. Eventually, the bones that meet at the joint rub against each other, which can be extremely painful and can severely reduce movement in the joint.

Physical activity plays a key role in treating almost all forms of arthritis. Exercises that help to alleviate arthritis are mobilising exercises and exercises to strengthen muscles. Mobilising exercise helps to keep the joints moving and prevent them becoming stiff. When a person takes part in mobilising exercises, they increase the production of synovial fluid into the joint, which helps to lubricate the joint. Mobilising exercises also increase blood flow to the tissues around the joint, which helps to keep the joint healthy. Muscle strengthening exercises help to build up the muscles around the joint and so help to protect the joints. Swimming and hydrotherapy are good examples of effective ways of strengthening muscles as well as mobilising joints. A person suffering with arthritis will usually have good days when they feel less pain, and bad days when they feel more pain. It is better to exercise on good days, although taking part in exercise every day may well help to prevent joints becoming stiff and painful, and keep muscles strong.

Osteoporosis and physical activity

Osteoporosis is a disease in which the mineral density of bones is decreased, resulting in the bones becoming fragile and more likely to break. Women are four times more likely than men to develop the disease. Osteoporosis is largely preventable for most people and requires a healthy diet with the recommended daily amount of calcium and vitamin D, together with appropriate exercise.

Prevention is very important because, while there are treatments for osteoporosis, there is currently no cure. If a person has exercised regularly in childhood and adolescence, they are more likely to build strong, dense bones, which will stand them in good stead for the rest of their life. The best exercise to build bone density is weight-bearing exercise such as walking, jogging, aerobics, racket sports and hiking.

Psychological benefits of physical activity

A number of studies have attempted to explore the effects of exercise on depression and found that exercise increases self-esteem, improves mood, reduces anxiety levels, increases the ability to handle stress and generally makes people happier than those who do not exercise. It is thought that one cause of depression may be due to a decreased production of certain chemicals in the brain, specifically adrenaline, dopamine and serotonin. Exercise has been shown to increase the levels of these substances, which may have the effect of improving a person's mood after taking part in exercise. For the last decade or so, exercise has been prescribed as a method of combating depression.

Smoking

You are probably aware that smoking is bad for you. It actually kills around 14,000 people in the UK each year, and 300 people die in the UK every day as a result of smoking. These deaths occur through a range of diseases caused by smoking and include a variety of cancers, cardiovascular disease and an array of chronic lung diseases.

Fig 12.03 A normal lung (left) beside the lung of a smoker

The products in a cigarette that appear to do the most damage include tar, nicotine and carbon monoxide.

Smokers are making themselves much more likely to suffer from a range of cancers; 90 per cent of people suffering with lung cancer have the disease because they smoke or have smoked. You are also four times more likely to contract mouth cancer if you are a smoker. Other forms of cancer that have been linked to smoking include cancer of the bladder, the oesophagus, the kidneys, the pancreas and cervical cancer.

Cardiovascular disease

Cardiovascular disease is the main cause of death in smokers. The excess cholesterol produced from smoking narrows the blood vessels.

When the blood vessels become narrower, blood clots are more likely to form which can then block the coronary blood vessels. A blockage in these vessels can lead to a heart attack. It is estimated that 30 per cent of these heart attacks are due to smoking.

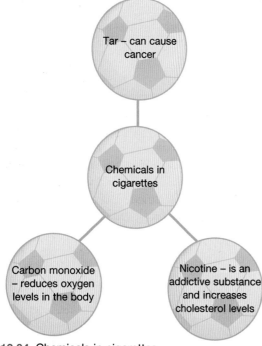

Fig 12.04 Chemicals in cigarettes

> **definition**
>
> Coronary blood vessels: **blood vessels that supply blood to the heart.**

Alternatively, the blood clot may travel to the brain, which can lead to a stroke; or it could travel to the kidneys, which could result in kidney failure; or the block may occur in the legs, which can lead to gangrene for which the main treatment is amputation.

Chronic lung disease

The following diseases are more prevalent in smokers:

- emphysema – a disease that causes breathlessness due to damaged alveoli
- bronchitis – makes the person cough excessively because of increased mucus production in the lungs.

Smoking is responsible for 80 per cent of these conditions, which basically block air flow to and from the lungs making breathing more difficult. These diseases tend to start between the ages of 35 and 45.

> **definition**
>
> Alveoli: **air sacs in the lungs in which gaseous exchange takes place.**

Other smoking-related health risks

Smoking can also damage health in a variety of other ways. A person who smokes may suffer from some of the following:

- high blood pressure
- impotence
- fertility problems
- eye problems
- discoloured teeth and gums
- mouth ulcers
- skin more prone to wrinkles.

LEARNER ACTIVITY
Government campaigns against smoking

Find out how the government is trying to make people aware of the dangers of smoking. Things that you may like to consider include:

- messages written on cigarette boxes or advertising
- adverts on the TV
- national non-smoking day (when is the next one?).

Alcohol

Alcohol is a legal drug that may be consumed by people aged 18 or over, but by the age of 16, over 80 per cent of young people in the UK have tried alcohol. In fact, in the UK people aged between 16 and 24 are the heaviest drinking group of the population. Studies reveal that one in two men and one in four women drink more than the recommended daily benchmarks, and over a quarter of males and females drink more than double the recommended daily amount.

The recommended daily benchmarks for alcohol consumption are based upon adults drinking, as there are no recommendations for children and young people as they should legally be refraining from alcohol consumption.

Recommended daily intake

The Health Education Authority recommends that women should drink no more than two units of alcohol per day and males should drink no more than three units per day. Both males and females should have at least two alcohol-free days per week.

It takes around an hour for the adult body to get rid of one unit of alcohol, and this may well be slower in young people.

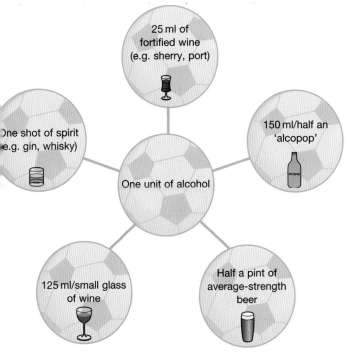

Fig 12.05 One unit of alcohol

Effects of alcohol on the body

Alcohol affects the brain so that it compromises our judgement and suppresses our inhibitions. It decreases our physical coordination and sense of balance, and makes our vision blurred and speech slurred. Excessive drinking can lead to alcohol poisoning, which can cause unconsciousness, coma and even death. Excessive alcohol consumption can often make a person vomit, and vomiting while unconscious can lead to death by suffocation as the vomit can block the air flow to and from the lungs. The effects of alcohol have also been implicated in a large proportion of fatal road accidents, assaults and incidents of domestic violence.

Diseases associated with excess alcohol consumption

Alcohol consumption in excess of the recommended daily guidelines will often cause physical damage to the body and increase the likelihood of getting diseases such as cancer, cirrhosis, high blood pressure, strokes and depression.

Cirrhosis: excessive alcohol consumption can result in cirrhosis of the liver. The liver is the largest organ in the body. It is responsible for getting rid of poisons from the blood, helps our immune system in fighting infection, makes proteins that helps our blood to clot and produces bile, which helps with the breakdown of fats. The disease damages the liver and produces scar tissue. The scar tissue replaces the normal tissue and prevents it from working as it should. Cirrhosis is the 12th leading cause of death by disease and causes 26,000 deaths per year.

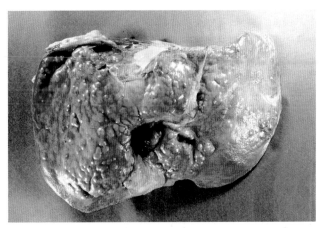

Fig 12.06 A liver affected by cirrhosis

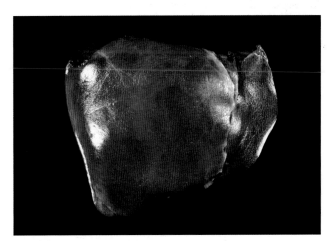

Fig 12.07 A healthy liver

Cancer: around 6 per cent of deaths from cancer in the UK are caused by alcohol (*Oxford Textbook of Medicine*, 2003). A range of cancers have been linked with excess alcohol consumption, these include:

- cancer of the mouth
- cancer of the larynx
- cancer of the oesophagus
- liver cancer
- breast cancer
- bowel cancer.

Depression: alcohol consumption has been linked with anxiety and depression; one in three young people who have committed suicide drank alcohol before they died, and more than two out of three people who attempt suicide have drunk excessively.

Stress

When we perceive ourselves to be in a situation that is dangerous, our stress response is activated. This has been developed as a means of ensuring our survival by making us respond to danger. For example, if we are walking home at night along dark streets and we hear noises behind us our body will instigate physiological changes, called the 'fight or flight' response, as the body is preparing to turn and fight the danger or run away as fast as it can.

Adrenaline is the main hormone released when we are stressed, which has the effect of:

- increasing the heart rate
- increasing the breathing rate
- decreasing the rate of digestion.

It is not healthy for the body to be in a constant state of stress because of the excess production of adrenaline. This results in excess cholesterol production that raises blood cholesterol levels and is a risk factor for coronary heart disease (CHD).

Stress and cardiovascular disease

If the excess hormones and chemicals released during stressful periods are not 'used up' through physical exertion, the increased heart rate and high blood pressure place excess strain on our blood vessels. This can lead to vascular damage. Damaged blood vessels are thicker than healthy blood vessels and have a reduced ability to stretch. This can have the effect of reducing the supply of blood and oxygen to the heart.

Stress and the immune system

Stress can decrease our body's ability to fight infection, which makes us more susceptible to suffering from illnesses. This explains why we catch more colds when we are stressed.

Stress and depression

Stress is also associated with mental health problems and, in particular, anxiety and depression. Here the relationship is fairly clear. The negative thinking that is associated with stress also contributes to these.

Diet

Our diets have changed significantly over the years. Today we have the largest range of foods available to us, but we are choosing to eat foods that are high in saturated fats and simple carbohydrates. Fast-food restaurants are flourishing because they are used so regularly by our society. Today, the nation's diet tends to be lacking in a number of important nutrients, including fibre, calcium, vitamins and iron. This is because a high proportion of the population relies on snacks and fast foods as their main source of nutritional intake. As a result, the western diet is generally high in fat and sugars, resulting in a huge increase in obesity.

Estimates in 1990 suggested that one in twenty children aged nine to eleven could be classified as clinically obese. If a person is obese they are much more likely to suffer from coronary heart disease, currently the biggest killer in Britain. As we are continuing to rely on foods that do not give us the right balance of vital nutrients, a number of people are suffering from poor nutrition. This not only impairs physical and mental functioning, but can also increase the risk of suffering from a range of diseases including anaemia, diabetes and osteoporosis. A number of nutrition experts have also linked poor nutrition to emotional and behavioural problems, such as hyperactivity and attention deficit, that are seen to occur much more frequently among children today.

A healthy diet contains lots of fruit and vegetables. It is based on starchy foods, such as wholegrain bread, pasta and rice, and is low in fat (especially saturated fat), salt and sugar. Current recommendations for a healthy diet are shown in Table 12.01.

Table 12.01 Recommendations for a healthy diet

Food	Amount we should eat	Function	Examples of food sources
Carbohydrates	50–60%	Provide energy for sports performance	
Sugars		Provide short bursts of energy	Jam, sweets, fruit, fizzy drinks, sports drinks
Starch		Provide energy for longer periods	Pasta, rice, bread, potatoes, breakfast cereals
Fat	25–30%	Provides energy for low-intensity exercise, e.g. walking	
Saturated fats		Insulates the body against the cold	Mainly animal sources: cream, lard, cheese, meat
Unsaturated fats		Helps to protect internal organs	Mainly plant sources: nuts, soya, tofu
Protein	10–15%	For growth and repair	Meat, eggs, nuts, fish, poultry

Vitamin	Food sources	Function
A	Carrots, liver, dark green vegetables, mackerel	Maintains good vision, skin and hair
B group	Cereals, liver, yeast, eggs, beef, beans	Helps to break down food to produce energy
C	Most fresh fruits and vegetables, especially citrus fruits	Fights infection, maintains healthy skin and gums, wound healing
D	Oily fish, eggs	Helps to build bones and teeth
E	Nuts, whole grains, dark green leaf vegetables	Antioxidant that prevents damage to cells
K	Leafy green vegetables, peas, milk, egg yolk	Helps to form blood clots

Mineral	Food sources	Function
Iron	Liver, lean meats, eggs, dried fruits	Blood production
Calcium	Milk, fish bones, green leafy vegetables	Helps to build strong bones and teeth, helps to form blood clots
Sodium	Salt, seafood, processed foods, celery	Maintains fluid balance in cells, helps in muscle contraction
Potassium	Bananas	Works with sodium to maintain fluid balance, aids muscle contraction, maintains blood pressure
Zinc	Meats, fish	Tissue growth and repair

Key learning points

- People are much more sedentary today and many are not meeting national recommended guidelines.
- Children should be physically active for at least 60 to 90 minutes per day.
- Adults should be physically active for at least 30 minutes five times per week.
- People who take part in physical activity are less likely to suffer from CHD, hypertension, diabetes, obesity and depression.
- Smoking has been shown to cause cancer, chronic lung disease and cardiovascular disease in some people.
- Adult males should have no more than three units of alcohol per day and adult females should have no more than two. Males and females should both have at least two alcohol-free days per week.

- Excess alcohol consumption has been shown to cause cirrhosis, cancer and depression in some people.
- Stress can cause cardiovascular disease, decrease the immune system's response to infection and cause depression in some people.
- Today, many people are eating fast food and not taking in the right quantities of macronutrients, vitamins and minerals.
- A healthy diet contains lots of fruit and vegetables, is based on starchy foods, such as wholegrain bread, pasta and rice, and is low in fat (especially saturated fat), salt and sugar.

Assessing the lifestyle of an individual

When assessing the lifestyle of an individual you will need to gather as much information as is possible on them. This can be done effectively through a comprehensive questionnaire. It will be part of an initial consultation and must cover at least the following:

- medical history
- activity history
- lifestyle factors
- nutritional status
- any other factors that will affect the person's health.

LEARNER ACTIVITY
Information gathering

Visit a local health and fitness club and find out how it gathers information on its clients' training needs and requirements. If possible, ask for the questionnaire it uses.

Key learning points

- A lifestyle questionnaire should address levels of activity, alcohol consumption, smoking, stress levels and diet. A one-to-one consultation should follow up a lifestyle questionnaire.

Lifestyle questionnaire

Section 1: Personal details

Name

Address

Home telephone _____ Mobile telephone

Email

Occupation

Date of birth

Section 2: Physical activity levels

1 Does your occupation require you to take part in physical activity? If so, what?

2 What are your medium-term goals over the next three months?

3 What are your short-term goals over the next four weeks?

Section 3: Current training status

1 What are your main training requirements?

✓ Muscular strength
✓ Muscular endurance
✓ Speed
✓ Flexibility
✓ Aerobic fitness
✓ Power
✓ Weight loss or gain
✓ Skill-related fitness
✓ Other (please state) _____

2 How would you describe your current fitness status?

3 How many times a week will you train?

4 How long have you got for each training session?

Section 4: Your nutritional status

1 On a scale of 1 to 10 (1 being very low quality and 10 being very high quality) how would you rate the quality of your diet?_____

2 Do you follow any particular diet?

✓ Vegetarian
✓ Vegan
✓ Vegetarian plus fish
✓ Gluten-free
✓ Dairy-free

3 How often do you eat? Note down a typical day's intake.

4 Do you take any supplements? If so, which ones?

Section 5: Your lifestyle

1 How many units of alcohol do you drink in a typical week?_____

2 Do you smoke?_____ If yes, how many a day?_____

3 Do you experience stress on a daily basis?_____

4 If yes, what causes you stress (if you know)?

5 What techniques do you use to deal with your stress?

Section 6: Your physical health

1 Do you experience any of the following?

✓ Back pain or injury
✓ Knee pain or injury
✓ Ankle pain or injury
✓ Swollen joints
✓ Shoulder pain or injury
✓ Hip or pelvic pain or injury
✓ Nerve damage
✓ Head injuries

2 If yes, please give details

3 Are any of these injuries made worse by exercise?_____

4 If yes, what movements in particular cause pain?

5 Are you currently receiving any treatment for any injuries? If so, what?

Section 7: Medical history

1 Do you have, or have you had, any of the following medical conditions?

✓ Asthma
✓ Bronchitis
✓ Heart problems
✓ Chest pains
✓ Diabetes
✓ High blood pressure
✓ Epilepsy
✓ Other _____

2 Are you taking any medication? (If yes, state what, how much and why)

Name:

Signature: Date:

Consultation

It is always a good idea to follow up a lifestyle questionnaire with a consultation with the individual. The person running the consultation must know when to ask questions and prompt the client, and when to listen and take notes. The main rule of thumb is that, in a consultation, the client should be doing most of the talking; the consultant's role is to ensure that questions are answered accurately and fully. The client should be made aware that their lifestyle questionnaire and the follow-up consultation is confidential, and the questionnaire stored in a secure place.

Lifestyle improvement through physical activity

When designing a physical activity programme it is important to make the programme as personal as possible. It must meet the needs of the individual it is written for or it will result in the person being unhappy or unsuccessful. The key to this is gathering as much information as possible on the individual, by asking questions such as:

- What activities do they like to take part in?
- What have they done in the past that they enjoyed?
- Do they like to exercise alone or with other people?

You should take into account the facilities in the person's area. Do they live near a gym or leisure centre? One of the biggest factors to put people off going to a gym is if it is quite some distance away and takes them a while to get there. If the gym is close to where they live or work, this makes it a much more viable option. They could go to the gym in their lunch break or on the way to or from work.

Increasing daily activity

It is actually unnecessary to join a gym or go to a swimming pool to increase physical activity levels. There are lots of ways to attain the benefits of physical activity by just adapting everyday life. If a person takes the bus or train to work, they could get off one or two stops earlier and walk the remaining distance. If a person drives to work, they could park further away from their workplace and walk the remaining distance. If cycling to work is a viable option, it is not only good for you but is also cheaper and better for the environment. Many new cycle paths are being constructed to encourage people to cycle. Choosing options such as walking up a flight of stairs instead of taking a lift or escalator also help to increase a person's activity levels.

Housework and gardening are productive ways of increasing daily activity levels. Vacuum cleaning and dusting the home, or digging the garden or mowing

Fig 12.08 Gardening can increase heart rate and help tone muscles

the lawn will increase heart rate and help tone muscles.

Reducing alcohol consumption

If a person is dependent on alcohol they must seek help to prevent the damage it does to their body and mind and to those around them.

In order to determine if a person is drinking more than the government recommended amounts of alcohol, it is a good idea to keep a 'drinking diary'. This involves noting what, how much and when that person drinks alcohol. If the person is just over the limit, simple changes could help them cut down. If they usually drink strong lager they could opt for one that contains less alcohol. Or if they usually drink wine, they could have a spritzer instead, as this will make their drink last longer and help them to drink less. If they regularly meet up with friends in pubs, they could try to find alternative venues such as a juice bar or coffee shop.

A GP can give confidential advice and support. In order to help to prevent the withdrawal symptoms of drinking, they may be prescribed anti-depressants (e.g. Valium). Two drug treatments are also available to help a person stop drinking. Once drug called Disulfiram makes the person feel very ill if they drink even a small amount of alcohol. Another drug called Acamprosate helps to reduce a person's craving for alcohol, but it does have many unpleasant side-effects. A person may attend organisations such as Alcohol Concern and Alcoholics Anonymous to help them stop drinking alcohol.

Stopping smoking

Smokers have both a physical addiction to smoking and a psychological addiction. The combination of these two factors makes cigarettes one of the most addictive drugs used today. Determining whether you are more physiologically than psychologically addicted to smoking will help to decide the best course of action in trying to stop smoking.

First of all, a person needs to think about why they smoke and identify the things they do that always make them want to light up. Once these triggers have been identified, the person can attempt to remove themselves from them. The next step is to decrease the person's dependence on nicotine. Either they can slowly decrease the amount of cigarettes they smoke over a set period or they could use a nicotine replacement therapy, such as a nicotine patch and/or nicotine gum. This process helps the person break the cigarette habit and also slowly reduces the amount of nicotine being taken into the body.

The NHS has set up a smoking helpline and runs clinics to help advise people on how to give up smoking. Each year there is a national no smoking day, which has also been effective in making people think about giving up smoking and giving them a clear target day to attempt to stop.

Reducing stress through stress-management techniques

The main methods of stress management are:

- progressive muscular relaxation
- mind-to-muscle relaxation
- meditation/centring.

Progressive muscular relaxation (PMR) involves a person tensing and relaxing the muscle groups individually and sequentially to relax their whole body and mind. It is also called 'muscle-to-mind' relaxation, as muscles are tensed and relaxed to induce complete relaxation. Each muscle is tensed and relaxed to teach the person the difference between a tense muscle and a relaxed muscle. After a muscle is tensed, the relaxation effect is deepened, which also has an effect on the involuntary muscles.

The technique is practised using a series of taped instructions, or with the psychologist giving the instructions. It usually starts at the hands by making a tight fist and then relaxing. The tensing and relaxing carries on up the arms into the shoulders, the face and neck, then down to the stomach and through the hips and legs.

These sessions last between 20 and 30 minutes, and need to be practised about five times a day to gain the maximum effect. Each time they are practised they have an increased effect and a person can relax more quickly and more deeply. The aim is that when they need to use the relaxation technique quickly they can induce relaxation using a trigger, such as tensing the hand or the shoulders.

Mind-to-muscle relaxation is also called imagery and involves the use of a mental room or a mental place. This is a place where a person can quickly picture themselves to produce feelings of relaxation when they need to relax.

Again, it involves the person using a taped script or a psychologist giving instructions. Usually the psychologist asks a person to build a mental picture of a room. This is a room where they can feel relaxed and where there is somewhere to sit or lie down. It should be decorated in a pleasing manner. Alternatively, the person may imagine a relaxing place, such as somewhere they went on their holidays or a beach or quiet place where they feel calm and relaxed. They are taught to vividly imagine this place and feel the sensations associated with being there. They do this about five times, so that eventually they can go there when they need to and are able to relax more quickly and deeply. As the person relaxes their mind, they feel the sensations transferring to their muscle groups and they can achieve overall body relaxation. It tends to work best for individuals who have good skills of imagery. Other people may feel that PMR is more effective for them.

Centring/meditation techniques involve the person focusing on one thing, such as their breathing (centring) or a mantra (meditation). By focusing their attention they become more and more relaxed. Again, these feelings of relaxation can eventually be produced when needed.

Lifestyle improvement through diet

Food preparation

The way food is prepared has a huge impact on its nutritional value. We should eat a fair amount of potatoes, but if you fry the potatoes to make chips the food then belongs in the fats and oils food group as it now has such a high concentration of fat.

You can prepare foods in certain ways to make them much healthier.

Breads and grains: pasta dishes can be prepared using lots of wholemeal pasta and a small portion of sauce. You can make sandwiches out of thick slices of wholemeal bread. You can mash sweet potatoes and regular potatoes in larger than usual quantities for a shepherd's pie topping.

Fruits and vegetables: it's healthy to eat dried fruit, fresh fruit or vegetable sticks (e.g. carrot sticks) as snacks. A selection of vegetables or salads can accompany each main meal. You can make fruit-based puddings, such as poached pears or apple and blackberry crumble. Add dried or fresh fruit to breakfast cereals. Include more vegetables in casserole dishes.

Meat, fish and vegetarian alternatives: you should use lean meat and remove skin and fat where possible.

Then grill meats wherever possible. You can include pulses in meat dishes to reduce the fat content and increase the fibre content, such as kidney beans in a chilli. Also try to eat two portions of oily fish per week.

Milk and dairy foods: choose semi-skimmed or skimmed milk and low-fat or reduced-fat cheeses. You can replace cream with fromage frais or yoghurt. Use strong-tasting cheese in cooking and then you will require smaller amounts.

Foods containing fat and foods containing sugar: do not fry these foods as it will just add more fat to them. Instead, grill or dry bake them (without oil) in the oven. Use small amounts of plant-based cooking oils (e.g. olive oil or rapeseed) when frying foods. Try making salad dressings with a balsamic vinegar base instead of oil. You can sweeten puddings with dried or fresh fruits, and drink fresh water instead of fizzy drinks.

LEARNER ACTIVITY
Your own diet
Write down the last three meals you have eaten. Try to work out how you could have made these meals healthier by using the principles shown above.

Timing of food intake

There is a saying that you should 'Eat breakfast like a king, lunch like a prince and dinner like a pauper.' This basically means that you should have your main meal at breakfast time, have a good-sized lunch and then eat your smallest meal at dinner time. The reasoning behind this saying is to have enough energy for the day and then to digest the food properly before going to bed. Heavy meals eaten before bedtime, such as a curry, take a long time to digest, which may disturb sleep. Any excess calories eaten during this meal will most probably be turned into body fat as very few people actually take any form of exercise after a late heavy meal.

Planning a health-related physical activity programme

Collecting information

When a trainer sits down to design a physical activity programme they need to consider a range of factors to ensure that the programme is appropriate and that it will benefit the person rather than harm them. They will need to consider the following factors.

- PAR-Q responses – have any contraindications to exercise been identified?
- Medical history – do they have any conditions which may affect the training programme and choice of exercises?
- Current and previous exercise history – this will give an idea about the current fitness level of the client.
- Barriers to exercise – do they have constraints such as time, cost, family responsibilities or work commitments?
- Motives and goals – what is the participant aiming to achieve and what is their time scale?
- Occupation – hours worked and whether work is manual or office-based.
- Activity levels – amount of movement they do on a daily basis.
- Leisure time activities – whether these are active or inactive.
- Diet – what, how much and when they eat.
- Stress levels – either through work or their home life and how they deal with it.
- Alcohol intake – how much they consume and how often.
- Smoking – whether they are a smoker or ex-smoker and the amount they smoke.
- Time available – the client needs to fit the training into their schedule and the trainer needs to be realistic when planning the programme.

LEARNER ACTIVITY
Lifestyle questionnaire

Find a person that you know who is wanting to change their lifestyle and incorporate more physical activity into their life. Ask them to complete a lifestyle questionnaire. Then assess whether your participant has any of the following:

- contraindications
- specific areas in their lifestyle that need addressing
- types of physical activity that would be suitable for them to participate in.

Goal setting

Short-term goals are set over a brief period of time, usually from one day to one month. A short-term goal may relate to what you want to achieve in one training session or where you want to be by the end of the month.

Long-term goals run from three months to over a period of several years. You may even set some lifetime goals which run until you retire from your sport. In sport we set long-term goals to cover a season or a sporting year. The period between one and three months would be called medium-term goals.

Usually short-term goals are set to help achieve the long-term goals. It is important to set both short- and

---

Key learning points

- Ways to increase physical activity – lifestyle changes, organised physical activities.
- Reducing alcohol intake – complete a drinking diary, choose drinks with reduced alcohol, seek help from GP, attend meetings designed to help people control their alcohol intake.
- Stopping smoking – identify triggers for smoking, use nicotine patches or nicotine gum, use NHS smoking helpline, seek help from GP.
- Stress-management techniques – progressive muscular relaxation, mind-to-muscle relaxation, meditation/centring.
- Diet – food preparation and timing of food intake.

long-term goals, particularly short-term goals because they will give a person more motivation to act immediately.

When goals are set you need to use the SMART principle to make them workable. SMART stands for:

- Specific
- Measurable
- Achievable
- Realistic
- Time-constrained.

Specific: the goal must be specific to what you want to achieve. It is not enough to say 'I want to get fitter', you need to say I want to improve strength, speed or stamina.

Measurable: goals must be stated in a way that is measurable, so a goal needs to state figures. For example, 'I want to cut down my alcohol intake to five units per week'.

Achievable: it must be possible to actually achieve the goal.

Realistic: we need to be realistic in our setting of goals and look at what factors may stop us achieving them.

Time-constrained: there must be a timescale or deadline on the goal. This means you can review your success. It is best to give a date by which you wish to achieve the goal.

Strategies to achieve goals

Some commonly used and effective strategies are as follows.

- **Using a decision balance sheet:** an individual writes down all the gains they will make by exercising and all the things they may lose through taking up exercise. Hopefully the gains will outweigh the losses and this list will help to motivate them at difficult times.
- **Prompts:** an individual puts up posters or reminders around the house which will keep giving them reminders to exercise. This could also be done with little coloured dots on mirrors or other places where they regularly look.
- **Rewards for attendance/completing goals:** the individual is provided with an extrinsic reward for completing the goal or attending the gym regularly. This may be something to pamper themselves, such

as a massage, and should not be something that conflicts with the goal – such as a slap-up meal!

- **Social support approaches:** you can help people exercise regularly by developing a social support group of like-minded people with similar fitness goals, so that they can arrange to meet at the gym at certain times. This makes it more difficult for people to miss their exercise session. Also, try to gain the backing of the people they live with to support them rather than tease or criticise them.

Principles of training

In order to develop a safe and effective training programme you will need to consider the principles of training. These principles are a set of guidelines to help you understand the requirements of programme design. They are:

- Frequency
- Intensity
- Time
- Type
- Overload
- Reversibility
- Specificity.

LEARNER ACTIVITY
Goal setting

With the participant chosen in the previous activity, set some short- and long-term goals.

- Ask your participant to complete a decision balance sheet.
- Devise some prompts for your participant to put up in their home and/or around their working environment.
- Determine what sort of rewards your participant would like and match these with the short-term goals you have devised.

Frequency: this means how often the person will train per week.

Intensity: this is how hard the person will work. It is usually expressed as a percentage of maximum intensity.

Time: this will indicate how long they train for in each session.

Type: this shows the type of training they will perform and needs to be individual to each person.

Overload: this shows that to make an improvement a muscle or system must work slightly harder than it is used to. This may be as simple as getting a sedentary person to walk for ten minutes or getting an athlete to squat more weight than they have previously.

Reversibility: this says that if a fitness gain is not used regularly the body will reverse it and go back to its previous fitness level. The rule is commonly known as 'use it or lose it'.

Specificity: this principle states that any fitness gain will be specific to the muscles or system to which the overload is applied. Put simply, this says that different types of training will produce different results. To make a programme specific you need to look at the needs of the person and then train them accordingly. For example, a person who was overweight would need to take part in lots of low intensity cardiovascular training in order to burn fat.

Appropriate activities

When you are devising your training programme you need to be sure that you are including activities that are appropriate to your client. If your client is obese, a training programme that includes jogging would probably not be appropriate. This kind of exercise is a high-impact exercise which places a lot of stress on the joints. If a person is obese, they will be stressing their joints to a greater degree which means they would be much more likely to injure or damage their joints. Therefore, walking or swimming would be much more appropriate as these place much less stress on the joints.

You should also try to include activities that you know your client enjoys. That way, they will be much more likely to continue their exercise programme.

LEARNER ACTIVITY
Training programme

Devise a training programme for your participant that you have used in the previous learning activities. Ensure that you take into account the training principles and your participant's preferred activities.

Exercise intensity

The intensity of exercise can be monitored by expressing it as a percentage of maximum heart rate. Your maximum heart rate is the maximum number of times your heart could beat. To find this out you would have to work to your maximum intensity, which for most people would clearly be unsafe. Therefore, we estimate the maximum heart rate by using the following formula:

Maximum heart rate = 220 – age

So, for a 17 year old their maximum heart rate would be 220 – 17 = 203 beats per minute (bpm).

To work out the heart rate training zone we take percentages of heart rate maximum. If we work between 60 and 90 per cent we would be working in the aerobic training zone, where the exercise we are performing is effective in improving aerobic fitness without being dangerous. However, it is still a wide range for a heart rate to be within, so we change the zone depending upon the fitness level of the participant.

Effective zones for different groups as % of maximum heart rate (MHR)

Beginners	60–70% of MHR
Intermediate	70–80% of MHR
Advanced	80–90% of MHR

Rate of perceived exertion (RPE) is another measure used to monitor exercise. RPE is scale that can be used by the participant to rate how hard they feel they are working between two extremes. Rather than monitoring heart rate the participant is introduced to the scale and then asked during the aerobic session where they feel they are. Below is Borg's modified RPE scale.

1	Extremely light
2	Very light
3	Moderate
4	
5	Somewhat hard
6	
7	Hard
8	Very hard
9	Extremely hard
10	Maximal exertion

To achieve aerobic fitness gains the participant needs to be working at around 6 to 7 on the modified scale.

LEARNER ACTIVITY
Monitoring exercise intensity

Working in pairs, one person is to exercise, while the other monitors them. The exercising person should wear a heart rate monitor if available.

The exercising person should start to exercise on a treadmill or fixed cycle at a low intensity. After every five minutes of exercising at the same intensity, ask them to rate their perceived exertion on Borg's modified RPE scale and check their heart rate.

Increase the intensity and, after five minutes, repeat your measurements.

Repeat this process until the exercising person wishes to terminate the test.

Look at your data and determine if the heart rate recorded relates to the RPE. Try to explain your answer.

Key learning points

- Ensure you collect all relevant information from your client to assess their lifestyle and determine any contraindications.
- Ensure you set short- and long-term goals.
- Apply the principles of training to your training programme.
- Ensure your training programme incorporates appropriate activities.
- Ensure your client exercises at the appropriate intensity.

Review questions

1 Explain why people are less physically active today than was the case 30 years ago.
2 What are the national recommended guidelines for physical activity?
3 What are the health benefits of physical activity? Discuss in relation to common conditions.
4 What is the Health Education Authority recommended alcohol intake for males and females?
5 Explain the short-term effects of alcohol on the body.
6 What is stress and how does it affect the body?
7 Describe ways in which a person can reduce their alcohol consumption.
8 Explain the principles of training.
9 Explain different methods of measuring exercise intensity.

References

Baechle, T. and Earle, R. (2000) *Essentials of Strength Training and Conditioning*, Human Kinetics.

Dalgleish, J. and Dollery, S. (2001) *The Health and Fitness Handbook*, Longman.

Elphinstone, J. and Pook, P. (1999) *The Core Workout – A Definitive Guide to Swiss Ball Training for Athletes, Coaches and Fitness Professionals.*

Stafford-Brown, J., Rea, S. and Chance, J. (2003) *BTEC National in Sport and Exercise Science*, Hodder Arnold.

Stafford-Brown, J., Rea, S., Janaway, L. and Manley, C. (2006) *BTEC First Sport*, Hodder Arnold.

Wesson, K., Wiggins-James, N., Thompson, G. and Hartigan, S. (2005) *Sport and PE: A Complete Guide to Advanced Level Study*, Hodder Arnold.

Goals

By the end of this chapter you should:

- understand the principles of an effective exercise session and exercise programming
- be able to plan an exercise session
- be able to assist in instructing an exercise session
- be able to review an exercise session and exercise programme.

The fitness industry continues to expand in a rapid manner and so does the demand for fitness trainers and instructors. The increasing competition has meant that customers are also looking for quality instructors who are knowledgeable and professional in their approach. This chapter looks at the knowledge and technical skills which are required to become an effective instructor of physical activity and exercise.

Principles of safe and effective exercise sessions

Components of fitness

Fitness is a wide-reaching concept and the instructor needs to be able answer the following question: 'What does this client need to be fit for? or 'What daily functions do they need to able to perform?'

Any of the following answers may apply:

- lose a bit of weight to look and feel better
- improve my endurance so I can play with my children
- put on some muscle so I can do more tasks
- improve my golf
- stop feeling this back pain
- be more effective at work

- have more energy on a daily basis
- be able to run a marathon.

Fig 13.01 Playing with children

Each of these activities will involve a range of the components of fitness, which are the different aspects of fitness.

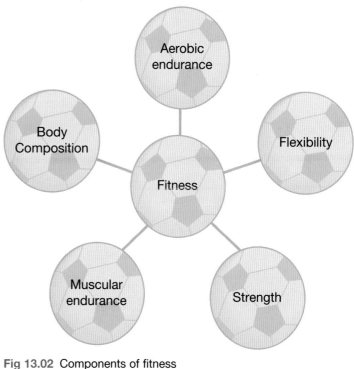

Fig 13.02 Components of fitness

Aerobic endurance

Also called cardiovascular fitness, this is the ability of the body to take in, transport and use oxygen. It depends upon the efficiency of the lungs in taking on oxygen, the heart in transporting oxygen and the working muscles in using oxygen. Examples of activities needing aerobic endurance fitness include long-distance running, swimming and cycling.

Flexibility

This is the range of movement available at a joint or group of joints. Examples of activities needing flexibility include dancing, gymnastics, running and most everyday functions.

Strength

This is the maximum force that a muscle or group of muscles can produce. Examples of activities needing strength include weight lifting and scrummaging in rugby.

Muscular endurance

This is the ability of a muscles or group of muscles to produce low-intensity forces repeatedly for long periods of time. Examples of activities needing muscular endurance include running, aerobics and carrying bags of shopping.

Body composition

This is the make-up of the body in terms of how much of the body weight is fat and how much is not fat, which we call lean body weight (LBW). Many people would like to lose excess body fat and/or gain

muscle bulk as they feel that this will make them look better.

Fig 13.03 Running

Adaptations to training

Our participant will start training because they are unhappy with their current position and they want to change something. They will be looking for 'training adaptations' or for their body's systems to adapt to the stimulus of training. Cardiovascular and resistance training will cause slightly different changes to occur.

Adaptations to aerobic endurance training

Lungs

- Respiratory muscles become stronger
- Lungs become more efficient
- Lungs are able to extract more oxygen from the air

LEARNER ACTIVITY Components of fitness

Using the following table decide, by giving a score from 1 to 10, the extent to which each component of fitness is required by the performer.

Component	Rugby union	Sprinting	Gymnastics
Aerobic endurance			
Flexibility			
Strength			
Muscular endurance			
Body composition			

Heart

- Heart muscle becomes larger
- Increase in the amount of blood pumped in each beat (stroke volume)
- Increase in amount of blood pumped per minute (cardiac output)
- Fall in resting heart rate

Blood and blood vessels

- Increase in number of capillaries (capillarisation)
- Increase in size of blood vessels
- Decrease blood pressure
- Increase in blood volume and red blood cell count

Muscles

- Increase in number and size of mitochondria (energy-producing parts of cells)
- Increases tolerance to lactic acid
- Increased aerobic enzyme production (muscles will become better at producing energy using oxygen)
- Muscular endurance increases

Bones

- Bone density increases (if activity is weight bearing, like running)

Adaptations to resistance training

- Increase in muscle size (hypertrophy)
- Increase in strength of ligaments and tendons
- Increase in bone density
- Improved nervous system function
- Decreased body fat
- Improved body composition (ratio of muscle to fat)
- Increased resting metabolic rate
- Improved posture
- Less risk of injury

Principles of training

When designing an effective training programme you must take into account a range of factors to make sure that the programme is effective. These are called the 'principles of training'. When designing a training programme these principles of training must always be applied.

Frequency: this means how often the participant will train. This may be three times a week.

Intensity: this means how hard the participant will be training. Intensity is usually stated in terms of what percentage of their maximum heart rate they will work at or by using the rate of perceived exertion.

Time: this means the length of each training session.

Type: this refers to the type of training they will be performing. For example, cardiovascular or resistance training.

Overload: this means applying intensity to the participant's training which is slightly higher than they are used to. The exact intensity of overload depends upon the individual's level of fitness and it can be produced by changing time, intensity or type.

Reversibility: this means that any adaptation which can be gained can also be lost if the training stops. It is commonly known as the 'use it or lose it' principle because if you don't use the fitness gain you will quickly lose it.

Specificity: this means that any adaptations that occur will be specific to the training that has been performed. When designing a training programme every exercise must be specific to the needs of the individual, whether they are a golfer, a runner or want to lose some fat. If a programme is not specific the individual will not get the gains they require.

The principles of training spell the acronym FITTORS:

- Frequency
- Intensity
- Time
- Type
- Overload
- Reversibility
- Specificity.

Health and safety for exercise sessions

The health and safety of the individuals we are instructing in exercise environments is of paramount importance to a gym instructor. This is to ensure that they work within the law of the country and ensure the safety of participants, themselves, colleagues, employers and employees. We are living in an

LEARNER ACTIVITY Principles of training

Match the definitions to the terms.

Term	Definition
Frequency	How long the session lasts
Intensity	Working a system harder than it is used to
Time	How many times a week they will train
Type	Fitness gains can be lost as well as achieved
Overload	Fitness gains will depend upon the type of training done
Reversibility	How hard a person works
Specificity	Description of the training performed

increasingly litigious society where there is always blame to be apportioned.

Health and Safety at Work Act 1974

This Act is the basis of the British health and safety legislation and it clearly sets out the duties of employers and employees in implementing safety for themselves and the public. The Act says that employers must do everything that is 'reasonably practical' to ensure safety. This includes:

- providing a safe working environment
- the safe use, storage and handling of dangerous substances
- production of a written health and safety policy
- maintaining a safe working environment, and appropriate health and safety equipment and facilities.

The Act also covers employees in the following ways:

- to take reasonable care of their own health and safety, and use the safety equipment provided
- to inform the employer of any potential risks to health
- to report any accidents and incidents.

Therefore we need to minimise this risk by doing several things before training our participant.

- Fill out a detailed medical questionnaire and lifestyle form. This is called a PAR-Q or

participation questionnaire and identifies any medical conditions and injuries a person may have; it helps us in our programme design.

- Fill out an informed consent form where the client is made to understand the risks of exercise and sign that they are willing to accept these risks.
- Check the training environment before every session to ensure all equipment is working properly and that there are no injury risks.
- Ensure the trainer is appropriately qualified and insured against personal injury.
- Check the client before every session to ensure they have no injuries and are dressed properly.
- Conduct a full warm-up and cool-down with the client.

Physical activity readiness questionnaire (PAR-Q)

There are a range of questionnaires available but they all ask similar questions. An example is shown on the opposite page.

The Exercise and Fitness Code of Ethics

The Exercise and Fitness Code of Ethics is a document produced by an organisation called the Register of Exercise Professionals (REPs). The code ensures that we deal with our clients in an appropriate manner and that we make their safety our priority. The code of ethics covers four main areas.

Physical activity readiness questionnaire (PAR-Q)

	Yes	No
1. Do you have a bone or joint problem which could be made worse by exercise?		
2. Has your doctor ever said that you have a heart condition?		
3. Do you experience chest pains on physical exertion?		
4. Do you experience light-headedness or dizziness on exertion?		
5. Do you experience shortness of breath on light exertion?		
6. Has your doctor ever said that you have a raised cholesterol level?		
7. Are you currently taking any prescription medication?		
8. Is there a history of coronary heart disease in your family?		
9. Do you smoke, and if so, how many?		
10. Do you drink more than 21 units of alcohol for a male, and 14 units for a female?		
11. Are you diabetic?		
12. Do you take physical activity less than three times a week?		
13. Are you pregnant?		
14. Are you asthmatic?		
15. Do you know of any other reason why you should not exercise?		

If you have answered yes to any questions please give more details_____

_____

_____

If you have answered yes to one or more questions you will have to consult with your doctor before taking part in a programme of physical exercise.

If you have answered no to all questions you are ready to start a suitable exercise programme.

I have read, understood and answered all questions honestly and confirm that I am willing to engage in a programme of exercise that has been prescribed to me.

Name _____   Signature _____

Trainer's name _____   Trainer's signature _____

Date _____

Principle 1 – Rights

- Promote the rights of every individual to participate in exercise, and recognise that people should be treated as individuals.
- Not condone or allow to go unchallenged any form of discrimination, nor to publicly criticise in demeaning descriptions of others.

Principle 2 – Relationships

- Develop a relationship with customers based on openness, honesty, mutual trust and respect.
- Ensure that physical contact is appropriate and necessary and is carried out with within the recommended guidelines and with the participant's full consent and approval.

Principle 3 – Personal responsibilities

- Demonstrate proper personal behaviour and conduct at all times.
- Project an image of health, cleanliness and functional efficiency, and display high standards in use of language, manner, punctuality, preparation and presentation.

Principle 4 – Professional standards

- Work towards attaining a high level of competence through qualifications and a commitment to ongoing training that ensures safe and correct practice, which will maximise benefits and minimise risks to the participant.
- Promote the execution of safe and effective practice and plan all sessions so that they meet the needs of participants and are progressive and appropriate.

(Adapted from *The Code of Ethical Practice* (2005), produced by the Register of Exercise Professionals)

Contraindications

A contraindication is any factor which will prevent a person from exercising or make an exercise unsafe. The aim of the PAR-Q and the initial consultation is to identify any potential contraindications and then decide what needs to be done about them to minimise their chances of being a risk.

Common contraindications to exercise are:

- blood pressure higher than 160/100
- body fat higher than 30 per cent for a male and 40 per cent for a female

- diabetes mellitus
- resting heart rate higher than 100
- lung disorders
- blood pressure medications and blood thinners
- coronary heart disease
- angina pectoris
- joint conditions.

There are many more contraindications and the rule to follow is that if you are in doubt then refer the participant to a doctor prior to training.

Warm-up

A warm-up is performed to make sure that the heart, lungs, muscles and joints are prepared for the activities which will follow. The warm-up also helps to activate the nervous system. A warm-up can be specific to the training session which is being performed or it can be more general.

A warm-up involves general body movements of the large muscle groups in a rhythmical, continuous manner. For example, you may use running or cycling to warm up the muscles for a weight training session. The limitation of this is that it does not prepare for the movements which are to follow and the neuromuscular pathways have not been activated. This would be particularly dangerous for an athlete.

A specific warm-up involves the rehearsal of the exercises which are to follow. This may be through replicating the movement with dynamic stretches or using low-intensity resistance training exercises to prepare for the heavier weights to follow.

A warm-up can be summarised as having three main objectives:

- to raise the heart rate
- to increase the temperature of the body
- to mobilise the major joints of the body.

By gradually raising the temperature it will give the heart time to increase stroke volume and thus cardiac output. As the warm-up continues we start to experience a widening of the blood vessels within the muscles (vasodilation). The capillary beds within the muscles will open up and allow more oxygen and nutrients to flow through the muscles. Also, the warm-up should involve some of the movements that the person will perform in their main session. This gives the warm-up 'specificity' and acts as a rehearsal for the exercises to come.

A typical warm-up will involve the following components:

- a pulse raiser
- joint mobility
- dynamic stretching for muscles.

The **pulse raiser** involves rhythmical movements of the large muscle groups in a continuous manner. This would involve CV-type activity such as running, rowing or cycling. The pulse raiser should gradually increase in intensity as time goes on. A pulse raiser would typically last for around five minutes but may go on for ten minutes. At the end of the warm-up the heart rate should be just below the rate that will be achieved during the main session. A person who is fitter is able to warm up more quickly as their body is used to it, while an unfit person will take longer and needs to warm up more gradually.

A warm-up for a run may involve one minute walking, one minute brisk walking, one minute jogging, one minute running and then one minute fast running. An advanced performer could progress to running very quickly.

Joint mobility is used to enable the joints to become lubricated by releasing more synovial fluid on to the joints and then warming it up so it becomes more efficient. This means moving joints through their full range of movement. The movements will start off through a small range and slowly move through a larger range until the full range of movement is achieved. The joints that need to be mobilised are shoulders, elbows, spine, hips, knees and ankles. If a trainer is clever they can use the pulse-raising movements to also mobilise the joints. For example, rowing will have the effect of raising the pulse and mobilising all the joints.

Dynamic stretching is a relatively recent introduction but is very important for the specific preparation of the muscles for the movements which are due to follow.

> **definition**
>
> Dynamic stretching: **stretching the muscles through their full range of movement in a controlled manner.**

Static stretching, where a muscle is stretched and held, has been proved to be of limited value in a warm-up. The reasons being that static stretching causes a fall in heart rate and tends to relax the muscles. It can also act to desensitise the muscle spindles which protect the muscle against injury. Static stretching has a role to play in a warm-up because a short, tight muscle may prevent the participant from performing some of the exercises in their main session with perfect technique. For example, tight hamstrings make squatting and bent-over rows very difficult to perform well.

The benefits of dynamic stretching are that it:

- keeps the heart rate raised
- stretches muscles specifically through the range of movements they will be doing
- activates the nervous system and improves synchronisation between the nerves and muscles.

To perform dynamic stretching you need to copy the movements in the session you will perform. These movements are repeated in a steady and controlled fashion. In performing a set of ten repetitions you slowly speed up the movement as the set progresses. Figures 13.04, 13.05 and 13.06 show dynamic stretches.

Fig 13.04 Squat and press

Fig 13.05 Rear lunge with arm swing

Fig 13.06 Chest stretch

Main component

Content

The content of the main component can vary and is specific to the needs of the client. It may involve some of the following:

- CV training
- resistance training
- aerobics
- mixture of CV training and resistance training.

The main component will last around 40 minutes dependent on the length of the warm-up and main session (a training session generally will last an hour).

Resistance training

The participant should aim for around eight to ten exercises covering all muscle groups at least once. The larger muscle groups may be worked more than once. The design of a resistance training programme is covered later in this chapter.

Aerobic training

An aerobic session may last between 20 and 60 minutes, although it is agreed that 35 minutes is a good target to aim for. Designing aerobic training programmes is also covered later in this chapter.

Methods of monitoring exertion

When you are training aerobically it is important that the intensity worked at is closely monitored. This can be done by a number of methods:

- heart rate training zones
- rate of perceived exertion
- Karvonen formula.

Heart rate training zones: the intensity of exercise can be monitored by expressing it as a percentage of maximum heart rate. Your maximum heart rate is the maximum number of times your heart could beat. To find this out you would have to work to your maximum intensity which for most people would clearly be unsafe. Therefore, we estimate the maximum heart rate by using the following formula:

Maximum heart rate = 220 − age

For a 20 year old their maximum heart rate would be 220 − 20 = 200 bpm.

This is clearly a theoretical maximum heart rate because it is unlikely that every 20 year old in the country would have the same maximum heart rate. In reality there will be a massive variation but it can be useful as a guideline.

To work out the heart rate training zone we take percentages of heart rate maximum. If we work between 60 and 90 per cent we would be working in the aerobic training zone, where the exercise we are performing is effective in improving aerobic fitness without being dangerous. It is still a wide range for a heart rate to be within, so we change the zone depending upon the fitness level of the participant.

Rate of perceived exertion (RPE): this was developed by Gunnar Borg and is a scale which can be used by the participant to rate how hard they feel they are working between two extremes. Rather than monitoring heart rate the participant is introduced to

Effective zones for different groups as % of maximum heart rate (MHR)

Beginners	60–70% of MHR
Intermediate	70–80% of MHR
Advanced	80–90% of MHR

the scale and then asked during the aerobic session where they feel they are on the scale of 1–15 (see Table 13.01).

Table 13.01 Borg's 15-point scale

1	Rest
2	Extremely light
3	
4	Very light
5	
6	Light
7	
8	Somewhat hard
9	
10	Hard
11	
12	Very hard
13	
14	Very, very hard
15	Exhaustion

Borg's scale has been modified to a ten-point scale (see Table 13.02) because some participant's have found working between 1 and 15 difficult.

To achieve aerobic fitness gains the participant needs to be working around 12 to 15 on the 15-point scale and around 6 to 7 on the modified scale.

Karvonen formula: this is a more advanced way of working out a heart rate training zone. To find out the participant's heart rate training zone you need to know the following information first:

- age
- resting heart rate
- required exercise intensity (percentage of maximum intensity).

Age predicted maximum heart rate (APMHR) = 220 – age

Table 13.02 Borg's modified RPE scale

1	Extremely light
2	Very light
3	Moderate
4	
5	Somewhat hard
6	
7	Hard
8	Very hard
9	Extremely hard
10	Maximal exertion

Heart rate reserve (HRR) = APMHR – resting heart rate (RHR)
Target heart rate (THR) = HRR × exercise intensity + RHR

A participant, 20 years old, has a resting heart rate of 60 and wants to work at 70 to 80 per cent of their maximum intensity. They would have the following heart rate training zone:

APMHR = 220 – 20 = 200 bpm

HRR = 200 – 60 = 140

Target heart rate reserve = 140 × 0.70 + 60 = 158 bpm
Target heart rate reserve = 140 × 0.80 + 60 = 172 bpm

We get a training zone of between 158 and 172 bpm for this participant.

Cool-down

A cool-down is performed to return the body to its pre-exercise state. If you consider that once you have finished training your heart rate is still high and the blood is still being pumped to your working muscles you will need to slowly bring the heart rate back to normal.

The cool-down has four main objectives:

- to return the heart to normal
- to get rid of any waste products built up during exercise
- to return muscles to their original pre-exercise length
- to prevent venous pooling.

The aim of the cool-down is opposite to the aim of the warm-up in that the pulse will lower slowly and waste products such as carbon dioxide and lactic acid are washed out of the muscles. Also, as the muscles work during the main session they continually shorten to produce force and they end up in a shortened position. Therefore, they need to be stretched out so they do not remain shortened. Also, as the heart pumps blood around the body, circulation is assisted by the action of skeletal muscles. The skeletal muscles act as a 'muscle pump' to help return the blood to the heart against gravity. If the participant stops suddenly the heart will keep pumping blood to the legs, but because the muscle pump has stopped the blood will pool in the legs. This causes the participant to become light-headed and they may pass out.

The cool-down consists of the following activities:

- lower the heart rate
- maintenance stretching on muscles worked
- developmental stretching on short muscles.

Lowering the heart rate

To lower the heart rate you need to do the reverse of the pulse raiser. First, choose a CV-type exercise involving rhythmical movements and the large muscle groups. This time the intensity starts high and slowly drops to cause a drop in heart rate. This part should last around five minutes and an exercise bike is a good choice because it enables the client to sit down and relax as well. The gradual lowering of the intensity allows the muscle pump to work and avoid venous pooling. You want to ensure the pulse rate is around 100 to 110 bpm at the end of the pulse lowerer.

Stretching

Two types of stretching can be used in the cool-down: maintenance and developmental. A maintenance stretch is used to return the muscles worked to their pre-exercise state. During training they will be continuously shortened and they need to be stretched out to prevent shortening. Stretching will also help eliminate waste products from the muscles and also prevent soreness the next day. A maintenance stretch is one where the muscle is stretched to the point of discomfort and then is held for around ten seconds or until the muscle relaxes and the stretch goes off. All

muscles worked in the main session will need at least a maintenance stretch.

Developmental stretching is used on muscles which have become short and tight. They may be short because they have been overtrained or due to the positions adopted on a daily basis. If a person is sat down all day, either in front of a computer or driving, they may develop shortened pectorals, hamstrings, hip flexors and adductors.

Developmental stretching involves stretching a muscle and then holding it for around ten seconds until it relaxes. Once it has relaxed the stretch is increased and held for ten seconds; this is repeated three times.

LEARNER ACTIVITY
Possible questions

In your own words write down what you would say to a participant who asked the following questions.

- Why do I need to warm up?
- Can I just cool down when I have a shower?
- Does it matter how hard I work during my training session?
- How can I tell if I am working hard enough?

Designing and planning an exercise programme

To ensure that participants are happy with their progress and will keep training it is important that the trainer is able to design exercise programmes and session plans which are relevant to the specific needs of the participant. This section looks at the process you need to go through in order to write an effective training session for the participant.

Stage 1 – Gathering information

To enable the trainer to design a specific exercise programme you need to carry out a comprehensive initial consultation. This will involve the participant filling out a questionnaire about their health, medical conditions, goals and lifestyle. This is followed up by a face-to-face discussion to find out more information about the participant. The trainer will be building up

Key learning points

Cardiovascular fitness (CV) is the ability of the body to take in, transport and use oxygen.

Flexibility is the range of movement available at a joint or group of joints.

Speed is the rate at which we can move our limbs or our body.

Strength is the maximum force that a muscle or group of muscles can produce.

Muscular endurance is the ability of a muscle or group of muscles to produce low-intensity forces repeatedly for long periods of time.

Power is the production of strength at speed.

Frequency is how often the participant will train. This may be three times a week.

Intensity means how hard the participant will be training.

Time is the length of each training session.

Type refers to the type of training they will be performing.

Overload means applying intensity to the participant's training which is slightly higher than they are used to.

Reversibility means that any adaptation that can be gained can also be lost if the training stops.

Specificity means that any adaptations that occur will be specific to the training that has been performed.

A typical warm-up will involve the following components:

- a pulse raiser
- joint mobility
- dynamic stretching for muscles.

The cool-down consists of the following activities:

- lowering the heart rate
- maintenance stretching on muscles worked
- developmental stretching on short muscles.

a detailed picture of this participant and their life so that the exercises they choose and the programme they design will have the best chance of succeeding.

Factors to consider

When the trainer sits down to design the programme they need to consider a range of factors to ensure that the programme is appropriate and that it will benefit the participant rather than harm them. The trainer will need to consider the following.

- PAR-Q responses – have any contraindications to exercise been identified?
- Medical history – do they have any conditions which may affect the training programme and choice of exercises?
- Current and previous exercise history – this will give an idea about the current fitness level of the client.
- Barriers to exercise – do they have constraints such as time, cost, family responsibilities or work commitments?
- Motives and goals – what is the participant aiming to achieve and what is their timescale?
- Occupation – hours worked and whether work is manual or office-based.
- Activity levels – amount of movement they do on a daily basis.

- Leisure time activities – whether these are active or inactive.
- Diet – what, how much and when they eat.
- Stress levels – either through work or their home life, and how they deal with it.
- Alcohol intake – how much they consume and how often.
- Smoking – whether they are a smoker or ex-smoker and the amount they smoke.
- Time available – the client needs to fit the training into their schedule and the trainer needs to be realistic when planning the programme.

LEARNER ACTIVITY
PAR-Q questionnaire

- In pairs using a PAR-Q run a consultation with a partner. First, ask the questions on the PAR-Q and then prepare a series of other topics that you may want to find information about.
- Identify five actions you will recommend to the participant.

Client groups

Clients are the central focus of the fitness industry and it is essential that we understand the individual needs and goals of each one. Each person needs to be treated as an individual to ensure they remain on their training programme. Clients will come from a range of backgrounds, ages, fitness levels, shapes and sizes. You may see the following groups of people as clients:

- varied ability levels – beginners, intermediates, advanced
- varied fitness levels – low, moderate or high
- elderly
- juniors
- athletes
- people with specific goals, such as running a marathon or weight loss
- pregnant women
- people with medical conditions such as asthma or diabetes.

When you meet a new client it is important that you consider what this person is feeling and thinking. You need to place yourself in their shoes to consider what it is they need. We call this 'walking a mile in their shoes'.

Fig 13.07 A young gymnast

Activity selection

When we have gathered information about the participant we select an appropriate intervention in terms of the exercises we choose. You need to consider the following factors.

- Likes and dislikes – What is the participant comfortable doing? Why do they not like certain exercises?
- Accessibility – Where can they get to for their training? This may be physical or limited by cost.
- Culture – Are they limited by their culture in terms of expected roles and responsibilities, and also dress codes?
- Equipment available – Are activities limited by the venue and what it has to offer? You may be training in a gym or maybe at the client's home or in a park.

LEARNER ACTIVITY
Training activities
Prepare a list of activities that you could perform if you were training your participant in the park or at their home.

Stage 2 – Establishing objectives

To ensure the success of the programme it needs to be specific to the outcome a client wants. Therefore, it is important to find out exactly what this is. If you ask them what they want to achieve they will say that they want to get fit. You need to question them further and find out what this means to them. You may need to make suggestions as they may not know themselves. Their objectives could be any of the following:

- CV fitness
- flexibility
- weight loss
- improved health
- muscular strength
- muscular size
- muscle tone
- power.

Once you have established the objectives it is time to plan the programme.

Stage 3 – Planning the programme

Programme design is an area of controversy, and different trainers have different ideas about what is right and wrong. Usually the programme will use the structure shown in the box below and in Table 13.03.

The training programme will usually last for one hour. The length of each component will depend upon the objectives of the client and the importance they place on each.

Programme design rules

When designing the programme you need to follow rules and then check that you have done so.

Rule 1: Work muscles in pairs to keep them balanced. All muscles work in pairs and if they are not worked as pairs the body can become unbalanced. This means that joints will move out of their correct place, causing a change in posture and possibly pain. It also increases the chances of injury. The body works as a complete unit and it must be trained in this way too. Many gym programmes focus on a few muscle groups – usually the chest, arms and abdominals – as these are seen to make a person more attractive.

The main pairs of muscles are:

- pectorals and trapezius
- latissimus dorsi and deltoids
- biceps and triceps
- abdominals and erector spinae
- quadriceps and hamstrings.

A check must be made to ensure that all muscle pairs have been worked equally.

Rule 2: Large muscle groups should be trained first. If you are training several muscles in one session it is

---

Programme structure

Warm-up	Raise pulse Mobilise joints Dynamic stretches	5–10 minutes
Resistance component	6–10 free weight or resistance machine exercises	30–45 minutes
CV component	Walking, running, cycling or rowing	20–60 minutes
Abdominal training	Abdominals and lower back	5 minutes
Cool-down	Lower the pulse Developmental stretches Maintenance stretches	5–15 minutes

---

Table 13.03 Meeting the objectives

Objective	Strength	Muscle size	Endurance	CV
Repetitions or duration	1–5	6–12	12–20	20 mins+
Recovery period	3–5 mins	1–2 mins	30–60 secs	N/A
Sets per exercise	2–6	3–6	2–3	1
Frequency per week	1–2 on each muscle group	1–2 on each muscle group	2–3 on each muscle group	3 session a week

(Adapted from Baechle and Earle, 2000)

important that the large muscle groups are trained first. The large muscles are the gluteus maximus, quadriceps and hamstrings, pectorals, latissimus dorsi and trapezius.

These muscles need to be worked first because they require the most effort to work and are best exercised when the client is feeling fresh. Second, if the smaller muscles become tired early on in the session it will be difficult to work the large muscles as hard.

Rule 3: Do the difficult exercises first. Each exercise will have a difficulty rating and this depends upon two main issues: how many joints are moving and how much balance is needed. An exercise where only one joint moves can be seen as simple, while an exercise with two or more joints moving will be complex. Also, the more balance that is needed the more difficult an exercise becomes. The most difficult exercises need the most skill and should be done early on in the exercise session.

Rule 4: Work the abdominals and lower back at the end of the session. The abdominals and lower back are called the core muscles and these keep the body's posture correct. If they are tired out early on it increases the risk of the spine becoming injured. They should be exercised after the resistance and CV work have been done.

Following these rules will make sure that the programme is performed in a safe and effective way.

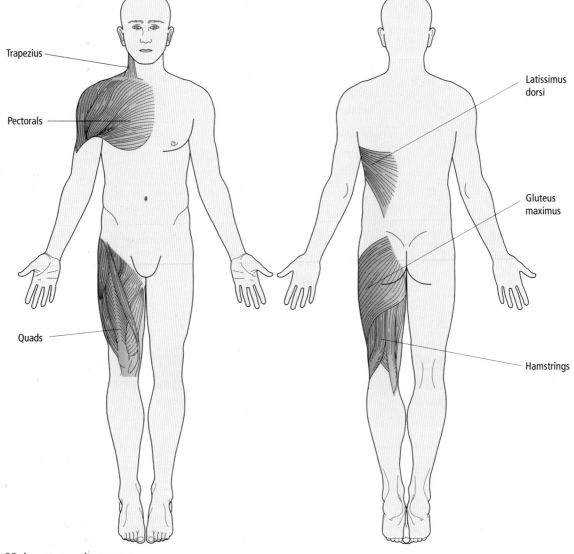

Fig 13.08 Large muscle groups

Considerations for aerobic training

It is important to consider that not everyone will want to go to a gym to improve their fitness. You will need to be flexible in finding ways to make them more active in their daily lives. The Health Education Authority (HEA) has offered guidelines concerning health and fitness.

To improve cardiovascular fitness you need to train three times a week for between 20 and 60 minutes at 60 to 90 per cent of your maximum heart rate – jogging, running, swimming, cycling or rowing.

To improve health you need to be involved in an activity which makes you slightly warmer and slightly out of breath for 30 minutes between five and seven times a week.

This can involve activities such as brisk walking, gardening, mowing the lawn or recreational swimming. Also you can look at extra ways to increase activity levels, such as walking rather than taking the car, taking the stairs instead of the lift, getting off the bus at an earlier stop or parking the car in the furthest away parking spot!

Leading an exercise session

Preparation of the session

When you take a participant through their exercise programme you need to follow a clear structure to ensure the training session is safe and that good customer care is applied.

Before the session starts you need to check the equipment and the environment:

- availability of equipment
- equipment is in working order
- all cables are strong
- floor is clear of equipment and cables
- temperature
- ventilation.

Questions and explanations

The session will start when you meet the participant. At this point you need to explain some safety issues and procedures. The following questions are appropriate to screen the participant prior to the session.

Key learning points

There are a range of factors which will need to be considered when designing an exercise programme, including: medical history, exercise history, barriers, motives and goals, occupation, activity levels, leisure time activities, diet, stress levels, alcohol intake, smoking, time available, current and previous training history.

An exercise programme should have the following components:

- warm-up
- resistance component
- CV component
- abdominal training
- cool-down.

When designing an exercise programme you need to follow four rules.

Rule 1: Work muscles in pairs to keep muscles balanced.

Rule 2: Large muscle groups should be trained first.

Rule 3: Do the difficult exercises first.

Rule 4: Work the abdominals and lower back at the end of the session.

According to the HEA recommendations, to improve cardiovascular fitness you need to train three times a week for between 20 and 60 minutes at 60 to 90 per cent of your maximum heart rate. To improve health you need to be involved in an activity which makes you slightly warmer and slightly out of breath for 30 minutes between five and seven times a week.

- Have you any illnesses or injuries I need to be aware of?
- Have you eaten today?
- Is your clothing appropriate and have you taken off your jewellery?

Then you need to explain some procedures:

- fire exits and fire drill
- first-aid kit, first aider and nearest telephone
- position of water.

Finally explain:

- the training programme and its demands
- the aims and objectives of the session
- the process of instruction.

Delivery of the session

The aim of the exercise session is to get the participant working for as much time as possible in a safe and effective manner. It is important that the participant is supported and pushed to work as hard as they can within their limits.

The instructor will perform the following roles.

Communicate effectively

It is important that the client is able to understand you and respond in the way you would like them to. We communicate mainly through the words we use and also how we deliver these words and the body language we use. It is good practice to listen to your client and assess their level of knowledge before deciding how you will deliver your instructions. If a person is new to the gym you should keep things simple and use less technical language. The more experienced client will be able to communicate using more technical language.

Give instructions

An instruction is providing information on how to perform a technique. When providing instructions you must say what you want the client to do rather than what not to do. If you use the word 'don't' as in 'don't lock your knees', it increases the chances that they will actually do it!

Demonstrate

The instructor needs to give demonstrations to show the participant how to perform the technique. Once a demonstration has been give the instructor can explain the technique to the client and then let them practise to get the feel of the movement.

Provide motivation

The reason most people do not achieve the results they want is because their motivation is too low. They give up when the going gets tough. You will motivate them with what you say, how you say it and by using positive body language. This will push them to work as hard as they can within the limits of their fitness.

Fig 13.10 Trainer and participant

Observe and correct techniques

The instructor needs to observe the client's technique from a variety of positions by moving around the client. Once they have observed for a short period, feedback needs to be given about what they are doing right and then what parts need to be corrected.

Modify exercises

If an exercise is too easy or too hard it can be modified in a variety of ways: changing the length of the lever used, getting them to stand up and resist the force of gravity, change the range of movement or the speed of movement (tempo).

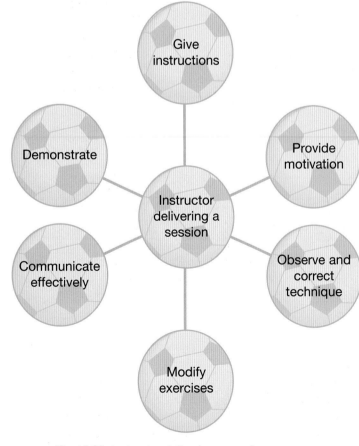

Fig 13.09 Instructor delivering a session

Key learning points

Before a session starts you need to check the environment, the client and tell them about the safety procedures.

During the session you need to be supporting the client in the following way:

- communicate effectively
- give instructions
- demonstrate
- provide motivation
- observe and correct
- respond to the client's needs.

At the end of the session ask your client for feedback about the session.

End of session

Once the session is finished you have two roles to perform.

- **Gain feedback**: it is important to ask the participant how they felt the session went and what they liked or did not like. Also, ask about the intensity of the session – whether it was too easy or too hard. This is vital when you reflect on your work and assess whether there are any changes that need to be made for next time to make your session even more effective.
- **Put equipment away and check for damage**: it is important to tidy up your equipment and leave the environment in a safe and acceptable state for the next person. Also, if any damage has occurred, it must be reported so that repairs can be made.

Reviewing an exercise session

The purpose of reviewing sessions

To improve as a trainer and a person it is vital to regularly review your performance and identify any changes that need to be made. We can receive feedback from a range of sources and it is all useful.

Feedback is information about performance. It is neither good nor bad, it is just information. It allows us to improve our performance in the following ways.

- **Track progression:** we can assess whether our training is having the desired effect on the participant. This can be done through fitness testing or from their own perspective.
- **Adapt sessions:** if we are not achieving our aim or an exercise has had a negative response we can adapt the programme to achieve a different response.
- **Improve own performance:** we need to identify any weaknesses we may have as then we can improve how we work with our participants. Our strengths will always work for us but we will only improve if we address our weaknesses.

Codes of practice

We must always be sure that what we do is ethical. Reflecting on how we act, talk and work with our clients will ensure we stay within accepted codes of behaviour.

Continued professional development

For a trainer to continue to improve their skills they need to be continually attending conferences and taking courses. This development should work on improving our weaknesses. It is also a requirement of the Register of Exercise Professionals (REPs) that each trainer who is a member of the Register must achieve 24 points for training per year.

Conducting a review

The ideal time to conduct a review is as soon as you can after a session while the issues are still fresh in your own mind and your participant's. You may even be able to ask the participant some questions during the cool-down period, as the work is less intense and they will be starting to relax. You need to ask them specific questions regarding the session and its outcomes.

You could use a form like the one shown overleaf and cover the following detail.

Self-evaluation

The client may not pick up things you see or feel yourself so you must ask yourself the same questions and answer them in an honest manner. Particularly, you must assess yourself in terms of the safety of the session and then whether it was effective. Did it really meet the aims that you have set for your session?

The benefits of self-evaluation are as follows.

- You can plan future sessions to ensure they are enjoyable and effective.
- Good evaluation is likely to increase the chances of the client sticking to their training programme.
- The client will stay interested and motivated.
- The client will keep progressing.
- You are able to identify any training needs you may have.
- You can set yourself goals for personal development and any training needs you may have.

Peer evaluation

As part of your support group you may work with a colleague and observe each other's training sessions. This may give a third perspective on the training and highlight issues you would not have considered yourself.

Modifying an exercise programme

There are many ways to change a participant's training programme to ensure they continue to achieve overload and keep interested and motivated:

- change a training principle
- frequency – increase the number of times they train a week
- intensity – make the programme harder by increasing speeds or resistance
- time – make each session longer

- type – change the training they do from aerobic to resistance training.

The body is expert at adapting and will only gain benefit from an exercise for a limited period. Therefore, if we change an exercise we gain a new stimulus for the body to adapt to. So change from resistance machines to free weights or cable exercises and a change will occur.

You can also give the participant a new target each week to continue to push them – cycle 5 km in under ten minutes or run 5 km in 25 minutes.

SMART targets

Regular evaluation can lead to improvements in performance. If you set yourself specific goals then you can monitor your actual performance. Achieving goals relies on effective goal setting using the SMART principle. This stands for:

- **S**pecific
- **M**easurable
- **A**chievable
- **R**ealistic
- **T**ime-constrained.

As you continue to evaluate yourself and improve your training skills, communication skills and motivation skills, you will see yourself become a more professional and effective trainer.

Review form

1. Did you think the programme was effective in meeting your aims?

2. What did you enjoy and not enjoy about the training session?

3. To what extent did you feel safe?

4. Could the session be improved in any way?

Review questions

1. Define five components of fitness and give an example of an activity for each one.
2. Give three adaptations for each of the following systems of the body: respiratory (lungs), cardiovascular (heart and blood vessels) and muscular.
3. Give four adaptations to regular resistance training.
4. What is the Health and Safety at Work Act and what general areas does it cover?
5. What is a contraindication and list five of them.
6. What are the three objectives of a warm-up?
7. Describe the differences between static and dynamic stretches.
8. Give three methods of monitoring intensity and briefly describe each one.
9. What activities should be performed in a cool-down?
10. How can the following factors impact upon the design of a training programme: medical history, current exercise level, occupation and stress levels?
11. Explain the four main rules of programme design.
12. Explain five roles an instructor will perform during a training session.
13. Why is it vital to review your performance after every training session?
14. Give two ways you could modify a participant's training session.

References

Baechle, T. and Earle, R. (2000) *Essentials of Strength Training and Conditioning*, Human Kinetics.

Dalgleish, J. and Dollery, S. (2001) *The Health and Fitness Handbook*, Longman.

Stafford-Brown J., Rea, S., Janaway, L. and Manley, C. (2006) *BTEC First Sport*, Hodder Arnold.

Exercise for specific groups

Goals

By the end of this chapter you should:
- know about the provision of exercise for specific groups
- understand the benefits of exercise for different specific groups
- know about exercise referral schemes
- be able to plan and deliver an exercise session for a specific group.

In today's society people are living longer and experiencing an increase in the prevalence of medical diseases and disorders. It is generally understood that there is no medical condition that cannot benefit from some form of physical exercise or activity. The government is well aware of this link and is assigning money to the management of medical conditions through the establishment of exercise referral schemes and schemes through the National Health Service.

For fitness trainers, it is becoming increasingly rare to find people who are completely free of all medical conditions or injuries. Thus, it is important to have an appreciation of these medical conditions, enabling you to discuss the condition and then deal with the person in a safe and effective manner.

The provision of exercise for specific groups

When we discuss specific groups we need to have something to compare them with to make them specific. We have two clear types of specific group:

- those who are in a specific stage in life
- those who have medical conditions.

The special groups examined are:

- older people
- children
- pre- and post-natal women
- disabled people
- obese people
- heart disease such as high blood pressure and coronary heart disease
- pulmonary disorders such as asthma
- diabetics
- arthritis
- osteoporosis.

Provision for sport in Britain is a joint effort between sectors of provision:

- private – individuals investing their own money in sport to make a profit
- public – government or local authority investment in sport to provide a low-cost service
- voluntary – like-minded individuals working together to create opportunities for each other.

With regard to special groups, as listed above, the majority of the provision comes from the public sector. This is due to the motives of each provider. The private sector is mainly motivated by investing money to make a return as profit. The voluntary sector involves volunteers giving their time to create opportunities to play competitive sport.

The public sector invests its money to improve the quality of life of its taxpayers and to benefit society in general. This includes promoting the health and well-being of each person. Thus, the aims of the public sector fit in with the aims of the schemes provided. That is not to say that the private sector will not be involved, rather that it will be less involved. All sports facilities are covered by the law of the land, which stipulates that all buildings must be adapted to the needs of disabled people and be sensitive to their requirements.

Meeting the needs of people is done through a range of measures:

- appropriate facilities
- provision of classes and activities for different groups

- appropriate equipment or adaptations to equipment for specific groups.

LEARNER ACTIVITY Meeting user needs

In groups of three or four visit a sports or leisure centre and find out the following information.

- Which sector of provision does it fall into?
- What activities has it targeted at each specific group (get hold of a programme of classes and activities)?
- How have the facilities been modified to cater for the needs of each group (you can do this by looking around the facilities and questioning)?

When you look at the programme of classes and activities look out for activities with special names as they are rarely as simple as 'Exercise class for 50+'. The class list may have a guide which describes what each class entails and who the target market may be. If in doubt ask a member of staff.

Exercise referral schemes

The aim of an exercise referral scheme is to provide an alternative to treating a patient by giving them a prescription for medication. The belief is that exercise has a role to play in managing medical conditions and improving health. Therefore, rather than being given a prescription for medicine the doctor will give them a prescription for exercise in the form of a referral to a sports centre. The patient will take the prescription along and be dealt with by the fitness trainer who is qualified to work with such individuals.

All schemes will have variations but follow the same basic format. A scheme lasts for ten to twelve weeks and takes place either in groups or on an individual basis. Each patient has to have written referral from their GP and will have to pay a nominal fee. The fee is usually around £1 a week or £12 for the full course. This is to make the programme available to all members of society and promote equality. The nominal fee also help to keep the person on the exercise programme as they have made a financial commitment. The programme starts with an initial assessment by the qualified trainer, who will then design a specific training programme for the patient. There will be follow-up reassessments at the mid- and end-points. Once the programme is complete the patient may be prescribed another 12

weeks of training on the programme or encouraged to keep themselves active and join the gym. This is at the discretion of all the health professionals involved.

There can be regional variations in the exercise referral schemes provided, due to the staffing and facilities available. However, they will all be working towards achieving the same outcomes. A set of guidelines has been developed to ensure that the schemes maintain some common features in their operation. In 2001 the government developed guidelines called the National Quality Assurance Framework (NQAF) to allow local authorities to base their schemes on common criteria.

All exercise referral schemes are based on a development model which has five distinct stages.

1 Selection of the patient by the GP
2 Physical assessment of the patient and appropriate intervention applied
3 Long-term support to help the patient stay physically active
4 Evaluation of the patient experience and health outcome
5 Return into the community.

Stage 1: Selection of the patient by the GP – there are seven guidelines which are given to the individual GP and nurses to consider when they are making their decision to refer a patient. The seven guidelines are as follows:

- The scheme should cater for adults (over the age of 16) except in exceptional situations. The scheme also needs to address issues of equality and social inclusion. This means it needs to be cheap enough to be affordable by all groups in society.
- The scheme should be aimed at people who are sedentary. This means they are doing less than 30 minutes of moderate-intensity activity per week. Moderate intensity is activity which makes you slightly out of breath and slightly sweaty.
- Serious medical conditions, such as coronary heart disease (CHD) and mental health problems, should have clear measures for them to be identified.
- The scheme needs to develop strategies to promote the uptake of provision by all groups – for example, laying on transport for the elderly and isolated groups, and reduced costs for the unemployed and old age pensioners.
- The scheme must ensure that the needs of high-risk patients are catered for by staff with the appropriate qualifications and experience.

- The scheme must employ a model of behaviour change to take a person through the stages of change. When a person starts exercising they may move through five distinct stages. The stages are contemplation (thinking about exercise), preparation (putting in place preparations to become active), and action (actually made the change to become active), maintenance (keeping up their current activity) and relapse (they have stopped exercising).
- The exercise referral scheme should reflect the values of the health improvement programme of the care trust in that area.

Stage 2: Assessment of the patient and intervention applied – all schemes should consider the following.

- For each patient there must be a written activity plan which clearly outlines the aim of the referral, details of the medical condition and how it is being managed (medication) and the effect these will have on the patient's training and daily activity.
- The patient must give written consent to the trainer that they agree to undertake an assessment and a programme of exercise.
- The physical assessment must be specific to the needs of that patient and the tests selected appropriately.
- A copy of the exercise plan devised by the trainer should be sent to the GP to be placed in the patient's file.
- The trainer must inform the patient how the scheme operates and what is expected of them.
- The trainer must make sure that a copy of the GP referral form, the patient's consent form and their programme of activity are filed in a secure and confidential place. They also must be available for inspection by the health trust.
- The content of the exercise programme must be specific to the individual needs of the patient.
- The trainer must ensure that the patient is involved in the decision-making process to help them develop a healthy lifestyle.
- The trainer needs to closely monitor the attendance of the patient and investigate the situation if they do not train for two weeks. If a patient does not train for three weeks a letter needs to be sent to the GP, and likewise if the patient drops out of the exercise referral scheme. This is because the patient's medication and care may have changed when they are exercising and they may be in danger if it is not adjusted.
- An assessment needs to be conducted at the mid-point of the scheme to monitor the patient's progress.

- An assessment needs to be done at the end of the scheme to assess the outcomes.
- Once the programme is complete, the GP and the exercise professional will consult to decide upon the next step. The choices are to prescribe another programme of exercise or to return the patient to the community.

Stage 3: Long term support to help the patient stay physically active

- The patient is encouraged to keep a record of their progress through the use of a diary or by setting goals.

Stage 4: Evaluation of the patient by the GP

- Once the 12-week programme is complete the patient will take part in an evaluation to assess the outcomes of the programme.

Stage 5: Return into the community

- The patient can either continue on the scheme or they can return to finding a way to exercise in the wider community.

LEARNER ACTIVITY Exercise referral scheme

In groups of two prepare a list of benefits and drawbacks for the trainer of working within an exercise referral scheme. Think beyond any financial gains or losses.

Legal considerations

When dealing with specific groups we are faced with people who are at greater risk than the general public. Their conditions may be unstable and their symptoms may set in quickly. Therefore, we have to be clear about who is responsible for the well-being of the patient while they are training.

All people involved in the network of care for the patient have a legal responsibility. When we train any client we owe them 'a duty of care', which means we must do everything reasonably possible to keep them safe. The same applies for a patient with a specific need and there will be more people involved in the network who owe a duty of care. This will include the GP who referred them and other people supporting them. When they are training with the trainer it is the trainer's full responsibility that they are kept safe. This is why it is imperative to keep detailed records of everything that is done with each patient in case something does happen. You may need to show that you were not negligent in any of your dealings with the patient to prevent yourself being sued.

Benefits of exercise and appropriate forms of exercise

You will look at each specific group in the following manner:

- a brief summary of the condition and the factors you will need to consider
- any associated risks with the group
- the benefits of exercise for the group
- recommendations of exercise for the group.

Prior to exercise, factors such as screening participants, completion of informed consent forms and planning of the exercise sessions should be considered. During the delivery of each session, you should ensure the participant is appropriately warmed up, appropriate motivation and feedback is given during the session, and that the session ends with an appropriate cool-down.

You should aim to carry out a review process at the end of each session so that you can determine your strengths and areas for improvement. This is covered in Chapter 14: Instructing physical activity and exercise. If you are not going to or have not already studied this chapter, ensure that you read the sections on designing, planning and reviewing an exercise programme.

LEARNER ACTIVITY Working with special groups

In groups of four consider the following questions.

- What do you think are the benefits of working with special groups?
- What problems may you face when working with special groups?
- What do you think you need before you would be ready to work with special groups?

Older adults

Up to the age of 35 the structures of our body such as muscle and bone are building up. After this age we start to lose muscle and bone, and the tendons and ligaments become weaker. The loss of bone is called osteopenia and the loss of muscle is called sarcopenia. In particular the ageing adult will lose their type 2 muscle fibres and as a result strength will be decreased.

The amount of muscle we have affects the speed of our metabolism. Metabolism is the number of calories we use on a daily basis and if it is lowered we are more likely to lay down fat. Unless we keep active we will lose around 1 lb of muscle a year and lay down around 2 lbs of fat a year. This results in a creeping fat gain over time. The main effects of ageing are:

- loss of muscle mass
- loss of bone density
- gain in body fat
- loss of muscular strength
- loss of muscular endurance
- decline in cardiovascular fitness
- lower ability to maintain balance
- changes in posture.

All these effects of ageing can be reversed through a programme of resistance training with some cardiovascular work. In particular, resistance training is very important.

> **Both aerobic and resistance exercise are beneficial for older adults, but only resistance training can increase muscle strength and muscle mass.**
>
> (Baechle and Earle, 2000)

Here are some safety guidelines for training older adults.

- Always have a thorough consultation with the person and ensure you use a medical questionnaire (PAR-Q) to identify any medical conditions.
- If there are any medical conditions present or concerns, always refer to their GP before training using a written letter.
- Older adults take longer to warm up – at least five to ten minutes is recommended.
- When using resistance training the intensity should be relevant to their level of strength; overload should be applied progressively.
- Allow periods of between 48 and 72 hours between training sessions to allow for recovery.
- All exercises should be pain free; if there is pain then change the range of movement or change the exercise.

Fig 14.01 Older people exercising

The benefits of exercise for older adults are:

- increases in muscle strength and endurance
- less risk of falling due to improved balance
- improved body composition
- improved cardiovascular function
- increased bone density
- reduced symptoms of medical diseases
- greater ability to perform daily activities and functions.

Exercise recommendations

Cardiovascular fitness

Frequency	3–5 times a week
Intensity	Resting heart rate + 20 bpm up to 40–70 of max heart rate
Time	20–30 minutes
Type	Walking, swimming or cycling (depending on structural health status)

The equipment should be chosen to avoid excess stress on bones and joints. Walking is a good choice for most older adults. Exercise in water is a good option for those who need to avoid weight-bearing exercise, and stationary cycling would have the same effect. Group training makes the session more sociable and may improve retention over time. When increasing the training load increase duration before intensity.

Resistance training

Frequency	2–3 times a week
Intensity	10–15 repetitions until loss of good technique
Time	8–10 exercises, at least one set of each for 20–30 minutes in total

Type	Machines and free weights depending upon individual ability and mobility

Initially use low resistance to allow the older person to adapt. Perform large movements involving more than one joint. Ensure normal breathing patterns are maintained and that breath holding is avoided. Always ensure good technique and that exercises are performed in a controlled manner.

Flexibility training

Frequency	2–3 times a week
Intensity	Take to the point of discomfort
Time	10–15 seconds per stretch
Type	All major muscles and those which are shorter than their functional length

Keep stretching pain free. Slowly stretch the muscle into position and avoid any bouncing or jerky movements.

(All these guidelines are adapted from the American College of Sports Medicine's guidelines for exercise prescription (2006).)

Young people

When considering how to train a young person you will need to consider both their chronological age and their biological age. Chronological age is their age in years and months and biological age looks at their stage of development and maturity. Clearly, biological age is much more important to us as there can be large variations in the maturity levels between two 11-year-old children. Biological age will consider their muscular strength and development of their skeleton.

The main considerations in training young people are their bone and muscle development. When a long bone develops the growth occurs at each diaphysis in the growth cartilage which is present predominantly at the epiphyseal plate. Once the epiphyseal plate has completely hardened (ossification) then the bone will stop growing. If this growth cartilage becomes damaged bone growth may be impaired.

> A particular concern in children is the vulnerability of the growth cartilage to trauma and overuse.
>
> (Baechle and Earle, 2000)

The concern is that trauma to the bone can affect the supply of blood to the bone. The blood will deliver a steady supply of oxygen and nutrients to the bone, and without this supply the bone will not develop.

As the child grows their muscle mass will steadily increase. At birth muscle mass accounts for around 25 per cent of the baby's body weight and once they have reached adulthood it makes up around 40 per cent. As muscle mass increases strength will also increase. Strength will peak soon after their peak height has been reached.

- overuse injuries to underdeveloped joints
- lower tolerance of anaerobic exercise
- less developed systems for dissipating heat (less able to sweat)
- less able to deal with cold environments
- faster to fatigue during aerobic exercise.

Exercise recommendations

'Young people' covers a wide variation within stages of development and this must be considered before applying the guidelines.

Cardiovascular fitness

Frequency	5–7 times a week
Intensity	Moderate
Time	Up to 60 minutes a day in periods of 15 minutes
Type	Age-appropriate activities promoting fun and enjoyment

Resistance training

Frequency	2–3 times a week (with rest days in between)
Intensity	Light loads initially (increasing by 5–10 per cent as strength increases)
Time	20–30 minutes per session
Type	Exercises focusing on movements involving several joints (6–15 repetitions)

Flexibility training

Frequency	2–3 times a week
Intensity	Until slight discomfort is felt
Time	Hold for 8–10 seconds
Type	Maintenance stretching only; all major muscle groups

Fig 14.02 Children enjoying exercise

The benefits of training for young age groups are:

- increased muscular strength and endurance
- reduced risk of injury
- improved motor skills
- improved sporting performance
- reduction of body fat
- decreased mental stress
- less chance of developing future adult diseases.

The risks of training young people are:

LEARNER ACTIVITY Working with young people

In groups of four complete the following tasks.

- What activities could you do which would be suitable for a group of eight to nine year olds?
- Design a circuit training session for a mixed group of 12 to 13 year olds.

Pre-natal women

Pregnancy is a time of rapid physiological change for the female. As a trainer it is vital to understand the physiology behind what is happening to the female's body. More and more women have become wise to the benefits of exercising when pregnant, for themselves and their babies. However, the medical profession has always had a conservative approach to training when pregnant due to the instability of the situation and the changes occurring. The view is generally not to put yourself at risk unnecessarily. As a trainer it is vital to understand the following:

- the physiological changes occurring
- the risks of exercise
- the benefits of exercise
- how to prescribe exercise.

The period of a pregnancy is divided into three trimesters:

- the first is 0 to 3 months
- the second is 4 to 6 months
- the third is 7 to 9 months.

During the first trimester we refer to the developing baby as an embryo and during the second and third trimesters we refer to it as a fetus. It only becomes a baby when it has been born. The fetus/embryo is attached to the wall of the uterus via the placenta, which is a large structure full of blood vessels providing oxygen, nutrients and a means to exchange waste. It also provides a protective barrier against disease and produces hormones to maintain the pregnancy. The fetus/embryo develops in a fluid-filled sac, which contains amniotic fluid to keep the fetus at a stable temperature, provide for some shock absorbency and offer protection.

Clearly, a trainer will have some concerns about training a pregnant woman, most of which come from a lack of understanding or knowledge. The following is a list of concerns a trainer may have:

- risk of miscarriage
- physical damage to the fetus/embryo
- morning sickness and nausea
- joint problems, back pain and ligament damage
- changes in posture
- overheating of the mother and fetus
- loss of oxygen to the fetus.

To limit these risks the American College of Gynaecologists (ACOG) has produced a series of guidelines for trainers to work within:

- Choose regular, moderate-intensity exercise.
- Stationary cycling, swimming, walking and stretching are recommended.
- Avoid exercises which have jerky, bouncy movements and involve jumping or sudden changes in direction.
- Don't exercise lying on your back after the fourth month.
- Use longer periods of warming up and cooling down.
- Stop exercise when fatigued and consult a doctor if any unusual symptoms occur.
- Increase intake of calories to cover the energy cost of exercise.
- Keep well hydrated by taking on fluid before, during and after exercise.
- Avoid hot and humid environments.

(Adapted from ACOG, 1994)

Training considerations

During the first trimester the hormone progesterone will cause blood vessels to dilate (expand) and this will cause the following effects:

- lower blood pressure
- increased heart rate
- feelings of sickness, fatigue and dizziness.

This loss of blood pressure is called 'vascular underfill' and means that the pregnant woman has the same amount of blood in a larger blood vessel and thus there is underfill in the blood vessel. This causes the symptoms of light-headedness and fatigue.

During the second trimester the blood volume starts to increase, although it is mainly plasma. The red blood cell count will start to rise towards the end of the second trimester, causing the following effects:

- blood pressure returns to normal
- heart rate returns to normal
- mother starts to feel less nauseous and fatigued.

The mother will also experience a change in their centre of gravity due to the developing bump at the front. Also, after about the fourth month of the pregnancy the hormone relaxin is released which has the effect of making the joints more mobile. Its role is to allow the pelvis greater movement for when the head of the baby passes through it. It will also affect every other joint in the body and cause the mother to become less stable.

During the third trimester the mother becomes much larger in weight and size and this becomes a problem. She will experience the following effects:

- rise in blood pressure
- lowered heart rate
- difficulty raising heart rate.

The mother will become even less stable and have difficulty balancing. She may also be fairly breathless and have back pain. She will experience difficulty getting up from and down to the floor.

The pelvic floor muscles are a group of muscles which run across the pelvis and hold up the contents of the abdomen. When a woman becomes pregnant the contents of the abdomen become heavier due to the increased size of the uterus. There is increased pressure placed on the pelvic floor muscles and they become stretched and weak. If this happens the mother can become incontinent (leaking urine) because these muscles control the action of the bladder. There are specific sets of exercises which can be performed to work these muscles. They involve lifting the pelvic floor muscles – stopping yourself going to the toilet and then holding them there for ten seconds.

The mother needs to be realistic that the aim of pre-natal exercise is to make the pregnancy and the delivery of the baby easier. It is not a time to worry about increasing their level of fitness or minimising weight gain. They can expect a whole host of benefits through training:

- improved circulation
- less fluid accumulation in the lower limbs
- fewer leg cramps
- strengthening of weaker muscles
- reduced risk of incontinence
- reduced feelings of sickness
- less chance of constipation
- improved self-image
- easier and less complicated labour.

Exercise recommendations

When deciding upon what exercises to perform you must consider the following issues.

- What stage of pregnancy is the mother in?
- What size is she?
- What is her current level of fitness?
- Has she any contraindications to exercise?
- What is the potential for injury of the chosen exercise?
- Can she still lie on her back (up to four months)?
- Will the exercise place extra stress on the pelvic floor?

Cardiovascular fitness

Frequency	3–5 sessions a week
Intensity	40–70 per cent of maximum intensity
Time	20–30 minutes per session
Type	Low-impact, rhythmical activity, such as swimming, cycling or walking

Resistance training

Frequency	2–3 sessions a week
Intensity	15–20 repetitions to form failure
Time	8–10 exercises with one or two sets
Type	Exercises to cover all major muscle groups

Flexibility training

Frequency	2–3 sessions a week
Intensity	To the point where mild discomfort is felt
Time	Hold for 8–10 seconds
Type	Maintenance stretches on all major muscle groups

General recommendations are to keep well hydrated. Ensure an extra 250–300 calories a day to cover the energy cost of exercise. All sessions should include pelvic floor exercises.

Post-natal women

After the birth of the baby the mother may be keen to return to exercise as she feels that her body has changed due to the pregnancy. Having said that, we need to consider that there is now a baby to be looked after and the mother may feel overwhelmed by the experience. Also, the woman's body has experienced a major trauma and there is damage to many structures.

The benefits of exercise are:

- promote weight loss
- improve self-image
- return tone to abdominal muscles

LEARNER ACTIVITY Exercise during pregnancy

In groups of three prepare a small five-minute presentation to give to the other two members of the group.

- Learner 1 explains the issues a pregnant women in her first trimester faces, and designs a suitable training programme for her.
- Learner 2 explains the issues a pregnant women in her second trimester faces, and designs a suitable training programme for her.
- Learner 3 explains the issues a pregnant women in her third trimester faces, and designs a suitable training programme for her.

- return strength to stretched muscles
- return flexibility to shortened muscles
- improve posture.

Due to the massive stress that the body has undergone, it is recommended by ACOG that the mother lifts nothing heavier than the baby for the first two weeks. Then at six weeks the mother will have a GP check-up, after which she can start to resume normal daily activities, including training. The only exception to this is if she has delivered the baby through Caesarean section in which case she should not exercise for eight to ten weeks.

Post-natal concerns are as follows.

- **Joint instability and injury**: there will be relaxin present in the body for three to twelve months and thus the joints are still unstable and prone to injury.
- **Injury due to weak abdominal muscles**: the abdominal muscles may either be stretched or even split and thus weaken the core of the body.
- **Damage to pelvic muscles**: as the baby's head passes through the pelvis it will stretch and tear the surrounding tissue, the result being that it can make it sore for the mother to sit, or change the position of the pelvic bones.

Exercise recommendations are:

- choose low-impact aerobic exercise
- use only maintenance stretching
- start off with very gentle stomach exercises, such as stomach tightening
- ensure good posture and work to loss of form on resistance exercises
- include pelvic floor exercises in every session.

Obesity

One of the most popular subjects is obesity and growth of obesity levels in children.

definition

Obesity: 'Excess body fat frequently resulting in a significant impairment of health.' (Wallace, in Durstine and Moore, 2003)

Only recently has obesity been recognised as a disease in its own right. The problem has always been that obesity brings on other medical conditions due to the stress it causes to the organs and structures of the body. In the National Health Survey 2003 of adults in England, the figures showed that 22.2 per cent of men and 23 per cent of women were classified as clinically obese. Childhood obesity stood at 16 per cent with 32 per cent of children being overweight. It is a burgeoning problem in our society.

Obesity can bring on the medical conditions depicted in Fig 14.03.

This is important because when we come to design a training programme for an obese person we may also have to consider that they have other medical conditions to further complicate the issue.

The concerns of training obese people are:

- very low levels of fitness
- poor cardiovascular fitness
- low body strength in relation to weight
- stress on weight-bearing joints of the hip, knee and ankle

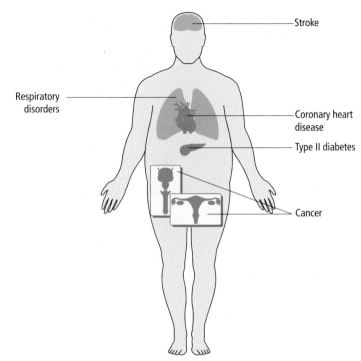

Fig 14.03 Medical conditions brought on by obesity

- less mobility and awareness of their lower limbs
- difficulty getting up from and down to the floor
- certain machines may not be suitable due to their design
- poorer sense of balance.

Any intervention applied must be combined with nutritional advice. The best way to lose weight in a sustainable way is to reduce calorie intake by around 250 kcals a day and increase activity level by 30 minutes a day. This should result in a loss of around 1 lb of body fat a week.

The benefits of exercise are:

- loss of body fat
- increase in muscle
- improvements in body composition
- raised metabolic rate
- improvements in medical conditions
- more energy
- better able to perform daily functions
- improved self-esteem and body image.

Exercise recommendations

Cardiovascular exercise

Frequency	5–7 times a week
Intensity	60–70 per cent of maximum
Time	20–60 minutes
Type	Non-weight bearing, low impact such as rowing, cycling or walking

Resistance training

Frequency	2–3 times a week
Intensity	10–15 reps to form failure
Time	8–10 exercises, one or two sets
Type	Large muscle groups, limit weight bearing on the lower limb

Flexibility training

Frequency	5–7 times a week
Intensity	To point of mild discomfort
Time	6–8 stretches on all major muscle groups
Type	Use standing stretches if they have trouble with mobility

(Adapted from ACSM, 2006)

Water activity or aerobics can be a good choice as water creates a non-weight-bearing environment and provides considerable resistance to work against.

Fig 14.04 Exercising in water

LEARNER ACTIVITY Health risks and obesity

- In groups of four prepare an educational poster showing the health risks faced by obese clients.
- Then show four things they could do to decrease their weight.

Heart disease and hypertension

Heart disease is a catch-all term which refers to disorders of the heart muscle and blood vessels of the heart, and problems with the valves and the nerve supply (sino-atrial node). The treatment of these is conducted by medical professionals, although there is a role for fitness professionals in cardiac rehabilitation. The most common disorder that is dealt with is high blood pressure (hypertension).

definition

Blood pressure: the pressure blood exerts on the artery walls.

As the blood leaves the left ventricle it is pumped under great pressure into the aorta to give it the power to be distributed around the body. A wave of pressure passes through the arterial system each time the heart beats. This pressure falls when the heart relaxes. This is called blood pressure and there are two readings:

- systolic blood pressure – the pressure of blood in the arteries during the contraction of the heart
- diastolic blood pressure – the pressure of blood in the arteries during the relaxation phase of the heart.

Normal blood pressure would be expressed as 120/80 meaning a systolic reading of 120 mmHg and a diastolic reading of 80 mmHg:

Category	Systolic reading	Diastolic reading
Normal	120	80
High blood pressure	160	100
Mild hypertension	140	90
Low blood pressure	90	60

High blood pressure has no obvious symptoms and people can live without realising they have it. As a result, it is called 'the silent killer' and needs to be detected using a sphygmomanometer and stethoscope. High blood pressure causes structural changes to the arteries that supply blood to the organs of the body. As a result, it can affect blood supply to organs such as the brain, liver, kidneys and the heart itself.

Any person who is diagnosed with high blood pressure needs to receive clearance from their GP before being allowed to start training. This is because exercise will raise blood pressure even further and could lead to a heart attack.

Low blood pressure is less dangerous as it will not place such stress on the organs of the body. It needs to be managed because it can cause spells of dizziness and fainting.

The benefits of training hypertensives are:

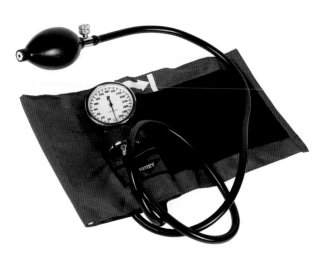

Fig 14.05 A sphygmomanometer (blood pressure meter)

- lowering of systolic and diastolic blood pressure
- loss of weight
- decrease in medication needed to control hypertension.

Exercise recommendations

The following exercise precautions need to be taken.

- Hypertensives need longer periods of warming up and cooling down because their circulation may be poor.
- Ensure they breathe regularly as breath-holding raises blood pressure.
- Avoid any isometric muscle contractions or heavy power work.
- If blood pressure is taken as over 200/115 on that day do not train.

Cardiovascular training

Frequency	3–5 times a week
Intensity	50–70 of max HR
Time	20–60 minutes
Type	Walking, jogging, cycling, rowing and swimming

Resistance training

Frequency	2–3 times a week
Intensity	15–20 reps to form failure
Time	8–10 exercises, one or two sets
Type	All major muscle groups

Flexibility training

Frequency	2–3 times a week
Intensity	Hold stretch at point of discomfort
Time	10–15 seconds per stretch
Type	All major muscles

Other considerations are:

- reduce the weight when working above the shoulders
- work to loss of form rather than failure
- modify lifestyle to reduce smoking and drinking alcohol, and reduce weight.

Asthma sufferers

Asthma is a disorder affecting the respiratory system where the airways become obstructed and resist the flow of air. This obstruction may be due to inflammation, mucus production or contraction of the smooth muscle in the airways. An asthma attack is characterised by an inability to breathe out. The asthmatic may be able to breathe in but not out. An asthma attack is defined as 'a period of difficult breathing'. Asthma affects around 3 million people in Britain.

There are three characteristics of an asthma attack.

- Contraction of the smooth muscle, causing a narrowing of the airway. The bronchioles are lined with smooth muscle which assists the passage of the air through the airways. During an asthma attack these go into spasm, which means they do not relax after a contraction and make breathing out difficult.
- Inflammation – the bronchioles are lined with structures called mucus membranes which produce mucus to keep the air clean. They can become irritated and inflamed, causing the airway to narrow.
- Increased mucus production – as the mucus membranes become inflamed they start to produce more mucus, which causes congestion in the airways.

During an asthma attack the asthmatic experiences a tightening of the chest, shortness of breath, wheezing when they breathe, coughing and coughing up mucus. They may also experience anxiety and panic.

Asthma is managed through the use of inhalers of which there are two types:

- relievers – these tend to be blue in colour and are used when the asthmatic becomes short of breath; they will relax the contraction of the smooth muscle.
- preventers – these tend to be brown in colour and are used morning and night to reduce the inflammation of the mucus membranes.

Fig 14.06 Asthma reliever

Fig 14.07 Asthma preventer

The benefits of exercise are:

- increased strength of the respiratory muscles
- improved lung function
- less occurrence of smooth muscle contraction
- greater tolerance to exercise
- less medication needed.

Exercise recommendations

Cardiovascular training

Frequency	3–7 times a week
Intensity	Light to moderate activity (60–70 per cent of max)
Time	30 minutes per session
Type	Walking, jogging, cycling or rowing

Resistance training

Frequency	2–3 times a week
Intensity	15–20 reps to form failure
Time	6–8 exercises, one or two sets
Type	All major muscle groups

Flexibility training

Frequency	2–3 times a week
Intensity	Hold stretch at point of discomfort
Time	10–15 seconds per stretch
Type	All major muscle groups

Other considerations are:

- training should be conducted in a warm, dust-free environment
- medication should be taken around ten minutes before training
- keep well hydrated as this reduces mucus production
- stop immediately if symptoms of breathlessness occur.

Diabetes

Diabetes mellitus is a metabolic disorder where the person is no longer able to deal with carbohydrate-based foods such as bread, pasta and rice. Carbohydrates are always broken down into their smallest unit which is glucose and then glucose is used as energy immediately or stored in the muscles and liver. A diabetic experiences high levels of glucose in their bloodstream because they cannot store the glucose in their muscles and liver. This is due to the action or inaction of the hormone insulin.

Insulin is a hormone which is produced in the pancreas (a gland just under the stomach). As soon as we eat carbohydrate foods the pancreas releases insulin into the bloodstream. Insulin acts to open the cells of the muscles and liver to allow glucose to flow into them and be stored. It acts like the key to the door of the cells. If there is no insulin or less insulin produced the glucose will remain in the bloodstream and this is what happens to a diabetic. Unfortunately, high levels of glucose will cause damage to many structures of the body.

There are two main types of diabetes, as follows.

- **Type 1 diabetes:** this occurs when the pancreas does not produce any insulin. It is the result of the insulin-producing cells of the pancreas being destroyed and is described as being an auto-immune disorder. This means that the body's immune or defence system has become overactive and has destroyed these cells by mistake. It usually occurs in childhood after the body has been dealing with a childhood illness such as chicken pox or mumps. This type of diabetic has to inject insulin and is called an IDDM: insulin-dependent diabetes mellitus.
- **Type 2 diabetes:** this occurs when the pancreas produces less insulin or poorer-quality insulin so that the cells of the muscles and liver no longer recognise the insulin and do not act upon it. In effect, the cells become resistant to the effects of insulin and this is called 'insulin resistance'. It is common in obese people when the effect of obesity is to place stress on the body's systems and cause the cells to become insulin-resistant. This type of diabetic may take a diabetic pill or control their condition through their diet and is called a NIDDM: non-insulin-dependent diabetes mellitus.

In the short term diabetes is characterised by either very high levels of blood glucose (hyperglycaemia) or very low levels of blood glucose (hypoglycaemia).

- Hyperglycaemia is caused by missing an insulin injection or eating the wrong types of food –

something high in sugar. The high levels of sugar damage the structures of the body and can lead to a person entering a coma.
- Hypoglycaemia is caused by low levels of glucose as the result of missing a meal, taking too much exercise or injecting too much insulin. As blood glucose levels fall the diabetic may feel dizzy and start to shake, feel hungry and thirsty, find it difficult to concentrate and have severe mood swings.

In the long term poorly controlled hyperglycaemia in diabetics can cause the following problems.

- **Eye problems:** the glucose in the blood can block the small capillaries in the retina at the back of the eye, causing blurred vision and even blindness.
- **Circulatory disorders:** the glucose can stick to the artery walls making them more attractive for fats to become attached. This causes a narrowing and even blockage of the artery resulting in high blood pressure and heart disease.
- **Nerve damage:** the glucose can damage the myelin sheath surrounding the nerves, causing a loss of sensation, particularly in the hands and feet.
- **Kidney damage:** the excess urine has to be excreted out and this puts strain on the kidneys.

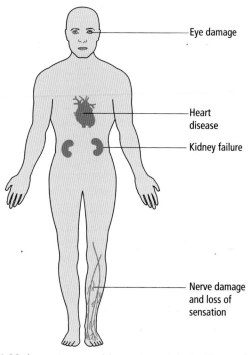

Fig 14.08 Long-term problems associated with poorly controlled diabetes

The benefits of exercise are as follows.

- It will burn off any excess glucose.
- It has an insulin-like effect and means the sufferer needs to inject less insulin.
- It will help to control weight which contributes to insulin resistance.
- It will help to prevent the long-term damage which occurs.

Exercise recommendations

Cardiovascular training

Frequency	3–5 times a week
Intensity	40–70 per cent of max
Time	20–40 minutes
Type	Low-impact, non-weight-bearing rhythmical exercise, such as cycling or rowing

Resistance training

Frequency	2–3 times a week
Intensity	15–20 reps to form failure
Time	6–8 exercises, one or two sets
Type	All major muscle groups

Flexibility training

Frequency	2–3 times a week
Intensity	Hold at a position of mild discomfort
Time	10–15 seconds per stretch
Type	All major muscle groups

The advice to diabetics about training is:

- always wear med alert identification
- train at the same time each day
- set up a routine of injecting, eating and training
- wear comfortable shoes to prevent foot damage.

LEARNER ACTIVITY Working with people with diabetes

In groups of two prepare a brief talk to educate your partner on the following.

- Learner 1 will explain what diabetes is and the two different types of diabetics.
- Learner 2 will explain the short- and long-term risks of diabetes, why the diabetic needs to exercise and what they should do.

Arthritis

Arthritis is a general term meaning inflammation of joints. There are many types of arthritis, the two main ones being osteoarthritis and rheumatoid arthritis.

Osteoarthritis is a condition which occurs mainly in the weight-bearing joints of the hip, knee and ankle. It can occur in a joint where there has been a previous injury, or when a person is obese or is older. It is a result of 'wear and tear' in a joint. As a joint becomes worn the cartilage will start to wear down and it becomes replaced by bone. This is especially the case if ligaments are stretched because they are less effective at holding the joint in place. This movement of bone on bone can cause friction and pain, and result in swelling of the joint as more synovial fluid is released on to it. The bone formation can also be irregular and create small, bony spurs. The joint can become misshapen and look red and swollen. It will cause pain and a loss of function.

Rheumatoid arthritis is an autoimmune disease (like type 1 diabetes) where the body's immune system breaks down cartilage and replaces it with bone. The process can start at any age but is most common between the ages of 30 and 50. It starts with the small peripheral joints such as the fingers and wrist or toes and feet, and moves up to the larger joints of the elbow, shoulder, knee and hip. It can also spread into the joints of the back and neck and even the jaw.

Rheumatoid arthritis causes a swelling and deformation of the joints, creating redness and pain. The bone-on-bone action causes changes in the synovial capsule and more synovial fluid is released, causing the swelling. It can go through periods where the symptoms disappear to periods where the pain is intense.

The benefits of exercise are:

- strengthening the surrounding muscles can take the pressure and pain out of the joint
- it maintains the mobility and flexibility of the joint and muscles
- it relieves symptoms and pain.

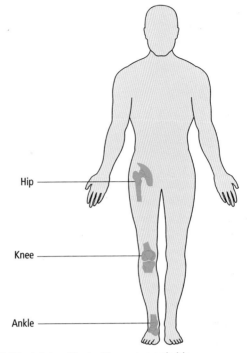

Fig 14.09 Joints affected by osteoarthritis

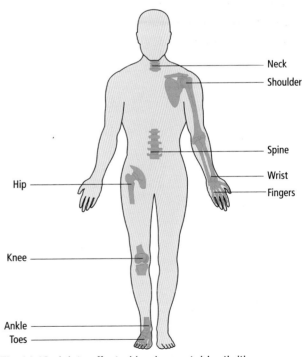

Fig 14.10 Joints affected by rheumatoid arthritis

Exercise recommendations

Cardiovascular training

Frequency	3–5 times a week
Intensity	40–60 per cent of max

Time   Start at 5 minutes and work up to 30 minutes

Type   Low-impact activity such as walking, cycling or swimming

Resistance training

Frequency   2–3 times a week

Intensity   Build up to 10–12 reps

Time   6–8 exercise; hold end position for up to 6 seconds

Type   Use isometric movements for affected joints (static contractions) and normal concentric contractions for unaffected joints

Flexibility training

Frequency   1–2 times a day

Intensity   Hold at a position of mild discomfort

Time   10–15 seconds per stretch

Type   All major muscle groups

Other considerations for arthritics are:

- ensure they have good-quality footwear to lessen impact
- do not train when joints are inflamed or painful
- train later in the day when joints are warmed up.

> ## LEARNER ACTIVITY Working with people with arthritis
>
> In groups of four prepare a poster which educates people on the two types of arthritis, the cause of arthritis and what type of training should be done by an arthritic.

Osteoporosis

Osteoporosis is a disease which affects the bones (osteo). The bones lose mass and become porous (porosis) or thinner. The effect of this is that they are more susceptible to fractures. The joints particularly affected are the hip, wrist and spine. It is predominantly, although not exclusively, a disorder that affects women. One in three women will experience an osteoporotic fracture compared with one in twelve men.

Osteoporosis occurs when more bone is destroyed than laid down. This is due to the action of osteoblasts and osteoclasts:

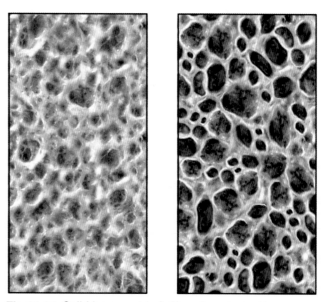

Fig 14.11 Solid bone matrix (left) and weakened bone matrix (right)

- osteoblasts build or lay down bone
- osteoclasts destroy or clean out old bone.

Up to the age of 35 the number of osteoblasts will be greater than the number of osteoclasts and thus we lay down more bone than we lose. However, after the age of 35 the number of osteoblasts falls and the number of osteoclasts increases, which causes a steady loss of bone and bone density.

This loss of bone is accelerated by various factors:

- family history
- female gender
- post-menopause in women
- low body weight
- lack of activity
- smoking
- excess alcohol intake
- poor diet (especially low in calcium and vitamin D).

Exercise is undertaken to protect against the possibility of osteoporosis occurring rather than when osteoporosis has been diagnosed. If a person has a number of the risk factors it is advised they train to offset the effects of bone loss from their mid-thirties. The benefits are:

- development of bone through weight-bearing exercise

- strengthening of muscles around potential fracture sites
- improved balance and coordination prevents falls leading to fractures
- improved posture.

Exercise recommendations

Cardiovascular training

Frequency	3–5 times a week
Intensity	40–70 per cent of max
Time	20–30 minutes per session
Type	Weight-bearing activity such as walking, jogging or step aerobics

Resistance training

Frequency	2–3 times a week
Intensity	8–10 reps, two or three sets of exercises putting forces through bones (squats, lunges, bench press, shoulder press)
Time	6–8 exercises
Type	All major muscles, weight bearing and around potential fracture sights

Flexibility training

Frequency	2–3 times a week
Intensity	To the point of mild discomfort
Time	10–15 seconds per stretch
Type	All major muscle groups

Other considerations are as follows.

- The potential osteoporotic may also consider hormone replacement therapy to replace the oestrogen lost after their menopause. Oestrogen promotes the activity of the osteoblasts.
- Nutritional advice should be given to ensure the person receives enough protein, calcium, vitamin D, phosphorous and magnesium to ensure the ingredients for bone-building are present.

Conclusion

Specific groups are a new and developing area in the health and fitness industry and may offer considerable challenges to the trainer. Before dealing with any of these groups you need to be appropriately qualified to REPs Level 3. You also need to have the confidence and knowledge to show the client that they are safe in your hands and to reassure them.

The trainer must realise that when we talk about special groups we are talking in fairly general terms and no two clients will be identical. Therefore, it is important to look at each client individually and look at what we call the 'presenting factors', meaning 'How does this medical condition affect this person?' and 'What symptoms do they actually have and what can we do about it?'

It is most important to follow the relevant protocols and if in doubt to refer the client to a GP or other professional, rather than just trying something. In these terms it is important to have a network of people around you to help and reassure you. That said, working with specific groups can be a very interesting and rewarding experience.

Review questions

1 Explain why the public sector is most likely to be involved in exercise referral schemes.
2 List and briefly explain the five stages of an exercise referral scheme development model.
3 Give four criteria used to select patients for exercise referral schemes.
4 Explain five effects of the ageing process.
5 Why is training young people of particular concern to the trainer?
6 Name three risks involved in training pregnant women.
7 Explain what happens to blood pressure, blood volume and heart rate in the three trimesters of pregnancy.
8 What are the benefits of a mother training during the post-natal period?
9 Define obesity and explain the effect it has on the body.
10 What issues may obese people face when training?
11 What are the categories for normal, high, mild hypertension and low blood pressure?
12 What are the three characteristics of an asthma attack?
13 Explain the two different types of diabetes.
14 Give the four long-term complications of uncontrolled diabetes.
15 Differentiate between osteo and rheumatoid arthritis.
16 What type of training should a potential osteoporotic perform?

References

American College of Obstetricians and Gynaecologists (ACOG) (1994) Exercise during pregnancy and the post partum period, *Technical Bulletin* 189, ACOG.

American College of Sports Medicine (ACSM) (2006) *Guidelines for Exercise Testing and Prescription*, Lippincott, Williams and Wilkins.

Baechle, T. and Earle, R. (2000) *Essentials of Strength Training and Conditioning*, Human Kinetics.

Durstine, J. and Moore, G. (2003) *Exercise Management for Persons with Chronic Diseases and Disabilities*, Human Kinetics.

Psychology for sports performance

Goals

By the end of this chapter you should:

- understand the effect of personality on sports performance
- understand the relationship between stress, arousal and anxiety and sports performance
- understand group dynamics in sports teams
- be able to plan a psychological skills training programme to enhance sporting performance.

Success in sport is derived from a series of variable factors. The athlete must be prepared physically, have the correct nutritional strategy, and ensure that they are appropriately recovered and in a positive mental state. Sport psychology deals with ensuring that the performer has this correct mental state and is able to control this state during training and training periods.

Sport psychology can be defined as:

> The scientific study of individuals and how they behave in sport and exercise environments, and how this knowledge can be applied in a practical and beneficial way.

Through the systematic research and study of individuals in sporting environments it has been possible to gain an insight into what makes certain performers successful. By 'modelling' these effective techniques it has been possible to improve their performance and gain an insight into excellence. Sport psychologists have developed a body of techniques to assist performers in improving their performances and developing consistency.

Sport psychology techniques can be applied to all levels of athletes, from giving a beginner the confidence to jump the high jump bar to helping a professional footballer score a penalty in the World Cup final; they can help coaches to produce the best performances from their athletes and stay calm as they watch their performances; they can be used by fitness trainers to motivate their clients and ensure they keep performing their training routines. They can even be used in business to ensure that employees always produce their best performances at work.

Literally speaking, psychology means study of (ology) the human mind (psyche). The recent work of Bill Beswick in football, Stephen Bull with the English cricket team during the successful 2005 Ashes series, and Jos Vanstiphort with golfers Ernie Els and Retief Goosen has shown the value of psychologically preparing athletes.

The key in preparing performers mentally is understanding that we actually have control over our mind and how we think and, because we have control, we can use it either to our advantage or disadvantage. Consider the situation when we buy a new computer and it comes with a long manual about how to assemble it and then how to work it. Some people will throw away the manual and work it out for themselves; this may or may not be successful and they will certainly never use the computer to its full capability. Other people will spend time and effort reading the manual and then applying this information to the computer. They will have a much better understanding of how it functions and its capacity. Sport psychology has been called 'a user's manual for the brain' because it helps us to understand how the brain works and what it is capable of doing for us. Once we gain control over our brain then the possibilities are limitless.

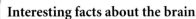

Interesting facts about the brain

- 95 per cent of all we know about how the brain works has been discovered in the last ten years.
- Brain cells are so tiny you can fit 10,000 of them on to a single pinhead.
- Each of your brain cells is more powerful than a standard computer.
- If we represented the size of the world's most powerful computer as a two-storey house then the potential power of your brain would be represented by a building reaching to the moon and ten blocks square at the bottom.
- The human brain can generate thousands of new brain cells every day.

(Adapted from *The Ultimate Book of Mind Maps* by Tony Buzan, Thorsons, 2005)

Personality

The key concept that underpins all studies in sport psychology is the personality. It is clear that each person has the same brain structure and that their senses will all work in the same way to provide the brain with information. However, each person appears to be different in the decisions they make and how they behave in specific situations. Personality looks at these individual differences and how they affect performance.

Definitions of personality

There is a range of definitions of personality, each with their merits and drawbacks. It has been suggested that we all have traits and behaviour that we share with other people but we also have some particular to ourselves. However, this idea does lack depth of information, as does Cattell's (1965) attempt to define personality: 'that which tells what a man will do when placed in a given situation'. This suggests that if we know an individual's personality, we can predict behaviour. However, human beings tend to be less than predictable and can act out of character, depending upon the situation. Their behaviour may also be affected by their mood, fatigue or emotions.

Hans Eysenck (1960) sought to address the limitations of previous definitions: 'the more or less stable and enduring organisation of an individual's character, temperament, intellect and physique which determines their unique adjustment to the environment'. Eysenck's

statement that personality is more or less stable allows the human element to enter the equation and explain the unpredictable. He also makes the important point that personality is 'unique'. We may have behaviour in common with other people, but ultimately every person has a set of characteristics unique to themselves.

In summary, most personality theories state the following:

> Personality is the set of individual characteristics that make a person unique and will determine their relatively consistent patterns of behaviour.

By giving labels to a person's character and behaviour, you have started to assess personality. By observing sportspeople we are using a behavioural approach, i.e. assessing what they are like by assessing their responses to various situations. In reality, our observations may be unreliable because we see sportspeople in only one environment, and although we see them interviewed as well, we do not know what they are truly like. A cognitive psychologist believes we need to understand an individual's thoughts and emotions as well as watching their behaviour. This we cannot do without the use of a questionnaire or an interview.

Introduction to personality theories

Matt Jarvis (2006) identifies four factors that will determine how an individual responds in a specific situation:

1. our genetic make-up
2. our past experiences
3. the nature of the situation in which we find ourselves
4. free will.

Our genetic make-up refers to the innate aspect of our personality which we inherit from our parents. Past experiences are important because if we have acted in a certain way in the past and it had a successful outcome, then it is likely we will act the same way in the future. Or if we have had a negative experience in the past then the same experience in the future will be seen as threatening or stressful. The nature of the situation and how we perceive it will cause us to adapt our behaviour in a way that suits the situation. Free will is a difficult concept in psychology and it suggests we have control over our thinking and thus our behaviour. It can be difficult to separate whether a person has chosen to behave in that way or is programmed by their genetics or past experiences.

LEARNER ACTIVITY

Choose one of the following groups of sports people and discuss in pairs what personality characteristics each person has, based on your observations of their behaviour and interviews you have seen with them.

- Are there personality characteristics they have in common?
- Are these characteristics important in their sport?
- Can these characteristics explain their success?

Football	Golf	Athletics
Wayne Rooney	Colin Montgomery	Paula Radcliffe
John Terry	Tiger Woods	Mark Lewis-Francis
Steven Gerrard	Sergio Garcia	Marlon Devonish
Rio Ferdinand	Phil Mickelson	Ashia Hansen
Joe Cole	Darren Clarke	Phillips Idowu

Tennis	Rugby Union
Roger Federer	Matt Stevens
Andrew Murray	Paul O'Connell
Maria Sharapova	Danny Grewcock
Rafael Nadal	Brian O'Driscoll
Amelie Mauresmo	Shane Williams

LEARNER ACTIVITY

Consider your own personality and give an example of one time you felt your behaviour was the result of:

- your genetic make-up
- your past experiences
- the situation in which you found yourself
- free will.

Trait theory

The trait approach to personality relates to the first factor of personality. Jarvis (2006) identifies that personality is based in genetics. This is called the nature approach and says we inherit personality at birth; this has some validity – for example, we can observe how different babies have different personalities from a young age. A trait is defined as 'a relatively stable way of behaving', suggesting if a person shows a trait of shyness in one situation then they will be shy across a range of situations. Across a population the traits people have are the same; however, they show them to a greater or lesser extent and this dictates their personality. This theory was very popular in the 1960s; however, it continues to be criticised for not considering that the situation may influence an individual's behaviour.

Social learning theory (situational approach)

Social learning theory, or the situational approach, takes the view that personality is determined by the environment and the experiences a person has as they grow up.

Richard Cox (1998) outlines the two mechanisms of learning: modelling and social reinforcement.

1 **Modelling** – as we grow up we observe and imitate the behaviour of significant others in our lives. At first, this is our parents and siblings, then our friends, teachers, sports stars and anyone we regard as a role model. We often hear sportspeople, such as Michael Owen and David Beckham, being praised for being good role models to young people, meaning that their conduct is good to observe and imitate.

2 **Social reinforcement** – this means that when behaviour is rewarded positively it is more likely that it will be repeated. Conversely, behaviour negatively rewarded is less likely to be repeated. At an early age our parents teach us right and wrong by positively or negatively rewarding behaviour.

In sport there is a system of negative reinforcement to discourage negative behaviour on the sports field. Thus, rugby players get sent to the sin bin, cricketers get fined part of their match fee, and footballers get yellow and red cards as a means of social reinforcement.

In particular this theory shows why people behave differently in different situations. For example, an athlete may be confident and outgoing in a sporting setting but shy and quiet in an educational setting. The athlete may have chosen positive role models in the sporting environment and had their successful performances rewarded. In the educational setting they may have modelled less appropriate behaviour and had their behaviour negatively rewarded.

The interactional approach

The trait theory of personality is criticised for not taking into account the situation which determines behaviour; the situational approach is criticised because research shows that while situation influences some people's behaviour, other people will not be influenced in the same way. The interactional approach considers the person's psychological traits and the situation they are in as equal predictors of behaviour:

Behaviour = f (personality, environment)

Thus, we can understand an individual's behaviour by assessing their personality traits and the specific situation they find themselves in. Bowers (1973) says the interaction between a person and their situation could give twice as much information as traits or the situational approach alone.

An interactional psychologist would use a trait–state approach to assess an individual's personality traits and then assess how these traits affect their behaviour in a situation (state). For example, an athlete who exhibited high anxiety levels as a personality trait would then have an exaggerated response to a specific situation.

Neither personality traits nor situations alone are enough to predict an individual's behaviour. We must consider both to get a real picture.

Other personality measurements: type A and type B personalities

A questionnaire written by Friedman and Rosenman (1959) was initially developed to identify people who were prone to stress and stress-related illnesses. However, it has some application to sport and exercise.

Type A behaviour:

- highly competitive and strong desire to succeed
- achievement orientated
- eat fast, walk fast, talk fast and have a strong sense of urgency
- aggressive, restless and impatient
- find it difficult to delegate and need to be in control
- experience high levels of stress.

Type B behaviour:

- less competitive
- more relaxed
- delegate work easily
- take time to complete their tasks
- calm, laid back and patient
- experience low levels of stress.

Type Bs will exhibit the opposite types of behaviour to type As.

In sport we see both personality types being equally successful. However, with people exercising recreationally, we see higher levels of retention on their exercise programmes. Type As would benefit from exercise as it promotes type B-related behaviour. Type A behaviour is seen as causing a rise in a person's blood pressure and then increasing the risk of coronary heart disease (CHD).

Personality and sports performance

The majority of research using trait theory was done in the 1970s and 1980s (Table 15.01 gives a summary).

Table 15.01 Summary of trait theory research

Name of researcher/s	Questionnaire used and groups studied	Research findings
Schurr, Ashley and Joy (1977)	16PF – 1500 American students	Athletes versus non-athletes – athletes were more: • independent • objective • relaxed Athletes who played team sports were: • more outgoing and warm hearted (A) • less intelligent (B) • more group dependent (Q2) • less emotionally stable (C) Athletes who played individual sports were: • more group dependent (Q2) • less anxious (Q4) • less intelligent (B)
Francis *et al* (1998)	EPQ – 133 female hockey players versus non-athlete students	Hockey players were: • more extroverted
Ogilvie (1968)	16PF – athletes versus non-athletes	Athletic performance is related to: • emotional stability • tough mindedness • conscientiousness • self-discipline • self-assurance • trust • extroversion • low tension
Breivik (1996)	16PF – 38 elite Norwegian climbers	Research showed: • high levels of stability • extroversion • adventure seeking
Williams (1980)	Female athletes versus female non-athletes	Athletes were: • more independent • more aggressive and dominant • more emotionally stable

Motivation

If a sport psychologist were asked why athletes of similar talents achieve different levels of performance, they would consider several factors, such as personality and ability to cope with stress. However, if one subject could be said to influence everything in sport psychology it would be motivation – the reasons why we do what we do, and behave and respond in the manner particular to us.

Psychologists would say that there is a reason for everything we do in life; some of these motives are conscious and some are unconscious – as a result it can be difficult to assess our own motivating factors, let alone anyone else's.

Motivation is important to coaches and managers as they seek to get the best performances out of their athletes. Jose Mourinho and Alex Ferguson are two managers who are seen as being great motivators of people.

Motivation can be a difficult subject to pin down and deal with, because it is not steady and constant and depends on many factors. Most people will experience fluctuations in motivation in that some days they are fully prepared for the competition mentally, and on other days they just cannot seem to get themselves in the right frame of mind. This applies to all those things we may do in a day, as sometimes it takes all our powers of motivation just to get out of bed!

Here are a number of definitions of motivation as put forward by various psychologists:

> **Motive – a desire to fulfil a need**
>
> *(Cox, 1998)*

> **The internal mechanisms which arouse and direct behaviour**
>
> *(Sage, 1974)*

> **The direction and intensity of one's effort**
>
> *(Sage, 1974)*

When examining motivation five terms seem to come up again and again.

1 **Fulfilling a need** – all motivation arises as we seek to fulfil our needs; these may be basic biological needs such as finding food and shelter, or more sophisticated needs such as self-esteem or the need to belong and be loved.

2 **Internal state** – a state is 'how we feel at any point in time' and this will be subject to change. As we see and feel things they will trigger an internal state which will need actions to fulfil any needs.

3 **Direction** – the direction of effort refers to the actions we take to move towards what we feel motivated by and feel we need.

4 **Intensity** – the intensity of effort refers to how much effort the person puts in to achieving their goal or in to a certain situation.

5 **Energise behaviour** – this shows how the power of the brain and the thoughts we have can give us the energy we need to produce the behaviour that is required to be successful in a certain situation.

Intrinsic and extrinsic motivation

To expand on Sage's definition, we can see motivation as coming from internal mechanisms or sources inside the body. We can call these intrinsic factors, or rewards coming from the activity itself. These include motives such as fun, pleasure, enjoyment, feelings of self-worth, excitement and self-mastery. They are the reasons why we do a sport and keep doing it.

> **Those who are intrinsically motivated engage in an activity for the pleasure and satisfaction they experience while learning, exploring or trying to understand something new.**
>
> *(Weinberg and Gould, 2003)*

External stimuli can be called extrinsic rewards; they come from sources outside the activity. This would include the recognition and praise we get from other people, such as our coach, friends and family. It could also be the approval we get from the crowd who support us. Extrinsic motivating factors would also include trophies, medals, prizes, records and any money derived from success.

> **Those who are extrinsically motivated engage in the activity because of the valued outcome rather than the interest in the activity solely for itself.**
>
> *(Weinberg and Gould, 2003)*

LEARNER ACTIVITY

Consider each of the following statements made by athletes as to why they are motivated, and decide whether it is an intrinsic or extrinsic motivating factor.

- I want to win medals.
- I want to earn an England cap.
- I want to reach my full potential.
- I want to make money.
- I want to play in a good team.
- I want to play in front of large crowds.
- I want to give the public enjoyment.
- I want to feel good about my performance.
- I want to be recognised by the public for my ability.
- I want to feel mastery in my own ability.
- I want to feel the joy of winning.

Achievement motivation

> I do not play to win; I play to fight against the idea of losing.

(Eric Cantona, Manchester United, 1997)

Achievement motivation is seen as a personality factor and describes our persistence to keep striving for success, irrespective of the bad experiences and obstacles that are put in our way. It can be seen as our level of 'competitiveness' or desire for success. Achievement motivation is not that simple, however, as the quote from Eric Cantona shows. Some people are driven to success and have no fear of failure, while others are driven to succeed because they have a deep-rooted fear of failure. This paradox was addressed by McClelland and Atkinson in their theory of need for achievement.

When in a certain sporting situation, we may have conflicting feelings: on one hand, we want to take part and achieve success; on the other hand, we are motivated to avoid the situation by our need to avoid failure. The relative strength of these emotions influences our achievement motivation:

$$\text{Achievement motivation} =$$
$$\text{need to achieve (nACH)} - \text{need to avoid failure (naF)}$$

If our nACH outweighs our naF, then we are said to be high in achievement motivation; if our naF outweighs our nACH, we are said to be low in achievement motivation. This will influence our behaviour in sport and the types of challenges we seek.

A sportsperson with a high need to achieve will choose competitive situations and opponents close to their skill level who will challenge them. A person with a high fear of failure will choose opponents of much higher skill or much lower skill because these are less threatening to them; they will also tend to avoid situations involving personal challenges.

The situation will also affect achievement motivation. If the probability of success is high, it tends to weaken the need to achieve because the reward for success is low; on the other hand, if the probability of success is low and failure is likely, it tends to weaken the need to avoid failure.

LEARNER ACTIVITY

Think about the following situations.

- You play well, but lose to an opponent who is better than you.
- You play well and beat a tough opponent.
- You play badly and still manage to win against a weak opponent.
- You play badly and lose to an opponent you know you can beat.

1 Number the situations from 1 to 4 starting with the one which you find most satisfying (1), and ending with the one you find least satisfying (4).
2 Take the situation ranked first and explain why it is most satisfying. Why may this result have occurred?
3 Take the situation ranked fourth and explain why it is least satisfying. Why may this result have occurred?

Weiner's attribution theory

The reasons we give for an outcome are called attributions. We are attributing that outcome to a certain factor. We all make attributions about our own performances as well as those of other people. It is important for us to make attributions because:

- they affect our motivation levels
- we need to understand the outcome so that we can learn from our experiences
- they will affect our future expectations of success and failure.

Attributions fall into four categories.

1 **Ability or skill** – a performer's capability in performing skills.
2 **Effort** – the amount of physical or mental effort put into a task.
3 **Task difficulty** – the problems posed by the task, e.g. strength of the opposition or difficulty of a move.
4 **Luck** – factors attributed to chance, such as the effect of the weather, the referee or the run of the ball.

LEARNER ACTIVITY

1 Look at the following statements and decide which of the four attribution categories each one fits into.

Reasons for success
'I played well today, the training is paying off'
'I think I've got a natural talent for running – it comes easily to me'
'I tried like mad in the final set – that's what pulled me through'
'I was lucky to get away with that one'

Reasons for failure
'I played like an idiot! I deserved to lose'
'I can't play this game – it's impossible'
'I was really lazy today'
'I didn't get the rub of the green today'

2 Now that you know what attributions are, do a piece of your own research. Look through the newspapers on a Monday morning and try to find the reasons sportspeople and coaches give for their successes or failures. Also, think why they are choosing to make these particular attributions.

As shown in Table 15.02, these four categories can be classified as internal (inside an individual), external (outside the individual), stable (not subject to change) or unstable (continually changing).

Table 15.02 Locus of control

	Internal	External
Stable	Ability	Task difficulty
Unstable	Effort	Luck

Research findings

Research shows that winners tend to give internal attributions and take responsibility for their successes. They will usually say 'I won because I tried hard' or, 'I am more talented'. Losers, on the other hand, tend to give external attributions and distance themselves from their failures. For example, they will say 'the task was too difficult' or 'the referee was against me'. These attributions can be seen as ego enhancing and ego protective respectively. Winners give internal attributions to make themselves feel even better; losers give external attributions so they do not feel so bad.

Attributions and self-confidence

If we make a more stable attribution, i.e. to ability or task difficulty, it is more realistic and gives a clearer indication of future expectations and confidence.

Fig 15.01 Attributions and self-confidence model

However, attribution to unstable factors can act to protect the ego and reduce loss of self-confidence.

This is important because confidence levels will influence motivation – the more confidence we have the more motivation we will have for a task.

Stress, arousal and anxiety
Stress

Stress is usually talked about in negative terms. People complain that they have too much stress or are 'stressed out'; sportspeople claim the stress of competition is too much for them. However, we should not see stress as an entirely negative thing because it provides us with the mental and physical energy to motivate us into doing things and doing them well. Stressors are anything that causes us to have a stress response, and these are invariably different for different people.

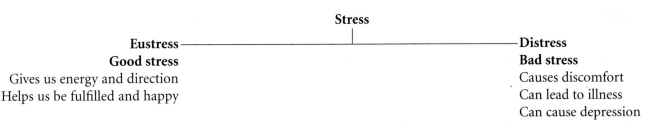

Stress

Eustress ——————————————— Distress
Good stress   **Bad stress**
Gives us energy and direction   Causes discomfort
Helps us be fulfilled and happy   Can lead to illness
                                                   Can cause depression

If we did not have any stress in our lives, we might not bother to do anything all day. We need stressors to give us the energy and direction to get things done. Without any stress we would become bored and psychologically stale. This type of positive stress is called eustress (good stress), however, if we have too much stress is can become damaging and we call this distress (bad stress).

Too much stress in our lives over a long period of time can seriously damage our health, causing things like coronary heart disease, high blood pressure, ulcers, impotence, substance addiction, mental health problems and suicidal tendencies.

Sport is a source of stress for some sportspeople. This is related to the experience of the performer, the importance of the competition, the quality of the opposition, the size of the crowd, or previous events. The stress response will be specific to the individual.

> ## LEARNER ACTIVITY
>
> Think of a recent competition that you very much wanted to win. Try to recall how you felt before this competition started.
> The feelings you had are the symptoms of stress, and they can be separated into physical (the effects on your body), mental (the effect on your brain) and behavioural (how your behaviour changed).

> **definition**
>
> Stress: 'any influence which disturbs the natural equilibrium of the body' (Wingate, 1982)

The classic definition of stress sees the body as having a natural equilibrium, or balance, when the heart rate is at its resting level, the breathing rate at its resting level, and blood pressure at normal levels. Anything that changes these natural levels is a stressor. Theoretically, we could say we become stressed as soon as we get out of bed, as our heart rate, breathing rate and blood pressure all rise. Indeed, to some people the alarm going off is a real source of stress!

The stress process

McGrath (1970) sees the stress response as a process and defines stress as:

> **a substantial imbalance between demand (physical and psychological) and response capability, under conditions where failure to meet the demand has important consequences**

Stress will occur when the person does not feel they have the resources to deal with the situation and that this will have negative consequences.

Causes of stress

The causes of stress are many and varied, but crucially they are specific to an individual. For example, you can have two people in the same event, each with a different stress response.

> ## LEARNER ACTIVITY
>
> Make a list of things that cause you stress. These may be related to the sports you play or other things in general life.

The sources of stress can generally be divided into four categories.

1 **Internal** – things we think about, such as past memories and experiences, current injuries, past injuries, our own feelings of self-worth, and so on.
2 **External** – things in our surroundings and our environment, such as competition, our opponents, the crowd, the weather, spiders and snakes, transport problems.
3 **Personal factors** – people we share our lives with, such as friends, family and partners, and life factors such as money and health.

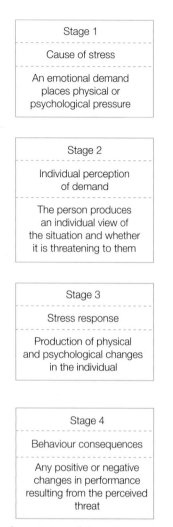

Stage 1
Cause of stress
An emotional demand places physical or psychological pressure

Stage 2
Individual perception of demand
The person produces an individual view of the situation and whether it is threatening to them

Stage 3
Stress response
Production of physical and psychological changes in the individual

Stage 4
Behaviour consequences
Any positive or negative changes in performance resulting from the perceived threat

Fig 15.02 The four stages of the stress process

4 **Occupational factors** – the job we do, the people we work with (the boss) and our working conditions. In sport it could include our relationships with team-mates and coaches/managers.

Stress levels also depend upon personality. Those people who have a predominantly type A personality will find more situations stressful, as will people who have a high N score using Eysenck's personality inventory.

The physiology of stress

When we perceive ourselves to be in a situation which is dangerous, our stress response is activated. This has been developed as a means of ensuring our survival by making us respond to danger. For example, if we are walking home at night through dark woods and we hear noises behind us our body will instigate physiological changes, called the 'fight or flight' response, as we prepare to turn and fight the danger or run away as fast as we can.

The response varies depending upon how serious we perceive the threat to be. The changes take place in our involuntary nervous system which consists of two major branches (as shown in Fig 15.03 below):

- the sympathetic nervous system
- the parasympathetic nervous system.

The sympathetic nervous system produces the stress response and its aim is to provide the body with as

INVOLUNTARY NERVOUS SYSTEM

SYMPATHETIC NERVOUS SYSTEM	PARASYMPATHETIC NERVOUS SYSTEM
Increased adrenaline production	Decreased adrenaline production
Increase in heart rate	Slowed heart rate
Increase in breathing rate	Slower breathing rate
Increased metabolism	Slower metabolism
Increased heat production	Lower body temperature
Muscle tension	Muscle relaxation
Dry mouth	Dry skin
Dilated pupils	Smaller pupils
Hairs on the skin stand on end (to make us look bigger)	
Digestive system slows down	Digestion speeded up
Diversion of blood away from internal organs to the working muscles	

Fig 15.03 Involuntary nervous system

much energy as it can to confront the threat or run away from it; it works by releasing the stress hormones, adrenaline and cortisol, into the bloodstream. The parasympathetic nervous system produces the relaxation response, its aim being to conserve energy. It is activated once the stressor has passed.

It is not healthy for the body to be in a constant state of stress because of the activation of the sympathetic nervous system. The excess production of adrenaline is dangerous because the body requires more cholesterol to synthesise adrenaline. This excess cholesterol production raises blood cholesterol levels and is a risk factor for coronary heart disease (CHD).

Symptoms of stress

Stress will have a threefold effect on the body, causing cognitive (mental), somatic (physical) and behavioural responses as outlined in Table 15.03.

Arousal and anxiety

Arousal and anxiety are terms related to stress. Arousal is seen as being a positive aspect of stress and shows how motivated we are by a situation. The more aroused we become the more interested in and excited we are by a situation. We can see this when we watch a football match involving a team we support: we are so aroused that we are engrossed in the action to the point where we do not hear noises around us and time seems to go very quickly. During a match that does not arouse us to the same extent we find that our attention drifts in and out as we are distracted by things happening around us.

Arousal continuum

We can look at levels of arousal on a continuum that shows the varying degrees of arousal:

Deep sleep   Mild interest   Attentive   Absorbed   Engrossed   Frenzied

Arousal and attention span

As arousal levels increase, they can affect a performer's attention span. If a performer has a broad attention span they are able to pick up information from a wide field of vision. The more narrow the attention span becomes then the less information the performer will pick up and the more they will miss. The attention span can also be too broad and performer may try to pick up too much information.

Anxiety

Anxiety can be seen as a negative aspect of stress; it may accompany high levels of arousal. It is not pleasant to be anxious and anxiety is characterised by feelings of nervousness and worry. Again, the stress and anxiety responses are unique to each individual.

Trait and state anxiety

Trait anxiety means that a person generally experiences high levels of anxiety as part of their personality; they tend to worry and feel nervous in a range of situations and find them threatening. State anxiety is anxiety felt in response to a specific situation; it is anxiety related to a specific mood state. Usually, a person who has high trait anxiety will also

Table 15.03 Effects of stress

Cognitive response	Somatic response	Behavioural response
Reduced concentration	Racing heart rate	Talking, eating and walking quickly
Less interested	Faster breathing	Interrupting conversations
Unable to make decisions	Headaches	Increased smoking, drinking and eating
Sleep disturbances	Butterflies in the stomach	Fidgeting
Making mistakes	Chest tightness and pains	Lethargy
Unable to relax	Dry cotton mouth	Moodiness and grudge-bearing
Quick losses of temper	Constant colds and illness	Accidents and clumsiness
Loss of sense of humour	Muscular aches and pains	Poor personal presentation
Loss of self-esteem	Increased sweating	Nervous habits
Loss of enthusiasm	Skin irritations	

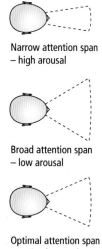

Narrow attention span
– high arousal

Broad attention span
– low arousal

Optimal attention span
– optimal arousal

Fig 15.04 The three attentional spans

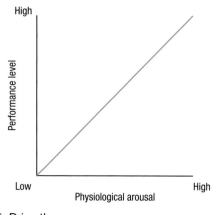

Fig 15.05 Drive theory

experience higher levels of state anxiety. This is important for athletes because their levels of trait anxiety will determine their state anxiety in competition and as a result their performance.

Key learning points

- Stress is any factor which has the effect of changing the natural balance of the body in a physical, mental or behavioural manner.
- Arousal is how interested or excited we become in a given situation.
- Anxiety is a negative emotional response where an individual feels nervous and worried.

Arousal and performance

Arousal levels will have an influence on performance, but it is not always clear what this relationship is. The following theories help to explain the relationship.

Drive theory

This theory, initially the work of Hull (1943), states that, as arousal levels rise, so do performance levels. This happens in linear fashion and can be described as a straight line (see Figure 15.05).

The actual performance also depends on the arousal level and the skill level of the performer. Arousal will exaggerate the individual's dominant response, meaning that if they have learnt the skill well their dominant response will be exaggerated positively. However, if they are a novice performer their skill level will drop to produce a worse performance.

The inverted U hypothesis

This theory is based on the Yerkes and Dodson Law (1908) and seeks to address some of the criticisms of the drive theory. This theory agrees that arousal does improve performance, but only up to a point, and once arousal goes beyond this point performance starts to decline. Figure 15.06 shows the curve looking like an upside-down U.

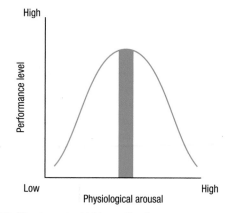

Fig 15.06 The inverted U hypothesis

This theory's main point is that there is an optimum level of arousal before performance starts to diminish. This is also called the ideal performing state (IPS) and is often referred to as 'the zone'. At this point the arousal level meets the demands of the task, and everything feels good and is going well.

Catastrophe theory

This theory has been taken a step further by Fazey and Hardy (1988), who agree with the inverted U hypothesis, but say that once the arousal level has passed a certain point, the IPS will drop off drastically, rather than steadily (see Figure 15.07). The point where performance drops is called the point of catastrophe. The Americans refer to this phenomenon, when performance drops, as 'choking', and the history of sport is littered with examples of people or teams throwing away seemingly unassailable positions.

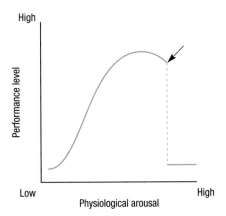

Fig 15.07 Catastrophe theory

Individualised zones of functioning

This theory was developed by Yuri Hanin. He found that each individual athlete will have a level of state anxiety which is most comfortable for them and in which they produce the best performance. If a performer is outside this zone then they will experience a loss in performance. The important point being that each performer is individual and needs to find their own individual zone of functioning (IZOF) to produce their best performance.

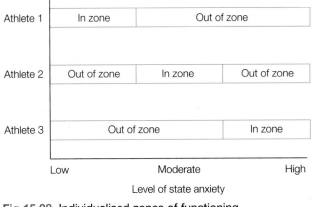

Fig 15.08 Individualised zones of functioning

Group dynamics

Group processes

Throughout our sporting and social lives we are involved in working in groups, such as our families, our school groups, our friendship groups and the sports teams in which we play. Sports teams have different characteristics; for example, an athletics team will have different teamwork demands to a rugby team or a cricket team. However, all groups rely on the fundamental characteristics of teamwork. In 1991 the British 4×400 m relay team beat the highly favoured Americans at the World Championships and Roger Black made the following comments:

> On paper we were not capable of winning the gold medal, but we had a shared belief – that the greater good of the team was more important than any individual ego. That is the secret of teamwork.

Defining a group is not easy; however, the minimum number required for a group is two people. A group can be seen as two or more likeminded people interacting to produce an outcome they could not achieve on their own. Groups involve interaction or working with other people in order to influence the behaviour of other people and in turn be influenced by them.

To define a group we can use the distinguishing characteristics of groups as devised by Weinberg and Gould (2003). A group should have:

- a collective identity
- a sense of shared purpose or objectives
- structured modes of communication
- personal and/or task interdependence
- interpersonal attraction.

The difference between a group and a team

Generally speaking, an instructor will call people who are involved in an exercise class or dance class a group, while people playing cricket or rugby will be called a team. The people involved in the group may have a similar sense of purpose and may share common objectives; however, a team's members will actually be dependent on one another to achieve their shared goals and will need to support each other.

So why is the outcome of the group not always equal to the sum of its parts? For example, we can see in football that the teams with the best players do not always get the results they should. In 2006 the very talented Brazilian and Argentinian teams were knocked out at the quarter-final stage of the World Cup, and in 2004 the European Championships were won by Greece rather than the individually talented Portugal team. In cricket the England one-day side is continually changing its players as it seeks to find a team rather than a group of individuals. We can even see the importance of a team when individual players come together in an event such as the Ryder Cup in golf. In 2006 the British and European team beat the Americans emphatically due to the team feeling that had developed.

Stages of group development

A group of people coming together does not form a team. Becoming a team demands a process of development. Tuckman and Jensen (1977) proposed a five-stage model of group development:

- forming
- storming
- norming
- performing
- adjourning.

Each group will go through the five stages; however, the length of time they spend in each stage is variable.

1 **Forming** – the group comes together, with individuals meeting and familiarising themselves with the other members of the group. The structure and relationships within the group are formed and tested. If it is a team, the coach may develop strategies or games to 'break the ice' between the group members. At this point the individuals are seeing whether they fit in with this group.
2 **Storming** – a period of conflict will follow the forming stage as individuals seek their roles and status within the group. This may involve conflict between individual members, rebellion against the leader or resistance to the way the team is being developed or managed, or the tactics it is adopting. This is also a period of intense inter-group competition, as group members compete for their positions within the team.
3 **Norming** – once the hostility and fighting have been overcome, either by athletes leaving the group or accepting the common goals and values of the group, a period of norming occurs. Here, the group

members start to cooperate and work together to reach common goals. The group pulls together and the roles are established and become stable.
4 **Performing** – in this stage, the group members work together to achieve their mutual goals. The relationships within the group have become well established, as have issues of leadership and strategies for play. It is unrealistic to see the group as being stable and performing in a steady way. The relationships within the group will change and develop with time, sometimes for the good of the group and sometimes to its detriment. As new members join the group there will be a new period of storming and norming, as each person is either accepted or rejected. This re-evaluation of the group is often beneficial and stops the group becoming stale. Successful teams seem to be settled and assimilate two or three new players a year to keep them fresh. Bringing in too many new players can disrupt the group and change the nature of the group completely.
5 **Adjourning** – once the group has achieved its goals or come to the end of its useful purpose then the team may break up. This may also be caused by a considerable change in the personnel involved or the management and leadership of the group.

Group effectiveness

The aim of a group is to be effective by using the strengths of each person to better the effectiveness of the group. However, the outcome is often not equal to the sum of its parts.

Steiner (1972) proposed the following model of group effectiveness:

Actual productivity = potential productivity − process losses

Where: actual productivity = the actual performance achieved
potential productivity = the best possible performance achievable by that group based on its resources (ability, knowledge, skills)
process losses = losses due to working as part of a group (coordination losses, communication problems, losses in motivation)

For example, in a tug-of-war team each member can pull 100 kg individually; as a team of four they pull 360 kg in total. Why do you think this would happen?

Social loafing

One of the problems of working in groups is that it tends to affect motivation. People do not seem to work as hard in groups as they do on their own. Research shows that rowers in larger teams give less effort than those in smaller teams:

1 person = 100% effort
2 people = 90% effort
4 people = 80% effort
8 people = 65% effort

This phenomenon is called the Ringelmann effect, or social loafing, and is defined as the tendency of individuals to lessen their effort when part of a group.

> **definition**
>
> The Ringelmann effect: the tendency for individuals to lessen their effort when working as part of a group.

Cohesion

Cohesion is concerned with the extent to which a team is willing to stick together and work together. Cohesion is defined as:

> ❝ **the total field of forces which act on members to remain in the group** ❞
>
> *(Festinger et al., 1950)*

The forces mentioned in the definition will tend to cover two areas:

- the attractiveness of the group to individual members
- the extent to which members are willing to work together to achieve group goals.

To be successful in its goals, a group has to be cohesive. The extent to which cohesion is important depends upon the sport and the level of interaction needed.

There seem to be two definite types of cohesion within a group:

- **task cohesion** – the willingness of a team to work together to achieve their goals
- **social cohesion** – the willingness of a team to socialise together.

It would appear that task cohesion comes first as this is why the team has formed in the first place. If the group is lucky they will find that they develop social

cohesion as well, and this usually has a beneficial effect on performance. This is because if you feel good about your team-mates you are more likely to want success for each other as well as yourself.

> **LEARNER ACTIVITY**
>
> Place the following ten team sports in order depending upon the level of interaction and thus cohesion needed to be successful.
>
> Rowing eights   Cricket team
> Tennis doubles   Volleyball team
> 4 × 100 m relay   Cycling team
> Golf team   Curling team
> Bobsleigh four   Synchronised swimming team

Research says that cohesion is important in successful teams, but that task cohesion is more important than social cohesion. It does depend upon the sport being played, as groups that need high levels of interaction need higher levels of cohesion.

Research also suggests that success will produce increased cohesion rather than cohesion coming before performance. Being successful helps to develop feelings of group attraction, and this will help to develop more success, and so on. This can be seen by the cycle of success, in that once a team has been successful, it tends to continue being successful, i.e. success breeds success.

> **LEARNER ACTIVITY**
>
> Before reading the section on leadership, take time to answer the following questions.
>
> 1 How would you define 'leadership'?
> 2 Make a list of eight people you consider to be effective leaders. Choose four from sport and four from other areas.
> 3 List eight personality qualities or traits that you think are needed to make an effective leader.
> 4 Are the leadership qualities needed to lead in sport the same as in all leadership situations?
> 5 Do you think an effective leader will be effective in all situations? Why?

Leadership in sport

The choice of a manager, coach or captain is often the most important decision a club's members have to make. They see it as crucial in influencing the club's chances of success. Great leaders in sport are held in the highest regard, irrespective of their talent on the pitch. Sportspeople such as Martin Johnson, Clive Woodward, Alex Ferguson, Michael Vaughan and Linford Christie are all regarded as 'great' leaders.

Leadership can be defined as:

> The behavioural process of influencing individuals and groups towards goals

(Barron, 1977)

Leadership behaviour covers a variety of activities, hence we call it multidimensional; it includes:

- decision-making processes
- motivational techniques
- giving feedback
- establishing interpersonal relationships
- confidently directing the group.

Leaders are different from managers: managers will plan, organise, budget, schedule and recruit; leaders determine how a task is completed.

People become leaders in different ways; not all are appointed. Prescribed leaders are appointed by a person in authority, e.g. a chairman appoints a manager, a manager appoints a coach, a principal appoints a teacher. Emergent leaders emerge from a group and take over responsibility, e.g. John Terry emerged to become the leader of the England football team, just as Steve McLaren emerged to become the new England manager. Emergent leaders are often more effective as they have the respect of their group members.

Theories of leadership

Sport psychologists have sought to explain leadership effectiveness for many years and they have used the following theories to help understand effective leadership behaviour.

Trait approach

In the 1920s researchers tried to show that characteristics or personality traits were stable and common to all leaders. Thus, to be a good leader you needed to have intelligence, assertiveness, independence and self-confidence. Therefore, a person who is a good leader in one situation will be a good leader in all situations.

Behavioural approach

The trait approach says that leaders are 'born', but the behavioural approach says that anyone can become a good leader by learning the behaviour of effective leaders. Thus, this approach supports the view that leadership skills can be developed through experience and training.

Interactional approach

Trait and behavioural approaches look at personality traits. The interactional approach looks at the interaction between the person and the situation. It stresses the following points.

- Effective leaders cannot be predicted solely on personality.
- Effective leadership fits specific situations, as some leaders function better in certain circumstances than others.
- Leadership style needs to change to match the demands of the situation. For example, relationship-orientated leaders develop interpersonal relationships, provide good communication and ensure everyone is feeling good within the group. However, task-orientated leaders are concerned with getting the work done and meeting objectives.

The multidimensional model of sport leadership

The three models previously discussed were adapted from non-sporting examples. Although they help us understand leadership behaviour, each model has its shortcomings. In 1980, Chelladurai and Saleh presented a sport-specific model (see Fig 15.09). They proposed the view that effective leadership will vary depending on the characteristics of the athletes, the leader and the situation.

1. **Situational characteristics** – characteristics such as size, type of sport, winning or losing, the situation the group is in.
2. **Leader characteristics** – the personal qualities of the leader. Some of the qualities needed are confidence, intelligence, assertiveness and self-motivation.
3. **Member characteristics** – the different personality types of different groups of athletes. These characteristics include age, gender, ability level and experience.

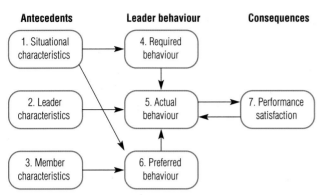

Fig 15.09 Leadership model

4 **Required behaviour** – the type of behaviour required of a leader in a particular situation. For example, if a team is losing with five minutes to go, it is best for the leader to make a decision themselves rather than discuss it with their teammates.

5 **Actual behaviour** – the behaviour the leader actually displays.

6 **Preferred behaviour** – the preferred leadership of the group, depending on their characteristics.

7 **Performance satisfaction** – the extent to which the group members are satisfied with the leader's behaviour and with the outcome of the competition.

The model says that if a leader behaves appropriately for the particular situation and this behaviour matches the preferences of the group members, then they will achieve their best performance and feel satisfied.

The leadership scale for sport

The leadership scale for sport was developed by Chelladurai and Saleh (1980) to assess the five main types of behaviour of coaches in their positions of leadership, and to evaluate how often they use each.

1 **Training and instruction** – information is provided by the coach, aimed at improving the performance of the athlete in terms of technique and strategy.

2 **Democratic behaviour** – the athlete is involved in reaching decisions regarding group goals and group strategy.

3 **Autocratic behaviour** – the coach acts independently, forcing decisions on the group.

4 **Social support behaviour** – this is aimed at improving the well-being and welfare of the athletes and developing group relationships.

5 **Positive feedback behaviour** – this rewards individual and group actions through acknowledging athletes' efforts and performance.

Leadership in sport is a complex subject as it involves the process of influencing people towards achieving their personal goals and the goals of the group. Individuals will respond to different types of leader and different types of leadership behaviour. Different leaders have different strengths and ways of leading, and may find that what was successful in one situation is not so effective in another.

Planning a psychological skills training programme to enhance sporting performance

Identifying psychological strengths and weaknesses

An assessment of an individual's mental strengths and weaknesses can be made in different ways. We will look first at the use of a questionnaire but it could also be done through performance profiling.

Example questionnaire

Name:

Sport played:

- Explain any past experience you have of psychological skills training.
- Explain your involvement in sport and any important competitions or events coming up.
- What do you consider to be your psychological strengths and weaknesses?

Below is a list of statements, circle the answer appropriate to your experience

1. **I always feel motivated to succeed, whatever activity I am doing.**
   Don't know   Never   Sometimes   Usually   Alway

2. **I always work towards clear goals.**
   Don't know   Never   Sometimes   Usually   Alway

3. **I set myself goals on a weekly basis.**
   Don't know   Never   Sometimes   Usually   Always

4. **I always make full use of my skills and abilities.**
   Don't know   Never   Sometimes   Usually   Alway

5. **When I am involved in my physical activity, I often find my attention wavering.**
   Don't know   Never   Sometimes   Usually   Alway

6. **I am easily distracted during whatever activity I am involved in.**
   Don't know   Never   Sometimes   Usually   Always

7. **I perform much better when I am under a lot of pressure.**
   Don't know   Never   Sometimes   Usually   Always

8. **I become very anxious when I am under pressure.**
   Don't know   Never   Sometimes   Usually   Always

9. **If I start to become tense, I can quickly relax myself and calm down.**
   Don't know   Never   Sometimes   Usually   Always

10. **I find it easy to control my emotions, whatever the situation.**
    Don't know   Never   Sometimes   Usually   Always

11. **I am always able to remain upbeat and positive, whatever the situation.**
    Don't know   Never   Sometimes   Usually   Always

12. **If I am criticised by a coach or trainer I tend to take it very badly.**
    Don't know   Never   Sometimes   Usually   Always

13. **I am easily able to deal with unforeseen situations.**
    Don't know   Never   Sometimes   Usually   Always

14. **I have my own set of strategies for dealing with difficult situations.**
    Don't know   Never   Sometimes   Usually   Always

Analysing the results

Questions 1–4 relate to motivation

Questions 5–6 relate to concentration

Questions 7–10 relate to arousal and anxiety

Questions 11–14 relate to self-confidence

There is no scoring system as such, but the questions are designed for you to establish areas of strength and areas of weakness.

Identifying the psychological demands of a sport

Each sport will have an individual psychological demand on it which is also constantly open to change. The main categories of psychological demands are shown in Fig 15.10.

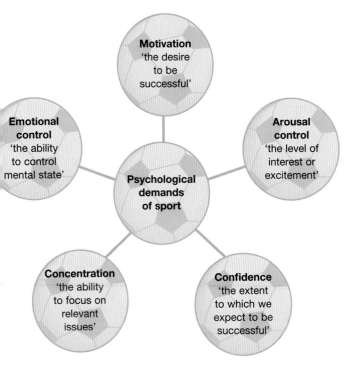

Fig 15.10 Psychological demands of sport

By using techniques such as performance profiling we can assess why each one of these is important in our sport, how important it is and our current level of competence at the skill. Once our current competence level and the importance of the skill to the sport have been identified then you can lay down the aims of the training programme and begin to identify the content and the techniques needed to address these skills.

Techniques to influence motivation: goal setting

The main way that sports psychologists develop motivation is through the use of goal setting.

> A goal: what an individual is aiming to achieve. It is the outcome they desire from their actions.

In reality they are the dreams we have for ourselves but goal setting gives these dreams legs and starts moving us towards them. A goal usually represents a situation we want to be in, which involves us moving away from the situation we are currently in.

Why does goal setting work?

Goal setting works because it gives our wants and desires a specific outcome and gives us the steps we need to move towards this outcome. It gives our daily actions a meaning or framework to work within and gives us direction in life. Goals will work to direct our energy and efforts.

What you focus on you will move towards

Short-term, medium-term and long-term goals

Short-term goals are set over a brief period of time, usually from one day to one month. A short-term goal may relate to what you want to achieve in one training session or where you want to be by the end of the month.

Short-term goals can be:

- one session
- one day
- one week
- one month.

Medium-term goals will bridge the gap between short- and long-term goals and are set from one to three months.

Long-term goals will run from three months to over several years. You may even set some lifetime goals which run until you retire from your sport. In sport we set long-term goals to cover a season or a sporting year.

Long-term goals can be:

- four months
- six months
- nine months
- one year
- one season
- three years
- lifetime.

Usually short-term goals are set to help achieve the long-term goals. It is important to set both short-term and long-term goals, particularly short-term goals because they will give a person more motivation to act now. If you have to give in a piece of coursework tomorrow it will make you work hard tonight but if you have to submit it in one month then you are unlikely to stay in tonight and complete the work!

Outcome and process goals

An outcome goal focuses on the outcome of an event or performance, such as winning a race or beating an opponent.

A process goal focuses on the process or actions that an individual must produce to perform well – for example, train three times a week or get eight hours' sleep a night.

Both types of goal are important and we find that short-term goals are normally process goals while long-term goals are outcome goals.

The process goals will be the small steps we take towards the big outcome or goal. A marathon race is the result of millions of small steps and it is each individual step which is most important at that time.

SMART goals

When goals are set you need to use the SMART principle to make them workable. SMART stands for the following:

- **Specific**
- **Measurable**
- **Achievable**
- **Realistic**
- **Time-constrained.**

- **Specific** – the goal must be specific to what you want to achieve. This may be an aspect of performance of fitness. It is not enough to say 'I want to get fitter', you need to say 'I want to improve strength, speed or stamina, etc.'
- **Measurable** – goals must be stated in a way that is measurable, so they need to state figures. For example, I want to improve my first serve percentage is not measurable. However, if you say I want to improve my first serve success by 20 per cent it is measurable.
- **Achievable** – it must be possible to actually achieve the goal.
- **Realistic** – we need to be realistic in our setting and look at what factors may stop us achieving the goal.
- **Time-constrained** – there must be a timescale or deadline on the goal. This means you can review your success. It is best to state a date by which you wish to achieve the goal.

How to set goals

The best way to do this is to answer three questions.

1 What do I want to achieve? (Desired state)
2 Where am I now? (Present state)
3 What do I need to do to move from my present state to my desired state?

Then present this on a scale:

Present state   Desired state
| | | | | |
1   2   3   4   5

1 Write in your goal at point 5 and your present position at point 1.
2 Decide what would be halfway between points 1 and 5; this is your goal for point 3.
3 Then decide what would be halfway between your present state and point 3; this is your short-term goal for point 2.
4 Then decide what would be halfway between point 3 and the desired state; this is your goal for point 4.
5 All these goals are outcome goals and must be set using the SMART principle.
6 Work out what needs to be done to move from point 1 to point 2. These are your process goals and must again use the SMART principle.

It is best to use a goal-setting diary to keep all goal-setting information in the same place, and to review the goals on a weekly basis.

LEARNER ACTIVITY

1 Think about your own sport and set yourself a goal which you would like to achieve in the next year.
2 Using the process above set yourself outcome goals and then work out the process goals to get you from point 1 to point 2.

Techniques to influence motivation: performance profiling

Performance profiling is a way of getting the athlete to analyse their own strengths and weaknesses. It can be a way of monitoring improvements in psychological skills as well as being used to motivate and energise athletes.

The benefits of performance profiling are as follows.

- It considers what the individual feels is important.
- The individual is actively involved and will feel some sense of possession of their performances.
- It is used to motivate and monitor improvements.

- It is specific for each athlete.
- The visual display helps to give it more power.
- It enables the athlete and coach to identify areas of weakness.

Process of performance profiling

1 Introduce the idea of performance profiling

This may be a new concept for the athlete and a period of explaining the process will be valuable. You will need to cover the following information:

- explain performance profiling
- explain the benefits and how the results can be applied
- emphasise there are no wrong or right answers and what is important is the individual's view
- show them examples of completed performance profiles (they should be anonymous).

2 Elicit the constructs

The sport psychologist will need to ask the athlete to come up with ten psychological factors that are vital to their performance. You may ask a question such as 'What psychological factors do you consider to be most important in helping you to achieve your best performance?'

The sport psychologist may assist the process by making relevant suggestions if the athlete is struggling to come up with good responses.

The ten factors they come up with are called 'constructs'.

3 Assess the constructs

The athlete is asked to complete the following tasks.

- Rate themselves on a scale of 1–10 to show their current level of competence at each construct. A rating of 10 would represent their idea of perfection.
- Rate how far they would like to progress towards their idea of perfection; they may feel that a score of 10 is not necessary and they would be happy to get to 7.

4 Plot the performance profile

Once the above tasks have been completed, you can present the information on a grid such as the one below. The dark bars show current levels of competence and the lighter bars show desired levels.

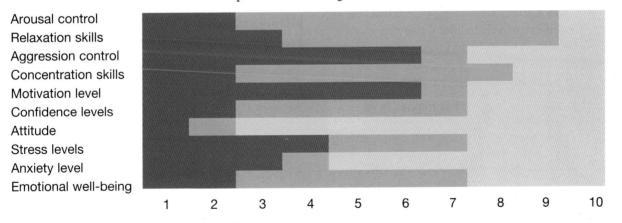

You can then use this information in different ways.

- Assess their strengths and weaknesses.
- See what they feel is important in their sport.

- As their coach you may have different ideas about what is important and their level of skill. This exercise will highlight any differences in your points of view.

You can identify the following information from the profile.

- Areas of perceived strength – where they score 5 or more (e.g. Aggression control).
- Areas of perceived weakness – where they score less than 5 (e.g. Arousal control).
- Areas resistant to change – where there is little difference between their current rating and the rating they would like to achieve (e.g. Attitude).

LEARNER ACTIVITY

1 Complete a performance profile regarding your psychological skills by following the above process.
2 Once it is complete write down the following:
   - areas of strength
   - areas of weakness
   - areas resistant to change
   - prioritise which psychological skills you need to work on first.

Imagery

Imagery is one of the most important techniques in sport psychology because the pictures and thoughts that we have in our head will influence how we feel and then how we behave. If we can have positive thoughts and images it is going to be beneficial to our performance.

What is imagery?

Imagery is the creation or re-creation of an image or experience in your mind rather than physically practising the skill. It will involve the employment of all the senses in actually re-creating the experience. Imagery is used extensively by many athletes, particularly golfers and track and field athletes. Jack Nicklaus, one of the most successful golfers of all time, explains how he uses visualisation:

> Before every shot I go to the movies in my head. Here is what I see. First I see the ball where I want it to finish, nice and white, sitting up high on the bright green grass. Then I see the ball going there; its path and trajectory and even its behaviour on landing. The next scene shows me making the kind of swing that will turn the previous image into reality. These home images are the key to my concentration and to my positive approach to every shot.

Imagery is a skill and some people will be better at it than others. If you find developing images difficult then you will need to use the practices later to help you with this skill.

Why does imagery work?

Imagery works because when you imagine yourself performing a skill the brain is unable to differentiate between a real experience and an imagined experience. As a result the brain sends impulses to the muscles via the nervous system; these impulses are not strong enough to produce a muscular contraction, although you may see twitches. As the impulses are passed down the nervous system so the pattern becomes imprinted on the nervous system and is there for whenever you physically perform the skill. It is as if you have been there without actually going there.

Imagery can be used for the following skills:

- management of mental state
- mental rehearsal
- relaxation techniques
- developing confidence
- concentration skills.

Mental rehearsal

Mental rehearsal is taking time to sit down and think about your sport. It is seeing, feeling and hearing yourself playing your sport. It can be utilised in different ways:

- developing and practising skills
- reducing anxiety about an event
- practising 'what if . . .' scenarios
- developing confidence before an event
- to replay and review performance.

Rather than just physical practice mental rehearsal can complement your skill development. However, you need to have well-developed imagery skills to be able to perform mental rehearsal effectively.

Developing and practising skills

Mental rehearsal can be used before, during and after competitions to ensure the best performance. Roger Black, who won the 400 m silver medal in the 1996 Olympics, talks about the power of mental rehearsal:

> For the Olympic Games I walked around the stadium four months prior and I kept that picture in my mind every day. I ran it from every lane. I could close my eyes now and run the 400 m race and I would feel how I would feel.

Guidelines for mental rehearsal

1 Precede the activity with a short relaxation session.
2 Bring up the picture and make sure it is big, colourful, sharply focused and bright, as in a movie.
3 Employ all your senses by hearing the sounds associated and also the feelings of performing.
4 Visualise at the correct speed (same speed as the action).
5 Always visualise yourself successfully executing the skills.
6 Visualise from inside your head looking out.
7 Practise in intervals of 5–10 minutes a day.

LEARNER ACTIVITY

Choose five skills from your sport and spend one minute rehearsing each in your mind.

Developing confidence before an event

Self-confidence is the extent to which you expect to be successful. If you can, use imagery to recall times when you were sure about being successful or you can use the following activity to help you experience what it would be like to be completely self-confident.

Techniques to control arousal levels

According to the inverted U hypothesis our performance is related to our arousal level. If we are over-aroused then we need to reduce arousal by using relaxation techniques; conversely if we find ourselves under-aroused then we need to use energising techniques to raise our arousal level.

LEARNER ACTIVITY

Use a role model to develop confidence through the following steps.

1 Think of a sportsperson who is totally self-confident.
2 Observe their posture, their facial expressions and their behaviour.
3 Now go over to your role model and float into their body. Experience their posture, what they see, hear and feel.
4 Then take yourself back into your body and keep the feeling of self-confidence.
5 See yourself acting and feeling confident in specific situations.
6 Keep repeating this activity until the feelings are locked in.

Relaxation techniques

There is a range of relaxation techniques which address different aspects of the effects of stress and anxiety. They are:

- progressive muscular relaxation (PMR)
- mind to muscle techniques (imagery)
- breathing control.

Certainly relaxation techniques will control arousal before and during performance, and they can also be used for other purposes:

- to lower levels of trait and state anxiety
- to help the athlete fall into a deep sleep before or after a competition
- to keep the athlete calm and reduce energy lost through nervous worry before a competition
- to relax and recover during breaks in play or between races or matches
- to help recovery from illness and injury
- to help them enjoy their life in general.

When performing relaxation techniques it is important to follow these instructions.

1 Find a place where you will not be disturbed.
2 Sit or lie down in a comfortable place.
3 Close your eyes and turn down the lighting.
4 Put on some relaxing music.
5 Enjoy the experience.

- **Progressive muscular relaxation (PMR)** – this technique is excellent for people who are experiencing the symptoms of somatic anxiety such as tension in the muscles and butterflies in the stomach. PMR involves listening to a recording of a script or a psychologist reading out a script where muscle groups are sequentially contracted and then relaxed. This starts from the hands and arms, up to the face, upper body and then lower body.
- **Mind to muscle techniques (imagery)** – these techniques will work with a person who is experiencing cognitive anxiety. It works best with people who have well-developed imagery skills. This technique involves listening to a recording of a script or a psychologist reading out a script where you develop pictures in your head. These pictures will be of a relaxing place or room where you can go to rest and relax when you need to.
- **Breathing control** – breathing control is a method often used by athletes to reduce muscle tension and lower anxiety levels. When we become stressed and anxious we will experience short and shallow breathing; when we are relaxed our breathing deepens.

  To aid relaxation we can teach the athlete to breathe deeply and slowly from the diaphragm to produce mental and physical relaxation. If they are focusing on their breathing it will shift their attention from whatever is causing them stress. It can be done in a standing or sitting position. Get the individual to place their hands on their stomach; see how the hands move out and fall back as they breathe in and out.

  Once they have learnt how to breathe properly they can use it at the appropriate time during a competition.

Energising techniques

If the athlete is feeling under-aroused there are ways of raising the arousal level. For example, many coaches will use music to psych their athletes up and raise their energy levels. This can be a personal choice or a team may develop a theme tune which they play before performing to lift them. Also scripts, similar in style to relaxation scripts, can be employed to raise arousal and energy levels.

- **Self-talk to develop confidence** – self-talk is what we say to ourselves when we have internal conversations, and this affects our mental state at any time. If we have positive thoughts and say positive things to ourselves then we will maintain high levels of confidence. However, if we say to ourselves that we are useless and no good then that is how we will act and we will get poor outcomes as a result. We need to keep building our confidence by reframing any negative thoughts we have in a positive way. For example, rather than saying 'I always perform poorly against Sheena' you might say 'Playing Sheena is a good challenge for me.'

LEARNER ACTIVITY

Reframe these statements in a positive way to boost confidence:

- 'I find I lose concentration in the second half'
- 'I am not good enough to beat Sian'
- 'I always run badly in the rain'
- 'If I don't get one set up on Becky she always beats me'

Review questions

1. What is meant by the term 'personality'?
2. How do trait theories and social learning theories of personality differ?
3. Discuss the two ways a social theorist says that we learn our personality.
4. Explain how stress can be a positive and negative influence on people.
5. What is meant by the terms 'arousal' and 'anxiety', and how do they influence performance?
6. Explain the term 'motivation' and the differences between intrinsic and extrinsic motivation.
7. What is meant by the term 'group'?
8. Discuss the five stages of group development.
9. What is cohesion, and explain the two types of cohesion.
10. Discuss the multidimensional model of leadership and how it explains group success and failure.
11. Why is goal setting of interest to a sport psychologist and their athletes?
12. Explain the use of the acronym SMART in goal setting.
13. Briefly explain how you would implement the technique of performance profiling.
14. Explain how imagery can be used to improve sporting performance and why it works.
15. Explain two techniques to reduce arousal levels.
16. What five psychological areas can be developed through a psychological skills training programme?

References

Bandura, A. (1973) *Aggression: A Social Learning Analysis,* Prentice Hall.

Bandura, A. (1977a), *Social Learning Theory,* Prentice Hall.

Bandura, A. (1977b) (Self-efficacy: toward a unifying theory of behavioural change). *Psychological Review,* 84, 191–215.

Bandura, A. (1986) *Social Foundations of Thought and Action,* Prentice Hall.

Bandura, A. (1997) *Self Efficacy: The Exercise of Control,* Freeman.

Baron and Richardson (1994) *Human Aggression,* Plenum.

Beashel, P. and Taylor, J. (1996) *Advanced Studies in Physical Education and Sport,* Nelson.

Berkowitz, L. (1969) *Roots of Aggression,* Atherton Press.

Berkowitz, L. (1989) *Aggression: Its Causes and Consequences and Control,* Temple University Press.

Bowers, K. S. (1973) Situationism in psychology: an analysis and a critique, *Psychological Review,* 80, 307–36.

Buzan, T. (2005) *The Ultimate Book of Mind Maps,* Thorsons.

Cattell, R. B. (1965) *The Scientific Analysis of Personality,* Penguin.

Chelladurai, P. and Carron, A. V. (1978) *Leadership,* Sociology of Sport Monograph Series.

Chelladurai, P. and Saleh, S. D. (1980) Dimensions of leadership behaviour in sport: development of a leadership behaviour scale. *Journal of Sport Psychology,* 2, 34–45.

Cottrell, N. B. (1968) Performance in the presence of other human beings. Mere presence, audience and affiliation effects, in E. Simmell, R. Hoppe and G. Milton (eds) *Social Facilitation and Imitative Behaviour,* Allyn & Bacon.

Cox, R. (1998) *Sports Psychology: Concepts and Applications,* Wm C. Brown Communications.

Davis, R. J., Bull, C. R., Roscoe, J. V. and Roscoe, D. A. (2000) *Physical Education and the Study of Sport,* Mosby.

Dollard, J., Doob, J. Miller, N., Mowrer, O. and Sears, R. (1939) *Frustration and Aggression,* Yale University Press.

Fazey, J. and Hardy, L. (1988) *The inverted U hypothesis: a catastrophe for sport psychology?* British Association of Sports Sciences Monograph, no. 1. NCF.

Festinger, L. A., Schachter, S. and Back, K. (1950) *Social Pressures in Informal Groups: A Study of Human Factors in Housing,* Harper.

Hollander, E. P. (1971) *Principles and Methods of Social Psychology,* Oxford University Press.

Hull, C. L. (1943) *Principles of Behaviour,* Appleton Century Crofts.

Jarvis, M. (2000) *Sport Psychology,* Routledge.

Jarvis, M. (2006) *A Student's Handbook,* Routledge.

Latane, B., Harkins, S. G. and Williams, K. D. (1980) *Many Hands make Light Work: Social Loafing as a Social Disease*. Unpublished manuscript, Ohio State University.

Martens, R. (1977) *Sport Competitive Anxiety Test*, Human Kinetics.

McGrath, J. E. (1970) Major methodological issues, in J. E. McGrath (ed.) *Social and Psychological Factors in Stress*, Holt, Rinehart & Winston.

Oxendine, C. B. (1970) Emotional arousal and motor performance. *Quest*, 13, 23–30.

Prochaska, J. and Di Clemente, C. (1983) Stages and processes of self change of smoking. *Journal of Consulting and Clinical Psychology*, 51, 390–5.

Sage, G. (1974) *Sport and American Society*, Addison Wesley.

Schurr, K., Ashley, M. and Joy, K. (1977) A multivariate analysis of male athlete characteristics: sport type and success. *Multivariate Experimental Clinical Research*, 3, 53–68.

Smith, M. D. (1988) Interpersonal sources of violence in hockey: the influence of parents, coaches and teammates, in F. M. Smoll, R. A. Magill and M. J. Ash (eds) *Children in Sport* (3rd edn), Human Kinetics.

Steiner, I. D. (1972) *Group Processes and Productivity*, Academic Press.

Triplett, N. (1898) The dynamogenic factors in pacemaking and competition. *American Journal of Psychology*, 9, 507–33.

Tuckman, L. and Jensen, M. (1977) *Stages of Small Group Development Revisited*, Group and Organisational Studies.

Weinberg, R. S. and Gould, D. (2003) *Foundations of Sport and Exercise Psychology*, Human Kinetics.

Wesson, K., Wiggins, N., Thompson, G. and Hartigan, S. (2000) *Sport and PE: A Complete Guide to Advanced Level Study*, Hodder Arnold.

Williams, J. M. (1980) Personality characteristics of the successful female athlete, in W. M. Straub, *Sport Psychology: An Analysis of Athlete Behavior*, Movement.

Woods, B. (1998) *Applying Psychology to Sport*, Hodder & Stoughton.

Yerkes, R. M. and Dodson, J. D. (1908) The relationship of strength and stimulus to rapid habit formation. *Journal of Comparative Neurology and Psychology*, 18, 459–82.

Zajonc, R. B. (1965) Social facilitation. *Science*, 149, 269–74.

16

Goals

By the end of this chapter you should:

- understand how common sports injuries can be prevented by the correct identification of risk factors
- know about a range of sports injuries and their symptoms
- know how to apply methods of treating sports injuries
- be able to plan and construct treatment and rehabilitation programmes for two common sports injuries.

While participation in sport and physical activity has a lot of positive aspects, such as improving fitness levels and being involved in a social group who share common interests, it also has a negative aspect in the form of incurring physical injury. This chapter will identify different types of sports injuries and how they can occur. It will consider both physiological and psychological responses to injury and then suggest some methods to prevent and treat sports injuries. Finally, the chapter will outline a range of rehabilitation procedures that can be considered, together with important information on tracking and documenting injuries and their treatment.

Risk factors and prevention of sports injuries

Taking part in sport can result in injury to any part of the body. These injuries can be caused by a variety of factors which can be grouped into two categories:

- extrinsic risk factors
- intrinsic risk factors.

Extrinsic risk factors

An extrinsic risk factor is something external to the body that can cause an injury. These include:

- inappropriate coaching or instruction
- incorrect technique
- environmental conditions
- other sports players
- equipment, clothing and footwear issues.

Inappropriate coaching or instruction

Inappropriate instruction given by a coach or a trainer is an obvious way in which sports participants can easily become injured. It is vital that all instruction is given by someone who has an up-to-date depth of knowledge about the sport and is also able to communicate this appropriately and effectively. It is essential that the rules and regulations for the sport, as laid down by the specific governing body, have been correctly interpreted and are appropriately enforced. Likewise, during training activities, it is important that the information given by the coach/trainer is reliable. For this reason, many governing bodies have coaching schemes that are constantly reviewed so that coaching qualifications can be maintained at the highest and safest of standards.

Incorrect technique

The technique of performing an action or specific sport skill is usually dictated by the guidance that the sports participant has received from the PE teacher, coach, trainer or instructor. This being the case, the above is particularly relevant. But it is very easy for individuals to start to slip from these standards if they are not reinforced at the right time. If correction does not occur the participant can soon start to adopt bad habits in terms of skill level and performance. This incorrect performance of skill can in turn lead to injury problems. An obvious example is weight lifting, where back injuries particularly occur due to incorrect and bad or poor technique.

Environmental conditions

The environment in which we perform sports can also have a big impact on the likelihood of sustaining an injury. The environment encompasses the area in which a sport is played, so if you were playing basketball the environment would consist of the sports hall, and include the playing surface, the lighting and the temperature. If the lighting was poor, a player may be more likely to misjudge attacking or defensive moves and injure themselves or another player. If the surface was wet, a player would be more likely to slip over because the surface becomes much more dangerous when it is wet.

Other sports players

Some sports are obviously more susceptible to incurring sports injuries as the rules of the sport allow for tackles, scrums, etc. These are called contact sports. For instance, after a rugby game players will often come away with at least a few bruises from tackling or being tackled by other players. In non-contact games, players can also sustain sports injuries from other players from foul tackles or accidental collisions.

Equipment, clothing and footwear issues

It is important to remember to always use the equipment needed to play a particular sport correctly or this too can increase the chances of injury to either the player themselves or to other players. For example, if a javelin, shot-put or a discus are not held and thrown correctly any improper use could cause serious damage to an individual.

The use of appropriate clothing can also be an issue. Certain sports require, as stipulated by the respective governing body of the sport, certain pieces of protective clothing, such as shin pads for football, pads, gloves and helmets for cricket and hockey.

Other sports, by their very nature, need to have clothing which is very flexible and allows a full range of movement. For example, gymnasts wear clothing which allows them to perform complex movements on the floor and on specialised equipment. If restrictive clothing was worn this could greatly reduce the range of movement allowed and therefore cause injury.

Correct footwear for the correct surface that the sport is to be played on is a must. There is a phenomenal array of specialised footwear for all sports including running, basketball, tennis/squash, gymnastics, football and rugby. All these specialised pieces of footwear are made to be supportive to the player and totally suitable for the surface required for the sport. Football has grass, artificial turf and sports hall floors as its main playing areas and there are specialised shoes and boots for each surface. However, although a sportsperson may be wearing the correct footwear, certain types of footwear make a person more susceptible to injury. For instance, the studs on a footballer's or rugby player's boot can make the wearer more susceptible to leg injuries because the studs plant the foot in the ground, so if the person is turning on a planted foot they are more likely to twist their knee.

Incorrect footwear can also be a factor in causing a person to injure themselves while playing sport. For example, a marathon runner needs a lot of cushioning in their trainers to absorb the repeated impact of running. If they were to wear trainers with little padding they would be much more likely to sustain an overuse sport injury.

Intrinsic risk factors

An intrinsic risk factor is a physical aspect of the athlete's body that can cause an injury.

These include:

- inadequate warm-up
- muscle imbalance
- poor preparation
- postural defects
- poor technique
- overuse
- age.

Inadequate warm-up

This is a very common cause of sports injury. The warm-up prepares both the body and the mind for the exercise that is to come by gradually taking the body from its non-active state to being ready for the exercise. How long it takes to warm up will vary from person to person, and will depend on their level of fitness. The environment will also affect the length of the warm-up. In cold surroundings it will be necessary to carry out a longer warm-up than in hot surroundings.

A warm-up should consist of three components:

- a pulse raiser to get the blood flowing more quickly around the body and so help to warm up the muscle tissues and make them more pliable

- a mobiliser, in which the joints are taken through their range of movement, such as arm circles, to mobilise the shoulder joint
- the main muscles that are going to be used in the sport should be stretched.

LEARNER ACTIVITY Warm-up

Devise a warm up for a sport of your choice that consists of the following components:

- a pulse raiser
- a mobiliser
- a stretch.

Muscle imbalance

A muscle imbalance means that one muscle in an antagonistic pair is stronger than the other. This is often seen in footballers who have strong quadriceps muscles from extending their knee to kick the ball, but their hamstring muscles are not as strong. This can result in knee injuries because the hamstring muscles are not strong enough to put a brake on the kicking action of the knee. As a result, when a striker goes to score a goal they can over-kick, so that their knee hyperextends and gets injured.

Poor preparation

This includes a player's fitness levels specific to the sport they are going to take part in. If a person is not fit to take part in a sport they are more likely to injure themselves because they are so tired that they develop a poor sports technique. A sportsperson must also acclimatise to the environment in which they are going to play. For example, if a marathon runner living in England takes part in a race in Australia in the summer time, they have to train in hot conditions to get their body used to the heat.

Postural defects

Most people are born with a slight postural defect, such as having one leg slightly longer than the other. If there is a large difference between the two legs, this can affect the person's running technique, which may then place more strain on one side of the body, which would make the person more likely to sustain injuries after long periods of exercising.

Poor technique

If a person is not using the correct methods for exercising, they are more likely to sustain a sports injury. For example, if a swimmer continues to perform the front crawl stroke incorrectly with their arms, they may be prone to shoulder or elbow injuries. Note how this differs from the description of incorrect technique in the extrinsic factors section. Poor technique is related to the individual's performance without the use of equipment as opposed to incorrect techniques related to the misuse of equipment to perform a movement.

Overuse

An overuse injury is caused because a sportsperson does not take time to recover after exercise. Every time we exercise we place our body under strain, which means the body has to repair itself afterwards. If a person does not allow their body to repair itself it will become weaker until eventually parts of the body become injured. Also, if we continue to use specific parts of the body over a long period of time the repair is sometimes difficult to manage. A runner puts a lot of pressure and strain through their body and particularly through the knees. Injuries to the knee joint can start to be a problem if a runner has trained or competed for a long period of time, even allowing for rest periods within training.

Age

The type of injury that is most common varies with the age of the subject and also the level of competition. In young children most injuries are due to falling. In older children injuries that result from collisions and violence are more common. In older age groups and in top-level sportsmen and women there are less acute injuries and more overuse injuries and those that are due to intrinsic factors.

Preventative measures

Besides maintaining fitness and doing a warm-up, an important way to prevent sports injuries is to wear protective clothing. As already noted, some sports require their use by the governing body in order to minimise injury. Some sports do not have these but an individual can still consider protecting themselves with the use of certain items such as a gum shield or knee pads.

Suitable clothing minimises the risk of sustaining an injury in any sport. At the very least, people should wear loose-fitting or stretchy clothing and appropriate footwear. Jewellery should always be removed.

Supervision by a suitably qualified coach will also help to prevent injuries. Supervision should ensure that the sports performer is using the correct techniques for their sport. They will also be able to design training programmes that can adapt with the performer's needs. For example, if the sports performer is not training to the best of their ability,

the coach may include more rest during one week of the training programme to ensure the person has recovered suitably from their training. A coach will also ensure that the equipment and environment is appropriate for training and, if not, they would ensure that either protective clothing or equipment is used or an alternative safe training session is carried out.

Sports injuries and their symptoms

The repair of injured soft tissue, such as muscle, actually commences within the first 24 hours following injury. One of the first signs that soft tissue is injured is the appearance of swelling. When the injured area starts to swell it will feel painful. This is due to the swelling creating pressure on the nerves surrounding the damaged tissue. The swelling occurs because the surrounding blood vessels are ruptured, allowing blood to bleed into the area and tissue fluid to gather around the injury site. The injured area will usually look red because the blood vessels surrounding the site dilate, which also has the effect of making the injured area feel hot. The injured area

LEARNER ACTIVITY

Identify the pieces of protective equipment that sportspeople wear during competition in order to minimise the risk of incurring an injury for the following sports:

- football
- cricket
- fencing
- hockey
- rock climbing
- weight lifting
- rugby
- boxing
- canoeing
- gymnastics.

LEARNER ACTIVITY

In the following sports injuries an extrinsic or intrinsic factor has been identified that might be the cause. Suggest what preventative measures you would take to avoid the injury.

Injury	Extrinsic factor	Preventative measure	Intrinsic factor	Preventative measure
Dislocated finger	Ball hitting finger			
Hamstring pull			Muscle imbalance	
Concussion	Tripped and slipped on wet sports hall floor			
Ankle strain			Poor/inappropriate warm-up/training/overuse injury	

will show a reduced function or a total inability to function because of the pain and swelling.

The level of the above signs and symptoms will be directly related to the degree of the injury – the greater the degree of damage, the greater the effects of inflammation.

It is over a period of between 48 and 72 hours and up to 21 days that the repair is carried out with vigour by the body. The body's clotting mechanism seals the end of the torn blood vessels so that further blood plasma cannot escape into the surrounding tissues.

As the immediate effects of injury subside the healing/repair process begins. This consists of:

- absorption of swelling
- removal of debris and blood clot
- growth of new blood capillaries
- development of initial fibrous scar tissue.

After 12 hours, and for the first four days, the cells soon become active and new capillary blood vessel buds form and gradually grow to establish a new circulation in the area. With the new blood supply the debris of dead cell tissues and the initial blood clot that was formed is cleared.

Scar tissue

The damaged tissue is repaired by scar tissue. It is important to remember that scar tissue has 'plastic' properties.

Scar tissue is not elastic like muscle. It will form in a haphazard pattern of 'kinks and curls' and will contract or shorten if not carefully stretched daily for many months after the injury.

There is a great need for the new scar tissue to form in parallel 'lines' to give it strength. Correct 'stretching'

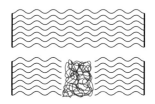

Fig 16.01 Scar tissue (bottom)

causes the scar tissue to line up along the line of stress of the injured structure. Therefore injured muscles or ligaments should be carefully mobilised and stretched daily (beginning five days after the initial injury).

The stretching will ensure that the scar is moulded to the desired length and improve the strength of the healed area (scar), and thus reduce a recurrence of damage to the scarred area and injured structure.

Muscular system

For a detailed discussion of skeletal muscular structure and function read Chapter 1: The body in action.

Ligaments and tendons

Other tissues that are frequently damaged during sport are ligaments and tendons. These are also soft tissue and are primarily made out of collagen. Ligaments connect bone to bone and tendons connect muscles to bone. Ligaments and tendons can adapt to changes in their mechanical environment due to injury, disease or exercise. A ligament or tendon is made up of fascicles.

Each fascicle contains the basic fibril of the ligament or tendon and the fibroblasts, the cells that make the ligament or tendon.

Unlike normal ligaments, healed ligaments are partly made up of a different type of collagen, which has fibrils with a smaller diameter, and are therefore a mechanically inferior structure. As a result, the healed ligament often fails to provide adequate joint stability which can then lead to re-injury or a chronically lax (permanently slightly unstable) joint.

Classification of injuries

There are many ways in which we can classify the severity of an injury. One example is that there are three general stages of injury which can be applied to most sports injuries:

1 acute stage (0 to 72 hours after injury)
2 sub-acute stage (72 hours to 21 days after injury)
3 chronic continuum (21 days after injury).

Note that the severity of the injury will dictate stages 2 and 3 of the above model – less severe will reach stage 3 sometime before day 21, more severe may take longer than 21 days.

The following are examples of specific injuries and how they can be classified.

Haematomas

A haematoma is bleeding either into or around a muscle. If the bleeding is within the muscle it is called an 'intramuscular' haematoma. This type of haematoma will lead to a pressure build-up within the muscle tissue as the blood is trapped within the muscle sheath. This will result in a marked decrease in strength of the injured muscle, a significant decrease in muscle stretch and a long recovery period.

Fig 16.02 An intramuscular haematoma

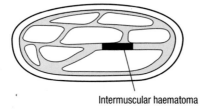

Fig 16.03 An intermuscular haematoma

Bleeding around the muscle tissue is called an intermuscular haematoma. This type of haematoma is much less severe than an intramuscular haematoma because the blood can escape from the damaged muscle and into the surrounding tissues, so there is less pressure in the area and the injury recovers much more quickly.

Sprained ankle

Injuries to the ligaments of the ankle are usually graded into three categories.

- A first-degree sprain is the least severe. It is the result of some minor stretching of the ligaments, and is accompanied by mild pain, some swelling and joint stiffness. There is usually very little loss of joint stability.

- A second-degree sprain is the result of both stretching and some tearing of the ligaments. There is increased swelling and pain and a moderate loss of stability at the ankle joint.

- A third-degree sprain is the most severe of the three. It is the result of a complete tear or rupture of one or more of the ligaments that make up the ankle joint. A third-degree sprain will result in massive swelling, severe pain and gross instability. With a third-degree sprain, shortly after the injury most of the localised pain will disappear. This is a result of the nerve endings being severed, which causes a lack of feeling at the injury site.

From the explanations above, you can see that pain and swelling are the two most common symptoms associated with an ankle sprain. You can also expect some bruising to occur at the injury site. The associated swelling and bruising are the result of ruptured blood vessels and this in turn will produce heat or inflammation.

Psychological responses to injury

The response to injury varies from individual to individual. It may vary within an individual alone dependent on when the injury occurs – at the start of a training session, middle of a season, during a major competition.

The reaction initially is negative in the main but positive attitudes can be formed. For example, it may give an individual more personal time to spend with family and friends, or time to develop new skills such as coaching, or to work on other aspects of their performance. Generally, though, the reaction is negative.

In reality, while some individuals struggle with the negative feelings that they experience, most cope without great difficulty, particularly if the injury is not so severe.

Various theoretical models have been proposed to explain the response to injury. These all include as early reactions:

- shock
- disbelief
- denial.

These are followed by possible further responses:

- anger
- depression

- tension
- helplessness
- acceptance
- adaptation
- reorganisation.

After the initial shock is over, many athletes tend to play down the significance of the injury. However, as the injury becomes more apparent, shock is often replaced by anger directed towards themselves or towards other people. The responses can vary in intensity depending on situational and personal factors but can be especially strong in individuals whose self-concept and personal identity are based on being 'an athlete/a player/a competitor'. The loss of this identity due to the inability to perform can cause much distress.

Following anger, the injured athlete might try bargaining or rationalising to avoid the reality of the situation. A runner may promise to train extra hard on return to training. By confronting reality, and realising and understanding the consequences of the injury, an individual can become depressed at the uncertainty of the future. An injured individual who belongs to a team may start to feel isolated from the 'group' and this in turn can lead to depression. It must be noted, however, that depression is not inevitable and has not always been observed during the grief reaction in research studies.

Tension and helplessness are then generated as the individual becomes frustrated at not being able to continue as normal with training or playing. Again, the isolation that injury causes, from a normal routine or from being with 'the team' can be difficult for some people to accept.

Finally, the individual starts to move towards an acceptance of the injury and adaptation of lifestyle while injured. The focus is then turned to rehabilitation and a return to sports activity. This stage tends to mark the transition from an emotional stage to a problem-coping stage as the individual realises what needs to be done to aid recovery. The timescale for progression through these stages can vary considerably depending on the individual and the severity of the injury, and setbacks during rehabilitation can lead to further emotional disturbance. In cases of very serious injury and ones in which the emotional reactions are prolonged, the skills of a clinical psychologist might be required.

It must be stressed that this process may not be a linear one for all individuals who experience some of these feelings.

Motivations and goal-setting strategies have been shown to help some people. It is possible as a coach, trainer or parent to help an injured individual recover sensibly, effectively and more positively by encouraging them to follow professional advice relating to physical rehabilitation. You can also reassure them that the feelings they are experiencing are not uncommon.

The channelling of a positive attitude can ease the rehabilitation for not just the injured player but also those around them!

Key learning points

- Physiological responses to injury – how the body reacts to an injury immediately after its occurrence and how it adapts over a period of time.
- Physical signs of injury may include swelling, blood, damaged tissue, discoloration, abnormal alignment of a limb or joint.
- Non-physical signs may include pain and heat (inflammation).
- Adaptation over time will include:

  absorption of swelling

  removal of debris and blood clots

  growth of new blood capillaries

  development of initial fibrous scar tissue.

Psychological responses to injury – how the sports person mentally reacts and copes with the physical injury. This response can vary from individual to individual; be determined by the severity of the injury; be different dependent on when the injury occurs, e.g. start of the playing season; and can change within an individual during the course of rehabilitation.

Injuries can be categorised into soft tissue and hard tissue injuries. Soft tissue refers to the muscles, tendons, ligaments and skin, whereas hard tissue refers to the skeleton, including joints, bones and cartilage.

Soft tissue injuries

Strains

A strain is a twist, pull and/or tear to a muscle or tendon, and is often caused by overuse, force or over-stretching. If a tear in the muscle occurs, surgical repair may be necessary. Muscle strains can also be classified into three categories.

First-degree strains commonly exhibit the following symptoms:

- few muscle fibres are torn
- mild pain
- little swelling
- some muscle stiffness.

Second-degree strains commonly exhibit the following symptoms:

- minimal to moderate tearing of the muscle fibres
- moderate to severe pain
- swelling and stiffness.

Third-degree strains commonly exhibit the following symptoms:

- total rupture of the muscle
- severe pain
- severe swelling.

Sprains

A sprain is a stretch and/or tear to a ligament and is often caused by a trauma that knocks a joint out of position, and over-stretches or ruptures the supporting ligaments. Sprains often affect the ankles, knees or wrists.

Muscle contusions or haematomas occur due to direct trauma, commonly a blow to the outer part of the thigh or back of the calf; this injury is commonly referred to as a 'dead leg' – it is a bruising of muscle tissue caused by the muscle being squashed between the object causing the impact and the underlying bone. The muscle fibres are squashed and associated capillaries are torn. This results in bleeding into the area with resultant haematoma formation. Usually the haematoma formed is fairly small. But in some circumstances the bleeding may be extensive and can cause a 'pressure problem'.

Oedema is swelling in the tissue due to trauma. The swelling may be a combination of tissue fluid and blood. The blood comes from local damage to capillaries at the injury site.

LEARNER ACTIVITY

In small groups discuss the types of injuries you and your colleagues have sustained while playing different sports.

Fill in the table below with your answers to highlight both the main physiological condition (fractured tibia) and the psychological response to that injury (upset, angry).

Sport	Injury sustained	Cause	Preventative measure	Psychological response

Having completed the table, compare the following categories:

- the severity of the injury (i.e. how severe or not the injury sustained was) and the type of psychological response
- the cause of injury (i.e. extrinsic or intrinsic) and the psychological response.

Are there any similarities or differences dependent on the nature of the injury?

An **abrasion** is when the surface of the skin is grazed so that the top layer is scraped off, leaving a raw, tender area. This type of injury often occurs as a result of a sliding fall.

Fig 16.04 Oedema (swelling)

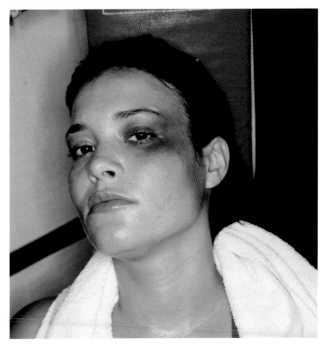

Fig 16.05 Contusion (bruising)

Bursitis is inflammation or irritation of a bursa. Bursae are small sacs of fluid that are located between bone and other moving structures such as muscles, skin or tendons. The bursa allows smooth gliding between these structures. If the bursa becomes inflamed it will feel painful and restrict movement within that area. Bursitis is an injury that usually results from overuse.

Tendonitis is inflammation or irritation of a tendon. It causes pain and stiffness around the inflamed tendon, which is made worse by movement. Almost any tendon can be affected with tendonitis, but those located around a joint tend to be more prone to inflammation. Tendonitis usually results from overuse.

A **contusion** is the technical term for a bruise. Contusions are often produced by a blunt force such as a kick, fall or blow. The result will be pain, swelling and discoloration.

Hard tissue injuries
Dislocation

Dislocation is the displacement of a joint from its normal location. It occurs when a joint is over-stressed, which makes the bones that meet at that joint disconnect. This usually causes the joint capsule to tear, together with the ligaments holding the joint in place. Most dislocations are caused by a blow or a fall. If a person has dislocated a joint then it will usually look out of place, discoloured and/or misshapen. Movement is limited, and there is usually swelling and intense pain.

Subluxation

A subluxation is when one or more of the bones of the spine moves out of position and creates pressure on, or irritates, the spinal nerves. This interferes with the signals travelling along these spinal nerves, which means some parts of the body will not be working properly.

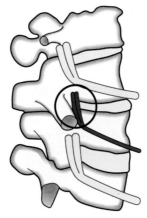

Fig 16.06 A subluxation

Cartilage damage

Normal synovial joint function requires a smooth-gliding cartilage surface on the ends of the bones. This cartilage also acts to distribute force during repetitive pounding movements, such as running or jumping. Cartilage injury can result in locking, localised pain and swelling around the affected area. It appears as a hole in the cartilage surface. As cartilage has minimal ability to repair itself, it needs treatment in order to minimise the deterioration to the joint surface.

Haemarthrosis

Haemarthrosis is where there is bleeding into the joint. It is a serious injury, and swelling of the injury site occurs very rapidly. The swelling works to protect the joint structures by limiting or preventing movement of the injured joint.

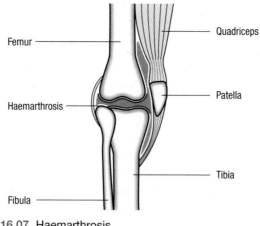

Fig 16.07 Haemarthrosis

Fractures

A fracture is the technical term for a broken bone. They result whenever a bone is hit with enough force to make it break, creating either a small crack or, in a serious fracture, a complete break. There are five main types of fracture.

- **Transverse fractures** are usually the result of a direct blow or force being applied at a sideways angle to the bone. The resultant shape of the bone ends helps transverse fractures stay in alignment more easily than those of other fractures, where the resultant ends do not line up so readily.

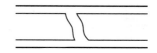

Fig 16.08 A transverse fracture

- **Spiral fractures** are also known as **oblique fractures**. They usually occur as a result of a twisting movement being applied about the long axis of the bone, for example, the foot being held trapped by football boot studs while the leg twists around it.

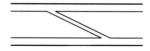

Fig 16.09 A spiral fracture

- A **comminuted fracture** is where there is splintering of the bone so that the bone is broken into a number of pieces. This type of fracture can take longer than others to heal, and is usually caused by direct trauma.

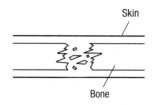

Fig 16.10 A comminuted fracture

- A **stress fracture** is an overuse injury. It occurs when muscles become fatigued and are unable to absorb added shock. Eventually, the fatigued muscle transfers the overload of stress to the bone, causing a tiny crack called a stress fracture. Stress fractures usually occur because of a rapid increase in the amount or intensity of training. The impact of an unfamiliar surface or incorrect trainers can also cause stress fractures.

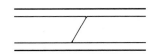

Fig 16.11 A stress fracture

- An **open fracture** is also called a **compound fracture**. It is generally a more serious type of injury because the bone breaks through the skin. The break causes considerable damage to surrounding tissue and can cause serious bleeding if a large artery is ruptured. It also exposes the broken bone to the possibility of infection, which can interfere with healing.

Fig 16.12 An open fracture

First aid

First aid is the immediate treatment given to an injured person. When a suitably qualified person arrives on the scene they then take over the care of the person. Anyone with some knowledge of first aid can have a huge impact on the health of an injured person, so it is always useful to know some basics. By completing a recognised first-aid qualification you will gain a very good basic knowledge of what to do in an emergency situation. It is not in the scope of this book to cover all aspects of first aid because practical work is required to complement the theoretical principles of first aid. Therefore this section will cover only some very basic aspects of first aid.

Immediate treatments

It is necessary to establish what is wrong with the person. If they are lying on the ground you should follow the guidelines below.

1 Assess the situation – identify any risks to yourself and to the casualty.
2 Make the area safe, such as turning off an electric switch.
3 Assess the casualty and give first aid if appropriate. Establish if the person is conscious and then check

their ABC. This would be thoroughly covered in a first-aid course:

- **A**irway – they have an open airway
- **B**reathing – they are breathing
- **C**irculation – check their circulation by assessing if they have a pulse.

4 Try to get help as soon as possible.
5 Deal with the aftermath – complete an accident or incident report.

If you follow a first-aid course you will be taught how to:

- check the ABC
- open a person's airway
- deal with them if they are not breathing by performing artificial resuscitation
- check if a person has a pulse and how to administer cardiac compressions if they do not.

Calling for an ambulance

If a person is injured and you believe the injury requires professional attention, you must ensure that someone calls for an ambulance. If you are dealing with a casualty by yourself, minimise the risk to them by taking any vital action first (check their airway, breathing and circulation), then make a short but accurate call.

- Dial 999 and ask for an ambulance.
- Give your exact location.
- Give clear details of the accident and the severity of the injuries your casualty has sustained.
- Give the telephone number you are calling from and the sex and approximate age of the casualty.

If you get someone else to make the call, always ask them to report back to you to confirm that the call has been made.

When the paramedics arrive, tell them as much as possible about how the casualty has behaved, such as if they are unconscious, if they needed artificial resuscitation, and so on.

Contents of a first-aid box

A first-aid box should contain a number of items in order for a person to effectively administer first aid. The contents of a first-aid box for a workplace or leisure centre must conform to legal requirements and must also be clearly marked and readily accessible. Below is a list of materials that *most* first-aid kits contain:

- sterile adhesive dressings (plasters) – there should be a range of sizes for dressing minor wounds
- sterile eye pads – a sterile pad with a bandage attached to it to cover the eye following eye injuries
- triangular bandages – these can be used as a pad to stop bleeding, or to make slings, or used as a sterile covering for large injuries such as burns
- large and medium wound dressings – a sterile, non-medicated dressing pad with a bandage attached to it
- disposable gloves – these should be worn at all times when dealing with blood or body fluids
- face shield for resuscitation – this may be used to prevent contamination by the casualty's vomit, blood or other body fluids.

Bleeding

A person may suffer from external bleeding, which is usually obvious to the first aider as blood flows out from the site of injury. Internal bleeding, however, is not so obvious – it is not visible as the blood is flowing out of the injury site into the body. The first aider should ensure they are adequately protected when dealing with a casualty who is bleeding to ensure that they do not expose themselves to any blood-borne viruses such as HIV.

External bleeding should be treated in the following manner.

- Lay casualty down.
- Apply direct pressure with a gloved hand or finger to the site of bleeding. As soon as possible, place a clean dressing over the wound.
- Elevate and rest the injured part when possible.
- Seek medical assistance.

Internal bleeding is difficult to diagnose, but some of the potential signs and symptoms are:

- coughing up red frothy blood
- vomiting blood
- faintness or dizziness
- weak, rapid pulse
- cold, clammy skin
- rapid, gasping breathing.

The treatment for a person you suspect has internal bleeding is as follows.

- Lay the casualty down.
- Raise the legs or bend the knees.
- Loosen tight clothing.
- Urgently seek medical assistance.
- Give nothing by mouth.
- Reassure the casualty.

Shock

When a person is suffering from shock, there is not enough blood going to the major organs of the body. Shock can be caused by number of things, including burns, electric shock, allergic shock or severe injuries. A person suffering from shock will usually have cool, moist skin, a weak, rapid pulse and shallow breathing. Other symptoms may include nausea, vomiting or trembling. The treatment for a conscious casualty suffering from shock is to reassure them, then try to find and treat the cause of shock, such as control any bleeding. Keep the casualty lying down and check for neck, spine, head or abdomen injuries. If none of these injuries is apparent then the casualty's feet should be raised so that they are higher than their head.

Unconscious adult casualty

If you see a person lying on the ground, talk to them first to see if they respond – they may just be asleep! If they do not respond, speak to them with a louder voice, asking them if they are all right. If you still receive no response, gently shake them. If the person is not injured but is unconscious, they should be placed in the recovery position, see Figure 16.13. This position helps a semi-conscious or unconscious person breathe and allows fluids to drain from the nose and throat so that they do not choke. The casualty should not be moved into the recovery position if you suspect that they have a major injury, such as a back or neck injury.

Fractures

There are five different types of fracture. All the closed fractures can be treated in a similar manner, but an open fracture needs special attention. A person can be diagnosed as having a fracture if the injured area looks deformed or is tender, if there is swelling in the area, if the casualty cannot move the injured part, or

Fig 16.13 The recovery position

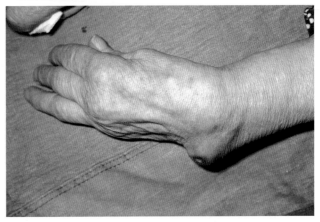

Fig 16.14 A fracture

if there is a protruding bone, bleeding or discoloured skin at the injury site. A sharp pain when the individual attempts to move the injured body part is also a sign of a fracture. The casualty should be told firmly not to move the injured part, since such movement could cause further damage to surrounding tissues and make the casualty go into shock.

A fracture should be immobilised in order to prevent the sharp edges of the bone from moving and cutting tissue, muscle, blood vessels and nerves. The injured body part can be immobilised using splints or slings. If a casualty has an open fracture, the first aider should never attempt to push the bones back under the skin. A dressing should be applied to the injury site to protect the area and pressure should be applied in order to try to limit the external bleeding. A splint can be applied, but should not be placed over the protruding bone.

SALTAPS

The sooner an injury is treated, the greater the chances of a complete recovery and the faster the rehabilitation. The immediate treatment can be summarised by the acronym SALTAPS:

- **S**ee the injury occur and the mechanism of injury
- **A**sk the casualty what is wrong and where they have pain

- **L**ook for signs of bleeding, deformity of limbs, inflammation, swelling and redness
- **T**ouch the injury or close to the injury for signs of heat, tenderness, loss or change of sensation and pain
- **A**ctive movement – ask the casualty to move the injured area; if they are able to, ask them to move it through its full range of movements
- **P**assive movement – try to move the injured site only if a good range of movement is available
- **S**trength – if the casualty has been taken through the steps above with no pain, use resisted movements to assess loss of function; for example, with an injured ankle you would assist the casualty to their feet, then ask them to stand unaided, then progress the test to walking and running.

This process will determine the extent and severity of the injury, although it may be obvious. Treatment at this stage should consist of protect, rest, ice, compression and elevation (PRICE), which is described below.

In minor injuries all stages of SALTAPS can usually be completed. But if a person sustains a serious sports injury, such as a fracture or dislocation, the assessment should not be completed because further injury may occur.

PRICE

If a person has suffered from a soft tissue injury such as a strain or a sprain, ensuring that they follow the **PRICE** regime will help to limit the severity of their injury:

- **P**rotect the injured body part from further injury
- **R**est – as soon as a person has injured themselves they should be told to discontinue their activity;

further activity could cause further injury, delay healing, increase pain and stimulate bleeding

- **Ice** – an ice pack or cold compress should be applied to the injured area; this will help to reduce the swelling and pain of the injury
- **Compression** – gentle pressure should be applied to the injury site by surrounding the area with padding, a compressive bandage or a cloth; compressing the injured area will reduce blood flowing to the injury site and also help to control swelling by decreasing fluid seeping into the injured area from adjacent tissue; after applying a compression bandage, the casualty's circulation should be checked by squeezing the nail beds of the injured limb; if blood is seen to return to the nail bed on release, the compression bandage is not too tight; the compression bandage should be reapplied after 24 hours in order to maintain compression over the injury site
- **Elevation** – the injured area should be supported in a raised position above the level of the heart in order to reduce the blood flow to the injury, which will further help to minimise swelling and bruising at the injury site.

Cold application

Cooling an injured body part to minimise the swelling and bruising of an injured area and to reduce pain is essential. When a person sustains a soft tissue injury, blood vessels are torn and blood cells and fluid escape into the spaces among the muscle fibres. By cooling the injury site, the local blood vessels are constricted, so blood flow to the area is reduced. The application of something that is cold to the injured area not only has the effect of decreasing the flow of this fluid into the tissues but also helps to slow the release of chemicals that cause pain and inflammation. Cold also decreases the feeling of pain by reducing the ability of the nerve endings to conduct impulses.

Because cold reduces bleeding and swelling within injured tissue, it is best used immediately after injury has occurred, and for up to 48 to 72 hours after an injury.

Ice bags (plastic bags with ice cubes in, a bag of frozen vegetables or chemical cold packs) can be used. Never apply ice directly on to the skin. The injured area should be covered with a cloth towel in order to prevent direct contact of the ice with the skin, which

could cause a blister or 'ice burn'. The cold application should be applied to the injured area for no more than ten minutes. During this time the person's skin will pass through four stages of sensation:

1 cold
2 burning
3 aching
4 numbness – as soon as the skin feels numb the cold therapy should be stopped.

The cooling procedure should be repeated every two waking hours. There are a number of methods of cold treatments (cryotherapy) on the market, including ice and gel packs, ice bath immersion and cans of spray.

Heat treatments

The application of heat to an injury site will act to dilate the local blood vessels, thus increasing the blood flow to the area. This type of treatment should only be given in the sub-acute stage in order to aid in the healing process. The increased blood supply will have the effect of absorbing the swelling and removing the dead cells from the injury site. It will also help to increase the growth of new blood vessels in the area and help scar tissue to form. The application of heat to muscles allows them to relax and aids in pain relief. Heat treatment would not be suitable during the early stages of injury, on an open wound or where tissues are very sensitive, such as the genital region.

Contrast bathing

Contrast bathing is the process by which alternating treatments of both hot and cold therapy are applied to the injury site and should be used during the sub-acute phase. The application of a hot treatment will increase the blood flow to the area and, when this is followed by a cold treatment, the blood flow to the area will decrease and take with it the debris from the injury site. The injured site should be immersed in alternating hot and cold water for periods ranging from one to four minutes, with increased time initially in the cold water.

Support mechanisms

In order to help protect and support some injuries it is possible to use a variety of products that are readily available at chemists, sports retailers and via the internet including tubigrip, tape and neoprene support.

Bandaging and taping can be carried out in order to prevent injury, or to treat or rehabilitate an injured joint. Both are performed in order to increase the stability of a joint when there has been an injury to the ligaments that normally support it. They limit unwanted joint movement, support the injury site during strengthening exercises and protect the injury site from further damage.

Taping involves the use of adhesive tape (e.g. zinc oxide tape), whereas bandaging uses strips of cotton and/or specialised pressure bandages. Their purpose is to restrict the joint movement to within safe limits. Taping should not be carried out if the joint is swollen or painful, or if there are any lesions around the taping area. The person who applies the taping/bandaging should be careful to ensure that they do not bind the injury site too tightly so that circulation is affected.

It should also be noted that some individuals have an allergic reaction to some types of tape, such as zinc oxide. Ideally, they should be asked about this possibility before application of the tape. If there is any uncertainty, an underwrap can be applied to provide a protective barrier between the skin and the tape. Unfortunately this can impair the tape's performance as tape also provides a proprioceptive response mechanism by having its contact directly with the skin. It reminds the individual that it is there to protect and maintain a joint within a range of movement.

The use of tape may well provide support and comfort for a sportsperson, but the benefits of use over approximately 20 minutes are diminished due to the material properties. This said, it is often used for time periods well beyond the 20-minute mark and its proprioceptive response declines after this amount of time. The psychological value of tape is valuable for a lot of players at all levels of competition, to the extent that it may even be applied to an injury that has fully recovered but the player still feels 'comforted' by the application of the tape!

Bandaging can be used to create pressure around the injury site in order to restrict swelling.

Key learning points

- Soft tissue injury – injury to muscles, tendons, ligaments and skin.
- Hard tissue injury – injury to the skeleton, i.e. bones, joints and cartilage.
- First aid – the immediate treatment given to an injured person, preferably by a qualified first aider.
- SALTAPS – See, Ask, Look, Touch, Active movement, Passive movement, Strength.
- PRICE – Protect, Rest, Ice, Compression, Elevation.

LEARNER ACTIVITY
Assessing an injury

- Imagine you are a player for a successful local sport club (you can contextualise this scenario to your sport), and you are also a qualified first aider. One of the players in your team sustains an injury (again of your choice) during a training session.
- Run through the series of steps you would follow in order to assess where the injury had occurred and the extent of the damage.
- Remember to stop the process of SALTAPS in the appropriate section if your player has a serious injury.

Rehabilitation considerations

Rehabilitation is the restoration of the ability to function in a normal or near-normal manner following an injury. It usually involves reducing pain and swelling, restoring range of motion and increasing strength with the use of manual therapy (massage and manipulation), therapeutic methods such as ultrasound and an exercise programme.

If a sportsperson does not rehabilitate their injury effectively, they are much more likely to sustain another injury to the same area.

It should be taken into consideration that as well as the physical rehabilitation of the player, the psychological rehabilitation may also need to be considered. The trauma of the injury itself and the resulting exclusion from training/coaching sessions, competitions, matches and after-competition social events can be very difficult for some individuals to come to terms with. In some cases this alone can force injured players to try to start playing again much too soon.

Physical rehabilitation process

For rehabilitation to occur, an accurate and immediate diagnosis is needed to help establish effective treatment and rehabilitation management of an injury. Therefore it is essential that an appropriately qualified person diagnoses the injury as early as possible. This may include a sports therapist, a physiotherapist, a doctor or some other suitably qualified person.

The diagnosis relies on accurate information given by either the injured person or someone who saw the injury happen. The smallest of details can make a difference to how accurate a diagnosis can be. So all information, including information regarding the environment, previous injury history, as well as the actual injury event is very important to communicate.

Post-injury treatment and rehabilitation

There are numerous ways in which to classify injury and its management. The following is a commonly accepted role model. This is called the 'stepladder approach' to rehabilitation.

Phase 1: The aim of treatment at this stage is to:

- prevent as much of the initial swelling as is possible (e.g. if sprained ankle injury do not remove footwear at this stage – it will help with compression)
- protect the injured part from any further damage (e.g. remove from field of play)

Phase 1	Immediate post-injury phase (0–20 mins post-injury)
Phase 2	Acute phase (up to 48–72 hrs post-injury)
Phase 3	Sub-acute phase (3–10 days)
Phase 4	Active rehabilitation stage Mobilising exercises for joint range Strengthening exercises
Phase 5	Functional rehabilitation/training stage

(Football Association)

- control any bleeding (apply cover and add pressure)
- help to relieve the pain (help support or position the injured part in a comfortable position – non-weight-bearing).

So the use of cold compression, elevation and rest are vital.

Phase 2: The aim of treatment at this stage is to:

- control any bleeding and swelling (maintain sterile cover and cold compress, elevate)
- relieve pain (cold compress and elevation)
- protect from further damage (advise to refrain from using as much as possible)
- give advice for home treatment (do not wear compression bandages throughout the night, correct use of ice, PRICE etc.).

Phase 3: During this stage the injury should be in the early stages of recovery:

- absorption of swelling
- removal of debris/dead cells from the area
- growth of new blood vessels
- development of scar tissue.

The use of treatments such as contrast bathing, elevation and massage, and passive exercises, such as non-weight bearing exercises, will help to disperse the products of inflammation. The joint should be moved through its pain-free range in order to increase the range of movement, help to strengthen and lengthen the muscles around the injury, and also to help the scar tissue to form in alignment. Throughout these exercises the person should feel no pain.

Contrast bathing as well as the use of heat packs may also aid the healing process. It may be necessary to use walking aids to protect from further injury or bandages for added support. The use of strengthening exercises specific to the injured area will help the tone of muscle and encourage stability around a joint. Attention to scar tissue development is essential during this stage

Phase 4: Before starting active rehabilitation it is important to make sure that the following applies to the injured part.

- There is no significant inflammation.
- There is no significant swelling.
- While there may be some joint stiffness, there is some range of movement free from pain.

There is the ability to undertake some weight-bearing.

Initially the range of movement needs to be improved as there may have been some weakening of muscles through injury. For every week of immobilisation, a person may lose up to 20 per cent of their muscle strength. Therefore it is important to start to encourage movement first through non-weight-bearing exercises and then to progress to weight-bearing activities.

The use of supports may still be necessary in the early part of this stage. Prolonged immobilisation will lead to stiffness of the joints in the injury area and a decrease in ligament strength. However, if the injured area is mobilised early on in the rehabilitation process, regrowth of the damaged tissues is encouraged and sports ability and skills are maintained.

A selection of exercises used for the injured part should be encouraged on a regular basis as well as continuing to exercise the rest of the body without undue pressure on the injury. Care should be taken to avoid over-exercising, which may result in more damage and therefore a delay in rehabilitation.

The two main types of exercises that should be used throughout this stage are:

- mobilisation activities to improve the range of movement and reduce joint stiffness
- strengthening activities that will help stability of joints and strengthen the weakened muscles.

Phase 5: The aim of treatment at this stage is to:

- improve balance and movement coordination
- restore specific skills and movement patterns to pre-injury level
- provide psychological reassurance of function.

Progression to a functional phase is dependent on the ability to repeatedly perform a task at the level below.

Here are some examples of exercises in the stepladder approach.

Phase 1: play/exercise should cease as soon as injury occurs. 'Playing on through the pain' is not the best advice. Immediate treatment should be given as specified earlier.

Phase 2: very little exercise should be performed during this stage as the aim of the treatment is to control the bleeding and swelling, and protect the injured body part from further damage. PRICE is recommended at this stage for up to 72 hours.

Phase 3: contrast bathing and massage are used during this phase along with stretching. Stretching the injured body part is very important in order to help ensure that the new tissue is laid down in the correct orientation. If there are any signs that the injured body part is not ready to commence this stage, such as heat or swelling around the injury, then stretching should not be started. When stretching, the person should have their injured body part made as warm as possible. This can be done through the use of a thermal heat pack or soaking in a hot bath. Stretches should be held (static stretches) to the onset of discomfort for 15 to 20 seconds. However, a person should never stretch to the extent that they are in pain. Stretching should be performed for short periods of time and frequently throughout the day.

Phase 4: the strengthening exercises that can be used start with isometric exercises. This is where the muscle contracts but no joint movement occurs. Once these have been carried out and no pain has been felt, concentric muscle contractions can be introduced. This is where the muscle shortens – for example, the biceps shortening in a biceps curl.

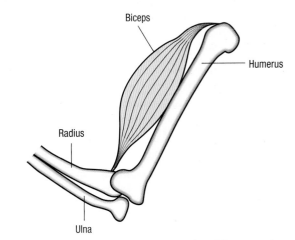

Fig 16.15 Concentric muscle contraction in a biceps curl

Once this type of muscle contraction can be carried out with no pain, eccentric muscle contractions can be performed. This involves the muscle lengthening under tension. An example of this is the quadriceps muscle lengthening as the knee flexes into the sitting position.

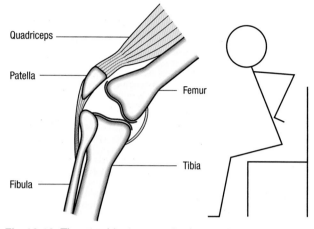

Quadriceps

Patella

Femur

Tibia

Fibula

Fig 16.16 The quadriceps muscle demonstrates an eccentric muscle contraction when getting into a sitting position

If the person has injured their leg(s), initially all the strength-training exercises should be carried out in a non-weight-bearing position, so the injured body part should not take the weight of the body. Instead, the person should be sitting down, lying down or standing on their good leg. The next stage is partial weight-bearing, where the arms are used to help support the body weight. Lastly, the exercises can be carried out with the full body weight on the injured body part.

Phase 5: initially this stage should involve the very basic elements of the sportsperson's usual sport. For example, a footballer would start with running on the spot or in a straight line. Then they would progress to running up and down hills, then on a diagonal and changing direction. This would then progress to skill training. Once they are able to complete these exercises with no problems, they can commence full training and eventually be ready for competitive play.

Psychological rehabilitation

Throughout the injured player's physical rehabilitation programme alongside it must run a psychological rehabilitation programme to deal with the feelings and emotions of the individual during the altering stages and phases of recovery to full fitness.

Frequently athletes react to injuries with a wide range of emotions including denial, anger and even depression. An injury often seems unfair to anyone who has been physically active and otherwise healthy. Although these feelings are real, it is important to move beyond the negative and find more positive

strategies to cope with this setback. In many cases dealing positively with an injury will make for a more focused, flexible and resilient athlete/player.

The following are some suggestions that can help form a psychological coping strategy alongside the physical rehabilitation of an injury.

Learn about the injury

The individual should learn as much as possible about the cause, treatment and prevention of their injury. Not fully understanding an injury can cause fear or anxiety. The professional treating the individual should be aware of this, but if the nature of the injury is not explained there is some uncertainty about the recovery as far as the injured player is concerned. Identification of the facts is a good starting point in the psychological rehabilitation process.

At the start of the physical rehabilitation process, diagnosis is key. If the individual knows *and* understands the answers to some of the following questions a lot of uncertainty can be removed before the related feelings have time to develop.

- What is the diagnosis (what type of injury is it)?
- How long will recovery take?
- What type of treatment is available?
- What is the purpose of the treatment?
- What should be expected during rehabilitation?
- Can alternative exercise help?
- What are the warning signs that rehabilitation is not progressing?

By understanding the injury and knowing what to expect during the rehabilitation process, an individual will feel less anxious and may also feel that they have a greater sense of control over their recovery.

Responsibility for the injury

This does not mean that the individual should blame themselves or anyone else for the injury that they have sustained. What it means is that they accept that they *have* an injury and that they can be in control of their own recovery. By taking on responsibility for the recovery process individuals tend to find a greater sense of control and some go through the process quickly, rather than dwelling on the past or blaming the injury on an outside factor.

Monitor attitude

Just as the person dealing with the physical rehabilitation will keep records on the progress of the individual, it is also important that the psychological aspects are considered and recorded. If an individual has accepted their injury and is positive at the start of rehabilitation, it does not mean that they will stay like this, feeling exactly the same over a period of time. Particularly if the recovery does not go as planned it can be very easy for an individual to become disillusioned.

Using support

A common response after an injury is to feel isolated and to withdraw from being around team-mates, coaches and friends. It is important to maintain contact with others during recover from an injury. Team-mates, friends and coaches need to be good at listening when there is emotion to vent, or able to offer advice or encouragement. Simply realising that others around the injured player care and are willing to help so that the injury does not have to be faced alone can also be a tremendous comfort. So, it might be that the injured player is encouraged to go along to training, to matches, remain around the gym and the weight room, or be visible and included by being an active member of the group – for example, scoring or compiling data, such as the number of tackles, etc.

Set goals

When not injured most sports people set themselves targets and goals to achieve, perhaps in training, or in a match, or by the end of a season. Injury does not mean that this should stop. Planning or setting goals can be a very positive focus. Rather than viewing the injury as a crisis, it can be made another training challenge. The goal is now focused on recovery rather than performance. This will help keep the individual motivated. By monitoring these goals it becomes easier to notice small improvements in the rehabilitation of the injury. This in turn encourages confidence in the recovery process. It is important that realistic goals and targets are set so this should always be done in conjunction with the person in charge of the physical rehabilitation process. Most athletes have a tendency to try to speed up their recovery by doing too much too soon. It is important that the injury is accepted and that the individual takes professional advice and knows their own limits.

Training to stay fit

Depending upon the type of injury incurred, it may be possible to continue training to some extent and maintain cardiovascular conditioning or strength. This is vitally important to how quickly someone can go back to playing after the injury. If their overall fitness has dropped during the rehabilitation phase while the injury has been dealt with, the individual is not at an appropriate level of fitness to return to playing. A good alternative training programme should be devised between the coach/trainer, the therapist and the injured player to ensure appropriateness throughout.

With the right knowledge, support and patience, an injury can be overcome without it being a totally negative experience. By taking things slowly, setting realistic goals and maintaining a positive, focused approach most athletes can overcome minor injuries quickly and major injuries in time.

Recording data

With any accident or incident resulting in a person being injured it is important to keep accurate and up-to-date records to help prevent, where possible, the injury happening again.

This information will normally be maintained by a coach, a teacher or a sports centre, or wherever the injury took place. This information is necessary to protect individuals from being sued for malpractice but also helps to highlight issues which may prevent other similar injuries.

It may help to make sports environments safer, and more importantly, for the coach/trainer, it can help to log the process of injury–treatment–rehabilitation. This can become an accurate record to be used as a template for similar injuries on other players or to identify the recurrence in the same player which may lead to taking into account why the injury is happening regularly. This could be down to inappropriate training regimes, inappropriate fitness levels and/or insufficient time to rehabilitate through the differing phases.

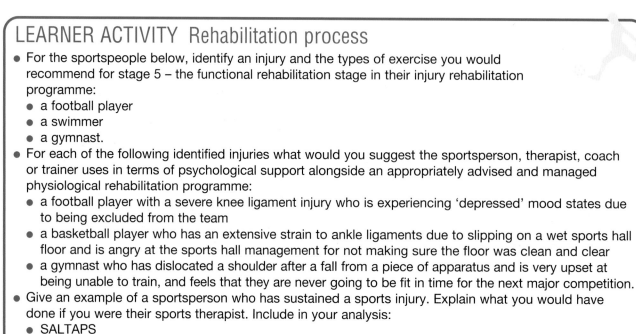

LEARNER ACTIVITY Rehabilitation process

- For the sportspeople below, identify an injury and the types of exercise you would recommend for stage 5 – the functional rehabilitation stage in their injury rehabilitation programme:
  - a football player
  - a swimmer
  - a gymnast.
- For each of the following identified injuries what would you suggest the sportsperson, therapist, coach or trainer uses in terms of psychological support alongside an appropriately advised and managed physiological rehabilitation programme:
  - a football player with a severe knee ligament injury who is experiencing 'depressed' mood states due to being excluded from the team
  - a basketball player who has an extensive strain to ankle ligaments due to slipping on a wet sports hall floor and is angry at the sports hall management for not making sure the floor was clean and clear
  - a gymnast who has dislocated a shoulder after a fall from a piece of apparatus and is very upset at being unable to train, and feels that they are never going to be fit in time for the next major competition.
- Give an example of a sportsperson who has sustained a sports injury. Explain what you would have done if you were their sports therapist. Include in your analysis:
  - SALTAPS
  - PRICE
  - methods of rehabilitation, both physiological and psychological.

Review questions

1 What is an extrinsic risk factor?
2 Why is a warm-up necessary in order to help avoid sustaining a sports injury?
3 What is an intrinsic risk factor? Give three examples.
4 What are the main methods of preventing sports injuries?
5 Identify and explain three possible reasons why a sportsperson may sustain a soft tissue sports injury.
6 Identify and explain three possible reasons why a sportsperson may sustain a hard tissue sports injury.
7 Identify various psychological responses to an injury and suggest why these may be different depending on:
   - the severity of the injury
   - the cause of the injury
   - the individual who has sustained the injury.
8 Why are sportspeople more likely to injure an area that has previously been injured?
9 What is the purpose of scar tissue?
10 Explain why it is difficult to identify an exact timescale for each stage of injury.
11 Explain what SALTAPS is and when you would use it.
12 What does PRICE stand for and when would you use it?
13 What is the purpose of first aid?
14 What does ABC stand for in relation to first aid?
15 Name six things that a first-aid box should contain.
16 What is cryotherapy?
17 What is contrast bathing and what is its purpose?
18 Why would you use taping on a sports injury?
19 What are the five stages of injury treatment and rehabilitation in the stepladder approach?
20 What psychological issues are faced by some sportspeople after sustaining a sports injury?
21 How might the psychological factors associated with the time of injury be managed alongside the physiological issues facing a sportsperson's rehabilitation?

References

Crossman, J. (2001) *Coping with Sports Injuries: Psychological Strategies for Rehabilitation*, OUP.

Flegal, M. J. (2004) *Sport First Aid* (3rd edn), Human Kinetics.

Heil, J. (1995) *Psychology of Sport Injury*, Human Kinetics.

O'Connor, B., Budgett, R., Wells, C. L. and Lewis, J. (2001) *Sports Injuries and Illnesses: Their Prevention & Treatment*, Crowood Press Ltd.

Peterson, L. and Renstrom, P. (2000) *Sports Injuries: Their Prevention & Treatment*, 3rd edn, Taylor and Francis.

Rubin, A. (2003) *Sports Injuries and Emergencies: A Quick Response*, McGraw-Hill Education.

Shamus, E. and Shamus, J. (2001) *Sports Injury – Prevention & Rehabilitation*, McGraw-Hill Education.

Sneyd, S. (technical adviser for Sports Coach UK) (2003) *How To Coach Sports Safely*, Coachwise Solutions.

sports coach UK (1999) *Sports Injury: Prevention and First Aid Management*, Coachwise Solutions.

sports coach UK (2000) *Emergency First Aid For Sport*, Coachwise Solutions.

Taylor, J. and Taylor, S. (1997) *Psychological Approaches to Sports Injury Rehabilitation*, Lippincott Williams & Wilkins.

Analysis of sports performance

Goals

By the end of this chapter you should:

- understand the performance profile of a sporting activity
- be able to analyse a sporting performance
- be able to provide feedback to athletes regarding performance
- understand the analysis required for different levels of sporting performance.

Every sportsperson is aiming to improve their performance in terms of their technical ability, physiological fitness, psychological strength and biomechanical efficiency. We tend to become even more reflective and ask more questions when things are not going well and we are losing competitions. In order to analyse our performances we need a structure or framework in which to work. This chapter provides a structure for athletes to interpret their performances and their successes and failures.

The performance profile of a sporting activity

The performance profile is a visual method of looking at performance in a broad manner. It is used by the athlete and coach to pinpoint strengths and weaknesses and this information is then used to design future actions. When a coach works with an athlete the coach can make decisions on techniques and changes, with the methods being imposed on the athlete by the coach. In this method the success or failure of the training programme is viewed by the athlete as being dependent upon the effectiveness of the coach in meeting their needs.

However, the coach only has the 'outsider' view. Butler and Hardy (1992) identified that this was a

major weakness as it affected an individual's intrinsic motivation. Bull (1991) agreed that an athlete's commitment to their training schedule and the accompanying educational work would be affected if the coach who had imposed the schedules was not always present. It would seem to be a more productive relationship if the expertise of two people was utilised. The coach is the expert in terms of 'the outsider' view of the athlete's performance, while the athlete is the expert in terms of 'the insider' view of their experiences and how they are feeling.

Butler (2000) described the athlete's role as follows:

> The athlete's assertions, discriminations and insights are not only valid but valuable. They make a significant contribution to the development of an effective training programme.

The performance profile gives the coach and athlete a tool to provide a visual display of the areas of performance that are perceived to be important in working towards a top performance, and their assessment of the current position in relation to this.

Using a performance profile

First, you need to choose the sporting activity you want to examine and then you can look at any of the following:

- technical and tactical (shooting, passing, tackling)
- physiological fitness (strength, power, flexibility)
- psychological (motivation, arousal, confidence)
- biomechanical (speed, motion, momentum).

To construct a performance profile you would do the following.

- The athlete is asked to think about the qualities or skills which are shown by those athletes who perform at the top level of their sport in the same position, role or event as themselves.

- These qualities or skills are called the 'constructs' and they are then placed on the performance profile.
- The athlete then describes their current position in terms of their competency by giving themselves a mark out of 10. This score of 10 is in comparison to an athlete they consider to be excellent in their chosen sport.
- The coach may do the same exercise to provide the 'outsider viewpoint'.

These scores can be filled in on the performance profile and used to:

- identify their current level of competence
- identify areas of strength and weakness
- monitor progress and any changes occurring
- monitor effectiveness of training programmes
- identify any differences in the viewpoints of athlete and coach
- provide a basis for designing a training programme.

Technical analysis of a sporting activity

You can analyse a sporting activity in terms of the whole activity, an individual position or an individual aspect of the game.

Whole activity

Snooker, for example, can be broken down into the following constructs:

- stance
- cueing action
- bridging
- striking
- long potting
- short potting
- cushion shots
- snookering
- back spin
- top spin
- side spin
- deep screw
- follow through.

Positional activity

A midfielder in football would perform the following techniques:

- short passing
- long passing
- crossing
- dead ball work
- throwing in
- tackling
- blocking
- long-range shooting
- close-range shooting
- defensive heading
- attacking heading.

Individual aspect of an activity

A tennis player would perform the following backhand shots:

- smash
- volley
- half volley
- drop volley
- lob
- flat drive
- topspin drive
- slice.

	1	2	3	4	5	6	7	8	9	10
Short passing										
Long passing										
Crossing										
Dead ball work										
Throwing in										
Tackling										
Blocking										
Long-range shooting										
Close-range shooting										
Defensive heading										
Attacking heading										

Fig 17.01 Performance profile for a midfielder

LEARNER ACTIVITY
Constructs

Put together eight to ten constructs for the following sporting activities:

- 100 m sprinting
- goalkeeping
- tennis serve.

Physiological analysis of a sporting activity

This is completed in the same manner as the technical analysis except the constructs will be different (see Fig 17.02).

Psychological constructs

This is also completed in the same manner as the technical analysis, except the constructs will be different (see Fig 17.03).

	1	2	3	4	5	6	7	8	9	10
CV fitness										
Anaerobic fitness										
Speed										
Strength										
Power										
Muscular endurance										
Flexibility										
Lung function										
Body composition										
Agility										
Reaction times										
Core stability										

Fig 17.02 Physiological constructs for a tennis player

	1	2	3	4	5	6	7	8	9	10
Intrinsic motivation										
Extrinsic motivation										
Arousal control										
Anxiety levels										
Attentional focus										
Confidence										
Controlling agression										
State management										
Concentration skills										
Relaxation skills										
Emotional well-being										
Mental rehearsal										
Imagery skills										

Fig 17.03 Psychological constructs for a boxer

	1	2	3	4	5	6	7	8	9	10
Development of velocity										
Velocity at release										
Acceleration										
Application of force										
Use of levers										

Fig 17.04 Biomechanical constructs for a javelin thrower

Biomechanical constructs

A fourth analysis can be completed of the biomechanical demands of a sporting activity (see Fig 17.04).

Benefits of performance profiling

As a technique for analysing performance, profiling works very well because it can take into account a vast amount of information for analysis by coach and athlete. It also considers the roles of coach and athlete as equally important with their different viewpoints on performance. Crucially, it takes into account the opinion of the athlete and gives them an active role in the analysis process, allowing them to take ownership of their performance and outcomes. It also allows the coach and athlete to identify any areas of mismatch where there is a differing opinion, and provides a basis for discussion. It can act as a process of education for the athlete as they become self-aware of the varying demands on them as well as their relative importance.

Performance profiles can form the basis of a review of progress on a monthly basis as the athlete and coach track their progress. They can also inform the process of goal setting to set the way forward.

Key learning points

- Performance profiling is a way of looking at performance in a broad sense.
- It involves the opinion of the athlete as well as that of the coach.
- It can be used to identify strengths and weaknesses.
- Performance profiling can be applied to technical, physiological, psychological and biomechanical components of performance.

Analysing sporting performance

The effectiveness of an individual's sporting performance comes down to a range of factors, which can be split into two categories:

- intrinsic – factors within the body
- extrinsic – factors outside the body.

Intrinsic factors would include:

- age
- health
- diet
- previous training
- motivation
- confidence
- ability level.

Extrinsic factors would include:

- group dynamics
- group cohesion
- temperature
- time of the day.

Intrinsic factors

Age

It is generally accepted that performance declines after the age of 35. Up to the age of 35 the body is building up in terms of bone and muscle strength and cardiovascular fitness. After the age of 35 these structures of the body slowly start to lose their efficiency with a resulting performance decrement, although, having said that, training will slow down this decline and maintain strength, flexibility and cardiovascular fitness. We have seen many sportspeople remain at the top level despite being over the age of 35. Martina Navratilova was winning tennis titles into her fifties. Stephen Redgrave, Steve Davis, Teddy Sheringham, Shane Warne and Gary Speed are all still able to perform at the top level in their sports despite their age.

Health

The health of an individual's organs and systems are all vital in gaining their adaptations from training and then producing top-level performances. The body functions as a whole organism made up of many systems and organs, and poor function in one area will affect the functioning of the whole organism.

Diet

There is a clear link between nutrition and health. When we eat we are ultimately feeding the cells of the body with nutrients to allow them to function and give them the basic building blocks to remain healthy. If we feed our cells with fresh, nutritious foods we will have healthy cells, contributing to our health. But if we feed our cells with poor-quality nutrients from processed or fast foods we will end up with unhealthy and ultimately diseased cells, contributing to illness.

Previous training

Our current position is the result of all the activity we have or have not done in our lives. The performance the athlete is able to produce depends upon the quality of their training programme and the fine balance between training and rest periods.

Motivation

Motivation is the amount of drive and energy that we possess at any point in time. It influences our desire to win. If we have trained hard and looked after our nutrition and rest patterns we will feel better and subsequently more motivated.

Confidence

Our confidence is the extent to which we feel we will be successful. It is affected by a range of factors. These will include our previous experiences and our perception of these experiences as either successful or otherwise. In addition, there is our perception of our opponents and our ability to deal with the environment in which we are placed. For example, we may feel more confident when we compete on our home territory and slightly intimidated when we go away. Our confidence level is closely related to our anxiety levels and if we are anxious about our performance this will start to erode our confidence levels.

Ability level

Our ability is the natural level of skills we possess and is the basis for developing further skills. Our performance is clearly the result of the ability and skills we possess.

Extrinsic factors

Group dynamics

Group dynamics refers to the sum of the processes occurring within the group that will influence its effectiveness. The most successful groups have a high level of attractiveness for the individual members, and the members will also share the same goals and work towards achieving these objectives.

Group cohesion

Group cohesion is the extent to which the individual members of the group have an attraction to the group and keep the group together. Cohesion can be task-related or socially related. Task cohesion is the extent to which you are willing to work together in the sporting environment, and social cohesion is how well you get on away from the sporting field. Task cohesion is the most important factor but it can be boosted by social cohesion.

Temperature

Extremes of temperature can have a negative effect on performance due to the effect on the physiological systems of the body. Heat can cause excess sweating, dehydration and heat exhaustion, while cold can make it difficult for the cardiovascular and muscular systems to achieve the correct temperature for optimal functioning.

Time of day

The time of day can influence performance in terms of nutritional and fatigue status. In the morning before a person has eaten they will be in a dehydrated state with low blood sugar and in a far from optimal state to perform effectively. Depending upon when they eat and drink they will fluctuate in terms of their nutritional status through the day. Other physical factors can change through the day. Mobility and flexibility will be lowest in the morning due to the inactivity of the joints and the lack of synovial fluid that has been excreted into the joint.

Performance profile analysis

The performance profile relies on the respective viewpoints of the athlete and coach. It is also useful to gather information to be used in rating the score for each construct. The opinions of the athlete and coach would be qualitative data, while the information gathered from testing would be quantitative data.

The four aspects of the performance profile could be analysed using the following quantitative data

Technical constructs:

- notational analysis
- tally charts.

Physical constructs:

- multi-stage fitness test
- 40 m sprint
- 1 rep max
- 15 rep max
- sit and reach test
- peak flow test
- skinfold calipers
- T-test.

Psychological constructs:

- questionnaires
- interviews
- observation of behaviour.

Biomechanical analysis:

- video recording
- computer packages.

Notational analysis

Notational analysis is the tracking of the actions of an individual performer through the course of a game or match to see the frequency with which they perform a particular technique. It can be done through a computer package or by hand using tally charts.

A tally chart for football is reproduced on page 342.

This information is of limited value as you also need to look at where this action occurs. This can be done by sectionalising the area of play (see Fig 17.05) and giving areas labels. This will elicit more valuable information.

This can be done with a cricket pitch, tennis or netball court. You can then track where each type of skill occurs and its outcome.

An example of tracking the passing of a footballer is also reproduced on page 343.

The uses of notational analysis are to:

- identify individual strengths and weaknesses
- analyse all the actions of a player
- build up information to rate score on performance profile
- develop an action plan to improve performance.

Tally chart: football

Skill	Successful completion	Unsuccessful completion
Short-range pass (< 5m)		
Medium-range pass (5–15m)		
Long-range pass (> 15m)		
Dribble		
Short-range shot (< 6m)		
Medium-range shot (7–18m)		
Long-range shot (> 18m)		
Tackle		
Block		
Defensive header		
Attacking header		
Throw-in		
Free kick		
Corner		
Penalty kick		

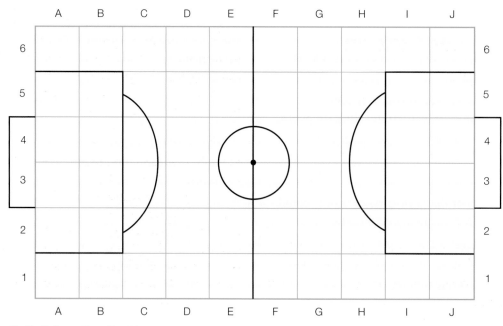

Fig 17.05 Football pitch sectionalised into areas

Passing record		
Skill	Successful completion	Unsuccessful completion
Short-range pass (< 5m)	G5–F5 D3–D2 I6–J5	F4–F3 C3–C4
Medium-range pass (5–15m)	G2–E4 C6–A6 H1–F3	D5–B4
Long-range pass (> 15m)	I4–E3 C1–B5	F6–D1 I5–D3 F1–C4

Key learning points

- The effectiveness of an individual's sporting performance is dependent upon intrinsic and extrinsic factors.
- Notational analysis involves identifying and then analysing the individual actions of each player and the outcome each achieved.
- Each component of performance is identified and each time it is performed the outcome is recorded.
- Tally charts are used to record the outcomes and frequency of each component.
- This information is used to identify strengths and weaknesses.

Providing feedback on performance

It is impossible for anyone to improve or change unless they receive feedback.

definition

Feedback: **information about performance.**

It has no value judgement attached to it as it is not positive or negative. It is simply information. The information is provided and the athlete has the choice of doing something about it or not.

Types of feedback

There are different categories of feedback regarding its timing and the type of feedback given. They are:

- knowledge of performance and results
- immediate and delayed
- internal and external
- concurrent and terminal.

Knowledge of performance and results

Knowledge of performance (KP) is information regarding how well skills were performed in a technical sense and will involve qualitative judgements. Knowledge of results (KR) is information regarding the outcome of the skill – whether the action produced success or failure – this is a quantitative judgement. It is possible to perform a skill well (KP) and have a negative outcome (KR) or have a poor performance (KP) and a positive outcome (KR). It is generally regarded that experienced performers are more interested in knowledge of performance, while novices are more interested in knowledge of results.

Immediate and delayed

Immediate means that the feedback is given immediately after the skill has been performed, while delayed means feedback is provided at a time after the event – this could be a day or an hour later. The coach needs to consider the impact that the feedback will have on the athlete's motivation and how important it is for the athlete to receive it. Once they have considered those two questions they can decide when to give the feedback.

Internal and external

Internal feedback is generated within the body of the athlete. As you perform a skill you will feel whether you have performed it correctly or not due to the nervous pathways you have set down to produce the movement and judge its correctness. As we hit a tennis ball we feel whether we have struck it sweetly or not. External feedback is provided by an external party who observes the performance. For example, the coach will observe the performance of the skill and offer feedback as to how it looked and how effective it was. External feedback may also be provided by using video recordings or other recording devices.

Concurrent and terminal

Concurrent means literally 'running together'. This type of feedback is provided during the performance of the skill in terms of how it feels and often the outcome as well. Concurrent feedback is usually internal in nature and clearly immediate in when it is provided. Terminal means 'at the end'. This type of feedback is provided at the end of the performance. It is usually external and is always delayed.

Delivering the feedback

Once the coach has decided on what feedback is necessary to address the individual's strengths and areas for improvement they will need to decide when, where and how to deliver it. How the feedback is received depends upon how it is delivered.

Structure

When giving feedback you should use the sandwich technique. Feedback should have this structure:

- tell them what they are doing right
- tell them what they need to improve on
- tell them something else they did right.

This means that the feedback ends on a high note and the athlete understands what needs to be improved.

Non-verbal communication

Feedback can be given visually and through gestures as well as verbally. The use of facial expressions, posture and hand gestures will convey more than the actual words used. The delivery of the message should match the message being given. This is called being 'congruent'. Also, gestures such as a pat on the back or a hand on the arm will convey information which cannot be imparted in words.

Avoiding negative approaches

Avoid any negative approaches or comments.

- Intimidation: 'If you don't improve you can find a new coach.'
- Sarcasm: 'My granny could have caught that!'
- Physical abuse: 'Unless you listen to what I say you will be doing press-ups.'
- Guilt: 'You should be ashamed of yourselves the way you played out there. It was gutless and you let your supporters down.'

Private and confidential

Ensure feedback is given in a private area as it may be sensitive and is not relevant for anyone else.

Focus on behaviour

Focus on the behaviour rather than identity. This is the difference between a coach saying 'You are an aggressive person and this is not acceptable' and 'Your aggressive actions are not acceptable.' One addresses the behaviour, which can be changed, and the other addresses the identity of the person, which is long term and relatively stable.

Using the feedback provided

Once the feedback has been received and processed by the athlete, they have to decide how to use the information. It may be used in the following ways:

- to set SMART targets combining short-, medium- and long-term goals
- to develop or change a training programme to include technical, physiological and psychological components of performance
- to inform the process of performance profiling and assessment of scoring the individual constructs.

Analysis for different levels of sporting performance

Sport England has identified four different levels of sporting performance, as follows.

Key learning points

Feedback is information about an individual's performance.

Feedback can be categorised in two ways: knowledge of performance (KP) and knowledge of results (KR). KP is information about how well the skill was performed and KR is information about the outcome of the skill.

Immediate feedback is given as soon as the skill has been performed, while delayed feedback is given at a period after the performance.

Internal feedback is derived from sources inside the body and external feedback comes from sources inside the body.

Concurrent feedback occurs as the skill is being performed and terminal feedback occurs after the completion of the skill.

When providing feedback keep in mind the following:

- using the sandwich approach of positive/negative/positive
- providing it visually as well as verbally through body language
- avoiding sarcasm, intimidation, abuse and guilt
- ensuring it is delivered in a private area
- focus on behaviour rather than identity.

Foundation level

At foundation level focus is on the participants learning and understanding basic movement skills and developing a positive attitude to physical activity. This level is concerned with giving school children positive and meaningful experiences of sport.

Beginner or participation level

At participation or beginner levels the participants will be taking part in sport for a range of reasons, such as health, fitness and social. They may also be attracted by the competitive aspects of sport. This level of participation would involve out-of-school sports teams and Saturday league players.

Performance level

At performance level the participants will be active in improving standards of performance through coaching, competition and training. This would involve the participants playing at county or national standard.

Elite or excellence level

Elite and excellence levels involve the participants reaching national standards of performance up to Olympic or world-class performances.

Purpose of analysis and resources required

Foundation level

At this level the emphasis is on fun and enjoyment, and learning the basic skills and techniques. Analysis will be limited to identifying the strengths and weaknesses of the children and giving them feedback to improve their enjoyment of the sports. The resources required are limited to support from teachers and parents.

Beginner level

At beginner level there is an emphasis on developing techniques and improving weaknesses along with developing strengths. This is a point where talent may be assessed for further development through coaching and physical training. Analysis is again done in a fairly informal manner through recommendations or even talent scouting.

Performance level

Analysis starts to become very important at this level as it is about achieving standards of performance to reach county or national level. Analysis will be conducted to:

- identify talent
- form the basis for squad selection at county and national level
- assess current level of performance
- identify strengths and weaknesses
- assess fitness level and health status
- inform the process of goal setting.

In terms of resources required there is a need to put in time and effort on behalf of personnel. This is a key stage in moving people towards becoming athletes and to ultimately developing elite potential. Equipment required will include fitness testing equipment, sport science facilities, expertise from sport scientists and time devoted to each individual.

Elite level

At elite level every aspect of an athlete's performance is analysed to the smallest degree as they seek to gain all the advantages they possibly can to improve their chances of success. At this level aspects of health, fitness and performance are analysed on a daily basis. Indeed, the athlete may be professional or training on a full-time basis. The purpose of analysis at this level is to:

- assess current health and fitness status
- identify strengths and weaknesses
- assess current level of performance
- inform the process of goal setting
- identify any future issues or problems.

As athletes at this level may have contact with their support team at facilities such as a national sports centre, they are heavily dependent on resources. These resources are human in terms of sport scientists with various expertise, and physical resources for assessing fitness levels and analysing skills and techniques.

Key learning points

- At foundation level focus is on the participant's learning and understanding basic movement skills and developing a positive attitude to physical activity. Analysis is provided at this level to help participants improve their skills.

- At participation or beginner levels the participants will be taking part in sport for a range of reasons, such as health, fitness and social and competitive reasons. Analysis is used at beginner level to improve performance and identify talent.

- At performance level the participants will be active in improving standards of performance through coaching, competition and training. Analysis is provided to assess current level of performance and how to improve it, as well as identify talent to move to a higher level.

- Elite and excellence levels involve the participants reaching national standards of performance up to Olympic or world-class performances. Analysis is done at elite level to identify any area where the athlete could improve so they can compete at the very highest level.

Revision questions

1 What is a performance profile?
2 What are the benefits of using a performance profile?
3 Why is it important to have an 'insider' view on performance as well as an 'outsider' view?
4 What is meant by technical, physiological, psychological and biomechanical analyses of performance?
5 What is meant by 'notational analysis' and what information does it provide?
6 What is the difference between an intrinsic and extrinsic factor affecting sporting performance?
7 Why is age a factor in influencing sporting performance?
8 How can diet be an influence in sporting performance?
9 What is feedback and why is it different from criticism?
10 Explain three types of feedback.
11 What is the 'sandwich technique' of providing feedback and why should it be used?
12 Explain how feedback can be given visually as well as verbally.
13 Explain briefly the four levels of participation in sport.
14 At which level is talent identified?

References

Bull, S. J. (1991) *Sport Psychology: A Self-help Guide*, Crowood.

Butler, R. J. (2000) *Sport Psychology in Performance*, Arnold.

Butler, R. J. and Hardy, L. (1992) The performance profile: theory and application. *The Sport Psychologist*, 6, 253–264.

Davis, R. J. (2003) *Physical Education and the Study of Sport*, Mosby.

Martens, R. (1997) *Successful Coaching*, Human Kinetics.

Weinberg, R. and Gould, S. (2003) *Foundations of Sport and Exercise Psychology*, Human Kinetics.

Talent identification and development in sport

Goals

By the end of this chapter you should:

- understand the key predictors of talent for individuals in sport
- be able to design a talent identification programme for a chosen sport
- understand key factors in talent development in sport
- be able to design a talent development programme for a chosen sport.

At a time when all sports look for the 'secret formula' for effective talent identification and player and team development plans, it is often down to the scout, the coach or the teacher whose speciality is identifying talented individuals. Who is the next David Beckham? Scouts and teachers strive to find the 'one', the next player who will play for his country and develop through the ages. It is often a predictor or measured opinion when scouts look at young players. It would defy most scientific rules if a scout could identify top-quality players at seven or eight years of age. It is a ten-year cycle and a golden age of learning where players develop, learn and meet the challenges faced at every age group barrier.

This chapter examines the key predictors of talent including physical, physiological and psychological factors. Methods of designing talent identification programmes will be explored, together with the key factors in talent development in sport.

Professional sports clubs and organisations invest heavily in talent identification and development. Potential talent may not be obvious at an early age, but there will normally be some indicators that enable trained individuals to identify it. However, even in the eyes of trained experts, talent in sport is difficult to assess. There is a worldwide industry built around talent recognition and development, and many people are employed in both finding gifted individuals and developing the talent they possess.

Key predictors of talent for individuals in sport

Types of talent

Within any sport that you watch and support, the players must have a high degree of talent. In uni-dimensional sports only one type of talent is required, for example the ability to run fast in a straight line over a given distance.

definition

> Uni-dimensional: where only one type of talent is required.

Michael Johnson and Veronica Campbell are both Olympic champions who are known throughout the world as talented sprinters within their chosen event. As athletes they represent the upper end of elite sporting talent but as a talent they are described as uni-dimensional. Sprinting from start to finish requires several ingredients, such as speed, balance, coordination, flexibility, strength and power, however there is only one goal – to be as fast as possible.

definition

> Multi-dimensional: where many different types of talent are required.

As a scrum half, a player combines a variety of physical components and skills for the entire length of the game or session. As a player they are rarely seen running quickly at pace in a straight line. Their role involves having to make multiple decisions, i.e. catching, passing, calling plays, handling, directional change and tackling. Multiple outcomes in the broad sense, but there can be opportunities where uni-dimensional attributes are evident.

Sport is developed through schools, clubs, external organisations and play. There does come a point where individual players choose to specialise. Tiger Woods was targeted at the age of four years old as a special talent. He may be an exception. In the modern world Tiger Woods is known as the best golfer on the planet but not as an all-round sports athlete; he would be classed as a 'uni-sport' talent. In comparison, Daley Thompson (Olympic decathlete) would be classed as a multi-sport talent. He specialised in a huge variety of events with a high skill requirement to each.

Fig 18.01 Tiger Woods

Predictors of talent

Within the English language talent signifies some attribute that is either innate or learnt.

> definition
>
> **Innate:** something that you are born with, for example having a natural talent in kicking a football.

- T = Technique
- A = Athleticism
- L = Leadership
- E = Effective
- N = Natural speed
- T = Team player
- I = Individual
- D = Desire

These are guidelines for sporting scouts who are looking for the next player. The selection process is split into categories of physical, technical, psychological and social ability. These are the four corners of learning (FA learning), where players are assessed.

- **Physical** – anthropometric measures which relate to age groups and development.
- **Technical** – specific skill requirements at each development age group.
- **Psychological** – how do players seem; confident, social, what is their emotional state?
- **Social** – interaction from the family, friends and peers.

The main areas to consider in relation to the physical parameters of the player are their individual make-up.

Physical

Players differ depending upon their age and the development stage they are in. However, if a player is below a predictor height in relation to his chronological age this suggests only that he is undersized, a little weaker than other players and therefore lacking in some of the physical fitness components such as speed and endurance. It does not mean that there is no talent. In contrast, some players develop and grow early; you might hear coaches talk about a 12 year old who is physically better than those around him and who can run the length of the field at pace. This however leads to concerns about the 'what happens next' scenario. What happens when the underdeveloped yet talented players grow?

Talent identification is designed to help sports teams and coaches identify talented athletes and prepare them for participation in domestic, national and eventually international competition. Many sports programmes utilise information across all sports science disciplines to identify young athletes with characteristics associated with elite performance. Athletes are then guided to sports that best suit their attributes and are provided with the opportunity to realise their potential in a high-quality talent development programme. There is, however, an important ingredient that is often overlooked. Talent is often the capture and development of 'accelerated expertise'. An individual may possess a certain quality, whether innate or learnt, but it is the ability to manage and develop this in the right manner that is important.

Growth, maturation and development are key components in any talent assessment criteria. Growth is a dominant biological activity that occurs during the first 20 years of life. It starts at conception and continues late into the teenage years. The term growth relates to the increase in size of the body either as a whole or as individual body parts. Growth of the body is traditionally measured in a standing position using various stadiometers. Individual limb lengths are measured using anthropometric techniques. This process allows the accurate measurement of each individual body part length.

Development is an interesting concept taking in all areas of growth, maturation, learning and experience. Maturation refers to the instance of biological maturation which can be seen through sexual maturity, skeletal maturity and physical maturity.

Weight relates to the individual body mass measured in kilograms. In simple terms a person's body weight can be divided into two components: fat mass (FM) and fat free mass (FFM). These components are the principles behind body composition and assessment. Fat mass includes both the internal and the external fat or adipose tissue and fat free mass includes muscle, bone and the vital internal organs.

A child's body make-up or shape can have a major influence on a scout or coach in all ages of the development spectrum. Somatotyping relates to the make-up of the human body in terms of shape and its composition. There are three general components that relate to somatotyping.

1 **Endomorph** – this component refers to the degree of fatness on the body, wherever it may be found. As a shape an endomorph stature would be rounded in appearance.
2 **Mesomorph** – this component relates to the relative musculoskeletal development of the body. In its appearance the body shape is muscular and toned.
3 **Ectomorph** – this component describes the slenderness of the body with an absence of any muscular size and bulk.

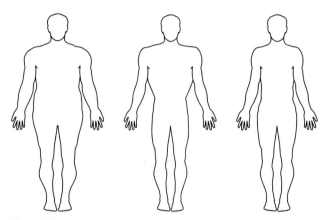

Fig 18.02 Endomorph, mesomorph and ectomorph

LEARNER ACTIVITY

From the list below, state which body type is the most prevalent for each sport:

- long-distance running
- shot-put
- swimming
- football
- rugby (scrum half)
- horse racing.

Anthropometric measures are requisites that all medical teams will carry out on a regular basis with players who enter into a full-time development programme. All the components mentioned above are taken as part of the individual player profile. In addition the medical teams will also look at girth measurements.

Girth relates to the maximal muscle circumference. It is measured at varied sites through flexion and extension. This is a valued tool, especially in relation to biological and skeletal age.

Physiological

Within some sports the main criteria for assessing talent would be a player's fitness. We are aware there are several components that can be targeted and assessed by eye. Aerobic endurance when measured in young children forms a pattern. Boys tend to continually improve with age whereas girls can display a peak and drop off in their late teens. At any age it is easy to see how a player moves, with what tempo and intensity and, most importantly, how quickly they recover. Without physically carrying out performance tests a lot of the fitness components are compared visually among talented players. If the sport requires testing to determine aerobic endurance then you would assess a player's aerobic capacity, aerobic power and, probably the most important in terms of player identification, their movement analysis. The physiological components play a vital part in continued assessment but initial assessment relies on performance indicators such as 'How does the player move?'

Sociological

A child growing up in the world will see and experience new things every day. It is the social support that they have that will allow them to develop at the appropriate speed. When children play in sports teams, the referee will make decisions for or against a team as well as an individual. Any experience of success or failure will have an effect on the player. It is the role of the parents, the coaches and the friends to recognise the stressors and strains that are being placed on the child. With parental and external support the player has a security blanket that allows them to try new things, and express themselves knowing that they will have love and support regardless of the outcome. With this support the child will accelerate and develop at a faster rate than a

player who does not have the same supporting network. This is the same for a child's education. If a young player enjoys the sessions or lessons and takes positive experiences from them then they will learn and develop in an appropriate way. If the experiences they go through are negative in any way then this may well result in reduced performance.

Psychological

Psychological ability is probably one of the most important factors in relation to the complete player but probably the most overlooked. Psychological analysis in terms of performance is often difficult to quantify but it defines what you would be looking for. When assessing players psychology tends to refer to how the players train and play in relation to their sport. Within team sports do the players make positive decisions at the right time either through anticipation or through their individual game intelligence? In a sense this relates to individual sportspeople as well but the traits that scouts look for in a psychological analysis tend to focus mainly on the individual – their level of personal control, for example. Is the player composed and confident among his peers? Do they show good levels of concentration? Is there an under 9 years player who has positive traits within his group but would probably be defined as an accelerated player in terms of understanding and application?

Key learning points

- Uni- and multi-dimensional talent have a major impact on their chosen sports. By having multi-dimensional characteristics a player can achieve most of their goals, whereas uni-dimensional sports tend to have one goal.
- Anthropometric measurements such as height, weight and somatotyping create an individual profile for every player.
- Talent is often said to be within the genes we have and were born with. What is important then is how these genes are developed and taught to bring about accelerated learning.

Designing a talent identification programme for a chosen sport

Identifying, developing and nurturing talented players are key priorities in a systematic long-term plan for success at elite level. People who make a living from spotting and discovering talented players understand that the potential to excel in sport depends upon several factors. A combination of physical, environmental, mental and emotional factors will go a long way but this does not guarantee elite success.

> **definition**
>
> Systematic: **a planned and organised approach.**

There are several identifications that many sports, sports academies and even governing bodies rely on to find, develop and nurture new talent. Within many sports you often hear the phrase 'he/she looks and moves like a professional player'. Scouts use and adopt many different processes to assess players in games and sessions. Visual information is the first real point of contact – for example, 'he moves like a player'. However, scouts will look for and consider other qualities and requirements of the modern game.

- **Pace and mobility** – does the player have it now or lack it due to age and strength?
- **Game understanding and awareness** – this includes when, where and how to pass, run, receive, tackle, or simply change the play.
- **Attitude and application** – for example, do the players seem to be actually enjoying playing the game?
- **Determination** – will the player work hard to get the ball and work harder to get it back?
- **Technical qualities** – does the player have a good touch, passing range and ability, defending principles and attacking qualities?

When assessing a potential player, you will no doubt see some of these attributes in the very young players, however a scout will look closer if the players are hoping to enter a talent development programme. There are several talent identification programmes that are used by many sports today. In reviewing and

evaluating the processes that are in place talent identification assessment is paramount in finding the right players.

Many of the current assessment programmes look at different specific components but all cover the following three elements:

- technical
- physical
- mental.

Talent programmes

TIPS

One of the most common talent programmes is TIPS. Tips can be applied to all sports and predominantly to most major sports.

TIPS is broken down into four key areas in which scouts will score and reflect a player's overall potential.

1. **T**alent – player's technical ability within their chosen sport.
2. **I**ntelligence – player and game understanding. This is often judged when the player has the ball and also when they have not got the ball.
3. **P**ersonality – this includes the player as a person, as a learner and in varied practices; how they react and learn as well as how they take onboard specific and relevant information.
4. **S**peed – speed can be broken down into various components but ultimately the players are looked at in terms of reaction speed to and from the ball, and it includes pure speed, both with and without the ball, and acceleration.

TIPS is a very common method and is a valuable tool for coaches, scouts and teachers within the game.

TABS

A second programme is TABS. TABS examines the technical, the personal and the physical elements of the player:

- **T**echnical
- **A**ttitude
- **B**alance
- **S**peed.

Here the emphasis is placed on the player's technical understanding and their ability. The next component relates to the player's attitude. Attitude can be assessed in training, in games, in the changing room and to an extent away from the sport. Balance is the first physical element that TABS looks at. In terms of player development, the work of Dr Istvan Balyi (2004) describes development as key learning stages and windows of opportunity. The first stage concentrates on the development of players aged between six and nine years, and concentrates on the FUNdamentals of the game (for this age, the 'fun' element should be included as part of the training programmes). It also includes ensuring the players understand the rules as well as learning the ABCs.

The ABCs are the physical components in which players are trained: Agility, Balance and Coordination. Even at this early stage of development balance is vital in some development programmes. To an extent as the players progress through the ages and go through the training windows and opportunities it is harder to train a specific movement pattern. The final component is speed and, again through Balyi's work, the six- to nine-year age group offers a great opportunity to not only develop speed but incorporate specific sessions into the player's development programme.

SUPS

The final development programme is SUPS:

- **S**peed
- **U**nderstanding
- **P**ersonality
- **S**kill.

Even though in a different order to the previous two programmes the key requirements follow the same trend.

Here the emphasis is placed on the physical pace of the player. If the player has pace then often the mindset of the scouts is that he/she can develop technique and skill. Within these two criteria the emphasis is placed on the understanding players show within small-sided games and their own individuality and what they bring to the game.

Structure of a talent identification programme

So what happens now? By using the above programmes and scoring players accordingly you are left with a group of players who have stood out on

several fronts: speed, technique, personality, understanding, etc.

Many professional football clubs are recruiting the best players within their catchment area from as early as six years old. This recruitment and development process continues on a cycle up until 16 years, when the players then enter a full-time training programme.

So how good are they? How can we measure them? Once clubs have players within their systems it is ultimately down to them as a club and their coaches to develop them in the right way. Some clubs follow testing protocols throughout the season where players through every age group are tested both physically and technically. These tests produce a BASE result which can then be used within the development programme but more importantly as a recruitment tool. We now know what we are looking for within a player's make-up but we can also test and compare an under-8 or an under-12 player against last year's technical and physical component tests. By testing and re-testing the clubs then build up a database or norm data. These data can then be used not only to monitor individual progression through each age group but also in comparisons.

Comparisons relate to a test score which is classed as good for that particular age group. If you have identified a player through your identification assessment programmes you then have a valid test which can be compared within the age group and also with positional players.

Understanding key factors in talent development in sport

In every sport and game there is a search to find and recruit young individuals with the potential for achieving excellent results in the future. At an early age youngsters show suitability for training and become more successful through basic training and practice. The purpose of identifying young talent is to predict with a high degree of probability whether or not a young athlete or player will be at the required level to successfully complete the sport training programme. In the world of competitive football and performance, to produce a top footballer, identification of talent is of the utmost importance. Youth team management and recruitment of young players cannot be separated from one another. The coach or trainer works alongside the chief scout of the club and is involved in his scouting network so that the supply of young players is both an effective and continuous one. The chief scout and his associates must establish a good relationship with the local schools, the teachers and parents so that they can select the best schoolboy footballers. The club which fails to recruit the best of the local schoolboy talent creates difficulties for itself. In order for this to function effectively, clubs should have a youth development policy.

Specialisation in football can begin only when an academy or club has prepared the young player's system; this includes their physical foundation, a high mental capacity and the ability to consciously master the specific practical and theoretical knowledge of football. Clubs will need to cater for the general preparation of the child which includes the whole process of laying the foundation for the development of the body's many-sided physical capabilities and psychological consistency, as well as general movement ability. It is also difficult to determine the lower age limit for children's general preparation, but body preparation begins from the age of three in pre-school, especially in the physical education classes. This is the development of general motor abilities such as balance, agility and coordination, as well as the strengthening of the child's muscular system.

In general, from the age of ten upwards it is possible to begin to teach the young players the technical elements of the game. However, careful consideration must be given to the mental capacity of the 10–12-year-old player. At this age it is still too early to teach tactical and position-specific skills. General and special preparations for young football players start at an early age with informal ball play and physical movements brought into their sessions. Around the age of ten children start to learn the fundamental skills – various types of kicks, ball receiving, dribbling, tackling, heading, goalkeeping techniques, etc.

They apply the skills in friendly and competitive matches. At this age, the inborn quality and partly developed prerequisites of the game possessed by the individuals most likely to achieve high performance in the future can be objectively spotted by scouts or professionals within the chosen sport or field.

Nowadays highly developed systematic scientific research works are needed for spotting and determining the combination of talent factors and various parameters responsible for achieving the ultimate goal in competitive football. Football scientists, top coaches, trainers and physical educators need to dedicate time to constructing a variety of test batteries to find out, challenge and help in the spotting of the best talented young football players in this early age bracket. Spotting of young talent is a difficult task. It involves physical, psychological, physiological, social and total motor variables. These are the performance-limiting factors responsible for talent identification.

Within the increasingly popular game in the UK, there is this great need for effective spotting and selection of young footballers in the school levels in order to develop their football prowess so as to produce future developing players. In talent identification, good cooperation from parents, teachers and highly motivated students to participate in playing football is indispensable to a club's scouting team. This network relationship between scouting team, parents, teachers and young footballers should be maintained carefully to promote the development of talent in the correct way. Various basic test batteries can be applied to the youngsters to check their football potentiality.

On this basis, talent identification and its development in the early years has become an important area of research. In this international footballing world, scientists try to spot talented young players on the basis of fitness and performance areas such as fundamental skills, motor abilities, psychological and physiological parameters. Hence, it is recommended that screening of potential talent from early identification at the younger age group become a matter of national urgency within the professional game.

> If something exists, it exists in some amount. If it exists in some amount, then it is capable of being measured.
>
> (*Rene Descartes*, Principles of Philosophy, *1644*)

A group of respected professionals in the field of gifted children suggest a definition based on the gifted child's differences from the norm:

> Assessing gifted children is similar to and different from assessing other types of children. Though areas to be assessed are similar for all, for gifted children, the assessment techniques and tests require special characteristics. While most professionals are trained to assess many kinds of children, few are specifically trained to assess in this particular area. The general perception is that these youngsters, with abilities and strengths in many areas, have no special needs, educational or otherwise, that merit serious clinical attention. For this reason, it is important that parents who suspect that their child may be gifted search for a professional with experience in working with this population …
>
> Gifted and talented children are those identified by professionally qualified persons who by virtue of outstanding abilities are capable of high performance. These are children who require differentiated educational programs and/or services beyond those normally provided by the regular school program in order to realize their contribution to self and society.

A lack of success at a young age does not mean a child will not become a champion; deliberate practice is as important as innate talent, and the acquisition of basic motor skills in early childhood is crucial.

Physiological factors that influence sporting performance can be assessed by administering tests such as speed over varied distances. Further in-depth assessment can be achieved by using such equipment as the cybex dynamometer to give physical data which will influence sporting performance.

Some sports rely on anthropometric measures as a valuable tool, e.g. for height for football during the younger ages. Utilising this information can help the scouts and the assessors. Height, weight and limb lengths can be a real contributory factor in enhancing sport performance. During the early ages of talent identification taking anthropometric measurements such as height, weight, limb length, skinfolds and girth measurements can aid the talent identification process, especially when these results are compared.

Comparative testing can occur when the players develop and grow. The Australian Institute carried out a study looking at the general population and its national rowers. The results showed that on average the rowers were taller with longer leg and arm lengths.

Research on the influence of psychological factors has shown that it has as much a positive contribution as do the physiological factors. Heredity is another area that we should consider when looking further into talent identification. Children tend to inherit physiological and psychological factors from their parents. Some of the inherited factors such as height, limb length, speed and coordination cannot be changed through the environment, however factors such as weight, strength and endurance can be developed through the right education and specific training. The sociological side within talented individuals is huge in terms of the overall development plan. To many children their parents are role models, friends, motivators, teachers and critics. Having this parental support allows the innate talent to come out more. Any child involved in sport will experience lots of highs and lows through the early years. It is the support of the parents that plays a massive role in the development of that child. By praising and encouraging the child, he or she is nutured in the sport they love and will continue to play. By adding tangible support such as hugs and the sense of feeling loved the child has a comfort zone as well as a safety net. Without this support the development will be negative, i.e. if there is little or no sign of affection or praise. Parents cannot live their childhood through their children. They have to encourage and be there when they are needed most, and offer the support and love that go alongside developing a superstar.

It is the dream of any developing player in whatever their chosen sport to be the next find. There are many demands placed both on the player and their support network. This support is vital for players when obstacles are placed in their development path. The most common obstacle for players is injury. Depending on the seriousness, injury can also be a big psychological blow to a player at any age. By having the correct tangible support and the correct treatment the player can survive and still be developing at the same time. If this process is neglected or negated then the injury can be the reason why players fall short of the next level.

Key learning points

- Every player within any development age is special. What they see or hear or feel on a regular basis has an impact on their overall make-up, which at times runs alongside their actual playing ability.
- At every age and for any gender the player is assessed as an individual and also against other players in the same development year or age group.
- Many young footballers display very good individual key factors, however the football clubs will examine the application of these factors in specific sport-related situations in order to assess their suitability for the club.

Designing a talent development programme for a chosen sport

There are a number of talent identification programmes and models that currently exist and are used in the UK. Among these are:

- the World Class Performance Programme
- TASS (Talented Athlete Scholarship Schemes)
- Gifted and Talented
- the World Class Pathway programmes
- ECFA (English Colleges Football Association)
- Football Development Centres
- LTAD (Long Term Athlete Development) model.

Talent identification programmes
World Class Performance Programme

The World Class Performance Programme is aimed at providing support for the UK's top athletes in the Olympic sports. It is a Lottery-funded programme administered by UK Sport, with funding currently in the region of £25 million per annum. UK Sport is a QuaNGO. In his budget statement in March 2006, the Chancellor of the Exchequer announced a further £200 million of Exchequer funding for this programme for the period up to the London Olympics in 2012. He also called on the private/corporate sector to contribute £100 million over the same period. The programme is managed through the appropriate sports governing bodies.

> **definition**
>
> QuaNGO: the term originated as a shortening of Quasi-NGO, which is a non-governmental organisation that performs governmental functions, often with government funding or other support.

UK Sport has full responsibility for all Olympic and Paralympic performance-related support in England since 1 April 2006. This spans talent identification through to Olympic and Paralympic performance levels. However, non-Olympic sports have not been entirely left out. It will also provide consultancy for non-Olympic sports to improve performance and develop future success.

UK Sport currently operates a World Class Performance Pathway at three key levels, as described below.

World Class Podium

This programme will support sports with realistic medal capabilities at the next Olympic/Paralympic Games.

World Class Development

This programme is designed to support the stage of the pathway immediately beneath the Podium pathway.

World Class Talent

This programme is designed to support the identification and confirmation of athletes who have the potential to progress through the World Class pathway, with the help of targeted investment.

TASS (Talented Athlete Scholarship Scheme)

The Talented Athlete Scholarship Scheme (TASS) is a government initiative that is aimed at providing support for talented athletes who may be in danger of dropping out of sport due to their commitment to both competitive sport and education. The initiative is operated through a partnership between sport and further/higher education institutions. Awards are granted to talented athletes to enable them to continue with their studies while training and competing at a high level.

TASS is specifically aimed at talented 16–25-year-old sportspeople who want to remain in education. It helps them to fulfil their sporting potential by enabling them to develop and maintain a sensible balance between academic life, employment, training and competing as a performance athlete. Awards are distributed to performers who show a commitment to combine sport and education in a sensible manner. TASS aims to reduce the number who drop out from sport because of the financial demands of study, training and competing.

National Governing Bodies are asked to nominate the athletes who they would like to receive a TASS award. There are currently 50 sports that are eligible for TASS, of which 16 are disability sports.

In England, TASS operates through a regional structure of nine consortia. Each consortium consists of a small number of further and higher education institutes that provide services to athletes. Each performer is assigned to an individual institute that offers support for that performer. You can visit the TASS website at www.tass.gov.uk.

Table 18.01 TASS sports

Archery	Athletics	Badminton	Boxing
Canoeing	Cricket	Cycling	Diving
Equestrian	Fencing	Football (women)	Golf
Gymnastics	Hockey	Judo	Modern pentathlon
Netball	Orienteering	Rowing	Rugby league
Rugby union	Sailing	Shooting	Skeleton
Snow sports	Speed skating	Squash	Swimming
Synchronised swimming	Table tennis	Tae kwon do	Tennis
Triathlon	Volleyball	Water skiing	

Table 18.02 TASS disability sports

Alpine	Archery	Athletics	Boccia	Cycling	Equestrian
Fencing	Judo	Power lifting	Sailing	Shooting	Swimming
Table tennis	Wheelchair basketball	Wheelchair rugby	Wheelchair tennis		

Gifted and Talented

The Gifted and Talented in PE and sport programme is part of the Department for Education and Skills' (DfES) PE, School Sport and Club Link (PESSCL) strategy. It aims to support talented (and potentially talented) young people who are still involved in full-time compulsory education (under 16 years of age). It is, in that sense, a junior version of TASS. However, it does not provide direct funding to the performer, but seeks to develop pathways through PE and club links to enable the performer to develop their talent fully.

World Class Pathway

The World Class Pathway programmes are Sport England Lottery-funded programmes with the following aims:

- to identify exceptionally talented young performers and give them a comprehensive basis on which to build future world-class success
- to select performers with world-class potential and develop their talents in order to give them the greatest chance of achieving major senior international success.

Amateur Rowing Association

One example of this is the Amateur Rowing Association (ARA) World Class Start programme sponsored by Siemens. The ARA is the National Governing Body for rowing.

The ARA World Class Start programme is aimed at the untrained athlete; the vision is to build the future

definition

National Governing Body: This title refers to an organisation that represents and organizes a particular sport at a national level. For example, The Football Association (FA) or Rugby Football Union (RFU).

of rowing in Great Britain by identifying and developing potential Olympians.

This talent identification programme is applied to local networks and delivered via clubs, universities and schools in partnership with the ARA. The selection procedure involves a proven battery of tests designed to estimate the long-term (Olympic) ability to be successful in rowing. Tests are administered by the World Class Start team.

ECFA and Football Development Centres

The English Colleges Football Association (ECFA) was formed in 2002. ECFA developed the English Colleges Football League (sanctioned by the Football Association). It provides a competitive environment for young, talented footballers who have been recruited by Football Development

Centres based in further education colleges around the country.

Each college must meet strict criteria before membership to the league is approved. These criteria ensure that an effective, planned programme is delivered. All coaches involved must be UEFA 'A' or 'B' licensed coaches and players receive a minimum of six hours of coaching per week.

Long Term Athlete Development (LTAD) model, Istvan Balyi (2004)

This model is based on the principle of periodisation. In other words, a specific and well-planned practice, training, competition and recovery regime will ensure optimum development throughout an athlete's career. Ultimately, sustained success comes from training and performing well over the long term rather than winning in the short term. There is no short-cut to success in athletic preparation. An over-emphasis on competition in the early phases of training will usually cause shortcomings in athletic abilities later in an athlete's career. Child development is taken into consideration and care taken in planning coaching. For example, optimal windows of trainability appear at various stages of the child's development and these are taken into consideration when planning coaching and training.

> **definition**
>
> Periodisation: this is the organisation of a training schedule aimed at peaking the athlete(s) at a specified time range in a competitive period (Dick, 1997).

> **definition**
>
> Optimal windows of trainability: during certain periods of a child's development, accelerated adaptation to training can occur, given appropriate training. If these windows are not recognised and taken advantage of, opportunities to maximise potential may be lost.

Balyi's model states that it takes 10,000 hours over eight to twelve years of deliberate practice for a talented athlete to reach elite levels of performance.

> **definition**
>
> Deliberate practice: activities designed, typically by a teacher or coach, for the sole purpose of effectively improving specific aspects of an individual's performance.

Sports are classified as early or late specialisation. Sports such as gymnastics, figure skating, diving and table tennis require early sport-specific training and specialisation. Other sports, such as team sports, combat sports and cycling, require a generalised training regime in the early years.

> ## LEARNER ACTIVITY
>
> Calculate the average amount of deliberate practice per day required for a talented athlete to reach elite levels of performance.

Four-stage model (early specialisation)	**Six-stage model** (late specialisation)
	FUNdamental
	learning to train
training to train	training to train
training to compete	training to compete
training to win	training to win
retirement/retaining	retirement/retaining

> ## LEARNER ACTIVITY
>
> 1 Apart from those listed above, what other sports can be described as (a) early specialisation, (b) late specialisation?
> 2 Why do you think they are described as such? Why does it matter?

The LTAD has been described as the golden thread that permeates the 2004 National Framework for Sport. It appeared as the preferred model (in fact the only model) in the government's (2002) Game Plan National Sports Policy document. However, there has been some criticism:

> www.Sportdevelopment.org.uk states that, scientific interrogation of the model remains impossible since the **LTAD** refers to virtually no science and includes no research data, just a few examples of people who might fit the idea ... good science is reviewed by respected scientists [peers], the results published in proper [peer reviewed] journals – i.e. the science is verified as far as it can be! The **LTAD** model appears in [up to 2004] no journals in seminal form.

Even so, it forms a major part of the Canadian coach education programme and has been exported worldwide. It is now being used by many NGBs in this country to remodel their talent-development pathways.

Structure of talent-identification programmes

When designing a talent-identification and development programme a number of issues must be taken into consideration.

Programme aims

What is (are) the aim(s) of the programme? Establishing clear aims will guide the whole process. The aims of the programme, for example, might be to (a) identify talented performers and (b) provide opportunities or funding for them.

Programme purpose

What is the purpose of the programme? Following on from the example above, the purpose of the programme might be to produce performers for a specific event such as the London Olympics in 2012 or the FIFA World Cup in 2014.

How do we define programmes as successful? This relates directly back to the aims and purposes of the programme. If these are met, then the programme is successful. Therefore much care must be taken when deciding on the aims and purpose. For example, if the aim is to produce two gold medal performances at a particular championship and we achieve four silver medals, have we been successful?

Programme format

The format of the programme will be partly determined by the aims and purpose of the programme. But it will also be determined by finance, political and geographical factors. It might be that the programme concentrates solely on identifying potential medal hopefuls and providing financial support. Or it could be much more comprehensive and offer fitness testing and training support, lifestyle management assistance, access to top coaches and facilities, etc. If its purpose is to target a range of sports it could be operated through NGBs or through a central body.

There are also a number of questions of detail that need to be considered. How do we establish normative values for classifying performers as talented or potentially talented? Should we use batteries of tests? What tests should we use? Should this be limited to fitness testing or should medical and psychological screening be used? Do we use generic testing or sport-specific testing? Will the programme have phases? What determines whether performers stay in the programme? For example, is their inclusion based on (a) the need to win medals or reach finals at certain championships or (b) are they guaranteed support for a set time?

As stated above, the ARA operates a World Class Start programme. Here is a summary of its approach. The ARA operates testing camps rather than training camps. These take place nine times per year. The aim of these camps is to test the athletes' technical and physiological progress and then monitor improvement from camp to camp. The athletes are tested in three main areas: sculling skills, technique/performance, and physiology. The athlete and coach can objectively test the effectiveness of the past training programme and set goals for the next camp. Goal setting on a regular basis is key to the development of any performer.

As rowing is a sport that is dominated by physique and physical capability, the emphasis is on testing these aspects. The ARA uses comparisons of test results with international champions to provide realistic feedback to each athlete and coach. Regular anthropometric measures of height, arm span and body mass provide insight into growth and development factors, particularly for the younger athletes.

Education is a major factor at the camps too. Information is provided on nutrition, lifestyle, fitness, psychology, etc. This informs the training of the athletes and helps them to use the latest developments from sport science.

The rowers are tracked throughout their time on the programme so that their progress can be charted against existing data from elite rowers. This is known as the Rower Performance Development Model. Progress against this model, on an annual basis, determines whether rowers move into or out of the programmes.

Key learning points

- There are a number of talent-identification and development programmes in operation in the UK. Most are funded by the National Lottery and central government:
  - World Class Performance Programme
  - TASS (Talented Athlete Scholarship Schemes)
  - World Class Pathway programmes
  - Gifted and Talented
  - ECFA (English Colleges Football Association)
  - Football Development Centres
  - LTAD (Long Term Athlete Development) models.
- These programmes are mostly operated by government departments and QuaNGOs, and delivered through NGBs and educational institutes.

- There is currently only one recognised talent-development programme: the Long Term Athlete Development (LTAD) model, being widely used in the UK. However, this model has come in for some criticism.
- Designing a talent-identification and development model is an extremely complex process and requires much planning.
- The aims and purposes of the programme must be well thought out as they will determine the success of the programme and influence the format for delivery.

Review questions

1. What are the key assessment criteria that development scouts identify early?
2. Why is it important to have a development structure and plan in place for talented individuals?
3. Talent identification often refers to broad-based sports. What does this mean in terms of multi-talented and uni-talented players
4. What physiological components would you measure as players enter a development programme, and why?
5. Why is battery testing important in talent identification?
6. What predictors could I use to identify a talented player from any sport?
7. At early ages in the ten-year cycle categorise the importance of technique, speed, power and skill.
8. What current development plans have an impact on your sport?
9. As a country we are lucky to be hosting the 2012 Olympic Games. What key areas would you look to develop now to ensure we have participants within these Games?
10. Why is talent identification an important tool for player recruitment?
11. List as many current UK talent-identification and development programmes as you can.
12. How much extra funding has been promised to the World Class Performance Programme between 2006 and 2012?
13. Who developed the LTAD?
14. UK Sport currently operates a World Class Performance Pathway at three key levels: name them.
15. At what age range is the TASS programme aimed?
16. Name five of the sports included in the TASS programme.
17. At what age range is the Talented and Gifted programme aimed?
18. Name the four stages of the LTAD early specialisation model.
19. Name the two extra stages included in LTAD late specialisation model.
20. What are the differences between the aim(s) and the purpose of a talent identification and development programme?

References

Balyi, I. (2004) *Long Term Athlete Development: Trainability in Childhood and Adolescence*, National Coaching Institute.

Dick, F. W. (1997) *Sports Training Principles*, Black.

Websites

www.ara-rowing.org – Amateur Rowing Association

www.ecfaleague.co.uk – English Colleges Football Association

www.talentladder.org – Talent Ladder

www.tass.gov.uk – Talented Athlete Scholarship Fund

www.uksport.gov.uk – UK Sport

Sport and exercise massage

Goals

By the end of this chapter you should:

- understand the effects and benefits of sports massage
- understand the role of sports massage professionals
- be able to identify the sports massage needs of athletes
- be able to demonstrate different sports massage techniques.

Massage can be used both to remedy problems and enhance an athlete's performance. It can also be used to treat problems arising from non-athletic, yet still physical activities such as gardening and walking. In reality most of us would benefit from massage therapy as it can promote relaxation, correct physical dysfunction and create a feeling of well-being.

The history of massage

Although there are indications that massage was used in China more than 5000 years ago, in the western hemisphere recorded history dates sports massage back to the Ancient Greeks and the original Olympic Games. Hippocrates, the Greek physician generally considered as the father of physical medicine, used massage as one of his vital therapies.

The principles behind current massage techniques were developed by Per Henrik Ling of Sweden in the nineteenth century. These techniques became known as Swedish massage and spread throughout Europe and then the world. In the 1924 Paris Olympics runner Paavo Nurmi, the 'Flying Finn', won five gold medals including two in one day with only a 30-minute break between events. Nurmi had his own personal massage therapist and he credited special massage treatments as a vital component of his

training programme. In the 1972 Munich Olympics the modern-day 'Flying Finn' Lasse Viren won two gold medals with the aid of daily massage.

As participation in sport and exercise becomes increasingly popular, greater demands are placed on today's athletes as the rewards for success increase. As they continue to improve their performances, the athletes push themselves to their physical and psychological limits. If the inevitable injuries are ignored and become chronic, they not only hinder rehabilitation but also affect performance, which makes the athlete susceptible to further injury.

definition

Chronic: **long term.**

Sports massage is therefore an expanding industry which aims to aid an athlete's recovery and enhance performance. It can now be seen at most major sporting events around the world.

definition

Sports massage: **the systematic manipulation of the soft tissues of the body for therapeutic purposes to aid individuals participating in physical activity.**
Soft tissues: **ligaments, tendons, muscles, connective tissue and skin.**

The effects and benefits of sports massage

The aims of sports massage are to restore normal functional activity to the musculoskeletal system. Massage should therefore be an integral part of every athlete's pre- and post-training and competition routines, and should be viewed with similar importance to warming up and cooling down.

The general benefits of massage can be said to fall into three specific categories:

- mechanical
- physiological
- psychological.

Mechanical benefits to the athlete are:

- stimulation of soft tissues
- stretching of soft tissue to improve flexibility
- breaking down scar tissue
- correction of posture and limb alignment to improve body awareness
- reducing tension and associated pain
- reducing soreness and pain after an activity.

Physiological benefits to the athlete are:

- improved circulation via stimulation of the sympathetic nervous system to increase the supply of oxygen and nutrients to the injured tissue, thereby promoting healing
- improved circulation to remove waste products from the soft tissues via the lymphatic system
- improved circulation to reduce swelling post-injury
- sedative effect on the parasympathetic nervous system to reduce tension, induce relaxation and relieve pain
- stimulation of the nervous system to prepare the muscles for activity.

Psychological benefits to the athlete are:

- promoting relaxation
- creating a sense of well-being
- increasing confidence pre-competition.

In summary, the above effects will allow athletes to train more often, at a higher intensity and with fewer physical problems. It is therefore an essential part of an overall training programme.

The indications for sports massage

The following problems would indicate a need for sports massage based on the above benefits it can offer:

- pain post-injury or following training and competition
- swelling
- reduced flexibility
- reduced strength

- muscle tension
- pre-event nerves
- post-event fatigue or soreness
- routine part of training schedule to minimise the chance of the above situations arising
- injury prevention.

The contraindications for sports massage

Under certain circumstances, conditions may be present that sports massage may make worse and hence it should not be carried out. These conditions are collectively known as contraindications. The massage therapist needs to know what they are and how to deal with them.

- **A body temperature over 100 degrees Fahrenheit, or feeling unwell:** these symptoms suggest a period of illness, and as massage improves circulation, it may also spread toxins and potentially make the condition worse.
- **Skin diseases and disorders:** the skin may become inflamed due to allergies or medical conditions such as eczema and psoriasis. Infections can be recognised by swelling, redness, pain and heat. Massage can cause further irritation and may spread the infection through the client, on to the therapist, or even to a subsequent client.
- **Vascular diseases:** phlebitis is the inflammation of veins, and can often accompany a blood clot called a thrombosis. The clot may be disturbed by massage causing a blockage elsewhere in the blood vessels of the heart, lungs or brains, all with serious consequences. Caution should be taken if there is swelling, increased temperature and pain in the calf muscles. If a clot is suspected, urgent medical attention should be sought. Attempts to massage an area where varicose veins are present could also cause further damage and pain.

definition

Vascular: relating to the blood vessels.

- **Recently injured areas:** the site of an injury may be acutely inflamed with swelling, heat, redness, pain and probable dysfunction. Massage may act to disturb the healing process, thus making the condition worse by increasing circulation and therefore causing further swelling.

The above conditions may need a medical opinion and the client should be advised to see a doctor.

- **Pregnancy:** care should be taken if the client is experiencing nausea and vomiting. Massage of the back and abdomen must be avoided during the first 16 weeks of pregnancy as friction could promote miscarriage. In the later stages of pregnancy, massage of the lower limbs may reduce swelling and aid relaxation in areas such as the upper back and shoulders.
- **Other medical conditions:** clients presenting with a medical history of cancer, diabetes, tuberculosis, multiple sclerosis or other serious medical conditions should be advised to gain medical clearance from their doctor prior to treatment.

LEARNER ACTIVITY
Indications and contraindications

1 Which conditions would benefit from massage and which would be contraindicated.

Broken leg	Tight muscle
Anxiety	Post-training fatigue
Feeling unwell	Thrombosis
Psoriasis	Recent injury

2 List two mechanical, two physiological and two psychological benefits of massage.
3 What is phlebitis?
4 You should never perform massage on a pregnant client. True or false?

Key learning points

- The aim of sports massage is to restore normal function. Its benefits can be divided into mechanical, physiological and psychological.
- The indications for sports massage are wide-ranging and need to be known by both the therapist and client.
- Be aware of the contraindications to avoid making the client feel worse; seek medical advice if you are not certain whether to proceed.

The role of the sports massage professional

A sports massage professional has a varied job: preparing athletes for competition, helping them warm down after competition, and then dealing with any injuries or symptoms they may have. They can also treat other people who are active but not athletes.

In order to practise, the therapist ideally requires a sports therapy diploma, accredited by the Vocational Training Charitable Trust (VTCT), which can be studied at most further education colleges. It is also possible to do degrees at a limited number of universities, and private training organisations offer an excellent range of courses and career opportunities. Details of all these can be found on the internet.

To be an effective sports therapist you need a thorough base of knowledge and a range of physical and personal skills:

- **knowledge** of anatomy and physiology, exercise physiology, massage techniques and effects
- **physical** skills in massage techniques, strapping, stretching, resistance training, first aid and modalities such as heat, ice and electrotherapy
- **personal** attributes and skills – professional, honest and reliable, as well as listening and communication skills.

The therapist also needs to know their limits and when to seek advice or refer a client to a medical colleague. This is because the diagnosis of certain conditions may require more extensive training and expertise. Treatment could be provided once the all-clear was given. For this reason many therapists work alongside other specialists, such as physiotherapists, and this relationship is often of mutual benefit. Sports massage professionals may be required to perform a range of treatments in addition to the basic sports massage techniques, including strapping and electrotherapy.

The sports massage professional usually has to deal with administration and may choose to set up their own business. This business could be located anywhere, but usually they are at sports clubs, leisure centres, gyms and medical centres. Some will travel to clients' homes and others will diversify, offering additional personal training services. To this end, it is useful to have a sound knowledge of sport-specific techniques and the rigours of competition.

In summary, they have a huge role to play in the treatment of sports injuries, the conditioning of athletes and the treatment of the general public.

> ### LEARNER ACTIVITY Attributes of a therapist
>
> List three physical and three personal attributes that the sports massage therapist needs.

Key learning points

- The career is varied and rewarding, with high levels of satisfaction.
- Qualifications are necessary to become a sports therapist, as is a thorough knowledge base.
- Certain personal and physical attributes are needed if you are considering a career as a sports therapist.

Sports massage requirements

Client assessment

Once you are clear about the effects of massage and know when massage is both indicated and contraindicated, you can proceed to the assessment. This initial consultation is as important as the treatment itself, and an accurate record must be kept along with details of the subsequent physical examination.

The questioning of a client is known as the subjective assessment. It enables the therapist to build up a picture of the current issues, the client's history and what they aim to achieve from treatment.

Prior to any questioning, you should make your client aware of any health and safety issues that are specific to your facility, and the location of fire exits, fire procedures, etc.

The initial questions will establish the cause, nature and irritability of their symptoms:

- What is your presenting problem?
- If there has been an injury, how and when did it occur?
- If there has been no injury, how long have you had the problem?

- Did the problem occur immediately or gradually?
- How would you describe the symptoms, e.g. dull ache, sharp pain?
- Has there been any swelling, redness or increased temperature?
- Is the problem improving, remaining the same or getting worse?
- How is this currently affecting your function and performance?

Once you have this detailed information about the client's current status you need to build up a picture of their history:

- How is your general health?
- Have you any history of medical problems?
- Are you taking any medication?
- What physical activities are you involved in?
- At what level are you competing?
- What is your training schedule?
- What injuries, if any, have you previously suffered?
- What treatments have you previously had?

The information that you are given needs to be recorded on a record form similar to that shown on the opposite page.

At this point you may have identified a contra-indication, or may have concern beyond your level of expertise. If so, you may choose to refer your client to their doctor before progressing with treatment.

You should at this stage have a good idea of what their problem is, but you will need to verify this by examining the client. This is known as the 'objective assessment'. If appropriate, it may be necessary for the client to remove clothing, often down to their underwear, with their dignity being maintained at all times. A basic understanding of anatomy is essential for these next stages.

- You need to observe the client for limping, swelling, muscle wasting, bruising, haematomas, abrasions, redness or other abnormal signs.
- You then need to test the range of movement in the areas adjacent to their problem. First, ask the client

definition

> Haematoma: **bruising.**
> Abrasion: **grazed skin.**

Confidential medical history

Name:_____   Occupation: _____

Age: _____   D.O.B.: _____

Address:_____

Tel: Day: _____   Eve: _____   Mob: _____
Sex: _____   Height: _____   Weight: _____
Sport played: _____   Frequency/intensity: _____

GP name/address:

Medical history:

Present complaint:

History of injury:

I confirm that the information I have given is accurate to the best of my knowledge and I have not withheld any details. I accept that I will receive sports massage therapy at my own risk.

Signed:_____   Date: _____

Print name: _____   Therapist signature: _____

Notes – physical assessment

to move and assess their willingness (active movement), then move the area yourself within a comfortable range (passive movement). This will assess the flexibility of the tissues in question.

- You then need to assess any muscle weakness by resisting certain movements or asking them to perform certain functional tasks.
- Finally, you need to palpate (touch) the problem area to check for muscle spasm, increased temperature, tenderness or pain.

This will complete your client assessment and provide you with all the necessary information to move on to the treatment stage. The information you are given needs to be recorded on a form which also includes the client's details. This form is an accurate record of your assessment and subsequent treatment, and needs to be signed and dated on every entry. The information disclosed by the client is strictly confidential and should not be discussed without their authority.

Proposed treatment

The results of the assessment should be discussed with the client, along with how you intend to treat their problem and what this aims to achieve. Your plan will involve informing the client which treatments you propose to use and the number of treatments that may be required to achieve satisfactory results. This may include the client having to perform a home exercise programme such as guidance for stretches, on strengthening and posture, or how to use heat and ice.

LEARNER ACTIVITY Client assessment

- With a partner of the same gender, take the role of the client and then the therapist. Complete a subjective assessment as if it were a real situation. On completion, reflect on each other's performance and highlight both positive and negative aspects. If necessary repeat the activity.
- It can be embarrassing for a client to undress down to their underwear for treatment. With this in mind, each partner should remove clothing relevant to their injury or problem so that the assessment and treatment can be carried out. This will give you an insight into how the client may feel, making you think about another person's need for dignity.

Key learning points

- Perform a subjective examination and understand the relevance of the questions.
- Perform an objective examination based on the previous questioning, recognising the importance of maintaining client dignity.
- Understand the need to accurately document all information and to maintain confidentiality at all times.
- The assessment is essential to formulate a safe and effective treatment plan.

The client is then in a position to give you their informed consent for you to proceed. Any charges should be made clear prior to the assessment and any payments received should be accurately recorded.

Environment, appearance and equipment

You will often have to be flexible as to where you work. The environment will often be out of your control, especially if working at a sporting event. Care is essential to create an environment as near to the ideal as possible. This would involve the following:

- privacy for the client
- clean, tidy and well-ventilated room
- warmth to promote relaxation, especially if the client has to undress.

The therapist should have:

- a professional appearance, unhurried and confident
- clean hands – wash basin, soap, towels and waste disposal available
- short nails with no polish and no jewellery
- short sleeves and no wristwatch.

The following equipment should be available:

- massage couch with adjustable height and pillows
- privacy screens (for a private changing area)
- massage oils, creams or powders
- massage cologne to remove oils
- towels to cover areas not being massaged and to provide a comfortable temperature.

Client comfort is paramount, so the couch should ideally be adjustable with a face hole and a ready supply of pillows to support the head or limbs. It is also important for the therapist to be comfortable as they will adopt positions for sustained periods, day in day out, so the height of the plinth and your position requires careful attention to convey relaxation and confidence to the client.

Safe practice needs to be implemented, and an understanding of health, safety and hygiene regulations is important. You also need to note that massage is often a personal experience for both therapist and client, and although professionalism is adhered to and inappropriate behaviour does not occur, complaints may still arise. An awareness of consumer rights is therefore beneficial.

LEARNER ACTIVITY Hygiene and appearance

- Go to www.RCN.org.uk and discover how to correctly wash and dry your hands. Practise this with a partner.
- List five aspects of a therapist's appearance that would create a professional image.

Client preparation

Success depends not only on diagnosis, treatment and physical skills, but also on personal skills. It is essential that a professional rapport is developed with the client. This can be achieved by:

- relaxing the client and putting them at ease
- showing a caring attitude by listening to their concerns
- being professional at all times
- maintaining client confidentiality
- explaining the treatment course and the desired effect
- using tact and respecting their privacy and dignity.

Once the treatment has commenced, the client must be able to relax. Experience will allow you to work out whether the client wishes to talk or not.

Massage oils are used to allow smooth movement over the client's body and prevent friction. Vegetable oils such as olive and sunflower oils are commonly used as they have little fragrance and are easily absorbed by the skin. Aromatherapists use essential oils which have specific effects and should therefore only be used following appropriate training. If using oils, sports cologne should be applied post-treatment to remove any excess. The traditional lubricant for Swedish massage is talcum powder but this can cause extra friction and subsequent discomfort on dry skin. The finer powder may also be inhaled over time by the therapist, endangering their health. But as certain clients still prefer it, you should still consider using it with caution. Less frequently used are certain creams and lotions.

Massage techniques

The three main techniques used are:

- effleurage
- petrissage
- frictions.

> ## LEARNER ACTIVITY
> ### Clients at ease
> What are the vital components needed to make your client feel at ease?

Key learning points

- The assessment results and subsequent treatment plan should be shared with the client so they can offer their informed consent to treat.
- A considerable amount of organisation is needed to prepare the environment, equipment, the therapist and the client, in order to portray a professional image and strike up an appropriate rapport.
- Awareness of health and safety legislation and customer rights are essential, and hygiene and hand washing are of particular importance.
- It is important to understand which massage medium to use – oils, powders or creams.

Effleurage

This involves a variety of stroking movements and is used at the beginning and end of a massage. It can be applied with varying degrees of pressure and is broken into light and deep stroking. Light stroking is performed with the whole hand, keeping the fingers together and with the hand relaxed. The speed and pressure will vary as the massage proceeds. The initial light stroking enables the therapist to spread the oil and identify tension in the muscle, even starting to relax the muscle. Gradually more pressure is applied, with the aim of assisting fluid flow through the tissue spaces, vessels and veins. The movement should occur up the limb towards the superficial lymph glands which can be found in the groin, back of the knee and the armpit.

Pressure should be consistent throughout a stroke, but can be increased by placing one hand on top of another or using the heel of the hand, finger pads or thumbs. The aim is to relax and sedate initially, then to stretch tissues, increase flow and drainage, reduce swelling, reduce pain by nerve stimulation, and remove waste products.

Petrissage

This is also known as kneading as the basic movement involves compressing then releasing the tissues. Direct pressure is performed in a circular motion using the palm of the hand to compress muscle tissue on to underlying structures. More localised pressure can be applied using the fingertips, thumbs and even the elbows. The next stage is similar to kneading but is

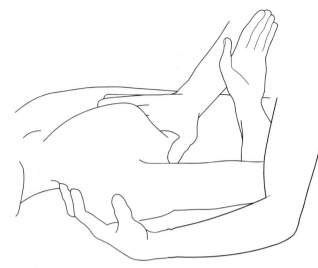

Fig 19.01 Effleurage

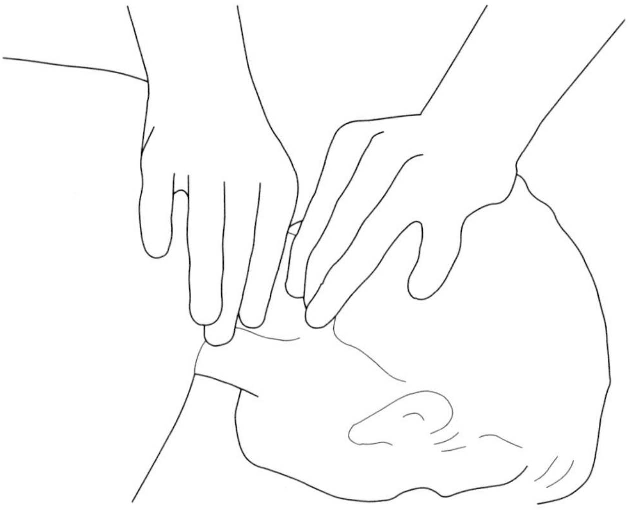

Fig 19.02 Petrissage

LEARNER ACTIVITY
Effleurage massage

Working in pairs, practise effleurage on each other's calf muscles, with strokes starting at the foot and ending at the back of the knee. Relax your partner with gentle stroking movements, warming the muscles and spreading the oils. Promote circulation, increase pressure and stimulate lymph drainage to the major superficial glands. Gradually end the massage using further gentle stroking techniques. Reflect on each other's performance and remember that practice makes perfect.

known as 'picking up' as it involves lifting the tissues up perpendicular to the underlying tissues then squeezing with the forefinger and thumb prior to release. Once the tissue is released, blood returns to it, bringing with it the essential oxygen and nutrients for healing. This technique also aims to mobilise tissues and reduce tension, promote lymph drainage and encourage relaxation.

Frictions

These are small movements over a localised area using the pads of the fingers or thumbs. Unlike other techniques they are often used where there is little soft tissue, such as the elbows, knees and ankles. Considerably more pressure is applied than during petrissage.

The action is initiated by bracing with the heels of the hands, then holding the thumbs steady and moving the fingers in a circular motion. The fingers do not move across the skin but they do move the skin across the deeper tissue. By increasing the pressure you can stimulate the deep muscle tissue and the breakdown of recently formed scar tissue by separating adhesions between repaired muscle fibres. There can be a degree of discomfort but only for a short time. The aims are to stimulate blood flow, separate adhesions, minimise the effects of scar tissue, promote flexibility and promote healing.

Although the above techniques form the basis of massage, there are other techniques in use, including tapotement, vibrations and trigger points.

LEARNER ACTIVITY
Petrissage massage

Practise this technique in a similar way to effleurage. This time decide for yourself which muscles would benefit most from this technique.

LEARNER ACTIVITY
Frictions massage

Practise this technique in the same way as the other two. Decide what injuries and which parts of your body would benefit most.

Fig 19.03 Frictions

Tapotement

This is also known as percussion and can be divided into cupping and hacking.

Cupping involves the therapist making a cup shape with their hands and, with the palms down, they strike the muscle making a dull thud, which should sound different from the slap of a flat palm. Moving the hands rapidly up and down the muscle this has the effect of improving superficial circulation and stimulating the muscle.

Hacking has a similar effect and involves using the outside of the hands with the palms facing each other to strike the muscle, usually targeting the larger muscle bulks such as the quadriceps.

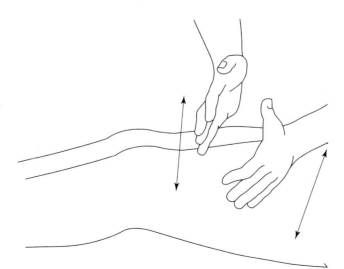

Fig 19.04 Tapotement (hacking)

Vibration

This is often used to finish off a massage. It involves the therapist supporting a muscle with one hand and vibrating the other hand from side to side as they move up and down the muscle. This aims to stimulate the muscle, and to promote blood flow and increase flexibility.

Trigger point

This massage involves the therapist applying sustained pressure in one specific place, using a finger, thumb or even an elbow. The trigger point is an area of high tension in the muscle where the fibres have failed to relax. It can cause local or referred pain where symptoms are felt at a distance away from the trigger point. Pressure is applied and the pain it creates will tend to subside after ten seconds, following which greater pressure can be applied and sustained for up to a minute. The aim is to gain relaxation and allow blood to return to the muscle.

Order of routine

Usually the techniques described above are performed in the order given, with the massage finishing with effleurage. The time you spend on each technique may vary depending on the needs of your client.

Evaluation

It is important to evaluate the effect of treatment by:

- asking for immediate feedback
- stretching and loading affected muscles
- performing specific tests
- getting client feedback once they return to sporting action.

Based on the feedback, you may prescribe more treatments or a change of technique. If symptoms persist, referral to another medical professional such as a doctor, physiotherapist, chiropractor or osteopath may be advised.

Key learning points

- There are three main massage techniques that are the basis of treatments; these need to be practised diligently in order to gain maximum benefit and to instil confidence in the client.

- Additional techniques are also available and it is important to learn when to use all the techniques

and for which body parts certain techniques are most suitable.

- An evaluation after the treatment is an essential part of the overall management.

Review questions

1 What benefits does sports massage provide?
2 Give three situations when sports massage should not be used.
3 What equipment does a sports massage therapist require?
4 Describe the procedures that need to be undertaken before treatment.
5 Explain the difference between effleurage, petrissage and frictions.
6 How would you create a professional image?

References

Cash, M. (1998) *Sports and Remedial Massage*, Mosby.

Dawson, L., Dawson, K. A. and Tiidius, P. M. (2004) Evaluating the influence of massage on leg strength, swelling and pain following a half marathon. *Journal of Sports Science Medicine*, 3, 37–43.

Lewis, M. and Johnson, M. I. (2006) The clinical effectiveness of therapeutic massage for musculoskeletal pain: a systematic review. *Physiotherapy*, 92(3), 146–58.

Paine, T. (2000) *The Complete Guide to Sports Massage*, A & C Black.

Preyde, M. (2000) Effectiveness of massage therapy for sub acute low back pain: a randomised controlled trial. *Canadian Medical Association Journal*, 162, 1815–20.

Tiidius, P. M. and Shoemaker, J. K. (1995) Effleurage massage, muscle blood flow and long term post exercise strength recovery. *International Journal of Sports Medicine*, 15, 478–83.

Van der Dolder, P. A. and Roberts, D. L. (2003) A trial in to the effectiveness of soft tissue massage in the treatment of shoulder pain. *Australian Journal of Physiotherapy*, 49, 183–8.

Watt, J. (1999) *Massage for Sport*, The Crowood Press.

Rules, regulations and officiating in sport

Goals

By the end of this chapter you should:

- understand the rules and regulations of a selected sport
- understand the roles and responsibilities of officials involved in a selected sport
- be able to analyse the performance of officials in a selected sport
- be able to officiate effectively in a selected sport.

British match officials are a national resource to be proud of and to nurture. They are often unsung heroes and heroines who provide the backbone of equity and fair play at every level of sport.

> At the highest level, their reputation and visible presence abroad is proportionally higher than that [of officials] from many other countries. In the final rounds of international competition, British officials are often still involved long after many of [their] teams have gone home.

(UK Sports Council, Officiating In Sport: An Investment in Fair Play, *cited in Pegg, 2005)*

Officials are essential to the success of sport at every level, whether in the international arena or at a local league match. Officials apply rules, maintain health and safety and generally work as part of a team. Officials need to have management skills, self-awareness, empathy, communication skills and a love for the sport.

Understanding the rules and regulations of a selected sport

The rules and regulations of any sport are normally set and amended by its National Governing Body (NGB) and the International Sports Federation (ISF). These are set to ensure that the sport is played fairly and that competitors are aware of how to win, and play fairly.

ISFs and NGBs may change the rules and regulations periodically as they look to improve the sport. For example, the Federation Internationale de Football Associations (FIFA) recently changed the offside law to encourage more attacking football. The English Football Association (the NGB for football) ensured that both referees and the teams playing in this country understood the change.

Other ISFs and NGBs are shown in Table 20.01.

Time

Many team sports have time constraints and are split into periods of play. The team with the most points or goals is declared the winner, while if the scores are tied then the game is normally declared a draw. Time can be stopped for minor stoppages such as injuries or the ball being out of play. In basketball the clock is stopped every time the ball is out of play. Some sports may have periods of extra time to declare a winner. In

Table 20.01 International Sports Federations and National Governing Bodies

Sport	NGB	ISF
Basketball	England Basketball (EB)	International Basketball Federation (FIBA)
Cricket	The England and Wales Cricket Board (ECB)	International Cricket Council (ICC)
Rugby	Rugby Football Union (RFU)	International Rugby Board (IRB)

other sports a winner can be declared before the allocated time has elapsed: in test match cricket, a team may have bowled out its opponents twice and scored the required number of runs before the five days are over. Time has a major effect on sports even if the sport does not have time constraints. The longer a game goes on the more tired the players will become and this can be a problem as players are normally

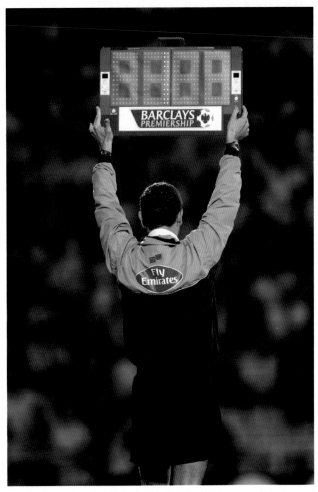

Fig 20.01 A fourth official in football holding up the time board

trained to withstand the usual time constraints of the game.

Scoring

Each sport has a different scoring system, with the team or individual with the most points usually being declared the winner. An exception to this is golf, where the player who has taken the fewest strokes is the winner. Scoring may include putting the ball into

the goal in football or handball, or downing the ball in rugby or hitting a shuttlecock into your opponent's court in badminton. Many sports give a different number of points for certain scoring actions. In rugby there are different methods of scoring and different points are given for tries, drop goals and conversions. In basketball successfully shooting outside the three-point arc will give you an extra point compared with scoring a lay-up. In cricket a batsman can score anywhere between one and six runs off a single ball.

Facilities and equipment

Specific sports require certain facilities to enable play to take place. Different surfaces can be used for different sports and often sports are played on a range of surfaces. Tennis is a good example of this as it can be played on grass, clay and hard surfaces, and can be played inside or outdoors. Occasionally rules may be adapted for sports played on different surfaces.

Many sports require the participants to wear or use specialist equipment. In football the laws of the game insist that all players must wear shin guards to protect their lower legs. In sports such as hockey, rugby and

LEARNER ACTIVITY

1 Select two sports from the following list: rugby league, volleyball, tennis, squash, cricket.
2 Design a set of simplified rules for that sport, including diagrams where necessary. Be sure to include scoring, timing, facilities and equipment.

cricket players may wear specific equipment to reduce the risk of injury; this could include arm guards, helmets and padding.

You can find out about the rules and regulations of each sport via its National Governing Body. The NGB looks after many aspects of a sport, including organising major competitions, running coaching schemes and dealing with the development of the sport at all levels.

Key learning points

- National Governing Bodies are responsible for establishing and maintaining the rules or laws of a sport.
- Sports differ in terms of the time they take, whether time is a factor and whether game time is stopped and restarted or is simply allowed to lapse.
- Usually the player or team that scores the most points will be successful.
- Sports are played on many different surfaces, inside and outside, and will require a range of different equipment and clothing.
- Many sports require competitors to wear/use protective or safety equipment that usually forms part of the rules or regulations of the sport.

Understanding the roles and responsibilities of officials involved in a selected sport

Officials go by many names: referees, umpires, judges, linesmen, starters, markers, marshals, touch judges, scorers, assessors, third umpires, fourth officials, etc. Some officials run on the field of play, others sit at the side.

Officials can be split into two categories.

1 **Performance controllers** regulate the sport on or close to the action, e.g. rugby, football or basketball.

2 **Performance managers** measure competitors against standards, e.g. trampolinists, long jumpers or snooker players.

Fig 20.02 A judo official

The roles of an official

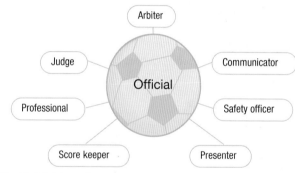

Fig 20.03 The roles of an official

Arbiter

It is essential that officials demonstrate a completely neutral standpoint and eliminate any bias, intended

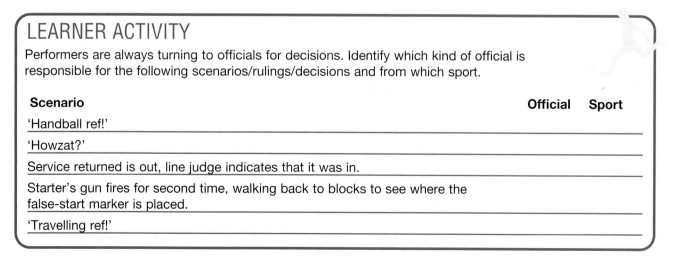

LEARNER ACTIVITY

Performers are always turning to officials for decisions. Identify which kind of official is responsible for the following scenarios/rulings/decisions and from which sport.

Scenario	Official	Sport
'Handball ref!'		
'Howzat?'		
Service returned is out, line judge indicates that it was in.		
Starter's gun fires for second time, walking back to blocks to see where the false-start marker is placed.		
'Travelling ref!'		

or otherwise. Equally nobody likes to play against opponents who have no respect for the rules or laws of the game.

Communicator

Officials are required to listen and provide information to a variety of people, performers, co-officials, support staff, spectators and the media. Development as an official will require a great deal of communication, ranging from discussion, meetings, and formal or informal training.

Safety officer

Sports that require participants to compete over the same object in the same space carry a risk of injury or physical danger. Every step should be made to ensure safety. An official must control these situations and identify ways of minimising danger.

Presenter

Officials present the sport to spectators. Some officials even have microphones to announce key decisions. Most sports have clearly defined signals that are as important to the spectators as the performers.

Scoring and timekeeping

Many officials are required to keep a score of the game that they are officiating in addition to their usual duties, e.g. football and netball. In some sports, such as gymnastics, officials are required to deduct scores before reporting the result.

Professional

It is essential that officials establish and maintain professional standards. This can be working effectively as part of a team, establishing effective working practices, updating knowledge of the rules and their interpretation, maintaining a professional appearance and managing people or situations.

Judge

In many situations it is necessary for officials to make judgements according to the rules/laws of the game and within the nature and spirit of the activity. Officials should also do their best to communicate their decisions to all concerned.

Responsibilities of officials in sport
Application of the rules

Knowledge of the rules is very important. Some would argue that the application of these rules is even more important. Picture the football referee who allows play to continue after a foul. Assuming that the fouled team retains possession and gains a useful advantage you could argue that this allows the game to flow uninterrupted. It would be just as correct to award a free kick for the foul. Which would you prefer? A balance should be struck between what is correct to the letter of the law and what constitutes unnecessary interference.

Health and safety

The role of the official in health and safety is significant. First, sports in which contact is not

---

LEARNER ACTIVITY

Using the example provided, demonstrate your understanding of the particular rules of the following sports that are designed mainly to help prevent physical harm.

Sport	Rule
Rugby	Binding rules in scrummages
Boxing	
Cricket	
Bowling	
Hockey	
Basketball	
Netball	

Fig 20.04 Responsibilities of officials in sport

allowed, e.g. basketball or netball, will require the official to make a judgement and if necessary penalise the offender. Other sports allow contact, e.g. rugby or football, and the role of the official is to decide which contact is fair and which is unfair. Other sports have physical contact as the whole point of the activity, e.g. martial arts or boxing. Even in the more passive sports such as badminton, umpires may be required to stop play, for example if the floor gets moist. Track marshals wave yellow flags as a warning.

Rugby has blood-bins which are off-the-field treatment areas used in the case of bleeding injuries.

In summary, officials have a duty of care to all participants.

In an ever more health and safety-conscious environment there are a number of related government acts concerning health and safety.

> **definition**
>
> Duty of care: is a legal obligation (Tort law), which implies that an official must exercise a reasonable amount of care while officiating any activity that may lead to harm.

In short, officials should do everything reasonable to foresee any dangers, warn of any risks and make sure that the sporting environment is as safe as possible.

Child protection

Once the realm of the sports coach, concern over the welfare of children has highlighted the need for officials to be aware of their role in the care and protection of children.

All sports governing bodies in the UK are required to have policies to ensure that all young people, regardless of age, culture, disability, gender, language, racial origin, religious belief and sexual identity, have the right to protection from abuse. Details of these policies are usually available on request, and on official websites.

Physical and mental fitness

Some sports demand a certain level of fitness of their officials, and will require them to train and maintain an acceptable level of fitness, e.g. football, basketball and rugby. It is important that officials prepare in the same way as athletes for the physical and mental demands of the sport. Mental preparation might include stress reduction, imagery, concentration, psyching up, etc.

LEARNER ACTIVITY

Complete the following checklist, using the last competitive match that you have officiated or participated in, from the point of view of the official.

1	Are the performers using appropriate protective equipment?	Yes/No
2	Do they have shin pads, gloves, goggles or other equipment recommended for that sport?	Yes/No
3	Are they aware of any safety rules and are they sticking to them?	Yes/No
4	Is the playing area safe?	Yes/No
5	Is there sufficient space between this event and the adjacent match?	Yes/No
6	Is first-aid equipment available?	Yes/No
7	Is the location of the nearest accident and emergency centre known?	Yes/No

LEARNER ACTIVITY

Read through the following scenarios and discuss what action you could take as an official (if any).

- Someone makes you aware that an individual is taking pictures of children changing in the changing rooms.
- A grandfather is video recording his granddaughter at a swimming gala.
- A parent loudly and publicly berates their child who has just lost a closely contested match.

Fig 20.05 A female basketball referee

Legal responsibilities

The growth of money and its influence is noticed in a number of sports. The elite sportspeople in many sports are millionaires or multimillionaires, and success in sport is often perceived as going hand in hand with financial success or gain. One of the results of this situation is the stress put on officials at the highest level. Pressure is also felt in a society where people increasingly take legal action against each other.

Sports performers who suffer injury can take legal action against whoever they feel is responsible. Criminal action may also be taken against performers who very obviously break the law in a sporting contest, e.g attack a spectator.

While the rules or laws of a sport will assist officials in ensuring that performers behave in an appropriate manner, there are times when officials will be required to make a judgement or decision that will be in the best interests of the competitors that is not covered by the rules, or where rules could be ambiguous in their interpretation.

When officiating at a competition an official may be considered as being under a contract, which implies a standard of performance and behaviour. Officials should be aware of the Acts of Parliament that apply to sporting events, e.g. Health and Safety Acts. In addition to this there are criminal laws regarding misconduct, and common laws that apply through the court system.

This may be one of the reasons why many sports struggle to find new officials. It is worth pointing out that there are in fact only a very few examples of successful prosecutions against sports officials. Generally speaking, and assuming that they are qualified, officials will have the support of the National or International Governing Bodies and often sports have their own officials' organisations, which will offer extra support and insurance.

Keep up to date

Most sports have changes to their rules on a regular basis. For the most part these are very slight changes, barely noticeable and usually to the benefit of the sport. In order to be consistent it is important that officials stay in touch with all changes to rules/laws. In basketball a world congress meets just after every summer Olympiad and discusses suggestions for rule changes. Thus every four years the rules of basketball change and some of these changes can be dramatic.

Well-organised sports hold national, regional and local conferences and seminars to update officials, along with bulletins made available to all that explain the changes to the rules or interpretation of those rules.

Managing people and situations

Perhaps the main difference between successful and unsuccessful officials is the way in which they deal with the people involved and the situation where the

LEARNER ACTIVITY

From the list of sports below, see it you can identify significant rule changes that have occurred in the last five years.

Sport	Rule change
Basketball	Game now played in 4 × 10-min quarters (and no longer 2 × 20 mins)
Rugby union	
Volleyball	
Badminton	
Cricket	

greatest emotions are involved. Officials at the highest level are generally the most experienced, which in itself does not mean that they will be the best. What it does mean is that the 'library of images' that they have relating to their sport is far greater than that available to their inexperienced technically superior colleagues. In any given situation for an official there is a range of options. If that official can draw from a 'database' of visual memories they are certainly better placed to make a quality decision.

Many officials are pleased if they are not remembered in a particular competition. While this at first might seem strange, it indicates that the official's actions were considered normal and were therefore not as well noticed. It is worth remembering that while they are an important part of the competition, officials should not become the central focus of attention as the nature and spirit of the competition should always be the key focus.

Managing performers

Officials should:

- try to influence behaviour rather than change personalities
- encourage and reward constructive behaviour
- say 'thank you' to people whenever it is necessary
- allow people the opportunity to express themselves where appropriate
- practise reading body language.

(Mahoney, 2005)

Maintain effective working relationships

It is essential for all officials that they establish and maintain good working relationships with all groups involved in sport: players, co-officials, spectators and, at a higher level, the media.

This includes acting professionally, communicating effectively, contributing to discussions with other officials, recognising the limits of their authority, treating everyone fairly and keeping an open mind.

Key learning points

- Officials can be classified as performance controllers or performance managers.
- The roles of an official are: judge, arbiter, communicator, professional, score keeper, presenter and safety officer.
- The responsibilities of officials can be summarised as:
  - child protection
  - application of the rules
  - maintaining working relationships
  - managing people and situations
  - keeping up to date
  - legal
  - physical and mental fitness
  - health and safety.

Analysing the performance of officials in a selected sport

One of the first things that a new official will experience after their first few competitions is the desire to improve their performance.

In the first instance, it is necessary to identity the important characteristics to be measured.

1 **Consistency** – this comes from both knowledge of the rules and the ability to apply them in a range of situations. Officials can be influenced by:

- spectators
- pressure from the performers
- feelings of empathy with the players
- overlooking transgressions from the side that is losing.

Consistent decisions need also to be applied to the context of the situation, so that the application of the rules is balanced with a good working knowledge of a 'feel' for the competition. Consistency will bring confidence and trust from performers.

2 **Decisiveness** – all good officials are decisive and keen to show that they are in control of a situation. The message for performers is that they must trust decisions made and that in being decisive the official is demonstrating a positive mental image. When new officials are trained in sport they are often given examples of the kinds of persuasion or reinforcement that help to 'sell' decisions. In basketball referees are encouraged to step closer to the place where fouls (illegal contact) occur in order to reinforce, or 'sell', the decision to the performer.

> ## LEARNER ACTIVITY
> Chose three sports and identify examples similar to the basketball example that assist officials in the presentation of their decision, in such a way as to help convince performers and others of their decision.

3 **Self-control** – increasingly in sport decisions are contested. Consider the football referee who, having awarded a penalty, is surrounded by players, or the tennis umpire repeatedly questioned over the quality of line decisions. Dealing with this kind of emotion is a skill that separates quality officials from average ones. It is important to maintain self-control in these instances. It is useful not to take comments and accusations personally, rather deal with their personal attacks with a sense of calmness and authority. Remaining without emotion is essential, all the while doing your best to remove the negative emotion that your decision has aggravated.

Evaluating the performance of officials

In order to improve at officiating it is important to evaluate your own performance or perhaps even have your own performance measured.

What needs to be measured? Officials could use the following list as the basis of their assessment.

1 Knowledge of the rules.
2 The governing body's rules for officials.
3 An understanding of the spirit of the game.
4 The ability to recognise tactics and techniques in a variety of situations from a performer's viewpoint.
5 The ability to work well with co-officials.
6 The ability to remain focused and concentrate.

> ## LEARNER ACTIVITY
> Officiate in a competition in a sport of your choice. Having done this complete the following performance evaluation.
>
> | | Good   Bad |
> |---|---|
> | How well did I do? | 1 2 3 4 5 6 7 |
> | Amount of mistakes made | = |
> | Communication with participants | = |
> | Dealing with distractions | = |
> | Conflict resolution | = |

Analysing officiating performance

It is useful to consider that in order to analyse the performance of officials it is important to first identify the desired behaviour, then compare it with the actual behaviour, determine how to change and develop that behaviour (modify it), and draw up an action plan to make that change.

An example of this is shown in Fig 20.07.

Methods of analysis

There are a number of ways in which it is possible to analyse officiating. Each of the following methods is recognised and used in a variety of sports and at all levels. It is important to point out that there is no one correct or necessarily more accurate method. It is simply best to select the method that provides you with the most useful information.

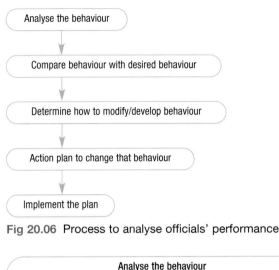

Fig 20.06 Process to analyse officials' performance

Fig 20.07 An example of analysing an official's performance

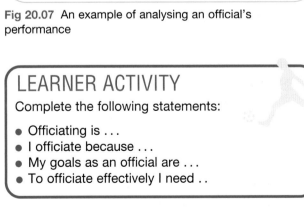

Using a diary or log

These can come in all shapes and sizes. Most people will have used a diary at some point and this will make them easy to use. Diaries can be useful tools in assisting self-reflection, planning and monitoring progress.

Tips for a good diary

- Write your diary soon after the event.
- Write in a form that suits you – notes, flow charts, etc.
- Write down what happened first, before attempting to analyse.
- Always focus on the positives first.
- Describe what was not so positive and how you might change it.
- Identify ways in which you could improve.
- Be patient with yourself.

The major benefits of diaries are that they provide a written record, over time, of progress. It is also easy to record emotions, feelings, etc.

Critical analysis and self-reflection

Everyone has experienced a certain amount of self-reflection. As an official it is possible to think back over a competition; situations in everyday life that you might reflect on include a driving test or an argument.

This can be a useful process if you review what happened and what you did and then suggest to yourself what you might have done better. This could lead you to determine what you might do in the future.

An example could be becoming frustrated or angry with a particular performer and the way that they challenged a critical decision. If you were less than pleased with your reaction you could reflect on that, decide that it was not beneficial and set about deciding how to avoid that reaction being repeated in similar circumstances. Quite often deciding what to do (action plan) will require help, perhaps in the form of a mentor or experienced colleague. The process of reflection has several stages, as illustrated in Fig 20.08.

Using video

This is an excellent way in which you can provide yourself with evidence of your performance as an official.

Simply having your performance filmed will provide you with an objective record of what happened, with the advantage of being able to analyse in slow motion or real time. You will see yourself as you see others and there is no need to try to remember everything as in the case of a diary.

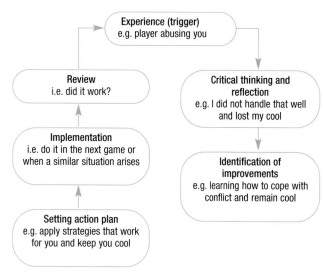

Fig 20.08 An example of the self-reflection process

Videos can also be used to form a point of reference. Watching an elite official in action can be beneficial and help demonstrate the techniques required to improve.

LEARNER ACTIVITY

Video a practical session with the camera focused on the official(s) and not the play. When you have completed filming, go to a quiet area and reflect on what went well and what may need development. You may need some help with this to start with, so don't be afraid to ask others to make comments on your performance.

You should be able to produce at least three action points for future developments.

Guidelines

- Make sure the person filming you is able to do so properly and understands what action they need to record.
- Picking up sound, particularly your voice or whistle, is an advantage.
- Camera positioning is crucial. It would be good to follow the officials in the course of the game, and try to pick up on body language, interaction with players, etc.

Checklist

A checklist is a simple and easy-to-use list that can be applied in real time by an observer and used to help provide you with feedback relating to your performance. You could also use a checklist after your performance as a self-analysis tool.

Your checklist, depending upon your sport, might include the following, which can be rated as good, excellent or in need of development:

- judgement
- communication
- fitness
- allowing the game to flow
- application of the rules/laws
- safety
- relationship with players
- dealing with conflict, etc.

Peer observation

Information from people in the same situation as you can be some of the most valuable information received. Often as a new official it is easier for peers to relate to the kinds of situations that you might be in, and offer you the benefit of their own experiences and ways in which they have dealt with challenging situations. It is very easy for an international official to state the easiest way to deal with a difficult situation, but it should be borne in mind that what works for them is most likely based on the relationships that they have established through years of experience and that an appropriate course of action for you could be completely different from the one that they might take.

Qualifications

To improve as an official it is necessary at some stage to become qualified. For some sports this may be the only way of receiving any kind of officiating training. A National Governing Body qualification as an official will not only allow you to train and gain a certification, it will also introduce you to peers and usually affiliate you in some way to the governing body, which will want to update you with all the relevant rules and scenarios relating to the rules. Membership of officials' associations and/or governing bodies usually helps provide the official with insurance and points of contact for assistance and development as an official.

Message boards/chat rooms

One fairly recent development on the internet is the use of message boards or chat rooms as a means of communication between officials. Officials are free to discuss issues relating to rules, interpretation of rules and even where to get specialised equipment. It should be pointed out that while this medium may be very useful it is open to abuse and you will need to be cautious about all content unless it is supported by the governing body.

Key learning points

- Officials could be assessed for: decisiveness, consistency, self-control, judgement, communication, fitness, allowing the game to flow, application of the rules/laws, safety, relationship with players and dealing with conflict.
- Officials should be measured against the following:
  - knowledge of the rules
  - the governing body's rules for officials
  - an understanding of the spirit of the game
  - the ability to recognise tactics and techniques in a variety of situations from a performer's viewpoint
  - the ability to work well with co-officials
  - the ability to remain focused and concentrate.
- There are a range of analysis tools available to the official:
  - critical analysis
  - self-reflection
  - diary
  - video
  - checklist
  - peer observation.

Officiating effectively in a selected sport

In order to work well as an official it is important to develop an understanding of what is required of an official or what skills are necessary and how they can be used in a competition setting.

As a minimum officials are expected to show automation or produce a tacit response. This skill is evident in all experienced officials who have drawn on their own knowledge and experiences in a range of circumstances and scenarios.

> **definition**
>
> **Automation or tacit response:** to have a knowledge of the rules in such a way as to need little troubling of the decision-making process, and to make decisions seem almost automatic.

The following is a kind of 'skills tool kit' that all officials should aim for in order to officiate effectively in their chosen sport:

- an in-depth knowledge of the rules
- excellent communication skills
- awareness and control of anxiety
- ability to monitor and control body language
- enhanced motivation, confidence and concentration
- ability to visualise
- people management skills
- ability to read players and 'feel' the game
- ability to anticipate
- mental toughness.

Dealing with conflict

Sports participation elicits powerful responses from competitors. The task of the official is to find the balance between acceptable confrontation and what should not be allowed.

The rules of sports have clear instructions for officials on how to deal with specific instances of conflict, and many carry strict penalties.

Officials should ask themselves the following questions concerning conflict resolution.

- Could the conflict have been prevented and, if so, how?
- What is the most appropriate action to take?
- Did I have alternative options?
- How would I resolve the situation, should it happen again?

Dealing with abuse and pressure

While not prevalent in every sport, unfortunately the amount and kind of abuse aimed at officials is extensive and many argue that this is the key reason new officials are not being developed.

First, it is important to consider the actions that performers and coaches take, sometimes in an atmosphere of passion, pressure and excitement. Often in this heightened state of arousal players make unfortunate choices, something many would not consider away from sport. This of course does not excuse their actions, but might help officials to understand certain actions.

Fig 20.09 Abusing the referee

Good officials will have developed a strategy for such instances. In other words they have thought through what they will do and say in these circumstances.

It is absolutely essential that officials learn to remain calm and in control, as in passionate situations poor emotional control will result in subsequent poor decision making, which will tend to exacerbate the situation.

Application of the rules

Perhaps the most important role of an official is the interpretation and application of the rules. In other words, to understand the purpose of a rule and apply it correctly is far more important than the simple enforcement of rules and penalties.

Good positioning or mechanics is an essential part of making good-quality decisions. A call or decision made from a distance is less likely to be accurate, and has less credibility with performers and spectators.

Knowing when not to interfere is also important. For example, applying the principle of allowing play to continue in spite of an obvious infringement, in favour of an advantage to the infringed team or competitor, is usually regarded as good practice.

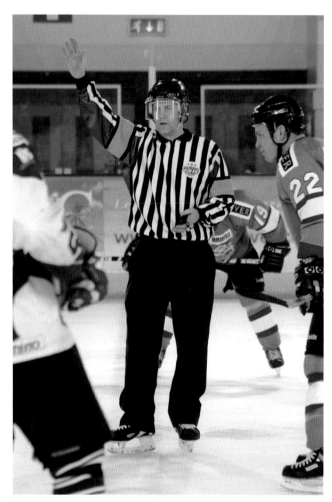

Fig 20.10 An ice hockey official making a clear signal

Control of the game

Keeping control of the game is essential for all officials. Being aware of certain situations, such as players who may feel aggrieved at opponents or at officials' decisions can help officials make better-informed judgements and actions. Maintaining self-control during a performance is also vital, as is communicating decisions clearly and to all involved.

Often officials have pre-planned actions or strategies for what they might say and do in particular circumstances, ways of dealing with situations that are likely to occur, and coping strategies for difficult situations.

Scoring systems

All sports have some kind of method for scoring. Some officials are required to simply rule on a score, others are

LEARNER ACTIVITY

1 Read the following scenarios, and consider what action you would take in those situations.

Scenario	Action
Cricket – you suspect that a player on the fielding team is tampering with the ball in a manner that will affect the way it plays, to the advantage of that team.	
Basketball – a player is continually verbally abusing a team-mate, but is not in breach of the rules.	
Tennis – a spectator is continually making fun of your performance, laughing and goading just about everyone about your decisions. That spectator happens to be a prominent local figure and one of the sponsors of the event.	

2 When you have done this, apply the following questions to the actions that you have chosen.
- Is this the best course of action for the contest?
- Does your action bear any resemblance to the rules?
- Are there any alternative actions that you could consider?

expected to keep a score, e.g. in football and netball. Some sports require performers to keep a score and then have that score confirmed by an official such as for golf.

Health and safety

Health and safety is a prerequisite of most everyday functions, and is equally important in sports. Rules and regulations are written in most sports that cover health and safety, usually outlining the required actions of officials in given situations.

Officials in many sports are responsible for making pre-match checks on facilities, equipment and the performers themselves.

In many sports, officials are required to assess risk and determine what action, if any, should be taken.

In addition it is absolutely essential that officials are aware of the guidelines and general practices involved in the protection of children and other vulnerable people.

Signals

Each sport has a range of signals that aid officials in effective communication. These signals can be to inform:

- players and performers
- co-officials
- coaching staff
- spectators.

Review

A review of performance is essential after every competition, in order that improvements can be made to future performances. Reviews and assessments can be either:

- **formative** – assist the official in the improvement of their own performance, and provide corrective advice and guidance for improvement
- **summative** – pass a judgement on performance and can be used as an assessment tool, such as in the assessment of an official's course or qualification, or in the grading of an official's performance, measured against a specification authorised by the governing body.

Feedback

Feedback in a review can be from:

- **peers** – other officials
- **mentors** – other experienced officials who are charged with the responsibility of supporting less experienced officials

LEARNER ACTIVITY

Look at the grid below, which is a performance profile for a team sports official. The darker column is the official's own assessment and the lighter column that of an observer or mentor.

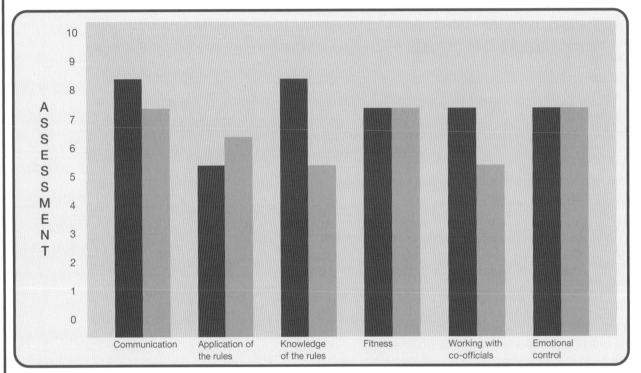

1 Identify the differences in opinion and say what you think may be the causes of those differences.
2 Copy and complete a similar profile for your own sport, substituting the measured components with the most appropriate ones for your sport.
3 Complete your own evaluation, immediately post-game, and collect an evaluation that someone suitable has completed for you.
4 Discuss any differences.
5 Suggest any changes that you may make for the next performance.

Key learning points

- Effective officials are usually able to make tacit responses concerning their sport.

- Officials must not only know the rules/laws of their sport, they must be proficient at applying them within the context of their sport.

- Health and safety is of primary concern to any official.

- Officials are required to know and practise all relevant decision signals, for the benefit of players, co-officials and spectators.

- Reviewing performance will be the best starting point for the improvement of an official's performance.

- **performers or club officials** – in most professional sports, feedback on the performance of officials is invited from the two teams or representatives of the two teams or individuals, usually in the form of a match report.

Strengths and areas for improvement

Officials are encouraged to review their own performance and identify strengths or areas for development.

Review questions

1 Who is responsible for setting rules and regulations for sports, both nationally and internationally? Provide two examples.
2 Describe the roles and responsibilities of a sports official.
3 Why is it important to analyse officiating performance?
4 What methods can be used to analyse sports-officiating performance?
5 Why should an official always remain calm?
6 Describe recent changes to a sport's rules that have meant changes to the way that sport is played.
7 How is application of the rules different to knowledge of the rules?
8 What are an official's legal responsibilities?
9 What should officials be assessed against?
10 How can an official keep up to date with rule changes to their sport?

References

Crisfield, P. (2001) *Analysing Your Coaching*, Coachwise.

Mahoney, C. (2005) *Managing People and Situations*, Coachwise.

Miles, A. (2004) *Coaching Practice*, Coachwise.

Pegg, Dr D. (2005) *An Introduction to Sports Officiating*, Coachwise.

Stafford-Brown, J., Rea, S. and Chance, J. (2006) *BTEC First Sport*, Hodder Arnold.

Goals

By the end of this chapter you should:

- know about different types of sports events
- understand the roles and responsibilities of people involved in planning and delivering sports events
- be able to plan a sports event
- be able to deliver a sports event
- be able to review the planning and delivery of a sports event.

Most people working in the sports industry will be involved in organising an event in some shape or form. Although there are a huge variety of types of event, the process of planning and coordinating any such event tends to be very similar.

In this chapter, it is expected that learners will choose an event they wish to organise and to participate in. The chapter will help to inform the learners on how to choose a suitable event, understand the various roles and responsibilities of planning the event, carry out a feasibility study and undertake the event.

The chapter finishes with ways in which learners may evaluate the success of the event, the performance of the project team and the performance of individuals in their specific roles within the team.

Different types of sports events

There are a huge variety of sports events. Some of these are listed in the box on the next page.

To help you decide which is the most appropriate sporting event for you, consider the main purpose of the event and the participants for whom you are running the event.

Purpose of the event

When planning an event, it is very important that you are clear about why the event is being held. It is a good idea to make a list of possible event objectives to help you determine the best event for you.

Possible reasons for running an event are to:

- raise funds for a charity or equipment for your college/school
- help the local community
- promote an activity to newcomers
- provide a competition
- improve sporting performance
- increase environmental awareness.

If you would like your event to raise money for charity or for your college/school then you may like to consider a sponsored event. While you could charge a fee for entering a tournament or competition, most of the money would be spent on prizes and refreshments for the competitors so these types of events are usually not the best method of fundraising.

If you would like to increase environmental awareness, which may help you with other units that you are studying or just for general interest, an expedition would be a good event to organise as this involves spending time in the countryside.

If you and your team would like to develop your sporting performance in a particular sport then a coaching course would be appropriate.

Participants

Every event needs to have participants. Think about the people who are living, going to school or working nearby – these are the ones who are most likely to want to attend your event. Participants you may wish to consider are as follows.

- Primary-aged school children: if you have a local primary school nearby, you may wish to invite these children to your event.

Sports events

Tournament

A tournament is a competition in which teams or individuals play each other in individual games. After each game, the losing team is either dropped from the tournament or plays a new team in the same 'round'. After each round, the winning team advances to play in the next round. The rounds continue until there are only two teams remaining. These teams play each other in the final, and the winner of the final is the winner of the entire tournament.

This type of event is good for large numbers of teams as well as smaller numbers; you will need at least three teams in order for a tournament to be viable.

Competition

A competition has two or more contestants or teams who compete against each other in order to win first place. Frequently the winner receives a prize of some sort; this prize could take the form of a sports trophy or a desired possession, which could take on many different forms such as a television or signed football shirt.

Sponsored event

A sponsored event is usually a good fundraising activity. Event participants will need to gather sponsors and then complete the event in order to receive the sponsorship money. The event should challenge the participants, such as walking or jogging a distance that they have not covered before. Sponsored events could also include a fun element, such as a sponsored three-legged walk.

Coaching courses

Many people would like to improve their performance in their favoured sport. It is possible to organise for a professional coach to lead a coaching course to improve participants' skills or even complete or work towards a proficiency award in that sport.

Expedition

An expedition usually involves hiking in the countryside. It costs very little money; however, participants would need to ensure they have the correct footwear and clothing, and such an event would need to be supervised by a qualified expedition leader.

- Older people: people living in a residential home.
- People of your own age: if you have a college or secondary school nearby you may wish to consider inviting these people to your event. Alternatively, you may wish to invite people from your own college or school or just have the people in your class participate in your event.

Roles and responsibilities of people involved in planning and delivering sports events

Once you are in your group, you must decide who is going to perform each of the different roles required to plan and run an event successfully.

There is a range of different types of role, all of which have their particular responsibilities, and it may be an idea to assign a role to each member of your team so that they know what they are responsible for. Once you are aware of the basic requirements of each role, you can determine to which role you are most suited. Some people in your team may need to take on more than one role in order to meet all the role requirements. If one person does need to take on more than one role, it is important that they take on the roles with slightly less responsibility, such as marketing officer and steward, as opposed to chairperson and secretary.

Chairperson

The chairperson is the main person who takes overall responsibility for organising the team and ensuring the event is planned effectively and runs smoothly. They will need to be an organised person who is able to take charge of the group and delegate work accordingly. They will also need to be a fair person to ensure each member of the team feels valued and is able to have their say. They are responsible for helping to determine how frequently meetings are held and ensuring that all people attending the meeting stay on task and discuss only the relevant topics. They must be a good listener and able to make decisions.

Secretary

The secretary is primarily responsible for writing and distributing information to the team. During meetings, the secretary will make notes in order to write the minutes for each meeting. The secretary is then responsible for ensuring that every member of the team has a copy of the minutes. If a person is unable to attend a meeting, they should contact the secretary so that an appropriate apology can be made and the meeting can start on time. The secretary is also responsible for informing the rest of the team when and where each meeting is to be held. A secretary may also be responsible for any correspondence you need to write. Therefore, a secretary would need to have good writing skills and good organisational skills.

Finance officer

In sports clubs, a finance officer has a significant accounting responsibility. However, as finance officer for your event, it is unlikely that you will have a huge amount of finances to deal with. The main things a finance officer would have to do would be to try to work

out how much the event would cost and how the event is going to be paid for. They would need to consider whether prizes need to be purchased for the event and, if so, how much money is available to spend on them.

For most centres, the person delegated as finance officer would liaise with a tutor and they would work together in this role. If the centre is providing the funding, the finance officer would need to write a plan to explain how much money is required and what it is going to be used for. For example:

Hire of hall for half a day = £50
Refreshments (squash, plastic cups, packet of crisps per person) = £10
Prize trophies (first prize, second prize, third prize) = £10

Therefore, your finance officer would have to be good at maths and have good communication skills in order to determine the costs of your event.

Marketing officer

The marketing officer is primarily responsible for ensuring that people know about your event; if you have no participants then the event will not be able to take place. Examples of how to market an event may involve putting up posters in your college, putting an advert in the local paper, putting up posters in local leisure centres or schools, and so on – you may even contact a local radio station and try to get a slot discussing your planned event with a DJ.

Often a marketing officer is quite creative as they need to devise eye-catching posters to try to entice people to come to your event. They may also need to be creative in the locations in which they choose to market the event to ensure they are attracting the sort of person who would be interested in participating in your event.

Steward

A steward is primarily concerned with the health and safety of the participants and ensuring that the event runs smoothly. They would carry out checks such as ensuring that the exits and entrances are clear, and that the facility is the right size for the number of people attending. They would ensure all participants are adhering to health and safety guidelines and be on hand to direct people to first-aid provision, toilets, refreshments, etc.

You will probably find that a number of your team will double up and take on the responsibility of, say, secretary for the planning phase of the event and then take on a second role as a steward during the event.

A steward should have good communication skills and interpersonal skills. They should be vigilant and able to remain focused during the event.

Planning and delivering a sports event

To ensure the event is planned thoroughly and appropriately, your team must hold regular meetings. Meetings are an essential part of organising an event as they help to maintain effective communication, and allow the team to share ideas and agree various decisions.

Every meeting should have an agenda. An agenda is basically a list of items that need to be discussed during the meeting. For example:

Date of meeting

1 Outcome of meeting with teacher from the primary school
2 Costs of prizes for the competition
3 Dates to choose for the competition
4 Possible sites for the competition
5 Any other business

Any other business leaves room for any person at the meeting to discuss any relevant topic or issue that they have at that time that has not already been covered in the meeting.

Agendas can be devised by the chairperson and handed out prior to the meeting. Alternatively, you can devise the agenda at the start of the meeting. Each person in the team must have thought of an issue they would like to discuss/resolve prior to the meeting and then the chairperson will make a note of each of these items before the start of the meeting. Another approach would be to place an agenda sheet on a convenient notice board. Your team could then

write on it items they would like raised at the next meeting.

Each meeting should be recorded. The process of recording meetings is called taking the minutes.

The minutes record the names of all the people who attended the meeting and record all information discussed during the meeting. Any person who could not attend the meeting and informed the team that this was the case has their name written next to the 'Apologies' section of the minutes. Here is an example of minutes:

---

1 **Attendance** – Roger Parker, Charlotte Smith, Gary Dixon, Richard Horner, Yvette Marshall, Scott Issacs, Charlotte Haffenden, Dan Stocks
2 **Apologies** – Greg Smith
3 **Minutes of the previous meeting** – this should include tasks that should have been completed.
4 **The outcome of discussions from each item on the agenda and from 'any other business'** – one primary school teacher agreed that a game of quick cricket with soft balls would be appropriate for groups of eight Year 6 children
5 **Date, time and venue for the next meeting**
6 **Closure** – there being no further business, the chairperson thanks members for attending and closes the meeting

---

Planning

When planning your event you must be clear as to what your aims and objectives are. You should be able to answer each of the following questions to help determine the exact purpose of your event.

- What type of event will it be?
- Who is going to participate in the event?
- What is the date of the event?
- Where will the event be held?
- What are the roles of each member of your team and what are they responsible for?
- What resources will be required for the event?
- Who will acquire these resources and how?
- What are the likely problems or barriers you may encounter?
- What contingency plans are in place?
- What is the cost of the event?
- How are you going to make money to pay for the event?

Targets

Your team or chairperson should set short-term and long-term goals to aim for to ensure that the planning runs smoothly. When goals are set you need to use the SMART principle to make them workable. SMART stands for:

- **S**pecific
- **M**easurable
- **A**chievable
- **R**ealistic
- **T**ime-constrained.

Specific

The goal must be specific to what you want to achieve. Your plan will include many specific goals – for example, recruit a group of participants for the event.

Measurable

Goals must be stated in a way that is measurable, so figures are needed – for example, we need to have 20 participants to make the tournament a viable option.

Achievable

It must be possible to actually achieve the goal – for example, setting yourself a goal to make much more money than is feasibly possible means that the team would probably be disappointed if they did not achieve this goal.

Realistic

The team need to be realistic in setting their goal and look at what factors may stop them achieving the goal.

Time-constrained

There must be a timescale or deadline on the goal. This means you can review your success. It is best to state a date by which you wish to achieve the goal; this will ensure that all the required preparation is carried out prior to the event.

Resources

You will need to think about all the things you will require in order to run the event properly and effectively. If you are running a football tournament, of course you will need all the appropriate football equipment. You would also need to consider how you plan to time the event, how you plan to display the results, how you will need to distinguish teams from one another, what refreshments you are going to provide, and so on.

You will also need to consider how many people you will require to run the event. You would of course need stewards, however you would also need referees and linesmen for each game that is being played.

On the day of the event, a person or people in the team should be responsible for checking that all the equipment is on site and has been checked to ensure it is working properly. If any person is sick and is unable to fulfil their role requirements, either one member of the team must take on the sick person's roles and responsibilities as well as their own, or a substitute must be found to replace the sick person.

Contingency plans

You should always plan to be able to run your event even when something unexpected happens. In order to do this you will need to think about all the things that could happen or go wrong, and make provision for them.

For example, if you were running an event outside, then a basic contingency plan would take into account what you would do if it rained. Could the event continue in the rain or would you need to provide shelter in some shape or form? How would you provide that shelter: would you have access to gazebos or to an indoor sports hall, and so on?

Contingency plans allow you to think clearly and to imagine what could go wrong, and then calculate what you would do and make provision for this in any given situation. On the day of the event if anything does go wrong or anything unexpected happens, you would then have to hand a contingency plan which would detail what you needed to do and how you needed to do it.

Health and safety

How you plan for the health and safety of your participants and your team is paramount. You should ensure that appropriate risk assessments have been carried out prior to the event. Ways in which to carry out risk assessments are discussed in Chapter 02: Health and Safety in Sport. You will need to ensure there is adequate first-aid provision – this would include first-aid equipment and also qualified first aiders. If the event is going to be very big, you may consider asking St John Ambulance to be present in order to help you provide adequate first aid.

On the event day, it is important that all members of your team have been told what to do in case of an accident or emergency. They should be shown where all the first-aid kits are placed and where the telephones are located so that they are able to phone for help if necessary.

The site of the event should be inspected carefully to ensure that there have been no changes from when the risk assessment was carried out. For example, an event was being held on a sports field and the original risk assessment was carried out when the field was dry. On the day of the event, there had been a lot of rain and the sports field was now wet. This wet sports field would result in exposing the participants to different hazards and risks. Therefore another risk assessment would have to be carried out and the contingency plan would have to be used if the risks and hazards could not be controlled adequately.

Legal considerations

You should always take into account any legislation that applies to you when running an event; if you do not adhere to this legislation you may be held liable if anything goes wrong or if somebody gets hurt.

If the people participating in your event are children then you should be aware of the Child Protection Act and be able to make suitable provision so that these children are looked after appropriately. It may be the case that you ask their school teacher to remain on site for the event so that they are there to help ensure the children's health and welfare is maintained at all times. Any person working with the children and over the age of 18 should have had a CRB check to ensure they are eligible to work with children.

Reviewing the planning and delivery of a sports event

In order to learn from your experience of planning and delivering a sports event, it is always a good idea to carry out a full review of the processes leading up to the event and the execution of the event.

First of all, you should assess your performance; did you fulfil your roles and responsibilities? You may like to prepare a list of all the things you were expected to do and then write down how successfully you think you achieved these goals. You should also try to get feedback from other people. It is a good idea to ask your team how they thought you performed, as well as asking the people who took part in the event. A good way to assess what people thought of the event is to hand out a questionnaire asking for their opinion on a number of aspects of the event.

Your assessment should examine your strengths, as well as areas for improvement. Questions that you should be asking yourself are: What went well? Did I meet my aims and objectives? Did I attain the goals I set out to achieve?

You will no doubt spot some areas for improvement; once these areas have been ascertained, it is a good idea to try to find out how you can go about improving your planning or delivery of the event. For example, you may find suitable courses that will help you to manage a team of people more efficiently. You should also consider any barriers that you face that may restrict your development. For example, you may have too many commitments and not be able to take on an extra course at the moment.

Review questions

1 Write a description of three different sports events.
2 What are the roles and responsibilities of: a chairperson, a secretary, a finance officer, a marketing officer and a steward?
3 Give an example of minutes taken from a team meeting.
4 What are SMART targets? Give examples of each.
5 What is a contingency plan? Give an example of when one may be needed.

References

Cox, D. (2002) *The Sailing Handbook*, New Holland Publishers.

Hanson, J. and Hanson, R. (1997) *Ragged Mountain Press Guide to Outdoor Sports*, McGraw-Hill.

Lockren, I. (1998) *Outdoor Pursuits*, Nelson Thornes.

Long, S. (2003) *Hill Walking: The Official Handbook of the Mountain Leader and Walking Group Leader Schemes*, UKMTB.

Rowe, R. (1989) *Canoeing Handbook: Official Handbook of the British Canoe Union*, Chameleon Press.

Stafford-Brown, J., Rea, S., Janaway, L. and Manley, C. (2006) *BTEC First Sport*, Hodder Arnold.

Websites

www.bcu.org – British Canoe Union
www.ramblers.org.uk – The Ramblers Association
www.rya.org – Royal Yachting Association
www.thebmc.co.uk – British Mountaineering Council

Working with children in sport 22

Goals

By the end of this chapter you should:

- understand the needs and rights of children
- understand the effects of sport in the development of children
- know about good practice in the protection of children in sport
- know about signs of potential child abuse and appropriate courses of action.

Sport has many positive influences on the physiological, psychological, social and emotional development of a child. Many people who wish to work in the sports industry will be involved in working with children at some point in their career. This chapter will explore some of the benefits of sport to the child, together with their needs and rights.

The skills required to lead sports activities in an appropriate and ethical manner are covered, together with relevant legislation and procedures for working with and protecting children. Any person working with children should also be aware of what to look out for if they think a child is suffering from some form of abuse; this chapter covers some signs of abuse that a person may look out for and how they may take appropriate action to deal with this issue.

The needs and rights of children

The needs of children

Children have many needs to help ensure they grow up to be happy and well-balanced adults. School, family, and the community in which they grow up are the three major contexts in which children grow and develop. Children learn from all of these environments.

Children need to have some form of education throughout their childhood. This will usually start at home and then progress into pre-school playgroups and then into school. Both physical and social skills are learnt through teaching and through play. The ability to catch and throw a ball is a physical skill that takes time to learn. This is because children need to build 'motor programmes' of performing that activity. This means that a child's brain needs to be able to send the right signals to move the appropriate body parts in the right way in order to perform an action. The more a child practises the activity, the stronger the motor programme becomes and the more likely the child is to catch or throw the ball effectively.

Research has also shown that regular sports participation is strongly linked to improvements in pupil behaviour, school attendance and attainment. Sports participation has also been shown to help children to develop social skills including teamwork and leadership skills.

Sporting activities allow children to mix with different children. Rather than always spending their time with their 'best friend' children will be placed into different sports teams and will 'mark' different players, which will help them to mix with and to meet new friends. This can help to break down barriers between individuals and groups of young people.

Sports participation can also help children to develop self-esteem and increase their confidence in themselves. This will help them to stand up for themselves and will therefore make them less likely to be bullied or feel pressured to take part in things they do not want to do – for example, some children may feel pressured to smoke because their friends smoke. Sports participation will also give children a place to go in their free time, which helps to combat anti-social behaviour. Taking part in sports can also help to increase the safety of children – for example, children who are taught how to swim will be less likely to drown.

Sports participation will also help children to remain healthy: it will help to strengthen the immune system, reduce the risk of the child becoming obese, and reduce the risk of coronary heart disease and cancers in later life. Taking part in high-quality and fun sports from an early age will motivate the child to develop good habits which they will hopefully continue with into their adult life.

> ### LEARNER ACTIVITY
> Carry out research to find out how local communities have benefited from organised sports. Find out what sort of sports schemes they have employed and how this has helped to combat anti-social behaviour.

The rights of children

All children, whatever their circumstances or abilities, should be able to participate in and enjoy physical education and sport. A number of laws and regulations are in place to help ensure all children have access to appropriately run sporting activities.

Every Child Matters

This is a government scheme devised to support children. Its main aims are to ensure that all children should have the support they need to:

- **be healthy** – this includes physical health, sexual health, mental health, emotional health
- **stay safe** – safe from abuse or neglect, accidental death, bullying, discrimination, anti-social behaviour
- **enjoy and achieve** – attend and enjoy school, personal and social development, meet national standards or higher
- **make a positive contribution** – support their community and environment, adopt positive behaviour in and out of school and develop self-confidence
- **achieve economic well-being** – progress into further education, employment or training, and live in decent homes with access to transport and material goods.

(Adapted from www.everychildmatters.gov.uk, 30.11.06)

The UN Convention on the Rights of the Child

This is a set of legal instructions which promotes the rights of children. Although all humans have rights,

children are more vulnerable than adults so they have this set of rights that takes into account their particular right for protection. It recognises the fact that children are human beings with their own rights and responsibilities that will develop as the child gets older. The convention promotes the fact that all children, regardless of race, gender, religion, ability or wealth, should be entitled to a basic quality of life including shelter and food, and that children should all be encouraged to reach their full potential.

This convention means that any organisation working with children or providing services for children will be able to share information and work together to protect children. In 2005 a children's Commissioner for England was appointed, which means that children's views will be sought and considered in relation to the organisations that work with them.

United Nations Children's Fund (UNICEF)

This is an international charity that promotes the protection of children's rights, and campaigns to help all children receive their basic needs and reach their full potential.

> ### LEARNER ACTIVITY
> Log on to the UNICEF website and find out how the charity helps children in different countries.

Playing for Success

Another government initiative, from the Department for Education and Skills, is called Playing for Success. This has helped to set up after-school clubs and weekend clubs held within top sports clubs. Through a sports medium, these clubs help to teach numeracy, literacy and ICT.

> ### LEARNER ACTIVITY
> Carry out research to determine where your nearest participating Playing for Success club is based.

It is the responsibility of any person caring for or working with children, both parents and coaches, to ensure they are taking into account the child or children's rights and helping them to fulfil their potential. Some parents or coaches may push a child to compete and train when the child is either not interested or not physically able to cope with the regime. This would be considered a form of abuse as the adults are pushing the child into doing things that they do not want to do. It may also give the child a 'win at all costs' attitude which could result in the child becoming aggressive and prone to foul play in their sport or even taking performance-enhancing drugs – all of which turn sports participation into a negative experience.

Key learning points

- Children need to have some form of education throughout their childhood. Sports participation helps to meet some of their needs, including skill development, motor programming, communication skills, confidence, social awareness and the promotion of good health.
- Every Child Matters and the UN Convention on the Rights of the Child are legislations that promote and protect the rights of children.

The effects of sport in the development of children

Social and psychological effects

Children's participation in sport is strongly believed to help them learn how to socialise with other people and also introduce them to the values and beliefs of society. The basis for this belief is the fact that sport introduces children to other children, rules, social values and the desire to improve their own skills in order to stay in the game and enjoy it. Children will learn to respect other children through sports participation. Research has shown that children automatically admire others who have a greater sporting ability than themselves, however a good teacher or coach will ensure that the all participating children with differing abilities are accepted and respected.

Other valuable social skills can be learnt through sport – these include leadership, communication, cooperation, independence and confidence. There has also been a significant amount of research that implies sports participation can help children to perform better academically.

Sports participation will help children to deal with failure. In most sports there are winners and losers, and a good coach or teacher will help to ensure children are placed on teams that will have their fair share of wins and losses. This will allow children to increase their confidence and self-esteem while on the wining team and then to accept failure and develop good sportsmanship skills when they are on the losing team.

> **definition**
>
> Sportsmanship: fair play, courtesy and grace in losing.

Physiological effects

The physiological benefit of children taking part in sports and exercise is an area that has not been researched thoroughly as yet. The general consensus however is that sport and exercise is beneficial to children as long as they do not exercise to excess and are supervised by suitably qualified trainers.

The National Association for Sports and Physical Education recommends that school-age children should take part in 60 minutes or more of physical activity every day. However, it is better for the child if the activity is broken down into bouts of around 15 minutes.

A child who takes part in regular physical activity will gain the same benefits as adults who exercise regularly. These benefits include:

- **improved immune system function** – which means they are better at fighting infections
- **improved fitness levels** – which means they will be able to take part in more activities and have more energy to play
- **better weight management** – which means they are less likely to have excess body fat.

However, despite the fact that children clearly do benefit from taking part in sports and exercise, it is very important that any person working with children is fully aware that they are not 'mini adults'. Any person supervising exercising children should be suitably qualified. Coaching qualifications for specific sports, combined with first aid and an awareness of children's exercising needs, is usually adequate. However, any person wishing to supervise children who are exercising in a gym using weights or taking exercise classes should have specialist knowledge and qualifications to demonstrate a sound understanding of children's physiology as a very minimum.

In order to appreciate the needs of a child you should be aware of the process of growth and maturation which may influence the types of training and exercise that are appropriate to the child. It is also important to be aware of the differences in children compared to adults and how a person working with children can take these differences into account and adapt sports sessions accordingly.

Bone growth

Bones grow linearly from areas called 'growth plates'.

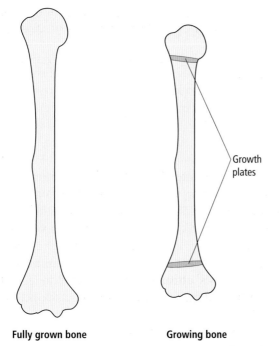

Growth plates

Fully grown bone   **Growing bone**

Fig 22.01 A fully grown bone with the growth plates fused and a growing bone still with growth plates

These growth plates are situated at both ends of a long bone. At the growth plates cells divide and produce more cells, which results in bone growth. Once the bones have stopped growing, the growth plates ossify and prevent further growth; however, not all parts of the skeleton reach maturity at the same time.

All studies to date suggest that physical exercise will increase bone density and inactivity will decrease

bone density. Problems may arise if the child injures a growth plate while exercising. If the growth plate is injured it can stimulate the plate to grow more quickly. This could then result in one limb being longer than the other.

As a child's skeleton is more pliable than an adult's, children are less likely to fracture a bone. There are three classifications of fractures for children: greenstick, complete and buckle.

- **A greenstick fracture** is when the bone does not fully break.
- **A complete fracture** is similar to an adult fracture in that the bone completely breaks into two or more pieces.
- **A buckle fracture** usually occurs when a child has fallen or jumped from a height and compressed their bone tissue. In adults, this compression would break the bone, however because children's bones are more resilient, the injured part of the bone will bulge outwards and not break.

Strength training for children

A child's strength training programme should not be a scaled-down version of an adult's weight-training programme. The reason behind this is the fact that children are still growing. An inappropriate strength training programme could damage the growth plates at the end of their bones, which could result in growth problems. A suitably qualified person should design a programme for the child. One of the most important aspects of this programme is to ensure that the child has the correct lifting techniques. Children should aim to lift lighter weights with a high number of repetitions. A strength training programme for children should not attempt to increase muscle bulk until the child has passed through puberty.

Thermoregulation and children

Children are much more prone to overheating than adults. This is partly because they do not have a fully developed sweating mechanism and also because they have a much higher surface area to volume ratio. This fact means that they will gain (and lose) heat much more quickly than adults. Therefore, if you are supervising children who are playing/exercising on a hot day, be sure to have lots of rest periods and lots of drinks, wear sun hats and sun cream, and try to stay out of the sun wherever possible.

Menstrual dysfunction

Female children who exercise for long periods of time and have little body fat may either have a delayed menarche or their normal menstrual cycle may stop. The main link appears to be the amount of body fat; a body fat percentage of 17 per cent or less is linked to an absence of a normal menstrual cycle (Frisch and McArthur, 1974). This may then impact on the bone density of the child and could result in problems in later life. This is due to the fact that oestrogen is an important hormone required to help bones take up calcium. Amenorrhoeic females have reduced levels of oestrogen which may lead to osteoporosis in later life.

> **definition**
>
> Amenorrhoea: **absence of a menstrual cycle.**
> Osteoporosis: **low bone mineral density.**

Coordination

Growth in children will affect their coordination as the length of their arms and legs, for example, is continually changing. However, as growth usually occurs gradually over a period of time, the child is usually able to adapt quite quickly to these changes. However, during adolescence, boys in particular tend to have 'growth spurts', which means their bones grow at a faster rate than normal. This means that the child will have less time to adjust to the changes in lever length and this often results in what appears to be 'clumsiness' as the child is no longer able to catch or kick a ball as skilfully as they could before the growth spurt. Continued sports participation will help the child to adjust to the changes in their body length more quickly. However, any person working with children should be aware that this 'clumsiness' is probably not due to the child putting any less effort into their sports – they are simply having to adapt to having longer levers than they are used to.

Good practice in the protection of children in sport

Good practice

In almost every sporting situation, children will look to their sports leader as their source of

Key learning points

- The majority of children will benefit socially, psychologically and physiologically from sports participation.
- Children will learn how to work as a team, accept failure, improve their communication skills, increase their self-esteem and confidence, and improve their motor skills by taking part in sports.
- Children who take part in exercise should be supervised by a suitably qualified instructor.
- A child's skeleton is still growing and their bones are less likely to fracture completely as in an adult.
- As children are smaller than adults they are more prone to overheating in hot weather conditions or losing more heat in cold weather.
- Female children who have low body fat are more likely to have delayed menarche or their periods may stop, which could affect bone density in later life.
- Children may lack coordination during growth spurts.

inspiration and knowledge. Children will frequently copy their instructor so it is imperative that the sports leader behaves in a suitable manner that would be appropriate for a child's role model. A sports leader should ensure that they encourage winning but do not encourage children to adopt a 'win at all costs' attitude. Children need to learn to lose with good grace and develop sportsmanship behaviour.

A person working with children should always follow these basic guidelines:

- ensure they work within the bounds of applicable codes of practice
- maintain safe and secure sporting environments
- establish good working relationships with the children and their parents
- control the behaviour of participants.

A sports leader should also be aware of the rights and needs of children; these are detailed in the section entitled 'The rights of children' (on page 398) and in the following pieces of information.

Good practice policy

A number of laws have been passed and agencies set up to promote the safety and welfare of children. Any person working with children should be aware of the relevant acts and agencies so that they can ensure they are working within the law and know how to get help and advice should they need it.

Recruitment

Any person recruited to work with children should have a CRB check prior to any contact with children. A CRB check will find out if a person has had any prior convictions, has been cautioned, has been given a reprimand or has been given a warning for a criminal offence.

In line with Child Protection: 'Preventing Unsuitable People from Working with Children in the Education Service' 2002, any person deemed inappropriate from the CRB check should then not be employed to work with children.

definition

CRB check: Criminal Record Bureau check.

The Children Act 1989

This basically puts the child first by promoting and safeguarding their welfare. It sets out rules and regulations for how a child should be treated that any person working with children should adhere to.

The Child Protection in Sport Unit (CPSU)

This was founded in 2001 as a partnership between the NSPCC and Sport England. The unit was set up in response to evidence that sport can provide access for a person to abuse children. As coaches often work with children over a long period of time, trust develops between the coach and the child. Research indicates that the majority of abuse is committed by a person who the child knows and has come to trust.

Therefore, the CPSU has been put in place to work with sport to help create a safe sporting environment for children. This is done through the promotion of good practice and encouraging people to confront practice that is harmful to children.

Key learning points

- Sports leaders should behave in a suitable manner that would be appropriate for a child's role model.
- Any person working with children should be CRB checked prior to employment.
- The Children Act 1989 sets out legislation that people working with children should adhere to.
- The Child Protection in Sport Unit promotes a safe sporting environment for children.

Signs of potential child abuse and appropriate courses of action

Child abuse

Child abuse can take many different forms, but it can basically be defined as any form of physical, emotional or sexual mistreatment or lack of care that leads to injury, harm or distress. Most people responsible for abusing a child are in a position of trust and are known by the child and the family. Abusers can be male or female adults, or other young people. Any person under the age of 18 is considered to be a child; if they are suffering from any kind of abuse, you should have an awareness of the different types of abuse and the signs to look out for – very few children will admit to suffering from some form of abuse.

The main types of child abuse are:

- physical abuse
- sexual abuse
- emotional abuse
- neglect
- bullying.

Physical abuse

Physical abuse is where a person physically hurts or injures a child. A syndrome called Munchausen's syndrome by proxy is classed as physical abuse.

Munchausen's syndrome by proxy: when an adult, usually a parent or carer, seeks medical intervention for their child who is not ill or the adult has deliberately caused ill health in a child they are looking after.

In sports, a coach may force a child to train or compete when they are physically not up to it, or give the child drugs to enhance their sporting ability; these are both forms of physical abuse.

Sexual abuse

Sexual abuse is where a person uses children to meet their own sexual needs. This includes any form of sexual physical contact, showing children pornography or talking to them in a sexual manner. Many coaches will make physical contact with the children they are coaching in order to help them with their techniques or ensure their safety. It is imperative that coaches do their very best to ensure that the children are happy with this handling and that all contact is entirely appropriate.

Emotional abuse

Emotional abuse is the consistent emotional ill-treatment of a child. This may involve telling the child that they are worthless, inadequate or unloved, or shouting and taunting the child which may well result in severe and long-lasting adverse effects on the child's emotional development. Emotional abuse can also take the form of having greater expectations for a child than are appropriate for their age and ability. In sport, a coach could be guilty of emotional abuse if they constantly criticise the child, are sarcastic to the child or bully them.

Neglect

Neglect is when a parent or carer does not meet a child's basic physical and/or psychological needs so that it could result in the child suffering from ill health or impaired development. Examples of neglect include inadequate provision of love, affection, food, shelter, clothing and medical care. Failing to protect a child from physical harm or danger is also a form of neglect. In sport, examples of how a coach could be guilty of neglect are if they do not ensure that the children are safe or if the environment is too hot or too cold.

Bullying

Younger people are often the perpetrators of bullying. Bullying can be verbal or physical and usually takes place over a period of time. This form of abuse can have a huge impact on a child's life and there have even been cases of children taking their own lives rather than face their bullies again.

A sports leader working with a group of children should make it explicit from the start that they will not tolerate any form of bullying and that it is the responsibility of every person to ensure that bullying does not happen. If any child is aware of any bullying they must be instructed to tell the sports leader immediately. Some sports leaders discuss with the children what they think bullying is and then draw up some conclusions so that all the children know how they are expected to behave with one another.

If bullying has taken place, a sports leader must find out the facts and individually talk to the bully(ies) and the victim(s). They should then take appropriate action – this should be detailed in the facility's policies and guidelines. If the bullying was a one-off incident and there is more than one bully, it may then be appropriate to break up the group dynamics and split the bullies into different groups – many groups of bullies lose their confidence if they are not with their friends.

Bullying should always be dealt with swiftly and effectively otherwise the bullies may gain confidence and it could become harder to put a stop to the bullying.

Effects of abuse

Any child who has suffered abuse in the past or is currently suffering from abuse will usually experience long-term physical and/or emotional, sometimes life-changing, effects as a direct result of that abuse. Extreme cases of child abuse may result in the death of that child. All forms of abuse usually leave a child with psychological, health and/or developmental difficulties.

Many children are left with feelings of low self-esteem and may also wet the bed and have frequent bad dreams. Some children develop a range of anti-social and/or self-destructive behaviours in an attempt to try to cope with the abuse. They may be excessively aggressive to other children or bully them, alternatively they may be very withdrawn and avoid communication and friendships with other children.

A child that is experiencing chronic abuse can experience behavioural changes. They may be easily startled and overreact to loud noises or a person shouting and sounding cross. Some children start to harm themselves as this somehow helps them to deal with the abuse they are receiving. Others may drink excessive amounts of alcohol or take drugs in an attempt to deal with the abuse they have received.

Signs of abuse

A sports leader can help to keep children and young people safe by watching for unexpected changes in their appearance and behaviour. A child subjected to some form of abuse may show some of the following signs.

- A change in their behaviour. For example, a bubbly happy child may suddenly or gradually become quiet and withdrawn.
- Distrust of a particular person.
- A sudden inability to concentrate or performance declines for no apparent reason.
- Refusal to attend school or club.
- Has no close friends.
- Refusal to get changed in front of other people, or wants to keep covered up even in warm weather.
- Inappropriate sexual awareness or behaviour for their age.
- Some form of injury on parts of the body which are not usually injured. For example, it is common for children to have cuts and bruises on their knees from falling over, however it is unusual to have injuries on parts of the body such as the stomach, chest or back.
- An unsatisfactory explanation for an injury, e.g. the child has a black eye and bruising to the chest and they say they walked into a door.
- Significant weight gain or weight loss over a short period of time.
- Poor personal hygiene.
- Constant hunger.
- Extremely passive or extremely aggressive.
- Discomfort in or near the genital area – this could be observed from an inability to perform a sporting technique because of discomfort in the genital area.

However, if a child is exhibiting some or all of these signs it does not necessarily mean that they are being abused – there may be another explanation. Alternatively, a child that is being abused or who has been abused may not show any of these signs.

Course of action

If you are working as a sports leader and you have any reason to believe a child is being abused you must take action. The organisation you are working in should have clear policies and guidelines on how to deal with this situation.

If the child is keen to talk to you, the best thing that you can do is to follow these guidelines.

- Give them your full attention and listen carefully.
- Tell the child that you will not be able to keep what they have said to you secret but that you will only tell people who are going to make their situation better and, if appropriate, that these people will help to stop the 'bad' things happening to them.
- Ensure that you respond to what the child says with sensitivity.
- Encourage the child to talk, e.g. ask 'Do you want to tell me about this?' Do not put any pressure on the child to talk to you.
- Keep calm and try not to appear shocked. You may find what the child is saying is upsetting but you should do your best to keep listening.
- Do not attempt to make any form of contact with the alleged abuser.
- If you believe the child's safety is in imminent danger, you should alert your sports facility's child welfare person and either they or you should contact the police or social services to take further action and help to ensure the health and welfare of the child.

When the child has finished talking to you, you should write a detailed account of what was said. If your centre has incident report forms, then this would be appropriate documentation to record the discussion on. If no incident report form is available an example of an incident report form is shown on the opposite page; you could copy and use this.

The report should remain confidential and only the people who need to know this information given access to it in order to help protect the child.

Child protection incident report form

Sports facility: _____   Child's address: _____

Your name: _____   Parents'/carers' names and address: _____

Your position: _____   Contact number: _____

Contact number: _____   Child's date of birth: _____

Child's name: _____   Date and time of any incident: _____

Your observations or details as reported to you: _____

_____

What the child said and what you said: _____

_____

If you are passing on someone else's concerns, record their name, address, position and contact number:_____

_____

Action taken so far: _____

External agencies contacted (date and time):

Police   If yes – which: _____

yes/no   Name and contact number: _____

                                                        Details of advice received: _____

                                                        _____

Social services   If yes – which: _____

yes/no   Name and contact number: _____

                                                        Details of advice received: _____

                                                        _____

Signature:_____

Print name: _____

Date: _____

(Adapted from www.nspcc.org.uk, 28.10.06)

Key learning points

- The main types of child abuse are:
  - physical abuse
  - sexual abuse
  - emotional abuse
  - neglect
  - bullying.
- People who abuse children are often people who the child and/or family trust.
- A child suffering from abuse may exhibit some or none of the typical signs of abuse.

- Any information a child discloses regarding abuse should be documented on an incident report form and reported to the appropriate people.
- If a child is deemed to be in imminent danger, immediate appropriate action should be carried out.
- Bullying should be dealt with swiftly and effectively.

Review questions

1. What are the basic needs of a child?
2. What are the rights of a child?
3. Which organisations promote the rights of a child?
4. How does sports participation develop a child's social and psychological skills?
5. What are the physiological benefits of sports participation for children?
6. What are the three types of fracture that can occur in children?
7. What agencies have been set up to promote the health and safety of children in sport?
8. Why have the agencies in question 7 been set up?
9. How should a person respond if an abused child confides in them?
10. What course of action should a person take if a child has told them that they are being abused?

References

Frisch, R. and McArthur, J. (1974) Menstrual cycles: fatness as a determinant of minimum weight for height necessary for their maintenance or onset. *Science Magazine*, September, 949–51.

Lee, M. (1997) *Coaching Children in Sport, Principles and Practice*, Spon Press.

Websites

www.nspcc.org.uk – National Society for the Prevention of Cruelty to Children

www.thecpsu.org.uk – Child Protection in Sport Unit

www.sportscoachuk.org – sports coachUK

Goals

By the end of this chapter you should:
- understand how businesses in sport are organised
- understand what makes a successful sports business
- understand the use of market research and marketing by sports businesses
- understand the legal and financial influences on sports businesses.

As you are probably well aware, sport is now a huge industry including sports participation, spectating, clothing and equipment. This chapter explores the factors that help to make a sports business successful. Organisation of sports businesses, including the structure of the staffing, is examined, followed by the different types of sports business. Methods of market research are then explored. The chapter concludes with a look at the various different types of legislation that apply to sports businesses, and financial influences upon sports businesses.

How businesses in sport are organised

Organisation

There is a range of different types of business; the main differences are determined by the number of people who own the business and how much of the business they own.

Sole trader

A sole trader business means that there is only one person in charge of the business. That person must be able to afford to set up the business or have a loan approved by a bank or building society. This person is then able to make all the decisions on how the business is to be managed. They must be able to keep records of all the money going into and out of the business, which can then be examined by an accountant to ensure that accurate books are kept on income and expenses, and correct payments of tax and VAT are made, etc. The sole trader is then able to keep all the profits; however, they are also personally liable for any debts.

Partnerships

This is very similar to a sole trader, but as the name suggests, in a business partnership two or more people own the business. In this way, the partners benefit by sharing the costs and responsibilities of the business. The profits of the business are then shared out between the partners. One partner may have put more money into the business, which would result in the profits being shared out in relation to the amount of money each person has put in. In most partnerships, each partner is involved in the decision-making process and all are liable for any debts. Some sports businesses may have 'sleeping' partners. This means that the sleeping partner has no say in how the business is run, however they are a partner because they have contributed money to the business.

As with a sole trader, a partnership business must keep books on money coming in and going out of the business, and the partners are responsible for paying the correct taxes and VAT, etc.

Limited companies

A limited company is a business that is registered on a government list called Companies House. There are two types of limited company: private limited companies and public limited companies. Both types of business have limited liability, which means if the business goes bankrupt, any debts are the debts of the company and not of the employees (unlike in a sole trader or partnership business). A limited company must complete a Memorandum of Association. Once this has been submitted, a Certificate of Incorporation is issued to the company, which allows it to begin trading. In a limited company at least one director is responsible for decision making and running the business.

A limited company must complete annual reports and an account summary and submit it to Companies House for filing. A limited company is owned by a number of people who hold 'shares'. Each person with shares in the company is called a shareholder. The profits of a limited company are divided out between the shareholders. People who own lots of shares will receive a greater percentage of the profits compared to shareholders who own a smaller number of shares.

- **Private limited companies** – in a private limited company, only certain individuals are able to buy shares. Many family-based businesses are private limited companies, and only family members are given access to buy shares. There are other much larger-scale companies that are private limited companies, such as Manchester United and Virgin.
- **Public limited companies** – a public limited company means that any person from the public can buy and sell its shares on the stock market.

Franchises

A franchise is when a person buys a business that is already successful and sets it up in a different location. A person wishing to buy a franchise would need to buy a licence to use the name, products and services of the business. They would also be given management support in setting up and running the business. The person buying the franchise would then be required to run the business in line with the franchise agreement drawn up between the franchiser and franchisee. Most franchises will be restricted to a certain location and will be for a limited period. A franchise may then pay ongoing fees to the original business or give the franchiser a share of its profits, or both. A franchise could exist as a sole trader, a partnership or a limited company; the type of company will determine the legal structure.

Organisational structure

Every organisation has a structure with various levels, which is often depicted as a staffing structure or organisational structure. The person at the top of the

chart is in charge and ultimately responsible for the success of the sports business and the welfare of staff and customers.

A typical hierarchal structure would look like the one shown in Fig 23.01.

Most people working in a sport or leisure facility will probably need to report to a duty manager. A duty manager will monitor the progress of the employees and ensure they are keeping to the rules and regulations of the job specification. The duty managers will then report to the general manager, who is responsible for monitoring their work.

Finances are dealt with by finance managers, who are usually in charge of an accountant or a team of accountants depending on the size of the facility. Their job role covers such aspects as profits and losses made by the facility, payment of staff, tax deductions, etc.

The human resource manager is responsible for recruiting new staff and ensuring current staff are being treated fairly and in accordance with the rules and regulations that are specific to the environment.

The Finance and Human Resource Departments provide a support service to the general manager and all three department managers report to the managing director. The managing director is accountable to the board of directors. The board of directors may consist of a range of people who include councillors, elected employees, trades union representatives and elected customer representatives. The board of directors oversee the running of the organisation with the aid of reports from their managers. They hold regular meetings to review the finances of the facility and make decisions on how to improve the facility and the services it has to offer.

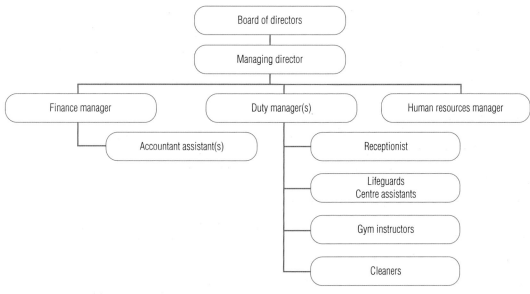

Fig 23.01 A typical hierarchal structure of a sports facility business

LEARNER ACTIVITY

If you work part-time in a sports business, try to find out the staffing structure of the business. If you do not have a part-time job, go to your local leisure centre and try to find out its staffing structure. Draw a hierarchal structure of the staffing structure of the business you have investigated in a similar fashion to the one shown in Fig 23.01.

Sports businesses

There are a range of different types of sports businesses. The majority aim to make money, however some are there to provide a service to the community and their focus is not on making a profit.

Public sports and leisure clubs

These sports facilities are funded by the government and do not aim to make a profit. These types of facilities usually offer lower-priced access to a variety of physical activities including swimming, badminton, five-a-side football, fitness classes, etc. Any person, who is receiving income support, is a senior citizen, is under the age of 16 or is a student will usually be given a discounted rate for whichever physical activity they choose to take part in.

Private sports and leisure clubs

These types of clubs aim to make a profit. They are often members-only and usually charge a joining fee to become a member. Thereafter, members are usually required to pay a monthly fee in order to stay a member and use all the centre's facilities. These types

of clubs frequently offer additional services compared with public sports clubs; for example, showers will often have shampoo and shower gel, towels are given out to members to use after their shower, etc. Jacuzzis and saunas are also commonplace in these sorts of clubs unlike many of the public clubs. Any person using these types of facilities will usually pay a lot more money than if they were to use public-sector facilities.

Professional sports clubs

Professional sports clubs pay their players for competing for them. Players will often receive a set salary for staying with the club and bonuses when they play particularly well; for example, football clubs may give their players a bonus if they score a goal. Professional sports clubs will usually offer their players good playing and training facilities, and some will offer rehabilitation services too. These days the majority of league football clubs are professional clubs.

Amateur sports clubs

An amateur sports club is open to the whole community and the club should offer no discriminations to membership. The cost of using the facilities should be of an affordable price so that most people are able to join and use its facilities. Many amateur sports clubs offer a range of different types of membership and discounted rates for children, students, the unemployed and retired people. The club should not aim to make a profit, but any excess money gained should be reinvested in the club, donated to charity or given to other amateur sports clubs. The club will usually reimburse players for any travel costs when they play at away games and may provide or pay for its members to go on coaching courses.

Up until 1995 rugby union was an amateur sport and players did not receive payment in the same way as professional sports players. They would have received expenses and other forms of benefits in order to ensure they remained with their club.

Fig 23.02 Success in a sports business

Key learning points

- The different types of business include: sole trader, partnerships, private limited companies, public limited companies and franchises.
- Every organisation has a structure with various levels, the person at the top of the hierarchy is in charge and ultimately responsible for the success of the sports business and the welfare of staff and customers.
- There is a range of sports businesses; these include public sports and leisure clubs, private sports and leisure clubs, professional sports clubs and amateur sports clubs.

What makes a successful sports business?

A number of factors will determine whether a sports business is successful; these factors are illustrated in Fig 23.02.

Income

This is the amount of money that the business makes. The business will then have to deduct money from its income to pay taxes, etc.

Profit

Profit literally means 'to make progress'. If a business is not making a profit after a certain period of time, it will usually have to close down. A business will make a profit if the money coming in to the company is more than the money that is going out. The money going out of the business includes staff salaries, cost of the product or services, tax deductions, rent, etc.

Growth

If a business is doing well, it will usually grow in some shape or form. Many successful businesses will grow by taking on more staff to cope with the greater demand for the product or service. Some businesses may open a branch in a different location so that they are able to sell to a larger market. Other businesses may grow by opening a website to either trade their product online or advertise their services.

Customer satisfaction

All sports businesses require customers to buy their products and/or services. Therefore, in order for the business to succeed it is vital that the customer is satisfied with the product or service they receive. If the customer is satisfied then the benefits your business will receive include the following.

1 **Customer loyalty** – customers will return to a business if they feel they have been treated well. If, however, they feel that they have been treated poorly, such as waiting too long for service or not having complaints dealt with effectively, then they are much less likely to return to the business.

2 **New customers** – new customers can be generated through word of mouth from existing customers. If someone is happy with a business they are more than likely to recommend it to other people.

3 **Increased sales and profits** – if customers are happy they will continue to use the products or services provided by the business which in turn increases the amount of money a business makes.

4 **A good image** – most sports businesses want to portray a good image to the public and this can be done through providing good customer care.

5 **Employee satisfaction** – employee satisfaction can be gained through ensuring the employees are given thorough training in customer care. This training will help to ensure that employees can handle complaints rather than becoming upset by them.

6 **A competitive edge** – a competitive edge is very important in sports business as there are usually a number of facilities that provide the same services in one area. If one business provides better customer satisfaction than another one, it is likely to have more customers.

Staff satisfaction

If staff are happy in their work, they will generally do their job well. Therefore, if the staff are satisfied, this usually has a knock-on effect which makes the customer satisfied. If staff are not satisfied, they may take time off sick or may not be very efficient at their jobs. The process of recruiting staff also costs time and money so it is in the employer's interest to do its best to ensure that staff are happy.

LEARNER ACTIVITY

When you are working, or if you are working now, think about the things you would like your employer to offer you that would help you to be satisfied in your place of work; try to think of realistic rewards such as a bonus for meeting targets, etc. Make a note of all the things you think of and explain how you think each would keep you happy in your work.

Key learning points

● The success of a business largely depends on whether it is making a profit.

● Other factors to consider include customer satisfaction, staff satisfaction, income and growth.

Use of market research and marketing by sports businesses

Marketing is basically the process of a business communicating with the public to make them aware of the product or service it is selling and to make this product or service sound as appealing as possible.

definition

Marketing: 'the process responsible for identifying, anticipating and satisfying customer requirements and profitably' (Institute of Marketing).

Its purpose is manyfold; Fig 23.03 gives examples of the different uses of marketing.

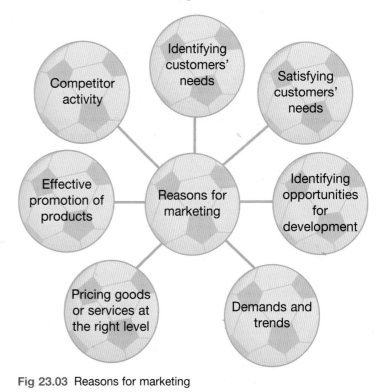

Fig 23.03 Reasons for marketing

Different uses of marketing

Identifying customers' needs

A business will want to find out what its potential customers need. Once this need has been identified, the business can produce the right products and services to meet it. For example, a leisure centre may not be offering the types of refreshments its customers would like. The customers would prefer freshly made hot drinks rather than machine-made ones, and more healthy snacks. The leisure centre could introduce a freshly made coffee stand which is staffed by a person who is also able to sell fruit and other healthy snacks.

Satisfying customers' needs

Once a customer's needs have been identified there need to be continual checks to ensure that the product and/or service offered has met these needs – for example, are the refreshments offered at the right price, is there enough variety. If customers' needs are satisfied then there is much more chance that they will continue to use the facility and therefore either help to maintain or improve current levels of business.

Identifying opportunities for development

Research carried out to determine customers' needs may also identify opportunities for the business to develop. For example, a customer survey may not only find out that the customers want different refreshments to be supplied by their leisure centre, but that they would also like some sort of crèche facility so that parents are able to take part in physical activity without having to take their pre-school child to a nursery, employ a childminder or make other childcare arrangements. This would then generate more income from the crèche facility and also more income from the parents paying to take part in their chosen physical activity.

Demands and trends

Many sports businesses are affected by a change in the market's demands because of new trends. This is clearly reflected in the continual new trends in exercise classes. For example, up until around six years ago, the exercise cycle was found only in the gym, now a 'spinning' cycle is commonplace in many aerobic studios; boxing gloves and pads would be used only by boxers, now 'boxercise' classes also use this type of

equipment. The different trends in exercise mean that a sports business has to determine if its customers demand this new exercise; if so, then it has to buy in the new equipment and either train staff to meet the needs of the new trends or employ other staff who fit the bill. If the business does not keep in touch with demands and trends then they may lose customers to other businesses who are in touch with and are meeting customers' changing needs.

Fig 23.04 Spinning bikes

Pricing

A sports business will need to ensure that it is charging enough money to make a profit, but it will have to ensure that it is not pricing its goods or services too high so that its customers are not able to afford to use the facility. The business will also have to ensure that its pricing is competitive – for example, if a similar business offers its goods and services at a much lower price then the customers will choose to go to the lower-priced business instead.

LEARNER ACTIVITY

Visit three similar sports facilities in your area. Choose three services they offer and make a note of the prices of each. Ensure that you also note down any concessions or price changes for different times of the day.
From this information determine:

- whether there is any difference between the pricing
- which facility provides the best value for money
- which facility is the most expensive
- why you think there may be differences in the pricing.

Promotion

A sports business will need to 'sell' itself to the public so that people will choose to go there. Most businesses take a lot of time and effort to promote a positive image of themselves and the products and services that they have to offer. Posters, leaflets and adverts in the local papers are used to promote the business. Many gyms advertise themselves using photos of good-looking and toned people using their facility. This is done to try and make people think that if they joined that particular gym then they too would look like the people in the advert. Many businesses will encourage customers to use their facility by offering various promotional discounts – for example, during the first few weeks of January when people are looking to keep to their 'New Year's resolution' of 'getting fit or losing weight', many gyms will offer a 'no joining fee' promotion to encourage potential new customers to join their gym.

LEARNER ACTIVITY

In groups of two or three, choose three gyms in your local area. Find out methods they use to promote themselves. Try to get hold of copies of the posters, leaflets or adverts they use.
Decide which gym has the best promotional material and explain why.

Competition

Virtually all sports businesses have some sort of competition – for example, think about the many different brands of sportswear: Adidas, Nike, Reebok, to name but a few. In the same way, you would rarely find one sports facility servicing the needs of a large community. Therefore, most sports business will need to keep a close eye on their competition to ensure that they are able to maintain their custom. Some businesses will strive to make themselves different from their competition; this is called the 'unique selling position' (USP). The business will then promote its exclusive products or services so that they appear very attractive, and therefore maintain its customers with the prospect of potentially attracting new ones. For example, if there are two leisure centres in close proximity and leisure centre A has tanning beds whereas leisure centre B does not, leisure centre A has the USP and could advertise to promote its tanning beds. It may further promote its USP by offering a 'swim and sun offer' whereby the customer is offered a discounted swim followed by a tanning session.

LEARNER ACTIVITY

Thinking about the three gyms in the previous activity, try to determine if any of these gyms has a USP. Find out and explain how the gym promotes this USP.

Methods of marketing

A business may use a number of different sources of information in order to carry out market research.

Primary sources

Any information that is gained directly from its current or potential customers is from a primary source. This type of information is usually gained from questionnaires or direct observation of the customers.

Secondary sources

This type of information is gained from studying information about customers, e.g. national statistics, sales records.

Selection of appropriate methods

The type of information used must be appropriate and relevant. The data should have been collected from a suitable time period, e.g. national statistics should be the most recent ones published.

Marketing activities

There is a huge array of different methods of marketing. Primary marketing research is very popular and in order to ensure the data collected are relevant and appropriate, the researcher must take a number of factors into account.

Whichever method you use to directly find out information about your customers you should ensure that it will be as quick and as easy as possible for the customer to complete. Occasionally businesses will offer incentives for customers to complete their market research, e.g. the name of every person who completes the questionnaire will be placed into a 'hat' and the person whose name is pulled out will win a year's free membership.

Sampling

Although it is not possible to collect data from every customer, the data collected are going to be used to represent the views of all the business's customers. Therefore, the sample of people used in the marketing activity should represent a cross-section of all the customers. For example, in a leisure centre, if the sample was taken between 10 am and 11 am on a Monday morning it would probably consist mainly of retired people and mothers and children, and would therefore not be a true representation of all the customers who use the facility. However, if the sampling took place throughout the day say, 6–7 am, 9–10 am, 12–1 pm, 3–4 pm, 6–7 pm and 9–10 pm, it would give a much clearer picture of the views of all the facility's customers.

Another method of sampling could be to pick every 20th customer throughout the day. This again would give a good representation of the customers who use this facility.

Surveys

Surveys are usually in a questionnaire format. They can be carried out in writing, face to face or by telephone.

The questionnaire should be brief so that it does not put the customer off. The questions should be relevant to the topic of interest. This information can then be examined and the business could alter its services and products accordingly.

> ### LEARNER ACTIVITY
> Think of a sports product or service that you are familiar with. Devise a questionnaire that you would use to find out what customers think of this product and how it could be improved.

Product testing

Most new products go through a pilot phase in which they are tested on a small scale. In this way, if there are any problems with the product, these can be brought to the business's attention and rectified. For example, many new sports drinks are tested on the public, before they are sold nationwide. A market researcher would invite people to taste the new product and complete a questionnaire on its taste, proposed pricing, etc. This research would then inform the sports drink manufacturer if the drink needed to be made sweeter, should be a different colour, is in the wrong price bracket, etc.

Marketing plan

A marketing plan is devised to help a business achieve its goals. The plan usually consists of four interlinked factors (see Fig 23.05).

The product

The product is basically what the business has to offer its customers. Many sports businesses will develop new products or redevelop existing products in order to meet customers' needs. Many businesses will brand their products. The process of branding a product will give a business's customers a good idea as to what to expect from that product and, if the brand is successful, customers will become loyal to it. For example, some people will choose to purchase sports clothing made by Adidas because they like the quality, style and cut of the clothing. Once a product is branded, various famous people can be sponsored by that brand and advertise the business's products. Customers that admire the sponsored celebrity may then choose to buy products from that particular

Fig 23.05 Marketing plan

brand as they feel it has been endorsed by their favoured celebrity. For example, David Beckham has been sponsored by a variety of brands including Adidas, Pepsi, Gillette, Police sunglasses and Vodafone.

The place

Once the product has been determined, the place in which it is available to the customer has to be decided.

The location of the business is very important; there is no point having a really good product if the customer is unable to get to it. Factors to consider when determining how a product reaches its consumer are:

- the location
- the type of facility used to distribute the product.

1 **Location**
Most gyms and leisure centres will be located close to good transport links such as roads, bus routes and possibly railway stations. They will also be placed close to where large numbers of people live and/or work. Many large gyms are located just outside town centres in their own retail complex which contains other leisure facilities such as cinemas and restaurants. By locating outside the town centre this usually means that the facility has lots of room for parking (usually free parking too,

unlike in most town centres) and is not unduly affected by excess traffic as in rush hours, etc.

2 **Type of facility**
Factors to consider when deciding on the type of facility include the size, the layout and the cost of the premises. The size of the facility should be able to accommodate the predicted number of customers and ideally have the potential to expand if the business takes off. The layout of the facility should be planned to satisfy the needs of the business. For example, the changing rooms for the swimming pool would be placed so that a person may change and walk directly from the changing room to the swimming pool. If the facility is to have a jacuzzi and sauna, then these too should be placed so that they are able to be accessed directly from the changing rooms.

The price

Factors to consider when pricing a product are as follows.

1 **The actual price of the product** – in order to make a profit, the business must charge more than the raw cost of the product.
2 **The price the competitor charges for the product** – the business should try to sell its product at a similar or cheaper price than its competitor.
3 **The demand for the product** – the number of people who want to buy the product should be monitored regularly as demand for products will vary throughout the year (for example, many people plan to join a gym and get fit during the New Year or before their summer holidays).
4 **The aims of the business** – the majority of businesses aim to make a profit, however some businesses, such as a public-sector businesses, primarily aim to provide a service to the community.

Promotion

In order to try to make customers aware of their product and encourage them to buy it, many businesses will spend a lot of time and money promoting themselves. The main aims of promotion are to remind customers of the products they are selling, to raise the profile of a product, to try to make their product seem more attractive than a competitor's product and to offer incentives to customers if they choose to buy the product.

Businesses will place adverts in papers and magazines that they think potential customers will

Key learning points

- Market research is carried out in order to: identify customers' needs, satisfy customers' needs, identify opportunities for development, determine demands, trends and pricing.
- A business may carry out market research by using primary or secondary sources.

- Marketing strategies should select an appropriate sample that will represent the views of all the customers.
- A marketing plan is devised to help a business achieve its goals and usually consists of four interlinked factors: product, price, promotion and place.

read; many promotions have a short, catchy slogan such as 'Just do it' for Nike.

Some businesses may contact potential new customers directly through letter or phone calls; they may also sponsor a well-known person to help promote the product.

Legal and financial influences on sports businesses

Legal influences

A number of laws have been passed to help protect employees and employers while at work. Some of these are included in Chapter 02: Health and safety in sport.

Discrimination

A number of laws have been passed which make it illegal for an employer to discriminate against a person on the grounds of their sex or marital status, sexual orientation, race, religion or disability. Therefore, employers must recruit and pay staff in accordance with their job specification. All staff should be able to be eligible for promotion, training and benefits in accordance with their working ability, and discrimination should not take place.

The following acts have been passed to prevent discrimination at work:

- Race Relations Act 1976 (amended and updated 2000)
- Equal Pay Act 1984
- Sex Discrimination Act 2000
- Employment Equality Regulations (Religion or Belief) 2003
- Disability Discrimination Act 1995.

Health and safety

The Health and Safety at Work Act has already been covered in Chapter 02: Health and safety in sport. However, there are additional health and safety issues that any person working in a sports business should be aware of.

- **The Display Screen Equipment Regulations 1992** set out clear guidelines for any people working with visual display units (VDUs) such as a computer screen. The business is eligible to pay for all of its employees who use a VDU to have an eyesight test. They must also make employees aware of the correct posture to assume when working at a computer, provide adjustable chairs for employees, the screen brightness and colour on the screen must be adjustable, and the employer should encourage employees to take regular breaks.
- **The Health, Safety and Welfare Regulations 1992** require every employer to provide free drinking water in the workplace, which is accessible to all employees. They should also provide proper toilet facilities and, where possible, there should be separate toilets for males and females. The number of toilets an employer should provide is determined by the number of employees it has.
- **The Management of Health and Safety at Work Regulations 1992** state that the employer must carry out risk assessments where necessary and if the business has more than five employees, these risk assessments must be filed. The employer should take extra precautions if its employees are pregnant or young; it must have procedures in place dealing with emergencies, and should employ health and safety specialists to carry out training and inform employees of the health and safety issues that are relevant to them.

Treatment of employees

- **The Employment Act 2002** provides guidelines for how employees should be treated. These guidelines include details on maternity and paternity leave entitlement, the rights of parents to request flexible working hours, disciplinary and grievance procedures and rules for fixed-term workers. Any person planning to start their own business and who will be employing people to work for them should ensure they examine this in its entirety so that they are aware of how the law expects them to treat their employees.
- **The Working Time Regulations 1989** detail the length of time employees are expected to work. These regulations state that employees should:
  - work an average of 48 hours per week
  - work for no more than 8 hours on a night shift in a 24-hour period
  - be entitled to at least one day off a week
  - be entitled to a break if their working day is longer than 6 hours
  - be entitled to 4 weeks' paid leave per year.
- **The Christmas Day Trading Act 2004** is a law that prohibits the opening of large shops on Christmas Day. It also places restrictions on the loading or unloading of goods at these shops on Christmas Day. One of the reasons this act was passed was to help ensure as many people as possible would be entitled to a day off on Christmas Day. This act is applicable only in England and Wales.

Consumers

- **The Fair Trading Act 1973** is there to protect consumers against businesses that continue to conduct themselves in a way that is detrimental to consumers' interests. Examples of this act include requiring businesses to give refunds for faulty goods, and ensuring the business provides accurate descriptions of the goods and services it is providing.

  If a business does not meet the needs of the employee as set out by the various guidelines and legislation, it may be deemed to be in 'breach of duty'. Breach of duty basically means that the business has failed to do what it 'reasonably' should be expected to do and has therefore been negligent in some way. An employee could then take their employer to court and sue them for any damages caused. The court would determine if it believed the business was indeed negligent and the extent of the damage caused, and award compensation to the employee.

Key learning points

- The following acts have been passed to prevent discrimination at work:
  - Race Relations Act 1976 (amended and updated 2000)
  - Equal Pay Act 1984
  - Sex Discrimination Act 2000
  - Employment Equality Regulations (Religion or Belief) 2003
  - Disability Discrimination Act 1995.
- The following legislation protects the health, safety and welfare of employees:
  - the Display Screen Equipment Regulations 1992 is a set of guidelines for any employees working with visual display units
  - the Health, Safety and Welfare Regulations 1992 require every employer to provide appropriate facilities for its workers
  - the Management of Health and Safety at Work Regulations 1992 require employers to carry out risk assessments.
- The following legislation relates to the treatment of employees:
  - the Employment Act 2002 provides guidelines for how employees should be treated
  - the Working Time Regulations 1989 detail the length of time employees are expected to work
  - the Christmas Day Trading Act 2004 is a law that prohibits the opening of large shops on Christmas Day.
- The Fair Trading Act 1973 is there to protect consumers against unfair trading.

Financial influences

As stated previously, the success of a business depends largely on the amount of profits the business makes. Profits are made when the amount of money coming into the business is greater than the money going out. Money goes out of the business for a variety of reasons. Most businesses will have to rent or pay a mortgage for the site that they use. They will also have to pay their staff or themselves a suitable salary. If the company is a limited company then the cost of the shares will help to determine if the business is successful. If a business is doing well, the cost of the shares will go up and investors will need to pay more money to buy shares. However, if the business is not doing well, then the cost of the shares will decrease and shareholders will lose money when they come to sell them on the stock market.

Review questions

1   Name the different types of business and state the advantages and disadvantages of each.
2   Which sports businesses do not set out to make a profit?
3   Draw an example of a typical sports business hierarchical organisational structure.
4   Explain the factors that contribute to a successful sports business.
5   What are the reasons for a business to use market research?
6   Give examples of the different types of sources used in market research.
7   Give examples of ways a business could carry out market research in order to gain information on the views of the majority of its customers.
8   What is a marketing plan?
9   Give examples of legislation that an employer should be aware of.

References

Stafford-Brown, J., Rea, S., Janaway, L. and Manley, C. (2006) *BTEC First Sport*, Hodder Arnold.

Websites
www.dti.gov.uk – Department of Trade and Industry
www.bcentral.co.uk – Microsoft's website for the UK's small business community

Goals

At the end of this chapter you should:

- know about the opportunities for work-based experience in sport
- be able to prepare for a work-based experience in sport
- be able to undertake a work-based experience in sport
- be able to evaluate a work-based experience in sport.

There is a huge variety of jobs in this sector so it is vital for learners to be aware of the range of occupations available and to gain first-hand experience of what the job entails. Not only will this give you a better picture of what is expected of you in your career of choice, it will also demonstrate your commitment to future employers.

This chapter gives information that will allow you to plan and carry out a practical work-based experience within the sports industry. It explores the different types of sports industry organisations, sources to locate jobs, how to apply for jobs, interview skills and how to evaluate your experience.

Opportunities for work-based experience in sport

The various sectors that provide opportunities for work-based experience in sport include:

- health and fitness – gyms, health clubs and leisure centres
- sport and recreation – football, hockey and swimming clubs
- outdoor education – outdoor pursuit centres, water sports centres and indoor ski slopes.

The provision of sports facilities and opportunities in Britain is the result of the interaction between the public, private and voluntary sectors.

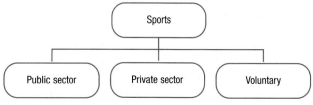

Fig 24.01 Sports provision

Public-sector provision

definition

The public sector: institutions funded by money collected from the public in the form of direct and indirect taxes.

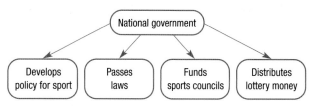

Fig 24.02 National government's responsibilities in sports provision

The public sector collects money through income tax, community charges, business taxes, valued added taxes on spending and national insurance. It then makes decisions on how to spend this money. These decisions are based on priorities and are seen as political decisions. The government may see the National Health Service and education system as priorities for spending and this position would be the basis for its decisions on spending. If the government does not see sport as being important it allocates only a relatively small amount of its budget to sports facilities, organisations and performers.

The public sector is made up of national government and local government (or local authorities), each of which has different responsibilities in sports provision.

National government is funded by taxes (income tax, VAT, business taxes) and receives money from the National Lottery (Lotto). Its role in sport is indirect, as it does not fund buildings or the running of facilities, but provides money to other organisations to spend on sport. It has a role as an 'enabler' and the main recipient is Sport England. National government provides grants and loans to local authorities, as well as offering technical assistance. Sport is the responsibility of the Department of Culture, Media and Sport (DCMS). It has the following roles in sport:

- represents interests of sport, arts, tourism and heritage
- promotes sporting success at the highest levels
- helps develop government sporting strategy
- funds the Sports Councils in Britain and Northern Ireland
- funds other agencies involved in sports provision
- distributes money raised by the National Lottery.

Sport England is responsible for the development of sport in England, while the Sports Councils for Scotland, Northern Ireland and Wales are responsible for the development of sport in their respective countries. Their main purpose is to:

- get more people involved in sport
- provide more places to play sport
- win more medals through higher standards of performance.

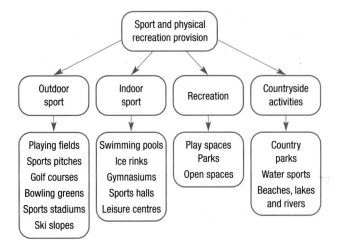

Fig 24.03 Local government's responsibilities in sports provision

Local government

Local government or local authorities are responsible for providing facilities for sport and physical recreation. Provision is usually divided into the areas shown in Fig 24.03.

Facilities in the public sector are usually named after the town or city they are in – e.g. Colchester Leisure Centre, Watford Baths, Wimbledon Recreation Centre.

LEARNER ACTIVITY Government role in sport

Find out the following information.

- Who is the Secretary of State for the Department of Culture, Media and Sport?
- Who is the Minister for Sport?
- Where is your local office of Sport England or Sports Council for Scotland, Northern Ireland or Wales?
- What is the address of your local office?

LEARNER ACTIVITY Sport and society

The government (national and local) spends around £1000 million a year on sport. There are many courses to study sport in Britain and there is a huge amount of media coverage of sport. Thus, we can assume that sport is significant in British society. But why? What are the benefits of playing, watching and talking about sport?

Answer the following questions.

- List the ways you can think of that sport contributes to the British economy.
- What benefits does sport have for participants and spectators? Consider why you participate in or watch sport.
- What are the social benefits of sports participation and watching sport? How does it improve the world we live in?
- What are the international benefits of sports participation?
- What are the educational benefits of sports participation?

The majority of funding comes from the council tax and will go to the county council, with the rest going to the local authority and some to the county police force. Other sources include receipts from trading, such as leisure centre entry fees, rents from council housing, loans from banks and grants from national government.

Private-sector provision

definition

Private sector: sport is provided by individuals or groups of individuals who invest their own money in the facilities with the main aim of making a profit.

Private-sector sport is provided by individuals or groups of individuals (companies) who invest their own money in facilities. As a result, these facilities are usually named after people, such as David Lloyd clubs, although some have a brand name, such as Virgin Active or Cannons.

The private sector provides sports facilities for two main reasons:

- to make a return on their investment for themselves and their shareholders
- to make a profit out of sport.

Claims are sometimes made that it is for other altruistic reasons, such as improving the standards of a sport or improving the community the facilities are in. However, they would not exist unless they could make a profit.

The private sector provides for sports increasing in demand. It is able to respond quickly to new trends or to instigate new trends. It provides facilities where it can attract large numbers of customers, or more exclusive facilities where it can attract fewer customers but charge more. It is involved in the following areas:

- active sports – tennis, golf, health and fitness suites, snooker and pool, water sports and ten-pin bowling
- spectator sport – stadiums for football, rugby, cricket, tennis, golf (football is by far the most popular spectator sport)
- sponsorship – this has risen dramatically over the last 15 years.

The role of the private sector can be well summarised by this quote from George Torkildsen (1991):

> The major difference between the commercial operator and the public or voluntary operator is the raison d'être of the business, the primary objective of the commercial operator being that of financial profit or adequate return on investment.

The voluntary sector

definition

The voluntary sector: clubs that operate as non-profit-making organisations and which are essentially managed by and for amateur sportsmen and women.

Most amateur clubs are run on a voluntary basis. Some voluntary clubs own facilities, but the majority hire facilities, usually provided by the public sector. Most clubs, such as football and athletics clubs, that people join to enable them to participate in competitive sport are in the voluntary sector. Voluntary-sector clubs often work in partnership with the private or public sector. They might use public-sector facilities or gain sponsorship from the private sector. In the evening you may find the swimming pool at your leisure centre being used for swimming club or kayaking club training.

Funding of voluntary clubs

The voluntary sector is funded primarily by its members in the form of subscriptions. Every club will have an annual subscription fee and match fees. This is to cover the costs of playing, travel and equipment. The club may try to raise some money in the form of sponsorship. This is often by a local company or by one of the players. Some clubs have local benefactors who put money into a club as a gesture of goodwill. Clubs also run fundraising events such as discos, race nights or jumble sales, particularly if they are trying to raise money for a tour or special event.

Clubs can apply for other sources of funding:

- National Lottery grants
- grants from national governing bodies
- grants from government
- grants from the local authority.

These types of grants are usually to enable clubs to build or improve their facilities.

Partnerships

Partnerships occur when two or more of the sectors come together to provide opportunities for sport. We have already seen how the public sector rents out its facilities to the voluntary sector to give them an opportunity to play sports. Sponsorship, which is primarily provided by the private sector, is given to the public and voluntary sectors.

Sports facilities are also built as partnerships. The new English National Stadium at Wembley is a private-sector initiative by Wembley plc, but it has received a National Lottery grant from the public sector. It will also go into partnership with other private-sector organisations to raise finance and gain sponsorship.

Compulsory competitive tendering (CCT), introduced to the leisure industry in 1990, was aimed at developing partnerships between the public and private sectors. The aim was to hand the management of sports centres to private-sector organisations while the ownership of the centres remained with the public sector (local authorities). The theory behind this arrangement was that the private-sector companies would aim to run the centers for profit and thus they would be run more efficiently. Today we can still see the benefits of this arrangement in our local sports facilities.

Types of occupation

There is a huge range of jobs available in the sports industry, from sports massage therapist to mountain leader. In order to gain the skills and qualifications you require, you may need to continue your studies to a higher level or complete a part-time course. The following list gives a range of different jobs available in the sports industry but is by no means exhaustive:

- fitness instructor
- leisure attendant
- sports centre manager
- kayak instructor
- sports coach
- sports development officer
- sports/PE teacher or lecturer
- mountain leader
- professional sports performer
- sports massage therapist
- sport and exercise scientist
- sports nutritionist
- sport psychologist
- sports groundsman
- sports retailer.

Fitness instructor

This involves assessing people's fitness levels, designing their exercise programmes and instructing these programmes in the gym. Fitness instructors may also teach aerobics classes and circuit classes, and supervise people in the gym.

Instructors need sound anatomy and physiology knowledge gained from a sport science course, and also a recognised fitness instructor's award from a training organisation such as Premier Training International, YMCA or Focus. To teach specific skills, such as aerobics, circuits or stability ball work, extra qualifications are required. First aid and CPR qualifications are also essential. Instructors must have good communication skills, be friendly and able to remain calm under pressure.

Leisure attendant

Leisure attendants are responsible for preparing and supervising the sports hall, swimming pool and changing rooms in a leisure facility. Most leisure attendants are also involved in coaching or supervising sports sessions in their sports hall.

A sports qualification is desirable but not essential. The National Pool Lifeguard Qualification is compulsory in order to work in a swimming pool. To coach sports, leisure attendants need specific national governing body coaching awards.

Leisure attendants need to be outgoing and people-orientated. Communication skills are important as you may have to deal with a range of people.

Sports centre manager

Managing a sports centre involves some of the following activities:

- managing and motivating staff
- programming facilities and organising activities
- establishing systems and procedures
- preparing and managing budgets
- monitoring sales and usage
- marketing and promoting the centre
- dealing with members and any complaints or incidents.

Managers may have been promoted into this position having qualified with a BTEC First or National Diploma or GNVQ. Most managers will hold higher-level qualifications such as a degree or HND in leisure management or business studies.

To be an effective manager you need the following personal qualities: confidence, enthusiasm, assertiveness, communication skills, self-motivation, presence and professionalism.

Kayak instructor

A kayak instructor is usually qualified in a range of outdoor pursuits and works at an outdoor pursuits centre. The role involves checking equipment, ensuring weather conditions are appropriate and then teaching a range of skills to kayak safely and effectively.

You will have to have a high level of personal proficiency (three-star minimum) and then attend an instructor training course. You also need to be qualified in rescue skills and first aid. You must have good communication skills, be able to withstand cold and wet working conditions, and also have very good safety awareness.

Sports coach

Sports coaches are usually former or current competitors in their sport. They are responsible for developing the physical fitness and skills of their athletes. They need to be able to evaluate their athletes' performances and offer feedback to improve these. As a result, they require knowledge of many aspects of sport science, such as anatomy and physiology, biomechanics, nutrition, psychology and sports injury.

Every sport has its own system for awarding coaching qualifications, and coaches must hold the relevant award. Many coaches also hold qualifications in sport or sport science.

Coaches need to be able to motivate athletes and have their trust. They need to be good communicators and listeners, and able to show patience and empathy towards their athletes.

Sports development officer

A sports development officer works to increase participation rates in sport and provide opportunities for people to play sport in a local area. They work for local authorities and may have responsibility for specific groups of people, such as ethnic minorities, women or disabled people.

Most sports development officers have at least a BTEC National in sport or sports science, and usually also hold a degree or HND in sport, sport science or leisure management, along with a range of coaching qualifications. You need an interest and knowledge in a range of sports and the needs of a community. You have to be able to communicate with people from different backgrounds and be sensitive to their needs. Good leadership, motivational skills and an organised approach to work are also necessary.

Sports/PE teacher or lecturer

You can teach PE in schools to children from the age of four to eighteen years. If you choose the younger-aged children you also usually have to teach a range of other subjects from the National Curriculum. If you teach PE in a secondary school this is usually the only subject you will be required to teach. A lecturer teaches in a college or university and usually specialises in a few subject areas, such as physiology or psychology.

A teacher needs to be educated to degree level and to be qualified as a teacher. There are two ways to do this:

- take a four-year teaching degree such as a Bachelor of Education (BEd) or a Batchelor of Arts with Qualified Teaching Status (BA (QTS))
- take a three-year degree in sport science or sport studies and then complete a one-year Postgraduate Certificate in Education (PGCE).

To study to become a teacher you must have passed GCSE English and maths (at grade C or above and a science if you wish to teach primary or key stages 2/3), and at least two A levels.

Teaching is a very demanding profession and you need to be patient and able to deal with young people and their various needs. Teachers need to be organised, and able to maintain discipline and adapt their communication skills to the group they are teaching. You should also have a good level of personal fitness and enjoy working with young people.

Mountain leader

A mountain leader may work in an outdoor pursuits centre and lead mountain walks or they may be involved in leading a venture scouting group and instruct the group on how to carry out an expedition.

A mountain leader must have gained a great deal of personal experience walking and navigating in the outdoors. They must then attend a mountain leader instructor course, which involves mountain walks, night walks and camping overnight. They must keep a logbook and then complete a mountain leader assessment to ensure they are proficient in all the skills required for mountain leading. They can then carry out a mountain leader course for winter conditions and undergo another assessment. A mountain leader must be able to withstand cold and wet conditions, have excellent navigational skills, a first aid qualification, good communication skills, and excellent health and safety knowledge.

Professional sports performer

Ultimately the goal of every sports performer would be to play their sport fulltime at a professional level. However, it is only the most talented who get this opportunity and there are only a limited number of sports where you can play professionally. Football,

cricket, rugby league, rugby union and golf have the largest number professional players. However, most professional players have a second job to ensure their income.

No formal qualifications are needed, although you need to investigate the best route into a sport as every sport will be slightly different in how it recruits young players.

Technical efficiency at the chosen sport, along with physical fitness, are the most important assets, as well as self-motivation, commitment and determination.

Sports massage therapist

A sports massage therapist has a varied job, using their massage skills to prepare athletes for competition, helping them to warm down after competition and then dealing with any injuries or soreness they may suffer. They can also treat the public who have injured themselves during non-sporting activities such as gardening.

A sports massage therapist needs to hold a sports therapy diploma. These courses are accredited by the Vocational Training and Charitable Trust (VTCT) and can be studied at most colleges of further education. Private training organisations, such as Premier Training International, also offer these courses in an intensive 12-week format. It is possible to do a degree in sports therapy or sports rehabilitation at a limited number of universities.

A sports massage therapist always needs to adopt a professional approach, as their job involves physical contact with people. They should be patient, caring and sensitive to an individual's needs. A high standard of personal hygiene and good communication skills will be important to be successful.

Sport and exercise scientist

The aim of the sport and exercise scientist is to maximise the performance of an individual in their care. This will involve applying their knowledge and skills in the subjects of physiology, biomechanics and psychology to give the performers any possible advantage. Physiology will involve fitness testing and monitoring physical condition; biomechanics will involve examining the performer's technique and equipment to analyse where improvements can be made; psychology will be applied to ensure the performer is correctly prepared mentally.

A sport scientist will hold a degree in sport science and possibly a master's degree or a PhD in their chosen field of expertise.

Sports nutritionist

A sports nutritionist gives an athlete advice about how to organise their diet to ensure they maximise the effects of their training and reach competition in the best possible shape. They may also provide advice on the use of supplements.

A sports nutritionist needs to be qualified as a dietician first. This will involve completing a three-year degree to become recognised as a state registered dietician. To specialise in sports nutrition you need at least one year's experience before completing a sports dietetics course run by the Sports Nutrition Foundation.

Sport psychologist

A sport psychologist is involved in mentally preparing athletes for competition. It is a varied job which will differ depending on the individual needs of performers. A psychologist is involved in helping teams and individuals set goals for the short and long term, learn strategies to control arousal levels and stay relaxed in stressful situations. They are also often involved in lecturing and conducting research, as well as actually practising their skills.

A sport psychologist would usually be a graduate or sport scientist who had then completed postgraduate training. This would involve a master's degree or a PhD in sport psychology.

Psychologists need to have good listening and interviewing skills in order to assess the needs of their athletes and to develop strategies to help them. A psychologist should be able to build up a relationship of trust and be seen as someone who the athlete can talk to confidentially.

Sports groundsman

A groundsman is responsible for preparing and maintaining the condition of outdoor facilities, such as golf courses, cricket pitches, football pitches and tennis courts.

Entrance qualifications are not essential. You can study for an NVQ in turf management, or go on to HND or degree level. These courses need to be recognised by the Institute of Groundsmanship (IOG).

Sports retailer

Sports retail involves working in a sports shop selling sports goods. This can involve using your knowledge of sport and matching a client's needs to specific products. Different types of runners require different types of running shoes and you need to be able to identify which shoes they need.

A knowledge of sport is needed, but many people working in retail need business skills and customer care skills. A qualification in business studies or leisure studies would be appropriate. If you have aspirations to run a sports shop, it may be necessary to hold an HND or degree in a management-based subject.

An ability to deal with members of the public and a willingness to meet their needs is necessary. You must be good at communicating and be able to stay calm under pressure.

Fig 24.04 Sports groundsman

LEARNER ACTIVITY Skills and qualifications

- Think about the career you would like to pursue.
- Make a list of all the skills and qualifications you have to date and what you will need in the future.
- Make a list of all the advantages and disadvantages of this career.

Work placement considerations

Before choosing your work placement, you will need to bear in mind a number of factors to ensure the location and the actual placement are suitable for you.

Location

While deciding where you would like to carry out your project you should also include in your decision-making the locality of the placement. If the sports facility is not within walking distance how are you going to get there? You will need to investigate methods of public transport and look at the cost and travel times. If the facility is too far away from home for you to travel in to every day you will have to see if the facility provides staff accommodation and if it would be available to you. Alternatively, you may have family living near to your chosen facility and be able to stay with them for the duration of the placement.

Placement requirements

You need to speak to your supervisor prior to the placement in order to see if you need to provide your own clothing and, if so, what is required. Most leisure centres provide their staff with a uniform but outdoor pursuit centres staff usually provide their own clothing. This could be quite expensive if you do not have any of your own already, so it may be worth asking your supervisor if they have any kit you could borrow for the duration of the placement.

Any equipment you require will usually be provided, such as a whistle for a lifeguard. Again, it is worth asking your supervisor if you need to buy anything and check that you can afford it prior to your placement.

Occupation information

The purpose of a work placement is to help you determine if the job you have chosen to undertake or observe is suitable for you. Therefore, once you have thought of a job you would like to perform you will need to find out if you have or are going to have the right qualifications to be accepted on this job.

If you would like to work in outdoor pursuits, you will need to have a good level of personal proficiency and/or be working towards water-based or land-based outdoor pursuits qualifications – mountain leader, kayak instructor, etc.

On top of the qualifications required, every job has a different set of roles and responsibilities that you must examine and check to see you are capable of carrying them out. Working in the sports industry often entails working unsociable hours. If you want to work only in the daytime you may have to consider a different job.

Regulations

There are a number of regulations in place to help protect employees, employers and customers whilst at work:

- Health and Safety at Work Act 1974
- Control of Substances Hazardous to Health Regulations (COSHH) 1994
- Health and Safety (First Aid) 1981
- Safety at Sports Ground Act 1975
- Fire Safety & Safety of Places of Sport Act 1987
- Children Act 1989.

Skills

While on your work placement you will probably realise that you already have a number of skills that are appropriate. You may realise that you have good interpersonal skills and find it easy to deal with customer's questions and/or complaints. But you will no doubt also find that there are some skills that need to be developed. You may find it difficult to meet deadlines or that you are always rushing to get to work on time. You would need to improve your time-management skills.

You will be taught a number of new practical skills such as putting up and taking down equipment. You will no doubt have some knowledge of this from practical units you have covered and find that you just need to adapt these skills to meet the requirements of the new apparatus.

Preparation for a work-based experience

Aims and objectives

You need to consider what your aims and objectives are prior to your work-based experience in sport.

Aim: the broad long-term target of your experience.
Objectives: a number of targets that, combined, will allow you to reach your aim.

Personal skills

A work placement is an opportunity to try out a job and start to understand what knowledge and skills are needed for that position. Answering the questions below will start to give you an idea of what your next step should be. You can discuss this audit with your tutor or work placement officer when you have a meeting with them to arrange your industrial placement. This will help you to gain a placement which is fulfilling, worthwhile and develops your skills and personal qualities.

Ask yourself the following questions.

- What skills have I at present? Look at practical skills of coaching and teaching, key skills such as written and verbal communication, problem-solving and application of number, IT and skills gained from previous work experiences such as clerical and administrative skills.
- What skills would I like to acquire? This is difficult because there may be skills you have not gained because you haven't been in a situation to gain them. As a result, you may not be aware that you need them. However, try to be realistic and think what skills you may need in a job, such as communicating with the general public.
- What qualifications have I gained? This is just a list of all the qualifications you currently hold. Also list here any qualifications you are hoping to gain.
- What personal qualities have I got? Think about personal qualities in the following areas.
  - **Working with other people**: are there particular people you would not like to work with? Do you prefer to work in large or small groups? How do you feel about working as part of a team? Are you happy dealing with the public?
  - **Leadership**: how good are you at leading groups? Do you prefer to lead large or small groups? How do you feel about selling to people?
  - **Responsibility:** how do you feel about responsibility in the following areas – cash, equipment, other people's work, meeting deadlines, other people's safety and welfare.
- What do you want from a job? Split this up into what you would want and what you would not want. Consider the following areas.
  - **Pay**: do you want enough to get by on or is getting a high wage important to you? Would you like to be paid by results? Would you like to be paid extra for extra work you have done?
  - **Hours**: do you want to work fixed hours (9 to 5), or do you not mind doing shift work? How do you feel about overtime?
  - **Prospects**: how important are the opportunities for promotion and the presence of a career structure?
  - **Location**: do you have a fixed idea of where you want to work, or are you willing to relocate to find the right job? How important is an easy journey to work to you?
  - **Working with others**: is it important for you to work as a part of a group, or would you rather work alone? How do you feel about managers and supervisors, and are you looking for a certain style of leadership?
  - **What the job entails**: are you looking for job satisfaction or a job that pays well? Are you keen to utilise certain skills and abilities? Do you want to help other people?

Targets

Once a decision has been made about your future career it is an appropriate time to think about setting targets. Remember, you may not be able to walk into your dream job immediately and while this remains your long-term goal it is important to set realistic short-term targets to lay the pathway to achieving your dream job.

When targets are set you need to use the SMART principle to make them workable. SMART stands for:

- **S**pecific
- **M**easurable
- **A**chievable
- **R**ealistic
- **T**ime-constrained.

Specific: the target must be specific to what you want to achieve. You may need to improve your lifesaving leg kick in order to pass your pool lifeguard award.

Measurable: targets must be stated in a way that is measurable, so they need to state figures. For example, I want to be able to tow a person 25 m in one minute.

Achievable: it must be possible to actually achieve the target.

Realistic: we need to be realistic in our setting and look at what factors may stop us achieving the target.

Time-constrained: there must be a timescale or deadline on the target. This means you can review your success. It is best to state a date by which you wish to achieve the goal.

Application process

After having read a job specification you can then decide if you would like to apply for the role. To apply for work you need to use a suitable method to approach a prospective employer. Most job advertisements will specify which method you should use. There are three main methods that you may be asked for.

- **Curriculum vitae (CV)** – a concise written document that summarises your skills, qualifications and experience to date for a prospective employer. It needs to be accompanied by a covering letter.
- **Application form** – some jobs will not accept a CV and will ask you to complete a pre-designed application form asking you to show why you are suitable for the job. This also needs to be accompanied by a covering letter.
- **Letter of application** – some jobs will require you to apply in writing. The information will be similar to that of a CV, but presented in a different format.

Curriculum vitae

A CV is used for a range of reasons:

- to demonstrate your value to the employer
- as a marketing tool to get an interview
- to sell yourself to the employer.

There are three main styles of CV.

- **Chronological** – this is the most common format and involves you presenting your experiences of education and work in date order.
- **Functional** – this type highlights your skills and is directed towards a certain career. You may be qualified in more than one subject, but you would highlight only the skills that are relevant for the type of work you are trying to gain.
- **Targeted** – this type of CV emphasises skills and abilities relevant to a specific job or company. It is tailor-made for one job. You would examine the job specification and then adapt your CV to show how you meet the it.

Preparing a CV

A CV needs to be prepared meticulously and you should spend time deciding what your main selling features are. If you are still a student, you may not have been involved in full-time work, but you will still have important features to highlight. You must include any work experiences, part-time and voluntary work you have undertaken. You will need to start by compiling a biography of your life with dates and events. You will also need to consider what skills you have at present, and which ones are transferable to the type of work you are seeking.

A CV should include the following information.

- **Personal details** – full name and address, home telephone number and mobile number, email address and date of birth.
- **Current position and employment** – if you are employed, your position and your main responsibilities.
- **Key personal skills** – highlight your main personal skills, attributes and abilities.
- **Education and qualifications** – the names and dates of all academic qualifications received, with the most recent first.
- **Training or work-related courses** – any additional vocational or on-the-job training you have received.
- **Previous employment** – all the past employment you have had with the following information: name of employer, job title and a brief summary of responsibilities. Also include any periods of work placement.
- **Leisure interests** – the interests you have outside the academic environment; the sports you play and at what level (it may be appropriate to list

some of your achievements in sport), and other hobbies and activities in which you are involved. It is particularly good to state any positions of responsibility you have held, such as club captain, scout leader or cadet force rank.

- **Other relevant information** – anything else you feel may be of value to the employer, such as an ability to drive.
- **References** – the name, addresses and phone numbers of two people (referees) who can vouch for you. If you have a current employer, they should be the first; if not, a past employer or someone else in a position of responsibility, such as a teacher, would be appropriate. It is important that you ask them before using them as a reference in case they are not willing to write you a reference.

Sample CV

An example CV is shown below.

Curriculum vitae

Name:	Rebecca Sewell
Date of birth:	17 October 1982
Address:	125 Mill Crescent, Reading, Berks RG6 3JS
Nationality:	British
Tel:	01345 245131 (home); 01345 684877 (work); 07754 759868 (mob)
Email:	racsewell@aol.com

Current employment

Fitness instructor at the Premier Gym in Reading (2004–6)

A graduate in Sport Science (BSc Hons) with specialist skills in fitness instruction, teaching circuits and aerobics and core conditioning training.

Main responsibilities:
- teaching aerobics and circuits
- conducting fitness assessments, designing exercise programmes and instructing workouts
- selling memberships and sports clothing.

Key skills include:
- fitness testing, programme design and instructional skills
- ability to teach exercise to music
- good communication skills
- good motivator of people
- financial management skills of budgeting and monitoring budgets
- computer and internet literate
- first aid and CPR competent
- selling and marketing skills.

Education and qualifications

2000–3	Thames University. BSc (Hons) Sport and Exercise Science (2:1 gained)
1998–2000	Reading College of Sport. BTEC ND Sport Science: 8 distinctions, 8 merits, 2 passes
1995–9	Campbell School, Reading. 10 GCSEs: PE (A), English Lang (A), English Lit (A), French (A), Biology (B), Maths (B), Chemistry (B), German (B), Geography (B), Physics (D)

Work-related courses

Fitness Trainers Award (2003)
NVQ RSA Exercise to Music (2002)
NPLQ (2004)

Curriculum vitae (continued)

First aid at work (2005)
Stability ball training (2006)

Previous employment
2003–4   Leisure attendant at Springfield Baths.
Main duties included pool supervision and lifeguarding, laying out equipment in the sports hall, coaching and teaching children's sport at weekends and during holidays.

Previous work experience
1999   Three-week placement at Hills Spa Health and Fitness Centre.
This involved shadowing the fitness trainers and duty manager, serving the members and advising them in the gym.

Hobbies and interests
I am involved in local athletics and am captain of the ladies' team. I run the 800 m and 1500 m and am currently the Berkshire county champion at 800 m.
I enjoy travelling overseas, particularly to Australia and New Zealand.
My hobbies are reading and going to the cinema.

Other relevant information
Full driving licence and own car.

Referees

Mr W. Samways	Miss J. Gatehouse
Fitness Manager	Head of Sport Science
Premier Gym	Thames University
Garfield Road	Stratton Way
Reading	Easthampton
Berks RG16 4LP	Bucks BK34 7BJ
01345 874098	0152 854339

LEARNER ACTIVITY
Prepare a CV

Using the example provided, prepare a CV for yourself which you could send to a prospective employer.

Completing an application form

Many employers will produce their own application form, which you need to fill in when applying for a position. They will use this form to select the candidates they wish to interview. It is important to give yourself plenty of time to complete the form. Forms that are completed incorrectly or untidily will probably be discarded without being read. If you complete the form properly, you will already have an advantage over your rivals. Remember, you get only one chance to make a first impression. Here are some useful tips on completing the form.

- Photocopy the form first and use the copy to practise on. Check over what you have written and, when you are satisfied, copy it on to the original.
- Read the instructions on the form carefully and follow them exactly. For example, it may ask you to use black ink or block capitals. This is important because the form may need to be photocopied and will copy well only in black ink.
- Even if some of the information on the form is given in the covering letter, you must still include it on the form. Never write 'refer to CV', as the reader may not bother.
- Think about answers very carefully and plan your responses. For example, questions such as 'Why do

you want to work for this company?' need to be researched and responded to appropriately.

- Check that your referees are willing to provide a reference for you before you put in their details.
- Take a photocopy of your form so that you can remind yourself what you wrote before an interview.
- Make sure you do not miss the closing date, and post the form well in advance.
- Include a covering letter with your application form.

Letter of application

A letter of application relates your experience to a specific company or job vacancy. It should always be sent with a CV and perhaps an application form. It should be businesslike and complement the information in your CV. If you are writing in response to an advertisement, make reference to the job title and where you saw the vacancy advertised, and ensure the letter is addressed to the correct person. Indicate why you are attracted to the position advertised, and highlight why you think you are suitable and what key personal skills and experiences you have that are relevant to the vacancy. Finish the letter by stating that you look forward to hearing from them soon and would be delighted to attend an interview at their convenience.

> **LEARNER ACTIVITY** Write a letter of application
>
> Use the template on the next page to draft a letter of application.

Preparation for interview

One of the most important parts of the interview is the preparation that takes place beforehand. Learn all you can about the company and the job role. This can be done via the internet or it would be even better if you actually went to visit the workplace. During the visit not only will you have worked out how to get there you will also be able to see how people dress, exactly what facilities are available and even ask some of the staff questions.

Questions

You should think about which questions you are likely to be asked. For example: Why are you interested in this job? What are your strengths? What are your weaknesses? What do you think this job entails? Why do you think you will be good at this job?

Once you have worked out suitable answers, practise answering them out loud either with a friend or in front of a mirror. You may wish to record yourself with a camcorder or tape recorder and then see or hear yourself 'in action' and make improvements where necessary. You should also study your body language, which includes your facial expressions, mannerisms and gestures. If you smile and look enthusiastic this will portray the right image. You may find that you slouch or have a blank facial expression without even being aware of it while answering questions.

Be prepared to discuss anything you have written on your CV or letter of application. You may be asked why you decided to study a BTEC qualification or to explain your choice of work placement, etc.

You should also prepare questions to ask the interviewers as this will show them that you are interested and want to know more about the company or job role. Be sure not to ask questions that have already been answered within the job role specifications or during the course of the interview.

Dress

You will need to decide what you are going to wear well in advance of the interview. If you are not sure what to wear, it is best to choose smart, dark-coloured clothes such as a suit or smart trousers or skirt and a shirt/blouse. Clothing that is too tight or revealing is rarely acceptable attire for an interview. Ensure that your clothes are clean and ironed and also comfortable. Ensure that your hair is clean and you have a suitable haircut or style for the interview. If you have lots of visible body piercings, you may wish to take some out in order to portray the image you think the company is looking for.

Location

If possible, go and visit the place you are going to for interview beforehand. Travel at the same time of day you will be leaving for your interview time so that you

---

(Your name) _____

(Your address) _____

(Name of person applying to) _____

(Address of company writing to) _____

Date _____

Dear _____ (person's name)

(First paragraph to explain why you are writing, i.e. for which job and where you saw the vacancy)

(Next paragraph to explain what you are currently doing, i.e. employment or education)

(Next paragraph to discuss why you are applying for the job and what you like about it)

(Next paragraph to justify why you are suitable for the position – relevant experience or skills)

(End your letter by saying that you can attend an interview and hope to hear from them soon)

Yours sincerely*

_____ (Sign your name)

_____ (Type your name)

* If you do not have a person's name and addressed the letter to 'Dear Sir or Madam', you should end with 'Yours faithfully'.

Fig 22.05 How to write a letter of application

can see if there are any issues with rush hour traffic, etc. You should always plan to arrive at your interview location at least ten minutes in advance to allow time to compose yourself.

Interview skills

Body language

Body language can say an awful lot about how we feel, how confident we are and how enthusiastic we are. People will often make a first impression about someone based upon their body language alone. Therefore, it is important to convey the right message by using appropriate body language.

- Greet your interviewer with a firm handshake.

- Maintain eye contact as this shows that you are interested in what the person has to say. You should not overdo the eye contact, though, as this can sometimes look threatening.
- When answering questions, emphasise key points by leaning forward and using expressive gestures.
- Speak with an expressive voice to convey your enthusiasm and interest rather than a monotone voice which suggests a lack of interest and boredom.
- You should sit with your back up straight as this communicates self-assurance and eagerness. Do not slouch as this gives the impression that you are not interested or are lacking in confidence.
- Do not fidget or twiddle your fingers while the interviewer is talking as this shows you are not paying attention.

- When the interviewer is talking, nod your head and smile in relevant places to demonstrate your interest in what they are saying.

Answering questions

You will have rehearsed many of the answers that you give during the interview and therefore know what you need to say and how to say it. However, you will undoubtedly be faced with a few questions that you have not prepared for. Give yourself a few seconds to sit and think about your answer and then respond honestly and as positively as possible. If you do not understand the question, ask the interviewer to repeat it. If you still do not understand the question you can respond in a variety of ways.

- Ask 'Do you mean …?', which shows that you understand some of what they said but need clarity.
- Ask them to explain their question in more detail.

LEARNER ACTIVITY Role play an interview

Imagine you are having an interview for a job of your choice. With a partner carry out a role play interview. The interviewer must have a copy of your CV and ask appropriate questions relating to your CV and the job role.

The interviewer should then give feedback as to what they thought was good and which areas need to be improved.

Undertake a work-based experience

While undertaking your work-based experience there are a number of situations and considerations you will need to think about prior to and during the experience.

Planned activities

While on your work-based experience you will probably participate in planned activities. These may include testing chlorine levels in the swimming pool, staff meetings, cleaning duties, setting up and checking equipment, etc. Ensure you know the timing of these events, have been shown exactly what needs to be done and have a supervisor where necessary to ensure you are carrying out these planned activities safely and effectively.

Wherever you work you are part of a team that is responsible for running a safe and secure environment. Most working environments have a manual that covers details on how every part of the facility should operate under normal conditions and what to do in an emergency situation. These are usually referred to as Normal Operating Procedures (NOP) and Emergency Operating Procedures (EOP).

The NOP gives instructions on how to deal with everyday situations, whereas the EOP gives instructions on how to deal with minor and major emergency situations such as disorderly behaviour from customers or dealing with a drowning incident.

Working in the sports industry usually means you deal with customers on a regular basis. You therefore need skills in dealing with the public. These skills are very important so that you can be sure you are giving the customers the treatment they deserve to ensure they keep coming back to your leisure facility. You will need to learn what the customers' needs are and how you can meet these requirements or even exceed them.

> **definition**
>
> Customer care: the level of assistance and courtesy given to those who use the facility.

Equal opportunities

Every person should ensure that they deal with the people that they meet in an unbiased and equal way whether it is at work, home or school. This means that you should not discriminate for reasons of race or ethnic origin, gender, culture, disability, sexual orientation or social differences.

Different age groups

In the leisure industry you can expect to deal with people of all ages, from babies and toddlers right through to the over-sixties. Therefore, you should be able to have an understanding of their needs – be aware of where the baby changing facilities are, ensure you know about reduced prices for the over-sixties, be aware of special swimming sessions for different groups, etc.

Different cultural backgrounds

You need to be aware of different cultural needs and be able to cater for them accordingly. Some cultures will not allow males to see females in their swimsuits. Therefore, you must be able to give these females details of when there are female-only swimming sessions. These sessions would also have to have only female lifeguards on duty too. You should be aware of people who use the facility who do not have English as their first language and ensure there are signs and promotional materials that they can understand.

Special needs

A good leisure facility is able to cater for every person in its local area, including people who have specific needs. An example of a person with a special need is someone with restricted mobility. These people may require the use of a walking stick or wheelchair. In these cases the facility should have appropriate access so that they may enter the building unaided. If the building is on two storeys there must be a lift or ramps to allow the person to move up to the next floor. If the facility has a swimming pool there must be some form of access available for people with disabilities, such as a chair hoist.

Record-keeping

You will need to record your activities while on placement so that you are able to assess exactly what you have done and how well you have performed these activities.

The best method of recording this information is to keep a daily diary of activities. Information that you may wish to include in your diary is as follows.

- Interview a member of staff and find out what the roles and responsibilities of their job are, and how they have come to be in their position. Also find out what qualifications they have and what skills they need to do their job effectively.
- Find out the organisation's operating procedures for a range of tasks. An operating procedure is how a company completes certain tasks. This will depend upon the type of organisation you work for, but try to find out how it deals with new customers, how it manages the work it does in the gym, how it deals with cash and cashing up, how it manages the pool, and so on.
- It is of utmost importance that you are inducted in health and safety procedures on your first day. Take a note of the following: what the evacuation procedure is, where the fire exits are, where the

assembly point is, where the first-aid kit is, who is a trained first aider, where the phone for emergencies is, where the fire extinguishers are, what safety equipment is available and when you need to use it.
- Make a record of what you did each day in the workplace and any new skills you gained.
- Every day ensure you record the objectives you have met or are close to meeting, and check them off against the SMART targets you have set for yourself prior to starting the work-based experience. You may find that you need to review the timescales or other factors in your SMART targets as you may be achieving some of your targets faster or slower than expected.

Evaluate a work-based experience

So that you and your tutor(s) are able to assess how well you have performed on your work-based experience, you should carry out a full review of your placement and present your evaluation to these people.

Monitor and review

In order to be able to assess your work placement project you should review your work periodically to ensure it is all going to plan. Try to evaluate your strengths – are you working well with the team? Then assess which areas you need to improve. For example, do your customer service skills need attention?

Always be vigilant to see if any opportunities arise that may improve your experience. This could be something as simple as asking to sit in on a staff meeting which may give you additional information for your job role.

Make a note of the skills you have acquired and developed while on the placement. You may wish to record this evidence on your CV as they will probably be transferable skills and therefore relevant for future employment.

From your time on the work placement you should have a good idea of what you need to do to develop your career in the sports industry. You may find that some organisations will pay for you to carry out any further training needs you require, while others will expect you to fund the training yourself.

You should also try to gain feedback from a variety of sources, including your supervisor, colleagues and possibly a customer or two that you have had regular contact with. Through interviews or questionnaires try to gauge their assessment of your performance. You can then use this information to determine the areas in which you excel and the areas in which you need to improve.

Presentation

Try to work out the best way of presenting your evaluation. Here are a few ideas:

- poster presentation
- oral presentation
- diary/logbook
- written assignment
- video presentation.

You may wish to use one form of presentation or a combination. This will depend on a variety of factors, including who you are delivering the presentation to and the facilities you have to use.

Review questions

1　Explain the three different sectors that provide for sport.
2　Which sector has the main aim of making money?
3　Describe the skills and qualifications required for three sports jobs of your choice.
4　Name five different places where you could look for jobs in the sports industry.
5　What is the purpose of a CV?
6　Explain how body language should be used effectively in an interview.
7　Explain how you can prepare yourself for an interview.
8　On a separate sheet of paper write a letter of application for a sports career of your choice.

References

Torkildsen, G. (1991) *Leisure and Recreation Management*, Spon Press.

Websites

www.bases.org.uk – British Association of Sport and Exercise Scientists
www.exercisecareers.com – Exercise Careers
www.jobswithballs.com – Jobs with Balls
www.leisureopportunities.co.uk – Leisure Opportunities
www.sportengland.org – Sport England

Index